Preface

Welcome to a revolutionary time in marketing. Today, dramatic changes ranging from an increasing emphasis on customer value to the globalization of markets to advances in the information technology industry are creating new boundaries for the marketing discipline. Combining these changes, with the sophisticated marketplace perspectives students bring to the classroom, can create an exciting and relevant learning experience. To accomplish this, *Marketing, Second Canadian Edition,* incorporates the most recent changes in our global business environment and their implications for the marketing function. This new edition also continues the tradition set by *Marketing, First Canadian Edition,* by encouraging readers to become active participants in the learning process. The challenges of the new environment and the benefits of involvement and interaction provide a powerful framework for your introduction to the dynamic field of marketing.

Although this edition of *Marketing* emphasizes many of the new developments in the marketing discipline, it also continues to utilize the innovative pedagogical approach we developed and introduced in 1991. Since then, thousands of students and hundreds of instructors have used *Marketing*. Their feedback has been the basis for our personal efforts to continually improve.

The increasing interest in our book convinces us that building on the strengths of the previous edition will provide you with one of the best marketing textbooks available today.

NEW IN THIS EDITION

To reflect the increasing importance of global marketing, we have added a chapter titled "Global Markets and Cross-Cultural Analysis" (Chapter 5). This chapter covers world trade, global competition, and related issues such as economic protectionism. In addition, this chapter provides a framework for cross-cultural analysis that identifies variables, such as cultural variability, values, customs, and language, as important dimensions for comparing nations or societies. When combined with the traditional chapters on the environment (Chapter 3) and consumer behaviour (Chapter 6), students are exposed to a truly global view of marketing. Global marketing practices and examples are also provided throughout the text whenever they are relevant and logically expand on the materials provided in Chapters 5 and 23.

Because of the centrality of ethics and social responsibility in marketing, a new chapter on these topics has been added (Chapter 4). Ethics and Social Responsibility Alert boxes have also been added to every chapter and linked to appropriate text material to allow continuity in reading and discussion.

The growing interest in customer value is now incorporated into each chapter. We have expanded Deming's concept of quality by linking quality and customer value (Chapter 1). Later chapters cover specific topics such as how to provide value and how to assess value. We believe customer value will become one of the predominant marketing issues of the 1990s.

Many new marketing topics, consumer trends, and changes in the business environment have also been added. These include the growing importance of integrated marketing communications, direct marketing, strategic alliances, cultural ethnocentricity, reverse marketing, relationship marketing, euro-branding, everyday low pricing (EDLP), retromarketing, marketing public relations, and information technology.

Finally, the package of supplements has been expanded, updated, and integrated to provide the most comprehensive set of learning and teaching tools for students and instructors. For example, the majority of cases found at the end of the text are new to this edition, and all are linked directly to corporate examples discussed in the chapters. Many of the cases also have an accompanying videotape.

PEDAGOGICAL FEATURES OF THE SECOND EDITION

Marketing Action Memo

Ethics and Social
Responsibility
Alert

As in the first edition, we want to involve you in the study of marketing by encouraging you to think about your personal experiences as a consumer and by asking you to take the role of a marketing decision maker. Examples of contemporary people and organizations and their marketing decisions appear in the chapter opening vignettes and Marketing Action Memos, while extended examples are included in the chapters and end-of-text cases. To help you understand potential explanations for the success or failure of marketing plans, each chapter also integrates research related to marketing decisions.

The icons, seen adjacent here, highlight the special Marketing Action Memos and the Ethics and Social Responsibility Alert boxes found in each chapter.

In addition, the book reinforces major concepts as they are introduced in each chapter to stimulate your understanding of them and foster your ability to apply them appropriately. At the end of each major chapter section, Concept Checks pose two or three questions to test your recall. The Learning Objectives at the beginning of each chapter and the Summary and Key Terms and Concepts at the close of each chapter provide further reinforcement.

We believe that the use of these unique learning aids lets you learn about, understand, and integrate the many marketing topics covered in our text and allows you to apply them in the constantly changing marketing environment you will encounter as a consumer and a marketing manager.

TEXT ORGANIZATION

Marketing, Second Canadian Edition, is divided in six main parts. Part I, "Initiating the Marketing Process," first looks at what marketing is and how it identifies and satisfies consumer needs (Chapter 1). Then, Chapter 2 provides an overview of the strategic marketing process that occurs in an organization. Chapter 3 analyzes the five environmental factors in our changing marketing environment, while Chapter 4 discusses the significance of ethics and social responsibility in marketing decisions.

Part II, "Understanding Buyers and Markets," first describes the nature and scope of world trade and the influence of cultural differences on global marketing practices in Chapter 5. Next, Chapter 6 describes how ultimate consumers reach buying decisions. Finally, since they are different than ultimate consumers, industrial and organizational buyers and how they make purchase decisions are covered in Chapter 7.

Part III, "Targeting Marketing Opportunities," the marketing research function is discussed in Chapter 8. The process of segmenting and targeting markets and positioning products appears in Chapter 9. The increasing importance of relationship marketing, how today's marketing managers use strategic information systems, and sales forecasting are described in Chapter 10.

Part IV, "Satisfying Marketing Opportunities," covers the four Ps—the marketing mix elements. Unlike most competitive textbooks, the product element is divided into the natural chronological sequence of first developing new products (Chapter 11) and then managing the existing products (Chapter 12). Pricing is covered in terms of underlying pricing analysis (Chapter 13), followed by actual price setting (Chapter 14) and the related Appendix A, "Financial Aspects of Marketing." Three chapters address the place (distribution) aspects of marketing: "Marketing Channels and Wholesaling" (Chapter 15), "Physical Distribution and Logistics Management" (Chapter 16), and "Retailing" (Chapter 17). Retailing is a separate chapter because of its importance and interest as a career for many of today's students. Promotion is also covered in three chapters. Chapter 18 discusses integrated marketing communications in general and presents in-depth treatment of sales promotion, direct marketing, and marketing public relations.

"Advertising" (Chapter 19) and "Personal Selling and Sales Management" (Chapter 20) complete the coverage of promotional activities.

Part V, "Managing the Marketing Process," expands on Chapter 2 to show how the four marketing mix elements are blended to plan (Chapter 21) and implement and control (Chapter 22) the marketing process. Because these topics can become abstract, both chapters provide many examples of how companies actually plan, implement, and control marketing plans.

Part VI, "Expanding Marketing Settings," devotes separate chapters to two marketing topics of increasing importance in today's business environment: "International Marketing" (Chapter 23) and "Marketing of Services" (Chapter 24). The part closes with Appendix B, "Career Planning in Marketing," which discusses marketing jobs themselves and how to get them.

Twenty-five cases, a detailed glossary, and three indexes (author, company and product, and subject) complete the book. As we observe in Chapter 1, we genuinely hope that somewhere in *Marketing* you will discover not only the challenge and excitement of marketing, but possibly a career as well.

SUPPLEMENTAL RESOURCE MATERIALS

Providing a comprehensive and integrated package of high-quality instructional supplements continues to be a priority for us. We have been involved, as authors and supervisors, in the production of all the supplements that now accompany our text. Much attention has been given to providing elements and features in these supplements that were requested by both inexperienced and experienced instructors. As a result, each supplement contains several features not offered with any other marketing text.

Instructor's Manual   The Instructor's Manual includes lecture notes, transparencies and transparency masters, a discussion of Marketing Action Memos and the Ethics and Social Responsibility Alerts, and answers to the end-of-chapter Problems and Applications questions. Supplemental Lecture Notes and In-Class Activities are also provided as well as case teaching notes.

Test Bank   Our Test Bank has been developed to provide an accurate and exhaustive source of test items for a variety of examination styles. It contains more than 2,000 questions, categorized by topic and level of learning (definitional, conceptual, or application).

A Test Item Table allows instructors to select questions from any section of a chapter at any of the three levels of learning. The Test Bank includes approximately 10 essay questions and 75 to 100 multiple-choice questions per chapter, making it one of the most comprehensive test packages on the market.

Irwin's Computerized Testing Software   In addition to the printed format, a computerized test bank is available free to adopters. The easy-to-use test bank includes all the questions contained in the printed version. Additional benefits include the ability to:

- Add or develop individual test items.
- Personalize individual questions.
- Generate several versions of the same exam.
- Maintain class files and test scores on disk.

Video•Cases   A unique series of 16 contemporary marketing cases is available on a videocassette. Each video•case corresponds to specific cases found in the end-of-text cases.

Study Guide   Coauthored by an educational consultant, the Study Guide enables the students to learn and apply marketing principles instead of memorizing facts for an examination.

New case problems and five types of exercises are used to accomplish this goal: application exercises, matching terms to definitions, matching concepts to examples, recognition and identification exercises, and chapter recall.

Computer-Problem Software   This software features short cases and problems that allow students to learn about and apply marketing concepts and to see the results of marketing decisions on a personal computer.

Marketing Planning Software   The marketing plan software disk is designed to help students use the strategic marketing process introduced in Chapter 2 and discussed in detail in Chapters 21 and 22. The software and accompanying handbook provide a personal and computer-based tool for involving students in the course.

ACKNOWLEDGMENTS

Designing and continually improving a textbook requires extensive feedback from current and potential users. To guide the modifications incorporated into *Marketing, Second Canadian Edition,* we utilized reviews and comments by faculty and students from colleges and universities across Canada.

We are deeply grateful to the numerous people who shared their ideas with us. Reviewing a book or supplement takes an incredible amount of energy and attention, and we are glad that the following people took the time to do it. Their comments have inspired us to do our best. Reviewers and case authors who contributed to this edition of the text include:

Chris Vaughan *Saint Mary's University*
Steve Grant *University of New Brunswick*
Peter Sianchuk *Mount Allison University*
Shannon Goodspeed *Mount Royal College*
Gerald Edwards *Douglas College*
Clifford Hurt *University of Guelph*
Michelle McCann *University of Lethbridge*
Steve Janisse *St. Clair College*
Ted Kahl *Dawson College*
Cathy Goodwin *University of Manitoba*

We were also fortunate to be able to call on the special expertise of Erica Michaels, who used her extensive experience to write the Study Guide. The business community also provided great help in making available cases and information that appear in the text and supplements—much of it being used for the first time in university or college materials.

Thanks are due to Canadian Tire, Molson Breweries (*thanks Catherine*); Ganong Brothers; Statistics Canada (*thanks Marie*); Clearly Canadian; McDonald's Canada; the Royal Canadian Mint; Second Harvest; Alcan Aluminium Limited; Goldfarb Consultants (*thanks Allison*); The National Hockey League; the Canadian Football League; IBM Canada; Apple Canada; Shoppers Drug Mart; Dellware (*thanks Bob*); Rollerblade Inc. and Benetton Sportsystems Canada; Cantel; AEI; Canada Trust; Bank of Montreal; Rudnicki Murphy; Ault Foods; Chrysler Canada; Reader's Digest; Labatt Breweries; McKim, Baker, Lovick/BBDO; Scali, McCabe, Sloves (Canada) Ltd.; Marketing Magazine; and QMA Consulting Group Limited. A very special thanks to Wendy Miles and Television Bureau of Canada.

Finally, we acknowledge the professional efforts of the Richard D. Irwin staff. Completion of our book and its many supplements required the attention and commitment of many editorial, production, marketing, and research personnel. Thanks to Rod Banister, Amy Lund, Milton Vacon, Elke Price, Laurie Kersch, Eurnice Harris, Jeanne Rivera, Charlene Breeden, and many others. Very special thanks is extended to Evelyn Veitch for her goodwill, sense of humour, and genuine care and support throughout the project.

Eric N. Berkowitz
Frederick G. Crane
Roger A. Kerin
Steven W. Hartley
William Rudelius

I am responsible for the Canadianization of this text, so any questions or concerns about the book should be directed to me. I would like to thank my coauthors for their support and feedback. I am dedicating this book to my beautiful wife, Doreen (thank you for showing me that love is still the greatest power in the world); to Erinn, Jacquelyn, and Brenna (I love you!); and to God for watching over me.

F. G. Crane

To the Student

"Why are textbook prices so high?"

This is, by far, the most frequently asked question heard in the college publishing industry. There are many factors that influence the price of your new textbook. Here are just a few:

Author Royalties   Authors are paid based on a percentage of new book sales and do not receive royalties on the sale of a used book. They are also deprived of their rightful royalties when their books are illegally photocopied.

The Cost of Instructor Support Materials   Your instructor may be making use of teaching supplements, many of which are provided by the publisher. Teaching supplements include videos, colour transparencies, instructor's manuals, software, computerized testing materials, and more. These supplements are designed as part of a learning package to enhance your educational experience.

Developmental Costs   These costs are associated with the extensive development of your textbook. Expenses include permissions fees, manuscript review costs, artwork, typesetting, printing and binding costs, and more.

Marketing Costs   Instructors need to be made aware of new textbooks. Marketing costs include academic conventions, remuneration of the publisher's representatives, promotional advertising pieces, and the provision of instructor's examination copies.

Bookstore Markups   In order to stay in business, your local bookstore must cover its costs. A textbook is a commodity, just like any other item your bookstore may sell, and bookstores are the most effective way to get the textbook from the publisher to you.

Publisher Profits   In order to continue to supply students with quality textbooks, publishers must make a profit to stay in business. Like the authors, publishers do not receive any compensation from the sale of a used book or the illegal photocopying of their textbooks.

We at Irwin Dorsey/Times Mirror Professional Publishing hope you will find this information useful and that it addresses some of your concerns. We also thank you for your purchase of this new textbook. If you have any questions that we can answer, please write to us at:

Times Mirror Professional Publishing
College Division
130 Flaska Drive
Markham, Ontario
L6G 1B8

Contents in Brief

Contents

PART I

*Initiating the Marketing
Process 2*

PART II
Understanding Buyers and Markets 100

PART IV

*Satisfying Marketing
Opportunities 256*

Marketing

Initiating the Marketing Process

Satisfying consumers in local, national, and global markets: This is the essence of the marketing process described in Part I. Chapter 1 introduces the marketing process by describing the actions of Rollerblade, Inc., and its introduction of in-line skates to create what Time *magazine calls "the sport of the 90s." Chapter 2 describes how organizations, such as Canadian Tire, develop marketing plans to attract and retain customers. In Chapter 3, the dimensions of the business environment and how it has changed and will change are presented. These changes include increasingly diverse markets: an expanded North American market with few barriers between Canada, the United States, and Mexico; and an evolving global market. Finally, Chapter 4 provides a framework for including ethical and social responsibility considerations in marketing decisions.*

Marketing: A Focus on the Consumer

AFTER READING THIS CHAPTER YOU SHOULD BE ABLE TO:

▸ Define marketing and explain the importance of (1) discovering and (2) satisfying consumer needs.

▸ Understand the marketing mix and environmental factors.

▸ Describe how today's market orientation era differs from prior eras oriented toward production and selling.

▸ Understand the meaning of ethics and social responsibility and how they relate to the individual, organizations, and society.

▸ Know what is required for marketing to occur and how it creates utilities for consumers.

▸ Understand the concept of customer value and quality.

How Do You Grow an Industry?

Suppose you joined a small company whose objective was to "grow" a new industry almost from scratch. How could it be done? This was the question that faced Rollerblade, Inc., not long ago when it decided to produce and market in-line skates. In-line skates are roller skates with the rollers in a row rather than set as two pairs. In fact, some of you probably refer to in-line skating as "rollerblading." But the use of the company's name as the generic name for the sport—and in-line skates generally—is a very mixed blessing for Rollerblade, Inc., as we'll see later.

Although Rollerblade, Inc., is a young company, in-line skates are almost three centuries old. While trying to simulate ice skating in the summer, a Dutch inventor in the early 1700s created the first roller skates by attaching spools to his shoes. His in-line arrangement was the standard design until 1863, when the first conventional roller skates, or "quads," appeared. This design became standard, and in-line skates virtually disappeared from the market.

In 1980, two hockey-playing brothers found an old pair of in-line skates while browsing through a sporting goods store. Working in their garage, they modified the design to add polyurethane wheels, a moulded boot shell, and a toe brake. They sold their new product, which they dubbed "Rollerblade skates," out of the back of their truck to hockey players and skiers, who could use them as a means of staying in shape during the summer. In the mid-1980s, an entrepreneur bought the company from the brothers and was then faced with the question of how to market these in-line skates to a larger market. The solution was to create and market a whole new sport—the sport of in-line skating. At that time, Rollerblade, Inc., was the only company producing the skates, and its management believed that building an interest in the sport (industry) was the way to get Rollerblade, Inc., to grow.[1] In this chapter, we will see how Rollerblade created a global industry.

Rollerblade Skates, Marketing, and You   The key to Rollerblade, Inc.'s, success lies in the work that is the subject of this book: marketing. In this chapter and the rest of the book, we'll introduce you to the people, organizations, ideas, activities, and jobs in marketing that have spawned the products and services that have been towering successes, shattering failures, or something in between. The successes we see, buy, and use every day. The failures fade from sight.

Where will Rollerblade, Inc., be in five years? Prospective buyers will decide. Later in this chapter you can read about some of the critical marketing decisions Rollerblade, Inc., made. Decide for yourself—along with millions of consumers—whether or not these decisions were the right ones.

Marketing doesn't happen in a vacuum: it affects all individuals, all organizations, all industries, and all countries. This text seeks not only to teach you marketing concepts, but also to demonstrate the many applications of marketing and how it affects our lives. This knowledge should make you a better consumer, help you in your career, and enable you to be a more informed citizen.

In this chapter and the ones that follow, you will feel the excitement of marketing. You will see both successes and disasters. You will be introduced to the dynamic changes that will affect all of us in the 1990s. You will also meet many very human, ordinary men and women whose marketing creativity sometimes achieved brilliant, extraordinary results. And who knows? Somewhere in these pages you may find a career.

WHAT IS MARKETING?

BEING A MARKETING EXPERT: GOOD NEWS—BAD NEWS

In many respects, you are a marketing expert already. But just to test your expertise, try the "marketing expert" questions in Figure 1–1. These questions—some of them easy, others mind boggling—show the diverse problems marketing executives grapple with every day. You'll find the answers to these questions in the next few pages.

The Good News: You Already Have Marketing Experience   You are somewhat of an expert because you do many marketing activities every day. You already know many marketing terms, concepts, and principles. For example, would you sell more Sony Walkmans at $500 or $50 each? The answer is $50, of course, so your experience in shopping for products—and maybe even selling them—already gives you great insights into the world of marketing. As a con-

Answer the questions below. The correct answers are given later in the chapter.

1 In a magazine article, a well-known actress said she often "Rollerbladed" for fun and exercise. What was Rollerblade, Inc.'s, reaction? (*a*) delighted, (*b*) upset, or (*c*) somewhere in between. Why?

2 What is Polavision? (*a*) a new breathable contact lens, (*b*) a new TV network, (*c*) special bifocal glasses, (*d*) instant movies, or (*e*) a political newspaper.

3 Right after World War II, International Business Machines Corporation (IBM) commissioned a study to estimate the total future market for electronic computers. The study's results indicated that the total future market size would be (*a*) less than 10, (*b*) 1,000, (*c*) 10,000, (*d*) 100,000, or (*e*) 10 million or more.

4 How could Rollerblade, Inc., find an inexpensive way to get prospective buyers to try its in-line skates?

5 True or false: A recent Canadian study of university students showed that over 10 percent of male students reported wearing mascara two to six times per week.

■ *Figure 1–1*
The see-if-you're-really-a-marketing-expert test.

sumer, you've already been involved in thousands of marketing decisions, but mainly on the buying, not the marketing, side.

The Bad News: Surprises about the Obvious Unfortunately, common sense doesn't always explain some marketing decisions and actions.

An actress's saying in a national magazine that she "often Rollerbladed" (question 1, Figure 1–1) sounds like great publicity, right? But Rollerblade, Inc., was upset. Legally, Rollerblade is a registered trademark of Rollerblade, Inc., and, as a brand name, should be used only to identify its products and services. With letters to offenders and advertisements like the accompanying one, Rollerblade, Inc., is trying to protect a precious asset: its own name.

Under trademark law, if consumers generally start using a brand name as the basic word to describe an entire class of products, then the company loses its exclusive rights to the name. "Rollerblade" skates would become "rollerblade"—just another English word to describe all kinds of in-line skating. That fate has already befallen some famous products such as linoleum, aspirin, cellophane, escalator, yo-yo, corn flakes, and trampoline. In fact, *Random House Webster's College Dictionary* says it's "almost 100 percent sure" that the word *Rollerblade* will appear in its next edition—but with a capital "R" to recognize it as a trademark.[2]

Today corporations are spending millions of dollars in both advertising and court cases to protect their important brand names. Examples are Kimberly-Clark's Kleenex and 3M's Scotch tape. Coca-Cola takes dozens of restaurants to court every year for serving another cola drink when a patron asks for a Coca-Cola or even a Coke. Because legal and ethical issues, such as the Rollerblade skates trademark problem, are central to many marketing decisions, they are addressed throughout the book. The point here is that although your

Rollerblade, Inc., ran this ad to communicate a specific message. It's also part of a "reminder" postcard to people who *slip*. What is the message? For the answer and why it is important, see the text.

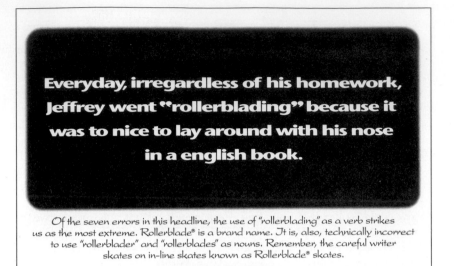

Everyday, irregardless of his homework, Jeffrey went "rollerblading" because it was to nice to lay around with his nose in a english book.

Of the seven errors in this headline, the use of "rollerblading" as a verb strikes us as the most extreme. Rollerblade® is a brand name. It is, also, technically incorrect to use "rollerblader" and "rollerblades" as nouns. Remember, the careful writer skates on in-line skates known as Rollerblade® skates.

Rollerblade.

© 1992 Rollerblade, Inc. Rollerblade and The Skate Logo are trademarks of Rollerblade, Inc.

common sense usually helps you in analyzing marketing problems, sometimes it can mislead you. This book's in-depth study of marketing augments your common sense with an understanding of marketing concepts to help you more effectively assess and make marketing decisions.

MARKETING: DEFINED

Many people, including some of you, have a misconception about what marketing is all about, and we know some of the misconceptions. But marketing is not a new ad campaign or this month's promotion at the local shopping center. It is not simply selling things and taking the customer's money; nor is it an attempt to fool the customer, or trick the customer. Marketing's ultimate assignment is to (1) discover and (2) satisfy customers' real needs.[3] The American Marketing Association, representing marketing professionals in the United States and Canada, states that "**marketing** is the process of planning and executing the conception, pricing, promotion, and distribution of ideas, goods, and services to create exchanges that satisfy individual and organizational objectives."[4]

This definition shows marketing to be a far broader concept than many people think. It also stresses the importance of beneficial exchanges that satisfy the objectives of both those who buy and those who sell ideas, goods, and services—whether they be individuals or organizations.

Exchange and Customer Value   The **exchange,** or the trading of things of *value* between buyer and seller so that each is better off than before, is central to marketing. The fact that successful firms gain loyal customers by providing value is not a new concept. But what is new to marketing is the attempt firms are now making to better understand how customers perceive value in their specific environment. The notion of customer value is *the* critical marketing issue for the 1990s and is discussed at the end of this chapter.

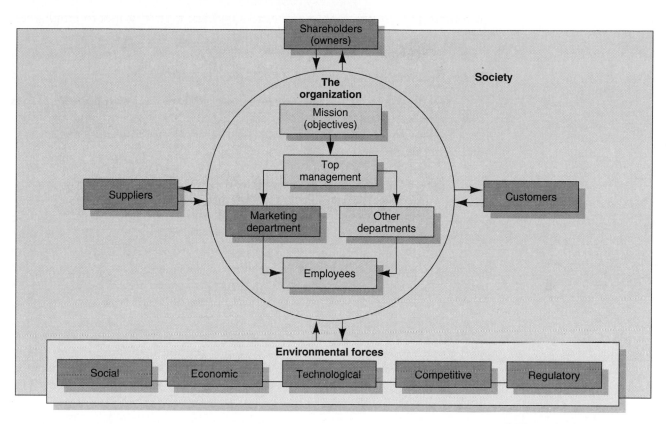

▍ *Figure 1–2*
**An organization's
marketing department
relates to many people,
groups, and forces.**

THE DIVERSE FACTORS INFLUENCING MARKETING ACTIVITIES

Although an organization's marketing activity focusses on assessing and satisfying consumer needs, countless other people, groups, and forces interact to shape it (Figure 1–2). Foremost is the organization itself, whose mission determines what business it is in and what objectives it seeks. Within the organization, top management is responsible for achieving these objectives. The marketing department works closely with other departments and employees to help provide the customer-satisfying products required for the organization to survive and prosper.[5]

Figure 1–2 also shows the key people, groups, and forces outside the organization that influence marketing activities. In addition to the customers, two groups with an important stake in the organization's success are its shareholders (or, if the organization is nonprofit, representatives of groups it serves) and its suppliers. Environmental forces, such as social, technological, economic, competitive, and regulatory factors, also shape an organization's marketing activities.

Finally, an organization's marketing decisions are affected by and in turn often have an important impact on society as a whole.

The organization must strike a continual balance among these individuals and groups, whose objectives sometimes conflict. For example, it is not possible to simultaneously provide the lowest-priced and highest-quality products to

How does your search
for a new diet cola show
what is needed for
marketing to occur? The
answer appears in the
text.

customers and pay the highest prices to suppliers, highest wages to employees, and maximum dividends to shareholders.

REQUIREMENTS FOR MARKETING TO OCCUR

For marketing to occur, at least four factors are required: (1) two or more parties (individuals or organizations) with unsatisfied needs, (2) a desire and an ability on their part to be satisfied, (3) a way for the parties to communicate, and (4) something to exchange.

Two or More Parties with Unsatisfied Needs   Suppose several months ago you had an unmet need—a desire for a different kind of diet, sugar-free cola that tasted like Pepsi—but you didn't yet know that Diet Crystal Pepsi existed. Also unknown to you was that several dozen bottles of Diet Crystal Pepsi were sitting on a shelf at your nearest supermarket, waiting to be bought. This is an example of two parties with unmet needs: you, with a need for a Pepsi-like diet drink, and your supermarket owner, needing someone to buy the Diet Crystal Pepsi.

Desire and Ability to Satisfy These Needs   Both you and the supermarket owner want to satisfy these unmet needs. Furthermore, you have the money to buy the item and the time to get to the supermarket. The store's owner has not only the desire to sell Diet Crystal Pepsi but also the ability to do so, since it's stocked on the shelves.

A Way for the Parties to Communicate   The marketing transaction of buying the Diet Crystal Pepsi will never occur unless you are aware that the product exists and know its location. Similarly, the store owner won't stock the new diet cola unless there's a market of potential consumers near the supermarket who are likely to buy. When you see your supermarket's newspaper ad for Diet Crystal Pepsi at half price, this communication barrier between you (the buyer) and your supermarket (the seller) is overcome.

Something to Exchange   Marketing occurs when the transaction takes place and both the buyer and seller exchange something of value. In this case, you exchange your money for the supermarket's Diet Crystal Pepsi. Both of you have gained something and also given up something, but you are both better off because you have each satisfied your unmet needs. You have the opportunity to drink Diet Crystal Pepsi, but you gave up some money; the store gave up the Diet Crystal Pepsi but received money, which enables it to remain in business. This exchange process is central to marketing.[6]

Concept Check

  1 **What is marketing?**

  2 **Marketing focusses on _____ and _____ consumer needs.**

  3 **What four factors are needed for marketing to occur?**

HOW MARKETING DISCOVERS AND SATISFIES CONSUMER NEEDS

The importance of discovering consumer needs and satisfying them is so critical to understanding marketing that we look at each of these two steps in detail below.

DISCOVERING CONSUMER NEEDS

The first objective in marketing is discovering the needs of prospective consumers. Sound simple? Well, it's not. In the abstract, discovering needs looks easy, but when you get down to the specifics of marketing, problems crop up.

Some Product Disasters With much fanfare, RCA Corporation introduced its Selecta Vision Videodisc player to the world in the early 1980s. Polaroid, flushed with the success of its instant still-photography business, introduced Polavision (question 2, Figure 1–1) as the first instant home movie in 1978. These firms quietly dropped or redirected these products a short time after their introduction, with RCA losing nearly $500 million on its venture and Polaroid losing $170 million.

These are two of the best-known product disasters in recent history, but thousands of lesser-known products fail in the marketplace every year. One major reason is that in each case the firm miscalculates consumers' wants and needs. In the RCA Videodisc case, consumers wanted to record TV programs, something videocassette recorders (VCRs) could do but Videodisc machines could not. Consumers also didn't want instant movies as much as they wanted instant still pictures, and Polavision failed in the consumer market. Today, of course, consumers are showing their "electric home movies" on their VCRs.

The solution to preventing such product failures seems embarrassingly obvious. First, find out what consumers need and want. Second, produce what they do need and want and don't produce what they don't need and want. This is much more difficult than it sounds.

It's frequently very difficult to get a precise reading on what consumers want and need when they are confronted with revolutionary ideas for new products. Right after World War II, IBM asked a prestigious management consulting firm to estimate the total future market for *all* electronic computers for *all* business, scientific, engineering, and government uses (question 3, Figure 1–1). The answer was less than 10! Fortunately, key IBM executives disagreed, so IBM started building electronic computers anyway. Where would IBM be today if it had assumed the market estimate was correct? Most of the firms that bought computers five years after the market study had not actually recognized they were prospective buyers because they had no understanding of what computers could do for them—they didn't recognize their own need for faster information processing.

Consumer Needs and Consumer Wants Should marketing try to satisfy consumer needs or consumer wants? The answer is both! Heated debates rage over this question, and a person's position in the debate usually depends on the definitions of needs and wants and the amount of freedom given to prospective customers to make their own buying decisions.

A *need* occurs when a person feels physiologically deprived of basic necessities like food, clothing, and shelter. A *want* is a felt need that is shaped by a person's knowledge, culture, and personality. So if you feel hungry, you have developed a basic need and desire to eat something. Let's say you then want to eat an apple or a candy bar because, based on your past experience and personality, you know these will satisfy your hunger need. Effective marketing, in the form of creating an awareness of good products at convenient locations, can clearly shape a person's wants. Diet Crystal Pepsi is an example.

At issue is whether marketing persuades prospective customers to buy the "wrong" things—say, a "bad" candy bar rather than a "good" apple—to satisfy hunger pangs. Certainly, marketing tries to influence what we buy. A question then arises: At what point do we want government and society to step in to protect consumers? Most Canadians would say they want government to protect them from harmful drugs and unsafe cars, but not from candy bars and soft drinks. The issue is not clear-cut, which is why legal and social issues are central to marketing. Because even psychologists and economists still debate the exact meanings of *need* and *want,* we shall avoid the semantic arguments and use the terms interchangeably in the rest of the book.

As shown in Figure 1–3, discovering needs involves looking carefully at prospective customers, whether they are children buying M&M's candy, college students buying Rollerblade in-line skates, or firms buying Xerox photocopying machines. A principal activity of a firm's marketing department is to carefully scrutinize the consumers to understand what they need, to study industry trends, to examine competitors' products, and even to analyze the needs of an industrial customer's customers.

What a Market Is   Potential consumers make up a **market,** which is (1) people (2) with the desire and (3) with the ability to buy a specific product. All markets ultimately are people. Even when we say a firm bought a Xerox copier, we mean one or several people in the firm decided to buy it. People who are

▌*Figure 1–3*
Marketing's first task: discovering consumer needs.

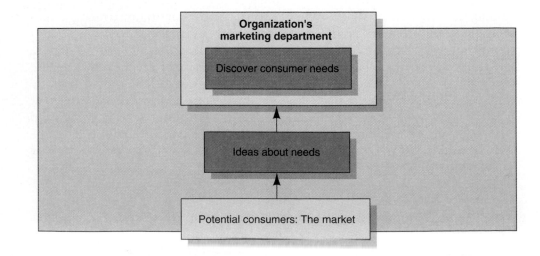

aware of their unmet needs may have the desire to buy the product, but that alone isn't sufficient. People must also have the ability to buy, such as the authority, time, and money. As we saw earlier in the definition of marketing, people may buy, or accept, more than just goods or services. For example, they may buy an idea that results in an action, such as having their blood pressure checked annually or turning down their thermostat to save energy.

SATISFYING CONSUMER NEEDS

Marketing doesn't stop with the ideas obtained from discovering consumer needs. Since the organization obviously can't satisfy all consumer needs, it must concentrate its efforts on certain needs of a specific group of potential consumers. This is the **target market,** one or more specific groups of potential consumers toward which an organization directs its marketing efforts.

The Four Ps: Controllable Marketing Mix Factors   Having selected the target market consumers, the firm must take steps to satisfy their needs. Someone in the organization's marketing department, often the marketing manager, must take action and develop a complete **marketing mix** designed to appeal to the target consumer. The marketing mix elements are called *controllable factors,* because they are under the control of the marketing department in the organization. The marketing mix consists of what are often called the *four Ps,* a shorthand term first published by Professor E. Jerome McCarthy.[7] The marketer constructs a mix by selecting appropriate aspects of each of the four Ps. The four Ps are:

- Product: a good, service, or idea to satisfy the consumer's needs.
- Price: what is exchanged for the product.
- Promotion (integrated marketing communications): a means of communicating between seller and buyer.
- Place (distribution): a means of getting the product into the consumer's hands.

The relationship between satisfying consumer needs and the development of the marketing mix is shown in Figure 1–4. After discovering what prospective customers need, the marketing manager must translate the ideas from consumers into some concepts for products the firm might develop. These ideas must then be converted into a tangible marketing mix. Prospective consumers then react to the mix offered, either favourably (by buying) or unfavourably (by not buying), and the process is repeated until the marketing mix is right and consumers respond favourably.

As shown in Figure 1–4, in an effective organization this process is continuous: consumer needs trigger product concepts that are translated into actual products that stimulate further discovery of consumer needs. We'll define each of the four Ps more carefully later in the book, but for now it's important to remember that they are the elements of the marketing mix designed to satisfy consumer needs.

The Uncontrollable, Environmental Factors   In addition to the controllable marketing factors, or marketing mix, there are a host of factors largely beyond

Figure 1–4
Marketing's second task: satisfying consumer needs.

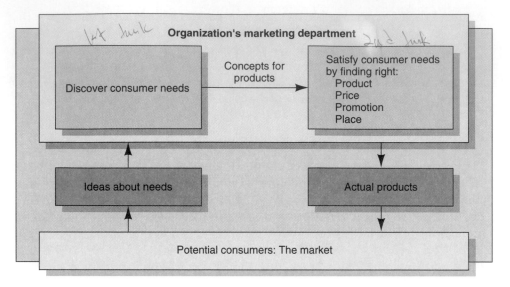

the control of the marketing department and its organization. These are called **uncontrollable, environmental factors** and can be placed into five groups (as shown in Figure 1–2): social, technological, economic, competitive, and regulatory forces.

Examples are what consumers themselves need and want, changing technology, whether the economy is expanding or contracting, actions that competitors take, and government restrictions. These five forces may serve as accelerators or brakes on marketing, sometimes expanding an organization's marketing opportunities and at other times restricting them.

Traditionally, many marketing executives have treated these environmental factors as rigid, absolute constraints that are entirely outside their influence.[8] However, recent studies and marketing successes have shown that a forward-looking action-oriented firm can often overcome some constraining environmental factors. IBM's technical and marketing breakthroughs gave birth to the entire digital electronic computer industry, even though initially consumers were apathetic. Apple did the same for personal computers. In 1990, after more than a decade of negotiations with Soviet bureaucrats, McDonald's Canada opened a 700-seat restaurant in Moscow and served more than 10 million customers in the first year. It now has two more restaurants there and has plans for up to 20 in the Russian city. Had environmental factors been viewed as rigid and uncontrollable, they might have forestalled productive marketing actions. Other marketers, recognizing the power and influence of environmental forces, do not fight those forces but instead use them to explore possible marketing opportunities. Environmental factors are covered in detail in Chapter 3.

Rollerblade, Inc.'s, Marketing Mix   To see the specifics of an actual marketing mix, let's return to the example that opened the chapter, Rollerblade, Inc., and its in-line skates. The company needed to develop the right marketing mix in order to get prospective buyers to put on its brand of skates and use them. In order to develop the appropriate mix, Rollerblade, Inc., started with some informal research that showed that using Rollerblade skates:

- Was incredible fun.
- Was a great aerobic workout and made the skater stronger and healthier.
- Was quite different from traditional roller skating, which was practised alone, mostly inside, and by young girls.
- Had great appeal to people other than just off-season ice skaters and skiers.

Rollerblade, Inc., then had to make some critical marketing decisions involving:

- *Finding the right group to target with its in-line skates.* Rollerblade, Inc.'s, marketing efforts focussed on 18- to 35-year-old men and women. They were active, were health- and sports-conscious, and had money to spend.
- *Changing the image.* Rollerblade, Inc., believed it had to build a new image for in-line roller skating. People knew about traditional roller skating, but Rollerblade, Inc., didn't want to be associated with that image. It also wanted to be sure that people didn't associate the product only with off-season ice skaters and skiers. The company wanted to build an image involving outdoor fun, freedom, and excitement. This proved to be a key element in its mix[9]
- *Stressing the right benefits.* The company chose to stress three benefits the product could offer the consumer: (1) fun, (2) fitness and health, and (3) excitement.

Rollerblade, Inc., made many specific marketing mix decisions. For the product, the company decided to improve the design to include such things as heel brakes. It also developed different versions of the product, including a lighter skate and a skate that buckled up like a pair of ski boots. Rollerblade, Inc., decided to offer the products at a range of prices from just under $100 to over $300 depending on the model. It also decided to concentrate on distributing its products through major sporting goods stores throughout the United States and Canada.

The big question concerned the promotional aspect of the marketing mix. Rollerblade, Inc., was a small company in the mid-1980s and as a result had a limited budget to use for promotion. Rollerblade, Inc., needed to make people aware of its skates and to get them to put them on. The company believed that if people tried the skates, they would fall in love with the sport. They came up with a simple and relatively inexpensive way to accomplish this task. They gave away hundreds of free skates where they would make people most aware of the new product and also enable key "opinion leaders" to try them. Entertainment celebrities, such as Michael J. Fox, Janet Jackson, Arnold Schwarzenegger, and cheerleaders for professional football teams, turned up wearing the skates in magazine photos or on television, giving Rollerblade, Inc., lots of free publicity.

The company also gave skates away to rental shops along the beaches of Southern California. Rollerblade, Inc., believed that major consumer trends in North America usually start on one coast and spread across the continent. Providing the skates to the rental shops increased awareness of the product and encouraged use. These "freebies" led to tens of thousands of converts to in-line skating, and sales of Rollerblades started to take off. This enabled Rollerblade, Inc.'s, marketing budget to expand and allowed for more ways to promote the

skates. These new ideas included sponsoring competitive in-line skating races and product endorsements from professional sports teams. The company also started Team Rollerblade, a group of skaters who performed on the skates everywhere from local shopping malls to the 1992 Winter Olympics in France.[10]

The company also filled up "demo vans" with skates and travelled across the United States and Canada allowing people to try the skates for free (question 4, Figure 1–1). Rollerblade, Inc., also produced a skating video that retailers could show on their VCRs, established Club Rollerblade for skaters, and published a how-to book. The company even did a joint promotion with General Mills that had Rollerblade skates displayed on millions of cereal boxes during a skate giveaway campaign. Finally, it promoted the findings of research studies showing that in-line skating could be as healthful for people as running or bicycling. The highlights of the marketing mix developed by Rollerblade are shown in Figure 1–5.

How did things work out for Rollerblade, Inc.? Fantastically! Rollerblade's sales doubled in each year during the late 1980s. In 1990, sales of in-line skates exploded, and *Time* magazine called in-line skating "the sport of the 90s." Today, Rollerblade, Inc., production lines often turn out more than 9,000 pairs of skates a day. So they succeeded in creating a new sport and a new industry. This means that they had no problems. Right? Not at all. In a free-market system, success encourages competition and imitations. Rollerblade, Inc., created the in-line skate industry, but it has now shifted its efforts from marketing the sport to marketing its Rollerblade brand against many new competitors.

MARKETING MIX ELEMENT	ROLLERBLADE'S MARKETING MIX	RATIONALE FOR MARKETING MIX
Product	Continuously improved products, such as the *heel* brake, the 2-lb-lighter Lightning skate, and the Macroblade with buckles like ski boots	Desire to make the highest-quality product necessitates continuing new product research and extensive testing to maintain and improve quality
Price	$99 to $325 a pair	Attempt to have prices that appeal to various market segments
Promotion	Free skates to key opinion leaders, 10-K races, Team Rollerblade, "demo vans," skating videos, Club Rollerblade, and book	Attempt to increase awareness of in-line skating and its benefits and to facilitate prospects' actual trial of skates
Place	Distribution and sales of Rollerblades at major sporting goods stores throughout Canada and the United States	Desire to make it easy for prospective buyers to buy skates

▌*Figure 1–5*
Rollerblade, Inc.'s, marketing mix.

Some of Rollerblade, Inc.'s, marketing efforts: demo vans, Team Rollerblade, packaging, and print ads.

1 An organization can't satisfy the needs of all consumers, so it must focus on one or more subgroups, which are its _____.

2 What are the four marketing mix elements?

3 What are uncontrollable variables?

HOW MARKETING BECAME SO IMPORTANT

Marketing is a driving force in the modern Canadian economy. To understand why this is so and some related ethical aspects, let us look at (1) the evolution of the market orientation, (2) ethics and social responsibility in marketing, and (3) the breadth and depth of marketing activities.

EVOLUTION OF THE MARKET ORIENTATION

Many market-oriented manufacturing organizations in North America have experienced four distinct stages in the life of their firms.

Production Era   Goods were scarce in the early years of North America, so buyers were willing to accept virtually any goods that were produced and make

■ *Figure 1–6*
**Four different
orientations in the
history of North
American businesses.**

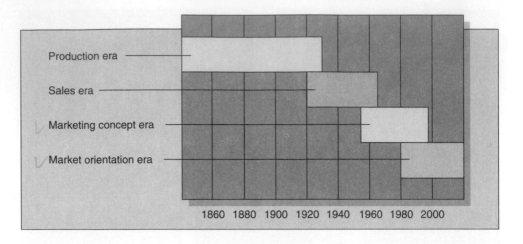

do with them as best they could. The French economist J. B. Say developed his law in the 19th century that described the prevailing business theory of the period: "Production creates its own demand." The central notion was that products would sell themselves, so the major concern of business firms was production, not marketing.[11] As shown in Figure 1–6, this production era generally continued in North America through the 1920s.

Sales Era   About that time, many firms discovered that they could produce more goods than their regular buyers could consume. Competition became more significant, and the problems of reaching the market became more complex. The usual solution was to hire more salespeople to find new markets and consumers. In simplified terms, the role of the sales force was to find consumers for the goods that a firm found it could produce best, given its existing resources. This era continued into the 1960s for many North American firms.

The Marketing Concept Era   In the 1960s, marketing became the motivating force for many companies. Many believe that the marketing concept grew, at least in part, as a result of the **consumerism** movement that also started in the 1960s. Consumers sought to obtain a greater say in the quality of products they bought and the information they received from sellers in order to increase their influence, power, and rights in dealing with institutions. As a result, the idea of the marketing concept started to take hold at this time. The **marketing concept** is the idea that an organization should (1) strive to satisfy the needs of consumers, (2) while also trying to achieve the organization's objectives. With the marketing concept, it was recognized that sales were just one element of marketing—that marketing includes a much broader range of activities. More important, the consumer became the focus of the marketing concept. The problem for many companies in the 1960s and 1970s was that they failed to implement the marketing concept effectively.

The Market Orientation Era   The 1980s saw many firms, such as McDonald's and Toyota, achieve great success in the marketplace by putting huge efforts into

MARKETING·ACTION·MEMO

Having a Marketing Orientation Means . . .

*F*or companies with a marketing orientation, marketing is not a simple business function; it is a way of doing business. Market-oriented firms know that marketing is not a new ad campaign or this month's promotion. To these companies, marketing is all-pervasive, part of everyone's job description in the organization from the receptionists to the board of directors. Market-oriented firms integrate the customer into the design of the product and design a process for buyer–seller interaction that will create substance in the exchange relationship.

Market-oriented firms reject the notion that marketing is selling things and collecting money. Marketing is not about fooling the customer, tricking the customer, or blaming the customer. To market-oriented firms, marketing is all about building relationships with customers. It is integrating the customer into the marketing decision process and creating customer value and satisfaction. In essence, marketing's ultimate assignment is to serve the customers' real needs.

Source: Adapted from R. McKenna, "Marketing Is Everything," *Harvard Business Review,* January–February 1991, pp. 65–79.

implementing the marketing concept, giving their firms what has been called a market orientation. An organization that has a **market orientation** has one or more departments (1) actively trying to understand customers' needs and the factors affecting them, (2) sharing this information across departments, and (3) using the information to meet customer needs.[12]

A key aspect of this marketing orientation is that understanding consumer needs goes far beyond talking to customers. Rather, marketing information or marketing intelligence is gleaned from many sources beyond the customer, such as observing broad industry trends, studying competitors, understanding the needs of an industrial customer's customers, and looking to likely future needs as well as present ones. It also means keeping an open mind and not allowing preconceived notions of customers to limit your opportunities. For example, remember question 5 in Figure 1–1? Well, it is true, more than 10 percent of male college students surveyed did report wearing mascara two to six times a week.[13] The information is surprising, and whether cosmetic companies would explore this finding further is another question. But it does illustrate that market-oriented firms must challenge assumptions and should not take customers or markets for granted. Research shows that firms having a demonstrated market orientation are more profitable than those lacking it.

Truly market-oriented firms design their entire organization so that everyone is involved in marketing, from the receptionist to the board of directors. In essence, it becomes everyone's job to help discover and satisfy customer needs. The accompanying Marketing Action Memo shows what it means to have a market orientation.

ETHICS AND SOCIAL RESPONSIBILITY: BALANCING CONFLICTING OBJECTIVES OF DIFFERENT GROUPS

In taking out a loan to buy a new car, should the buyer be told the total interest payments he will make over the period of the loan? Should a fast-food restaurant chain use polystyrene foam boxes to keep its hamburgers warm, thereby contributing to solid-waste problems? Or should a customer always be allowed to return merchandise she bought from a store, even if she misused the merchandise or didn't read the instructions properly? These questions pose dilemmas for buyers, for sellers, and for society as a whole. They also illustrate the complex ethical and societal issues that marketing decisions can involve.

Ethics   For example, take the issue of honouring a customer's complaint and request to return previously purchased merchandise. *Should* this request always be honoured, even if the buyer didn't follow instructions on the label and misused the merchandise? Of course not. Sellers should deal fairly with legitimate complaints to satisfy a customer, but they should not honour excessive demands of complaining customers, because the costs of doing so are eventually passed on to other customers in the form of higher prices. This marketing issue relates to **ethics,** the moral principles and values that govern the actions and decisions of an entire group. Many marketing issues go beyond legal dimensions to include ethical ones.

Social Responsibility   While many difficult ethical issues involve only the buyer and seller, others involve society as a whole. For example, suppose you buy your fast-food hamburger in a polystyrene foam warming box and put the box in the restaurant's rubbish can when you finish. Is this just a transaction between you and the restaurant? Not quite! Thrown in a rubbish dump, the plastic foam hamburger box probably won't degrade for centuries, so society will bear a portion of the cost of your hamburger purchase.

This example illustrates the issue of **social responsibility,** the idea that organizations are part of a larger society and are accountable to society for their actions. So to survive, an organization must balance ethics and social responsibility with the interests of its customers and those of other groups such as its employees, shareholders, and suppliers. Business firms must achieve this balance today under the most intense pressure they have ever known from competitors throughout the world. Because of the importance of ethical and social responsibility issues in marketing today, they—and related legal and regulatory actions—are discussed throughout this book. In addition, Chapter 4 focusses specifically on issues of ethics and social responsibility.

The well-being of society at large should also be recognized in an organization's marketing decisions.[14] In fact, some marketing experts stress the **societal marketing concept,** the view that an organization should discover and satisfy the needs of its consumers in a way that also provides for society's well-being. Western nations, as well as former communist-bloc and newly developing countries, are struggling with the issue of "sustainable development" for the benefit of their citizens, as discussed in the accompanying Ethics and Social Responsibility Alert box.

ETHICS AND SOCIAL RESPONSIBILITY ALERT

The Global Dilemma: How to Achieve Sustainable Development

World leaders and top-level conferences are increasingly using the phrase "sustainable development," a term that involves having each country find an ideal balance between protecting its environment and providing its citizens with the additional goods and services necessary to maintain and improve their standard of living.

Eastern Europe and the nations of the former Soviet Union provide an example. Tragically, poisoned air and dead rivers are the legacies of seven decades of communist rule. With over half of the households of many of these nations below the poverty level, should the immediate goal be a cleaner environment or more food, clothing, housing, and consumer goods immediately? What should the heads of these governments do? What should Western nations do to help? What should Western firms trying to enter these new, growing markets do?

Should the environment or economic growth come first? What are the societal trade-offs?

Sources: M. Simons, "Investors Shy Away from Polluted Eastern Europe," *The New York Times,* May 13, 1992, pp. A1, A4; J. O. Jackson, "Nuclear Time Bombs," *Time,* December 7, 1992, pp. 44–45; and M. Feshbach and A. Friendly, Jr., *Ecocide in the USSR* (New York: Basic Books, 1992).

This book focusses on **micromarketing,** how an individual organization directs its marketing activities and allocates its resources to benefit its customers. An overview of this approach appears in Chapter 2. This process contrasts with **macromarketing,** which looks at the aggregate flow of a nation's goods and services to benefit society.[15] Macromarketing addresses broader issues such as whether marketing costs too much, whether advertising is wasteful, and what resource scarcities and pollution side effects result from the marketing system. Macromarketing issues relate directly to the societal marketing concept and are addressed briefly in this book, but the book's main focus is on an organization's marketing activities, or micromarketing.

THE BREADTH AND DEPTH OF MARKETING

Marketing today affects every person and organization. To understand this, let's analyze (1) who markets, (2) what they market, (3) who buys and uses what is marketed, (4) who benefits from these marketing activities, and (5) how they benefit.

Who Markets? Every organization markets! It's obvious that business firms in manufacturing (Xerox, Alcan, Northern Telecom), retailing (The Bay, Toys "Я" Us, Canadian Tire), and providing services (Royal Bank, Canadian Broadcasting Corporation, Air Canada) market their offerings, as do colleges and universities (to attract good students and faculty members and donations) and government agencies (to encourage Canadians to quit smoking or stay fit). Individuals, such as entertainers or politicians, market themselves. Nonprofit organizations (Winnipeg Ballet, Canadian Museum of Civilization) also engage in marketing.[16]

Second Harvest, a charitable organization that locates and collects edible surplus food and delivers it to agencies that feed people in metropolitan Toronto, illustrates the diverse marketing-related activities of today's nonprofit organizations. The organization uses personal selling and public relations to encourage individuals and organizations to donate surplus food for redistribution to the hungry. The company has also produced a video and a newsletter to inform and educate individuals and organizations about the plight of the hungry in Toronto. The organization redistributes millions of pounds of food—food that would otherwise go wasted—to emergency food outlets in Toronto that try to feed some of the estimated 400,000 people who go hungry in Toronto every day. Second Harvest has taken other initiatives such as presenting self-help and educational programs for the poor in order to find a long-term solution to the hunger problem.

What Is Marketed?   Goods, services, and ideas are marketed. Goods are physical objects, such as toothpaste, cameras, or computers, that satisfy consumer needs. Services are intangible items such as airline trips, financial advice, or

Second Harvest, a nonprofit organization, uses marketing to achieve its goals.

telephone calls. Ideas are intangibles such as thoughts about actions or causes. Some of these goods, services, or ideas—such as lawn mowers, dry cleaning, and promotion of annual physical examinations—may be bought or accepted by individuals for their own use. Others, such as high-volume office copiers and vending machine repair services, are bought by organizations. Finally, the products marketed in today's shrinking globe are increasingly likely to cross a nation's boundaries and involve exports, imports, and international marketing (covered in Chapter 23).

Who Buys and Uses What Is Marketed?   Both individuals and organizations buy and use goods and services that are marketed. **Ultimate consumers** are people—whether 80 years or eight months old—who use the goods and services purchased for a household. A household may consist of 1 or 10 individuals. (The way one or more of the people in the household buy is the topic of consumer behaviour, discussed in Chapter 6.) In contrast, **organizational buyers** are units such as manufacturers, retailers, or government agencies that buy goods and services for their own use or for resale. (Industrial and organizational buyer behaviour is covered in Chapter 7.) The terms *consumers, buyers,* and *customers* may each be used for both ultimate consumers and organizations; there is no consistency. In this book, you will be able to tell from the example whether the buyers are ultimate consumers, organizations, or both.

Who Benefits?   In our free-enterprise society there are three specific groups that benefit from effective marketing: consumers who buy, organizations that sell, and society as a whole. True competition between products and services in the marketplace ensures that we consumers can obtain (1) the best products and services available (2) at the lowest price. Providing the maximum number of choices leads to the consumer satisfaction and quality of life that we have come to expect from our economic system.

Organizations that provide need-satisfying products with effective marketing actions—for example McDonald's, IBM, Avon, and the Royal Bank— have blossomed, but this competition creates problems for the ineffective competitors. For example, Osborne Computers and DeLorean cars were well-known names a few years back, but may now be unknown to you. Effective marketing actions result in rewards for organizations that serve consumers and in millions of marketing jobs such as those described in Appendix B.

Finally, effective marketing benefits the whole country. It enhances competition, which in turn both improves the quality of products and services and lowers their prices. This makes the country more competitive in world markets and provides jobs and a higher standard of living for its citizens.

How Do Consumers Benefit?   Marketing creates **utility,** the benefits or value received by users of the product. Utility is the result of the marketing exchange process. There are four different utilities: form, place, time, and possession. The production of the good or service constitutes *form utility. Place utility* means having the offering available where consumers need it, whereas *time utility* means having it available when needed. *Possession utility* is getting the product to consumers so they can use it.

General Electric's medical CAT scanners, Johnson & Johnson's Acuvue contact lenses, and Dell's personal computers have set world–class standards for customer value. For their strategies, see the Marketing Action Memo and text.

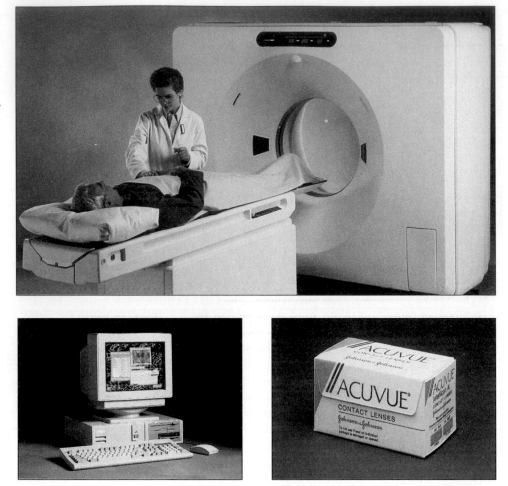

Thus, marketing provides consumers with place, time, and possession utilities by making the good or service available at the right place and right time for the right consumer. Although form utility usually arises in manufacturing activity and could be seen as outside the scope of marketing, an organization's marketing activities influence product features and packaging. Marketing creates its utilities by bridging space (place utility) and hours (time utility) to provide products (form utility) for consumers to own and use (possession utility).

Concept Check

1   Many firms have gone through four distinct orientations for their business: starting with the _____ era and ending with today's _____ era.

2   What are the two key characteristics of the marketing concept?

3   What three things are included in this book under the term *product?*

MARKETING · ACTION · MEMO

The 1990s as the "Value Decade": Learning a New Vocabulary

Until quite recently, it was assumed that customer value was how prospective buyers judged a good or service on some combination of quality and price. Today, value is a much broader concept that includes convenience, on-time delivery, both before-sale and after-sale service, and so on.

Curiously, to compete on customer value a manufacturer or retailer doesn't have to compete on all these dimensions. Management experts Michael Treacy and Fred Wiersema intensively studied 40 firms and concluded that firms often gain industry leadership by narrowing—not broadening—their focus. Instead, many successful firms have chosen to deliver outstanding customer value with one of three value strategies:

1 *A practical excellence:* providing customers with reliable offerings at competitive prices and with the most convenient delivery. While a college student in the mid-1980s, Michael Dell saw a strategy to outdo both IBM and Compaq by selling PCs through dealers to novices—a focus on the delivery system. Dell's annual revenues of almost $2 billion today attest to the success of the strategy.

2 *Customer intimacy:* segmenting and targeting markets precisely and then tailoring offerings to the exact demands of customers in those segments. General Electric's Medical Systems Department offers CAT scanners, from $350,000 to over $1 million each, that are targeted at customers with differing imaging needs.

3 *Product leadership:* providing customers with leading-edge offerings that enhance use by customers to make competitors' offerings obsolete. A Johnson & Johnson division produces specialty contact lenses. When one of its employees heard about a new Danish technology, Johnson & Johnson moved quickly and introduced the revolutionary Acuvue disposable contact lens.

A creative marketing manager in a firm tries to identify what "value" really means to the key segments of customers it seeks to serve and then tries to deliver that value.

Sources: M. Treacy and F. Wiersema, "Customer Intimacy and Other Value Disciplines," *Harvard Business Review*, January–February 1993, pp. 84–93; F. Rice, "What Intelligent Consumers Want," *Fortune*, December 28, 1992, pp. 56–60: S. Sherman, "How to Prosper in the Value Decade," *Fortune*, November 30, 1992, pp. 90–103; and C. Power, "Value Marketing," *Business Week*, November 11, 1991, pp. 132–40.

CUSTOMER VALUE: THE NEW MARKETING IMPERATIVE

Almost everyone agrees that creating and providing "customer value" is *the* critical marketing issue for the 1990s. Increased global competition, tremendous availability of product choices, and a growing population of better-informed, highly educated, professional consumers have pushed the concept of customer value to the forefront of the marketplace. Very simply, successful marketing involves obtaining and retaining customers. In today's marketplace, accomplishing these objectives will be primarily based on how well a firm can provide unique value to its customers. For our purposes, **customer value** is the combination of benefits received by targeted buyers that includes quality, price, convenience, on-time delivery, and both before- and after-sale service.

So, customer value is not just price, but a multifaceted concept. Moreover, it is the customer that ultimately determines what constitutes value. It is the marketer's job, then, to determine what value means to the customer and then deliver that value. The Marketing Action Memo on page 25 shows how Dell, General Electric, and Johnson & Johnson have followed very successful—but somewhat different—strategies in providing value to their targeted customers.[17]

QUALITY AND CUSTOMER VALUE

Quality is such a key element in today's concept of customer value that marketers must understand its dimensions, especially what quality means to the customer. **Quality** consists of three components: (1) conformance to standards or specifications; (2) design quality, or the intended degree of excellence; and (3) fitness for use, or the match between the product or service and the customer's needs.[18] Research shows that most product quality defects that occur are traceable to poor design quality and not to the production line as originally believed. When quality is viewed from the customer's perspective—as degree of fitness for use—a number of dimensions may be considered before the customer can judge the quality of a product or service, including (1) performance, (2) features, (3) reliability, (4) durability, (5) serviceability, (6) aesthetics, and (7) perceived quality (when quality cannot be judged accurately, the customer may rely on image, brand name, or advertising).

Marketers who place increased emphasis on quality will generally increase the customer's perception of value. But the marketer must focus on the dimensions of quality that are most meaningful and most valuable to the target customer. The success of Japanese products in world markets can be traced largely to Japan's preoccupation with all three dimensions of quality. For example, for over four decades, Japan has applied W. Edward Deming's simple chain-of-events model, linking quality, markets, and jobs (see Figure 1–7).

The Japanese focus not only on conformance to standards, or quality on the production line, but also on design quality, including simplicity of assembly and the match between the product and the way the customer uses the product. Most important, the Japanese stress the dimensions of quality most important to the customer, which would include reliability and durability in products such as automobiles. The results of the Japanese quest for quality have been staggering. Japan has risen from the ashes of World War II to become the wealthiest nation in the world. The Japanese provide, in many cases, better-quality products at lower prices than their Canadian and American competitors. The combination of quality and lower prices is extremely valuable to customers. A 1994 poll of consumers in 20 countries revealed that Japan was rated number one in terms of overall quality of manufactured goods. Canada ranked sixth in this poll and

▌ *Figure 1–7*
The Deming chain reaction linking quality, markets, and jobs.

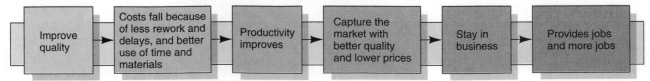

Source: Adapted from W. Edwards Deming, *Out of Crisis* (Cambridge, MA: MIT Center for Advanced Engineering Study, 1986).

Chrysler's focus on quality has made its minivan the leader in its category.

Russia was ranked last.[19] Even Canadian consumers in the same survey ranked the Japanese (as well as German) products higher in quality than their own domestically manufactured products.

But many Canadian companies are now following the Japanese lead and are placing increased emphasis on quality. Total quality control (TQC), total quality management (TQM), and quality improvement process (QIP) programs have become part of the competitive arsenal of many Canadian and American firms in an attempt to ensure that consumers receive quality products and the value they expect.

Chrysler Canada, for example, has won several awards for its minivan product, built in Windsor, Ontario, primarily because of its focus on design quality and its ability to meet customer needs. The concepts of "value-added" strategies and quality improvement as ways to achieve marketing success will be discussed throughout the book.

Summary

1 Combining personal experience with more formal marketing knowledge will enable us to identify and solve important marketing problems.

2 Marketing is the process of planning and executing the conception, pricing, promotion, and distribution of ideas, goods, and services to create exchanges that satisfy individual and organizational objectives. This definition relates to two primary goals of marketing: (*a*) assessing the needs of consumers and (*b*) satisfying them.

3 For marketing to occur, it is necessary to have (*a*) two or more parties with unmet needs, (*b*) a desire and an ability to satisfy them, (*c*) communication between the parties, and (*d*) something to exchange.

4 Because an organization doesn't have the resources to satisfy the needs of all consumers, it selects a target market of potential customers—a subset of the entire market—on which to focus its marketing mix.

5 The marketing mix is designed to satisfy customer needs and includes product, price, promotion, and place. These marketing mix elements (the *four Ps*) are called the *controllable variables,* because they are under the general control of the marketing department.

6 Environmental factors, also called *uncontrollable variables,* are largely beyond the organization's control. These include social, technological, economic, competitive, and regulatory forces.

7 In marketing terms, Canadian business history is divided into four periods: the production era, the sales era, the marketing concept era, and the current market orientation era.

8 Customer and organizational needs must be balanced against needs of employees, shareholders, suppliers, and society as a whole. This involves issues of ethics and social responsibility.

9 Both profit-making and nonprofit organizations perform marketing activities. They market products, services, and ideas that benefit all consumers, the organization, and the nation. Marketing creates utilities that give benefits, or customer value, to users.

10 Customer value, perhaps *the* critical marketing issue of the 1990s, is the unique combination of benefits received by targeted buyers that includes quality, price, convenience, on-time delivery, and both before-sale and after-sale service. Providing quality products and services, as defined by the customer, is a vital component of perceived customer value.

Key Terms and Concepts

marketing p. 8
exchange p. 8
market p. 12
target market p. 13
marketing mix p. 13
uncontrollable environmental factors p. 14
consumerism p. 18
marketing concept p. 18
market orientation p. 19
ethics p. 20

social responsibility p. 20
societal marketing concept p. 20
micromarketing p. 21
macromarketing p. 21
ultimate consumers p. 23
organizational buyers p. 23
utility p. 23
customer value p. 25
quality p. 26

Chapter Problems and Applications

1 What consumer wants (or benefits) are met by the following products or stores? (*a*) Carnation Instant Breakfast, (*b*) Adidas running shoes, (*c*) Hertz Rent A Car, and (*d*) catalogue showroom retail stores.

2 Each of the four products or stores in question 1 has substitutes. Respective examples are (*a*) a ham-and-egg breakfast, (*b*) regular tennis shoes, (*c*) taking a bus, and (*d*) a department store. What consumer benefits might these substitutes have in each case that some consumers might value more highly than those products mentioned in question 1?

3 What are the characteristics (e.g., age, income, education) of the target market customers for the following products or services? (*a*) *National Geographic* magazine, (*b*) *Playboy* magazine, (*c*) Blue Jays baseball team, and (*d*) the Canadian Open tennis tournament.

4 A college in a metropolitan area wishes to increase its evening-school offerings of business-related courses such as marketing, accounting, finance, and management. Who are the target market customers (students) for these courses?

5 What actions involving the four marketing mix elements might be used to reach the target market in question 4?

6 What environmental factors (uncontrollable variables) must the college in question 4 consider in designing its marketing mix?

7 Polaroid introduced instant still photography, which proved to be a tremendous success. Yet Polavision, its instant movie system, was a total disaster. (*a*) What wants and benefits does each provide to users? (*b*) Which of these do you think contributed to Polavision's failure? (*c*) What research could have been undertaken that might have revealed Polavision's drawbacks?

8 Rollerblade, Inc., is now trying to "grow" in-line skating—and the company—globally, just as it succeeded in doing in Canada and the United States. What are the advantages and disadvantages of trying to reach new global markets?

9 Does a firm have the right to "create" wants and try to persuade consumers to buy goods and services they didn't know about earlier? What are examples of "good" and "bad" want creation? Who should decide what is good and bad?

Marketing in the Organization: An Overview

AFTER READING THIS CHAPTER YOU SHOULD BE ABLE TO:

▼ Understand the relationship between strategic corporate planning and the strategic marketing process.

▼ Describe how an organization's mission, objectives, and corporate strategy set the stage for the strategic marketing process.

▼ Explain the importance of a situation analysis and SWOT in the strategic marketing process.

▼ Understand the nature of marketing strategy.

▼ Describe what is included in a good marketing plan.

Canadian Tire Has More Than Just Tires . . . It Has a New Marketing Plan, Too.

When Stephen Bachand took over the reins of Canadian Tire, his first order of business was to visit as many of the chain's 424 stores as possible in his first 100 days on the job. But it wasn't to glad-hand Canadian Tire's associate dealers (franchisees); it was to spread the message that the 71-year-old company needed to be invigorated. What it needed was a new strategy, a new plan. Canadian Tire had been slow to respond to the rapidly changing marketplace and now found itself being squeezed on one end by no-frills, warehouse-style competitors and on the other by more specialized, higher-end stores. But before any action could be taken, Bachand had to convince the fiercely independent dealers that change was necessary.

Sagging profits in the previous few years were a signal that change was needed and was needed quickly. Bachand believed that part of Canadian Tire's problem was that it failed to move decisively in an environment characterized by a shortening of the life cycle of retailing ideas, an environment where you must move quickly or be left behind. Canadian Tire had just developed a five-year marketing plan before Bachand took over as president, which included the introduction of large-format stores. Bachand reviewed the plan, kept what made sense, and introduced new changes designed to exploit available marketing opportunities.

For example, Bachand's plan included introducing a wider range of national brands, including tire and automotive products to augment Canadian

Tire's famous Motormaster house or private brands. Goodyear and Michelin already produced the store's Motormaster tires, but those companies' own national brands would now assume wall space next to the private label. Bachand said he wasn't diminishing the importance of the house brand; rather he was looking for another revenue stream. "There is a segment," Bachand argued, "that wants national brands, and we have denied ourselves of this opportunity to get any part of that business."[1] Bachand's objective was to take back the leadership role Canadian Tire had once had in its market.

This chapter introduces you to marketing's role in the organization. It describes how market-driven firms can develop and execute marketing plans that allow them to grow and prosper in a dynamic marketplace. It also introduces you to many of the important aspects of marketing covered in detail in the chapters that follow.

STRATEGIC CORPORATE PLANNING PROCESS

Key marketing decisions are made within limits set by the organization. Specifically, the organization's strategic corporate plan sets the framework for the strategic marketing process. The **strategic corporate planning process** involves the steps taken at an organization's corporate level to develop long-run master approaches for survival and growth. In contrast, the **strategic marketing process** involves the steps taken at the product and market levels to allocate resources to viable marketing opportunities and includes phases of planning, implementation, and control.[2] Key steps in these two processes are shown in Figure 2–1. Other units in the organization—assumed here to be a manufacturing firm—develop detailed plans based on directions from the strategic corporate planning process.

▌*Figure 2–1*
Steps in the strategic corporate planning and the strategic marketing processes.

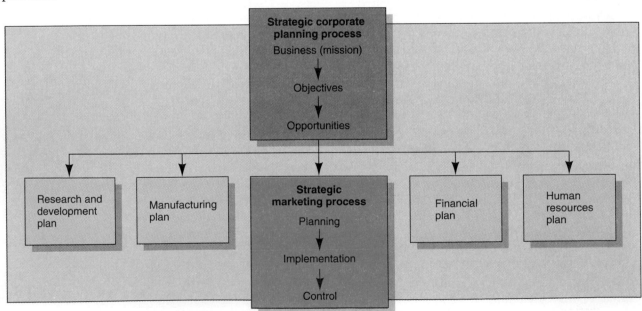

Senior executives—usually including a senior marketing person—within an organization are responsible for the development of the organization's mission, objectives, and strategic corporate direction. The strategic marketing process flows logically from the strategic corporate planning process, since corporate survival and growth are largely dependent on marketing strategy and activities. Thus, while marketing decisions are made within limits set by the organization, those decisions are a natural outgrowth of the strategic corporate planning process. In essence, objectives and strategy at the corporate level are "rolled into" synergistic objectives and strategy at the marketing level.

While Figure 2–1 provides a "hierarchical," or layered, depiction of the processes, they can be very "fluidlike" rather than hierarchical, especially in firms where marketing is accepted as a philosophy, or as a way of doing business. In such market-driven organizations, the strategic corporate plan is based largely on an external, or market, focus. Internal resources and skills are examined only in light of available opportunities in the external market environment.

Marketing, then, as a functional area of business within such organizations, takes on more importance. Marketing is recognized as being ultimately responsible for corporate revenue generation through the creation and provision of need-satisfying products to selected target markets. Therefore, marketing often becomes the focal point in the strategic corporate planning process. Naturally, other functional areas of business such as accounting, finance, human resources, production, and operations are important to corporate success, but in market-driven firms, marketing becomes everybody's business. Every area of the organization is designed and evaluated according to how well it supports the marketing function. In production-oriented firms, production dictates to marketing, but in market-driven firms, marketing dictates production.

Before we examine the strategic marketing process, let's briefly discuss some key elements of the strategic corporate planning process that set the framework or parameters for marketing in the organization.

DEFINING THE ORGANIZATION'S BUSINESS (MISSION)

Organizations that think and act strategically, such as Northern Telecom, 3M, Dow Canada, Bombardier, Canadian Tire, and Alcan Aluminum, often ask themselves, What "business"—in the broadest sense—are we in? The answer can dramatically narrow or broaden the range of marketing opportunities available to an organization. Railroads may have let other forms of transportation take business away from them because they saw themselves in the "railroad business" rather than the "transportation business."[3]

This narrow definition hurt railroads, because they failed to design effective marketing strategies to compete with a broad range of modes of transportation, including airlines, trucks, bus lines, and cars.

Focussing the Business with the Three Cs   Business theorists point out that three Cs—customers, competitors, and the company itself—interrelate to establish the basic character of an organization's business.[4] An **organizational business definition (mission)** is a statement of the type of customer the organization wishes to serve, the specific needs of its customers, and the means

M A R K E T I N G · A C T I O N · M E M O

The Mission as the Foundation of Corporate Strategy

Why is an organization's business definition, or mission, regarded as the foundation of corporate strategy? First, the mission reveals the true function or purpose of the business. If you follow Peter Drucker, who argued the only purpose of a business is to "create a customer," there has to be an explicit recognition of how the business satisfies the needs of its target customers. Second, the mission sets the boundaries of effort and the horizons for growth, or broad opportunities, to be sought. Third, it provides guidance and direction, while focusing the energies of all parts of the organization. As such, the mission is the basic starting point for strategy development. A change in mission may trigger dramatic changes in strategic direction, resource allocation, and performance measures.

Missions tend to evolve slowly as the organization expands its capabilities to serve new needs or related

market segments, develops or acquires new technologies, responds to changing customer expectations, or matches competitors' offerings. Missions are most likely to be reviewed when performance is lagging, new competitors are emerging, or a change in senior management leads to the questioning of old beliefs or conventional wisdom. Rather than wait for trouble, it is better to recognize that evolutionary expansions or contractions in mission have profound strategic implications and that the current mission may reflect only an uneasy compromise in the continuing trade-off between the benefits of breadth versus narrowness in the scope of the mission.

Source: Adapted from F. G. Crane, *Achieving Prosperity in Business*. Forthcoming. and G. S. Day, *Market Driven Strategy*, (New York: Free Press, 1990).

or technology by which it will serve these needs. In essence, it clarifies the nature of existing products, markets, and functions the organization presently provides. The business definition (mission) affects the organization's growth prospects by establishing guidelines for selecting opportunities in light of the organization's values, resources, and customer needs, its competitors' actions, and changes in other environmental factors. As the accompanying Marketing Action Memo points out, the mission is the foundation of an organization's corporate strategy. Many companies have also established corporate *core values* or *guiding principles* that reinforce their business definition and help clarify it to employees and customers (Figure 2–2).

SPECIFYING THE ORGANIZATION'S CORPORATE OBJECTIVES

An organization must translate the broad statement of its business (mission) into **corporate objectives**—specific, measurable goals it seeks to achieve and by which it can measure its performance. For our purposes, the terms *goals* and *objectives* mean the same thing.

How an Organization's Objectives Relate to Its Mission   An example of a precise policy statement of an organization's mission and objectives is that of Sara Lee Corporation (Figure 2–3), a firm with manufacturing operations in over 30 countries that markets its branded products in over 120 countries. Note

❚ *Figure 2–2*
**Example of core values
of Dow Chemical
Canada Inc.**

DOW CORE VALUES

Long-term profit growth is essential to ensure the prosperity and well-being of Dow employees, stockholders, and customers. How we achieve this objective is as important as the objective itself. Fundamental to our success are the core values we believe in and practice.

Employees are the source of Dow's success. We treat them with respect, promote teamwork, and encourage personal freedom and growth. Excellence in performance is sought and rewarded.

Customers will receive our strongest possible commitment to meet their needs with high-quality products and superior service.

Our products are based on continuing excellence and innovation in chemistry-related sciences and technology.

Our conduct demonstrates a deep concern for ethics, citizenship, safety, health, and the environment.

Source: Courtesy of Dow Chemical Canada Inc.

that the objectives are specific targets that flow directly from the broader statement about Sara Lee Corporation's business.

In fact, the mission statement is broad enough to cover four business units that produce well-known brand names like Chef Pierre, Sara Lee, Hanes Hosiery, L'eggs, and Kiwi. Even with this diversity of global products, Sara Lee Corporation's statement about its mission and objectives gives direction to its two growth strategies for the entire organization and its business units: (1) increase corporate returns by emphasizing profitable growth, and (2) accelerate growth by extending major brands and products globally.

All organizations, both profit and nonprofit, require objectives of some kind. A **business firm** is a privately owned organization that serves its customers in order to earn a profit. In contrast, a **nonprofit organization** is a nongovernmental organization that serves its customers but does not have profit as an objective. Objectives of these two different kinds of organizations are discussed briefly in the following sections. For simplicity in the rest of the book,

❚ *Figure 2–3*
**Mission and goals of
Sara Lee Corporation.**

BUSINESS (MISSION)

Sara Lee Corporation's mission is:

- To be a premier global-branded consumer packaged goods company.
- To aspire to have the leading position in each product category and in each world marketplace in which it participates.

GOALS

Sara Lee Corporation strives to achieve three financial goals:

- Real (inflation-adjusted) growth in earnings per share of 8 percent per year over time.
- A return on equity of at least 20 percent.
- A total-debt-to-capital ratio of no more than 40 percent.

Source: 1992 *Annual Report* (Chicago: Sara Lee Corporation, 1992).

the terms *firm, company, corporation,* and *organization* are used to cover both business and nonprofit operations.

Objectives of Business Firms   Business firms, with some exceptions cited later, must earn profits to survive. **Profit** is the reward to a business firm for the risk it undertakes in offering a product for sale: the money left over after a firm's total expenses are subtracted from its total revenues. As long as profits are earned fairly and ethically—and not through collusion, monopoly power, or other unfair business practices—they represent a reward for good performance. Thousands of firms fail every year because they are not run well enough and do not serve consumers thoroughly enough to make profits and continue operations. The profit of a business firm may be expressed in actual money earned during a time period ("an after-tax profit of $5 million") or in terms of the money earned as a percentage of invested capital ("an after-tax profit of 15 percent return on investment [ROI]").

Several different objectives have been identified that business firms can pursue, each of which has some limitations:

- *Survival.* A firm may choose a safe action with reasonable payoff instead of one with a large return that might endanger its future. It must survive today to be in business tomorrow.
- *Profit.* Classic economic theory assumes that a firm seeks to maximize long-run profit, achieving as high a financial return on its investment as possible. One difficulty with this is what is meant by *long run.* A year? Five years? Twenty years?
- *Social responsibility.* A firm may respond to advocates of corporate responsibility and seek to balance conflicting goals of consumers, employees, and shareholders to promote overall welfare of all these groups, even at the expense of profits. The Body Shop (discussed later in this chapter) is an example of such a firm.
- *Shareholder value.* Many business firms will determine objectives regarding value that shareholders (or stockholders) receive as a reward for investing in the company. Often shareholder value is tied directly to the profit objectives.
- *Customer value.* In market-driven organizations, a corporate objective of creating customer value is often defined. In market-driven firms, it is commonly accepted that the creation of customer value is what leads to the creation of shareholder value. In other words, providing customers with products they deem valuable leads to corporate profitability and greater returns to the shareholders. Shareholder value, on the other hand, doesn't necessarily create customer value.

Whatever its primary objective, a business must achieve a profit level that is high enough for it to remain in operation. Satisfactory profits are possible only if consumer needs are identified and satisfied. Procter & Gamble (P&G) is a good example. It has a corporate objective of a 10 percent after-tax profit from any given product. To achieve this objective, it uncovers needs and manufactures products that have developed tremendous consumer loyalty. Many of its high-visibility brands introduced decades ago still dominate the categories in which they compete: Ivory soap (introduced in 1879), Crisco (1912), Tide

(1947), Pampers (1956), and Crest (1966). The long market lives of these products are proof of P&G's ability to satisfy consumer needs.

Objectives of Nonprofit Organizations Many private organizations that do not seek profits also exist in Canada. Examples are museums, symphony orchestras, hospitals, social service organizations, and research institutes. These organizations strive to provide goods and services to consumers with the greatest efficiency and the least cost. The nonprofit organization's survival depends on meeting the needs of the consumers it serves. Although technically not falling under the definition of nonprofit organization, government agencies also perform marketing activities in trying to achieve their objective of serving the public good. Such organizations include all levels of federal, provincial, and local government, as well as publicly funded schools and universities. As discussed later, marketing is an important activity for nonprofit firms and government agencies, just as it is for profit-making businesses.

Pampers is an example of a profitable P&G product.

IDENTIFYING THE ORGANIZATION'S OPPORTUNITIES

To achieve corporate growth, an organization tries to find the right match between the market opportunities in its environment and its own resources and skills. Answers to three questions help an organization focus on key opportunities:[5]

1 *What might we do,* in terms of environmental opportunities we foresee?
2 *What do we do best,* in terms of our unique resources and special skills?
3 *What must we do,* in terms of achieving success in a market or with a product?

These questions are generally answered through the use of a situation analysis and a SWOT analysis. A **situation analysis** is an internal and external assessment of all the possible strategy-related factors that can mitigate or enhance an organization's opportunities for corporate survival and growth. An important output of the situation analysis is the construction of a SWOT analysis. The acronym **SWOT** refers to a simple, effective technique a firm can use to appraise its internal corporate *s*trengths and *w*eaknesses and external *o*pportunities and *t*hreats. It is the SWOT that allows the firm to examine only those *critical* factors that can have a major effect on its future.

Through the use of a situation analysis and SWOT, the organization can find a match between available opportunities and its unique resources and special skills (what it might do, and what it does best). These resources and skills (sometimes referred to as an organization's **distinctive competencies**) "drive," or form the basis for, the development of a firm's **sustainable competitive advantage (SCA)**—a strength, relative to competitors, to be used in the markets a firm serves or the products it offers. A firm's SCA is a pivotal part of "what the firm must do" in terms of achieving success in a particular market or with a specific product. The SCA concept will be further discussed later in this chapter. We will also discuss further the roles that a situation analysis and SWOT (conducted at the marketing level) play in completing the strategic marketing process.

General Electric used a situation analysis and SWOT to discover new growth opportunities such as its futuristic plastic home.

Concept Check

1 What are the three Cs that help define an organization's business or mission?

2 Which is more specific, an organization's business definition (mission) or its corporate objectives?

3 What is profit?

THE STRATEGIC MARKETING PROCESS

As we have seen, the strategic corporate planning process sets the stage for the organization's strategic marketing process. As mentioned earlier in the chapter, the strategic marketing process involves the steps taken at the product and market levels to allocate resources to viable marketing opportunities, and it includes phases of planning, implementation, and control.

Broad marketing strategies are, implicitly or explicitly, part of the strategic corporate planning process. But decisions regarding the specific scope and nature of the marketing strategies to be undertaken are generally dealt with in the strategic marketing process itself. For example, corporately, Canadian Tire decided it wanted to regain its market leadership role in its category, but how to do so, specifically, is a marketing strategy question and one that must be addressed on a marketing level. In market-driven firms, marketing strategy and corporate strategy are inextricably linked. In fact, marketing strategy sets the tone and direction for strategic decision making regarding other functional aspects of the business. In Canadian Tire's case, the new head of the company is a marketer, which makes it much easier to integrate both corporate and marketing strategy.

I SITUATION ANALYSIS	
Internal assessment	(Chapters 2, 21)
External assessment	(Chapters 2, 3)
II SWOT	(Chapter 2)
(Internal strengths and weaknesses, and external opportunities and threats)	
III MARKETING OBJECTIVES	(Chapter 2)
IV MARKETING STRATEGY	(Chapters 21–22)
Generic strategy options	(Chapter 21)
Target market (market segment)	(Chapter 9)
Sustainable competitive advantage and positioning	(Chapters 9, 21)
V MARKETING MIX	(Chapters 11–20)
Product	(Chapters 11–12)
Price	(Chapters 13–14)
Place (distribution)	(Chapters 15–17)
Promotion (integrated marketing communications)	(Chapters 18–20)
VI BUDGET	(Chapters 21–22)
Forecasts	(Chapter 10)
VII MARKETING ORGANIZATION	(Chapter 22)
VIII CONTROL AND EVALUATION	(Chapter 22)

▌ *Figure 2–4*
Format for a strategic marketing plan.

The essential output of the strategic marketing process is to produce a plan of action that will realize or achieve the corporate objectives set through the strategic corporate planning process, as well as specific marketing objectives determined through the strategic marketing process. This plan of action is generally committed to paper and is called a **marketing plan.**

The actual format, design, and structure of a marketing plan will vary from organization to organization, but every marketing plan should at least include:

- An analysis of the marketing situation (situation analysis and SWOT: internal strengths and weaknesses, and external opportunities and threats).
- Specific and measurable marketing objectives.
- Marketing strategy with identified target markets, and sustainable competitive advantage.
- The nature of the marketing mix being offered to the target segments.
- The marketing budget, including projected sales and expenses.
- A description of the marketing organization designed to execute the plan.
- Control and evaluation processes and procedures.

Figure 2–4 shows a format for a strategic marketing plan that could be used by almost any organization. Notice that we have indicated the chapters in the text that deal with the elements contained in the plan. While the later chapters provide in-depth coverage of most of the components contained in a marketing plan, we will now briefly discuss the elements of the plan, placing particular emphasis on the situation analysis and SWOT.

I SITUATION ANALYSIS

As we mentioned earlier, a situation analysis conducted at the corporate level involves an internal and external assessment of all the strategy-related factors that can mitigate or enhance an organization's opportunities for corporate survival and growth.

At the marketing level, a situation analysis involves (1) an internal assessment of the factors relevant to the development and execution of marketing strategies and (2) an external assessment of the market or industry as well as the overall environment in which the firm competes. The situation analysis also involves identifying and interpreting potential "trends" in the environment, sometimes referred to as the environmental scanning process, which is discussed in detail in Chapter 3. At the corporate level, the internal aspect of the situation analysis is sometimes called a **business audit.** At the marketing level, the internal assessment is commonly referred to as a **marketing audit** (often used in both the planning and control stages of the strategic marketing process).

Most marketing audits go beyond the marketing function to include other areas of the business, especially those that impact directly on the development and execution of possible marketing strategies (e.g., financial resources, production capabilities). The marketing audit is discussed in detail in Chapter 22.

▌ *Figure 2–5*
Situation analysis.

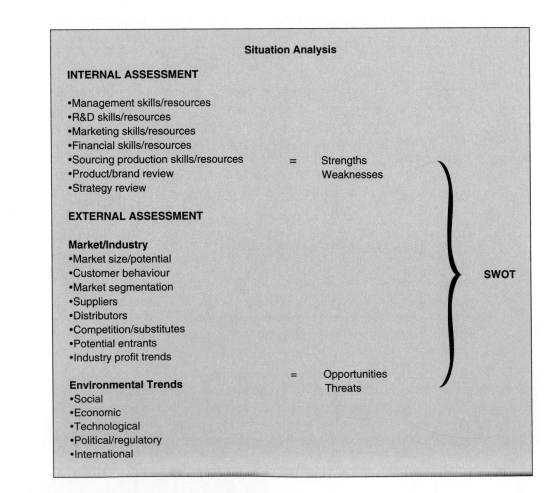

The situation analysis at the corporate level is most often completed by having each of the functional areas of the business, including marketing, making specific contributions. Since corporate strategy is strongly linked to marketing strategy, there is a strong relationship between the types of analysis conducted at both the corporate and marketing levels. Figure 2–5 shows what is examined in a situation analysis as well as the key output of such an analysis, a SWOT analysis.

II   SWOT

As we mentioned earlier, the most important output of a situation analysis is a SWOT analysis. Done at corporate level, the SWOT involves more than just marketing. But a corporate SWOT does provide valuable direct input into the SWOT that is conducted at the marketing level. By conducting a marketing-related SWOT, the firm can build on vital marketing strengths, correct glaring weaknesses, exploit significant marketing opportunities, and avoid disaster-laden threats.[6] Figure 2–6 shows what a marketing SWOT might look like for Canadian Tire.

The SWOT reveals that Canadian Tire has many strengths, but it does have some weaknesses, particularly with regard to a lack of customer orientation at the retail level, and the fact that some associate dealers (store managers) have to be convinced of the need for change, which can delay implementation of new market-driven initiatives. But given its new corporate leadership, financial

▌*Figure 2–6*
A "SWOT" at Canadian Tire.

INTERNAL	STRENGTHS	WEAKNESSES
	New corporate leadership Good geographic market coverage High corporate and brand name recognition Good supplier network Solid private-label product line Financial strength Strong core automotive supply and service business	Lack of customer focus at the retail level; product-oriented, not customer-oriented Some associate dealers sceptical of change; need to be sold on the concept of change Many smaller, older stores
EXTERNAL	OPPORTUNITIES	THREATS
	Potential to make over and expand many stores Wider, deeper product lines, augmented with national brands Cost reductions through electronic data interchange (EDI) Everyday low pricing (EDLP) to attract value-conscious customers New merchandising techniques Tool loan program for the do-it-yourself (DIY) segment	Fragmented, maturing market Aggressive, existing competition New potential entrants Customers more value-conscious Lack of consumer confidence in the economy, delaying purchases of larger-ticket items

resources, and name recognition and the strength of its "core" automotive supply and service component, Canadian Tire does have opportunities to exploit.

With electronic data interchange (EDI), Canadian Tire stores can track inventory and order directly from vendors. This will keep costs down and allow Canadian Tire to serve customers effectively. EDI also plays a role in the everyday low-price (EDLP) policy designed to attract the value-conscious consumer. To attract the do-it-yourself (DIY) segment, there is a tool loan program. Finally, in an effort to attract customers who want national brands, Canadian Tire is augmenting its strong line of house brands with some highly visible and sought-after national brands.

III   MARKETING OBJECTIVES

Marketing objectives, as mentioned earlier, should flow directly from the corporate objectives set by the organization. The most common marketing objectives include:

▌ *Figure 2–7*
Stating objectives: how to tell a "good" objective from a "bad" one.

For the managerial purpose of objectives to be fulfilled as well as they might, objectives need to meet five specifications:

1. An objective should relate to a single specific topic. (It should not be stated in the form of a vague abstraction or a pious platitude—"our objective is to be more aggressive marketers.")
2. An objective should relate to a result, not to an activity to be performed. (The objective is the result of the activity, not the performing of the activity.)
3. An objective should be measurable (stated in quantitative terms whenever feasible).
4. An objective should contain a time deadline for its achievement.
5. An objective should be challenging but achievable.

Consider the following examples:

- Poor: Our objective is to increase sales revenue and unit volume.

   Remarks: How much? Also, because the statement relates to two topics, it may be inconsistent. Increasing unit volume may require a price cut, and if demand is price inelastic, sales revenue would fall as unit volume rises. No time frame for achievement is indicated.

   Better: Our objective this calendar year is to increase sales revenues from $30 million to $35 million; we expect this to be accomplished by selling 1 million units at an average price of $35.
- Poor: Our objective in 1996 is to boost advertising expenditures by 15 percent.

   Remarks: Advertising is an activity, not a result. The advertising objective should be stated in terms of what result the extra advertising is intended to produce.

   Better: Our objective is to boost our market share from 8 percent to 10 percent in 1996 with the help of a 15 percent increase in advertising expenditures.

Source: Adapted from A. A. Thompson, Jr., and A. J. Strickland, *Strategic Management: Concepts and Cases* (Plano, TX: Business Publications Inc., 1984), pp. 24–25

- *Sales.* In general, most marketing objectives include an objective relative to sales, stated in terms of units sold or dollars.
- *Market share.* A firm may also state a marketing objective in terms of maintaining or increasing its market share. **Market share** is the ratio of sales revenue of the firm to the total sales revenue of all firms in the industry, including the firm itself.
- *Customer satisfaction.* If creating customer value is a stated corporate objective, a related marketing objective of achieving and maintaining customer satisfaction is also generally stated. The concepts of customer value and customer satisfaction are often directly related.

Other, more specific objectives are also defined at the marketing mix level: for example, levels of brand awareness to achieve through advertising, numbers of distributors carrying and stocking the product, and lowest prices compared with direct competitors. Figure 2–7 shows you how to tell a good marketing objective from a bad one.

IV   MARKETING STRATEGY

A **marketing strategy** is the means by which marketing objectives are to be achieved. One of the most crucial aspects of the strategic marketing process is selecting the best marketing strategy to use given the various alternatives available to the firm. Marketing strategy is characterized by determining *what* to do (generic marketing strategy), *who* will be the focus of the strategy (target market or market segment), and *how* to do it (sustainable competitive advantage and positioning). Determining marketing strategy is discussed in detail in Chapters 21 and 22, but here we will briefly highlight the fundamentals of marketing strategy.

Identifying Alternative Generic Marketing Strategies   Suppose the Coca-Cola Company's primary marketing objective was "to increase sales by 10 percent by the end of the fiscal year." Basically, there would be four specific generic marketing strategies they could use to achieve that objective: (1) market penetration, (2) market development, (3) product development, and (4) diversification. Any firm can pursue one or a combination of the four, even at the same time (see Figure 2–8).[7] For example, Coca-Cola can try to use a strategy of **market penetration,** which means increasing sales of present products in

| | PRODUCTS | |
MARKETS	PRESENT	NEW
Present	*Market penetration:* selling more Coca-Cola to Canadians	*Product development:* selling a new product like PowerAde to Canadians
New	*Market development:* selling Coca-Cola to the Chinese for the first time	*Diversification:* selling a new product like movies to Europeans

▌ *Figure 2–8*
Alternative generic marketing strategies.

For an explanation of what a product development strategy is and how Coca-Cola uses it with this sports drink, see the text.

existing markets—in other words, selling more Coca-Cola to Canadian consumers. There is no change in the product line, but increased sales are possible through marketing mix actions such as better advertising, more retail outlets, or lower prices. At the same time, Coca-Cola could use a **market development** strategy, which means selling existing products to a new market such as China or Russia. In fact, Coca-Cola believes opportunities for increased soft drink sales are greater in international markets from which it derives more than three-quarters of its profit already.

A strategy of **product development** involves selling a new product in an existing market. Coca-Cola has created numerous new products as a way of increasing sales, such as Fresca (1966), Diet Coke (1982), Cherry Coke (1986), and PowerAde—a sports drink to compete with Gatorade—(1990).[8] Diet Coke—a sugar-free, caffeinated soft drink—is an example of the difficult choice an organization faces in deciding to introduce a new product. In this case Coca-Cola was especially concerned about **product cannibalism**—a firm's new product gaining sales by stealing them from its other products. Coca-Cola managers were worried that Diet Coke would steal sales from Tab instead of reaching new customers, and that is exactly what happened. In response, the company introduced Clear Tab—with a modified taste and a clear colour—in 1993.

A final strategy Coca-Cola could use to increase sales is diversification. **Diversification** involves developing entirely new product categories or developing new businesses, often unrelated to existing businesses, and selling them in new markets. This is a potentially high-risk strategy for Coca-Cola, because the company has neither the previous production experience nor the marketing expertise on which to draw. In the early 1980s, Coca-Cola acquired Columbia Pictures, a producer of movies and TV programs. This acquisition represented a diversification strategy far removed from selling soft drinks. Coca-Cola had difficulty with this diversification move and in late 1989 sold Columbia Pictures to Sony.

Target Market When a marketer is considering selection of a marketing strategy, he must also focus on *who* will be the focus of that strategy. Marketers cannot be all things to all people. Customers are different and have different needs. Selecting target markets to serve involves the process of **market segmentation,** or aggregating prospective buyers into groups, or market segments (target markets) that (1) have common needs and (2) will respond similarly to a marketing action. Ideally, each segment can be reached by a specific marketing mix targeted to its needs. Coca-Cola Canada offers different versions of its Coca-Cola product to reach market segments that want or don't want sugar and want or don't want caffeine. It also offers the new-formula Coke for those wanting a sweeter taste. The decision to target soft drinks to these segments was a major one, because, until 1982, the name *Coca-Cola* was never allowed on any drink but the original Coca-Cola, now Coca-Cola Classic. We will discuss the market segmentation process in Chapter 9.

Sustainable Competitive Advantage and Positioning A critical aspect of marketing strategy is the concept of sustainable competitive advantage. As mentioned earlier in the chapter, an organization's distinctive competencies "drive," or form the basis for, the development of a sustainable competitive advantage (SCA), a strength, relative to competitors, to be used in the markets the firm serves or the products it offers. Simply put, a firm's SCA is its ability to do something better than its competition. Importantly, an SCA must be tough for competitors to imitate or copy (i.e., it must be sustainable), and it must also be valuable to the customer.[9] An SCA usually comes in the form of lowest cost of production (giving a low-price advantage), or an advantage in some area other than cost, such as (1) the product (e.g., product quality), (2) distribution (e.g., locational convenience), (3) promotion (e.g., better use of media), or (4) customer service. In essence, the SCA most often involves leveraging one or more aspects of the marketing mix such as the ability to offer the lowest price and/or the highest-quality product.

Once a firm determines its sustainable competitive advantage, it must *position* itself in the minds of the consumer on that competitive dimension. In other words, the consumer must see the firm or its product or brand as "better" in some way compared with the competition. When Coca-Cola created Diet Coke, it believed it had a competitive advantage, something that consumers wanted: a diet cola that tasted great. Coca-Cola positioned Diet Coke, single-mindedly, on the *taste* dimension, something no other diet soft drink had done before. Their "Just for the taste of it" positioning theme made Diet Coke one of the top-selling soft drinks in the world.

The concept of positioning is discussed in Chapter 9, and the concept of competitive advantage is discussed again in Chapter 21.

The concept of marketing strategy is often difficult to grasp, not just for students but also for seasoned marketers. Some marketers believe that an easy way to understand strategy formulation is to consider it a triangulation process. The three sides making up the triangle should be (1) a generic marketing strategy option, (2) a target market, and (3) a sustainable competitive advantage, with all sides mutually reinforcing, as shown in Figure 2–9. Frameworks for making effective marketing strategy decisions are discussed in detail in Chapters 21 and 22.

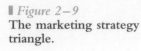

■ *Figure 2—9*
The marketing strategy
triangle.

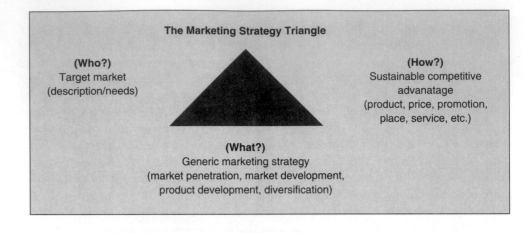

The Marketing Strategy Triangle

(Who?)
Target market
(description/needs)

(How?)
Sustainable competitive
advanatage
(product, price, promotion,
place, service, etc.)

(What?)
Generic marketing strategy
(market penetration, market development,
product development, diversification)

Concept Check

1 When Coca-Cola decided to produce Fresca and Clear Tab and sell them to
its existing customers, which marketing strategy was it following?

√ 2 What is market segmentation?

√3 What is sustainable competitive advantage?

V   THE MARKETING MIX

With the marketing strategy determined, the target markets selected, and the competitive advantage finalized, the task of developing the overall proper marketing mix needs to be completed. Since a firm's competitive advantage generally involves an area of the marketing mix, at least some aspects of the mix may already be clear to the organization at this stage of the process.

For example, if lowest price is to be a firm's competitive advantage, the price component of the marketing mix has been addressed in a strategic manner. However, developing the overall marketing mix, including price specifics, may still require tens or hundreds of hours of planning. Developing and executing a marketing mix successfully involves detailed decision making such as selecting when to use promotion, writing advertising copy, or selecting the outlets to carry the product. These decisions, called **marketing tactics,** are detailed day-to-day operational decisions essential to the overall success of a marketing strategy. While strategy provides the framework and direction for the marketing effort, marketing tactics involve all the immediate and ongoing actions to carry out the strategy and the marketing plan.

Figure 2—10 shows the components of each marketing mix element and shows all four elements combined in a cohesive manner in order for the marketing plan to be effective.

To be sure you understand the difference between marketing strategies and marketing tactics, let's examine the strategies and tactics of The Body Shop International, a global cosmetics company headquartered in Great Britain. The Body Shop markets more than 350 naturally based hair and skin preparations

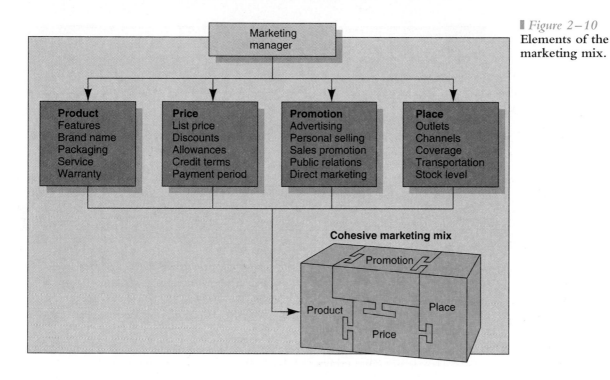

Elements of the marketing mix.

through its more than 900 retail stores in over 40 countries by means of partnerships and franchises.[10] As illustrated in the accompanying Ethics and Social Responsibility Alert, The Body Shop was founded on several key principles and values: close-to-source ingredients, no advertising, no animal testing, minimal packaging, plus honesty and respect for people and the environment.

Marketing Strategies for The Body Shop in the 1990s   *Time* magazine said that The Body Shop's cofounder Anita Roddick "may be Britain's best-known female entrepreneur—and someone who went from being penniless to become one of England's five wealthiest women.[11] As The Body Shop's key spokesperson, Roddick is called on to make some of the critical strategic decisions to take the firm into the next century. Examples include: What key new products

How do marketing strategies and marketing tactics differ for The Body Shop? For some ideas, see the text.

ETHICS AND SOCIAL RESPONSIBILITY ALERT

"Trade Not Aid": The Body Shop Buys from the Third World

When Anita Roddick, along with husband Gordon, started The Body Shop International in 1976, her idea was the ultimate in simplicity: package cosmetics made from natural ingredients in small containers. Today it's a little more complex than that.

As a part of The Body Shop's recent Trade Not Aid project, Anita Roddick searches the world for indigenous people who can provide natural ingredients that can go into her firm's products—from cosmetics with Brazil nut oil to back scrubbers woven out of cactus fibre. The Body Shop's goal is to pay First World prices for Third World products in countries such as Brazil, Nepal, and Bangladesh. The goal: Help local communities acquire the tools and resources to support themselves that, in turn, will help their developing nations become more politically stable.

How does The Body Shop's Trade Not Aid project affect its customers, employees, owners, and suppliers?

Source: P. Elmer-DeWitt, "Anita the Agitator," *Time*, January 25, 1993, pp. 52–54; *Anita Roddick & the Body Shop* and *Trade Not Aid in a Nutshell* (The Body Shop Communications Office: Cedar Knolls, NJ, 1992).

should we add to—or possibly delete from—our present product line? Should we start opening shops in Eastern Europe? What new, socially responsible activities should we initiate? Answers to questions like these will set The Body Shop's direction for years to come, a characteristic of strategic marketing decisions.

Marketing Tactics for The Body Shop in the 1990s   There are countless day-to-day decisions involving operations of The Body Shop corporation and its stores. Most of these are delegated by Roddick to her corporate and store managers. Many are important but don't set the strategic direction for the organization. For example, the exact location of the next retail store is important, but it is a tactical decision: with one new outlet opening somewhere on the globe every two and one-half days, Roddick must delegate that decision to others. Details of store layout, retail displays, and The Body Shop signs and posters are also vital decisions, but ones that store managers make. Regardless, decisions on marketing tactics, such as retail displays and truck signs, follow directly from higher-level marketing strategy decisions that Roddick and the firm's other top executives make. One possible exception is Roddick's current favourite slogan seen on the side of The Body Shop's delivery trucks: "If you think you're too small to have an impact, try going to bed with a mosquito."

VI   MARKETING BUDGET

The **marketing budget** must spell out the sales, expenses, and profit levels that can be expected as a result of the marketing plan. The firm normally establishes a sales forecast that indicates what it expects to sell under specified conditions for the marketing mix (e.g., at what price and with what level of promotion support) and under certain environmental factors such as reaction by competition. Forecasting of demand and sales is discussed in Chapter 10. The budget also includes a statement of expenses, margins, and profits, sometimes at different estimated sales levels, in order to account for possible changes in the marketing mix or environmental factors. The budget aspect of the plan is designed to show management that revenues should exceed expenses and result in increased profits under the strategy and marketing mix conditions specified in the plan.

VII   THE MARKETING ORGANIZATION

The **marketing organization** is responsible for converting marketing plans to reality. Figure 2–11 is an organization chart of a typical manufacturing firm, giving some details of the marketing department's structure. Four managers of marketing activities are shown to report to the vice president of marketing: the managers of (1) product planning, (2) marketing research, (3) sales, and (4) advertising and promotion. Depending on the size of the organization, there may be several product planning managers, each responsible for a separate product line. Also, several regional sales managers and an international sales manager may report to the manager of sales. We will discuss the marketing organization and the role of the product manager in detail in Chapter 22.

▌ *Figure 2–11*
Organization of a typical manufacturing firm, showing a breakdown of the marketing department.

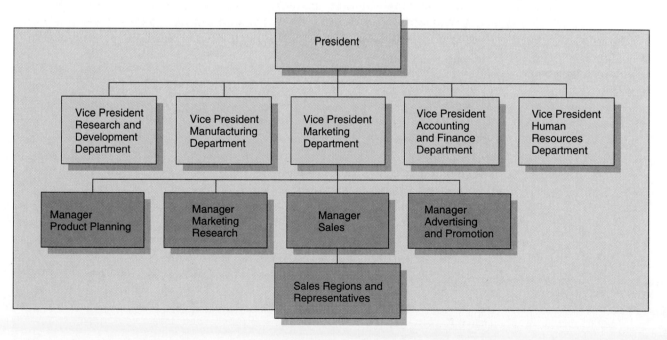

VIII   CONTROL AND EVALUATION

The **control and evaluation** phase of the marketing plan seeks to keep the marketing plan moving in the direction set for it. Accomplishing this requires the marketing manager (1) to compare the results of the marketing plan with the marketing objectives to identify deviations and (2) to act on these deviations, correcting negative deviations and exploiting positive ones.

Comparing Results with Plans to Identify Deviations   Early in 1990 Eastman Kodak wanted to set sales targets for the coming five years, from 1991 through 1995. It saw that its sales from 1989 to 1990 had started to flatten (Figure 2–12). Technological innovations were redefining the entire amateur photographic market, and product lines like instant cameras and movie film were faltering. Also, Fuji was providing far greater competition than expected in Kodak's traditional film and photographic markets.

Extending the 1988-to-1989 sales increase to the year 1995 would have resulted in the sales shown by line *AB* in Figure 2–11, an unacceptable, low-growth strategy. To equal its sales growth from 1987 to 1988, Kodak needed to increase sales by about 15 percent per year and follow the target sales shown by line *AC* in Figure 2–12; the large, wedge-shaped space between the two lines would then be Kodak's **planning gap.** But continued competition could result in sales far less than the targeted level. This is the essence of the control and evaluation phase of marketing—comparing actual results with planned objectives.

Acting on Deviations   When the control and evaluation phase shows that actual performance is not up to expectations, a corrective action is usually needed to adjust and improve the marketing plan and help it achieve the

▌*Figure 2–12*
Evaluation and control of Kodak's marketing program.

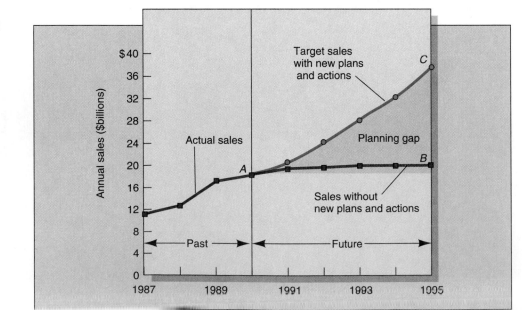

specified objectives. In contrast, comparing results with plans may sometimes reveal that actual performance is far better than the plan called for. In this case the marketing manager wants to uncover the reason for the good performance and exploit it further.

Kodak had assumed that the slowdown in its core photographic market in the 1980s was only temporary and that traditional growth would return.[12] By 1990, it realized that this wasn't likely to happen, so Kodak's evaluation of its likely future performance showed that it would need a new strategy that involved developing important new products.[13] Kodak executives increasingly fretted about what impact electronic or digital imaging would have on its photographic business. For example, if a digital camera can capture an image instantly, would anyone need traditional camera film, paper, and chemicals?

To move Kodak's growth toward line *AC* in Figure 2–11, these executives concluded that Kodak must also be able to "go electronic," and Kodak put millions of dollars into electronic imaging research. Kodak's first major product using this technology was its Photo CD (compact disc) System, which it introduced in 1992.[14] This permits a photographer's picture to be scanned by a computer, stored on a compact disc, and shown on a TV or home computer. Also, through cost cutting and greater focus, Kodak is continuing to bring its marketing plan under control and back in the right direction.

We will discuss the concepts of marketing control and evaluation again, in some detail, in Chapter 22.

Kodak is betting on its new Photo CD System to help fill its planning gap.

---

1 **What are marketing tactics?**

2 **What is the purpose of the control and evaluation part of the marketing plan?**

Concept Check

Summary

1 Strategic corporate planning is the process by which an organization examines its capabilities and its outside environment in order to identify its mission, corporate objectives, and long-run strategies for survival and growth.

2 The strategic marketing process involves the steps taken at the product and market levels to allocate resources to viable marketing opportunities, and includes phases of planning, implementation, and control.

3 A firm's marketing plan, or plan of action, should include (1) an analysis of the current marketing situation (situation analysis and SWOT), (2) specific and measurable marketing objectives, (3) marketing strategy with identified target markets, sustainable competitive advantage, and positioning, (4) the nature of the marketing mix being offered to the target segments, (5) the marketing budget including projected sales and expenses, (6) a description of the marketing organization designed to execute the plan, and (7) control and evaluation processes and procedures.

4 Marketing strategy is characterized by determining *what* to do (generic marketing strategy), *who* will be the focus of the strategy (target market or market segment), and *how* to do it (sustainable competitive advantage and positioning).

5 Four specific generic marketing strategies that could be used to achieve growth are (1) market penetration, (2) market development, (3) product development, and (4) diversification.

6 Marketing tactics are detailed day-to-day operational decisions essential to the overall success of a marketing strategy.

7 The marketing organization is responsible for converting marketing plans to reality.

8 The control and evaluation part of the marketing plan involves comparing results with established objectives, identifying deviations, and taking action to correct negative deviations or exploit positive ones.

Key Terms and Concepts

strategic corporate planning
   process p. 32
strategic marketing process p. 32
organizational business definition
   (mission) p. 33
corporate objectives p. 34
business firm p. 35
nonprofit organization p. 35
profit p. 36

situation analysis p. 37
SWOT p. 37
distinctive competencies p. 37
sustainable competitive advantage
   (SCA) p. 37
marketing plan p. 39
business audit p. 40
marketing audit p. 40
marketing objectives p. 42

Chapter Problems and Applications

1 What are some external threats to Canadian Tire's business that the company should consider when developing a marketing plan for the future?

2 Suppose you headed up General Motors Canada today. Develop a simple SWOT for the company based on what you know about its cars and external environmental factors.

3 Which of these three objectives is a "good" one? (1) We will increase our promotion budget by 15 percent this year. (2) Our objective is to maximize sales in fiscal year 1996. (3) Our sales target for 1996 is $1.5 million. Why are the other two objectives "bad"?

4 Many Canadian liberal arts colleges have traditionally offered an undergraduate degree in liberal arts to full-time 18- to 22-year-old students. How might such a college use the generic marketing strategies shown in Figure 2–8 to grow and prosper in the 1990s?

5 What are some of the problems a firm may experience if it uses new products as a way to obtain market growth?

6 Which element of the marketing mix do you think is leveraged or used most often by firms to obtain a competitive advantage? Is it possible to use more than one aspect of the marketing mix to achieve a competitive advantage?

7 What generic marketing strategies (Figure 2–8) do you feel McDonald's Canada uses to survive and prosper in the Canadian market?

8 If you selected a marketing strategy of market penetration, or selling more products in existing markets, which marketing tactics could you use to execute the strategy?

The Changing Marketing Environment

AFTER READING THIS CHAPTER YOU SHOULD BE ABLE TO:

▼ Understand how environmental scanning studies social, economic, technological, competitive, and regulatory forces.

▼ Explain how social forces like demographics and culture and economic forces like macroeconomic conditions and consumer income affect marketing.

▼ Describe how technological changes can affect marketing.

▼ Understand the competitive structures that exist in a market, the role of marketing within each, and the key components of competition.

▼ Recognize the major legislative and regulatory forces designed to protect consumers and ensure competition in the Canadian marketplace.

"Kidfluence" . . . a New Force in the Marketplace

Today, with the increase in dual-income and single-parent households, children and adolescents are taking on a greater role in the marketplace. A study has shown that 85 percent of teens said they regularly influence family buying decisions.[1] They influence purchase decisions ranging from cereal and automobiles to computers and vacations. In fact, many parents select a brand or an outlet on the basis of what the child wants, and this is especially true for fast food and clothing. Some have called this phenomenon **"kidfluence."** Young people exercise their kidfluence through (1) influencing their parents' buying decisions, (2) actually carrying out family purchase tasks, (3) having and spending money on their own needs and wants, and (4) forming habits that will affect their buying patterns as adults.[2]

Some marketers are actually targeting children, directly or indirectly, at a very early age, recognizing that kids wield considerable clout in family purchase decisions. For example, IBM Canada decided not to use the US parent's strategy when marketing its PS/1 computer in Canada. The company's research had shown that kids were strong influencers when it came to computer purchases. IBM found that parents may be interested in a computer for the home, but it was the kids who pushed them into the computer store. As a result, IBM has positioned the product as the "first computer for the whole family."[3]

The marketing landscape is changing; greater competition, new technology, changing buyer demographics, the new service economy, and an evolving regulatory climate are all part of the emerging marketing environment. Mar-

The IBM PS/1 is marketed as a computer for the whole family.

keters must anticipate further change in the environment and learn to respond to it. Scientist Buck Fuller has said, "You don't fight forces, you use them." This should be the new marketing axiom for the 1990s for firms wanting to achieve prosperity. This chapter describes how the environment for marketing has changed and will change in the years to come.

ENVIRONMENTAL SCANNING IN THE 1990s

The environment for marketing is a source of opportunities to be capitalized on and threats to be avoided or managed. The process of continually acquiring information on events occurring outside the organization in order to identify and interpret potential trends is called **environmental scanning.**

TRACKING ENVIRONMENTAL TRENDS

Environmental trends typically arise from five sources: social, economic, technological, competitive, and regulatory forces. As shown in Figure 3–1 and described later in this chapter, these forces affect the marketing activities of a firm in numerous ways.

To illustrate how environmental scanning is used, consider the following trend. Think about how it affects different kinds of firms and try to explain why it exists.

> Food marketers have observed that the percentage of total expenditures for food prepared at home in Canadian households has been declining, while expenditures for food eaten at restaurants and for takeout has been increasing. In the 1970s, 90 percent of food expenditures were for food prepared at home; 10 percent was spent for food prepared away from home. Currently, 70 percent of food expenditures are for food prepared at home; 30 percent is spent for food prepared away from home.

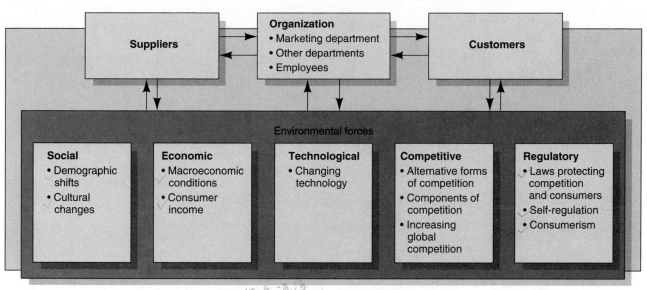

❚ *Figure 3–1*
Environmental forces affecting the organization, as well as its suppliers and customers.

This trend represents a two-edged sword. While supermarket executives are concerned that their sales will further erode, executives at McDonald's, Pizza Hut, and Kentucky Fried Chicken are elated. Not to be outdone, supermarkets now offer prepared foods for takeout and express checkout to woo customers.

Environmental scanning also involves explaining trends. Could it be that food prepared elsewhere is continually getting better than food prepared at home? Perhaps. Another explanation is that the growth of two-career households leaves consumers with little time or inclination for at-home food preparation. Still another explanation is that there is no one to cook for—more than 20 percent of all Canadian households are single households.

AN ENVIRONMENTAL SCAN OF THE 1990s

What other trends might affect marketing in the 1990s? A firm conducting an environmental scan of Canada in the 1990s might uncover key trends such as those listed in Figure 3–2 for each of the five environmental factors. Although the list of trends is far from complete, it reveals the breadth of an environmental scan—from identifying changing consumer tastes such as "high-tech and high touch" and the desire for improved product quality and customer service, to technological breakthroughs in biotechnology and competitive challenges in restructuring Canadian corporations. These trends affect consumers and the businesses and nonprofit organizations that serve them. Trends such as these are covered as the five environmental forces are described in the following pages.

SOCIAL FORCES

The **social forces** of the environment include the characteristics of the population, its income, and its values. Changes in these can have a dramatic impact on marketing strategy.

❚ *Figure 3–2*
An environmental scan of Canada in the 1990s.

ENVIRONMENTAL FORCE	TREND IDENTIFIED BY AN ENVIRONMENTAL SCAN
Social	• Growing number and importance of older Canadians • Continuing population shifts to urban areas • Desire for "high-tech and high touch": gadgets plus human interaction • Greater desire for product quality and customer service • Greater role for women in jobs and purchase decisions
Economic	• Concern that Canadian government deficit can trigger inflation • Increased number of Canadian firms looking to foreign markets for growth • Continuing decline in real per capita income of Canadians • Less consumer acceptance of debt
Technological	• Increased use of massive computer databases and networks • Major breakthroughs in biotechnology and superconductivity • More problems with pollution and solid waste
Competitive	• More employment in small, innovative firms • Downsizing and restructuring of many corporations • Reduced economies of scale resulting from flexible manufacturing • More international competition from Europe and Asia
Regulatory	• Less regulation of Canadian firms competing in international markets • More protection for firms owning patents • Greater concern for ethics and social responsibility in business • Renewed emphasis on self-regulation

DEMOGRAPHICS

Describing the distribution of the population according to selected characteristics—where people are, their numbers, and who they are, such as their age, sex, ethnicity, income, and occupation—is referred to as **demographics.**

The Population Trend   Population growth in Canada was relatively slow during the 1980s. However, the growth rate in the population in the early 1990s was the highest since 1975. This growth rate can be attributed to natural increase (more births) and higher immigration levels. Still, the growth rate is expected to average only about 1 percent per year between now and the year 2000. Given this trend, the population in Canada in 1996 will be slightly more than 28 million.[4] Without higher immigration levels, Canada's population is expected to decline by the year 2011. Many businesspeople are urging the government to increase the number of immigrants entering the country as a way to ensure future economic growth.[5]

AGE	1994	2000
0–9	13.5	12.3
10–19	13.4	13.1
20–29	14.7	13.6
30–49	31.8	31.4
50+	26.6	29.6

▌ *Figure 3–3*
Canadian population by age, 1994 and 2000.

Source: Adapted from Statistics Canada, 91–520 and Ernst & Young. Used with permission.

The distribution of Canada's population by age for the years 1994 and 2000 is shown in Figure 3–3. As you can see, Canadians are getting older. Currently, the median age of the population is 33 years, which means that 50 percent of the population is below that age but 50 percent is also above 33 years of age. The median age in Canada will reach almost 40 years by the year 2000.[6] The key age cohorts that are of interest to marketers are shown in Figure 3–3 and are dicussed below.

The Mature Market   The **mature market** consists of people aged 50 years and older, the fastest-growing segment of the Canadian population. By 2000, over 8 million Canadians, or almost 30 percent of the population, will be over 50 years old, and more than 13 percent will be over 65. The number of Canadians aged 75 and over has increased 140 percent in 10 years and currently stands at more than 1 million.[7]

Mature, or over-50, consumers are often split into two main segments: those between 50 and 64, and those 65 and over. The 65-plus group are considered different in that they usually are retired, live on fixed incomes, and have more leisure time. The over-50 segment controls much of the **accumulated wealth**—the value of net assets accumulated by households in the form of real property, financial securities, deposits, and pension assets—in this country. This wealthy "greying market" is a key niche for many marketers in Canada. Many manufacturers and retailers have developed products and marketing mixes especially designed for the over-50 and 65-plus consumer. Lederle, a vitamin manufacturer, was one of the first to launch a vitamin product, Centrum Select, for the over-50 consumer. The mature market is also a key segment for the travel, vacation, entertainment, health care, and personal and professional services industries.

The Baby Boom Market   **Baby boomers** are those Canadians born between 1946 and 1964. One in three Canadians is a baby boomer. Younger boomers, aged 34 to 44, are entering their prime asset-accumulation years. The first of the older boomers will be entering their 50s by 1996. The baby boomers are a diverse group with different lifestyles and income and education levels. However, this group in general buys more and saves less than do other age groups and is a prime target for consumer electronics, household services, second cars, and other luxuries.

The aging baby boom market has caught many marketers off guard and will continue to do so. For example, Levi Strauss was riding the wave in the

If you really want to relax, maybe it's your jeans that should loosen up.

Wearing jeans should make it easier to relax. But there's nothing easy about the way most jeans fit.
That's why Lee makes Easy Riders, jeans that always fit right, because they're built the way you're
built. Easy Riders. Because if you're going to stop and catch your breath, you have to be able to breathe.

E A S Y · R I D E R S

Lee
The brand that fits

Lee features its
loose-fitting jeans for
aging baby boomers.

1970s when baby boomers made jeans an integral part of their lifestyle. By the 1980s, however, Levi's sales dropped like a stone. Plants were closed and workers laid off. Levi Strauss refocussed its efforts on the maturing baby boomers and launched Dockers slacks for the male boomer and sold millions. Levi Strauss and other companies such as Lee are now offering "relaxed-fit" jeans to this same segment in recognition that the boomers are aging.

Generation X   **Generation X** is the label often given to people born in the mid–1960s to the late 1970s.[8] Sometimes this 20- to 29-year-old age group is referred to as the "twentysomethings"; they represent less than 15 percent of the Canadian population but are important to marketers because they spend money on clothing, entertainment, consumer electronics, and food away from home. Many still live at home and will be entering their peak earning years by the year 2000. However, this group has attitudes and opinions that are often different from their baby boomer parents. They are generally pessimistic about their future economic prospects and are not prone to extravagance. Marketers are now tracking this generation to identify the dominant consumption values of the 21st century.

The Youth Market   The **youth market** consists of pre-teens, "tweens," and teenagers. This 10- to 19-year-old group represents less than 15 percent of the population.[9] But this group is important to marketers. They are the primary kidfluence segment that we talked about in the chapter opener. They have their own spending power and influence many household expenditures as well. This group spends over $6 billion on consumer products alone. Many of the teens have discretionary income because they have part-time or full-time jobs. The youth market is an important global consumer group, representing more than 25 percent of the world's population. Many global companies are able to use a global strategy to appeal to this group because of their similarities in values worldwide. Coca-Cola ("The Real Thing" campaign) and Swatch watches have successfully targeted this youth market on a global basis.

The Canadian Family   The types of families in this country are changing in both size and structure. The average family size in Canada is 3.1 persons, and that figure is likely to decline further by the year 2000. In 1971, one in three Canadian families consisted of the once-typical husband working outside the home, with the wife working inside the home with children. By 1981, only one in five fell into this category. The figure is now one in seven. The dual-income family is now the norm in Canada, representing over 61 percent of all husband–wife families. The percentage of single-earner families in which the husband works outside the home while the wife does not is at an all-time low of 19 percent. Families in which the wife is the sole earner are almost 5 percent of the total, and the percentage of families in which neither spouse works is about 15 percent.

About 50 percent of all first marriages in Canada end in divorce. The majority of divorced people eventually remarry, giving rise to the **blended family,** in which two previously separate families are merged into one unit. Hallmark Cards now specially designs cards and verses for such blended families.[10] Still, many people do not remarry, and single-parent families represent over 13 percent of all family units in Canada.

Population Shifts   Since the mid-1970s, there has been a major shift in the Canadian population, from rural to urban areas. It is estimated that close to 80 percent of Canadians are urban dwellers.[11] Evidence that Canadians are urban dwellers can be seen in the growth of **census metropolitan areas** (CMAs), geographic labour market areas having a population of 100,000 persons or more. Just the top 25 CMAs account for more than 60 percent of the population.

The top five—Toronto, Montreal, Vancouver, Ottawa, and Edmonton— account for about 40 percent of the Canadian population. Even though the census metropolitan areas have been growing steadily, the growth has not necessarily been in the established city cores. Most of the growth has occurred in the suburban areas. With the concentration of population in or near the CMAs, a marketer can reach large segments of the market efficiently in terms of promotion and distribution. Some experts suggest that hyperurbanization is likely to occur in Canada and that most Canadians will be reachable by marketers in only seven or eight "city-states" that will emerge by about 2005.

There hasn't been much of a shift in how the population is distributed across the country. More than 60 percent of Canadians still live in two provinces, Ontario and Quebec. The 10-year outlook for population growth across

MARKETING · ACTION · MEMO

Regional Marketing

*I*f a region in Canada—like Quebec, for example—offers the possibility of major growth, a marketer may consider exploiting opportunities there through a regional marketing approach. Specific programs that will capitalize on fundamental differences such as levels of awareness, culture, purchase habits, and demographics may be developed. The programs will fall into the area of consumer promotions, merchandising, public relations, trade promotions, or sponsorships.

While a marketer's national campaign may serve as an umbrella for these regional activities (and reinforce them), these regional programs can help turn a business opportunity into sales and market share. In order to determine the relative focus on national versus regional marketing, the marketer must (1) evaluate the sales volume potential of the region, (2) evaluate the level of disparity from the national

norms, and (3) evaluate the resources needed to properly implement a regional program. In Canada, Quebec usually represents an opportunity for regional marketing. Quebec is a large market, and its 7 million potential consumers often talk, think, and purchase differently from the rest of Canada. History shows that successful national marketers have allowed for much marketing autonomy in this region.

Regional offices create strong local presence, and this translates into an image of the national company as "local." Regional marketing takes more time, more effort, and more resources, but its reward, if it is done properly, is not only more market share but greater customer and employee satisfaction.

Source: Adapted from B. Cote, "Rewards of Regionalism," *Marketing,* February 28, 1994, p. 19.

all provinces is for slight growth in all, with the biggest increases occurring in Ontario, Quebec, Alberta, and British Columbia.

Regional Marketing A new trend within marketing focusses not only on the shifting of consumers geographically, such as the move from rural to urban areas, but also on the differences in their product preferences based on where they live. This concept has been referred to as **regional marketing,** which is the developing of marketing mixes designed to reflect specific area differences in tastes, perceived needs, or interests. Given the vastness of Canada, many marketers view the country as composed of regions such as Atlantic Canada, Quebec, Ontario, western Canada, and British Columbia.

Because of differences in economics, topography, and natural resources, consumption patterns in regions tend to differ. Products and brands may sell well in one region but not in another. Strategies and tactics to sell them successfully may also differ. Colgate-Palmolive found that marketing its Arctic Power "cold-water" clothes detergent on an "energy savings" dimension worked well in Quebec but not in the west, where cold-water washing to protect clothing was more important. The company adjusted its marketing strategy accordingly.

With the aid of technology, marketers have begun to understand the variations in regional preferences. Computerized cash registers, for example, have allowed companies to coordinate and analyze sales data for geographic regions, determining what sells well and what doesn't in various regions. Pepsi-Cola can be a market leader in one region while Coca-Cola is the leader in

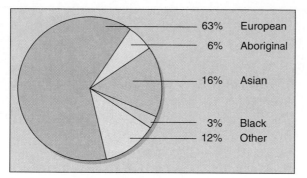

▌ *Figure 3—4*
**Ethnic origins of the
non-British and
non-French Canadian
population.**

Source: Statistics Canada, *1990 Census of Canada.*

another. The ability to market on a regional basis depends not only on the variance in regional preferences, but on the sufficiency of size of the region and the cost of localized efforts. Often, regional or localized efforts can be more costly than one simple national effort. But a better understanding of the geographic regions of Canada and any resultant differences in consumer preferences can lead to more successful marketing (see the accompanying Marketing Action Memo).

Ethnic Diversity   While we often think of Canada as consisting of French or English Canadians, close to 3 out of 10 Canadians are neither of French nor of British descent. While the majority of the non-British, non-French population are of European descent, there has been growth in other ethnic groups and visible minorities.

In fact, close to 70 percent of all immigrants to Canada today are classified as visible minorities, primarily people from China, Southeast Asia, Africa, and India. Hong Kong Chinese and Southeast Asian immigrants are the fastest-growing ethnic groups in Canada, representing close to 3 percent of the Canadian population. Contrary to what many believe, members of this group will make a higher-than-average contribution to Canada's gross domestic product than the average Caucasian Canadian. For example, the total assets of 10,000 Hong Kong Chinese granted business immigrant visas in 1992 were valued at $5 billion. Visible minorities are projected to represent close to 18 percent of the Canadian population by the year 2001, or over 5.5 million consumers.[12] Much of the ethnic population including Chinese, Asian, Italians, Portuguese, and blacks can be found in the major metropolitan areas of Toronto, Vancouver, Montreal, Calgary, and Edmonton. Close to 20 percent of the populations in these areas register their native tongue as something other than English or French. Figure 3—4 shows the ethnic origins of the non-British and non-French Canadian population.

These consumers cannot be ignored by marketers. Many Canadian companies, such as Bell Canada, the Royal Bank, and Ultramar, are putting "ethnic faces" on mainstream advertising. But some experts believe that marketers need to use "niche strategies" to appeal to the ethnic population, such as speaking their language and respecting their cultural values and heritage. The accompanying Marketing Action Memo shows the emerging importance of the ethnic markets, especially the Chinese-Canadian market. We will talk more about Canada's growing ethnic diversity when we deal with the issues of culture and subcultures as influencing factors in consumer behaviour (Chapter 6).

MARKETING · ACTION · MEMO

The Chinese-Canadian Market: A Sleeping Dragon for Marketers

Ask any Canadian marketer with a pulse: Chinese-Canadians are the proverbial key to Fort Knox. Convince the fastest-growing immigrant group in the nation (33,000 people from Hong Kong arrived in Canada last year alone) that you've got what they need, and the gates of consumer heaven will swing wide in your favour. The numbers speak for themselves. A consumer preference study shows that the average Chinese-Canadian consumer has a higher income than the general population, is better educated and less likely to be unemployed, and is significantly younger than the general population. The Royal Bank, a company consistently ranked number one in serving the Asian population (as indicated through a survey by the Toronto paper *Sing Tao*), believes this market to be a very sophisticated segment and one that is a good target for RSPs and mutual funds. The Royal Canadian Mint is also courting the Chinese-

Canadian segment. The Canadian marketplace, in general, has not responded well to gold bullion Maple Leaf coins, but these have sold well in the Asian market. Cantel, a cellular phone company, is also having success with this segment. The Chinese prefer cellular phones to answering machines, according to a Cantel spokesperson. Cantel argues that Chinese-Canadians will do business anytime and want the convenience of the cellular phone.

To deal successfully with Chinese-Canadians, or other segments with different backgrounds and cultures, Canadian companies must understand both their language and their cultural values, as we will see later in this chapter and in Chapters 5 and 6.

Source: Adapted from D. Bell, "The Chinese Market: A Sleeping Dragon for Advertisers," *Marketing*, July 19, 1993, p. 16.

CULTURE

A second social force, **culture,** incorporates the set of values, ideas, and attitudes of a homogeneous group of people that are transmitted from one generation to the next. Culture includes both material and abstract elements, so monitoring cultural trends in Canada is difficult but important for marketing. Cross-cultural analysis needed for global marketing is discussed in Chapter 5.

The Changing Roles of Women and Men   One of the most notable changes in Canada over the past three decades has been the change in the roles of women and men in society. These changes have had a significant impact on marketing practices. Distinctions between the traditional gender roles assigned to females and males have become blurred. One of the major trends has been the emergence of women as an integral part of the workforce. Nationally, more than 65 percent of women work outside the home. This figure is expected to rise to 73 percent by the year 2000.[13] With more women working outside the home, the number of tasks to do is expanding and the time available to do them is shrinking. This phenomenon is often referred to as **time poverty.** As a result, the male spouse has had to assume certain tasks. For example, more men than ever before are making grocery purchases. Many men are also assuming a greater role in child care and housekeeping duties. Marketers are becoming more aware of the necessity not to stereotype female or male behaviour and preferences.

Labatt's Wildcat beer for the "value-conscious" consumer.

Changing Attitudes   In recent years, there has been a shift in Canadians' attitudes toward work, lifestyles, and consumption. The Puritan work ethic of "I live to work" is now redefined by many as "I work to live." Work is now more likely to be seen as a means to an end—recreation, leisure, and entertainment. Canadian consumers are placing more emphasis on quality of life as opposed to work, which has contributed to a growth in sales of products such as video-cassette recorders and easily prepared foods.

There is greater concern for health and well-being, as evidenced by the level of fitness and sports participation in Canada. Firms like Nike and Reebok are profiting from this trend. Canadians are also more concerned about their diets, especially because of the linkage between diet and health. Growth in sales of no-fat, or lowfat, and cholesterol-free foods is evidence of this concern.

Value Consciousness   A change in consumers' attitudes toward consumption is also apparent. Conspicuous consumption, which marked much of the 1970s and 1980s, has been replaced by the search for value, as we discussed in Chapter 1. Instead of simply seeking highly visible brands or labels, consumers are more concerned about obtaining the best quality, features, and performance that a product or service can offer. Innovative marketers are responding to this new orientation by offering better pricing on products or offering value-added enhancements. Club Price, a food warehouse-style food discounter, has been very successful appealing to Quebec consumers seeking better value. Research in that province shows that in an effort to save money, many consumers are looking for bargains and are dropping their favourite brands for alternatives that offer better value.[14] Canada's two largest breweries now offer lower-cost brews to the value-conscious: Labatt markets the Wildcat brand, and Molson sells Carling.

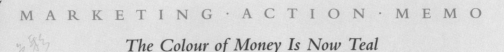

MARKETING · ACTION · MEMO

The Colour of Money Is Now Teal

You can call it calypso, ocean reef, cayman, empire, or just plain teal. But to marketers, the blue-green hue that's all the rage these days is the colour of money. The hard-to-describe colour is everywhere, driving sales in everything from cars to carpets to cosmetic packaging. As a marketing trend, colour analysts say, the use of teal is inspired by the environment, and it's here to stay for at least another three or four years.

According to Bob Daily, colour expert at Du Pont, the colour green is a big seller across all automotive categories; "Green is hot and it's going to stay hot." But the importance of teal in marketing is not restricted to the automotive industries. It is big in home furnishings and fashion including towels, linens, and floor coverings. Colour experts suggest that one of the first things consumers notice about products is the colour. If marketers offer products in the right colours, it increases the chances the products will be purchased. Teal is also used in packaging and in advertising for goods that are never coloured green, blue, or any shade in between. Procter & Gamble repackaged its Cover Girl Clarifying Pressed Powder in a teal compact. Gillette brought out its white-and-teal Sensor shaver for women in a teal package, and Bristol-Myers Squibb introduced a clear Ban deodorant in a teal-coloured package. Reebok also used teal to create a "new-age mood" look in its print advertising for the "Planet Reebok" campaign.

While there is no agreement on how to name the colour teal, experts use the same descriptive terms to describe the colour's appeal. They refer to teal as "safe," "comforting," "familiar," "easy to live with," and "soft." But without exception, they also connect the success of the colour with the environment. Experts also predict growth in the use of all colours that are considered to be "environmental colours."

Source: Adapted from M. Bream, "The Color of Money," *Marketing*, January 24, 1994, pp. 10–11.

Loblaw's (the supermarket chain) also offers its popular-priced President's Choice Premium Draft.

Environmental Consciousness   There is growing recognition that decisions today on use of the earth's resources have long-term consequences to society. Canadians are becoming more ecologically or environmentally conscious. A recent study shows that caring for the environment is a pervasive and deeply felt social responsibility for 80 percent of the population. This concern for the environment also spills over into marketplace behaviour. In a Canadian study, 45 percent of people surveyed said a product's environmental friendliness is an important factor in their purchasing decisions.[15] Many Canadian companies are already responding to the consumers' environmental concerns through what is termed **green marketing**—marketing efforts to produce, promote, and reclaim environmentally sensitive products. Loblaw's, Canada's largest food distributor, sells a line of environmentally friendly products. The 100-item line includes foam plates without chlorofluorocarbons, motor oil processed from recycled oils, and bathroom tissue made of recycled paper. Coca-Cola, Pepsi-Cola, and Procter & Gamble have introduced bottles made from recycled plastic. Sears Canada recycles its catalogues. Over 650 tons of paper were reprocessed into newsprint and fertilizer in 1993. Quaker Oats Canada has also substantially reduced its use of packaging and its garbage output.

Examples of
environmentally friendly
products.

Some environmental groups debate the effectiveness of the environmental
efforts and measures taken by many companies. Others suggest companies are
simply using the environment as a way to sell more products. (The accompanying Marketing Action Memo demonstrates that even the use of environmental colours is becoming popular with marketers.) But it is apparent that environmental considerations will be genuinely important for marketers in the
1990s, and this topic is discussed further in Chapter 4 in connection with social
responsibility.

---

1 Explain the term *regional marketing.*

2 What are blended families?

3 The work ethic of today may best be stated as "I work _____."

Concept Check

ECONOMIC FORCES

The third component of the environmental scan, the **economy,** pertains to the
income, expenditures, and resources that affect the cost of running a business or
a household. We'll consider two aspects of these economic forces: a macroeconomic view, and a microeconomic perspective of consumer income.

MACROECONOMIC CONDITIONS

Of particular concern at the macroeconomic level is the inflationary or recessionary state of the economy, whether actual or perceived by consumers or
businesses. In an inflationary economy, the cost to produce and buy products

and services escalates as prices increase. From a marketing standpoint, if prices rise faster than consumer incomes, the number of items consumers can buy decreases.

Whereas inflation is a period of price increases, recession is a time of slow economic activity. Business decreases production, unemployment rises, and many consumers have less money to spend. The Canadian economy experienced recessions in the early 1970s, early 1980s, and early 1990s.

Consumer expectations of an inflationary or recessionary Canadian economy are an important element of environmental scanning. Consumer spending, which accounts for the lion's share of Canadian economic activity, is affected by expectations for the future. Surveys of consumer expectations are often tracked over time by researchers, who ask questions such as "Do you expect to be better or worse off financially a year from now?" Pollsters record the share of positive and negative responses to this question and related ones to develop an index, sometimes called a consumer confidence or consumer sentiment index. The higher the index, the more favourable are consumer expectations. Many firms evaluate such indexes in order to plan production levels. Chrysler, for example, reduced its planned production level at the onset of the recession in 1991, when consumer confidence in the economy was found to be low.

CONSUMER INCOME

The microeconomic trends in terms of consumer income are important issues for marketers. Having a product that meets the needs of consumers may be of little value if they are unable to purchase it. A consumer's ability to buy is related to income, which consists of gross, disposable, and discretionary components.

Gross Income   The total amount of money made in one year by a person, household, or family unit is referred to as **gross income.** Gross income disparities in Canada are evident by gender, family, province, education, profession, and age. On average, men earn almost twice as much as women; moreover, 9 out of 10 Canadians earning more than $100,000 annually are male.[16] Average gross family income in Canada is a little more than $51,000, but it was highest in Ontario, more than $57,000 and lowest in Prince Edward Island, at slightly less than $40,000.[17] The percentage distribution of Canadian families, by income groups, is shown in Figure 3–5.

Disposable Income   The second income component, **disposable income,** is money a consumer has left after paying taxes to use for necessities such as food, shelter, and clothing. The single largest expense for families in Canada in 1994 was income tax, with over 18 percent of average family income going to just income tax. If taxes rise at a faster rate than does disposable income, consumers must economize. Figure 3–6 shows the distribution of family income in Canada by major expenditure category. This is the overall figure for all income classes. There is a wide variance in the percentage of income spent on necessities by the various income classes. Families making under $10,000 spend over 60 percent of their income on food, shelter, and clothing, while those making

INCOME GROUP	PERCENTAGE DISTRIBUTION OF FAMILIES
Under $10,000	3.3
$10,000–19,999	13.2
$20,000–29,999	15.1
$30,000–39,999	16.4
$40,000–44,999	7.7
$45,000–54,999	14.3
$55,000–64,999	9.9
$65,000–74,999	6.9
$75,000 and over	13.0

Source: "Income Distribution by Size in Canada," Statistics Canada, (Ottawa, 1994), 13–207.

▌ *Figure 3–5*
Percentage distribution of Canadian families by income group.

$60,000 and over spend only 30 percent of their income on such necessities. This leaves the higher income group with much more discretionary income, the third component of income, than lower income classes.

Discretionary Income   The third component of income is **discretionary income,** the money that remains after paying for taxes and necessities. Discretionary income could be used for luxury items such as a vacation at a Hyatt resort. An obvious problem in defining discretionary versus disposable income is determining what is a luxury and what is a necessity. Observation can be a way to determine who has discretionary income; if a family has Royal Doulton china, Rolex watches, and Lexus automobiles, one could assume that they have, or had, discretionary income.

There has been a general erosion of spending power for the majority of Canadians since the mid-1980s. This has led to cutbacks in discretionary purchases and to growth in demand for no-frills brands, do-it-yourself products,

EXPENDITURE CATEGORY	PERCENTAGE DISTRIBUTION
Personal taxes	18.5
Shelter	16.1
Food	14.2
Transportation	13.2
Clothing	6.3
Recreation	5.0
Security	4.5
Household operation	4.3
Household furnishings and equipment	3.6
Tobacco and alcohol	3.2
Gifts and contributions	3.2
Personal care	1.9
Health care	1.8
Other	4.0

Source: *Family Expenditure in Canada*, Statistics Canada (Ottawa, 1994), 62–555.

▌ *Figure 3–6*
Distribution of family income in Canada by major expenditure category.

As consumers' discretionary income increases, so does the enjoyment of pleasure travel.

and smaller and more efficient automobiles. Real income growth in the future is expected to be slow for most Canadians. However, the upper 20 percent of income earners, or the affluent market, will experience even more expansion of their spending power.

The affluent segment is attractive to many marketers. This 20 percent of income earners accounts for over 45 percent of education expenditures, over 40 percent of savings and financial security expenditures, over 40 percent of recreation spending, and over 40 percent of gifts and charitable contributions.

TECHNOLOGICAL FORCES

Our society is in the age of technological change. **Technology,** a major environmental force, refers to inventions or innovations from applied science or engineering research. Each new wave of technological innovation can replace existing products and companies. Do you recognize the items pictured on page 71 and what products they have replaced?

THE FUTURE OF TECHNOLOGY

Technological change is the result of research, so it is difficult to predict the timing of new developments. The Battelle Corporation, an internationally recognized research and consulting company, has made the following projections regarding technological change to the year 2000:[18]

1 Continued advances in development and refinement of microprocessors.
2 Advanced telecommunications systems and techniques.
3 Greater use and refinement of robots.
4 Improvement in materials technology, resulting in greater strength-to-weight ratios.

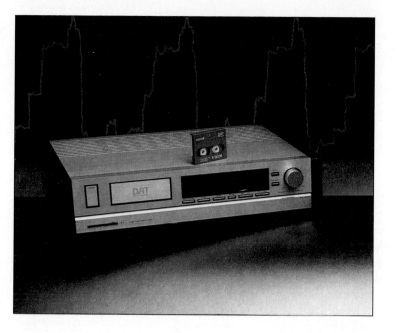

These trends in technology are seen in today's marketplace. The digital audio-tape player may soon replace the compact disc player, and, based on research by Kodak, electronic imaging may soon eliminate the need for film for cameras. Advanced communications systems have spawned a growing industry in cellular radiotelephones, and companies compete aggressively to get their phone in every car and everyone's hand!

TECHNOLOGY'S IMPACT ON MARKETING

Advanced technology, particularly the development of computers, is having a significant impact on marketing. In the supermarket, computerized checkout scanners allow retailers to monitor which products are selling and at what price level. Hand-held computers are being used by companies like Frito-Lay to allow delivery people to monitor in-store promotions and send a sales report directly to company headquarters. Customer service, an important ingredient in the marketing of services (as discussed in Chapter 24), is also being helped by computer technology. Both Avis and Hertz use hand-held computers to speed up the return of rental cars. Hertz personnel can provide the driver with a receipt while still in the parking lot.

Technology can also help in the development of new products.[19] BMW has developed a Heading Control System that tracks the centre stripe and the line on the right side of the road. If a driver gets too close to either, the car's steering self-corrects. Warner–Lambert Company, the manufacturer of Trident gum and Rolaids, has developed a biodegradable plastic by using a starch derived from corn, rice, or wheat. This application can be used in a host of products and will be a potential help in reducing solid waste in landfills.

Ultimately, the benefit of technology for marketers will be in allowing them to better understand and serve the consumer. But often marketers em-

MARKETING · ACTION · MEMO

Marketing and Technology

Technological advances are fundamentally changing marketing by helping companies target the right products to the right consumers at lower costs. Using everything from desktop personal computers to satellites in space, industries are using technology to improve research and to reduce costs of production and distribution, and to control inventory. George Harvey of Unitel suggests that new telecommunications technology helps companies such as Benetton gather information about consumer purchases, carrying data instantly over high-speed fibre-optic lines. Unitel itself has invested heavily in database marketing to pitch a variety of products to precisely defined markets. One example is its new 800 phone card offering free service to one dedicated phone number—a product targeted to university students calling home.

Technologies are also creating new alliances between packaged goods companies and retailers. To provide a value-priced product attractive to consumers, packaged goods companies are working with retailers to better understand their markets and reduce distribution costs. New technologies such as retail scanning equipment provide specific information on consumer purchases that can be used in new product development research. Wal-Mart is expected to use its technology to help it develop strong partnership arrangements with its suppliers in the Canadian market. Through the use of technology, Wal-Mart can ensure open and direct communications with suppliers at reduced costs, passing its savings on to consumers. The cost of new technology is often high, but most companies believe the payoff can be measured in increased competitiveness.

Source: Adapted from "Marketers Praise the Blessings of Technology," *Marketing,* February 7, 1994, p. 4; and J. Pollock, "Faster, Cheaper, Better," *Marketing,* February 7, 1994, p. 11.

brace new technology but fail to use it to their advantage in beating the competition. For example, many plumbers are sole proprietors. In the past, many used answering machines or answering services to take their calls when they were out on service calls. A customer with a flooded bathroom who called a plumber was often greeted by a recorded voice or by an answering service that could do nothing but take a message. Today, most plumbers have cellular phones, a new technology. But in general, most of them leave them in their vehicles and use them to call their answering services. They have failed to use the technology appropriately. The plumber who carries the cellular phone around all the time, even when she is crawling under houses, is using the technology the correct way. The customer wants to talk to a live plumber in an emergency situation, and the plumber who can be reached quickly and directly is the one who will have the edge. Technology is not just for the marketer's convenience. It should be used to make the customer's life easier and to build better relationships with customers.

To see how technology is impacting on marketing, read the accompanying Marketing Action Memo.

COMPETITIVE FORCES

The fourth component of the environmental scan, **competition,** refers to the alternative firms that could provide a product to satisfy a specific market's needs.

Rice: a commodity representative of pure competition.

There are various forms of competition, and each company must consider its present and potential competitors in designing its marketing strategy.

ALTERNATIVE FORMS OF COMPETITION

There are four basic forms of competition that form a continuum: pure competition, monopolistic competition, oligopoly, and monopoly. Chapter 13 contains further discussions on pricing practices under these four items of competition.

At one end of the continuum is *pure competition,* in which every company has a similar product. Companies that deal in commodities common to agribusiness (for example, wheat, rice, and other grains) are often in a pure competition position in which distribution (in the sense of shipping products) is important but other elements of the marketing mix have little impact.

In the second point on the continuum, *monopolistic competition,* the many sellers compete with their products on a substitutable basis. For example, if the price of coffee rises too much, consumers may switch to tea. Coupons or frequent sales are marketing tactics often used in a situation of monopolistic competition.

Oligopoly, a common industry structure, occurs when a few companies control the majority of industry sales. Canada is often referred to as the "land of oligopoly," with some of the highest levels of industrial concentration in the Western world. This high level of concentration refers to a few major producers controlling major sectors of the economy. For example, two airlines in this country control the bulk of the market in that industry sector, and the financial services industry is controlled largely by the chartered banks, particularly the "big five," as they are commonly known. Because there are few sellers in an oligopolistic situation, price competition among firms would lead to reduced revenue for all producers and thus is not desirable. Instead, in an oligopolistic situation, nonprice competition is common, which means competing on other dimensions of the marketing mix such as product quality, distribution, and/or promotion.

The final point on the continuum, *monopoly,* occurs when only one firm sells the product or service. It has been common for companies providing products or services considered essential to a community—water, electricity, or telephone—to be in a monopoly situation, usually granted by government regulation. Typically, marketing plays a small role in a monopolistic setting because of the regulation imposed by the provincial or federal government. Government control usually seeks to ensure price protection for the buyer. Until recently, there was no competition in the long-distance telephone business, but deregulation has given rise to new entrants such as Unitel. Bell Canada now must compete in a different marketing environment, a monopolistic competitive one.

COMPONENTS OF COMPETITION

In developing a marketing strategy, companies must consider the components that drive competition: entry, bargaining power of buyers and suppliers, existing rivalries, and substitution possibilities.[20] Scanning the environment requires a look at all of them. These relate to a firm's marketing mix decisions and may be used to develop a new entrant, create a barrier to entry, or intensify a fight for market share.

Entry   In considering competition, a firm must assess the likelihood of new entrants. Additional producers increase industry capacity and tend to lower prices. A company scanning its environment must consider the possible **barriers to entry** for other firms, which are business practices or conditions that make it difficult for new firms to enter the market.

Barriers to entry can be in the form of capital requirements, promotional expenditures, product identity, distribution access, or switching. The higher the expense of the barrier, the more likely it will deter new entrants. For example, IBM once created a switching cost barrier for companies that considered Apple Computer equipment because IBM had a different programming language for its machines.

Power of Buyers and Suppliers   A competitive analysis must consider the power of buyers and suppliers. Buyers are powerful when they are few in number, switching costs are low, or the product represents a significant share of the buyer's total cost. This last factor leads the buyer to exert significant pressure for price competition. A supplier gains power when the product is critical to the buyer and when it has built up the switching costs.

Existing Competition and Substitutes   Competitive pressures among existing firms depend on the rate of industry growth. In slow-growth settings, competition is more heated for any possible gains in market share. High fixed costs also create competitive pressures for firms to fill production capacity. For example, many Canadian universities are increasing their advertising and public relations activities to fill classrooms, which represent a high fixed cost.

GLOBAL COMPETITION

Global competition has become a central topic in the environmental scan for many Canadian industries. **Global competition** exists when firms originate, produce, and market their products and services worldwide.

The automobile, pharmaceutical, apparel, electronics, aerospace, and telecommunications fields represent well-known global industries with sellers and buyers on every continent. Other industries that are increasingly global in scope include soft drinks, beer, shaving supplies, ready-to-eat cereals, snack chips, and retailing.

Global competition broadens the competitive landscape for marketers and often produces novel competitive forms and forces. A significant trend has been toward the creation of **strategic alliances,** or agreements between two or more independent firms to cooperate for the purpose of achieving common goals. General Mills and Nestlé of Switzerland created Cereal Partners Worldwide for the purpose of fine-tuning Nestlé's European cereal marketing and distributing General Mills cereals worldwide. This alliance is expected to produce global sales of $1 billion by the year 2000. Molson Breweries has taken a giant step toward becoming a major brand in the US beer market through an agreement with Milwaukee-based Miller Brewing Company, an agreement Molson calls a North American strategic brewing alliance. Miller intends to use its marketing and distribution muscle to make Molson a mainstream US brand.[21] In another strategic alliance, Sleeman Brewing of Guelph, Ontario, along with Detroit-based Stroh, set up a new company called Great Northern Imports to introduce Michigan drinkers to Sleeman's brew.[22]

Global competition affects world trade and the wealth of nations, as will be discussed in Chapter 5. It also represents unique challenges for individual firms seeking to enter and compete in global markets, as discussed in Chapter 23.

THE NEW LOOK IN CANADIAN CORPORATIONS

Global competition has had two other important effects on corporate Canada: (1) the restructuring of corporations, and (2) the birth and growth of many small businesses.

Restructuring Corporations   Although the process is known by various names—downsizing, streamlining, or **restructuring**—the result is the same: striving for more efficient corporations that can compete globally by selling off unsatisfactory product lines and divisions, closing down unprofitable plants, and often laying off hundreds or thousands of employees. For example, General Motors shut down many plants and laid off thousands of workers over the past few years. Xerox Canada also went through a restructuring including large-scale layoffs and a reduction in the internal hierarchy to just four layers. The result was painful for those laid off, and employees still working for these companies have found their jobs are far different, sometimes with one person doing what two did before restructuring. Often restructuring also results in far different employment opportunities for those entering the workforce, and far greater problems for restructured companies in gaining loyalty from their employees.[23]

Restructuring frequently happens fast. It often involves a *corporate takeover,* meaning the purchase of a firm by outsiders, or a cooperative merger of two or more companies. Many firms have been restructured as a result of takeovers or mergers. Kraft and General Foods merged to create Kraft–General Foods Canada, and as a result many employees were terminated or reassigned. But this merger does give the new company more marketing and distribution clout in the Canadian market.

Startup and Growth of Small Business   One effect restructuring has on corporations is their increased reliance on **outsourcing**—contracting work that formerly was done in house by employees in marketing research, advertising, public relations, data processing, and training departments to small, outside firms. This has been a factor triggering a major growth in new business startups and in employment in small business. Many economists believe that entrepreneurs in these small businesses are the key to Canadian employment growth in the 1990s.

Concept Check

1 **What is the difference between a consumer's disposable and discretionary income?**

2 **In pure competition there are** _____ **numbers of sellers.**

3 **What does restructuring a firm mean?**

REGULATORY FORCES

For any organization, marketing and broader business decisions are constrained, directed, and influenced by regulatory forces. **Regulation** consists of restrictions the provincial and federal laws place on business with regard to the conduct of its activities. Regulation exists to protect companies as well as consumers. Much of the regulation from the federal and provincial levels has been passed to ensure competition and fair business practices. For consumers, the focus of legislation is to protect them from unfair trade practices and ensure their safety.

PROTECTING COMPETITION AND CONSUMERS

Legislation and regulations exist in Canada, at all three levels of government—federal, provincial, and municipal—to protect and encourage a competitive environment, which is deemed desirable because it permits the consumer to determine which competitor will succeed and which will fail.

The Competition Act   The key legislation designed to protect competition and consumers in Canada is the **Competition Act,** which replaced the Combines Investigation Act. The Combines Act, in effect since 1923, had been found to be ineffectual. The Competition Act was introduced in two stages in 1975 and 1986. The purpose of the Competition Act is:

> to maintain and encourage competition in Canada in order to promote the efficiency and adaptability of the Canadian economy, in order to expand opportunities for Canadian participation in world markets while at the same time recognizing the role of foreign competition in Canada, in order to ensure that small and medium-sized

enterprises have an equitable opportunity to participate in the Canadian economy and in order to provide consumers with competitive prices and product choices.

In essence, the act is designed to protect and to balance the interests of competitors and consumers. The Bureau of Competition Policy, which is part of the federal department of Consumer and Corporate Affairs, is responsible for administering and enforcing the provisions of the act. The act contains both criminal and noncriminal provisions.

Criminal offences under Part VI of the act include conspiracy (e.g., price fixing), bid rigging, discriminatory and predatory pricing, price maintenance, and misleading or deceptive marketing practices such as double ticketing or bait-and-switch selling.

Noncriminal reviewable matters under Part VIII of the act include mergers, abuse of dominant position, refusal to deal, consignment selling, exclusive dealing, tied selling, market restriction, and delivered pricing. The director of the Bureau of Competition Policy refers these matters to the Competition Tribunal under noncriminal law standards. The tribunal was established when the act took effect and is governed by the Competition Tribunal Act. The tribunal adjudicates all reviewable matters under the act.

Consumer and Corporate Affairs Canada is responsible for most of the legislation affecting business practices in Canada. Figure 3−7 lists the more significant federal legislation that protects competition and consumers in Canada. Marketers must also be cognizant of the fact that, in addition to federal laws and regulations, there are many more at the provincial level. Many provinces have their own departments of consumer affairs in order to administer any such legislation and regulations enacted on the provincial government level. Unfortunately, the laws and regulations at the provincial level vary from province to province. A marketer may find it necessary to adapt some aspect of the marketing mix or some broader business practice depending on the province.

Bank Cost Borrowing Act	Fish Inspection Act
Bankruptcy Act	Food and Drugs Act
Bills of Exchange Act	Hazardous Products Act
Board of Trade Act	Income Tax Act
Broadcasting Act	Industrial Design Act
Canada Agricultural Products Standards Act	Maple Products Industry Act
	Motor Vehicle Safety Act
Canada Cooperative Association Act	Official Languages Act
Canada Corporations Act	Patent Act
Canada Dairy Products Act	Precious Metals Marketing Act
Canadian Human Rights Act	Small Loans Act
Competition Act	Standards Council of Canada Act
Consumer Packaging and Labelling Act	Textile Labelling Act
Copyright Act	The Interest Act
Criminal Code	Timber Marking Act
Department of Consumer and Corporate Affairs Act	Trade Marks Act
	True Labelling Act
Electricity Inspection Act and Gas Inspection Act	Weights and Measures Act
	Winding-up Act

Figure 3−7
Major federal legislation designed to protect competition and consumers.

For example, in Quebec there are specific laws dealing with store signage, packaging, and labelling. Additionally, advertising directed toward children is prohibited in Quebec. Many provinces, including Quebec, also have consumer protection acts and/or business or trade practices acts.

SELF-REGULATION

The government has provided much legislation to create a competitive business climate and protect the consumer. An alternative to government control is **self-regulation,** under which an industry attempts to police itself. The Canadian Broadcasting Association, whose members include major television networks and radio stations across the country, has a code of ethics that helps govern the conduct of its members in terms of protecting the consumer against deceptive trade practices such as misleading advertising. Similarly, the Advertising Standards

ETHICS AND SOCIAL RESPONSIBILITY ALERT

The Canadian Code of Advertising Standards

The Advertising Standards Council, the self-regulatory arm of the Canadian Advertising Foundation, established the Canadian Code of Advertising Standards for its members to follow. The members of this organization consist of major advertising agencies that control much of the advertising you see and hear in this country. The code is designed to merit and enhance public confidence in advertising. This code of standards, approved by all participating organizations, helps set and maintain standards of honesty, truth, accuracy, and fairness in the marketplace. Advertising prepared by participating agencies must adhere in letter and in spirit to the regulatory clauses.

There are 16 different clauses in this code covering a wide range of issues, including (1) accuracy and clarity of advertising, (2) the prohibition of disguised advertising techniques such as subliminal advertising, (3) the banning of deceptive price claims, (4) the proper and genuine use of testimonials, (5) the prohibition of "bait-and-switch" techniques, (6) the use of comparative advertising, (7) the proper use of professional and scientific claims, (8) slimming or weight-loss claims, (9) the offering of guarantees, (10) prohibition of imitation of another advertiser's copy, slogan, or other illustrations, (11) regard for public safety, (12) prohibition of the exploitation of human misery, (13) banning the use of superstition and fears to mislead the public, (14) the imposition of a special responsibility in preparing advertisements to children, (15) advertising to minors, and (16) the standards of good taste and public decency.

The underlying principles of the code are meant to ensure that participating organizations act in an ethical and socially responsible manner in preparing and executing advertisements directed toward the Canadian consumer.

Source: Adapted from the *Canadian Code of Advertising Standards* (Toronto: Canadian Advertising Foundation, 1986).

Council, the self-regulatory arm of the Canadian Advertising Foundation, has established the Canadian Code of Advertising Standards for its members to follow. The members of this organization consist of major advertising agencies that are responsible for allocating the bulk of advertising dollars in Canada (see the accompanying Ethics and Social Responsibility Alert). The Canadian Radio-Television Commission, the federal agency responsible for licensing and regulating broadcasting in Canada, is in favour of greater industry self-regulation.

Another well-known self-regulatory group is the Better Business Bureau (BBB). This organization is a voluntary alliance of companies whose goal is to help maintain fair business practices. Although the BBB has no legal power, it does try to use "moral suasion" to get members to comply with its regulations. However, there are critics of self-regulation. These critics complain that there are two basic problems with self-regulation: noncompliance by members and enforcement.

CONSUMERISM

Regulation by government and self-regulation by industry help in protecting the consumer in the marketplace. But the consumer can also play a direct and active role. As discussed in Chapter 1, **consumerism** is a movement to increase the influence, power, and rights of consumers in dealing with institutions. Modern consumerism in Canada and the United States really began in the 1960s. President John F. Kennedy of the United States, in a speech entitled "Consumer Bill of Rights," outlined four basic consumer rights: (1) the right to safety, (2) the right to be informed, (3) the right to choose, and (4) the right to be heard. Although not passed as laws, these proclaimed rights serve as the basis for modern consumerism. Shortly after President Kennedy's consumer bill of rights was unveiled in the United States, the Canadian government formed the Department of Consumer and Corporate Affairs, making it the agency responsible for protecting consumers and regulating corporate activities.

Canada also has many independent consumer organizations that advance the cause of consumerism. The Consumers Association of Canada (CAC) is the largest consumer group working on behalf of the Canadian consumer. The CAC serves as a channel for supplying consumers' views to government and industry, providing consumer information, and studying consumer problems and presenting recommended solutions to those problems. In addition to ensuring that the four original consumer rights are protected, the consumer movement of the 1990s also includes consumer demands for environmentally safe products and ethical and socially responsible business practices.

1 The _____ Act is the key legislation designed to protect competition and consumers in Canada.

2 An alternative to legislation protecting competition and consumers is self-_____.

3 What is consumerism?

Concept Check

Summary

1 The population in Canada in 1996 will be slightly more than 28 million. Canada is experiencing an age-wave phenomenon. Four key waves are emerging: the mature market, the baby boom market, generation X, and the youth market.

2 The dual-income family is now the norm in Canada, representing over 61 percent of all husband-wife families. Also, a blended family structure is becoming more common. Children and adolescents are exerting more influence ("kidfluence") in purchase decision making.

3 It is estimated that close to 80 percent of Canadians are urban dwellers, with most living in census metropolitan areas (CMAs). Regional marketing, developing marketing mixes designed to reflect the specific geographic area's differences in tastes, perceived needs, or interests, is something Canadian marketers must consider.

4 Canada is becoming more ethnically diverse, as evidenced in recent growth in the population of visible minorities.

5 Culture incorporates abstract values and attitudes about material possessions. Attitudes are changing toward work, quality of life, the roles of women and men, and consumption. Value consciousness and environmental consciousness are growing concerns among consumers.

6 Disposable income is the number of dollars left after taxes. Discretionary income is the money consumers have after purchasing their necessities. Most Canadians are experiencing slow real growth in gross income.

7 There are various forms of competition, and each company must consider its present and potential competitors in designing its marketing strategy. Global competition, for example, is affecting Canadian companies. Many are restructuring in an effort to improve efficiency in order to compete in the global arena.

8 For any organization, marketing and broader business decisions are constrained, directed, and influenced by regulatory forces. The key legislation in Canada designed to protect competition and consumers is the Competition Act.

9 An alternative to government control is self-regulation, under which an industry attempts to police itself. The effectiveness of self-regulation is coming under greater scrutiny.

10 The consumer can also play a direct and active role in influencing what happens in the marketplace. Consumerism is a movement to increase the influence, power, and rights of consumers in dealing with institutions. Modern consumers are demanding more environmentally safe products and ethical and socially responsible business practices.

Key Terms and Concepts

kidfluence p. 55

environmental scanning p. 56

social forces p. 57

demographics p. 58

mature market p. 59

accumulated wealth p. 59

baby boomers p. 59

generation X p. 60

youth market p. 60

blended family p. 61

census metropolitan area p. 61

regional marketing p. 62

culture p. 64

time poverty p. 64

green marketing p. 66

economy p. 67

gross income p. 68

disposable income p. 68

discretionary income p. 69

technology p. 70

competition p. 72

barriers to entry p. 74

global competition p. 75

strategic alliances p. 75

restructuring p. 75

outsourcing p. 76

regulation p. 76

Competition Act p. 76

self-regulation p. 78

consumerism p. 79

Chapter Problems and Applications

1 Marketers recognize the role that children now play in influencing family purchases. Many marketers advertise directly to children, and now some want to get into the classroom with in-class advertising or through sponsorship of various academic or extracurricular activities. What do you think of these tactics? Are they appropriate? Why or why not?

2 Describe the target market for a luxury item such as the Mercedes-Benz 190 (the lowest-priced Mercedes). List three or four magazines in which you would advertise to appeal to this target market.

3 The growing concern with the environment was discussed in this chapter. Marketing in an ecologically or environmentally sensitive manner is more important to firms. Suggest how the following companies and products might respond to environmental concerns: (*a*) Gillette safety razor division, (*b*) Kentucky Fried Chicken restaurants, (*c*) Hallmark greeting cards.

4 In the Canadian brewing industry, two large firms control most of the beer sales in Canada (Labatt and Molson). But they are now facing competition from many smaller regional brands. In terms of the continuum of competition, how would you explain this change?

5 With the deregulation of the Canadian long-distance telephone industry, how do you think the role of marketing in the industry will change? What elements of the marketing mix are more or less important since deregulation?

6 When dual-income families are time-starved (i.e., experience time poverty), they simply have too many things to do and too little time to do them. How can marketers help dual-income families that want to balance work and family?

7 What type of impact has a new technology like inexpensive fax machines had on traditional delivery or courier companies? How can couriers respond to this technological threat to their business?

8 Today's consumer is more value-conscious. How could a retail home improvement centre sell the exact same products but still offer the consumer greater perceived value? What specific things could the retailer do?

"Planning every run
is the mark of a good skier,
even the run home. So think ahead
and don't drink and drive."

Brian Stemmle
NATIONAL SKI TEAM MEMBER

Take Care
MOLSON Ⓜ

Ethics and Social Responsibility in Marketing

AFTER READING THIS CHAPTER YOU SHOULD BE ABLE TO:

▸ Appreciate the nature and significance of ethics in marketing.

▸ Understand the differences between legal and ethical behaviour in marketing.

▸ Identify factors that influence ethical and unethical marketing decisions.

▸ Distinguish among the different concepts of ethics and social responsibility.

▸ Recognize the importance of ethical and socially responsible consumer behaviour.

There Is More to Molson Than Meets the Palate

Why would a company spend millions of dollars trying to convince people not to abuse its products? Ask Molson, one of Canada's largest brewers and a leader in the campaign for responsible drinking. "Take Care" is the latest Molson initiative in the company's ongoing commitment to encourage responsible drinking. As one of Canada's leading corporate citizens, Molson recognizes the need to support meaningful public dialogue and programs to raise community awareness about the responsible use of alcohol. The "Take Care" program is a multimillion-dollar national communications program that goes beyond conventional drinking-and-driving campaigns. It puts responsible drinking in a broader context—of work, health, and quality of life.

The program includes broadcast, print, and outdoor advertising, promotions tied to Molson sports and entertainment properties across the country, educational initiatives in schools and colleges, and support to community and interest groups.

Molson acts on what it views as an ethical obligation to its customers with its "Take Care" campaign. At the same time, the company is also involved in multifaceted efforts to support the communities in which it operates and to protect our natural environment. Molson has a long history of supporting countless charities and has founded some of the country's major health, educational, and cultural institutions. In the spirit of this commitment to social responsibility, the Molson Companies Donations Fund was incorporated in the 1970s to focus the corporation's philanthropic activities. Molson has also made the protection of the environment a high priority. For example, over 98 percent of its bottles and 75 percent of its cans are returned to points of sale, to be retrieved for reuse or recycling. Molson ensures that its breweries are environmentally efficient throughout all stages of the brewing process, and its offices have recycling programs. The company also supports a variety of environmental initiatives across Canada including Pollution Probe Foundation and the Centre for the Great Lakes.[1]

This chapter focusses on ethics and social responsibility in marketing. You will see how some companies recognize that while ethically and socially responsible behaviour often comes with a price tag, the price for unethical and socially irresponsible behaviour is often much higher. In essence, in this marketplace, companies can "do well by doing good."

NATURE AND SIGNIFICANCE OF MARKETING ETHICS

Ethics are the moral principles and values that govern the actions and decisions of an individual or a group.[2] They serve as guidelines on how to act rightly and justly when faced with moral dilemmas.

ETHICAL AND LEGAL FRAMEWORK IN MARKETING

A good starting point for understanding the nature and significance of ethics is the distinction between legality and ethicality of marketing decisions. Figure 4–1 helps you visualize the relationship between laws and ethics.[3] While ethics deal with personal and moral principles and values, **laws** are society's values and standards that are enforceable in the courts.[4] This distinction can sometimes lead to the rationalization that if a behaviour is within legal limits, then it is not really unethical. When a recent survey asked the question, Is it OK to get around the

▌ *Figure 4–1*
Classifying marketing decisions according to ethical and legal relationships.

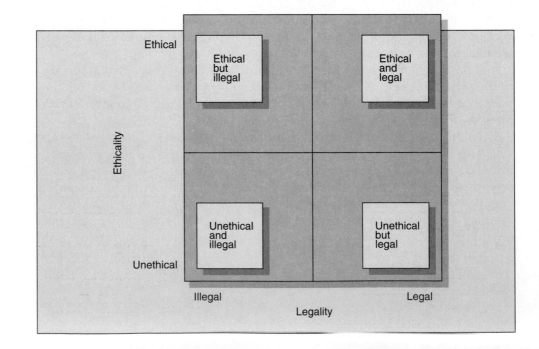

law if you don't actually break it?, 61 percent of businesspeople who took part responded yes.[5] How would you answer this question?

There are numerous situations where judgment plays a large role in defining ethical and legal boundaries. Consider the following situations. After reading each, assign it to the cell in Figure 4−1 that you think best fits the situation along the ethical-legal continuum.

1 Assume several companies meet and agree to bid rigging for sealed tendered government contract work. Bid rigging is illegal under the Competition Act, since it eliminates free and open competition.

2 Assume a company sells a computer program to auto dealers showing that car buyers should finance their purchase rather than pay cash. The program misstates the interest earned on savings earned over the loan period. The finance option always provides a net benefit over the cash option. Company employees agree that the program does mislead the buyers but say that the company will provide what the car dealers want as long as it is not against the law.

3 Assume a tobacco company decides to market a smaller package of cigarettes, a package containing 10 cigarettes versus the regular 20 or 25. They suggest that this offering will provide some of their customers a cheaper alternative. Health officials argue that the smaller, cheaper package will encourage minors to smoke. The company suggests this is not its intention and that stores cannot legally sell cigarettes to minors anyway, so it intends to market the new size package.

4 Assume a real estate agent sells a high-rise condo unit to a customer, primarily on the basis of the city view from the windows, which the customer loves. The agent knows that in one year another high-rise will be built, effectively blocking the view so important to the customer. The agent decides not to tell the customer, since there is no legal obligation to do so.

Do these situations fit neatly into Figure 4−1 as clearly defined ethical and legal or unethical and illegal practices? Some probably do not. As you read further in this chapter, you will be asked again to consider these and other ethical dilemmas.

CURRENT STATUS OF ETHICAL BEHAVIOUR

There has been much discussion over the deterioration of personal morality and ethical standards on a global scale. The news media offer well-publicized examples of personal dishonesty, hypocrisy, cheating, and greed. The ethical conduct of business is also coming under closer scrutiny. Most public opinion surveys as well as other research show that most adults believe the ethical standards of business have declined over the years.[6] A recent survey of senior corporate executives confirms this public perception. Two-thirds of these executives think people are "occasionally" unethical in their business dealings, 15 percent believe they are "often" unethical, and 16 percent consider people "seldom" without ethics.[7]

There are at least four possible reasons why the state of perceived ethical business conduct is at its present level. First, there is increased pressure on

MARKETING · ACTION · MEMO

MBAs and Their Views on Ethics: A Cross-National Examination

Recent cross-national research investigated MBA students and their views on ethics. Students from Canadian, American, and British universities were surveyed to determine their perceptions of ethics in society and business. The research revealed that these students believed current ethical standards do not meet the needs of society and that the majority of students believed business ethics have deteriorated over the years. While the majority of students believed that business ethics could be improved, fewer than 30 percent of students believed business ethics would actually get better in the future.

Over 60 percent of students surveyed believed that an ethics course should be required in business schools. Close to 20 percent of Canadian and American students, and about 40 percent of British students, felt that they have difficulty in determining what is ethical or unethical behaviour and believed

the teaching of ethics would help in improving business behaviour. The vast majority of students do believe that it is possible to be successful without compromising your ethical principles and that ethical standards have not deteriorated to the point of "anything goes." The researchers concluded that (1) there is a need for ethical awareness building among business students, (2) students are interested in and receptive to information about ethics, and (3) ethics education and training can help provide a framework for "handling ethical problems and dilemmas that can develop in business." This generation of MBA students may become the corporate leaders of tomorrow and must be equipped to demonstrate both business and ethical leadership.

Source: Adapted from F. G. Crane, J. E. Lynch, and T. K. Clarke, "Tomorrow's Business Leaders: MBAs and Their Views on Ethics: A Cross-National Examination," Working Paper, Dalhousie University, 1993.

businesspeople to make decisions in a society characterized by diverse value systems.[8] Consider the ethics of using animals for testing the safety of products. In one survey, 60 percent of respondents opposed using animals to test the safety of cosmetics, 43 percent opposed this practice for common medical products such as headache remedies, and 20 percent opposed testing to combat life-threatening illnesses such as cancer. A decade or so ago, this issue was rarely, if ever, raised.[9] Second, there is a growing tendency for business decisions to be judged publicly by groups with different values and interests. Third, the public's expectations of ethical business behaviour have increased. Finally, and most disturbing, ethical business conduct may have declined.

To read about MBA students' views on ethics, see the accompanying Marketing Action Memo.

Concept Check	1 What are ethics?
	2 **What are four possible reasons for the present perception of the ethical conduct of business?**

UNDERSTANDING ETHICAL BEHAVIOUR

Researchers have identified numerous factors that influence ethical behaviour.[10] Figure 4–2 presents a framework that shows these factors and their relationships.

SOCIETAL CULTURE AND NORMS

As described in Chapter 3, culture refers to the set of values, ideas, and attitudes of a homogeneous group of people that are transmitted from one generation to the next.

Culture also affects ethical relationships between individuals, groups, and the institutions and organizations they create. In this way, culture serves as a socializing force that dictates what is morally right and just. This means that moral standards are relative to particular societies. These standards often reflect the laws and regulations that affect social and economic behaviour, including business practices, which can create moral dilemmas. For example, Levi Strauss became aware that its contractor in Bangladesh was routinely using child labour to make its products—a customary practice in that country. Should the company abide by local or by Canadian customs? Levi Strauss chose to prohibit the contractor from using child labour, noting that such conditions "are not consistent with [their] values and fairness."[11] Also, Levi Strauss has recently pulled its operations out of China, citing that country's human rights violations as the primary reason (see the accompanying Ethics and Social Responsibility Alert).

Actions that restrain trade, fix prices, deceive buyers, or result in unsafe products are considered morally wrong in Canada and other countries. However, different cultures view marketing practices differently. Consider the use of another's ideas, copyright, trademark, or patent. In Canada, these are viewed as intellectual property, and unauthorized use is illegal and unethical. Hallmark Cards, Inc., was charged with copying ideas of a smaller card company without its consent. The courts ruled that Hallmark must stop publishing the cards, buy back existing cards from Hallmark stores, and pay damages to the owners of the company.[12]

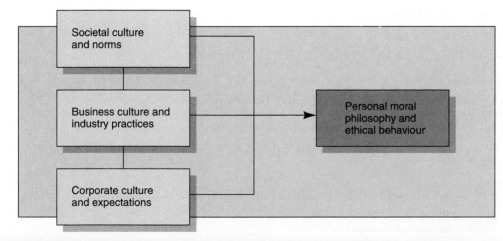

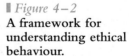

| *Figure 4–2*
A framework for understanding ethical behaviour.

ETHICS AND SOCIAL RESPONSIBILITY ALERT

Levi Strauss Drops China on Human Rights Breaches

Levi Strauss has announced it is pulling out of China for ethical reasons. It has cited persistent human rights violations in that country as the main grounds for its decision. The jeans manufacturer, which has direct and indirect investments in 60 countries around the globe, has been producing about $60 million worth of goods in China annually, using several local contractors to sew more than 5 million jeans and shirts for export.

Linda Butler, a Levi Strauss spokesperson, says the company's decision to walk away from its investment came after a six-month study of human rights in the country. Chinese officials have downplayed the Levi Strauss move, noting that companies can come and go as they please. A spokesperson for China's foreign ministry suggested, "Tens of thousands of foreign companies invest in China and if some individual ones want to withdraw, please do." Levi Strauss will be leaving behind other major international marketers who haven't made an issue of China's human rights record and vowed to continue doing business and marketing their products there. Nike and Coca-Cola, for example, have made public statements of their desire to maintain their business ties with China.

Source: Adapted from F. Kelly, "Levi Strauss Drops China on Human Rights Breaches," *Marketing*, May 31, 1993, p. 34.

Outside Canada, however, there is another story. Unauthorized use of copyrights, trademarks, and patents is routine in countries such as Taiwan, Mexico, and Korea and costs the authorized owners billions of dollars annually. In Korea, for instance, copying is partly rooted in the culture. According to international trade officials, many Koreans have the idea that the thoughts of one person should benefit all, and the Korean government rarely prosecutes infringements.[13] Thinking again about the ethical and legal framework in Figure 4-1, where would you place the practice of using another's trademark if you were Korean?

BUSINESS CULTURE AND INDUSTRY PRACTICES

Societal culture provides a foundation for understanding moral and ethical behaviour in business activities. *Business cultures* set rules, establishing boundaries between the competitive and the unethical, through codes of conduct for business dealings.[14] Business culture affects ethical conduct both in the exchange relationship between sellers and buyers and in the competitive behaviour among sellers.

Ethics of Exchange   The exchange process is central to the marketing concept. Ethical exchanges between sellers and buyers should result in both parties' being better off after a transaction.[15]

Prior to the 1960s, the legal concept of **caveat emptor**—let the buyer beware—was pervasive in Canadian business culture. The growth and strength of the consumer movement caused this concept to become an unacceptable marketplace philosophy. A codification of ethics between buyers and sellers was established, with consumers recognizing their rights to safety, to be informed, to choose, and to be heard. Consumers expect and often demand that these rights be protected. Most businesses comply, but exceptions exist. As an example of failure to ensure consumer safety, A. H. Robins sold the Dalkon Shield, an intrauterine device that was known to be potentially harmful to women. The company has since established a $2.5 billion fund to compensate women harmed by the device.[16] In a similar case, Dow Corning sold silicone breast implants that were found to be defective. The company is now going through litigation with women who have been harmed by the product.

The consumer's right to be informed means that marketers have an obligation to give consumers complete and accurate information about products and services, but they do not always do so. Remember the example of the real estate agent selling the condo with the great city view? The real estate agent knew the view would be blocked by another new building within the year and yet decided not to disclose this fact, even though the consumer was buying the condo primarily because of the view.

Relating to the right to choose, today many supermarket chains demand "slotting allowances" from manufacturers, in the form of cash rebates or free goods, to stock new products. This practice could limit the number of new products available to consumers and interfere with their right to choose. One critic of this practice remarked, "If we had had slotting allowances a few years ago, we might not have had granola, herbal tea, or yogourt."[17]

Finally, the right to be heard means consumers should have access to company and/or public policymakers regarding comments or complaints about products and services. Many Canadian companies have set up customer service departments to deal with customer comments or complaints. Some companies, such as Procter & Gamble, actually put toll-free phone numbers directly on the packaging of their products inviting customers to call if they have questions, comments, or complaints about the products.

Ethics of Competition   Business culture also affects ethical behaviour in competition. Two kinds of unethical behaviour are most common: (1) industrial espionage and (2) bribery.

Industrial espionage is the clandestine collection of trade secrets or proprietary information about a company's competitors. Many Canadian and American firms have uncovered espionage in some form that has cost them billions of dollars a years.[18] This practice is most prevalent in high-technology industries, such as electronics, specialty chemicals, industrial equipment, aerospace, and pharmaceuticals, where technical know-how and secrets separate industry leaders from followers. For example, Hitachi pleaded guilty to stealing confidential IBM documents describing one of its computer systems.[19] But espionage can occur anywhere—the toy industry and even the ready-to-eat cookie industry! Procter & Gamble charged that competitors photographed its plants and production lines, stole a sample of its cookie dough, and infiltrated a confidential sales presentation to learn about its technology, recipe, and marketing plan. The competitors paid Procter & Gamble $120 million in damages after a lengthy dispute.[20]

The second form of unethical competitive behaviour is giving and receiving bribes and kickbacks. Bribes and kickbacks are often disguised as gifts, consultant fees, and favours. This practice is more common in business-to-business and government marketing than consumer marketing.

In general, ethical standards are more likely to be compromised in industries experiencing intense competition and in countries in earlier stages of economic development. For example, bribery of government officials or political parties in developing countries by international companies is very prevalent. These bribes are paid to obtain or retain business in the country or to receive special exemptions from regulations or taxes.

CORPORATE CULTURE AND EXPECTATIONS

A third influence on ethical practices is corporate culture. *Corporate culture* reflects the shared values, beliefs, and purpose of employees that affect individual and group behaviour. The culture of a company demonstrates itself in the dress ("we don't wear ties"), sayings ("the IBM way"), and the manner of work (team efforts) of employees. Culture is also apparent in the expectations for ethical behaviour present in formal codes of ethics and the ethical actions of top management and co-workers.

Codes of Ethics   A **code of ethics** is a formal statement of ethical principles and rules of conduct. Ethics codes and committees typically address contributions to government officials and political parties, relations with customers and suppliers, conflicts of interest, and accurate recordkeeping.[21] For example, General Mills provides guidelines for dealing with suppliers, competitors, and customers and recruits new employees who share its views. However, an ethics code is rarely enough to ensure ethical behaviour. Boeing Company, one of the world's largest aerospace manufacturers, has had an ethics code, ethics advisors, and a corporate office for employees to report infractions since the mid-1960s, yet Boeing was recently charged with using inside information to win a government contract and was fined over $5 million.[22]

The lack of specificity is one of the major reasons for the violation of ethics codes. Employees must often judge whether a specific behaviour is really unethical. The American Marketing Association, representing Canadian and American marketing professionals, has addressed this issue by providing a detailed code of ethics, which all members agree to follow. This code is shown in Figure 4–3.

Ethical Behaviour of Management and Co-Workers   A second reason for violating ethics codes rests in the perceived behaviour of top management and co-workers. Observing peers and top management and gauging responses to unethical behaviour plays an important role in individual actions. A recent study of business executives reported that 40 percent had been implicitly or explicitly rewarded for engaging in ethically troubling behaviour. Moreover, 31 percent of those who refused to engage in unethical behaviour were penalized, either

CODE OF ETHICS

Members of the American Marketing Association (AMA) are committed to ethical professional conduct. They have joined together in subscribing to this Code of Ethics embracing the following topics:

Responsibilities of the Marketer

Marketers must accept responsibility for the consequence of their activities and make every effort to ensure that their decisions, recommendations, and actions function to identify, serve, and satisfy all relevant publics: customers, organizations, and society.
   Marketers' professional conduct must be guided by:

1 The basic rule of professional ethics: not knowingly to do harm.
2 The adherence to all applicable laws and regulations.
3 The accurate representation of their education, training and experience.
4 The active support, practice and promotion of this Code of Ethics.

Honesty and Fairness

Marketers shall uphold and advance the integrity, honor, and dignity of the marketing profession by:

1 Being honest in serving consumers, clients, employees, suppliers, distributors and the public.
2 Not knowingly participating in conflict of interest without prior notice to all parties involved.
3 Establishing equitable fee schedules including the payment or receipt of usual, customary and/or legal compensation or marketing exchanges.

Rights and Duties of Parties in the Marketing Exchange Process

Participants in the marketing exchange process should be able to expect that:

1 Products and services offered are safe and fit for their intended uses.
2 Communications about offered products and services are not deceptive.
3 All parties intend to discharge their obligations, financial and otherwise, in good faith.
4 Appropriate internal methods exist for equitable adjustment and/or redress of grievances concerning purchases.

   It is understood that the above would include, *but is not limited to,* the following responsibilities of the marketer:

In the area of product development and management

- Disclosure of all substantial risks associated with product or service usage.
- Identification of any product component substitution that might materially change the product or impact on the buyer's purchase decision.
- Identification of extra-cost added features.

In the area of promotions

- Avoidance of false and misleading advertising.
- Rejection of high pressure manipulation, or misleading sales tactics.
- Avoidance of sales promotions that use deception or manipulation.

(continued)

In the area of distribution

- Not manipulating the availability of a product for purpose of exploitation.
- Not using coercion in the marketing channel.
- Not exerting undue influence over the reseller's choice to handle the product.

In the area of pricing

- Not engaging in price fixing.
- Not practising predatory pricing.
- Disclosing the full price associated with any purchase.

In the area of marketing research

- Prohibiting selling or fund raising under the guise of conducting research.
- Maintaining research integrity by avoiding misrepresentation and omission of pertinent research data.
- Treating outside clients and suppliers fairly.

Organizational Relationships

Marketers should be aware of how their behaviour may influence or impact on the behavior of others in organizational relationships. They should not demand, encourage or apply coercion to obtain unethical behaviour in their relationships with others, such as employees, suppliers or customers.

1 Apply confidentiality and anonymity in professional relationships with regard to privileged information.
2 Meet their obligations and responsibilities in contracts and mutual agreements in a timely manner.
3 Avoid taking the work of others, in whole, or in part, and represent this work as their own or directly benefit from it without compensation or consent of the originator or owner.
4 Avoid manipulation to take advantage of situations to maximize personal welfare in a way that unfairly deprives or damages the organization or others.

Any AMA member found to be in violation of any provision of this Code of Ethics may have his or her Association membership suspended or revoked.

Source: Reprinted by permission of The American Marketing Association.

through outright punishment or a diminished status in the company.[23] Clearly, ethical dilemmas often bring personal and professional conflict.

PERSONAL MORAL PHILOSOPHY AND ETHICAL BEHAVIOUR

Ultimately, ethical choices are based on the personal moral philosophy of the decision maker. Moral philosophy is learned through the process of socialization with friends and family and by formal education. It is also influenced by the societal, business, and corporate culture in which a person finds himself. Moral philosophies are of two types: (1) moral idealism, and (2) utilitarianism.[24]

Moral Idealism   **Moral idealism** is a personal philosophy that considers certain individual rights or duties universal (e.g., right to freedom) regardless of the outcome. This philosophy is favoured by moral philosophers and consumer interest groups. This philosophy also applies to ethical duties such as informing the consumer about the safety hazards of a particular product—even conducting a large-scale recall of a defective product, regardless of cost, in order to uphold the consumer's right to safety.

Utilitarianism   An alternative perspective on moral philosophy is **utilitarianism,** which is a personal moral philosophy that focusses on "the greatest good for the greatest number," by assessing the costs and benefits of the consequences of behaviour. If the benefits exceed the costs, then the behaviour is considered ethical; if not, then the behaviour is deemed unethical. This philosophy underlies the economic tenets of capitalism[25] and, not surprisingly, is embraced by many business executives and students.[26]

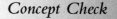

Some infants had allergic reactions to Nestlé's Good Start formula. Read the text to find out what the company did.

Utilitarian reasoning was apparent in Nestlé Food Corporation's marketing of Good Start infant formula, sold by Nestlé's Carnation Company. The formula, promoted as hypoallergenic, was designed to prevent or reduce colic caused by an infant's allergic reaction to cow's milk—a condition suffered by 2 percent of babies. However, some severely milk-allergic infants experienced serious side effects after using Good Start, including convulsive vomiting. Physicians and parents charged that the hypoallergenic claim was misleading. A Nestlé vice president defended the claim and product, saying, "I don't understand why our product should work in 100 percent of cases. If we wanted to say it was foolproof, we would have called it allergy-free. We call it hypo-, or less, allergenic."[27] Nestlé officials seemingly believed that most allergic infants would benefit from Good Start—"the greatest good for the greatest number." However, other views prevailed, and the claim was dropped from the product label.

An appreciation of the nature of ethics, coupled with a basic understanding of why unethical behaviour arises, alerts a person to when and how ethical issues exist in marketing decisions. Ultimately, ethical behaviour rests with the individual, but the consequences affect many.

---

1 **What is a code of ethics?**

2 **What is utilitarianism?**

3 **What is meant by moral idealism?**

Concept Check

UNDERSTANDING SOCIAL RESPONSIBILITY IN MARKETING

As we saw in Chapter 1, the societal marketing concept stresses marketing's social responsibility by not only satisfying the needs of consumers but also providing for society's welfare. **Social responsibility** means that organizations are part of a larger society and are accountable to that society for their actions. Like ethics, agreement on the nature and scope of social responsibility is often difficult to come by, given the diversity of values present in different societal, business, and organizational cultures.

CONCEPTS OF SOCIAL RESPONSIBILITY

Figure 4–4 shows three concepts of social responsibility: (1) profit responsibility, (2) stakeholder responsibility, and (3) societal responsibility.

Profit Responsibility   *Profit responsibility* holds that companies have a simple duty—to maximize profits for owners or stockholders. This view is expressed by the Nobel laureate Milton Friedman, who said, "There is one and only one social responsibility of business—to use its resources and engage in activities designed to increase its profits so long as it stays within the rules of the game, which is to say, engages in open and free competition without deception or fraud."[28] Burroughs Wellcome, the maker of AZT, a drug to treat people afflicted with AIDS, has been charged with unethical behaviour for adopting this view in its pricing practices. Critics claim that the company's high price for AZT ($6,500 per patient per year) was motivated by a desire to make as much profit as possible, since it holds the patent on the drug.[29]

Stakeholder Responsibility   Frequent criticism of the profit view has led to a broader concept of social responsibility. *Stakeholder responsibility* focusses on the obligations an organization has to those who enable it to achieve its objectives. These constituencies include customers, employees, suppliers, and distributors. Source Perrier S.A., the supplier of Perrier bottled water, exercised this responsibility when it recalled 160 million bottles of water in 120 countries after traces of benzene, a toxic chemical, were found in 13 bottles. The recall cost the

▌*Figure 4–4*
Three concepts of social responsibility.

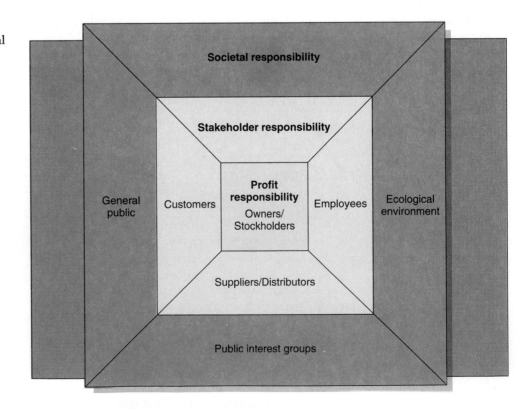

company $35 million, and $40 million more was lost in sales. Even though the chemical level was not harmful to humans, Source Perrier's president believed he was acting in the best interests of the firm's consumers, distributors, and employees by removing "the least doubt, as minimal as it might be, to weigh on the image of the quality and purity of our product."[30]

Perrier responsibly responded to its stakeholders when it pulled 160 million bottles of its water from the market at the first hint of quality problems.

Societal Responsibility   An even broader concept of social responsibility has emerged in recent years. *Societal responsibility* refers to obligations that organizations have to the (1) preservation of the ecological environment and (2) general public. Concerns about the environment and public welfare are represented by interest and advocacy groups such as Greenpeace, an international environmental organization.

Chapter 3 discussed the growing environmental consciousness of the consumer and the green marketing efforts of many companies as a response to those concerns. Many socially responsible companies are building environmental concerns into all aspects of their business. Black Photo of Markham, Ontario, leads the photofinishing industry in chemical waste management. The environment is factored into everything from product conception to manufacturing, distribution, and sales. Green behaviour has become institutionalized at Black's.

Other Canadian companies, such as Lever Brothers and Procter & Gamble, also exhibit green behaviour. Lever offers superconcentrated phosphate-free laundry detergent, which translates into more than a 30 percent reduction in packaging materials, as well as a parallel cost benefit to the company. Procter & Gamble has introduced Downy Refill liquid fabric softener, which reduces solid-waste pollution. The refill carton uses 75 percent less packaging material. Levi Strauss and Esprit have launched clothing lines using cotton that is naturally coloured, thus reducing the need for dyes, a source of water pollution. These voluntary responses to environmental issues were implemented with little or no additional cost to consumers.

Socially responsible efforts on behalf of the general public are becoming more common. A formal practice is **cause-related marketing** (CRM), which occurs when the charitable contributions of a firm are tied directly to the customer revenues produced through the promotion of one of its products.[31] This definition distinguishes CRM from a firm's standard charitable contributions, which are outright donations. When Kmart Canada sells one of its "Marty" stuffed toys (Marty is a cougar mascot who heads the Marty's Kids Club at Kmart), one dollar of sales is donated to the Kids Help Line.[32] Bank of Montreal markets its "Project Sunshine" calendars to its customers to raise money for children's hospitals in Canada. CRM programs incorporate all three concepts of social responsibility by addressing public concerns, satisfying customer needs, and increasing sales and profits. Many companies have also found that CRM provides another long-term benefit, enhancing corporate image (see the accompanying Marketing Action Memo).

THE SOCIAL AUDIT

Converting socially responsible ideas into actions involves careful planning and monitoring of programs. Many companies develop, implement, and evaluate their social responsibility efforts by means of a **social audit,** which is a sys-

M A R K E T I N G · A C T I O N · M E M O

Enhancing Corporate Image through Cause-Related Marketing

Many Canadian companies are discovering that good corporate citizenship goes hand in hand with effective marketing. Historically, Canadian companies have given little thought to the tie between social responsibility and the subsequent impact on their businesses. Indeed, many simply made donations to causes very quietly, for fear of looking opportunistic or self-serving. Today, however, charitable donations and cause-related marketing (CRM) efforts are often highly visible components of corporate cultures. Corporate philanthropy and CRM are now seen as complements to traditional marketing efforts. Although consumers do not usually choose between products or services solely on the basis of what "causes" a company supports, a company's visible stand or support of a cause may sway the buying decision with all other things—price, performance, perceived value—being equal. In fact, with many products and services now virtually indistinguishable from each other, how socially responsible a firm is perceived to be is often the "tie breaker" when a consumer is making a decision to buy.

Demonstrating social responsibility through cause-related marketing activities can encourage a new customer to buy as well as solidify relationships with existing customers. Many firms that have tried to build their corporate images solely through advertising and promotion are now finding CRM to be an effective tool in demonstrating the substance and character of a company. Some question the "true" altruism of some companies that engage in CRM activities, since they benefit from such behaviour in terms of enhanced image and customer loyalty. But the fact is, many worthwhile causes do benefit from this form of corporate behaviour and this should not be diminished simply because the corporation receives residual benefits. It is a win–win situation.

Source: Adapted from A. Mastromartino, "Giving Enhances Corporate Image," *Marketing*, June 28, 1993, p. 31.

tematic assessment of a firm's objectives, strategies, and performance in the domain of social responsibility.

Frequently, marketing and social responsibility programs are well integrated, as is the case with McDonald's. The company's concern for the needs of families with children who are chronically or terminally ill was converted into the concept of Ronald McDonald Houses. These facilities, located near treatment centres, enable families to stay together during the child's care. In this case, McDonald's is contributing to the welfare of a portion of its target market.

A social audit consists of five steps:[33]

1 Recognition of a firm's social expectations and the rationale for engaging in social responsibility endeavours.

2 Identification of social responsibility causes or programs consistent with the company's mission.

3 Determination of organizational objectives and priorities for programs and activities it will undertake.

4 Specification of the type and amount of resources necessary to achieve social responsibility objectives.

5 Evaluation of social responsibility programs and activities undertaken, and assessment of future involvement.

Ecological disasters such as the Exxon *Valdez* oil spill have moved environmental concerns to the forefront of corporate planning.

Attention to the social audit on environmental matters has increased since 1989, when the Exxon *Valdez* oil tanker spilled 11 million gallons of crude oil off the Canadian and American west coast. This spill killed tens of thousands of birds and mammals and fouled 1,000 miles of coastline. Soon after, the Coalition for Environmentally Responsible Economics drafted guidelines designed to focus attention on environmental concerns and corporate responsibility. These guidelines, called the **Valdez Principles,** encourage companies to (1) eliminate pollutants, minimize hazardous wastes, and conserve nonrenewable resources, (2) market environmentally safe products and services, (3) prepare for accidents and restore damaged environments, (4) provide protection for employees who report environmental hazards, and (5) appoint an environmentalist to their boards of directors, name an executive for environmental affairs, and develop an environmental audit of their global operations to be made available for public inspection. Numerous companies now embrace these guidelines, and firms such as S. C. Johnson & Sons and Colgate-Palmolive have environmental policy officers.[34] Nevertheless, environmental mishaps still occur.

Development and use of a social audit will depend on the extent to which a company's culture embraces social responsibility as part of its overall mission. 3M is considered an innovator in this regard. The company is investing $150 million in pollution controls for its manufacturing facilities, encourages employees to develop programs that prevent pollution, and now recycles trimmings from its famous Post-it pads.[35]

TURNING THE TABLE: CONSUMER ETHICS AND SOCIAL RESPONSIBILITY

Consumers also have an obligation to act ethically and responsibly in the exchange process and in the use and disposition of products. Unfortunately, consumer behaviour is spotty on both counts.

Unethical practices of consumers are a serious concern to marketers.[36] These practices include filing warranty claims after the claim period; misredeeming coupons; making fraudulent returns of merchandise; providing inaccurate information on credit applications; tampering with utility meters or tapping cable TV lines; recording copyrighted music, videocassettes, and computer software; and submitting phony insurance claims. The cost to marketers is lost revenue, and prevention expenses are huge.[37] For example, consumers who redeem coupons for unpurchased products or use coupons destined for other products cost manufacturers millions of dollars annually. The record industry loses hundreds of millions of dollars due to illegal recording, and many VCR owners who make illegal copies of videotapes cost producers millions of dollars in lost revenue.

Consumer purchase, use, and disposition of environmentally sensitive products relates to consumer social responsibility. Research indicates that consumers are sensitive to ecological or environmental issues.[38] However, research also shows that consumers (1) may be unwilling to sacrifice convenience or pay potentially higher prices to protect the environment and (2) lack the knowledge to make informed decisions dealing with the purchase, use, and disposition of products.[39]

Consumer confusion over which products are environmentally safe is also apparent, given marketers' rush to produce "green" products. For example, few consumers realize that nonaerosol "pump" hairsprays contribute to air pollution. And "biodegradable" claims on a variety of products, including trash bags, have not proven to be accurate, thus leading to buyer confusion.[40]

Ultimately, marketers and consumers are accountable for ethical and socially responsible behaviour. The mid-1990s will prove to be a testing period for both.

Concept Check

1 What is meant by social responsibility?

2 What is a social audit?

3 Unethical practices of consumers are a(n) _____ concern to marketers.

Summary

1 Ethics are the moral principles and values that govern the actions and decisions of an individual or a group. Laws are society's values and standards that are enforceable in the courts. Operating according to the law does not necessarily mean that a practice is ethical.

2 Ethical behaviour of businesspeople has come under severe criticism by the public. There are four possible reasons for this criticism: (1) increased pressure on businesspeople to make decisions in a society characterized by diverse value systems, (2) a growing tendency to have business decisions judged publicly by groups with different values and interests, (3) an increase in the public's expectations for ethical behaviour, and (4) a possible decline in business ethics.

3 Numerous external factors influence ethical behaviour of businesspeople. These include (1) societal culture and norms, (2) business culture and industry practices, and (3) corporate culture and expectations. Each factor influences the opportunity to engage in ethical or unethical behaviour.

4 Ultimately, ethical choices are based on the personal moral philosophy of the decision maker. Two moral philosophies are most prominent: (1) moral idealism and (2) utilitarianism.

5 Social responsibility means that organizations are part of a larger society and are accountable to that society for their actions.

6 There are three concepts of social responsibility: (1) profit responsibility, (2) stakeholder responsibility, and (3) societal responsibility.

7 Growing interest in societal responsibility has resulted in systematic efforts to assess a firm's objectives, strategies, and performance in the domain of social responsibility. This practice is called a *social audit*.

8 Consumer ethics and social responsibility are as important as business ethics and social responsibility.

Key Terms and Concepts

ethics p. 84
laws p. 84
caveat emptor p. 89
code of ethics p. 90
moral idealism p. 92

utilitarianism p. 93
social responsibility p. 93
cause-related marketing p. 95
social audit p. 95
Valdez Principles p. 97

Chapter Problems and Applications

1 What concept of moral philosophy and of social responsibility are applicable to Molson's practices described in the introduction to this chapter? Why?

2 Compare and contrast moral idealism and utilitarianism as alternative personal moral philosophies.

3 How would you evaluate Milton Friedman's view of the social responsibility of a firm?

4 The text lists several unethical practices of consumers. Can you name others? Why do you think consumers engage in unethical conduct?

5 Cause-related marketing programs have become popular. Describe two such programs that you are familiar with.

6 Is it ethical to charge one customer a higher price than you charge another for the same product simply because you think that customer will pay it?

7 Do you have any problem with people who phone work, occasionally, to say they are sick, even though they just want a day off?

8 When you are at the grocery store you often see people pick some grapes or an apple to munch on when they are shopping. But they don't tell the cashier about it or offer to pay for their munchies. A lot of people do it. Is this behaviour OK?

Understanding Buyers and Markets

*U*sing local and global perspectives to understand people as individual consumers and as members of companies that become organizational buyers is the focus of Part II. Chapter 5 describes world trade in the 1990s and examines global marketing activities such as Ganong's entry into the Japanese market. Chapter 6 examines the actions buyers take in purchasing and using products, and explains how they choose one product or brand over another. In Chapter 7, Bob Procsal, a product manager for fiber optics products at Honeywell, helps explain how manufacturers, retailers, and government agencies also buy goods and services for their own use or resale. Together these chapters help marketing students understand individual, family, and organizational purchases in a variety of cultural environments.

MAPLE CREAMS FROM CANADA

Canada

Net Weight 8 oz/225 g

Global Markets and Cross-Cultural Analysis

AFTER READING THIS CHAPTER YOU SHOULD BE ABLE TO:

▸ Describe the nature and scope of world trade from a global perspective and the implications for Canada.

▸ Understand why some companies and industries in a nation succeed globally while others lose ground or fail.

▸ Explain the effects of economic protectionism and the implications of economic, integration for global marketing practices.

▸ Recognize how cultures differ and appreciate why cultural values, customs, and symbols, coupled with language differences, make global marketing a challenging assignment.

▸ Understand why cultural ethnocentricity can spell disaster in a global marketplace.

Globetrotting in the 1990s

Canadian marketers cannot ignore the vast potential of global markets. Over 95 percent of the world's population lives outside of Canada. Not only are global markets substantial, but many are growing faster than comparable markets in Canada—a fact not lost on both large and small global-minded Canadian companies.

Successful Canadian marketers have responded to three challenges in the global marketplace. First, they have satisfied the needs of a discriminating global consumer who increasingly purchases goods and services on the basis of value. Ganong Brothers, a candy maker for over 100 years and based in St. Stephen, New Brunswick, has managed to penetrate the Japanese market by recognizing that country's growing taste for sweets and candies and by positioning its chocolates as a fine gift item. Second, these marketers have capitalized on trends favouring free trade among industrialized nations throughout the world. Finally, Canadian marketers have pursued opportunities in the newly emerging democracies in Eastern Europe and the former Soviet Union. McDonald's Restaurants of Canada, Ltd., has opened its third outlet in Moscow. McDonald's has invested over $65 million since 1990 to build its three restaurants, a modern food processing plant, and a 12-storey office tower in Moscow. McDonald's employs over 3,000 people and buys from 150 suppliers throughout Russia. It plans to build 20 outlets in Moscow and to expand into St. Petersburg in the near future.[1]

Pursuit of global markets by Canadian and foreign marketers ultimately results in world trade. The purpose of this chapter is to describe the nature and scope of world trade in the 1990s and highlight subtleties involved in marketing across cultures.

DYNAMICS OF WORLD TRADE

The dollar value of world trade has grown an average 13 percent per year since 1970 and will likely exceed $4 trillion in 1996. Manufactured goods and commodities account for 80 percent of world trade. Service industries, including telecommunications, transportation, insurance, education, banking, and tourism, represent the other 20 percent of world trade.

WORLD TRADE FLOWS

All nations and regions of the world do not participate equally in world trade. World trade flows reflect interdependencies among industries, countries, and regions and manifest themselves in country, company, industry, and regional exports and imports.

❚ *Figure 5–1*
Illustrative world trade flows.

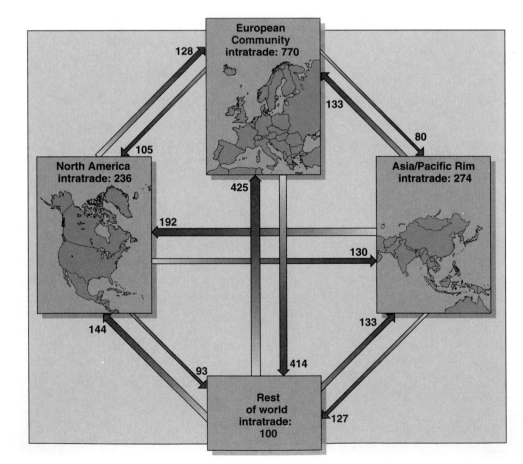

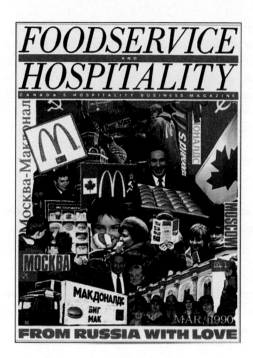

McDonald's Canada seized a marketing opportunity in Russia.

Global Perspective   Figure 5–1 shows the estimated dollar value (in billions) of exports and imports among North American countries, the 12-nation European Community, Asian and Pacific Rim countries, and the rest of the world, including intraregional trade flows.[2] As can be seen, the European Community is the world's largest exporter and importer of goods and services and the most active in intraregional trade.

Not all trade involves the exchange of money for goods or services.[3] In a world where 70 percent of all countries do not have convertible currencies or where government-owned enterprises lack sufficient cash or credit for imports, other means of payment are used. An estimated 10 to 15 percent of world trade involves **countertrade,** the practice of using barter rather than money for making international sales. As an example, PepsiCo trades its soft drink syrup concentrate in Russia in exchange for Stolichnaya vodka, which the company sells through Monsieur Henri Wines, Ltd., in North America. Initial shipments of vodka in 1973 totaled 20,000 cases; in 20 years, this countertrade had expanded to more than a million cases plus two oil tankers. Countertrade is popular with many Eastern European nations and developing countries.

A global perspective on world trade views exports and imports as complementary economic flows: a country's imports affect its exports and its exports affect its imports.[4] Every nation's imports arise from the exports of other nations. As the exports of one country increase, its national output and income rise, which in turn leads to an increase in the demand for imports. This nation's greater demand for imports stimulates the exports of other countries. Increased demand for exports of other nations energizes their economic activity, resulting in higher national income, which stimulates their demand for imports. In short, imports affect exports and vice versa. This phenomenon is called the **trade feedback effect** and is one argument for free trade among nations.

Continually rising consumer income in Japan, Taiwan, South Korea, Hong Kong, and other Asian and Pacific Rim countries, fueled by their growth in exports, has prompted demand for goods and services from Canada and the United States. Many North American companies are benefiting from rising consumer incomes in Asia and the Pacific Rim, including General Motors, which exports cars to Taiwan; Johnson & Johnson with its robust business for lotions and shampoos in South Korea; and Kodak, which dominates the $1 billion film market for professional photography in Japan.

Canadian Perspective   Canada's **gross domestic product** (GDP), which is the monetary value of all goods and services produced in the country during one year, is estimated at over $730 billion.[5] Canada is a trading nation; we export close to 25 percent of our GDP.

The difference between the monetary value of a nation's exports and imports is called its **balance of trade.** When imports exceed exports, a *trade deficit* has occurred. When exports exceed imports, a country has a *trade surplus*. Canada maintains a trade surplus at this time. The value of our exports to other countries is estimated at over $180 billion. However, the value of our imports has climbed dramatically over the past 10 years, and while Canada still enjoys a trade surplus, this surplus is estimated at only about $2 billion dollars, compared with over $4 billion in 1989.[6] Figure 5–2 shows the export–import trend for Canada over the past decade.

Almost every Canadian is affected by Canada's trading activity. The effects vary from the products we buy (Samsung computers from Korea, Waterford crystal from Ireland, wine from France) to those we sell (Ganong chocolates to Japan, Moosehead beer to Sweden) and the additional jobs and improved standard of living that can result from world trade.

World trade flows to and from Canada reflect demand and supply interdependencies for goods and services among nations and industries. While Canada trades with dozens of other countries, the three largest importers of

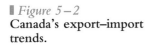

❚ *Figure 5–2*
Canada's export–import trends.

Source: Statistics Canada, Catalogue, 1994, 63-224.

Canadian goods and services are the United States (accounting for close to 75 percent), Japan, and the United Kingdom.

These countries are also the top three exporters to Canada, with both Japan and the United Kingdom enjoying a trade surplus with our country. While Canada's largest trading partner, the United States, is the world's perennial leader in terms of gross domestic product and is a leader in world exports, it is also the world's largest importer and has had successive trade deficits over the years. Canada has enjoyed a trade surplus with the United States over the past decade.

COMPETITIVE ADVANTAGE OF NATIONS

As Canadian companies in many industries find themselves competing against foreign competitors at home and abroad, Canadian government policymakers are increasingly asking why some companies and industries in a country succeed globally while others lose ground or fail. As summarized in Figure 5–3, Michael Porter suggests a "diamond" to explain a nation's competitive advantage and why some industries and firms become world leaders.[7] He identified four key elements, which appear in Figure 5–3:

1 *Factor conditions.* These reflect a nation's ability to turn its natural resources, education, and infrastructure into a competitive advantage. The Dutch lead the

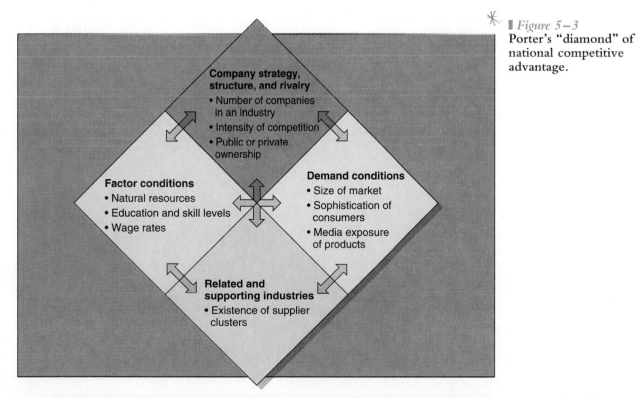

❚ *Figure 5–3*
Porter's "diamond" of national competitive advantage.

Sources: M. E. Porter, *The Competitive Advantage of Nations* (New York: Free Press, 1990); and M. E. Porter, "Why Nations Triumph," *Fortune,* March 12, 1990, pp. 94–108.

world in the cut-flower industry because of their research in flower cultivation, packaging, and shipping—not because of their weather.

2 *Demand conditions.* These include both the number and sophistication of domestic customers for an industry's product. Japan's sophisticated consumers demand quality in their TVs and radios, thereby making Japan's producers the world leaders in the electronics industry.

3 *Related and supporting industries.* Firms and industries seeking leadership in global markets need clusters of world-class suppliers that accelerate innovation. The German leadership in printing relates directly to the cluster of supporting German suppliers.

4 *Company strategy, structure, and rivalry.* These factors include the conditions governing the way a nation's businesses are organized and managed, along with the intensity of domestic competition. The Italian shoe industry has become the world leader because of intense domestic competition that enhances quality and innovation.

In Porter's study, case histories of firms in over 100 industries were analyzed. While the strategies employed by the most successful global competitors were different in many respects, a common theme emerged—a firm that succeeds in global markets has first succeeded in intense domestic competition. Hence competitive advantage for global firms grows out of relentless, continuing improvement, innovation, and change.

It is important to note, however, that it is not essential to be a giant company to gain benefits in global markets. Numerous small firms succeed in foreign markets by observing trends and capitalizing on them, through licensing arrangements, or by using unique technologies. As we saw in the chapter opener, Ganong Brothers observed a trend that the Japanese were increasing their intake of sweets and candies. Ganong also discovered that the Japanese

Ganong Brothers shows that even smaller firms can compete in global markets.

value family-owned businesses and respect firms with a history of providing quality products. Ganong was able to leverage these factors in order to secure entry into the Japanese market.[8]

Concept Check

1 The practice of using barter rather than money for making international sales is called _____.

2 What is the trade feedback effect?

3 What variables influence why some companies and industries in a country succeed globally while others lose ground or fail?

EMERGENCE OF A BORDERLESS ECONOMIC WORLD

Two trends in the late 20th century have significantly affected world trade. One trend has been a gradual decline of economic protectionism exercised by individual countries. The second trend is evident in the formal economic integration and free trade among nations.

DECLINE OF ECONOMIC PROTECTIONISM

Protectionism is the practice of shielding one or more sectors of a country's economy from foreign competition through the use of tariffs or quotas. The principal economic argument for protectionism is that it preserves jobs, protects a nation's political security, discourages economic dependency on other countries, and encourages the development of domestic industries. Read the accompanying Ethics and Social Responsibility Alert and ask yourself if protectionism has an ethical dimension.

Tariffs and quotas discourage world trade and often result in higher domestic prices on the goods and services produced by protected industries.[9] **Tariffs,** which are a government tax on goods and services entering a country, primarily serve to raise prices on imports. The average tariff on imported manufactured goods varies by country; in Japan tariffs average 2 percent, while Mexico's tariffs average 10 percent.

The effect of tariffs on world trade and consumer prices is substantial. Consider rice imports to Japan. Experts believe that if the Japanese rice market were opened to imports by lowering tariffs, lower prices would save Japanese consumers billions of dollars annually.

A **quota** is a restriction placed on the amount of a product allowed to enter or leave a country. Quotas can be mandatory or voluntary, and may be legislated or negotiated by governments. Import quotas seek to guarantee domestic industries access to a certain percentage of their domestic market. The best-known quota concerns the mandatory or voluntary limits on foreign automobile sales in many countries. Quotas imposed by European countries make cars imported to Europe 25 percent more expensive than similar models sold in Japan, costing European customers $40 billion per year.[10] Less visible quotas

ETHICS AND SOCIAL RESPONSIBILITY ALERT

Global Ethics and Global Economics: The Ethics of Protectionism

World trade benefits from free and fair trade among nations. Nevertheless, the governments of many countries continue to use tariffs and quotas to protect their various domestic industries through protectionism.

Sugar import quotas in the United States, automobile import quotas in many European countries, beer import tariffs in Canada, and rice import tariffs in Japan protect domestic industries, but also interfere with world trade for these products. Regional trade agreements such as those found in the provisions of the European Community and the North American Free Trade Agreement may also pose a situation where member nations can obtain preferential treatment in quotas and tariffs whereas nonmember nations do not. Protectionism, in its many forms, raises an interesting global ethical question: is protectionism, no matter how applied, an ethical practice?

Sources: Based on M. D. Lemonick, "The Big Green Payoff," *Time*, June 1, 1992, pp. 62–63; W. K. Stevens, "Economists Strive to Find Environment's Bottom Line," *The New York Times*, September 8, 1992, pp. B5, B8; and "The Green Giant? It May Be Japan," *Business Week*, February 24, 1992, pp. 74–75.

apply to the importation of many other products such as electronic and agricultural products.

Every country engages in some form of protectionism. However, protectionism has declined over the past 50 years, in large part because of the **General Agreement on Tariffs and Trade (GATT).**[11] This international treaty was intended to limit trade barriers and promote world trade through the reduction of tariffs. Since the inception of GATT in 1947, tariffs imposed by industrialized countries have declined from a country average of 40 percent to less than 5 percent today. However, GATT does not explicitly address nontariff trade barriers such as quotas or world trade in services.

RISE OF ECONOMIC INTEGRATION

In recent years a number of countries with similar economic objectives have formed transnational trade groups or signed trade agreements for the purpose of promoting free trade among member nations and enhancing their individual economies. Two of the most recent and best-known examples are the European Community (EC) and the North American Free Trade Agreement (NAFTA).

European Community   On January 1, 1993, twelve European countries effectively eliminated most of the barriers to the free flow of goods, services, capital, and labour across their borders. This event, after decades of negotiation, formed a single market composed of over 340 million consumers with a combined gross national product of over $6.5 trillion, or 28 percent of the world total.

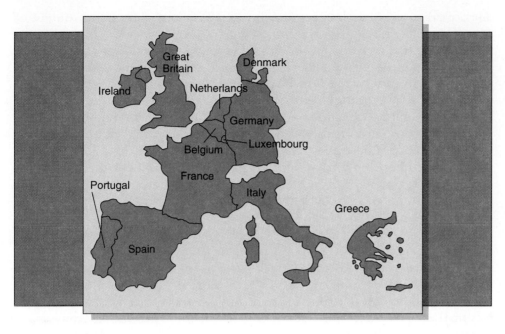

Country members in the European Community (EC) are Great Britain, Ireland, Denmark, Belgium, the Netherlands, Luxembourg, Germany, France, Italy, Greece, Portugal, and Spain (see Figure 5–4). Austria, Finland, Iceland, Norway, and Sweden have applied for membership. The Swiss voted not to join the EC.

Numerous marketing opportunities were made possible with the creation of the European Community. Most visibly, firms will no longer find it necessary to exclusively market their products and services on a nation-by-nation basis. Rather, pan-European marketing strategies are now possible because of greater uniformity in product and packaging standards, fewer differences in regulations countries impose on advertising and promotion, and removal of most tariffs that affect pricing practices. Distribution throughout Europe from a single location in one of the 12 countries will become more feasible given open borders. Specific implications for pan-European marketing strategies are discussed in later chapters. However, it is important to note that the removal of trade barriers will not overcome the unique product preferences of European consumers. As we will see later, cross-cultural differences between the countries are hurdles to be jumped by marketers in the European Community.

North American Free Trade Agreement   The **North American Free Trade Agreement** of 1992 (**NAFTA**) lifted many trade barriers between Canada, the United States, and Mexico. NAFTA was viewed by the Canadian government as a natural extension of the Canada–US Free Trade Agreement (FTA) established in 1988. At that time, the FTA was the largest and broadest trading agreement ever concluded between two countries, establishing a $250 billion-a-year economic relationship.

In transforming the FTA to NAFTA, one of the world's largest free trade zones was created. The United States, Canada, and Mexico collectively represent a market of 370 million consumers and a joint annual economic output of over $6.5 trillion. The FTA was important to Canada, since the United States is our largest trading partner. Canada's interest in a trilateral deal was rooted in a desire to protect and extend what it gained in the bilateral agreement. In particular, Canada wanted to avoid a loss of trade and investment with Mexico, which might have occurred had the United States become the sole North American country with tariff-free access to all three markets. Trade and investment flows between Canada and Mexico are not significant at this time and wouldn't warrant a bilateral agreement between the countries. However, Canadian companies would have faced greater competition from their US competitors if the United States was able to source its manufacturing components more cheaply in Mexico. With NAFTA, Canada obtains the same sourcing opportunities in Mexico as the United States.

There are other reasons why Canada wanted this trilateral agreement. Mexico is Canada's largest trading partner in Latin America. While two-way trade is valued at only $3 billion, total Mexican imports of Canadian products grew by 214 percent from 1987 to 1991.[12] Mexico still enjoys a trade surplus with Canada, but it is one of the fastest-growing markets in the world. Canada sees market opportunities in that country. Mexico is experiencing growing per capita income and increased demand for imported consumer goods. Mexico also needs imported technology especially in its transportation, financial services, and telecommunications industries, areas in which Canada has a competitive advantage. Agriculture, fishing, and mining are three other areas that are priority industries for Mexico and could represent other business opportunities for Canadian companies.[13]

Many people in Canada and the United States had opposed NAFTA. Much of this opposition focussed on Mexico's low-wage competitive advantage and the perceived threat it posed for certain Canadian and US labour-intensive industries. It is true that Mexican wage rates are extremely low by North American standards—one-sixth to one-seventh of Canadian and US rates in comparable industries. However, labour costs are but one of many potential determinants of a nation's competitive advantage, as we saw earlier (see Figure 5–3). The competitiveness of a nation depends on relative costs of all production inputs (natural resources, land, and capital, as well as labour); the degree of efficiency with which those factors are combined to produce marketable products (i.e., productivity); and the market appeal of the products. Over the past decade, productivity and noncost factors such as quality and image of products have come to play an increasingly important role in determining a competitive advantage on both an industry and a country-specific level.[14]

As the accompanying Marketing Action Memo shows, of the 15 sources of competitive advantage used to compare the NAFTA countries, only half relate to comparative costs. At present, Mexico's only source of competitive advantage is wages, and this advantage may not be sustainable over time. Mexico's 85 million inhabitants are becoming more sophisticated and have a marked preference for imported goods. Canada may have greater opportunities to compete on an "image" as opposed to price dimension in this new trade zone.

The tariff provisions of NAFTA have already resulted in some changes by manufacturing firms. For example, Whirlpool Corporation's Canadian subsid-

MARKETING · ACTION · MEMO

Evaluating the Competitive Advantage of the Three NAFTA Nations

Sources of competitive advantage vary among countries and change over time. Trade barriers are often designed to enhance, offset, and in some cases obliterate basic sources of competitive advantage. Trade patterns among the three North American economies reflect both their respective sources of competitive advantage and their trade barriers. With the NAFTA agreement much has been made of the relative competitive advantages of each of the participating nations under a free market access scenario. Particular emphasis has been placed on Mexico's wage advantage. As can be seen from the chart, Mexico's sole competitive advantage is its low wages. However, those low wages also reflect low levels of productivity, since Mexico experiences high absenteeism and labour turnover. Moreover, the maintenance of high tariffs through the late 1980s, and evidence of Mexico's widening trade deficit, show that Mexico's low wage levels have been only of limited use in securing and guarding markets. In the future, as Mexico's economy matures, it is likely to develop new sources of advantage but at the cost of losing its wage advantage. This is generally what happens in newly industrialized nations (NICs). For example, as countries like Hong Kong, Taiwan, and Korea prospered economically, wage levels rose closer to those of Western industrialized nations. Mexico would then have to develop new sources of advantage in order to stay competitive. For Canada, its resource endowment should be a substantial advantage for

years to come, particularly as it gains a more equal footing with the United States in other areas of potential competitive advantage. The United States still holds an advantage in terms of productivity, and, very importantly, in marketing.

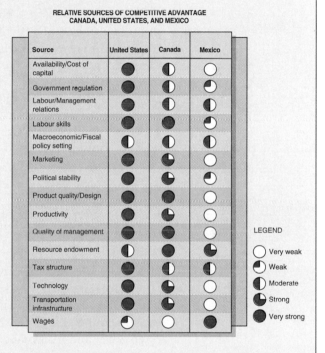

Source: Adapted from *The Search for Competitive Advantage: A New North American Free Trade Zone,* Bank of Montreal, Economics Department, April 1993.

iary stopped making washing machines in Canada and moved that operation to Ohio. Whirlpool then shifted production of household trash compactors, kitchen ranges, and compact dryers to Canada. While NAFTA creates an opportunity for freer trade between Canada, the United States, and Mexico, many interprovincial trade barriers exist in Canada that still restrict the movement of goods and services between the provinces. The federal government and many of the provincial governments are currently looking at ways to remove or lessen those trade barriers.

Concept Check	1 What is protectionism?
	2 What is GATT, what is its purpose, and what specific trade barriers does it not explicitly address?
	3 The North American Free Trade Agreement was designed to promote free trade among which countries?

CROSS-CULTURAL ANALYSIS IN A GLOBAL ECONOMY

World trade represents the sum of billions upon billions of exchanges between buyers and sellers across the globe. The exchange relationship ranges from the impulse purchase of a Big Mac for about 20 francs ($3.25) in Paris to the lengthy negotiation between Boeing Company and the Chinese government in Beijing for passenger airplanes costing millions of dollars each.

Marketers must be sensitive to the cultural underpinnings of different societies if they are to initiate and consummate mutually beneficial exchange relationships with global consumers. A necessary step in this process is **cross-cultural analysis,** which involves the study of similarities and differences among consumers in two or more nations or societies.[15]

CULTURAL VARIABILITY

Cultures differ in many respects. However, four dimensions have been identified that account for much of the variability among cultures.[16] These dimensions have important marketing implications.

1 *Power distance.* The way interpersonal relationships are formed when differences in power or influence are perceived. Some cultures emphasize strict, dependent interpersonal relationships (e.g., Japanese, Mexican, and Russian), while others, such as the Scandinavian countries, stress a greater degree of equality and informality.

2 *Uncertainty avoidance.* The extent to which people feel uncomfortable in uncertain and ambiguous situations. This characteristic affects how people respond to innovation and change and has been shown to be high in the newly emerging democracies of Eastern Europe.

3 *Masculinity.* The degree to which sex roles are defined. Many Asian and Latin American countries have traditionally emphasized clearly delineated sex roles (e.g., woman as wife and mother), while countries like Denmark, Finland, and Sweden have not. It is worth noting that sex roles are changing in all industrialized countries, including Canada.

4 *Individualism.* The extent to which the individual is valued over the group. In individualistic cultures, consumers attach importance to personal enjoyment and self-improvement. In collectivist cultures, people subordinate their personal ambitions and accept their position in life. Canada, Great Britain, and the United States represent individualistic cultures. Many Asian countries, Turkey, and Bulgaria are examples of collectivist cultures.

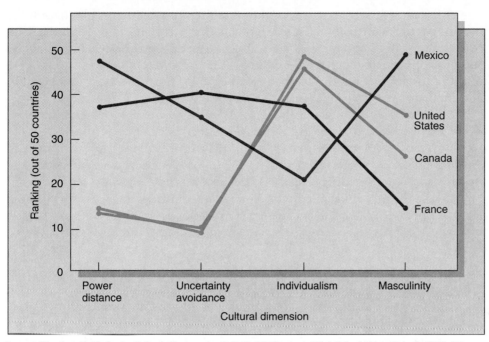

| Figure 5–5
**Profile of four countries
on four cultural
dimensions.**

Sources: Based on G. Hofstede, *Culture's Consequences: Individual Differences in Work Related Values* (Beverly Hills, CA: Sage Publications, 1980); and D. Hellriegel and J. W. Slocum, Jr., *Management,* 6th ed. (Reading, MA: Addison-Wesley Publishing Company, 1992).

Figure 5–5 profiles four countries on these cultural dimensions. As can be seen, the United States and Canada rank lowest on uncertainty avoidance, whereas Mexico ranks highest on masculinity. These dimensions have important implications for marketing across cultures. For example, a focus on group consensus and deference to others often observed among Japanese business negotiators is different from the Canadian style of negotiation. Similarly, societies prone to avoid uncertainty are less likely to adopt new products and services. Sex roles related to family decision making will determine the relative influence and independence of the spouses in making purchase decisions.

Cultural change along one or more of these dimensions is slow and often difficult. In some collectivist societies, evidence of individualistic tendencies is formally frowned upon. For example, the Malaysian government recently passed regulations warning that "advertisements must not project or promote an excessively aspirational lifestyle."[17]

ASPECTS OF CULTURE

A thorough cross-cultural analysis involves an understanding and appreciation of the values, customs, symbols, and language of other societies.

Values   A society's **values** represent personally or socially preferable modes of conduct or states of existence that are enduring. Understanding and working with these aspects of a society are important factors in successful global marketing. For example:[18]

▪ A door-to-door salesman would find selling in Italy impossible, because it is improper for a man to call on a woman if she is home alone. Similarly, a Procter & Gamble commercial for Camay soap that was popular in Western Europe flopped when it aired in Japan. The ad, which showed a husband interrupting his wife's bath, was thought to be in poor taste, since it is considered improper for a Japanese man to intrude on his wife.

▪ McDonald's does not sell hamburgers in its restaurants in India, because the cow is considered sacred by almost 85 percent of the population.

▪ Germans have not been overly receptive to the use of credit cards such as Visa or MasterCard and installment debt to purchase goods and services. Indeed, the German word for debt, *Schuld,* is the same as the German word for guilt.

▪ In the Arab world and Latin American countries, business-to-business negotiations are a social event where bargaining is an integral part of any transaction. Efforts to adhere to a strict agenda and impersonalize the negotiation could be viewed as an insult.

These examples illustrate how cultural values can influence behaviour in different societies. Cultural values become apparent in the personal values of individuals that affect their attitudes and beliefs, and the importance they assign to specific behaviours and attributes of goods and services. These personal values affect attitudes about consumption. For example, Canadian companies wanting to succeed in the global arena must become environmentally friendly, since "green behaviour" is already a well-entrenched value in many societies, particularly Europe. Accordingly, IBM is considering a global "cradle-to-grave" approach to green marketing, including having customers return their products for disposal, reuse, and/or recycling.

Customs   **Customs** are the norms and expectations about the way people do things in a specific country. Clearly, customs can vary significantly from country to country. Did you know that mothers in Tanzania don't serve their children eggs? They believe that eggs cause both baldness and impotence. General Mills designed a cake mix especially for preparation in the rice cookers used by Japanese consumers. It failed because of a lack of understanding of Japanese consumers and customs: Japanese take pride in the purity of their rice, which they thought would be contaminated if the cooker were used to prepare another food. Some other customs unusual to Canadians include the following:[19]

- In France, men wear more than twice the amount of cosmetics that women do.
- Japanese women give Japanese men chocolates on Valentine's Day.
- Businesspeople in Middle Eastern and Latin American countries prefer to negotiate within inches of their colleagues; Canadians who find this difficult can offend their potential associates and ruin a possible agreement.

Customs also relate to nonverbal behaviour of individuals in different cultural settings. For example, in many European countries it is considered impolite not to have both hands on the table in business meetings. A simple gesture in a commercial such as pointing a finger is perfectly acceptable in Western culture, but is perceived as an insult in Middle and Far Eastern countries. Direct eye contact is viewed positively in North and Latin America but

Tiffany & Company is sensitive to cultural symbols in its packaging.

negatively in Japan. Casual touching is also inappropriate in Japan, while men often hold hands in Middle Eastern countries as a sign of friendship.[20] Business executives in Japan like to hold their opinions, listen longer, and pause before responding in meetings. Sometimes the silence is misread by North American executives as nonresponsiveness.

Companies with worldwide operations are sensitive to how customs can make the difference between success and failure in global markets. For example, Colgate-Palmolive, General Electric, and Honda represent firms that place a high priority on cross-cultural training relating to customs.[21]

Cultural Symbols **Cultural symbols** are things that represent ideas and concepts to a society or nationality. Symbols and symbolism play an important role in cross-cultural analysis because different cultures ascribe different meanings to things. So important is the role of symbols that a field of study, called **semiotics,** has emerged that examines the correspondence between symbols and their role in the assignment of meaning for people. By adroitly using cultural symbols, global marketers can tie positive symbolism to their products and services to enhance their attractiveness to consumers. However, improper use of symbols can spell disaster. A culturally sensitive global marketer will know that Canadians are superstitious about the number 13 and Japanese feel the same way about the number 4. Shi, the Japanese word for four, is also the word for death. Knowing this, golf ball manufacturers do not sell golf balls in packages of four

Country of origin can be
a symbol of quality.

" THEY'RE MADE IN ITALY . "

in Japan, and Tiffany & Company sells its fine glassware and china in sets of five, not four, in that country.[22]

Cultural symbols can evoke deep feelings. Just ask executives at Coca-Cola Company's Italian office. In a series of advertisements directed at Italian vacationers, the Eiffel Tower and the Tower of Pisa were turned into the familiar Coca-Cola bottle. However, when, as part of the same ad campaign, the white marble columns in the Parthenon, which crowns Athens's Acropolis, were similarly turned into Coca-Cola bottles, the Greeks got word of it and were outraged. Greeks refer to the Acropolis as the "holy rock," and a government official said that the Parthenon is an "international symbol of excellence" and "whoever insults the Parthenon insults international culture." Coca-Cola apologized for the ad.[23]

Global marketers are also sensitive to the fact that the country of origin or manufacture of products and services can symbolize superior or poor quality in some countries. For example, Russian consumers believe products made in Japan and Germany are superior in quality to products from North America and the United Kingdom, and Japanese consumers believe Japanese products are superior to those made in Europe and North America.[24]

Language   Global marketers should know not only the native tongues of countries in which they market their products and services, but also the nuances and idioms of a language. Even though about 100 official languages exist in the world, anthropologists estimate that at least 3,000 different languages are spoken.[25]

There are nine official languages spoken in the 12-nation European Community, and Canada has two official languages (English and French). Fifteen major languages are spoken in India alone, although English is the official language.

English, French, and Spanish are the principal languages used in global diplomacy and commerce. However, the best language to communicate with consumers is their own, as any seasoned international marketer will attest. Unintended meanings of brand names and messages have ranged from the absurd to the obscene. For instance:[26]

- When an advertising agency set out to launch Procter & Gamble's successful Pert shampoo in Canada, it turned out that the name means "lost" in French. Procter & Gamble substituted the brand name Pret, which means "ready."
- In Italy, Cadbury Schweppes, the world's third-largest soft drink manufacturer, realized that its Schweppes Tonic Water brand had to be renamed Schweppes Tonica because "il water" turned out to be the idiom for a bathroom.
- The Vicks brand name common in Canada is German slang for sexual intimacy; therefore, Vicks is called Wicks in Germany.

Experienced global marketers use **back translation,** whereby a translated word or phrase is retranslated into the original language by a different interpreter to catch errors. Nevertheless, unintended meanings still occur in the most unlikely situations. Recently, a Japanese tire manufacturer found it necessary to publicly apologize in Brunei (a British-protected sultanate on the coast of Borneo) for the tread grooves on one of its tire brands. Some critics claimed the tread resembled a verse from the Koran, the sacred book of the Muslims written in Arabic.[27]

Cultural Ethnocentricity   The tendency for people to view their own values, customs, symbols, and language favourably is well known. However, the belief that aspects of one's culture are superior to another's is called **cultural ethnocentricity** and is a sure impediment to successful global marketing. Cultural ethnocentricity can often result in stereotyping others, including their behaviours, and result in a superficial understanding of and virtually no appreciation for the culture of another people.

An outgrowth of cultural ethnocentricity exists in the purchase and use of goods and services produced outside of a country. Global marketers are acutely aware that certain groups within countries disfavour imported products, not on the basis of price, features, or performance, but purely because of their foreign origin. **Consumer ethnocentrism** is the tendency to believe that it is inappropriate, indeed immoral, to purchase foreign-made products.[28] Ethnocentric consumers believe that buying imported products is wrong because such purchases are unpatriotic, harm domestic industries, and cause domestic unemployment. The prevalence of consumer ethnocentrism in the global marketplace is unknown. However, a recent study indicated that 5 percent of consumers in the United Kingdom and France and 6 percent of consumers in Germany said that knowing a product was made in their country was the single most important factor in considering the purchase of a product.[29]

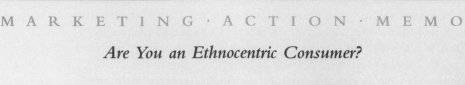

MARKETING · ACTION · MEMO

Are You an Ethnocentric Consumer?

Would you tend to agree or disagree with the following statements?

1 Buy Canadian products. Keep Canada working.
2 It is always best to purchase Canadian products.
3 It may cost me in the long run, but I prefer to support Canadian products.
4 Curbs should be put on all imports.

If you tended to agree with these 4 statements and 13 other, similar statements, you can call yourself an ethnocentric consumer.

Two researchers developed a 17-statement consumer ethnocentrism scale designed to identify the tendency of consumers to purchase foreign- versus domestic-made products. Frequent agreement with statements like those above means that a consumer would have a tendency to accentuate the positive aspects of domestic products and discount the virtues of foreign-made items. It is important to note that consumer ethnocentrism has been observed in many countries including France, Japan, and Germany. In these countries, it was found that the more ethnocentric a consumer was, the less likely he was to rate the quality of foreign-made products more highly

than domestic products. The prevalence of consumer ethnocentrism in a country has important marketing implications. Specifically, consumer resistance to foreign-made products will make the task of global marketers more difficult.

Sources: Based on J. Herche, "A Note on the Predictive Validity of the CETSCALE," *Journal of Marketing Science,* Summer 1992, pp. 261–64; R. G. Netemeyer, S. Durvasula, and D. R. Lichtenstein, "A Cross-National Assessment of the Reliability and Validity of the CETSCALE," *Journal of Marketing Research,* August 1991, pp. 320–27; T. A. Shimp and S. Sharma, "Consumer Ethnocentrism: Construction and Validation of the CETSCALE," *Journal of Marketing Research,* August 1987, pp. 280–89; and N. Giges, "Europeans Buy Outside Goods, but Like Local Ads," *Advertising Age,* April 27, 1992, pp. I-1, I-26.

Are you an ethnocentric consumer? The accompanying Marketing Action Memo might help you answer this question.

CULTURAL IMPLICATIONS FOR GLOBAL MARKETING

Values, customs, symbols, and language combine to create unique qualities of different cultures. Understanding cultural differences and similarities will become even more important to global marketers as artificial boundaries between societies crumble with the decline of economic protectionism. Successful global marketers will recognize (1) the potential for using cultural factors in devising their worldwide strategies and (2) the importance of anticipating cultural changes and linking these changes to consumption patterns.

Transnational Culture Groupings Cultures transcend national political boundaries. Accordingly, companies accustomed to using a sometimes ineffective and often inefficient nation-by-nation approach for marketing their products and services will look toward larger groupings of prospective buyers, often on the basis of subtle cultural similarities.

One recent study identified six clusters of Western Europeans that transcend national borders.[30] This research demonstrated that consumers living in different countries have similar cultural characteristics, consumers from different countries are often more similar to each other than they are to consumers in their own country, and it is feasible and possibly preferable to market to large European culture clusters. This research also suggests that the regional marketing strategies described in Chapter 3 have potential application in Western Europe. For example, L'Oreal, a pioneer of international marketing in the global health and beauty aids industry, has introduced the Golden Beauty brand of sun care products through its Helena Rubinstein subsidiary in Western Europe. Knowing that cultural differences related to skin care and tanning exist, Golden Beauty advertising features dark tanning for Northern Europeans, skin protection to avoid wrinkles among Latin Europeans, and beautiful skin for Europeans living along the Mediterranean Sea.[31]

Cultural Change Cultures change slowly. Nevertheless, overcoming impediments to world trade is likely to accelerate the rate of cultural change in societies around the world. A challenge facing global marketers is to anticipate how cultures are changing, particularly with respect to the purchase and use of goods and services.

An acknowledged master of anticipating cultural change and responding quickly is Nestlé, the world's largest packaged food manufacturer, coffee roaster, and chocolate maker. Nestlé derives 98 percent of its sales outside of its home country, Switzerland, because the company is always among the first to identify changing consumption patterns in diverse cultures. Consider Great Britain and Japan, with two very different cultures but a common passion—tea. Nestlé pioneered coffee marketing in both countries with its Nescafé instant coffee. The cultural preference for tea was changing, and Nestlé capitalized on this change. Today, Britons consume one cup of coffee for every two cups of tea. Twenty-five years ago, the ratio was one cup of coffee for every six cups of tea. The Japanese are now among the world's heaviest consumers of instant coffee on a per capita basis. Nestlé is a dominant coffee marketer in both countries.[32]

Concept Check

1 Cultures tend to vary along what four key dimensions?

2 Semiotics involves the study of _____.

3 Why might an ethnocentric consumer also tend to favour protectionist world trade policies?

Summary

1 The dollar value of world trade has grown an average of 13 percent per year since 1970 and is expected to exceed $4 trillion in 1996. Manufactured goods and commodities account for 80 percent of world trade, while services account for 20 percent.

2 Not all world trade involves the exchange of money for goods or services. About 10 to 15 percent of world trade involves countertrade, the practice of using barter rather than money for making international sales.

3 A global perspective on world trade views exports and imports as complementary economic flows. A country's exports affect its imports and vice versa. This phenomenon is called the *trade feedback effect*.

4 Canada is a trading nation, exporting 25 percent of its gross domestic product. Canada enjoys a trade surplus at this time. The United States is our largest trading partner.

5 The reason why some companies and some industries in a country succeed globally while others do not lies in their nation's competitive advantage. A nation's competitive advantage arises from specific conditions in a nation that foster success.

6 The 21st century holds the promise of a borderless economic world due to a decline in economic protectionism and the rise of transnational trade groups and free trade agreements.

7 Since world trade arises from exchanges between buyers and sellers across the globe, marketers must be sensitive to the cultural underpinnings of different societies. Careful cross-cultural analysis is necessary to initiate and consummate mutually beneficial exchange relationships with global consumers.

8 Successful global marketers understand how cultures around the world differ. They recognize how values, customs, symbols, and language affect consumer behaviour.

9 Cultural ethnocentricity is an impediment to successful global marketing.

Key Terms and Concepts

countertrade p. 105

trade feedback effect p. 106

gross domestic product p. 106

balance of trade p. 106

protectionism p. 109

tariffs p. 109

quota p. 109

General Agreement on Tariffs and Trade (GATT) p. 110

North American Free Trade Agreement (NAFTA) p. 111

cross-cultural analysis p. 114

values p. 115

customs p. 116

cultural symbols p. 117

semiotics p. 117

back translation p. 119

cultural ethnocentricity p. 119

consumer ethnocentrism p. 119

Chapter Problems and Applications

1 What is meant by this statement: "Quotas are a hidden tax on consumers, whereas tariffs are a more obvious one."

2 Would an ethnocentric consumer also favour economic protectionism? Why?

3 Is the trade feedback effect described in the text a long-run or a short-run view on world trade flows? Explain your answer.

4 Why would Canada have wanted to extend the FTA (Canada–US Free Trade Agreement) to include Mexico in NAFTA?

5 How successful would a television commercial in Japan be if it featured a husband surprising his wife in her dressing area on Valentine's Day with a small box of chocolates containing four candies? Why?

6 Merrill Lynch & Company, Inc., is the holding company for the world's largest securities brokerage firm, Merrill Lynch, Pierce, Fenner & Smith. The company ran a successful advertising campaign several years ago featuring a bull standing apart from a herd of cattle. The symbolism portrayed in the advertising was that Merrill Lynch was "a breed apart." How well would this advertising campaign be received in Asian countries?

7 What specific advice would you give to a group of Canadian executives planning to negotiate a business transaction with Latin American executives?

8 Is Mexico's competitive advantage of low labour costs likely to be maintained as its economy matures? Why?

Consumer Behaviour

AFTER READING THIS CHAPTER YOU SHOULD BE ABLE TO:

▼ Outline the stages in the consumer decision process.

▼ Distinguish between three variations of the consumer decision process: routine, limited, and extended problem solving.

▼ Explain how psychological influences affect consumer behaviour, particularly purchase decision processes.

▼ Identify major sociocultural influences on consumer behaviour and their effects on purchase decisions.

▼ Recognize how marketers can use knowledge of consumer behaviour to better understand and influence individual and family purchases.

It Just Feels Right

Who buys or influences 77 percent of all new car sales in Canada?[1] Who wasn't taken seriously by automobile manufacturers and dealers as recently as 10 years ago? Women—yes, women.

Automobile marketing has undergone a significant change in recent years as women have become an increasingly important part of the automobile market. Jan Thompson, vice president of sales operations for Mazda and one of the highest-ranking woman executives in the automobile industry, has made women her special consumer target.

After helping to draft the marketing plan for Lexus while an executive at Toyota, Thompson joined Mazda and participated in the launch of the successful Miata roadster with a nostalgic advertising campaign and the memorable theme, "It just feels right." Her sense of the market and timing couldn't have been better. Women purchase the majority of subcompact and compact cars, and a car's "feel" is important to them. Women prefer sleek, sporty exteriors. Interior designs that fit proportions of smaller drivers as well as opening ease of doors, trunks, and hoods are equally important. Auto manufacturers have also come to realize that designing vehicles for women often means attention to children as well. For instance, new designs in the popular minivans for families will better accommodate toddlers, via integrated child seats.

Recognition of women as important decision makers and influencers in car buying has also altered the behaviour of auto dealers. Many dealers now use a one-price policy and have stopped negotiating a car's price.[2] Industry research indicates that the majority of new car buyers dread the price negotiation process involved in buying a car, and women often refuse to do it at all. The one-price policy has proved very successful for Saturn, a car company that has a significant number of women buyers.

This chapter examines **consumer behaviour,** the actions a person takes in purchasing and using products and services and the mental and social processes that precede and follow these actions. Successful marketing begins with understanding how and why consumers behave as they do. This chapter will help answer these questions.

CONSUMER PURCHASE DECISION PROCESS

Behind the visible act of making a purchase lies an important decision process that must be investigated. The stages a buyer passes through in making choices about which products and services to buy is the **purchase decision process.** This process has the five stages shown in Figure 6–1: (1) problem recognition, (2) information search, (3) alternative evaluation, (4) purchase decision, and (5) postpurchase behaviour.

PROBLEM RECOGNITION: PERCEIVING A NEED

Problem recognition, the initial step in the purchase decision, is perceiving a difference between one's ideal and actual situations big enough to trigger a decision.[3] This can be as simple as finding an empty milk carton in the refrigerator; noting, as a first-year college student, that your high school clothes are not in the style that other students are wearing; or realizing that your stereo system may not be working properly.

In marketing, advertisements or salespeople can activate a consumer's decision process by showing the shortcomings of competing (or currently owned) products. For instance, an advertisement for a compact disc (CD) player could stimulate problem recognition because it emphasizes the sound quality of CD players over that of the conventional stereo system you may now own.

INFORMATION SEARCH: SEEKING VALUE

After recognizing a problem, a consumer begins to search for information, the next stage in the purchase decision process. First, you may scan your memory for previous experiences with products or brands.[4] This action is called *internal search.* For frequently purchased products such as shampoo, this may be enough. Or a consumer may undertake an *external search* for information.[5] This is espe-

❚ *Figure 6–1*
Purchase decision process.

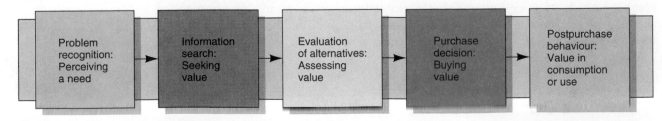

cially needed when past experience or knowledge is insufficient, the risk of making a wrong purchase decision is high, and the cost of gathering information is low. The primary sources of external information are (1) *personal sources,* such as relatives and friends whom the consumer trusts; (2) *public sources,* including various product-rating organizations such as *Consumer Reports,* government agencies, and TV "consumer programs"; and (3) *marketer-dominated sources,* such as information from sellers that includes advertising, salespeople, and point-of-purchase displays in stores.[6]

Suppose you consider buying an expensive or complex product, such as a CD player. You will probably tap several of these information sources: friends and relatives, CD player advertisements, and several stores carrying CD players (for demonstrations). You might study the comparative evaluation of single-play model CD players that appeared in *Consumer Reports,* published by a product-testing organization, a portion of which appears in Figure 6−2.

ALTERNATIVE EVALUATION: ASSESSING VALUE

The information search stage clarifies the problem for the consumer by (1) suggesting criteria to use for the purchase, (2) yielding brand names that might meet the criteria, and (3) developing consumer value perceptions. Based only on the information shown in Figure 6−2, what selection criteria would you use in buying a CD player? Would you use price, track-finding speed, taping convenience, or some combination of these and other criteria?

Figure 6−2
Consumer Reports' evaluation of low-price compact disc players (abridged).

BRAND AND MODEL	PRICE	CHANGER CAPACITY	PROGRAMMING CAPACITY	DISC-ERROR CORRECTION	TRACK-FINDING SPEED	BUMP IMMUNITY	TAPING CONVENIENCE
Technics SL-PD927	$269	5	32	◉	◉	◓	○
Philips CDC935	250	5	30	◉	◑	◉	◑
Sony CDP-C79ES	480	5	32	◉	◉	◉	◉
Carver SD/ A -350	345	5	32	◑	◑	◉	◒
JVC XL-F207TN, A Best Buy	220	5	32	◉	◑	◑	◒
Yamaha CDC-735	385	5	40	◑	◉	○	○
Denon DCM-520	420	5	20	◑	◑	○	◒
Onkyo DX-C606	400	6	40	◉	◑	◓	◑
Sony CDP-C725	335	5	32	◑	◉	○	◉
Denon DCM-320	275	5	20	◑	◑	○	◒

Rating: ◉   ◑   ○   ◒   ●
Better ◄ - - - - - - - - - - ► Worse

Source: "CD Players," *Consumer Reports,* March 1992, pp. 176−77.

For some of you, the information provided may be inadequate because it does not contain all the factors you might consider when evaluating CD players. These factors are a consumer's **evaluative criteria,** which represent both the objective attributes of a brand (such as bump immunity) and the subjective ones (such as prestige) you use to compare different products and brands.[7] Firms try to identify and capitalize on both types of criteria to create the best value for the money sought by you and other consumers.

Consumers often have several criteria for evaluating brands. (Didn't you, in the previous exercise?) Knowing this, companies seek to identify the most important evaluative criteria that consumers use when judging brands. For example, among the evaluative criteria shown in the columns of Figure 6−2, suppose that you use two in considering brands of CD players: (1) a list price under $300 (the price in column 2 of Figure 6−2) and (2) track-finding speed (column 6 in Figure 6−2). These criteria establish the brands in your **evoked set**—the group of brands you would consider acceptable from among all the brands in the product class of which you are aware.[8] Your two evaluative criteria result in only four models in your evoked set (Technics, Philips, JVC, and Denon). If these brands don't satisfy you, you can change your evaluative criteria to create a different evoked set of models.

PURCHASE DECISION: BUYING VALUE

Having examined the alternatives in the evoked set, you are almost ready to make a purchase decision. Two choices remain: (1) from whom to buy and (2) when to buy. For a product like a CD player, the information search process probably involved visiting retail stores, seeing different brands in catalogues, or viewing CD player promotions on a home shopping television channel. The choice of which seller to buy from will depend on such considerations as the terms of sale, your past experience buying from the seller, and the return policy. Often a purchase decision involves a simultaneous evaluation of both product attributes and seller characteristics. For example, you might choose the second-most preferred CD player brand at a store with a liberal credit and return policy versus the most preferred band at a store with more conservative policies.

Deciding when to buy is frequently determined by a number of factors. For instance, you might buy sooner if one of your preferred brands is on sale or its manufacturer offers a rebate. Other factors such as the store atmosphere, salesperson persuasiveness, and financial circumstances could also affect whether a purchase decision is made or postponed.

Many Canadians believe they can get better value by shopping across the border in the United States. Read the accompanying Marketing Action Memo to find out why Canadians do the border hop.

POSTPURCHASE BEHAVIOUR: VALUE IN CONSUMPTION OR USE

After buying a product, the consumer compares it with her expectations and is either satisfied or dissatisfied. If the consumer is dissatisfied, marketers must decide whether the product was deficient or consumer expectations too high.

MARKETING · ACTION · MEMO

Cross-Border Shopping: Canadians Seeking Value

The signs are all there. From Washington state to Maine, Canadians are flooding into the United States with cash and credit cards in hand. They are responding to the promise of greater value including lower prices and a wider selection of goods down south. The shopping lists of Canadians visiting the United States are pretty much the same. Gas is the most common purchase. Next on the list are groceries and other supermarket items including beer. Border hoppers say the savings on gas and groceries alone are enough to justify travelling an hour or more. But the further you travel, the more likely you are to pick up bigger-ticket items like clothes, footwear, toys, audio and video equipment, small appliances, and furniture.

Many experts believe that Canadians go across the border not only for lower prices and wider selection, but to escape taxes, including the dreaded GST. Still others believe that the perception of better service offered by American retailers is another reason. Many Canadian business organizations, as well as municipal governments, want to cap the flow of cross-border shopping. But do consumers want more cross-border shopping restrictions? No, according to an Angus Reid-Southam News Poll. Only 22 percent of Canadians want more restrictions on cross-border shopping, 31 percent want the border opened wider, and the rest are opposed to tighter regulations. Some experts believe there may be a silver lining behind cross-border shopping. Canadian businesses may become more efficient, lower their prices, and start offering better value if they know Canadians have the cross-border alternative.

Source: Adapted from D. Stevenson, "Cross-Border Dispute," *Canadian Consumer,* July–August 1991, pp. 8–15; and The Canadian Chamber of Commerce, *The Cross Border Shopping Issue: A Report by the Canadian Chamber of Commerce* (January 10, 1992).

Product deficiency may require a design change; if expectations are too high, perhaps the company's advertising or the salesperson oversold the product's features.

Sensitivity to a customer's consumption or use experience is extremely important in a consumer's value perception. Studies on automobile purchasing show that satisfaction or dissatisfaction affects consumer communications. Satisfied buyers tell eight other people about their experience. Dissatisfied buyers complain to 22 people.[9] Accordingly, firms like General Electric (GE), Johnson & Johnson, Coca-Cola, and British Airways focus attention on postpurchase behaviour to maximize customer satisfaction.[10] These firms, among many others, now provide toll-free telephone numbers, offer liberalized return and refund policies, and engage in staff training to handle complaints, answer questions, and record suggestions. Research has shown that such efforts produce positive postpurchase communications among consumers and contribute to relationship building between sellers and buyers.[11]

Often a consumer is faced with two or more highly attractive alternatives, such as a Technics or a Philips CD player. If you choose the Philips, you may think, "Should I have purchased the Technics?" This feeling of postpurchase psychological tension or anxiety is called **cognitive dissonance.** To alleviate it, consumers often attempt to applaud themselves for making the right choice. So after your purchase, you may seek information to confirm your choice by asking friends questions like, "Don't you like my CD player?" or by reading ads of the brand you chose. You might even look for negative information about the brand you didn't buy and decide that the taping convenience of the Technics, which was rated "acceptable" in Figure 6–2, was actually a serious deficiency. Firms often use ads or follow-up calls from salespeople in this postpurchase stage to try to convince buyers that they made the right decision. For many years, Buick ran an advertising campaign with the message, "Aren't you really glad you bought a Buick?"

INVOLVEMENT AND PROBLEM-SOLVING VARIATIONS

Sometimes consumers don't engage in the five-step purchase decision process. Instead, they skip or minimize one or more steps depending on the level of **involvement,** the personal, social, and economic significance of the purchase to the consumer.[12] High-involvement purchase occasions typically have at least one of three characteristics—the item to be purchased (1) is expensive, (2) can have serious personal consequences, or (3) could reflect on one's social image. For these occasions, consumers engage in extensive information search, consider many product attributes and brands, form attitudes, and participate in word-of-mouth communication.[13] Low-involvement purchases, such as toothpaste and soap, barely involve most of us, whereas stereo systems and automobiles are very involving. Researchers have identified three general variations in the consumer purchase process based on consumer involvement and product knowledge.[14] Figure 6–3 summarizes some of the important differences between the three problem-solving variations.[15]

Routine Problem Solving   For products such as toothpaste and milk, consumers recognize a problem, make a decision, and spend little effort seeking external information and evaluating alternatives. The purchase process for such items is virtually a habit and typifies low-involvement decision making. Routine problem solving is typically the case for low-priced, frequently purchased products. It is estimated that about 50 percent of all purchase occasions are of this kind.

❚ *Figure 6–3*
Comparison of problem-solving variations.

CHARACTERISTICS OF PURCHASE DECISION PROCESS	CONSUMER INVOLVEMENT HIGH < ————————— > LOW		
	EXTENDED PROBLEM SOLVING	LIMITED PROBLEM SOLVING	ROUTINE PROBLEM SOLVING
Number of brands examined	Many	Several	One
Number of sellers considered	Many	Several	Few
Number of product attributes evaluated	Many	Moderate	One
Number of external information sources used	Many	Few	None
Time spent searching	Considerable	Little	Minimal

Limited Problem Solving   In limited problem solving, consumers typically seek some information or rely on a friend to help them evaluate alternatives. In general, several brands might be evaluated using a moderate number of different attributes. You might use limited problem solving in choosing a toaster, a restaurant for dinner, and other purchase situations in which you have little time or effort to spend. Limited problem solving accounts for about 38 percent of purchase occasions.

Extended Problem Solving   In extended problem solving, each of the five stages of the consumer purchase decision process is used in the purchase, including considerable time and effort on external information search and in identifying and evaluating alternatives. Several brands are usually in the evoked set, and these are evaluated on many attributes. Extended problem solving exists in high-involvement purchase situations for items such as CD players, VCRs, and investments in stocks and bonds. Firms marketing these products put significant effort into informing and educating consumers. About 12 percent of purchase occasions fall into this category.

SITUATIONAL INFLUENCES

Often the purchase situation will affect the purchase decision process. Five **situational influences** have an impact on your purchase decision process: (1) the purchase task, (2) social surroundings, (3) physical surroundings, (4) temporal effects, and (5) antecedent states.[16] The purchase task is the reason for engaging in the decision in the first place. Information searching and evaluating alternatives may differ depending on whether the purchase is a gift, which often involves social visibility, or for the buyer's own use. Social surroundings, including the other people present when a purchase decision is made, may also affect what is purchased. Physical surroundings such as décor, music, and crowding in retail stores may alter how purchase decisions are made. Temporal effects such as time of day or the amount of time available will influence where consumers have breakfast and lunch and what is ordered. Finally, antecedent states, which include the consumer's mood or the amount of cash on hand, can influence purchase behaviour and choice.[17]

Figure 6–4 shows the many influences that affect the consumer purchase decision process. The decision to buy a product also involves important psychological and sociocultural influences, the two important topics discussed during the remainder of this chapter. Marketing mix influences are described in Chapters 11 through 22.

---

1 What is the first step in the consumer purchase decision process?   *Concept Check*

2 The brands a consumer considers buying out of the set of brands in a product class of which she is aware are called the _____ .

3 What is the term for postpurchase anxiety?

Figure 6–4
Influences on the consumer purchase decision process.

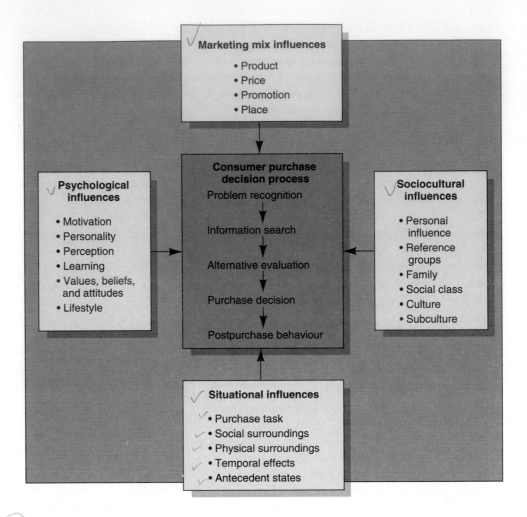

PSYCHOLOGICAL INFLUENCES ON CONSUMER BEHAVIOUR

Psychology helps marketers understand why and how consumers behave as they do. Particularly useful for interpreting buying processes and directing marketing efforts are concepts such as motivation and personality; perception; learning; values, beliefs, and attitudes; and lifestyle.

MOTIVATION AND PERSONALITY

Motivation and personality are two familiar psychological concepts that have specific meanings and marketing implications.[18] They are both used frequently to describe why people do some things and not others.

Motivation   **Motivation** is the energizing force that causes behaviour that satisfies a need. Because consumer needs are the focus of the marketing concept, marketers try to arouse these needs.

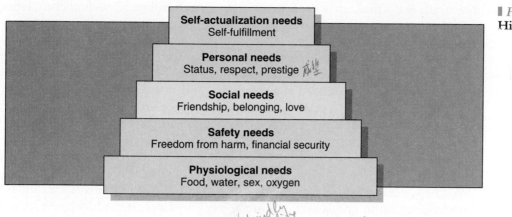

An individual's needs are boundless. People possess physiological needs for basics such as water, sex, and food. They also have learned needs, including esteem, achievement, and affection. Psychologists point out that these needs are hierarchical; that is, once physiological needs are met, people seek to satisfy their learned needs.

Figure 6—5 shows one need hierarchy and classification scheme that contains five need classes.[19] *Physiological needs* are basic to survival and must be satisfied first. A Burger King advertisement featuring a juicy hamburger attempts to activate the need for food. *Safety needs* involve self-preservation and physical well-being. Smoke detector and burglar alarm manufacturers focus on these needs. *Social needs* are concerned with love and friendship. Dating services and fragrance companies try to arouse these needs. *Personal needs* are represented by the need for achievement, status, prestige, and self-respect. Visa Gold Cards and Rolex watches appeal to these needs. Sometimes firms try to arouse multiple needs to stimulate problem recognition. Michelin combined security with parental love to promote tire replacement, as shown in the accompanying adver-

Michelin appeals to security and parental love needs in its advertising.

tisement. *Self-actualization needs* involve personal fulfillment, such as completing a higher education degree.

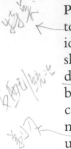

Personality   **Personality** refers to a person's consistent behaviours or responses to recurring situations. Although numerous personality theories exist, most identify key traits—enduring characteristics within a person or in his relationships with others. Such traits include assertiveness, extroversion, compliance, dominance, and aggression, among others. For example, cigarette smokers have been identified as having traits such as aggression and dominance, but not compliance.[20] Research suggests that compliant people prefer known brand names and use more mouthwash and toilet soaps. In contrast, aggressive types use razors, not electric shavers, apply more cologne and after-shave lotions, and purchase signature goods such as Gucci, Yves St. Laurent, and Donna Karan as an indicator of status.[21]

Cross-cultural analysis also suggests that residents of different countries have a **national character,** or a distinct set of personality characteristics common among people of a country or society.[22] For example, Canadians are relatively less aggressive than their American counterparts.

PERCEPTION

One person sees a Cadillac as a mark of achievement; another sees it as ostentatious. This is the result of **perception**—the process by which an individual selects, organizes, and interprets information to create a meaningful picture of the world.

Selective Perception   Because the average consumer operates in a complex environment, the human brain attempts to organize and interpret information through a filtering process called *selective perception.* The four stages of selective perception are selective exposure, selective attention, selective comprehension, and selective retention. Consumers are not exposed to all information or messages in the marketplace; there is *selective exposure.* Marketers cannot be successful unless they can get the consumer exposed to their messages.

But even if a consumer is exposed to a message, either by accident or by design, she may not attend to that message. In general, with *selective attention,* the consumer will pay attention only to messages that are consistent with her attitudes and beliefs and will ignore those that are inconsistent. Consumers are also more likely to attend to messages when they are relevant or of interest to them. For example, consumers are likely to pay attention to an ad about a product they have just bought, or to an ad for a product they are interested in buying.

Even if a marketer is successful in getting the consumer exposed to a message and to attend to it, the message is of little value if the consumer does not understand it. With *selective comprehension,* consumers interpret information so that it is consistent with their attitudes and beliefs. Thus, the same message may be interpreted differently by different people. For example, Sunlight liquid detergent was once marketed in a yellow bottle with a lemon on the label and it smelled like lemon when opened. While some people understood it was

MARKETING · ACTION · MEMO

It Keeps On Going . . . and Going . . . and Going: The Duracell—Or Is It the Eveready Bunny?

High atop the list of favourite and memorable commercials is the mechanical pink bunny powered by Duracell batteries. Or is it Eveready?

Research on the popular pink bunny commercials has uncovered a surprise. In a survey of 4,700 people, 60 percent said the bunny represented the Eveready Energizer brand. But wait—40 percent said the bunny was powered by Duracell! Which brand is it?

A spokesperson for the advertising agency that created the bunny advertisements for Eveready acknowledged that "there's going to be a lag time before people link [the bunny] to the actual product." In the meantime, makers of Duracell, the number-1-selling battery brand, are perfectly happy to be part of the confusion. According to a company spokesperson, "We thank Eveready for helping give us more impact from our advertising budget."

This example is more common than you might think. It has been frequently shown that customers remember a creative ad and the product category, but perceive the number-1-selling brand's name (Dura-

cell) rather than the name of the challenger—in this case, Eveready.

Sources: Based on J. Lipman, "Too Many Think the Bunny Is Duracell's, Not Eveready's," *The Wall Street Journal*, July 31, 1990, pp. B1, B4; J. Steinberg, "Be Sure to Leave 'Em Laughing," *Advertising Age*, February 5, 1990, p. 52; and "National Agency Report Card," *Adweek*, March 12, 1990, pp. 12–15.

detergent, other people thought it was lemonade and became ill as a result of drinking it. This type of selective miscomprehension is quite common in the marketplace.[23] The accompanying Marketing Action Memo details how the Eveready Energizer bunny is often "seen" as promoting Duracell—a case of selective miscomprehension.

Selective retention means that consumers do not remember all the information they see, read, or hear, even minutes after exposure to it. This affects the internal and external information search stage of the purchase decision process. This is why furniture and automobile retailers often give consumers product brochures to take home after they leave the showroom.

Since perception plays such an important role in consumer behaviour, it is not surprising that the topic of subliminal perception is a popular item for discussion. **Subliminal perception** means that you see or hear messages without being aware of them. The presence and effect of subliminal perception on behaviour is a hotly debated issue, with more popular appeal than scientific support. Indeed, evidence suggests that such messages have limited effects on behaviour.[24] If these messages did influence behaviour, would their use be an ethical practice? (See the accompanying Ethics and Social Responsibility Alert.)

ETHICS AND SOCIAL RESPONSIBILITY ALERT

The Ethics of Subliminal Messages

Although there is no substantive scientific support for the concept of subliminal perception, it is nevertheless popular. Even if consumers do see or hear messages without being aware of them, would it be ethical for marketers to pursue opportunities to create subliminal messages designed to change buying behaviour?

Perceived Risk   Perception plays a major role in the perceived risk in purchasing a product or service. **Perceived risk** represents the anxieties felt because the consumer cannot anticipate the outcomes of a purchase but believes that there may be negative consequences. Examples of possible negative consequences are the size of the financial outlay required to buy the product (can I afford $200 for those skis?), the risk of physical harm (is bungee jumping safe?), and the performance of the product (will the hair colouring work?). A more abstract form is psychosocial (what will my friends say if I wear that sweater?). Perceived risk affects information search because the greater the perceived risk, the more extensive the external search phase is likely to be.

Recognizing the importance of perceived risk, companies develop strategies to reduce the consumer's risk and encourage purchases. These strategies and examples of firms using them include:[25]

- Obtaining seals of approval: the Good Housekeeping seal or Canadian Standards Association (CSA) seal.
- Securing endorsements from influential people: Elizabeth Taylor's White Diamonds line of perfume.
- Providing free trials of the product: sample packages of Duncan Hines peanut butter cookies mailed by P&G.
- Giving extensive usage instructions: Clairol hair colouring.
- Providing warranties and guarantees: Cadillac's four-year, 50,000-mile, gold key bumper-to-bumper warranty.

LEARNING

Much consumer behaviour is learned. Consumers learn which information sources to use for information about products and services, which evaluative criteria to use when assessing alternatives, and, more generally, how to make purchase decisions. **Learning** refers to those behaviours that result from (1) repeated experience and (2) thinking.[26]

Behavioural Learning   *Behavioural learning* is the process of developing automatic responses to a situation through repeated exposure to it. Four variables are central to how consumers learn from repeated experience: drive, cue, response, and reinforcement. A *drive* is a need that moves an individual to action. Drives, such as hunger, might be represented by motives. A *cue* is a stimulus or symbol

perceived by consumers. A *response* is the action taken by a consumer to satisfy
the drive, and a *reinforcement* is the reward. Being hungry (drive), a consumer
sees a cue (a billboard), takes action (buys a hamburger), and receives a reward
(it tastes great!).

Marketers use two concepts from behavioural learning theory. *Stimulus
generalization* occurs when a response elicited by one stimulus (cue) is generalized to another stimulus. Using the same brand name for different products is an
application of this concept, such as Tylenol Cold & Flu and Tylenol P.M.
Stimulus discrimination refers to a person's ability to perceive differences in
stimuli. Consumers' tendency to perceive all light beers as being alike led to
Budweiser Light commercials that distinguished between many types of
"lights" and Bud Light.

Cognitive Learning   Consumers also learn through thinking, reasoning, and
mental problem solving without direct experience. This type of learning, called
cognitive learning, involves making connections between two or more ideas or
simply observing the outcomes of others' behaviours and adjusting your own
accordingly. Firms also influence this type of learning. Through repetition in
advertising, messages such as "Anacin is a headache remedy" attempt to link a
brand (Anacin) and an idea (headache remedy) by showing someone using the
brand and finding relief.

Brand Loyalty   Learning is also important because it relates to habit
formation—the basis of routine problem solving. Furthermore, there is a close
link between habits and **brand loyalty,** which is a favourable attitude toward
and consistent purchase of a single brand over time. Brand loyalty results from
the positive reinforcement of previous actions. A consumer reduces risk and
saves time by consistently purchasing the same brand over time. For example,

MARKETING · ACTION · MEMO

Shoppers Less Loyal, More Thrifty

Technological and social change are so rampant and fundamental, the two forces have created a landscape very foreign to marketers. Alan Gregg says a study by Decima Research in 1993 indicates that the double hit of a recession and a thorough change in consumer attitudes have made today's shopper a far different creature than the one who spent in the decadent 1980s. Today's shopper has less money to spend, is more concerned about saving, more circumspect about purchases, and no longer relies on material acquisitions to boost self-image.

The Decima survey revealed that 60 percent of consumers can't afford or don't want to make major purchases. Sixty-three percent say they replace large-ticket items less often than they once did; 29 percent just as often; and only 8 percent more often. Finding no particular joy in buying, the shopper is now focussed more on attaining what is needed at a good price, rather than on marginal purchases. Consumers are less loyal, with only 20 percent of shoppers knowing the brand they will buy when they enter the store. Consequently, they crave a wide selection of brands to choose from in order to select the best value. Marketers must become more concerned with providing customer value if they want to encourage brand loyalty.

Source: "Shoppers Less Loyal, More Thrifty," *Marketing*, June 14, 1993, p. 14.

if the brand of shampoo you buy gives you favourable results—healthy, shining hair—you are likely to continue to buy that brand. But there is some evidence that brand loyalty is declining, even for frequently used products.[27] The accompanying Marketing Action Memo focusses on this trend.

VALUES, BELIEFS, AND ATTITUDES

Values, beliefs, and attitudes play a central role in consumer decision making and related marketing actions.

Attitude Formation   An **attitude** is a learned predisposition to respond to an object or a class of objects in a consistently favourable or unfavourable way.[28] Attitudes are shaped by our values and beliefs, which are learned. Values vary by level of specificity. We speak of Canadian core values, including material well-being and humanitarianism. We also have personal values, such as thriftiness and ambition. Marketers are concerned with both, but focus mostly on personal values. Personal values affect attitudes by influencing the importance assigned to specific product attributes. Suppose thriftiness is one of your personal values. When you evaluate cars, fuel economy (a product attribute) becomes important. If you believe a specific car has this attribute, you are likely to have a favourable attitude toward it.

Beliefs also play a part in attitude formation. **Beliefs** are a consumer's subjective perception of *how well* a product or brand performs on different attributes. Beliefs are based on personal experience, advertising, and discussions with other people. Beliefs about product attributes are important because, along with personal values, they create the favourable or unfavourable attitude the consumer has toward certain products and services.

Attitude Change   Marketers use three approaches to try to change consumer attitudes toward products and brands, as shown in the following examples.[29]

1   *Changing beliefs about the extent to which a brand has certain attributes.* McDonald's ran an ad to allay consumer concerns about too much cholesterol in its french fries.
2   *Changing the perceived importance of attributes.* 7UP succeeded in building on its positively viewed "no-caffeine" attribute with its "never had it, never will" slogan to build market share.
3   *Adding new attributes to the product.* Chrylser added driver-side airbags in its vehicles, hoping consumers would perceive this new product attribute favourably.

LIFESTYLE

Lifestyle is a mode of living that is identified by how people spend their time and resources (activities), what they consider important in their environment (interests), and what they think of themselves and the world around them (opinions).[30] Moreover, lifestyle reflects consumers' **self-concept,** which is the way people see themselves and the way they believe others see them.[31]

The analysis of consumer lifestyles (also called *psychographics*) has produced many insights into consumers' behaviour. For example, lifestyle analysis has proven useful in segmenting and targeting consumers for new and existing products (see Chapter 9).

Lifestyle analysis typically focusses on identifying consumer profiles. The most prominent example of this type of analysis is the Values and Lifestyles (VALS) Program developed by SRI International.[32] The VALS Program has identified eight interconnected categories of adult lifestyles based on a person's self-orientation and resources. Self-orientation describes the patterns of attitudes and activities that help people reinforce their social self-image. Three patterns have been uncovered; they are oriented toward principles, status, and action. A person's resources encompass income, education, self-confidence, health, eagerness to buy, intelligence, and energy level. This dimension is a continuum ranging from minimal to abundant. Figure 6–6 shows the eight lifestyle types and their relationships, and highlights selected demographic and behavioural characteristics of each. While the VALS Program is the most widely known lifestyles or psychographics system in North America, it has only been used once or twice in Canada for commercial applications. Canada has a few home-grown systems, the most comprehensive being the Goldfarb Segments.

The Goldfarb Segments   Many experts believe that Canadians and Americans are different in their values and buying behaviour and that, therefore, an indigenous psychographic system would be more useful for the Canadian mar-

Figure 6–6
VALS 2 psychographic segments.

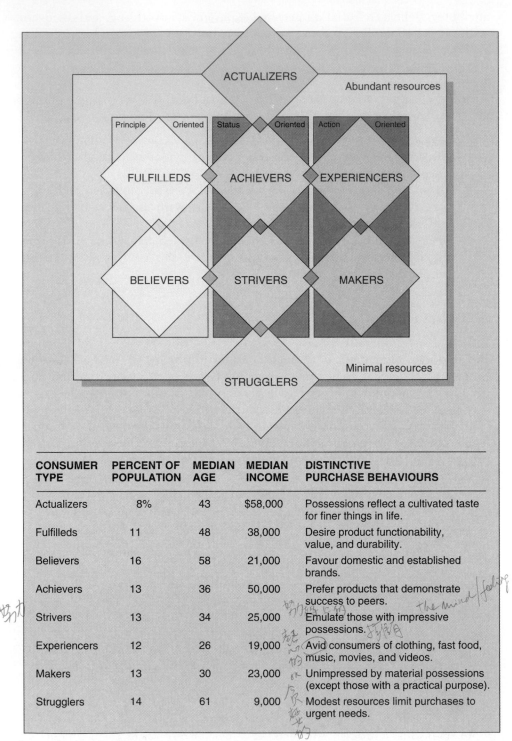

CONSUMER TYPE	PERCENT OF POPULATION	MEDIAN AGE	MEDIAN INCOME	DISTINCTIVE PURCHASE BEHAVIOURS
Actualizers	8%	43	$58,000	Possessions reflect a cultivated taste for finer things in life.
Fulfilleds	11	48	38,000	Desire product functionability, value, and durability.
Believers	16	58	21,000	Favour domestic and established brands.
Achievers	13	36	50,000	Prefer products that demonstrate success to peers.
Strivers	13	34	25,000	Emulate those with impressive possessions.
Experiencers	12	26	19,000	Avid consumers of clothing, fast food, music, movies, and videos.
Makers	13	30	23,000	Unimpressed by material possessions (except those with a practical purpose).
Strugglers	14	61	9,000	Modest resources limit purchases to urgent needs.

Source: SRI International.

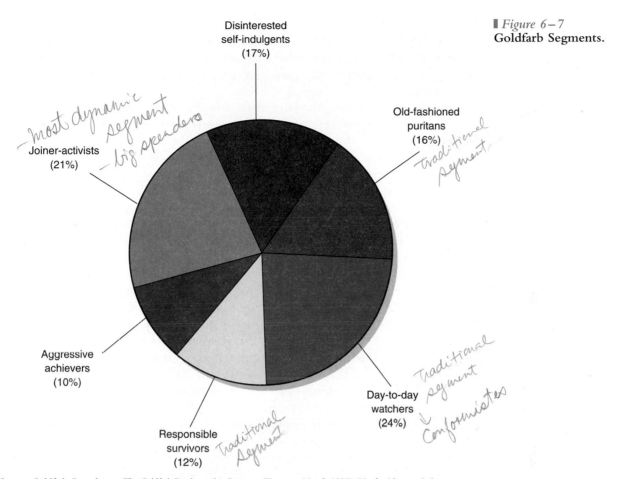

■ *Figure 6–7*
Goldfarb Segments.

Source: Goldfarb Consultants, *The Goldfarb Psychographic Segments* (Toronto, March 1992). Used with permission.

ketplace. The Goldfarb Segments were produced as a result of sampling 1,400 adult Canadians and examining their responses to approximately 200 questions. The questions dealt with attitudes toward life, goals, values, stands on moral issues, and life satisfaction. The results were subjected to various levels of analysis. An individual was assigned to a segment on the basis of his "dominant" attitudinal and behavioural characteristics. But, as is true with VALS 2, this does not mean that some of these characteristics will be completely dissimilar to those found in one or more of the other segments. However, the dominant characteristics are the primary factors that influence behaviour of individuals in a given segment.

Six lifestyle or psychographic segments emerged from this process, as shown in Figure 6–7.[33] The six are classified according to two broad categories: more traditional and less traditional. Let's talk briefly about the segments, including their key characteristics.

The *More Traditional Segments* include the day-to-day watchers, the old-fashioned puritans, and the responsible survivors. The day-to-day watchers (*conformistes*) segment is a realistic group, and its members are satisfied with what life has to offer. This group stands for and reflects some of the traditional, upstanding attitudes and values in Canada. This segment researches its purchases but gravitates toward the tried and true. They need to be comfortable with products before they buy and are not overly comfortable with new technology.

The old-fashioned puritan (*prudes démodés*) segment is conservative to the point of being defensive, and indifferent to the world to the point of apathy. They are terrified of new technology and rely heavily on others for guidance, living vicariously through others, particularly their families. They are least likely to try new brands and least likely to own credit cards, and are heavily insured and home oriented. The responsible survivors (*casaniers diligents*) are people who are not particularly confident about themselves or their own abilities. They are cautious and respect the status quo. They are likable, ethical, and good neighbours, but not particularly ambitious. They are open to advice, are very brand loyal, are heavy TV viewers, and enjoy video recorders and cameras.

The *Less Traditional Segments* include the disinterested self-indulgent, the joiner–activist, and the aggressive achievers. The disinterested self-indulgents (*hèdonistes non-engagés*) are an insular, self-centred group. They are not interested in the world's problems. They tend to indulge their desires and are interested in making their own lives easy and convenient. They are interested in self- and instant gratification; they are heavy lottery ticket buyers, tend to borrow a lot, and are impulse purchasers. They are prepared to take some risks such as being on the leading edge of product innovation.

The joiner–activist (*réformistes*) segment is a group of leading-edge thinkers. They are nonconformists who help shape current opinion. They tend to be global in their thinking and are involved in issues with a broad social or political impact. This is the most dynamic segment. They are interested in quality and intrigued by technology and are big spenders. Compared with other segments, this group eats out most, shops most for clothes, and is more convenience oriented. They are not sale oriented, are heavy pleasure-trip takers, use luxury accommodations, and like and buy new technology like computers.

The aggressive achievers (*conquérants aggressifs*) are success oriented, almost hungry for power and position. They need to demonstrate their success to others and do so through their consumption behaviour and the way they deal with others. They can lose sight of their ethical standards if they feel their own position is being threatened. They buy status-signalling goods, but can be bargain hunters too; they love to be noticed and flaunt their material possessions.

Many Canadian companies have used the Goldfarb Segments to assist them in making successful marketing decisions, including frozen food manufacturers, financial institutions, retailers, and fast-food companies. For example, Sears Canada (retail stores) recently turned to psychographic targeting using the Goldfarb Segments. It now tailors its messages and media campaigns to reach two groups, the day-to-day watchers and the joiner–activists. Sears Canada believes these are the two groups it must reach in order to stay competitive in the retail department store market.

1 The problem with the Sunlight detergent bottle was an example of selective _comprehension_ .

2 What three attitude-change approaches are most common?

3 What does lifestyle mean?

SOCIOCULTURAL INFLUENCES ON CONSUMER BEHAVIOUR

Sociocultural influences, which evolve from a consumer's formal and informal relationships with other people, also exert a significant impact on consumer behaviour. These influences include personal influence, reference groups, the family, social class, culture, and subculture.

PERSONAL INFLUENCE

A consumer's purchases are often influenced by the views, opinions, or behaviour of others. Two aspects of personal influence are important to marketing: opinion leadership and word-of-mouth activity.

Opinion Leadership   Individuals who exert direct or indirect social influence over others are called **opinion leaders.** Opinion leaders are more likely to be important for products that provide a form of self-expression. Automobiles, clothing, club memberships, home video equipment, and personal computers are products affected by opinion leaders, but appliances are not.[34]

Identifying, reaching, and influencing opinion leaders is a major challenge for companies. Some firms use sports figures or celebrities as spokespeople to represent their products, such as Wayne Gretzky for Thrifty Rent-a-Car, Sharp, and Coca-Cola, and Carolyn Waldo for Sears Canada. However, many consumers are starting to question the credibility of celebrity spokespeople, believing most are simply promoting the product for money.[35] Thus, some companies promote their products in media believed to reach opinion leaders. Still others use more direct approaches. For example, the Ford Motor Company invited executives and professional people to test-drive its new Thunderbird.[36] Although only 10 percent said they would purchase the car, 84 percent said they would recommend it to a friend.

Word of Mouth   People's influencing each other during their face-to-face conversations is called **word of mouth.** Word of mouth is perhaps the most powerful information source for consumers, because it typically involves friends viewed as trustworthy. When consumers were asked in a recent survey what most influences their buying decisions, 37 percent mentioned a friend's recommendation and 20 percent said advertising. When a similar question was posed to Russian consumers, 72 percent said advice from friends and 24 percent said advertising.[37]

Sears Canada sees
Carolyn Waldo as an
opinion leader and
features her in its
catalogue.

The power of personal influence has prompted firms to promote positive
and retard negative word of mouth.[38] For instance, "teaser" advertising campaigns are run in advance of new product introductions to stimulate conversations. Other techniques such as advertising slogans, music, and humour (Pepsi's
"uh-huh" campaign) also heighten positive word of mouth. On the other hand,
rumours about Kmart (snake eggs in clothing) or McDonald's (worms in hamburgers) have resulted in negative word of mouth, none of which was based on
fact. Overcoming or neutralizing negative word of mouth is difficult and costly.
Several food products in Indonesia, including some sold by Nestlé, were ru-
moured to contain pork, which is prohibited to the 160 million Muslim consumers in that country. Nestlé had to spend $250,000 in advertising to coun-
teract the rumour.[39] Firms have found that supplying factual information,
providing toll-free numbers for consumers to call the company, and giving
appropriate product demonstrations have also been helpful.

REFERENCE GROUPS

Reference groups are people to whom an individual looks as a basis for
self-appraisal or as a source of personal standards. Reference groups affect consumer purchases because they influence the information, attitudes, and aspiration levels that help set a consumer's standards.[40] For example, one of the first
questions one asks others when planning to attend a social occasion is, What are
you going to wear? Reference groups have an important influence on the
purchase of luxury products but not of necessities—reference groups exert a
strong influence on the brand chosen when its use or consumption is highly
visible to others.[41]

Consumers have many reference groups, but three groups have clear marketing implications. A *membership group* is one to which a person actually be-

Children as a Target Segment

Many companies are attempting to reach a new consumer group—children, and children as young as three years old. Why? Marketers recognize that not only do children have their own discretionary income, they also influence many areas of overall family spending. For example, Kmart Canada is using a cougar named Marty to boost the 124-store chain's image with kids 3 to 12 and their mothers, Kmart's key target segment. The furry mascot was selected by kids' focus groups. Marty will head the Marty's Kids Club. Club members receive free activity books and snacks and attend Marty birthday parties. A line of clothing and merchandise is also offered including T-shirts and educational games. The kid membership list will be used for direct mail offers.

Targeting children early is important to many other marketers. The Canadian Imperial Bank of Commerce (CIBC) sponsors a classroom edition of the *Globe and Mail,* and its motives are not strictly altruistic. CIBC wants to build relationships with the country's future leaders and consumers. Other companies such as Pepsi-Cola Canada and Clearly Canadian Beverages also see children as important targets for their products. Although kids are a primary target for traditional soft drinks, salty snacks, and sweets, they are responding to new products that are perceived as more healthy such as Crystal Pepsi and new-age beverages such as Clearly Canadian flavoured water. Most marketers agree that simply satisfying kids now is only one part of the plan; the other part is to develop a relationship with them so they will continue to buy those products in the future.

Sources: Adapted from *Marketing,* May 3, 1993, p. 5; D. Napier, "Building Relationship Loyalty in the Classroom," *Marketing,* February 8, 1993, p. 22; H. Skolnick, "Young People Eat Quick Nutrition," *Marketing,* June 14, 1993, p. 13.

longs, such as a fraternity, a social club, or the family. Such groups are easily identifiable and are targeted by firms selling insurance, insignia products, and charter vacations. An *aspiration group* is one that a person wishes to be a member of or wishes to be identified with, such as a professional society. Firms frequently rely on spokespeople or settings associated with their target market's aspiration group in their advertising. A *dissociative group* is one that a person wishes to maintain a distance from because of differences in values or behaviours. Believing that motorcycle ownership and usage has a "black leather–jacketed biker" stigma, Honda Motor Company has focussed its promotional efforts on disassociating its motorcycles from this group.[42]

FAMILY INFLUENCE

Family influences on consumer behaviour result from three sources: consumer socialization, passage through the family life cycle, and decision making within the family.

Consumer Socialization The process by which people acquire skills, knowledge, and attitudes necessary to function as consumers is **consumer socialization.** Children learn how to purchase by (1) interacting with adults in purchase situations and (2) their own purchasing and product usage experiences.[43] As

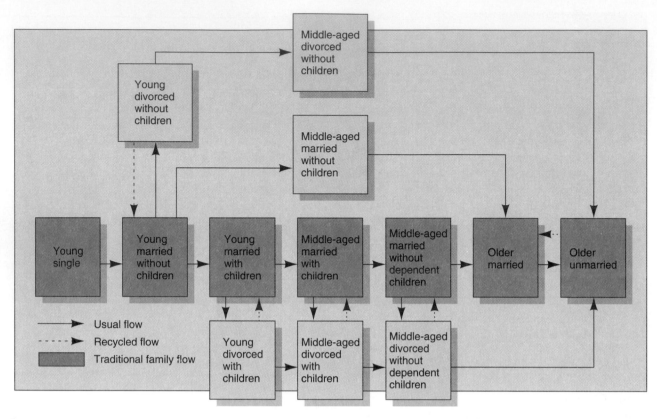

| Figure 6–8
Modern family life cycle.

children mature into adults, brand preferences emerge that may last a lifetime. As we saw in Chapter 3, children have become an important target for marketers not only because they often have their own purchasing power, but because they influence family purchase decisions ("kidfluence"). The accompanying Marketing Action Memo tells about some of the Canadian companies marketing to children.

Family Life Cycle   Consumers act and purchase differently as they go through life. The **family life cycle** concept describes the distinct phases that a family progresses through from formation to a couples old age, each phase bringing with it identifiable purchasing behaviours.[44] Figure 6–8 illustrates the traditional progression as well as contemporary variations of the family life cycle, including the prevalence of single households with and without children.

Young singles' buying preferences are for nondurable items, including prepared foods, clothing, personal care products, and entertainment. These people represent a target market for recreational travel, automobile, and consumer electronics firms. Young married couples without children are typically more affluent than young singles, because usually both spouses are employed. These couples exhibit preferences for furniture, housewares, and gift items for each other. Young marrieds with children are driven by the needs of their children. They make up a sizable market for life insurance, various children's products, and home furnishings.

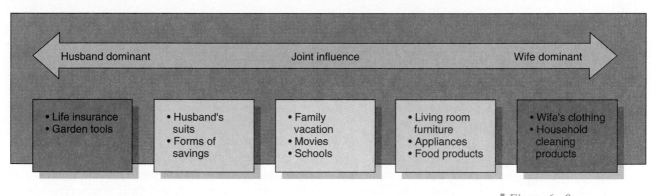

▌*Figure 6–9*
Influence continuum of spouse in family decision making.

Single parents with children are the least financially secure of households with children. Their buying preferences are affected by a limited economic status and tend toward convenience foods, child care services, and personal care items. Middle-aged married couples with children are typically better off financially than their younger counterparts. They are a significant market for leisure products and home improvement items and represent the fastest-growing life cycle stage in the 1990s. Middle aged couples without children typically have a large amount of discretionary income. These couples buy better furnishings, status automobiles, and financial services. Persons in the last two phases—older married and older unmarried—are a sizable market for prescription drugs, medical services, vacation trips, and gifts for younger relatives. These consumers are expected to represent the second-fastest-growing family life cycle stage in the 1990s.

Family Decision Making A third influence in the decision-making process occurs within the family. Two decision-making styles exist: spouse-dominant and joint decision making. With a joint decision-making style, most decisions are made by both husband and wife. Spouse-dominant decisions are those for which either the husband or the wife is responsible. The types of products and services associated with the decision-making styles are shown in Figure 6–9.[45] However, these tendencies are changing with the rise in dual-income families. Today, 40 percent of all food-shopping dollars are spent by male customers. Women now purchase 70 percent of men's dress shirts and 40 to 50 percent of all condoms purchased.

Roles of individual family members in the purchase process are another element of family decision making. Five roles exist: (1) information gatherer, (2) influencer, (3) decision maker, (4) purchaser, and (5) user. Family members assume different roles for different products and services. Knowledge of who plays which role is important to firms. Increasingly, teenagers are the information gatherers, decision makers, and purchasers of grocery items for the family, given the prevalence of working parents and single-parent households. General Mills, Nabisco, Kraft-General Foods Canada, and others advertise on the Much Music station to reach teens, while Pizza Hut advertises heavily on YTV to reach young consumers who can then convince their parents to go for pizza instead of preparing dinner.[46]

SOCIAL CLASS

A more subtle influence on consumer behaviour than direct contact with others is the social class to which people belong. **Social classes** may be defined as the relatively permanent, homogeneous divisions in a society into which people sharing similar values, interests, and behaviour can be grouped. Someone's occupation, source of income (not level of income), and education determine her social class.

Figure 6–10 compares the distribution by social class in Canada with that in the United States. This five-class categorization is consistent with how most marketers apply social class. The *upper class* consists of two groups, the "old rich" and the "new rich." The old rich have inherited wealth and have aristocratic status. The new rich are the new social elite—top professionals and corporate leaders. The *upper middle class* consists of successful professionals and businesspeople who are often referred to as the "technocrats," since they are the best educated in our society. The *middle class* consists of the typical white-collar worker, including small-business owners, middle managers, and minor professionals.

The *working class* represents the traditional blue-collar worker. The *lower class* consists of working poor and the underclass, including the underemployed, the unemployed, and those on welfare. As you can see from Figure 6–10, the bulk of Canadians and Americans fall into the middle- and working-class categories, with Canada having a higher proportion of middle-class consumers. Shifts in occupation to white-collaredness and more widespread higher education are reasons for the broadening of the middle class in Canada.

While no one has developed a completely accurate depiction of social class in Canada or the United States, Figure 6–10 does show the mainstream social classes to be the middle and the working class. The question for marketers is, Are they different in terms of consumer behaviour? The answer is yes. Research shows that the middle class and the working class do differ in many ways, including their concept of time, homes, personal appearance, work and leisure, money management, media habits, and actual shopping behaviour.[47]

The following comparisons are only the general characteristics and tendencies of each class, and exceptions to the behaviours outlined are possible.

The middle class is more future oriented and more time-conscious. The middle class is prepared to pay for a home in a neighbourhood that will provide

❚ *Figure 6–10*
Social class distribution in Canada and the United States.

CANADA	PERCENTAGE	UNITED STATES	PERCENTAGE
Upper	2.5	Upper	1.5
Upper middle	18.5	Upper middle	12.5
Middle	50.0	Middle	32.0
Working	20.0	Working	38.0
Lower	9.0	Lower	16.0
	100.0		100.0

Source: Adapted from R. P. Coleman, "The Continuing Significance of Social Class to Marketing," *Journal of Consumer Research* 10, no. 3 (December 1983), pp. 265–80; and S. Clarke, F. G. Crane, and T. K. Clarke, "Social Class and Adolescent Buying Behaviour," in *Proceedings of the Administrative Sciences Association of Canada*, vol. 7, ed. T. Muller (1986), pp. 309 16.

status, while the working class will choose a home that is convenient to work and schools. The middle class is more concerned with the mind and personality, and less with the body. Members of the middle class see work as part of their self-concept; the working class does not. The middle class prefers golf, tennis, and skiing while the working class prefers hunting, bowling, and fishing. The middle class is concerned about investment and tends to save regularly. The working class, on the other hand, tends to save less, and when members of this class do, it is usually for a short-term purpose such as Christmas shopping. The working class watches more television than the middle class and prefers game shows, talk shows, and sitcoms. The middle class is more likely to watch public broadcasting and late-night programming. The working class prefers AM radio, hard rock, and country, while the middle class prefers FM radio, jazz, and soft rock. The middle class tends to read magazines like *Good Housekeeping* and *MacLean's,* while the working class tends to read *Reader's Digest* and the *National Enquirer.*

The middle class tends to shop with a list and plans purchases more than the working class, which often buys on impulse. The middle class will use a variety of information sources when buying, while the working class will use word of mouth or information from salespeople. The middle class tends to use self-service outlets and will take a chance on generic brands, while the working class tends to use full-service outlets and remain loyal to national brands.

As the research shows, people within social classes exhibit common attitudes, lifestyles, and buying behaviours. Marketers use social class as a basis for identifying and reaching particularly good prospects for their products and services.

CULTURE AND SUBCULTURE

As described in Chapter 3, *culture* refers to the set of values, ideas, and attitudes that are accepted by a homogeneous group of people and transmitted to the next generation. Thus, we often refer to Canadian culture, American culture, British culture, or Japanese culture. Cultural underpinnings of Canadian buying patterns were described in Chapter 3; Chapter 5 explored the role of culture in global marketing.

Subcultures are subgroups within the larger, national culture that share unique values, ideas, and attitudes setting them apart from that larger culture. In the age of political correctness, many are now using the term *microculture* instead of subculture, since some believe the term *subculture* connotes inferiority. We do not subscribe to this line of thinking and do not use the term *subculture* in a negative or demeaning fashion. We suggest that the term *microculture* has no additive value and could be subject to the same criticism. The reality is, in any society, there are some groups that adhere to a distinct set of values that differentiates them from the larger society as a whole, and no one has the right to suggest that such differences are superior or inferior; they are just different. It is marketers' roles to deal with differences in people (segmentation) in order to create effective exchanges; it is never their role to make value judgments about any segment of the marketplace.

Marketers in Canada must be cognizant of the many subcultures that do exist in Canada. Such subcultures can be identified by age, geography, and ethnicity. We will focus on ethnic subcultures. An ethnic group is a segment of a larger society whose members are thought, by themselves and/or by others, to have a common origin and to participate in shared activities felt to be culturally significant.[48] Common traits, such as customs, language, religion, and values, hold ethnic subcultures together.

Because of Canada's pluralistic tradition, ethnic groups do not necessarily join the cultural mainstream. Some people have referred to this result as a **salad bowl** phenomenon, where a potpourri of people mix but do not blend. This allows for the maintenance of subcultural traditions and values. Because of the importance of the French Canadians as a subculture, we will discuss the French Canadian situation in detail. Then we will briefly discuss other important ethnic subcultures in Canada.

French Canadian Subculture   In Canada, French-speaking Canadians represent over 25 percent of the population, with 88 percent living in Quebec, 8 percent in Ontario, and 4 percent in New Brunswick. These 7 million French Canadians represent a sizable market force that should be taken seriously by marketers. There has been at least 20 years of research examining the consumption, buying, and media habits and patterns of French Canadians, and some have compared these patterns with the habits of English-speaking Canadians. Much of the research has been conflicting and contradictory in nature.

While many marketers agree that French Canadians are different from English Canadians, the reasons for their differences have not been fully explained. Some suggest that the differences are inherently cultural and language plays a key role in creating them. Others suggest demographic or lifestyle differences as the primary reasons for differences in consumption patterns between French and English Canadians. Some authors suggest that researchers have failed to define the French Canadian subculture effectively. Lumping together all people who speak French may not be a reasonable way to examine differences in consumption behaviour. This may be a partial explanation for the variance in findings of French Canadian consumption behaviour over the past two decades. However, recent research on the French Canadian market has found that use of language and self-identification are valid indicators of French Canadian ethnicity. In this case, an objective measure such as language, and a subjective measure such as an individual's belief that he belongs to the ethnic group, does allow researchers to group persons into a French Canadian subculture in order to examine their buying behaviour.[49]

Recent Canadian research shows that French-speaking Quebecers do exhibit different consumption behaviour from the rest of Canadians.[50] The data suggest among other things, that French Quebecers link price to perceived value but will pass on a buy rather than buy on credit. They are more willing to pay premium prices for convenience and premium brands, and they give greater credence to advertising than the average Canadian. They are cautious of new products and often postpone trial until the product has proven itself.

French Quebecers do exhibit brand loyalty but will switch for specials. Fewer French Quebecers go to food warehouses and local grocery stores; they prefer convenience and health food stores. While they are less concerned about nutritional value of food, they prefer low-calorie or light versions of food products. French Quebecers are less likely to drink tea or diet colas, or eat jam, tuna, cookies, and eggs on a daily basis compared with the average Canadian. They prefer instant coffee, preferably decaffeinated.

French Quebecers are more concerned with personal grooming and fashion, with 64 percent of French Quebecers going to specialized clothing boutiques, compared with 54 percent among other Canadians. They use less regular soap but more baby soap, as well as less acne medication.

French women in Quebec are big users of perfumed body spray, cologne, and toilet water as well as use more lipstick. They also buy more pantyhose, swimwear, and hair-colouring products. French Quebec women also buy more socks, but use smaller quantities of medicated throat lozenges and cold remedies. French Canadian women prefer Japanese cars, while English Canadian women prefer domestic cars.

French Quebec has a higher percentage of wine and beer drinkers and more smokers. However, French Quebecers do consume less hard liquor than the rest of Canada. There are fewer golfers, joggers, and gardeners in Quebec, and the proportion of people who go to movies or entertain at home is also lower. There are, however, more cyclists, skiers, woodworkers, dressmakers, and live theatre fans.

French Quebecers are big buyers of lottery tickets and more likely to subscribe to book clubs, but they make fewer long-distance phone calls. They travel less, whether for business or pleasure. More French Quebec adults hold life insurance policies (65 percent in Quebec versus 40 percent in the rest of Canada), but they are less likely to have a credit card. They also tend to use credit unions (*caisses populaires*) or trust companies more than banks. Self-perceived values are strong about family life, about having children in a marriage, and about giving them religious training. French Quebec women also feel it is important to keep a tidy house. Fewer Quebecers see taking an active role in politics as important, but more favour the free enterprise system.

Although many argue that French Canadian society can be characterized by a set of values that are traditional, consistent, and relatively static, changes were evident. Among other things, Quebecers, although predominantly Catholic, have increased their consumption of birth control pills, and Quebec's birth rate and marriage rate are both below the national average, while university enrollments are on the rise.

One marketer believes that the French Quebec consumer is different not because of language but because of differences in lifestyle values. In fact, according to the Goldfarb Segments, French Quebecers are different psychographically from other Canadians.[51] There are 60 percent more joiner–activists in Quebec compared with the rest of Canada, and this predominance of joiner–activists creates a unique character for French Quebec. Whatever the reasons, differences do exist between French and English Canadians, differences that affect consumption behaviour.

But some researchers argue that some powerful trends that transcend provincial and national boundaries, such as the return to traditional values of work and family, will have a greater impact on behaviour than other factors such as language or heritage. In this case, larger societal forces, or a homogenization of cultural values, may bring Canadians closer together, as opposed to further apart.[52]

Marketers must realize that certain products and other elements of a marketing mix may have to be modified if a marketer is to deal with the French Canadian market. Commercial advertising to children is prohibited in Quebec, and there are greater restrictions on alcohol and tobacco advertising. Products sold in Quebec must be perceived as being within the cultural norms of French Canadians. Products that are not will not sell well, simply because of their inappropriateness to French Canadian culture. New products or product variations may have to be designed for that market. It must be noted that, notwithstanding cultural differences, marketing in French Canada poses certain problems and opportunities for marketers. Because of bilingualism and Bill 101, marketers in Quebec must provide labels and packages in both French and English. Fascia or storefront signage in Quebec must be in French, not English, and other forms of advertising often must be altered to fit the French Canadian market there.

Other Ethnic Canadians   As we saw in Chapter 3, three out of ten Canadians are neither of French nor of British descent, and close to 70 percent of all immigrants to Canada today are classified as visible minorities, primarily people from Asia, Africa, and India.

Marketers in Canada are aware that most ethnic Canadians are found in major metropolitan areas such as Toronto, Vancouver, and Montreal. Some areas are known for their ethnic populations. For example, Kitchener–Waterloo has a large German Canadian population. Winnipeg has many Ukrainian Canadians, and Toronto has a large number of Italian Canadians. A common misconception is that ethnic Canadians have less spending power than Canadian-born people. However, a recent study showed that arriving immigrants are bringing in large amounts of capital. It has also been found that foreign-born Canadians earn more money, comparatively, than native-born Canadians.[53]

Chinese Canadians   The Chinese Canadian market comprises about 3 percent of Canada's population. This ethnic segment is made up predominantly of immigrants from Hong Kong and Taiwan and is concentrated in Toronto and Vancouver. It is a very affluent market with high disposable income. Chinese immigrants to Canada have unique values. While in the West we value straight-line thinking (logic), the Chinese value circular thinking (what goes around comes around). They value work, family, and education. They have different purchasing patterns and often perceive products differently. The difference in the way they think affects the way they communicate and the way they want to be communicated with. While either Mandarin or Cantonese can be used in a print campaign, radio or TV ads are better done in Cantonese.

These immigrants often experience cultural shock, and many do not change their habits. To reach them, marketers must use their language. A translation is not good enough; allowances must be made for cultural nuances. An understanding and respect for their culture is appreciated by this ethnic segment.[54] For example, American Express launched an awareness campaign designed to increase card membership among Chinese Canadians. Before starting the program, American Express studied the needs of this group and developed a special evaluation process for Chinese applicants. This program was

Benetton promotes the appropriateness of its products across subcultures.

supported by an effort to develop closer relations with Chinese retail outlets and restaurants that accept American Express.[55]

Acadians   Many Canadians assume that French Canadians are basically the same. Even though the majority of French-speaking Canadians reside in Quebec, there is another group of French-speaking Canadians who are a distinct group. These people are the Acadians, most of whom live in New Brunswick and are proud of their heritage and thus wish to be viewed as distinct from Quebec French. The Acadians are often referred to as the "forgotten French market."

Acadians are very fashion oriented and tend to dine out more often than their French counterparts in Quebec. Acadians are more price-conscious, and marketing strategies directed toward Acadians should do just that—specifically target them. The Acadians want the scope and nature of the marketing communications directed toward them to be French but not Québécois.

Summary

1 When a consumer buys a product, it is not an act but a process. There are five steps in the purchase decision process: problem recognition, information search, alternative evaluation, purchase decision, and postpurchase behaviour.
2 Consumers evaluate alternatives on the basis of attributes. Identifying which attributes are most important to consumers, along with understand-

ing consumer beliefs about how a brand performs on those attributes, can make the difference between successful and unsuccessful products.

3 Consumer involvement with what is bought affects whether the purchase decision process involves routine, limited, or extended problem solving. Situational influences also affect the process.

4 Perception is important to marketers because of the selectivity of what a consumer sees or hears, comprehends, and retains.

5 Much of the behaviour that consumers exhibit is learned. Consumers learn from repeated experience and reasoning. Brand loyalty is a result of learning.

6 Attitudes are learned predispositions to respond to an object or class of objects in a consistently favourable or unfavourable way. Attitudes are based on a person's values and beliefs concerning the attributes of objects.

7 Lifestyle is a mode of living reflected in someone's activities, interests, and opinions of herself and the world. Lifestyle is a manifestation of a person's self-concept.

8 Personal influence takes two forms: opinion leadership, and word-of-mouth activity. A specific type of personal influence exists in the form of reference groups.

9 Family influences on consumer behaviour result from three sources: consumer socialization, family life cycle, and decision making within the household.

10 Within Canada there are social classes and subcultures that affect consumers' values and behaviour. Marketers must be sensitive to these sociocultural influences when developing a marketing mix.

Key Terms and Concepts

consumer behaviour p. 126
purchase decision process p. 126
evaluative criteria p. 128
evoked set p. 128
cognitive dissonance p. 129
involvement p. 130
situational influences p. 131
motivation p. 132
personality p. 134
national character p. 134
perception p. 134
subliminal perception p. 135
perceived risk p. 136
learning p. 136

brand loyalty p. 137
attitude p. 138
beliefs p. 138
lifestyle p. 139
self-concept p. 139
opinion leaders p. 143
word of mouth p. 143
reference groups p. 144
consumer socialization p. 145
family life cycle p. 146
social class p. 148
subcultures p. 149
salad bowl p. 150

Chapter Problems and Applications

1 Review Figure 6–2 in the text, which shows the CD player attributes identified by *Consumer Reports*. Which attributes are important to you? What other attributes might you consider? Which brand would you prefer?

2 Suppose research at Apple Computer reveals that prospective buyers are anxious about buying personal computers for home use. What strategies might you recommend to the company to reduce consumer anxiety?

3 A Porsche salesperson was taking orders on new cars because he was unable to satisfy demand with the limited number of cars in the showroom and lot. Several persons had backed out of the contract within two weeks of signing the order. What explanation can you give for this behaviour, and what remedies would you recommend?

4 Which social class would you associate with each of the following items or actions? (*a*) Tennis club membership, (*b*) an arrangement of plastic flowers in the kitchen, (*c*) *True Romance* magazine, (*d*) *MacLean's* magazine, (*e*) formally dressing for dinner frequently, and (*f*) being a member of a bowling team.

5 Assign one or more levels of the hierarchy of needs and the motives described in Figure 6–5 to the following products: (*a*) life insurance, (*b*) cosmetics, (*c*) the *Financial Post* magazine, and (*d*) hamburgers.

6 With which stage in the family life cycle would the purchase of the following products and services be most closely identified? (*a*) Bedroom furniture, (*b*) life insurance, (*c*) a Caribbean cruise, (*d*) a house mortgage, and (*e*) children's toys.

7 " The greater the perceived risk in a purchase situation, the more likely that cognitive dissonance will result." Does this statement have any basis given the discussion in the text? Why?

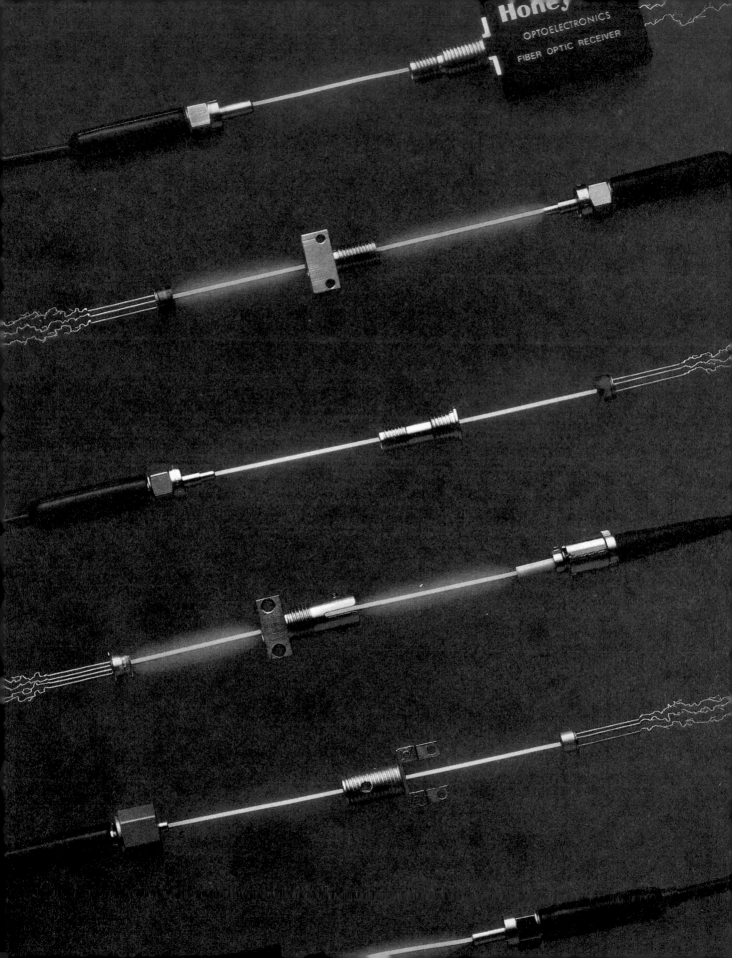

Organizational Markets and Buyer Behaviour

AFTER READING THIS CHAPTER YOU SHOULD BE ABLE TO:

▸ Distinguish among industrial, reseller, and government markets.

▸ Recognize key characteristics of organizational buying that make it different from consumer buying.

▸ Understand how types of buying situations influence organizational purchasing.

▸ Recognize similarities and differences in industrial, reseller, and government purchase behaviour.

Communicating through Light

Bob Procsal views light very differently from most people.

As product manager for fiber optic products at Honeywell, MICRO SWITCH Division, Procsal is responsible for fiber optic products (like those in the accompanying ad) that sense, modulate, and transmit infrared light for the data communications industry. Converting technology into products and bringing these products to market is part and parcel of his typical day.

Marketing fiber optic technology and products is a challenging assignment. Buyer experience with the technology is limited, even though potential applications are numerous in data communications, computer networks, and industrial automation. Honeywell's MICRO SWITCH Division and other suppliers such as Hewlett-Packard, Toshiba, Mitsubishi, and ABB HAFO (Sweden) must often convey the benefits of fiber optics technology and specific products through advertising, trade shows, personal selling, and demonstrations. This task often involves communicating with a diverse set of organizational buyers ranging from industrial firms to governmental agencies, throughout the world and in different languages. It also requires knowing which people influence the purchasing decision; what factors they consider important when choosing suppliers and products; and when, where, and how the buying decision is made.

Procsal believes Honeywell's MICRO SWITCH Division is poised to capture a significant share of the multibillion-dollar fiber optics market in 1996. Ultimate success will depend on continued product development and effective marketing to an ever-growing number of prospective buyers for fiber optic technology in the global marketplace.[1]

The challenge facing Procsal of marketing to organizations is often encountered by both small, startup corporations and large, well-established companies like Honeywell. Important issues in marketing to organizations are examined in this chapter, which examines the types of organizational buyers, key characteristics of organizational buying, and some typical buying decisions. The chapter concludes with how organizations can market to other organizations more effectively.

THE NATURE AND SIZE OF ORGANIZATIONAL MARKETS

Bob Procsal and Honeywell's MICRO SWITCH Division engage in business marketing. **Business marketing** is the marketing of goods and services to commercial enterprises, government, and other profit and not-for-profit organizations for use in the creation of goods and services that they then produce and market to other business customers, as well as to individuals and ultimate consumers.[2] Because many Canadian business school graduates take jobs in firms that engage in business marketing, it is important to understand the fundamental characteristics of organizational buyers and their buying behaviour.[3]

Organizational buyers are units such as manufacturers, retailers, and government agencies that buy goods and services for their own use or for resale. For example, all these organizations buy pencils and desks for their own use. However, manufacturers buy raw materials and parts that they reprocess into the finished goods they sell, whereas retailers resell goods they buy without reprocessing them. Organizational buyers include all the buyers in a nation except ultimate consumers. They purchase and lease tremendous volumes of capital equipment, raw materials, manufactured parts, supplies, and business services. In fact, because they often buy raw materials and parts, process them, and sell the upgraded product several times before it is purchased by the final organizational buyer or ultimate consumer, the aggregate purchases of organizational buyers in a year are far greater than those of ultimate consumers.

Organizational buyers are divided into three different markets: (1) industrial, (2) resellers, and (3) government markets.

INDUSTRIAL MARKETS

Industrial firms in some way reprocess a good or service they buy before selling it again to the next buyer. This is certainly true of a steel mill, which converts iron ore into steel. It is also true (if you stretch your imagination) of a firm selling services, such as a bank, which takes money from its depositors, reprocesses it, and "sells" it as loans to its borrowers. In fact, there has been a marked shift in the scope and nature of the industrial marketplace.

Service industries are growing and currently make the greatest contribution to Canada's gross domestic product (GDP). Because of the importance of service firms, service marketing is discussed in detail in Chapter 24. Industrial firms and primary industries (e.g., farming, mining, fishing, and forestry) currently contribute less than 25 percent to Canada's GDP. Nevertheless,

PROVINCE	$000,000	PERCENTAGE DISTRIBUTION
Canada	293,993	100.0%
Newfoundland	1,494	0.5
Prince Edward Island	458	0.2
Nova Scotia	6,015	2.0
New Brunswick	6,145	2.1
Quebec	72,940	24.8
Ontario	152,872	52.0
Manitoba	6,987	2.4
Saskatchewan	3,592	1.2
Alberta	18,952	6.4
British Columbia	24,538	8.3

▌ *Figure 7–1*
Estimated value of shipments in all manufacturing industries, by province of origin.

Source: Statistics Canada, *Inventories, Shipments and Orders in Manufacturing Industries*, 31-001, 1994. Reproduced with the permission of the Minister of Supply and Services Canada.

primary industries and the manufacturing sector are important components of Canada's economy. There are close to 40,000 manufacturers in Canada; their estimated value of shipments is about $300 billion. Figure 7–1 shows that manufacturing activity is highly concentrated in Ontario and Quebec, with over 75 percent of the total value of all shipments being produced in those two provinces.

RESELLER MARKETS

Wholesalers and retailers who buy physical products and resell them again without any reprocessing are **resellers.** There are over 220,000 retailers and over 65,000 wholesalers operating in Canada. In Chapters 15 through 17, we shall see how manufacturers use wholesalers and retailers in their distribution ("place") strategies as channels through which their products reach ultimate consumers. In this chapter, we look at these resellers mainly as organizational buyers in terms of how they make their own buying decisions and which products they choose to carry.

GOVERNMENT MARKETS

Government units are the federal, provincial, and local agencies that buy goods and services for the constituents they serve. Their annual purchases vary in size from billions of dollars for a federal department such as National Defence to millions or thousands of dollars for a local university or school. The bulk of the buying at the federal government level is done by the Department of Supply and Services Canada. Most provincial governments have a government services department that does the buying on the provincial level. Hundreds of government departments—including agencies and crown corporations such as CN and the Royal Canadian Mint—must purchase goods and services to operate. The federal government is a large organizational consumer, making total purchases of goods and services in excess of $100 billion annually.[4]

GLOBAL ORGANIZATIONAL MARKETS

Industrial, reseller, and government markets also exist on a global scale. In fact, many of Canada's top exporters, including Noranda, Abitibi-Price, and Pratt & Whitney, focus on organizational customers, not ultimate consumers. The majority of world trade involves manufacturers, resellers, and government agencies buying goods and services for their own use or for resale to others. The exchange relationships often involve numerous transactions spanning the globe. Honeywell's MICRO SWITCH Division sells its fibre optic technology and products to manufacturers of data communication systems worldwide, through electronic component resellers in more than 20 countries and directly to national governments in Europe and elsewhere.

MEASURING INDUSTRIAL, RESELLER, AND GOVERNMENT MARKETS

Measuring industrial, reseller, and government markets is an important first step for a firm interested in gauging the size of one, two, or all three markets. Fortunately, information is readily available from the federal government, through Statistics Canada, to do this. The federal government regularly collects, tabulates, and publishes data on these markets using the **Standard Industrial Classification (SIC) system.**[5] The SIC system groups organizations on the basis of major activity or the major product or service provided, which enables the federal government to publish the number of establishments, number of employees, and sales volumes of each group, designated by a numerical code. Geographic breakdowns are also provided where possible.

The Canadian SIC system consists of 18 major divisions (A through R). For example, Division A is agricultural and related industries, and Division J is retail trade industries. Within each division there are major groups, each identified by a two-digit code or category such as Major Group 60, food, beverage, and drug industries (retail), as found in Division J, retail trade industries. Often each of these two-digit categories is further divided into three-digit and four-digit categories, which represent subindustries within the broader two-digit category. Figure 7–2 presents a detailed breakdown of Major Group 60, food, beverage, and drug industries, found in Division J, retail trade industries, to illustrate the SIC system.

The SIC system permits a firm to find the SIC codes of its present customers and then obtain SIC-coded lists for similar firms that may want the same types of products and services. Also, SIC categories can be monitored to determine the growth in the number of establishments, number of employees, and sales volumes to identify promising marketing opportunities.

However, SIC codes have important limitations. The federal government assigns only one code to each organization based on its major activity or product, so large firms that engage in many different activities or provide different types of products and services are still given only one SIC code. A second limitation is that four-digit codes are not available for all industries in every geographic area, because Statistics Canada will not reveal data when only a few organizations exist in an area, in order to protect the confidentiality of the organizations.

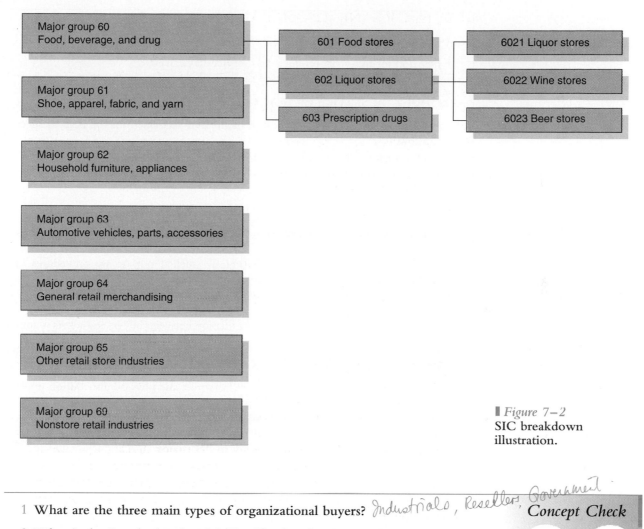

■ *Figure 7−2*
SIC breakdown illustration.

1 **What are the three main types of organizational buyers?** *Industrials, Resellers, Government*   *Concept Check*

2 **What is the Standard Industrial Classification (SIC) system?**

CHARACTERISTICS OF ORGANIZATIONAL BUYING

Organizations are different from individuals, so buying for an organization is different from buying for yourself or your family.[6] True, in both cases the objective in making the purchase is to solve the buyer's problem—to satisfy a need or want. But unique objectives and policies of an organization put special *to act* constraints on how it makes buying decisions. Understanding the characteristics *under* of organizational buying is essential in designing effective marketing programs to reach these buyers.

Organizational buying behaviour is the decision-making process that organizations use to establish the need for products and services and identify, evaluate, and choose among alternative brands and suppliers. Some key characteristics of organizational buying behaviour are listed in Figure 7−3 and discussed in the following pages.[7]

■ *Figure 7–3*
Key characteristics of industrial and organizational buying behaviour.

MARKET CHARACTERISTICS

- Demand for industrial products and services is derived.
- Few customers typically exist, and their purchase orders are large.

PRODUCT OR SERVICE CHARACTERISTICS

- Products or services are technical in nature and purchased on the basis of specifications.
- There is a predominance of raw and semifinished goods purchased.
- Heavy emphasis is placed on delivery time, technical assistance, postsale service, and financing assistance.

BUYING PROCESS CHARACTERISTICS

- Technically qualified and professional buyers exist and follow established purchasing policies and procedures.
- Buying objectives and criteria are typically spelled out, as are procedures for evaluating sellers and products (services).
- Multiple buying influences exist, and multiple parties participate in purchase decisions.
- Reciprocal arrangements exist, and negotiation between buyers and sellers is commonplace.

OTHER MARKETING MIX CHARACTERISTICS

- Direct selling to organizational buyers is the rule, and physical distribution is very important.
- Advertising and other forms of promotion are technical in nature.
- Price is often negotiated, evaluated as part of broader seller and product (service) qualities, typically inelastic owing to derived demand, and frequently affected by trade and quantity discounts.

DEMAND CHARACTERISTICS

Consumer demand for products and services is affected by their price and availability and by consumers' personal tastes and discretionary income. By comparison, industrial demand is derived. **Derived demand** means that the demand for industrial products and services is driven by, or derived from, demand for consumer products and services. For example, the demand for Alcan's aluminum products is based on consumer demand for beer, soft drinks, cars, and cameras. Derived demand is often based on expectations of future consumer demand. For instance, Whirlpool purchases parts for its washers and dryers in anticipation of consumer demand, which is affected by the replacement cycle for these products and by consumer income. Thus forecasting is very important in organizational buying, and it is discussed in Chapter 10.

NUMBER OF POTENTIAL BUYERS

Firms selling consumer products or services often try to reach thousands or millions of individuals or households. For example, your local supermarket or

Consumer needs and wants provide a derived demand for Alcan's aluminum products.

bank probably serves thousands of people, and Quaker Oats tries to reach 9 million Canadian households with its breakfast cereals and probably succeeds in selling to a third or half of these in any given year. In contrast, firms selling to organizations are often restricted to far fewer buyers. Cray Research can sell its supercomputers to fewer than 1,000 organizations throughout the world, and B. F. Goodrich sells its original equipment tires to fewer than 10 car manufacturers.

BUYING OBJECTIVES

Organizations buy products and services for one main reason: to help them achieve their objectives. For business firms the **buying objective** is usually to increase profits through reducing costs or increasing revenues. Southland Corporation buys automated inventory systems to increase the number of products that can be sold through its 7-Eleven outlets and to keep them fresh. Nissan Motor Company switched its advertising agency because it expected a more effective ad campaign than it was getting to help it sell more cars and increase revenues. To improve executive decision making, many firms buy advanced computer systems to process data. The objectives of nonprofit firms and government agencies are usually to meet the needs of the groups they serve. Thus a hospital buys a high-technology diagnostic device to serve its patients better, and Employment Canada buys pencils and paper to help run its office so it can assist Canadian workers.

Understanding buying objectives is a necessary first step in marketing to organizations. Recognizing the high costs of energy, Sylvania promotes cost savings and increased profits made possible by its new fluorescent lights to prospective buyers.

BUYING CRITERIA

In making a purchase, the buying organization must weigh key buying criteria that apply to the potential supplier and what it wants to sell. **Organizational buying criteria** are the objective attributes of the supplier's products and services and the capabilities of the supplier itself. These criteria serve the same purpose as the evaluative criteria used by consumers and described in Chapter 6. Seven of the most commonly used criteria are (1) price, (2) ability to meet the quality specifications required for the item, (3) ability to meet required delivery schedules, (4) technical capability, (5) warranties and claim policies in the event of poor performance, (6) past performance on previous contracts, and (7) production facilities and capacity.[8] Suppliers that meet or exceed these criteria create customer value.

Many organizational buyers today are transforming their buying criteria into specific requirements that are communicated to prospective suppliers. This practice, called **reverse marketing,** involves the deliberate effort by organizational buyers to build relationships that shape suppliers' products, services, and capabilities to fit a buyer's needs and those of its customers.[9] For example, Intel supports its suppliers by offering quality management programs and investing in supplier equipment that produces fewer defects.[10] Harley-Davidson requires its suppliers to provide written plans of their efforts to improve quality, and it monitors the progress of the suppliers toward achieving these goals.[11]

With many Canadian manufacturers adopting a "just-in-time" (JIT) inventory system that reduces the inventory of production parts to those to be used within hours or days, on-time delivery is becoming an even more important buying criterion and, in some instances, a requirement.[12] Caterpillar trains its key suppliers at its Quality Institute in JIT inventory systems and conducts

The success of Harley-Davidson motorcycles is due to continuous quality improvements with its suppliers.

supplier seminars on how to diagnose, correct, and implement continuous quality improvement programs.[13] The just-in-time inventory system is discussed further in Chapter 16.

SIZE OF THE ORDER OR PURCHASE

The size of the purchase involved in organizational buying is typically much larger than that in consumer buying. The dollar value of a single purchase made by an organization often runs into the thousands or millions of dollars. For example, IBM's worldwide purchases of electronic components, subassemblies, and assembly services is in the tens of billions annually. With so much money at stake, most organizations place constraints on their buyers in the form of purchasing policies or procedures. Buyers must often get competitive bids from at least three prospective suppliers when the order is above a specific amount, such as $5,000. When the order is above an even higher amount, such as $50,000, it may require the review and approval of a vice president or even the president. Knowing how the size of the order affects buying practices is important in determining who participates in the purchase decision and makes the final decision and also the length of time required to arrive at a purchase agreement.[14]

BUYER-SELLER RELATIONSHIPS

Another distinction between organizational and consumer buying behaviour lies in the nature of the relationships between organizational buyers and suppliers. Specifically, organizational buying is more likely to involve complex and lengthy negotiations concerning delivery schedules, price, technical specifications, warranties, and claim policies. These negotiations can last as long as five years, as was the case in GE's purchase of a $9.5 million Cray Research supercomputer.[15]

Reciprocal arrangements also exist in organizational buying. **Reciprocity** is an industrial buying practice in which two organizations agree to purchase each other's products and services. For example, GM purchases Borg-Warner transmissions, and Borg-Warner buys trucks and cars from GM.[16] Consumer

Scratching Each Other's Back: The Ethics of Reciprocity in Organizational Buying

Reciprocity, the buying practice in which two organizations agree to purchase each other's products and services, is frowned upon in many countries because it restricts the normal operation of the free market. Reciprocal buying practices do exist, however, in a variety of forms, including certain types of countertrade arrangements in international marketing. Furthermore, the extent to which reciprocity is viewed as an ethical issue varies across cultures.

Reciprocity is occasionally addressed in the ethics codes of companies. For instance, the Quaker Oats Company code of ethics states:

> In many instances, Quaker may purchase goods and/or services from a supplier who buys products or services from us. This practice is normal and acceptable, but suppliers may not be asked to buy our products and services in order to become or continue to be a supplier.

Do you think reciprocal buying is unethical?

Sources: Based on N. C. Smith and J. A. Quelch, *Ethics in Marketing* (Homewood, IL: Richard D. Irwin, 1993), p. 796; N. Gilbert, "The Case for Countertrade," *Across the Board,* May 1992, pp. 43–45; and A. J. Dubinsky, M. A. Jolson, M. Kotobe, and C. U. Lim, "A Cross-National Investigation of Industrial Salespeople's Ethical Perceptions," *Journal of International Business Studies,* Fourth Quarter 1991, pp. 651–70.

and Corporate Affairs Canada frowns on reciprocal buying because it restricts the normal operation of the free market. However, the practice exists and can limit the flexibility of organizational buyers in choosing alternative suppliers. (Regardless of the legality of reciprocal buying, do you believe this practice is ethical? See the accompanying Ethics and Social Responsibility Alert.) Long-term relationships are also prevalent. As an example, Shanghai Aviation Industrial Corporation, owned by the government of China, announced a $4.5 billion project to build 150 commercial airliners over 10 years. McDonnell Douglas, Boeing, and Europe's Airbus Industrie all vied for this lucrative, long-term project, with Boeing getting the initial order valued at $2 billion for the delivery of 33 aircraft. Boeing has sold aircraft to the Chinese government since 1972 and cited this factor as being important in getting the order.

THE BUYING CENTRE

For routine purchases with a small dollar value, a single buyer or purchasing manager often makes the purchase decision alone. In many instances, however, several people in the organization participate in the buying process. The individuals in this group, called a **buying centre,** share common objectives, risks, and knowledge important to the purchase decision. For most large multistore chain resellers such as Sears Canada, 7-Eleven convenience stores, Zellers, The Bay, or Safeway, the buying centre is highly formalized and is called a *buying*

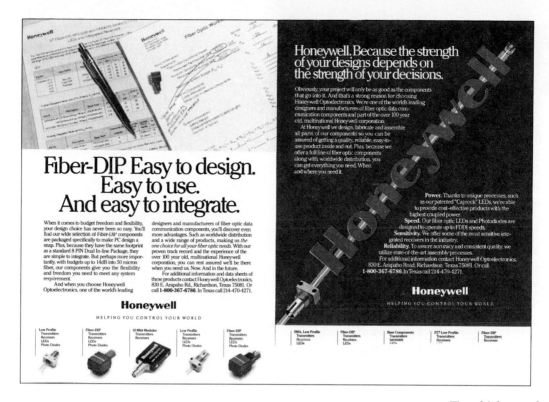

committee. However, most industrial firms or government units use informal groups of people or call meetings to arrive at buying decisions.

The importance of the buying centre requires that a firm marketing to many industrial firms and government units understand the structure and behaviour of these groups. One researcher has suggested four questions to provide guidance in understanding the buying centre in these organizations.[17] Which individuals are in the buying centre for the product or service? What is the relative influence of each member of the group? What are the buying criteria of each member? How does each member of the group perceive our firm, our products and services, and our salespeople?

Answers to these questions are difficult to come by, particularly in dealing with industrial firms, resellers, and government units outside Canada.[18] For example, Canadian firms are often frustrated by the fact that foreign buyers such as the Japanese or Chinese "ask a thousand questions" but give few answers, sometimes rely on third parties to convey views on proposals, are prone not to "talk business," and often say yes to be courteous when they mean no. Firms in the global chemical industry recognize that production engineering personnel have a great deal of influence in Hungarian buying groups, while purchasing agents in the Canadian chemical industry have relatively more influence in buying decisions.

People in the Buying Centre   The composition of the buying centre in a given organization depends on the specific item being bought. Although a buyer or purchasing manager is almost always a member of the buying centre, individuals

To which people in a prospective customer's buying centre are these ads targeted—(1) engineering management or (2) design and production engineers? To understand the situation and discover the answer, see the text and the accompanying Marketing Action Memo.

MARKETING·ACTION·MEMO

Reaching Different Members of a Buying Centre with Customized Advertisements

*D*ifferent members of a buying centre have different buying criteria for choosing suppliers and products. At Honeywell, MICRO SWITCH Division, the marketing staff responsible for fibre optics products develops customized advertisements for each person in a customer's buying centre—design engineers, production engineers, engineering management, and purchasing agents. Design and production engineers want new technologies and products that are easy to design, install, and use. Engineering management is concerned with supplier capabilities, including a proven track record and service. Purchasing agents often focus on cost and delivery.

Recognizing that different buying criteria exist, Bob Procsal, product manager for fibre optic prod-

ucts, carefully chooses different messages and media to communicate to each buying centre member. For instance, the left-hand side of the accompanying ad from Honeywell is directed toward design and production engineers and focusses on some specifics of their buying criteria. The right-hand side is designed for engineering management and deals at a more general level, with factors such as power, speed, and sensitivity.

Does the added effort and expense of customized advertisements pay off? Yes, it does! Inquiries about the company's line of fibre optics products increased 50 percent after this practice was implemented.

Source: Based on an interview with Bob Procsal, Honeywell, MICRO SWITCH Division.

from other functional areas are included depending on what is to be purchased. In buying a million-dollar machine tool, the president (because of the size of the purchase) and the production vice president or manager would probably be members. For key components to be incorporated in a final manufactured product, individuals from R&D, engineering, and quality control are likely to be added. For new word-processing equipment, experienced secretaries who will use the equipment would be members. Still, a major question in penetrating the buying centre is finding and reaching the people who will initiate, influence, and actually make the buying decision.[19] The accompanying Marketing Action Memo shows how Honeywell's MICRO SWITCH Division tailors its advertising to reach slightly different members of the buying centres in its customer organizations.

Roles in the Buying Centre   Researchers have identified five specific roles that an individual in a buying centre can play.[20] In some purchases the same person may perform two or more of these functions.

- *Users* are the people in the organization who actually use the product or service, such as a secretary who will use a new word processor.
- *Influencers* affect the buying decision, usually by helping define the specifications for what is bought. The information systems manager would be a key influencer in the purchase of a new mainframe computer.
- *Buyers* have formal authority and responsibility to select the supplier and negotiate the terms of the contract. The purchasing manager probably would perform this role in the purchase of a mainframe computer.

■ *Deciders* have the formal or informal power to select or approve the supplier that receives the contract. Whereas in routine orders the decider is usually the buyer or purchasing manager, in important technical purchases it is more likely to be someone from R&D, engineering, or quality control. The decider for a key component being incorporated in a final manufactured product might be any of these three people.

■ *Gatekeepers* control the flow of information in the buying centre. Purchasing personnel, technical experts, and secretaries can all keep salespeople or information from reaching people performing the other four roles.

STAGES IN AN ORGANIZATIONAL BUYING DECISION

As shown in Figure 7−4 (and covered in Chapter 6), the five stages a student might use in buying a CD player also apply to organizational purchases.[21] However, comparing the two right-hand columns in Figure 7−4 reveals some key differences. For example, when a CD player manufacturer buys headphones for its units from a supplier, more individuals are involved, supplier capability becomes more important, and the postpurchase evaluation behaviour is more formalized. The headphone-buying decision illustrated is typical of the steps in

9/30

■ *Figure 7−4*
Comparing the stages in consumer and organizational purchases.

STAGES IN THE BUYING DECISION PROCESS	CONSUMER PURCHASE: CD PLAYER FOR A STUDENT	ORGANIZATIONAL PURCHASE: HEADPHONES FOR A CD PLAYER
Problem recognition	Student doesn't like the sound of the stereo system now owned and desires a CD player.	Marketing research and sales departments observe that competitors are including headphones on their models. The firm decides to include headphones on its own new models, which will be purchased from an outside supplier.
Information search	Student uses past experience and that of friends, ads, and *Consumer Reports* to collect information and uncover alternatives.	Design and production engineers draft specifications for headphones. The purchasing department identifies suppliers of CD player headphones.
Alternative evaluation	Alternative CD players are evaluated on the basis of important attributes desired in a CD player.	Purchasing and engineering personnel visit with suppliers and assess (1) facilities, (2) capacity, (3) quality control, and (4) financial status. They drop any suppliers not satisfactory on these factors.
Purchase decision	A specific brand of CD player is selected, the price is paid, and it is installed in the student's room.	They use (1) quality, (2) price, (3) delivery, and (4) technical capability as key buying criteria to select a supplier. Then they negotiate terms and award a contract.
Postpurchase behaviour	Student reevaluates the purchase decision, may return the CD player to the store if it is unsatisfactory, and looks for supportive information to justify the purchase.	They evaluate suppliers using a formal vendor rating system and notify supplier if phones do not meet their quality standard. If problem is not corrected, they drop the firm as a future supplier.

M A R K E T I N G · A C T I O N · M E M O

How the Buying Situation Affects Buying Centre Behaviour

*H*ow does the buy-class situation influence the size and behaviour of the buying centre? Considerable research has examined this question and produced some consistent findings. The research findings are summarized below and illustrate that the buy-class situation affects buying centre tendencies in different ways. This research has important implications for industrial selling that are discussed in the text.

Sources: Based on J. M. Bristor, "Influence Strategies in Organizational Buying: The Importance of Connections to the Right People in the Right Places," *Journal of Business-to-Business Marketing,* vol. 1 (1993), pp. 63–98; E. Anderson, W. Chu, and B. Weitz, "Industrial Purchasing: An Empirical Exploration of the Buy-Class Framework," *Journal of Marketing,* July 1987, pp. 71–86; and R. D. McWilliams, E. Naumann, and S. Scott, "Determining Buying Center Size," *Industrial Marketing Management,* February 1992, pp. 43–49.

	BUY-CLASS SITUATION	
BUYING CENTRE DIMENSION	NEW BUY	STRAIGHT OR MODIFIED REBUY
People involved	Many	Few
Decision time	Long	Short
Problem definition	Uncertain	Well defined
Buying objective	Good solution	Low-price supplier
Suppliers considered	New and present	Present
Buying influence	Technical or operating personnel	Purchasing agent

a purchase made by an organization.[22] Later in the chapter we will analyze a more complex purchase made by an industrial organization.

TYPES OF BUYING SITUATIONS

The number of people in the buying centre and the length and complexity of the steps in the buying process largely depend on the specific buying situation. Researchers who have studied organizational buying identify three types of buying situations, which they have termed **buy classes.**[23] These buy classes vary from the routine reorder, or **straight rebuy,** to the completely new purchase, termed **new buy.** In between these extremes is the **modified rebuy.** Some examples will clarify the differences:

▪ *Straight rebuy.* Here the buyer or purchasing manager reorders an existing product or service from the list of acceptable suppliers, probably without even checking with users or influencers from the engineering, production, or quality control departments. Office supplies and maintenance services are usually obtained as straight rebuys.

▪ *Modified rebuy.* In this buying situation the users, influencers, or deciders in the buying centre want to change the product specifications, price, delivery schedule, or supplier. Although the item purchased is largely the same as with the straight rebuy, the changes usually necessitate enlarging the buying centre to include people outside the purchasing department.

- *New buy.* Here the organization is a first-time buyer of the product or service. This involves greater potential risks in the purchase, so the buying centre is enlarged to include all those who have a stake in the new buy. The purchase of CD player headphones was a new buy.

The marketing strategies of sellers facing each of these three buying situations can vary greatly because the importance of personnel from functional areas such as purchasing, engineering, production, and R&D varies with (1) the type of buying situation and (2) the stage of the purchasing process.[24] Read the accompanying Marketing Action Memo and suppose you are a sales representative selling a component part to a manufacturer for use in one of its products. How will your sales task differ depending on the purchase (buy-class) situation?

If it is a buy for the manufacturer, you should be prepared to act as a consultant to the buyer, work with technical personnel, and expect a long time for a buying decision to be reached. However, if the manufacturer has bought the component part from you before, so that it is a straight or modified rebuy, your sales task should emphasize low price and a reliable supply in meetings with the purchasing agent.

Concept Check

1 **What one department is almost always represented by a person in the buying centre?**

2 **What are the three types of buying situations, or buy classes?**

THE ORGANIZATIONAL NEW BUY DECISION

New buy purchase decisions are ones where the most purchasing expertise is needed and where both the benefits of good decisions and penalties of bad ones are likely to be greatest. This means that effective communication among people in the buying centre is especially important.[25] Tracing the stages in the buying decision made by an appliance manufacturer highlights some of the important aspects of organizational buying. It also illustrates the challenges involved in marketing to organizations.

AN INDUSTRIAL PURCHASE: AN ELECTRIC MOTOR

Suppose GE decides to design and build a new line of clothes dryers and needs an electric motor, a key component in the dryer. Let's track the five purchasing stages in this new buy situation.

Problem Recognition   After top management in GE's appliance division decides to introduce a new line of clothes dryers, engineering and R&D personnel come up with a workable design that is tested and approved. They meet with the purchasing manager to reach a **make–buy decision**—an evaluation of whether a product or its parts will be purchased from outside suppliers or built by the firm itself. The group concludes that the electric motor in each dryer should be bought, not made.

Information Search   The engineering and R&D personnel need to develop product specifications for the electric motor, which are detailed technical requirements the motor must meet such as its horsepower, life in hours, and ability to operate at a stated temperature and humidity. Members of the purchasing and production departments then perform a **value analysis** on the electric motor—a systematic appraisal of the design, quality, and performance requirements of the product to reduce purchasing costs. For example, suppose the GE engineers conclude that at least a ⅛-horsepower motor is needed to power the dryer. The purchasing department would recommend buying a ¼-horsepower motor, which is available as a standard item from many vendors, rather than a ⅛-horsepower motor, which must be made to order at a higher cost.

In its information search, the purchasing department also relies on the technical expertise of vendors in developing appropriate design specifications. Specifications are generally stated in terms of material, dimensions, and performance characteristics rather than brand name to maximize the number of qualified vendors available and to ensure genuine competition among bidders. A variety of other sources may be used by GE during the information search process (see Figure 7–5) in order to make an effective purchase decision.

Alternative Evaluation   The buying centre must develop the necessary buying criteria for the electric motor, which in this case are quality requirements, on-time delivery, and price, in that order. The purchasing manager is given the responsibility to select the supplier and negotiate a contract for the motors.

The next step in purchasing is soliciting bids from potential suppliers. This involves selecting the names of vendors from a **bidders list**—a list of firms believed to be qualified to supply a given item—and sending each vendor a quotation request form describing the desired quantity, delivery date, and specifications of the product.

Most purchasing departments maintain a separate bidders list for each general class of items they order. They update these lists continually by adding

Standardized electric motors are used in many applications.

INFORMATION SOURCE	DESCRIPTION
Salespeople	Sales personnel representing manufacturers or distributors of the product in question.
Technical sources	Engineering personnel internal or external to the subject's firm.
Personnel in buyer's firm	Peer group references (e.g., other purchasing agents in the subject's firm).
Purchasing agents in other companies	Peer group references external to the buyer's firm.
Trade association	Cooperatives voluntarily joined by business competitors designed to assist its members and industry in dealing with mutual problems (e.g., National Association of Purchasing Management).
Advertising in trade journals	Commercial messages placed by the manufacturer or distributor of the product in question.
Articles in trade journals	Messages relating to the product in question but not under the control of the manufacturer or distributor.
Vendor files	Information pertaining to the values of various sources of supply as developed and maintained by the buyer's firm.
Trade registers	Buyer guides providing listings of suppliers and other marketing information (e.g., *Fraser's Register*).
Product literature	Specific product and vendor information supplied by the manufacturing or distributing firm.

Source: Reprinted by permission of the publisher from "Achieving Seller Acceptability in Industrial Markets: Development of the Communication Mix," by H. L. Matthews, J. Robeson, and P. J. Banbic, in *Consumer and Industrial Buying Behavior,* ed. A. Woodside, J. N. Sheth, and P. D. Bennett, p. 223. Copyright 1977 by Elsevier Science Publishing Company, Inc.

the names of potential new vendors and deleting the names of unsatisfactory vendors. To further ensure competition, many firms require that at least three bids be solicited for purchases exceeding a specified dollar amount.

Purchase Decision Unlike the short purchase stage in a consumer purchase (such as buying a bag of potato chips), in organizations the purchase stage covers the period from vendor selection and placing the purchase order until the product is delivered, which often takes months or years. This period frequently involves performing vendor follow-up, expediting the order, and renegotiating the contract terms if specification changes are made after the initial contract is awarded.

Sometimes contracts are awarded directly to vendors on the basis of the data they provide in the quotation request forms. At other times the purchasing manager may wish to negotiate with one or more bidders, particularly on high-dollar, high-volume items. Eventually the GE purchasing manager selects two vendors and awards each a contract in the form of a purchase order—an authorization for the vendor to provide the items under the agreed-on terms and to bill the purchasing firm.

If the purchased item is of minor value and if no design or delivery changes are made in the order after it has been issued, the purchasing manager rarely follows up on the order. However, vendor follow-up is essential if conditions change or if an item is of high value, in short supply, or crucial to the firm. In the case of the electric motors, they are so critical to producing the new clothes dryers that the purchasing manager periodically checks with the two vendors to see that no problems arise.

Postpurchase Behaviour   When the electric motors are finally delivered, the quality control department tests them to ensure they meet specifications. If they are unsatisfactory, the purchasing manager negotiates with the supplier to rework the items according to specifications or arranges for an entirely new shipment.

Experienced buyers realize that evaluation of purchase decisions is essential. The vendor's performance is evaluated after final delivery of the purchased items. This information is often noted on a vendor rating sheet and is used to update the bidders lists kept by the purchasing department. Performance on past contracts determines a vendor's chances of being asked to bid on future purchases, and poor performance results in a vendor's name being dropped from the list.

Concept Check	1 **What kind of buying situation is GE's purchase of an electric motor?**
	2 **What types of information sources are available to GE in making a purchase decision?**

MARKETING TO ORGANIZATIONS MORE EFFECTIVELY

The preceding example of an organizational purchase suggests steps sellers can take to increase their chances of selling products and services to organizations. Firms selling to organizations must learn four key lessons to be successful in business marketing: (1) understand the organization's needs, (2) get on the bidders list, (3) find the right people in the buying centre, and (4) provide value to the organizational buyer.

UNDERSTAND THE ORGANIZATION'S NEEDS

As important and obvious as understanding the organization's needs seems, this guideline is violated as often with industrial products as with consumer products. Getting to know the organization's needs can be accomplished in several ways. A firm could simply review what an organization has purchased in the past. For example, a firm wanting to sell to the federal government can examine the "detailed expenditure accounts" of the government to see exactly what it has purchased over the past year. An important aspect of discovering needs is also determining if those needs are being met. To do so, a firm can obtain a copy of the successful bidders lists published by the government in order to determine who is currently supplying the government with goods and services. This information can allow the firm to investigate whether the government was satisfied with the existing goods and services and/or their suppliers. Marketing opportunities may exist where the organizational buyers have experienced some dissatisfaction.

Another way to understand the organization's needs is to *ask*. The firm can simply talk to organizational buyers to discuss their needs. In doing so, a firm may be able to work with potential customers to specifically design products that meet their requirements, rather than wait and hope for orders.

Global Upholstery Co., Ltd., of Downsview, Ontario, has been very successful with this strategy. Global is the sixth-largest office furniture manufacturer in North America, competing with such giants as Steelcase and Haworth. Very often Global will talk to customers to determine their exact requirements and then will make the product. David Feldberg, president of Global, says, "We'll have a customer in, and we'll show them a chair, and they'll say, 'Yeah, but I'd like the back a little bigger.' We say, 'Hold on,' and while we're out to lunch, we make a new chair. There's no way you'll lose a sale when you can do that."[26]

GET ON THE BIDDERS LIST

Understanding an organization's needs is vital, but a firm must also be considered a satisfactory or qualified supplier and get its name on the bidders lists of organizations to which it hopes to sell. A firm cannot compete unless its name is on the bidders list. This is often accomplished through personal selling and sending product samples to be tested by the organization. If the product and the supplier meet the organization's specifications, their name will get onto the list. For example, Global Upholstery met the rigid requirements of the Boeing Corporation and was selected to bid on a $20 million contract to refurbish Boeing's headquarters in Seattle, Washington. Global beat out a US competitor, Steelcase, for the contract.[27]

FIND THE RIGHT PEOPLE IN THE BUYING CENTRE

One of the most difficult parts of an industrial salesperson's job is finding the "right" people in the buying centre—the people who influence and make the decision to select the product and supplier. This information is critical to obtain, and it is often readily available. For example, one source that could be used is the *Canadian Trade Index* published by the Canadian Manufacturers Association. It lists Canadian manufacturers, contact people, telephone numbers, and addresses. Using this and other information can help the firm better direct its marketing efforts.

PROVIDE VALUE TO THE ORGANIZATIONAL BUYER

Obtaining the right or privilege to supply products or services to an organization is a marketing accomplishment. Now, however, the firm must satisfy the organization's needs and provide that customer with value. Providing value leads to repeat business and continued success. Global Upholstery attributes much of its success in providing value to its customers to its commitment to product design. Micheline Sanitar, an interior design consultant, says Global "is a real Canadian success story. When they started out calling themselves 'Global,' it seemed like a silly name, but now it's really appropriate."[28] The company has built a global business based on providing value to its customers. For example, in the low-end steno chair category, Global has been able to outshine its Italian and Chinese competitors by offering a nicer design, better detail, and better quality and at a price within 10 percent of its competitors.

To sell to the Canadian and US federal governments, Global has to meet demanding quality and durability standards, important ingredients in the concept of customer value. In order to meet these standards, the company created its own testing facility—one of only two manufacturing laboratories in Canada certified to do furniture testing. This investment has paid off for Global. It has built a reputation for providing value and now exports close to 45 percent of its total production, with one-third of its output going to the United States.[29]

Concept Check

1 Why is getting on the bidders list important to a prospective vendor?

2 How could a firm wanting to sell to the federal government discover the needs of that organization?

Summary

1 Organizational buyers are divided into three different markets: industrial, reseller, and government.

2 Measuring industrial, reseller, and government markets is an important first step for firms interested in gauging the size of one, two, or all three markets. The Standard Industrial Classification (SIC) system is a convenient starting point to begin this process.

3 Many aspects of organizational buying behaviour are different from consumer buying behaviour. Some key differences between the two include demand characteristics, number of potential buyers, buying objectives, buying criteria, size of the order or purchase, buyer–seller relationships, and multiple buying influences within companies.

4 The buying centre concept is central to understanding organizational buying behaviour. Knowing who composes the buying centre and the roles they play in making purchase decisions is important in marketing to organizations. The buying centre usually includes a person from the purchasing department and possibly representatives from R&D, engineering, and production, depending on what is being purchased. These people can play one or more of five roles in a purchase decision: user, influencer, buyer, decider, or gatekeeper.

5 The three types of buying situations, or buy classes, are the straight rebuy, the modified rebuy, and the new buy. These form a scale ranging from a routine reorder to a totally new purchase.

6 The stages in an organizational buying decision are the same as those for consumer buying decisions: problem recognition, information search, alternative evaluation, purchase decision, and postpurchase behaviour. An example of an organizational purchase described in the text is GE's purchase of an electric motor for its appliance division. To market more effectively to organizations, a firm must try to understand the organization's needs, get on the bidders list, reach the right people in the buying centre, and provide value to the organizational buyer.

Key Terms and Concepts

business marketing   p. 158
organizational buyers   p. 158
industrial firms   p. 158
resellers   p. 159
government units   p. 159
Standard Industrial Classification (SIC)
system   p. 160
organizational buying behaviour   p. 161
derived demand   p. 162
buying objective   p. 163
organizational buying criteria   p. 164

reverse marketing   p. 164
reciprocity   p. 165
buying centre   p. 166
buy classes   p. 170
straight rebuy   p. 170
new buy   p. 170
modified rebuy   p. 170
make–buy decision   p. 171
value analysis   p. 172
bidders list   p. 172

Chapter Problems and Applications

1 Describe the major differences among industrial firms, resellers, and government units in Canada.
2 Explain how the Standard Industrial Classification (SIC) system might be helpful in understanding industrial, reseller, and government markets, and discuss the limitations inherent in the SIC system.
3 List and discuss the key characteristics of organizational buying that make it different from consumer buying.
4 What is a buying centre? Describe the roles assumed by people in a buying centre and what useful questions should be raised to guide any analysis of the structure and behaviour of a buying centre.
5 Effective marketing is of increasing importance in today's competitive environment. How can firms more effectively market to organizations?
6 A foreign-based producer of apparel for men is interested in the sales volume for such products in Canada. The producer realizes that this is a difficult assignment but has given you a sizable fee to find these data. What information source would you examine first, and what kind of information would be found in this source?
7 If many of the federal government's purchases are classified as straight rebuys, how can a new firm wanting to do business with the government break into this market?

HOKKAIDO

Sapporo

JAPAN

HONSHU

Tokyo

Yokohama

Kyoto   Nagoya

Kobe

Osaka

Hiroshima

Kitakyushu

SHIKOKU

Fukuoka

KYUSHU

Targeting Marketing Opportunities

Part III describes how people with similar wants and needs become the target of marketing activities. The first step in this process, collecting information about prospective consumers, is discussed in Chapter 8. The information helps marketers focus their efforts on groups with common needs, or market segments. Chapter 9 describes how Reebok International develops specific products for diverse market segments such as runners, aerobic dancers, basketball players, cross-trainers, and others. Chapter 9 also describes how Japanese automobile manufacturers have reduced the number of products offered to focus on selected consumer segments. Finally, Chapter 10 explains how new information technologies facilitate information collection and use and help marketers develop long-term cost-effective relationships with individual consumers.

LOVE

NEVER

DIES

BRAM STOKER'S

Dracula

A FRANCIS FORD COPPOLA FILM

COLUMBIA PICTURES PRESENTS

AMERICAN ZOETROPE/OSIRIS FILMS PRODUCTION "BRAM STOKER'S DRACULA" GARY OLDMAN WINONA RYDER ANTHONY HOPKINS KEANU REEVES
PRODUCER JAMES V. HART VISUAL EFFECTS ROMAN COPPOLA MUSIC BY WOJCIECH KILAR COSTUMES DESIGNED BY EIKO ISHIOKA EDITED BY NICHOLAS C. SMITH GLEN SCANTLEBURY ANNE GOURSAUD,
PRODUCTION DESIGNER THOMAS SANDERS DIRECTOR OF PHOTOGRAPHY MICHAEL BALLHAUS, A.S.C. EXECUTIVE PRODUCERS MICHAEL APTED AND ROBERT O'CONNOR SCREENPLAY BY JAMES V. HART
PRODUCED BY FRANCIS FORD COPPOLA, FRED FUCHS AND CHARLES MULVEHILL DIRECTED BY FRANCIS FORD COPPOLA

READ THE SIGNET NOVELS
NEWMARKET PRESS & COLLINS PICTORIAL BOOKS

FROM
AMERICAN ZOETROPE

R RESTRICTED
UNDER 17 REQUIRES ACCOMPANYING
PARENT OR ADULT GUARDIAN

NOVEMBER 13

SOUNDTRACK AVAILABLE ON
COLUMBIA RECORDS CASSETTES AND COMPACT DISCS

DOLBY STEREO

A COLUMBIA PICTURES RELEASE

COLUMBI
PICTURE

Collecting and Using Marketing Information

AFTER READING THIS CHAPTER YOU SHOULD BE ABLE TO:

▶ Know what marketing research is and does.

▶ Identify the five steps in the marketing research process.

▶ Know how and when to collect secondary data.

▶ Understand the difference between qualitative and quantitative research.

▶ Know how observation, surveys, and experiments can be used to generate primary data.

▶ Understand how marketers analyze marketing research data.

Reducing Risk: Marketing Research for Movies

With today's typical movie costing $40 million to produce and market, how can motion picture studios use marketing research to reduce their risk of losses? One part of the answer: recruit people to attend sneak previews of a forthcoming movie and ask them questions that might bring about changes in the final edit of the movie.

Without reading ahead, think about answers to these questions:

- Whom would you recruit for these test screenings?
- What questions would you ask them, to help you in editing or modifying parts of the film?

Figure 8–1 summarizes some of the key questions that are used in test screenings—both to select the people for the screenings and to obtain the key reactions of those sitting in the screenings. Many motion picture studios have used sneak test screenings of movies and then made changes that led to more successful films.

Besides test screenings, motion picture studios also use marketing research to do concept tests of proposed plots and to design and test multimillion-dollar promotional campaigns that support a typical movie's introduction. This chapter shows how marketing research is linked to making effective marketing decisions.

Figure 8–1
Marketing research
questions asked in test
screenings of movies,
and how they are used.

WHEN ASKED	KEY QUESTIONS	USE OF QUESTION(S)
Before the test screening	• How old are you? • How frequently do you pay to see movies? • What movies have you seen in the last three months?	Decide if person fits profile of target audience for movie. If yes, invite to test screening. If not, don't invite.
After the test screening	• Were any characters too distasteful? Who? How? • Did any scenes offend you? Which ones? How? • How did you like the ending? If you didn't like it, how would you change it? • Would you recommend the movie to a friend?	Change aspects of some characters. Change scenes. Change or clarify ending. Overall indicator of liking and/or satisfaction with movie.

令人討厭 *使方改*

THE ROLE OF MARKETING RESEARCH

正確地觀察，透視

To place marketing research in perspective, we can describe what it is, some of the difficulties in carrying it out, and how marketing executives can use the marketing research process to make effective decisions.

WHAT MARKETING RESEARCH IS AND DOES

Marketing research is the process of defining a marketing problem or opportunity, systematically collecting and analyzing information, and recommending actions to improve an organization's marketing activities. Marketing research should be considered an ongoing process for acquiring routine and nonroutine information, internal as well as external, for marketing decision making.[1]

A Means of Reducing Risk and Uncertainty   Assessing the needs and wants of consumers and providing information to help design an organization's marketing mix to satisfy them is the principal role that marketing research performs. This means that marketing research attempts to identify and define both marketing problems and opportunities and to generate and evaluate marketing actions.[2] Although marketing research can provide few answers with complete assurance, it can reduce risk and uncertainty to increase the likelihood of the success of marketing decisions. It is a great help to the marketing managers who must make final decisions. Marketing research is useful in both problem diagnosis (identifying the cause of a problem) and problem prognosis (determining how to solve the problem). Conducted properly, marketing research can answer any pressing marketing-related question that an executive might have. However, marketing research should not be designed to simply replace an executive's good sense, experience, or intuition but should rather be used in conjunction with those skills and as a way of taking some of the guesswork out of the marketing decision-making process.

What are the difficulties in asking consumers if they would buy a ticket on a high-speed ICE (intercity express) train? To understand some of the problems faced by market researchers, see the text.

Judging the Value of Marketing Information   The value of marketing information should be judged by the extent to which it improves the marketing decision-making process. In other words, the marketing executive must ask, by gathering marketing information, will I increase my chances of making the correct decision? Think about it: would you make a decision when the probability of being wrong is 50 percent? Not many marketing executives like those odds, and that is why any new information that can increase the chances of making the correct decision is considered valuable. Marketing information is generally more valuable in a decision situation when (*a*) there is a high degree of uncertainty, (*b*) the consequences of a wrong decision are great, and (*c*) there are several alternatives and more than one is likely to be selected.

WHY GOOD MARKETING RESEARCH IS DIFFICULT

First of all, good research requires a clear understanding of the marketing problem to be investigated. Sometimes the nature of the problem appears obvious; other times it is much more difficult to identify and define. Collecting information for an inappropriately identified or poorly defined problem will not be of much help to the marketing executive.

When a marketing researcher must talk to consumers, other problems can arise, such as properly determining whom to talk to, deciding what to ask them, and how to ask them. Good marketing research requires great care—especially because of the inherent difficulties in asking consumers questions. For example:

- Do consumers really know whether they are likely to buy a particular product that they probably never thought about before? Can they really assess its advantages and disadvantages on the spur of the moment?
- Even if they know the answer, will they reveal it? When personal or status questions are involved, will people give honest answers?
- Will their actual purchase behaviour be the same as their stated interest or intentions? Will they buy the same brand they say they will? To appear aggressive, consumers often overstate their likelihood of buying a new product.

When people know they are being measured, the very measurement process itself can significantly affect their answers and behaviours. A task of marketing research is to overcome these difficulties to provide useful information on which marketing executives can act.

---

1 **What is marketing research?**

2 **How can you judge the value of marketing information?**

THE MARKETING RESEARCH PROCESS

Marketing research must always be conducted on the basis of the scientific method, a process of systematically collecting, organizing, and analyzing data in an unbiased, objective manner. Marketing research must meet two basic principles of the scientific method: reliability and validity. **Reliability** refers to the ability to replicate research results under identical environmental conditions. In other words, if a research project was to be conducted for the second, third, or fourth time, the results should be the same. Marketers need to have reliable information to make effective decisions. If results of a study are not reliable, the research can do more harm than no research at all. However, you should remember that sometimes identical research results are not replicated because conditions in the market have changed; the research then doesn't necessarily lack complete reliability, but its reliability under new conditions becomes a question.

Validity involves the notion of whether or not the research measured what it was intended to measure. In other words, does the research tell marketers what they needed to know? For example, sometimes a poorly worded question can mean different things to different people and the answers can lead to invalid results. You should keep the concepts of reliability and validity in mind as we discuss the steps in the marketing research process.

The marketing research process is generally considered to involve five basic steps as shown in Figure 8–2. The marketing researcher usually proceeds through the five steps in sequence. The research should proceed to successive steps only if a solution to the problem has not been found in the earlier steps. For example, exploratory research very often provides enough insight to solve the problem, thus saving the company from conducting more time-consuming and expensive research.

STEP 1: PROBLEM DEFINITION

The first step in the marketing research process is **problem definition,** or properly defining the scope and nature of the marketing problem to be investigated. What you must remember is that while we use the term *problem,* the marketing research process can also be undertaken to explore an *opportunity.* In this text, we will use the term *marketing problem* to include both problems and opportunities. Sometimes the problem is obvious, but in other cases the prob-

Step 1	Problem definition
Step 2	Exploratory research
	• Informal fact finding
	• Secondary data search
Step 3	Primary data generation
	• Sampling
	• Qualitative research
	• Quantitative research
Step 4	Data analysis and interpretation
Step 5	Recommendations and implementation

▌ *Figure 8–2*
The marketing research process.

lem may be more difficult to identify and define. Regardless, the marketing researcher must fully understand and properly identify the problem at hand.

The marketing research process is often initiated by the marketing manager, who will approach the marketing researcher with a problem that requires information for decision making. For example, the marketing manager might ask the researcher to find out why market share for the company's product is dropping in Alberta. But before any actions can be taken, the researcher needs to know what the manager really mans by market share. How is it defined and measured? By units? Dollars? Number of customers? Also, what does the manager mean by a *drop* in market share? Before the researcher can investigate the problem, these questions and many others must be answered.

An important part of the problem definition phase of the marketing research process is distinguishing between problem symptoms and problem causes. For example, the drop in market share in our example may not be the real problem but rather a result of some other problem.

Proper problem definition is critical, since research based on incorrect problem definition will be a waste of resources. Most researchers agree that when proper problem definition is completed, 50 percent of the marketing research task is already accomplished.

---

1 **What are reliability and validity?**

2 **What are the five steps in the marketing research process?**

Concept Check

STEP 2: EXPLORATORY RESEARCH

The next step in the marketing research process involves undertaking some exploratory research. **Exploratory research** is a preliminary examination of problem-specific information that may provide some insight into possible causes and solutions to the problem. This step helps the researcher determine why or how the marketing problem arose and to further solidify some alternatives to solving the problem. The extent of the exploratory research will depend on the magnitude of the problem as well as its complexity. While exploratory research appears informal and casual, it is a critical stage of the marketing research process. In many cases, good exploratory research can solve many marketing problems without the need to conduct further, more expensive research.

Exploratory research usually consists of informal fact finding, from discussions with informed sources inside the firm or customers and/or others outside the firm and an examination of secondary sources of information. The researcher is scanning for any readily available information that can offer insights into the problem as well as provide ideas about possible approaches and techniques to be applied or avoided in the later stages of the research process.

Secondary Data   Exploratory research almost always involves the use of secondary data. **Secondary data** means existing data not collected specifically for the research project but considered relevant and pertinent to the marketing problem. The researcher will usually first examine any internal documentation that may be relevant to the problem under investigation. This existing information is referred to as **internal secondary data.** Such data include financial statements, research reports, customer letters, sales reports, and customer lists. The researcher may also examine, simultaneously or in sequence, any useful outside information that may exist, or **external secondary data.** The federal government is a key source of such data. These data are made available through Statistics Canada or from local libraries. Statistics Canada completes the *Census of Canada* once every decade and updates certain census data every few years. The *Census of Canada* provides detailed information on Canadian households, such as number of people per household, their ages, their gender, household income, and education levels of those in the household. These are basic sources of information used by manufacturers and retailers to identify characteristics and trends of ultimate consumers.

Statistics Canada also prepares annual or biannual reports on the spending and eating habits of Canadians. One important publication it produces is called the *Family Expenditure Guide,* which provides a detailed breakdown of how families spent their money in the previous year. Statistics Canada produces many other census reports that are vital to business firms selling goods and services to organizations. The *Census of Manufacturers* is published annually and lists the number and size of manufacturing firms by industry group (the Standard Industrial Classification, described in Chapter 7), as well as other information including values of shipments and wages paid. Statistics Canada also provides the

Journals that can help a researcher examine techniques to solve marketing research problems.

reports *Retail Trade in Canada* and *Census Reports on Agriculture and Minerals.* A marketing researcher can obtain from Statistics Canada the annual *Marketing Research Handbook* or the *Canada Yearbook,* which includes a summary of key information often necessary to aid marketing decision making. Statistics Canada also has a database system known as CANSIM (Canadian Socio-Economic Information Management System), which marketers can access directly in order to examine aggregate data.

In addition to government-supplied data, trade associations, universities, and business periodicals provide detailed data of value to marketing researchers. For example, one business periodical is *Sales and Marketing Management* magazine, which publishes special issues each year that provide useful data for firms selling both consumer and industrial products. The most famous publication by *S&MM* is its *Annual Survey of Buying Power.*

A number of commercial organizations also serve the research needs of retailers and manufacturers. MacLean Hunter Research Bureau provides numerous reports on various industries. The *Financial Post* produces a publication called *Canadian Markets,* which provides information on demographic information and consumer spending power in provinces, cities, and towns across the country. Companies such as Compusearch and A. C. Nielsen offer both standard and customized information services to other firms on a subscription, or for-fee, basis. Compusearch can provide information on any geographic area of any size in Canada, highlighting population, income, and retail expenditure trends in that area.

Figure 8–3 shows some of the secondary data sources available to the marketer in Canada. There are also hundreds of useful computerized databases and specialized data services such as Dow Jones, Dialog, and Infoglobe that can be accessed by a telephone link from a personal computer on a marketer's desk. We will discuss these services in Chapter 10.

Advantages and disadvantages of secondary data   A general rule among marketing people is to use secondary data first before collecting primary data. Two important advantages of secondary data are (1) the tremendous time savings, since the data have already been collected and published, and (2) the low cost (e.g., most census reports are available for only a few dollars each). Furthermore, a greater level of detail is often available through secondary data. Because Statistics Canada can require business establishments to report information about themselves, its industry data are more complete than what a private organization would assemble if it attempted to collect them.

However, these advantages must be weighed against some significant disadvantages. First, the secondary data may be out of date. If you were working in 1995 on a project and you used 1990 census data, the data would already be five years old. Second, the definitions or categories of information that you find might not be quite right for your research purposes. For example, suppose you are interested in the age group from 13 to 16; many census age statistics appear only for the 10-to-14 and 15-to-19 age groupings. Finally, because the data are collected for another purpose, they may not be specific enough for your needs as a marketing researcher.

But what is critical to remember is that analysis of secondary data may be sufficient to solve the marketing problem and conclude the research process. All too often, marketers skip this stage of the marketing research process and start

▌ *Figure 8–3*
Secondary data sources
in Canada.

SELECTED GUIDES, INDEXES, AND DIRECTORIES
Business Periodical Index
Canadian Almanac and Directory
Canadian Business Index
Canadian News Index
Canadian Periodical Index
Canadian Statistics Index
Canadian Trade Index
Directory of Associations in Canada
Fraser's Canadian Trade Directory
Predicasts Index
Scott's Directories
Standards Periodical Directory
Ulrich's International Periodicals Directory

SELECTED PERIODICALS AND NEWSPAPERS
Advertising Age
Adweek
American Demographics
Business Horizons
Canadian Business
Canadian Consumer
Forbes
Fortune
Harvard Business Review
Journal of Advertising
Journal of Advertising Research
Journal of Consumer Research
Journal of Marketing
Journal of Marketing Management
Journal of Marketing Research
Journal of Personal Selling and Sales
  Management
Journal of Retailing
Journal of Small Business
Marketing Magazine

Marketing & Media Decisions
Marketing News
Progressive Grocer
Sales and Marketing Management
The Globe and Mail
The Financial Post
The Financial Post Magazine
The Wall Street Journal

SELECTED STATISTICS CANADA PUBLICATIONS
Annual Retail Trade
Canadian Economic Observer
Canada Yearbook
Family Expenditure Guide
Market Research Handbook
Statistics Canada Catalogue

SELECTED TRADE SOURCES
A. C. Nielsen
Compusearch
Conference Board of Canada
Dun & Bradstreet
Financial Post Publishing
Find/SVP
Gale Research
MacLean Hunter Research Bureau
Predicasts International
R. L. Polk

SELECTED DATABASES
CANSIM (Statistics Canada)
Dialog
Dow Jones
Infoglobe
Infomart
The Source

generating primary data. This is often a time-consuming and costly mistake. However, if the secondary data are not sufficient to solve the marketing problem, then it is necessary to generate primary data.

| *Concept Check* | 1 **What are secondary data?** |
| | 2 **What are some advantages and disadvantages of secondary data?** |

STEP 3: PRIMARY DATA GENERATION

When researchers have exhausted all secondary data sources and do not have sufficient information to solve their marketing problems, they will proceed to generate primary data. **Primary data** consist of "new" information that is problem-specific and necessary for the research project. In general, the secondary data research should have, at least, helped the researcher refine the scope and nature of the problem as well as filled in some of the information requirements about the problem. The objective at this stage is to proceed with new-information gathering until a sufficient amount of information is obtained to allow the company to make an informed and reasonable decision about the marketing problem.

Primary data can be classified as either qualitative or quantitative. Qualitative data are normally generated, as we shall see, through the use of depth interviews and focus groups. Methods normally used to generate quantitative data include observation, surveys, and experiments. However, these methods can also be used to obtain qualitative data, particularly observation and surveys. Ultimately, the type of primary data and the method used to generate the data should be largely driven by the type of information that needs to be obtained as well as time and cost considerations.

Before discussing the differences between qualitative and quantitative primary data and the methods used to generate such data, we need to discuss the concept of **sampling.**

Sampling   When primary data are to be generated, you must determine the appropriate population that should be the subject of the research. The population is the universe of people, places, or things to be investigated. To define the population or universe correctly, the researcher must know whom and what to study as well as where and when. Rarely does a research project involve a complete census of every person in the research population. This is because of the time and cost involved in conducting a census.

Since researchers will not be able to watch or communicate with every person they would like to, they must select a *sample* of people from the population relevant to the research project. A sample is a subset of the population that is intended to represent the whole population. When a sample is used instead of a census, marketers need to be concerned with sampling error. **Sampling error** is a measure of the discrepancy between results found researching the sampled group and the results that could have been expected had a census been conducted. In other words, it is the level of error in the research results because sampling was used instead of a census. In general, large samples, if selected correctly, have lower sampling errors than smaller samples.

Sampling techniques fall into two general categories: probability and nonprobability sampling. **Probability sampling** involves precise rules to select the sample such that each element of the population has a specific known chance of being selected. For example, if your college wants to know how last year's 1,000 graduates are doing, it can put their names in a bowl and randomly select 100 names of graduates to contact. The chance of being selected—100/1,000, or 0.10—is known in advance, and all graduates have an equal chance of being contacted. This procedure helps select a sample (100 graduates) that should be representative of the entire population (the 1,000 graduates) and allows conclusions to be drawn about the entire population. There are a variety of probability samples used by marketing researchers including (1) a **simple random**

sample, as illustrated in the preceding example; (2) a stratified random sample; (3) a cluster sample; and (4) a systematic sample.

A **stratified random sample** involves dividing the population into groups, or strata, and selecting a simple random sample of individuals from each group. These groups are related in some important way to the topic of the study. For example, restaurant patrons may be classified into heavy, moderate, and light user categories. Selecting a random sample from each of the three strata ensures that all types of customers are represented. A **cluster sample** involves dividing the population under study into subgroups or clusters and then drawing a random sample of the groups. A census of the elements within the sampled clusters is then completed. Thus, it is *groups* of respondents that are studied, not individuals. For example, a door-to-door survey project might involve interviewing a cluster of households in a neighbourhood of a specific geographic area. A **systematic sample** involves systematically selecting respondents from a list using a prescribed interval after a random start; thus every *n*th item on the list is selected from the random starting point. For example, a researcher could start by picking a telephone directory page at random and then select every *n*th name on every *n*th page.

Nonprobability samples are chosen on the basis of convenience or arbitrary judgment by the marketing researchers. With nonprobability samples, the chance of selecting a particular member of the population is either unknown or zero. If your college decided just to talk to 100 of last year's graduates who lived closest to the college, many class members would be arbitrarily eliminated. This has introduced a sampling bias, or possible lack of representativeness, which may make it difficult to draw conclusions about the entire population of the graduating class. With nonprobability samples, the probability that individual members of the population will be selected cannot be determined, and so the sampling errors of nonprobability samples cannot be measured.

Nonprobability samples are often used when time and budgets are limited and are most often used in qualitative research, where sampling error is not an issue. The basic types of nonprobability samples are convenience, judgment, and quota samples. A **convenience sample** is selected solely on the basis that it is convenient and readily accessible, as in person-on-the-street interviews. A **judgment sample** is one for which the researcher selects respondents on the belief that they will provide the needed information for study; it does not involve random selection of respondents. For example, the researcher may believe that women between 25 and 34 years of age are most likely to buy a particular product that may be under study and will seek to talk to women who fall into that age category. A **quota sample** is a type of convenience and judgment sample for which the researcher specifies a mix of characteristics of prospective respondents such as age, gender, income, or purchase volume. The researcher will attempt to find and talk to a prescribed number of respondents in these various categories. For example, the researcher may want to talk to a specific number of males and females as well as people in different age groupings and so will set out to fill a quota for each of the predetermined categories.

Once the researcher has determined the population or universe to be studied and determined whom or what should be sampled, a decision has to be made whether to conduct qualitative research, quantitative research, or both in order to generate primary data.

Qualitative Research   Very often, because of time and cost constraints, a researcher may elect to conduct only qualitative research when attempting to generate primary data. **Qualitative research** does not allow the researcher to make statistical inferences or quantitative statements. This is because the samples used are often selected on a nonprobability basis and are generally small. But qualitative research can play a valuable role in focussing quantitative research efforts and/or uncovering hypotheses that could be tested in a planned quantitative research activity. In fact, idea or **hypothesis generation** is a major reason for conducting qualitative research. Many marketing researchers conduct a two-stage primary data generation procedure. First, qualitative research is conducted. If this does not provide sufficient information to solve the problem, then quantitative research is undertaken. However, the use of qualitative research as a stand-alone method is growing in popularity as marketers learn more about the weaknesses and strengths of secondary research. As we mentioned earlier, qualitative research data are usually obtained through depth interviews and/or focus group sessions.

Depth interviews   **Depth interviews** are detailed individual interviews with people relevant to the research project. The researcher questions the individual at length in a free-flowing conversational style in order to discover information that may help solve the marketing problem being investigated. Sometimes the interviews can take a few hours, and they are often recorded on audio- or videotape.

Focus groups   **Focus groups** are informal interview sessions in which 6 to 10 people relevant to the research project are brought together in a room with a moderator to discuss topics surrounding the marketing research problem. The moderator poses questions and encourages the individuals to answer in their

own words and to discuss the issues with each other. Oftentimes, the focus group sessions are watched by observers through one-way mirrors and/or the sessions are videotaped. Of course, participants should be informed they are being observed and/or taped. Focus group sessions often provide the marketer with valuable information for decision making or can uncover other issues that should be researched in a more quantitative fashion.

Concept Check

1 **What are primary data?**

2 **What is sampling?**

3 **Depth interviews and focus groups represent what type of research?**

Quantitative Research **Quantitative research** differs from qualitative research because it allows conclusions to be drawn about the population under study through statistical inference. To draw accurate inferences about a population, either a census must be completed or a representative sample must be used. If the sample is not representative, it could lead to wrong conclusions and possibly bad marketing decisions. Quantitative research is typically used to *evaluate any hypotheses* that may have been generated in the qualitative research stage of the marketing research process. As we stated earlier, the three principal ways to generate quantitative primary data are observation, surveys, and experiments.

Observation   One way marketing researchers can obtain primary data is through observation. In general, **observation** means watching, either mechanically or in person, how people actually behave. In some circumstances, the speed of events or the number of events being observed make mechanical or electronic observation more appropriate than personal observation. Retailers, for example, can use electronic cameras to count the number of customers entering or leaving a store.

A classic instance of mechanical observation is A. C. Nielsen's "people meter," which is attached to television sets in selected households in Canada and the United States in order to determine the size of audiences watching the television programs delivered by the networks. When a household member watches TV, he or she is supposed to push a button on the box and to push it again when he or she stops watching. All information is sent automatically through phones to Nielsen each night. The people meter is supposed to measure who in the household is watching what program on a representative sample of TV sets owned.

Figure 8–4 shows an example of Nielsen data (average minute-audience) for the top 10 television programs in Canada during a given measurement period.

The people meter's limitations—like those of all observational data collected mechanically—relate to how its measurements are taken. Critics of people meters aren't so sure the devices are measuring what they are supposed to. They are concerned that household members, especially teenagers and the elderly, will find it annoying to hit the button every time they start or stop

A Nielsen "people meter" collects information about a household's TV viewing.

RANK	PROGRAM	NETWORK	AUDIENCE (ADULTS, THOUSANDS)
1	World Series (6*)	CTV	4,082
2	Election '93	CBC	2,591
3	AL Baseball Playoffs (6)	CTV	2,496
4	CFL: Grey Cup	CBC	2,304
5	Kurt Browning Special	CBC	2,265
6	The Boys of St. Vincent	CBC	2,177
7	Election '93	CTV	2,129
8	Anne Murray Special	CBC	2,118
9	Winter Olympics	CTV	1,953
10	Blanche	Radio-Canada	1,928

*Number of telecasts.

Source: Nielsen Marketing Research. For period August 30, 1993, to February 27, 1994.

■ *Figure 8–4*
Nielsen rating data—top 10 season-to-date programs.

watching TV. Yet, for television networks, precision in Nielsen data is critical, because advertisers pay rates based on the size of audience for a TV program. Programs with consistently low audience numbers often can't get advertisers and are dropped from the air. A "passive people meter" has now been developed to address some of these problems and is discussed in Chapter 10.[3]

Marketers can also rely on personal observations to collect primary data. For example, Procter & Gamble observes how consumers bake cakes in its Duncan Hines kitchens to see if the baking instructions on the cake mix box are understood and followed correctly. Chrysler watches how drivers sit behind the wheel of a car to see if they can operate the radio and air-conditioning controls easily. Fisher-Price uses its licensed nursery schools to observe children using and abusing toys in order to develop better products.[4] For example, Fisher-Price designers and marketers behind a one-way mirror watched children play with the original model of a classic Fisher-Price toy, the chatter telephone. At first it was a simple wooden phone with a dial that rang a bell. But observers noted that the children kept grabbing the receiver like a handle to pull the phone along behind them. So a designer added wheels, a noisemaker, and eyes that bobbed up and down. Kids liked this new design better, and so Fisher-Price introduced its noisemaking pull-toy telephone, which has become a classic and sold millions.

Personal observation is both useful and flexible, but it can be costly and unreliable, especially when different observers report different conclusions in watching the same activities. Also, although observation can reveal what people do, it cannot determine why they do it—why, for example, they are buying or not buying a product. In order to determine why consumers behave as they do, marketing researchers must talk with consumers and record their responses. This can be accomplished through the use of surveys.

Surveys Another way to obtain primary data is to ask people questions. **Surveys** are commonly used by marketers to provide information related to marketing problems. Surveys can be conducted by mail, telephone, or personal interview. In choosing among the three alternatives, the marketing researcher

Careful observation of
"toy testers" in
Fisher-Price's school
leads to better products.

has to make important trade-offs (as shown in Figure 8–5) to balance cost
against the expected quality of the information obtained. The figure shows that
personal interviews have a major advantage of enabling the interviewer to be
flexible in asking probing questions or to get reactions to visual materials. In
contrast, mail surveys usually have the lowest cost per completed survey of the
three data collection procedures. Telephone surveys lie in between in terms of
flexibility and cost.

    Sometimes marketers will survey the same sample of people over time,
commonly known as a survey **panel.** A panel can consist of a sample of consumers, stores, or experts from which researchers can take a series of measurements. For example, a consumer's switching from one brand of breakfast cereal
to another can be measured with panel data. The use of panels is becoming
more popular with marketers as they attempt to obtain continually updated
information about their constituents. The use of panel data is discussed further
in Chapter 10, where we deal with marketing information systems.

    When marketers decide to use surveys to ask questions, they make several
assumptions: that the right questions are being asked, that people will understand the questions being asked, that people know the answers to the questions,
that people will answer the questions truthfully, and that the researchers themselves will understand the answers provided. Marketers must concern themselves not only with asking the right questions but also with how to properly

■ *Figure 8–5*
Comparison of mail, telephone, and personal interview surveys.

BASIS OF COMPARISON	MAIL SURVEYS	TELEPHONE SURVEYS	PERSONAL INTERVIEW SURVEYS
Cost per completed survey	Usually the least expensive, assuming adequate return rate	Moderately expensive, assuming reasonable completion rate	Most expensive, because of interviewer's time and travel expenses
Ability to probe and ask complex questions	Little, since self-administered format must be short and simple	Some, since interviewer can probe and elaborate on questions to a degree	Much, since interviewer can show visual materials, gain rapport, and probe
Opportunity for interviewer to bias results	None, since form is completed without interviewer	Some, because of voice inflection of interviewer	Significant, because of voice and facial expressions of interviewer
Anonymity given to respondent	Complete, since no signature is required	Some, because of telephone contact	Little, because of face-to-face contact

Survey data being collected by personal interview.

▌ *Figure 8–6*
**Typical problems in
wording questions.**

PROBLEM	SAMPLE QUESTION	EXPLANATION
Leading question	Why do you like Wendy's fresh-meat hamburgers better than competitors' hamburgers made with frozen meat?	Consumer is led to make statement favouring Wendy's hamburgers.
Ambiguous question	Do you eat at fast-food restaurants regularly? ☐ Yes ☐ No	What is meant by word regularly—once a day, once a month, or what?
Unanswerable question	What was the occasion for your eating your first hamburger?	Who can remember the answer? Does it matter?
Two questions in one	Do you eat Wendy's hamburgers and chili? ☐ Yes ☐ No	How do you answer if you eat Wendy's hamburgers but not chili?
Nonexhaustive question	Where do you live? ☐ At home ☐ In dormitory	What do you check if you live in an apartment?
Nonmutually exclusive answers	What is your age? ☐ Under 20 ☐ 20–40 ☐ 40 and over	What answer does a 40-year-old check?

word those questions. Proper phrasing of a question is vital in uncovering useful marketing information.

Figure 8–6 shows typical problems to guard against in wording questions to obtain meaningful answers from respondents. For example, in a question whether you eat at fast-food restaurants regularly, the word *regularly* is ambiguous. Two people might answer yes to the question, but one might mean once a day while the other means once or twice a year. Both answers appear as yes to the researcher who tabulates them, but in reality dramatically different marketing actions may need to be directed to these two prospective consumers. Therefore, it is essential that marketing research questions be worded precisely so that all respondents interpret the same question similarly. Marketing researchers must also take great care not to use "leading" questions (questions worded in a way that ensures a particular response), which can lead to a very distorted picture of respondents' actual feelings or opinions.

In Figure 8–7 we can see the number of different formats that questions can take in a survey instrument. The questions presented are taken from a Wendy's survey that assessed fast-food preferences among present and prospective consumers. Question 1 is an example of an *open-end question,* which the respondent can answer in his own words. In contrast, questions in which the respondent simply checks an answer are *closed-end* or *fixed-alternative questions.* Question 2 is an example of the simplest fixed-alternative question, a *dichotomous question* that allows only a yes or a no answer. A fixed-alternative question

■ *Figure 8–7*
**Sample questions from
Wendy's survey.**

1 What things are most important to you when you decide to eat out and go to a restaurant?

_____

_____

_____

_____

_____

_____

open-ended question

2 Have you eaten fast-food restaurant food in the past three months?
☐ Yes   ☐ No

3 If you answered "yes" to question 2, how often do you eat fast food?
☐ Once a week or more   ☐ Two or three times a month
☐ Once a month or less

fix-alternative Q.

4 How important is it to you that a fast-food restaurant satisfy you on the following characteristics? Check the box that describes your feelings.

CHARACTERISTIC	VERY IMPORTANT	SOMEWHAT IMPORTANT	IMPORTANT	UNIMPORTANT	SOMEWHAT UNIMPORTANT	VERY UNIMPORTANT
Taste of food	☐	☐	☐	☐	☐	☐
Cleanliness	☐	☐	☐	☐	☐	☐
Price	☐	☐	☐	☐	☐	☐
Variety on menu	☐	☐	☐	☐	☐	☐

5 Check the space on the scale below that describes how you feel about Wendy's on the characteristics shown.

CHARACTERISTIC	CHECK THE SPACE DESCRIBING HOW WENDY'S IS		
Taste of food	Tasty	__ __ __ __ __ __ __	Not tasty
Cleanliness	Clean	__ __ __ __ __ __ __	Dirty
Price	Inexpensive	__ __ __ __ __ __ __	Expensive
Variety on menu	Wide	__ __ __ __ __ __ __	Narrow

semantic-differential scale

6 Check the box that describes your agreement with the statement.

STATEMENT	STRONGLY AGREE	AGREE	DON'T KNOW	DISAGREE	STRONGLY DISAGREE
Adults like to take their families to fast-food restaurants.	☐	☐	☐	☐	☐
Our children have a say in where the family eats.	☐	☐	☐	☐	☐

likert scale Q.

(continued)

▌ *Figure 8–7*
(concluded)

7 How important is this information about fast-food restaurants?

SOURCE OF INFORMATION	VERY IMPORTANT SOURCE	SOMEWHAT IMPORTANT SOURCE	NOT AN IMPORTANT SOURCE
Television	☐	☐	☐
Newspapers	☐	☐	☐
Billboards	☐	☐	☐
Mail	☐	☐	☐

8 In the past three months, how often have you eaten at each of these three fast-food restaurants?

RESTAURANT	ONCE A WEEK OR MORE	TWO OR THREE TIMES A MONTH	ONCE A MONTH OR LESS
Burger King	☐	☐	☐
McDonald's	☐	☐	☐
Wendy's	☐	☐	☐

9 Please answer the following questions about you and your household.
   a Are you   ☐ Male   ☐ Female
   b Are you   ☐ Single   ☐ Married   ☐ Other (widowed, divorced)
   c How many children under age 18 live in your home?
     ☐ 0   ☐ 1   ☐ 2   ☐ 3   ☐ 4   ☐ 5 or more
   d What is your age?
     ☐ 24 or under   ☐ 25–39   ☐ 40 or over
   e What is your approximate total annual household income?
     ☐ Less than $15,000   ☐ $15,000–$30,000   ☐ More than $30,000

Source: Adapted from a questionnaire developed by C. Scott and R. A. Hansen.

with three or more choices uses a scale. Question 5 is an example of a question that uses a *semantic differential scale,* a seven-point scale in which the opposite ends are marked by one- or two-word adjectives that have opposite meanings. For example, depending on how clean the respondent feels Wendy's is, she would check the left-hand space on the scale, the right-hand space, or one of the five intervening points. Question 6 uses a *Likert scale,* in which the respondent is asked to indicate the extent to which he agrees or disagrees with a statement.

The questionnaire in Figure 8–7 is an excerpt of a precisely worded survey that provides valuable information to marketing researchers at Wendy's. Questions 1 to 8 inform them about likes and dislikes in eating out, frequency of eating out at fast-food restaurants generally and at Wendy's specifically, and

sources of information used in making decisions about fast-food restaurants. Question 9 gives details about the personal characteristics of the respondent's household, which can be used in trying to segment the fast-food market, a topic discussed in Chapter 9.

Surveys of distributors—retailers and wholesalers in the marketing channel—are also very important for manufacturers. A reason given for the success of many Japanese consumer products in Canada and the United States, such as Sony Walkmans and Toyota automobiles, is the stress that Japanese marketers place on obtaining accurate information from their distributors.[5]

Constructing a survey instrument or questionnaire takes great skill. Moreover, good marketing researchers will always *pretest* the instrument in order to ensure that the questions being asked are the correct ones and are being asked properly. But even properly worded questionnaires may not get good response rates. In fact, a growing concern among market researchers today is the unwillingness of respondents to participate in surveys. Many marketers are looking for ways to improve this situation. For mailed questionnaires, there is some evidence to suggest that simply improving the design and format of the instrument itself can improve response rates (see the accompanying Marketing Action Memo).

Experiments   Another method that can be used by marketing researchers to generate primary data is the experiment. An **experiment** is a way of obtaining data by manipulating factors under tightly controlled conditions to test for cause

M A R K E T I N G · A C T I O N · M E M O

Questionnaire Design Affects Response Rate

One consideration that has not received adequate attention in stimulating good return rates with mailed questionnaires is the quality of the questionnaire. However, the design, format, and layout of the questionnaire have been found to affect response rates. While the average return rate for mailed questionnaires runs between 10 and 20 percent, one company obtained a response rate of 56 percent, which it attributes to a few simple factors pertaining to the data collection instrument itself. This company, Words and Numbers Research, Inc., offers five pointers that can help boost response rates. First, use nontraditional ways to structure questions on the questionnaire. For example, instead of using the traditional rating scale of measuring importance of product features, ask respondents to divide 100 points among all of the features, reflecting importance levels. Second, mix up the response formats on items you ask respondents to complete. Answering a survey that consists of all agree–disagree statements is like watching the same program on TV for nights in a row.

Third, questionnaires should have specific sets of directions for each group or section of items. Do not assume the respondents know what you want them to do. Be clear in stating directions. Fourth, pay attention to the visual appearance of the questionnaire. Putting boxes around groups of questions, using dark ink on light paper stock, shading multiple-response questions in the layout, selecting a clean, clear typeface, having a short, attractive cover letter, and using lines to take the respondent's eye from question to response make a difference in whether the individual will respond. Fifth, number all sections, and number all items in each section. When respondents see that section 1 has items 1 through 5, they are more likely to do all five.

These five pointers may make a difference in increasing the response rates of mailed questionnaires, and higher rates can mean better information.

Source: Adapted from S. Carroll, "Questionnaire Design Affects Response Rate," *Marketing News,* January 3, 1994, pp. 14, 23.

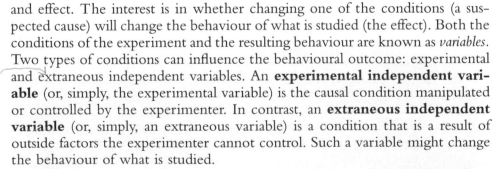

and effect. The interest is in whether changing one of the conditions (a suspected cause) will change the behaviour of what is studied (the effect). Both the conditions of the experiment and the resulting behaviour are known as *variables.* Two types of conditions can influence the behavioural outcome: experimental and extraneous independent variables. An **experimental independent variable** (or, simply, the experimental variable) is the causal condition manipulated or controlled by the experimenter. In contrast, an **extraneous independent variable** (or, simply, an extraneous variable) is a condition that is a result of outside factors the experimenter cannot control. Such a variable might change the behaviour of what is studied.

The change in the behaviour of what is studied is called the **dependent variable.** The experimenter tries to arrange a change in the independent variable and then measure the accompanying change, or absence of it, in the dependent variable. In marketing experiments the experimental independent variables are often one or more of the marketing mix variables, such as product

A successful test market led to the national rollout of Shoppers Drug Mart's Life brand cola.

features, price, or promotion used. An ideal dependent variable is usually a change in purchases of an individual, a household, or an entire organization. If actual purchases cannot be used as a dependent variable, factors that are believed to be highly related to purchases, such as preferences in a taste test or intentions to buy, are used.

A potential difficulty with experiments is that extraneous independent variables can distort the results of an experiment and affect the dependent variable. A researcher's task is to identify the effect of the experimental variable of interest on the dependent variable when the effects of the extraneous variables in an experiment might hide it.

Experiments can be conducted in the field or in a laboratory. In **field experiments,** the research is conducted in the real world—for example, in a store, in a bank, or on the street, or wherever the behaviour being studied occurs naturally. Field experiments can be expensive but are a good way to determine people's reactions to changes in the elements of the marketing mix. Test marketing is probably the most common form of field experiment. Shoppers Drug Mart used taste tests in the field to determine how consumers felt about its Life brand cola, compared with national brands such as Pepsi and Coke. The tests revealed that 33 percent of the consumers who participated like Life brand better than the competitive colas. Shoppers Drug Mart then put the product on the shelves of stores in Atlantic Canada to test the market's response to the product. A successful test market there led to a national rollout of the product in Shoppers stores across Canada.[6]

Because marketers cannot control all the conditions in the field, they sometimes turn to a laboratory setting. Laboratories are not the real world but do offer highly controlled environments. Unlike in the field, the marketer has greater control over the factors that may play a role in impacting on the behaviour under investigation. For example, in a field experiment the marketer may wish to examine the impact of a price reduction on sales of a particular product. The competition, however, may see the price reduction and offer its own price deal, thus interfering with the possible results of the field experiment. This does not occur in a lab setting. Many companies are using laboratory

ETHICS AND SOCIAL RESPONSIBILITY ALERT

What Is "Truth" in Reporting Survey Results?

Doctors were surveyed to find out what brand of butter substitute they recommend for their patients concerned about cholesterol. The results:

- Recommended no particular brand: 80%
- Recommended brand A: 5%
- Recommended brand B: 4%

No other brand is recommended by more than 2 percent of the doctors. The firm owning brand A runs an ad that states, "More doctors recommend brand A than any other brand." Is this ethical? Why or why not? What kind of ethical guideline, if any, should be used to address this issue?

Source: Adapted from D. S. Tull and D. I. Hawkins, *Marketing Research: Measurement and Method,* 5th ed. (New York: Macmillan Publishing Company, 1990), Chap. 23.

settings in which they can control conditions but can do so in a real-world fashion, such as through simulated supermarkets or test stores. Here they can experiment with changes in aisle displays, packaging changes, or other variables that may affect buyer behaviour without the fear of other extraneous factors influencing the results.

Advantages and Disadvantages of Primary Data   Compared with secondary data, primary data have the advantage of being more timely and specific to the problem under investigation. The main disadvantages are that primary data are usually far more costly and time-consuming to collect than secondary data.

Ethical Aspects of Collecting Primary Data   Professional marketing researchers have to make ethical decisions in collecting, using, and reporting primary data. Examples of unethical behaviour include failure to report problems with research results because of incomplete data, reporting only favourable but not unfavourable results, using deception to collect information, and breaching the confidentiality of respondents and/or their personal data if anonymity or non-disclosure was guaranteed.[7] Using formal statements on ethical policies and instituting rewards and punishments can increase ethical behaviour in marketing research. The accompanying Ethics and Social Responsibility Alert shows an example of an ethical issue in marketing research.

Concept Check

1 What are the three ways to generate quantitative data?

2 Survey data can be collected by three methods. What are they?

3 What is the difference between an independent and a dependent variable?

STEP 4: ANALYSIS AND INTERPRETATION

Mark Twain once observed, "Collecting data is like collecting garbage. You've got to know what you're going to do with the stuff before you collect it." The purpose of step 4 of the marketing research process is to analyze the collected data effectively to keep the data from having the value of garbage. This is the stage where data are transformed into valuable information for decision making.

In general, the researcher must evaluate and analyze both the sources and the nature of any secondary data being used, including how they were originally gathered. Relevant secondary data that have been collected are usually condensed and summarized by the researcher with a focus on how they relate to the marketing problem under investigation. If qualitative data have been collected (e.g., through depth interviews or focus groups), the marketing researcher must carefully analyze and interpret this information. However, no statistical interpretations or inferences can be made from such data. Instead, the researcher will analyze the verbatim responses provided by respondents while looking for any general "themes" that may have emerged from the data. The researcher evaluates the qualitative data in order to set the framework for any subsequent quantitative research that may have to be conducted.

The researcher tabulates the primary data that have been collected and makes calculations from these data in a quantitative or statistical manner. The level of analysis conducted on the data depends on the nature of the research and the information needed to provide a solution to the marketing problem. For survey data, frequency analysis is completed; the responses are calculated question by question. The researcher may then wish to identify patterns in the data or examine how some data pertaining to some questions may relate to data obtained from asking other questions.

Cross Tabulations   Probably the most widely used technique for organizing and analyzing marketing data is cross tabulation. A **cross tabulation,** or "cross tab," is a method of analyzing and relating data having two or more variables. It is used to discover the relationships in the data. In order to use cross tabs effectively, the marketing researcher must decide which variables should be paired together and how to form the resulting cross tabulations.

The Wendy's questionnaire in Figure 8−7 gave many questions that might be paired to understand the fast-food business better and help reach a decision about marketing actions to increase revenues. For example, secondary data and qualitative research may have led the researcher to believe that as age of household increases, patronage of fast-food restaurants declines. The researcher could test this hypothesis by cross-tabulating questions 9*d* and 3 in Figure 8−7. Using the answers to question 3 as the column headings and the answers to question 9*d* as the row headings gives a cross tabulation, as shown in Figure 8−8, of the answers that 586 respondents gave to both questions. The figure shows two forms of the cross tabulation:

- The raw data or answers to the specific questions are shown in Figure 8−8A. For example, this cross tab shows that 144 households whose head was 24 years old or younger ate at fast-food restaurants once a week or more.

Figure 8–8
Two forms of a cross tabulation relating age of head of household to fast-food restaurant patronage.

A. ABSOLUTE FREQUENCIES

AGE OF HEAD OF HOUSEHOLD (YEARS)	FREQUENCY			
	ONCE A WEEK OR MORE	2 OR 3 TIMES A MONTH	ONCE A MONTH OR LESS	TOTAL
24 or less	144	52	19	215
25 to 39	46	58	29	133
40 or over	82	69	87	238
Total	272	179	135	586

B. ROW PERCENTAGES: RUNNING PERCENTAGES HORIZONTALLY

AGE OF HEAD OF HOUSEHOLD (YEARS)	FREQUENCY			
	ONCE A WEEK OR MORE	2 OR 3 TIMES A MONTH	ONCE A MONTH OR LESS	TOTAL
24 or less	67.0%	24.2%	8.8%	100.0%
25 to 39	34.6	43.6	21.8	100.0
40 or over	34.4	29.0	36.6	100.0
Total	46.4%	30.6%	23.0%	100.0%

- Answers on a percentage basis, with the percentages running horizontally, are shown in Figure 8–8B. Of the 215 households headed by someone 24 years old or younger, 67.0 percent ate at a fast-food restaurant at least once a week and only 8.8 percent did so once a month or less.

A careful analysis of Figure 8–8 shows that patronage of fast-food restaurants is related to the age of the head of household. Note that as the age of the head of household increases, fast-food restaurant patronage declines, as shown by the boxed percentages on the diagonal in Figure 8–8B. This means if a fast-food restaurant wanted to reach a frequent user of fast food, it would direct its marketing effort to the 24-year-old or younger group.

Cross tabs offer a simple format that permits direct interpretation and an easy means of communicating data to management. They have great flexibility and can be used to summarize observational, survey, and experimental data. Also, cross tabulations may be easily generated on today's personal computers.

Cross tabulations also have some disadvantages. For example, they can be misleading if the percentages in the cross tabs are based on a small number of responses to given questions. Also, cross tabulations can hide some relations because each typically shows only two or three variables. By balancing both advantages and disadvantages, researchers probably make more marketing decisions using cross tabulations than any other method of analyzing data.[8] Good marketing researchers who have a solid understanding of all aspects of marketing as well as research are insightful and creative enough to use the proper level of analysis in this phase of the marketing research process.

M A R K E T I N G · A C T I O N · M E M O

Turning the Potential of Marketing Research into Reality

Stated in simplest terms, the job of marketing research is to help managers understand the voice of the customer. Unfortunately, in the increasing technical sophistication of many marketing research studies, that voice of the consumer is lost and fails to be translated into better products and product features. For example, only one-half of the market segmentation studies (see Chapter 9) done for six consumer goods companies over a four-year period were useful and helped companies reach strategic business decisions.

Here are some suggestions for increasing the value of marketing research:

1 *Keep key executives in touch with customers.* At age 82, J. Willard Marriott, Sr., still reads every complaint card from Marriott customers.
2 *Use observation research, not just questionnaire research.* Honda was the first carmaker to install coin trays in its cars. The reason: its founder insisted on it after his first visit to the United States, when he observed the hassle of trying to find change quickly at expressway tollbooths.
3 *Try "sequential recycling."* Use small samples to go out and learn a little bit, digest what you learn, and go back out again.
4 *Practise "backward marketing research."* Start by identifying the key marketing decisions to be reached, and work back to specify the marketing data and research useful for those decisions.

These ideas can convert marketing research to better products.

Sources: Adapted from C. L. Hodock, "The Decline and Fall of Marketing Research in Corporate America," *Marketing Research,* June 1991, pp. 12–22; and A. R. Andressen, "Backward Marketing Research," *Harvard Business Review,* May–June 1985, pp. 176–82.

STEP 5: RECOMMENDATIONS AND IMPLEMENTATION

At this stage of the process, the marketing researcher, often in conjunction with marketing management, must make suggestions for actions that should be taken by the organization that will solve the marketing problem. The potential solution(s) to the problem must be clearly identified. But identification of the potential solution(s) is not enough. Management must then make a commitment to act, to make decisions based on the research and on good judgment and knowledge of the situation. In other words, someone must "make something happen"—see that the solution is implemented. Failure to act on the research findings creates an appearance that the marketing research effort was of little value. Finally, once implemented, the proposed solution should be monitored to ensure that intended results do occur. The accompanying Marketing Action Memo identifies some techniques firms use to increase the usefulness of their marketing research.

The Need for Ongoing Marketing Research In this chapter, we have established why marketers need accurate and insightful information in order to make effective marketing decisions. Unfortunately, many believe that marketing research should be used situationally and for problem-specific reasons. In other words, marketing research should be used only when problems arise, and thus research projects should have a starting point and an end point. But more and more marketers are recognizing the need for continual collection and analysis of marketing information in order to avoid *potential* problems and to uncover possible future marketing opportunities.[9] This has led to the development of marketing information systems, which are discussed in Chapter 10.

When Not to Conduct Marketing Research   While marketing research can be of great value in aiding effective decision making, there are some situations when marketing research is not advisable. Marketing research should not be conducted when the cost of conducting the research is greater than the benefits that will be derived. If the cost of a marketing research project is $25,000 but the impact of a wrong decision on the organization is only $5,000, then the research is not economical. Research should not be conducted when it only supplies redundant information at needless cost. Finally, it should not be conducted if it is unlikely to be both reliable and valid.[10]

Concept Check

1 **What are cross tabs?**

2 **When would it be appropriate not to conduct marketing research?**

Summary

1 Marketing research is the process of defining a marketing problem or opportunity, systematically collecting and analyzing information, and recommending actions to improve an organization's marketing activities. The primary goal of marketing research is to assist in marketing decision making.

2 Marketing research must always be conducted on the basis of the scientific method, a process of systematically collecting, organizing, and analyzing data in an unbiased, objective manner. Marketing research must also meet two basic principles of the scientific method: reliability and validity.

3 The marketing research process consists of five steps: problem definition, exploratory research, primary data generation, data analysis and interpretation, and recommendations and implementation.

4 Step 1, proper problem definition, is critical, since research based on incorrect problem definition will be a waste of resources.

5 Step 2, exploratory research, involves informal fact finding, or discussions with informed sources inside the firm or customers and/or others outside the firm; and an examination of secondary sources of information. Secondary data are data that have been recorded prior to the research project and include data internal and external to the organization.

6 Step 3 is the generation of primary data, "new" information that is problem-specific. These data can be either qualitative or quantitative.

7 When generating primary data, the researcher will not be able to watch or communicate with every person she would like to. She must select a *sample* of people from the appropriate population relevant to the research project. A sample is a subset of the population that is intended to represent the whole population. Sampling techniques fall into two general categories: probability and nonprobability sampling.

8 Qualitative research (depth interviews, focus groups) is used for hypothesis generation, while quantitative research (observations, surveys, experiments) is used for hypothesis evaluation.

9 Primary data generated by surveys can be collected by mail, telephone, or personal interview.

10 An experiment is a way of obtaining data by manipulating factors under tightly controlled conditions to test for cause and effect. The interest is in whether changing one of the conditions (a suspected cause) will change the behaviour of what is studied (the effect).

11 The purpose of step 4 of the marketing research process is to analyze and interpret the collected data. It involves summarization, tabulation of data, and/or statistical analysis.

12 Step 5 involves making recommendations or suggestions for actions that should be taken by the organization to solve its marketing problem. The potential solution(s) to the problem must be clearly identified. Management must then make a commitment to act on or implement the recommendations.

Key Terms and Concepts

Chapter Problems and Applications

1 Before it introduced the people meter, Nielsen obtained TV rating data by using "audimeters" attached to TV sets. These devices measured whether the TV set was turned on and if so, to which channel. What are the limitations of this mechanical observation method?

2 Suppose Fisher-Price wants to run an experiment to evaluate a proposed chatter telephone design. It has two different groups of children on which to run an experiment for one week each. The control group has the old toy telephone, whereas the experimental group is exposed to the newly designed pull toy with wheels, a noise-maker, and bobbing eyes. The dependent variable is the average number of minutes during a two-hour play period that each child plays with the toy, and the results are as follows:

ELEMENT IN EXPERIMENT	EXPERIMENTAL GROUP	CONTROL GROUP
Experimental variable	New design	Old design
After measurement	62 minutes	13 minutes

Should Fisher-Price introduce the new design? Why?

3 As owner of a chain of supermarkets, you get the idea that you could sell more fresh strawberries by leaving them individually out on a tray and letting customers then fill their own pint or quart box with berries. (*a*) Describe an experiment to test this idea. (*b*) What are some possible measures to use in the experiment?

4 You plan to open an ice cream shop in your town. What type of exploratory research data would you collect to determine its feasibility? You find that the exploratory research doesn't answer all your questions. You decide to do a survey to determine whether or not you should open the shop. What kinds of questions will you ask? Whom do you ask?

5 You are a marketing researcher observing what people do when selecting bread in a supermarket. You are behind a one-way mirror, and none of the customers know they are being observed. During the course of the day, you observe several people shoplifting smaller snack products near the bread section. Two of the shoplifters you see you know personally. What are the ethical problems you face in this situation?

6 Suppose you are trying to determine shoppers' three favourite department stores in your area. You are concerned only with determining the shoppers' ranking from 1 to 3 (1 being the favourite). You decide to do a survey. What problems can go wrong with the survey?

7 You plan to open a new car rental business. You have drafted a survey you want to distribute to airline passengers. The survey will be left at airports, and respondents will mail questionnaires back in a prepaid envelope. Some of the questions you plan to use are shown on the next page. Use Figure 8–6 to (*a*) identify the problem with each question and (*b*) correct it. NOTE: With some of the questions, there may be more than one problem.

a Do you own your own car or usually rent one? _____ Yes _____ No

b What is your age? _____ 21–30 _____ 30–40 _____ 41–50 _____ 50+

c How much did you spend on rental cars last year?
_____ $100 or less _____ $101–$400 _____ $401–$800 _____ $800–$1,000 _____ $1,000 or more

d What is a good daily rental car rate?_____

CHAPTER 9

Market Segmentation, Targeting, and Positioning

AFTER READING THIS CHAPTER YOU SHOULD BE ABLE TO:

▸ Explain what market segmentation is, when to use it, and the five steps involved in segmentation.

▸ Recognize the different factors used to segment consumer and organizational markets.

▸ Understand the significance of heavy, medium, and light users and nonusers in targeting markets.

▸ Develop a market-product grid to use in segmenting and targeting a market.

▸ Understand how marketing managers position products in the marketplace.

Reebok: Putting Both Style and Wings on Your Feet

If you are an athlete—of sorts—and your thing is step training, running, or tennis, or if you just like comfortable, stylish shoes, Reebok may have changed what you have on your feet.[1] This is possible because of a very unlikely occurrence in 1979. That's the year when Paul Fireman, a camping equipment distributor, wandered through an international trade fair and saw Reebok's custom track shoes. He bought the North American licence from the British manufacturer and started producing top-of-the-line running shoes.

But Fireman then saw that the running boom had peaked and he needed other outlets for his shoes. In a brilliant marketing decision, Fireman introduced the first soft-leather aerobic dance shoe—the Reebok Freestyle—in 1982. The flamboyant colours of these Reebok designer sneakers captured the attention of aerobic dance instructors and students alike. This colour strategy still helps the sneakers get good display space in stores and attracts a lot of consumer attention.[2]

Today known as Reebok International, Ltd., the firm successively introduced tennis shoes, children's shoes (Weeboks), and basketball shoes in 1984 and walking shoes in 1986. For those who don't want to buy four different pairs of shoes to run, play tennis, shoot baskets, and walk in, Reebok introduced—of course—"cross-trainers" in 1988. This was followed the next year by the $170 Reebok Pump, a high-tech, high-top basketball sneaker with its own built-in air compressor located in the toe of the shoe. The Reebok Step Trainer appeared in 1991. And both Reebok and Nike are moving aggressively into the European sport shoe markets in the 1990s.[3]

The Reebok strategy, making shoes designed to satisfy needs of different customers, illustrates successful market segmentation, the main topic of this chapter. It also helps explain why Reebok's sales grew by more than 100,000 percent from the early 1980s to today.

After discussing why markets need to be segmented, this chapter covers the steps a firm uses in segmenting and targeting a market and then positioning its offering in the marketplace.

WHY SEGMENT MARKETS?

A business firm segments its markets so it can respond more effectively to the wants of groups of prospective buyers and thus increase its sales and profits. Nonprofit organizations also segment the clients they serve to satisfy client needs more effectively while achieving the organization's goals. Let's use the dilemma of sneaker buyers finding their ideal Reebok shoes to describe (1) what market segmentation is and (2) when it is necessary to segment markets.

WHAT MARKET SEGMENTATION MEANS

People have different needs and wants, even though it would be easier for marketers if they didn't. **Market segmentation** involves aggregating prospective buyers into groups that (1) have common needs and (2) will respond similarly to a marketing action. The groups that result from this process are **market segments,** a relatively homogeneous collection of prospective buyers.

The existence of different market segments has caused firms to use a marketing strategy of **product differentiation,** a strategy that has come to have two different but related meanings. In its broadest sense, product differentiation involves a firm's using different marketing mix activities, such as product features and advertising, to help consumers perceive the product as being different from and better than competing products. The perceived differences may be in physical features or nonphysical ones, such as image or price.

In a narrower sense, product differentiation involves a firm's selling two or more products with different features targeted to different market segments. A firm can get into trouble when its different products blend together in consumers' minds and don't reach distinct market segments successfully. The Reebok example that will be discussed shows both how a manufacturer has succeeded in using a product differentiation strategy to offer different products targeted to separate market segments and also how its success is forcing new efforts to separate two groups of its shoes in consumers' minds.

Segmentation: Linking Needs to Actions   The definition of market segmentation first stresses the importance of aggregating—or grouping—people or organizations in a market according to the similarity of their needs and the benefits they are looking for in making a purchase. Second, a firm must relate such needs and benefits to specific, tangible marketing actions it can take. These actions may involve separate products or other aspects of the marketing mix

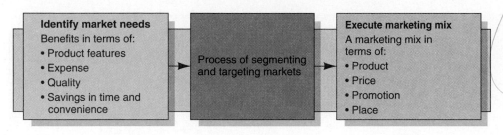

| Identify market needs
Benefits in terms of:
• Product features
• Expense
• Quality
• Savings in time and convenience | → | Process of segmenting and targeting markets | → | Execute marketing mix
A marketing mix in terms of:
• Product
• Price
• Promotion
• Place |

▌ *Figure 9–1*
Market segmentation links market needs to an organization's marketing mix.

such as price, advertising or personal selling activities, or distribution strategies—the four Ps (product, price, promotion, place).

The process of segmenting a market and selecting specific segments as targets is the link between the various buyers' needs and the organization's marketing mix (Figure 9–1). Market segmentation is only a means to an end: in an economist's terms, it relates supply (the organization's actions) to demand (customer needs). A basic test of the usefulness of the segmentation process is whether it leads to tangible marketing actions.

Using Market–Product Grids A **market–product grid** is a framework to relate the segments of a market to products offered or potential marketing actions by the firm. The grid in Figure 9–2 shows different markets of sneaker users as rows in the grid, while the columns show the different shoe products (or marketing actions) chosen by Reebok.

The darker-shaded cells in Figure 9–2, labeled P, represent the primary market segment that Reebok targeted when it introduced each shoe. The lightly shaded cells labeled S represent the secondary market segments that also started buying the shoe. In some cases, Reebok discovered that large numbers of people in a segment not originally targeted for a style of shoe bought it anyway. In fact, as many as 75 to 80 percent of the running shoes and aerobic dance shoes are bought by nonathletes represented by the (1) comfort- and style-conscious and (2) walker segments shown in Figure 9–2—although walkers may object to being labelled "nonathletes." When this trend became apparent to Reebok in 1986, it introduced its walking shoes targeted directly at the walker segment. Reebok also tries to reach not only the "serious athlete" market with its $150 Double Pump but also city outdoor-court players with its $70 Blacktop, designed to feature an extra-tough sole.[4]

Figure 9–2 also introduces one of the potential dangers of market segmentation for a firm: subdividing an entire market into two or more segments, thereby increasing the competition from other firms that focus their efforts on a single segment. Notice that Reebok's strategy is to reach both the performance (athletes) and fashion (nonathletes) segments. In the 1990s, Reebok finds itself trying to clarify its vague identity among consumers who see Nike as a "performance shoe" and L.A. Gear as a "fashion shoe." In trying to compete in both markets, Reebok runs the danger of being first in neither. To be more responsive to both markets, Reebok has divided its operations into two separate units: *technology,* targeted at athletes, performance-oriented consumers, and children; and *lifestyle,* targeted at style-conscious consumers.

MARKET SEGMENT		PRODUCT (Kind of shoes)							
GENERAL	GROUP WITH NEED	RUNNING (1981)	AEROBIC (1982)	TENNIS (1984)	BASKET-BALL (1984)	CHILDREN'S (1984)	WALKING (1986)	CROSS-TRAINERS (1988)	STEP-TRAINERS (1991)
Performance-conscious consumers (athletes)	Runners	P						P	
	Aerobic dancers		P					P	
	Tennis players			P				P	
	Basketball players				P			P	
	Step exercisers							S	P
Fashion-conscious consumers (nonathletes)	Comfort- and style-conscious	S	S	S	S		S	S	
	Walkers	S	S	S	S		P	P	
	Children					P			

Key: P = primary market; S = secondary market

▌ *Figure 9–2*
Market–product grid showing how eight different styles of Reebok shoes reach segments of customers with different needs.

WHEN TO SEGMENT MARKETS

A business firm goes to the trouble and expense of segmenting its markets when this increases its sales revenue, profit, and return on investment (ROI). When its expenses more than offset the potentially increased revenue from segmentation, it should not attempt to segment its market. The specific situations that illustrate this point are the cases of one product and multiple market segments and of multiple products and multiple market segments.

One Product and Multiple Market Segments   When a firm produces only a single product or service and attempts to sell it to two or more market segments, it avoids the extra cost of developing and producing additional versions of the product, which often entail extremely high research, engineering, and manufacturing expenses. In this case the incremental costs of taking the product into new market segments are typically those of a separate promotional campaign or new channel of distribution. Although these expenses can be high, they are rarely as large as those for developing an entirely new product.

Movies and magazines are single products frequently directed to two or more distinct market segments. Movie companies often run different TV commercials featuring different aspects of a newly released film (love, drama, or spectacular scenery) that are targeted to different market segments. *Time* magazine publishes different regional editions, each targeted at its own geographic and demographic segments and its own mix of advertisements. Although multiple TV commercials for movies and different editorial content for magazines are expensive, they are minor compared with the costs of producing an entirely new movie or magazine for another segment. Even Procter & Gamble is now marketing its Crest toothpaste with different advertising campaigns targeted at different market segments, including children and senior citizens.[5]

Multiple Products and Multiple Market Segments   Reebok's different styles of shoes, each targeted at a different type of user, are an example of multiple products aimed at multiple markets. Manufacturing these different styles of shoes is clearly more expensive than producing one but seems worthwhile if it serves customers' needs better, doesn't reduce quality or increase price, and adds to the sales revenues and profits.

Product differentiation is generally an effective strategy, as in the Reebok example, but it can be carried too far. For example, in some cases North American auto manufacturers have offered so many models and options to try to reach diverse market segments that sales revenue and profits have suffered in competition with imports.

Perhaps the extreme case occurred in 1982 when Ford Thunderbird had exactly 69,120 (including frames, engines, body styles, and colours) options compared with 32 on the 1982 Honda Accord. Japanese manufacturers did extensive marketing research on North American consumers and had selected a simple combination of options to meet the most typical needs. But by the late 1980s and early 1990s, these same Japanese manufacturers had forgotten this lesson, and their model and parts variations ballooned. Faced with huge losses in 1993, these manufacturers embarked on a new "simple is good" campaign. Some examples of the results: Nissan is reducing its 2,200 model variations by 35 percent, and both Toyota and Mitsubishi are following suit.[6]

North American car manufacturers are concluding that the costs of developing, producing, and servicing dozens of slightly different products probably outweigh the premium that consumers are willing to pay for the wider array of choices and are simplifying their product lines. For example, Ford's Thunderbird now has fewer options, and its sales brochures stress "preferred equipment packages" to simplify buying decisions for customers. In Ford's continuing emphasis on customer quality and value, its Thunderbird had more than 350 features evaluated in a "best-in-class" comparison with competing Mercedes and BMW models.[7] Although there are fewer choices, this provides two benefits to consumers: (1) lower prices through higher-volume production of fewer models, and (2) higher quality because of the ability to debug fewer basic designs.

Concept Check

1 Market segmentation involves aggregating prospective buyers into groups that have two key characteristics. What are they?

2 What is product differentiation?

3 The process of segmenting and targeting markets is a bridge between what two marketing activities?

STEPS IN SEGMENTING AND TARGETING MARKETS

The process of segmenting a market and then selecting and reaching the target segments is divided into the five steps discussed in this section (Figure 9–3). Segmenting a market is not a science—it requires large doses of common sense and managerial judgment.

Market segmentation and target markets can be abstract topics, so put on your entrepreneur's hat to experience the process. Suppose you own a Wendy's fast-food restaurant next to a large urban university that offers both day and evening classes. Your restaurant specializes in the Wendy's basics: hamburgers, french fries, Frosty milk shakes, and chili. Even though you are part of a chain and have some restrictions on menu and décor, you are free to set your hours of business and to undertake local advertising. How can market segmentation help?

FORM PROSPECTIVE BUYERS INTO SEGMENTS

Grouping prospective buyers into meaningful segments involves meeting some specific criteria for segmentation and finding specific variables to segment the consumer or industrial market being analyzed.[8]

Criteria to Use in Forming the Segments   A marketing manager should develop segments for a market that meet five principal criteria:

- *Potential for increased profit and ROI.* The best segmentation approach is the one that maximizes the opportunity for future profit and ROI. If this potential is maximized through no segmentation, don't segment. For nonprofit organizations, the analogous criterion is the potential for serving client users more effectively.
- *Similarity of needs of potential buyers within a segment.* Potential buyers within a segment should be similar in terms of a marketing activity, such as product features sought or advertising media used.
- *Difference of needs of buyers among segments.* If the needs of the various segments aren't appreciably different, combine them into fewer segments. A different segment usually requires a different marketing action that in turn means greater costs. If increased revenues don't offset extra costs, combine segments and reduce the number of marketing actions.
- *Feasibility of a marketing action to reach a segment.* Reaching a segment requires a simple but effective marketing action. If no such action exists, don't segment.

▌*Figure 9–3*
The process of
segmenting and targeting
markets connects the
firm's marketing actions
to its identification of
marketing needs.

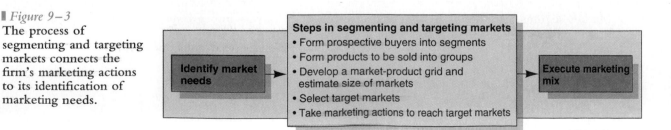

▪ *Simplicity and cost of assigning potential buyers to segments.* A marketing manager must be able to put a market segmentation plan into effect. This means being able to recognize the characteristics of potential buyers and assign them to a segment.

Ways to Segment Consumer Markets   Figure 9–4 shows a number of variables that can be used to segment consumer markets. They are divided into two

▪ *Figure 9–4*
Segmentation variables and breakdowns for consumer markets.

MAIN DIMENSION	SEGMENTATION VARIABLE	TYPICAL BREAKDOWNS
CUSTOMER CHARACTERISTICS		
Geographic	Region	Atlantic, Quebec, Ontario, Prairies, British Columbia
	City or census metropolitan area (CMA) size	Under 5,000; 5,000 to 19,999; 20,000 to 49,999; 50,000 to 99,999; 100,000 to 249,999; 250,000 to 499,999; 500,000 to 999,999; 1,000,000 to 3,999,999; 4,000,000 or over
	Density	Urban; suburban; rural
	Climate	East; west
Demographic	Age	Infant, under 6; 6 to 11; 12 to 17; 18 to 24; 25 to 34; 35 to 49; 50 to 64; 65 or over
	Sex	Male; female
	Family size	1 to 2; 3 to 4; 5 or over
	Stage of family life cycle	Young single; young married, no children; young married, youngest child under 6; young married, youngest child 6 or older; older married,with children; older married, no children under 18; older single; other older married, no children under 18
	Ages of children	No child under 18; youngest child 6 to 17; youngest child under 6
	Children under 18	0; 1; more than 1
	Income	Under $5,000; $5,000 to $14,999; $15,000 to $24,999; $25,000 to $34,999; $35,000 to $49,999; $50,000 or over
	Education	Grade school or less; some high school; high school graduate; some college; college graduate
	Race	White; Black; Asian; Native; other
	Home ownership	Own home; rent home
Psychographic	Personality	Gregarious; compulsive; extroverted; aggressive; ambitious
	Lifestyle	Use of one's time; values and importance; beliefs
BUYING SITUATIONS		
Benefits sought	Product features	Situation-specific; general
	Needs	Quality; service; economy
Usage	Rate of use	Light user; medium user; heavy user
	User states	Nonuser; ex-user; prospect; first-time user; regular user
Awareness and intentions	Readiness to buy	Unaware; aware; informed; interested; intending to buy
	Brand familiarity	Insistence; preference; recognition; nonrecognition; rejection
Buying condition	Type of buying activity	Minimum effort buying; comparison buying; special-effort buying
	Kind of store	Convenience; wide breadth; specialty

GE's extra-large
refrigerator caters to
large families.

general categories: customer characteristics, and buying situations. Some examples of how certain characteristics can be used to segment specific markets include the following:

- *Region* (a geographic customer characteristic). Colgate-Palmolive markets either different detergents or the same detergent using different messages in different parts of the country. Arctic Power, a cold-water detergent, is sold on an energy-cost–saving dimension in Quebec, but as a clothes saver (cold-water washing is better on clothes) in western Canada.
- *Family size* (a demographic customer characteristic). Many Canadian households are made up of only one or two people. Because smaller households have smaller kitchens, GE offers a downsized microwave oven that can be hung under a kitchen cabinet. However, GE also offers extra-large refrigerators for bigger family units, especially those at the beginning of their family life cycle.
- *Lifestyle* (a psychographic customer characteristic). Psychographic variables include consumers' activities, interests, and opinions. A Canadian frozen-food manufacturer discovered that 80 percent of its customers fell into the disinterested self-indulgent segment (of the Goldfarb Segments) and that convenience was more important to this segment than the taste of the food product. They pushed convenience in their advertising and were successful.[9]
- *Benefits offered* (a situation characteristic). Important benefits offered to different customers are often a useful way to segment markets because they can lead to specific marketing actions, such as a new product or service or new ad campaign. For example, Ault Foods developed the world's first pure low-fat butter, Pure & Simple, designed for Canadians looking for a low-fat, natural product.[10]
- *Usage rate* (which refers to quantity consumed or patronage—store visits—during a specific period, and varies significantly among different customer groups). Airlines have developed frequent-flyer programs to encourage passengers to use the same airline repeatedly—a technique sometimes called *frequency*

Ault Foods offers consumers the first pure lowfat butter, Pure & Simple.

marketing, which focusses on usage rate. The usage rate is often assumed to follow the **80/20 rule,** a concept that suggests that 80 percent of a firm's sales are obtained from 20 percent of its customers.

The percentages in the 80/20 rule are not really fixed at exactly 80 percent and 20 percent; rather, the rule suggests that a small fraction of customers provide a large fraction of a firm's sales. Segmentation based on product usage usually involves categorizing users as heavy, medium, or light. Marketers segmenting on the basis of product usage must also distinguish between users and two types of nonusers. Nonusers can be potential users, or **prospects,** those likely to become users; and **nonprospects,** those unlikely to ever become users. Prospects should be given some thought and marketing consideration, while nonprospects should receive little attention. For example, research has indicated that 90 percent of all households in Canada are users of milk and 10 percent are nonusers. The entire nonuser group consists of nonprospects, and no effort is spent by milk producers to convert this group. The research also revealed that 20 percent of milk user households in Canada could be classified as heavy users and were responsible for over 42 percent of all milk consumption.[11]

Research shows that there are heavy, medium, and light users for many product categories, including fast food. For example, for every $1.00 spent by a light user in a fast-food restaurant, each heavy user spends $5.22.[12] This is the reason for the emphasis in almost all marketing strategies on finding effective ways to reach the heavy users. Thus, as a Wendy's restaurant owner you would want to keep the heavy-user segment constantly in mind. Fortunately, many college students fall into the heavy-user segment for fast-food restaurants.

Remember Figure 8–8 in Chapter 8? Our "cross tab" example involving fast-food consumers showed that households headed by someone 24 years old or younger could be classified as heavy users of fast-food restaurants. But what if you discovered that many of these consumers, on a national level, preferred McDonald's or Burger King and used Wendy's only as a "secondary" choice? This information is important in developing your local strategy. To be successful in your local market you may have to target the customers of these two competitors and attempt to win them over. Now, what if you also discovered that there was a segment that ate fast food but didn't go to Wendy's at all? They are prospects, since they do dine out but at this time do not go to Wendy's.

New menu items or new promotional strategies might succeed in converting these prospects to users. One key conclusion emerges about usage: in market segmentation studies, some measure of usage or revenues derived from various segments is central to the analysis.

In determining one or two variables on which to segment the market for your Wendy's restaurant, very broadly we find that two main markets are appropriate to consider, given your location near the university: students and nonstudents. To segment students, we could try a variety of demographic variables such as age, sex, year in school, or college major; or psychographic variables, such as personality characteristics, attitudes, or interests. But none of the resulting segments really meets the five criteria listed previously—particularly the fourth criterion, feasibility of marketing actions to reach the various segments. Four student segments that do meet these criteria include the following:

- Students living in dormitories (college residence halls, sororities, fraternities).
- Students living near the college in apartments.
- Day commuter students living outside the area.
- Night commuter students living outside the area.

These segmentation variables are really a combination of where the student lives and the time he is on campus (and near the restaurant). For nonstudents who might be customers, similar variables might be used:

What variables might Panasonic use to segment the organizational markets for its Plain Paper Laser Fax? For the possible answer and related marketing actions, see the text.

- Faculty and staff members at the university.
- People who live in the area but aren't connected with the university.
- People who work in the area but aren't connected with the university.

People in each of these segments aren't quite as similar as those in the student segments, and so they are harder to reach with a particular marketing mix or action. Think about whether the needs of all these segments are different and how various promotional tools can be used to reach these groups effectively.

Ways to Segment Organizational Markets Variables for segmenting organizational markets are shown in Figure 9–5. A product manager at Panasonic responsible for its Plain Paper Laser Fax, which doubles as a personal copier, answering machine, and autodial phone, might use a number of these segmentation variables, as follows:

- *Location.* Firms located in a census metropolitan area (CMA) might receive a personal sales call, whereas those outside the CMA might be contacted by telephone.
- *SIC code.* Firms categorized by the Standard Industrial Classification (SIC) code as manufacturers that deal with customers throughout the world might have different fax and answering needs from retailers or lawyers serving local customers.
- *Number of employees.* The size of the firm is related to the volume of faxing and photocopying needs for a given industry or SIC, so firms with a specific size range of employees might be a specific target market for Panasonic.

▌ *Figure 9–5*
Segmentation variables and breakdowns for organizational markets.

MAIN DIMENSION	SEGMENTATION VARIABLE	TYPICAL BREAKDOWNS
CUSTOMER CHARACTERISTICS (Honeywell)		
Geographical	Region	British Columbia; Prairies; Ontario; Quebec; Atlantic
	Location	In a CMA; not in a CMA
Demographic	SIC code	2-digit; 3-digit; 4-digit categories
	Number of employees	1 to 19; 20 to 99; 100 to 249; 250 or over
	Number of production workers	1 to 19; 20 to 99; 100 to 249; 250 or over
	Annual sales volume	Less than $1 million; $1 million to $10 million; $10 million to $100 million; over $100 million
	Number of establishments	With 1 to 19 employees; with 20 or more employees
BUYING SITUATIONS		
Nature of good	Kind	Product or service
	Where used	Installation; component of final product; supplies
	Application	Office use; limited production use; heavy production use
Buying condition	Purchase location	Centralized; decentralized
	Who buys	Individual buyer; group
	Type of buy	New buy; modified rebuy; straight rebuy

FORM PRODUCTS TO BE SOLD INTO GROUPS

As important as grouping customers into segments is finding a means of grouping the products you're selling into meaningful categories. If the firm has only one product or service, this isn't a problem, but when it has dozens or hundreds, these must be grouped in some way so buyers can relate to them. This is why department stores and supermarkets are organized into product groups, with the departments or aisles containing related merchandise. Likewise, manufacturers have product lines that are the groupings they use in the catalogues sent to customers.

What are the groupings for your restaurant? It could be the item purchased, such as a Frosty, chili, hamburgers, and french fries, but this is where judgment—the qualitative aspect of marketing—comes in. Students really buy an eating experience, or a meal that satisfies a need at a particular time of day, so the product grouping can be defined by meal or time of day as breakfast, lunch, between-meal snack, dinner, and after-dinner snack. These groupings are more closely related to the way purchases are actually made and permit you to market the entire meal, not just your french fries or Frosties.

DEVELOP A MARKET–PRODUCT GRID AND ESTIMATE SIZE OF MARKETS

Developing a market–product grid means labelling the markets (or horizontal rows) and products (or vertical columns), as shown in Figure 9–6. In addition, the size of the market in each cell, or the market–product combination, must be estimated. For your restaurant this involves estimating the number of, or sales revenue obtained from, each kind of meal that can reasonably be expected to be sold to each market segment. This is a form of the usage rate analysis discussed earlier in the chapter.

The market sizes in Figure 9–6 may be simple "guesstimates" if you don't have time for formal marketing research (as discussed in Chapter 8). But even

▌ *Figure 9–6*
Selecting a target market for your fast-food restaurant next to a metropolitan college (target market is shaded).

	PRODUCTS: MEALS				
MARKETS	BREAKFAST	LUNCH	BETWEEN-MEAL SNACK	DINNER	AFTER-DINNER SNACK
STUDENT					
Dormitory	0	S	L	0	L
Apartment	S	L	L	S	S
Day commuter	0	L	M	S	0
Night commuter	0	0	S	L	M
NONSTUDENT					
Faculty or staff	0	L	S	S	0
Live in area	0	S	M	M	S
Work in area	S	L	0	S	0

Key: L, large market; M, medium market; S, small market; 0, no market.

such crude estimates of the size of specific markets using a market–product grid are far better than the usual estimates of the entire market.

SELECT TARGET MARKETS

A firm must take care to choose its target market segments carefully. If it picks too narrow a group of segments, it may fail to reach the volume of sales and profits it needs. If it selects too broad a group of segments, it may spread its marketing efforts so thin that the extra expenses more than offset the increased sales and profits.

Criteria to Use in Picking the Target Segments   There are two different kinds of criteria present in the market segmentation process: (1) those to use in dividing the market or forming the segments (discussed earlier), and (2) those to use in actually picking the target segments. Even experienced marketing executives often confuse these two different sets of criteria. The five criteria to use in actually selecting the target segments apply to your Wendy's restaurant this way:

- *Size.* The estimated size of the market in the segment is an important factor in deciding whether it's worth going after. There is really no market for breakfasts among dormitory students (Figure 9–6), so why devote any marketing effort toward reaching a small or nonexistent market?
- *Expected growth.* Although the size of the market in the segment may be small now, perhaps it is growing significantly or is expected to grow in the future. Night commuters may not look important now, but with the decline in traditional day students in many colleges, evening adult education programs are expected to expand in the future. Thus the future market among night commuters is probably more encouraging than the current picture shown in Figure 9–6.
- *Competitive position.* Is there a lot of competition in the segment now, or is there likely to be in the future? The less the competition, the more attractive the segment is. For example, if the college dormitories announce a new policy of no meals on weekends, the dormitory segment is suddenly more promising for your restaurant.
- *Cost of reaching the segment.* A segment that is inaccessible to a firm's marketing actions should not be pursued. For example, the few nonstudents who live in the area may not be economically reachable with ads in newspapers or other media. Therefore, do not waste money trying to advertise to them.
- *Compatibility with the organization's objectives and resources.* If your restaurant doesn't have the cooking equipment to make breakfasts and has a policy against spending more money on restaurant equipment, then don't try to reach the breakfast segment.

As is often the case in marketing decisions, a particular segment may appear attractive according to some criteria and very unattractive according to others.

Choose the Segments   Ultimately, a marketing executive has to use these criteria to choose the segments for special marketing efforts. As shown in Figure 9–6, let's assume you've written off the breakfast market for two reasons: too-small market size, and incompatibility with your objectives and resources.

In terms of competitive position and cost of reaching the segment, you choose to focus on the four student segments and not the three nonstudent segments (although you're certainly not going to turn away business from the nonstudent segments). This combination of market–product segments—your target market—is shaded in Figure 9–6.

TAKE MARKETING ACTIONS TO REACH TARGET MARKETS

The purpose of developing a market–product grid is to trigger marketing actions to increase revenues and profits. This means that someone must develop and execute an action plan.

Your Wendy's Segmentation Strategy   With your Wendy's restaurant you've already reached one significant decision: there is a limited market for breakfast, so you won't open for business until 10:30 AM. In fact, Wendy's attempt at a breakfast menu was a disaster and was discontinued in 1986. Wendy's evaluates possible new menu items continuously, to compete not only with McDonald's (and now its pizza), but with a complex array of supermarkets, convenience stores, and gas stations that sell reheatable packaged foods, as well as new "easy-lunch" products like Oscar Mayer's Lunchables and Hillshire Farms' Lunch 'n Munch.[13]

Another essential decision is where and what meals to promote to specific market segments. An ad in the student newspaper could reach all the student segments, but you might consider this "shotgun approach" too expensive and want a more focussed "rifle approach" to reach smaller segments. If you choose three segments for special actions (Figure 9–7), promotional activities to reach them might include:

- *Day commuters* (an entire market segment). Run ads inside commuter buses and put flyers under the windshield wipers of cars in parking lots used by day commuters. These ads and flyers promote all the meals at your restaurant to a single segment of students—a horizontal cut through the market–product grid.

Wendy's expanded menu.

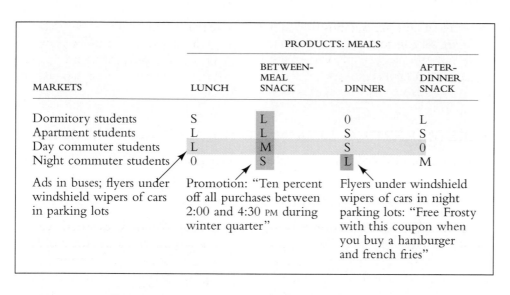

- *Between-meal snacks* (directed to all four student markets). To promote eating during this downtime for your restaurant, offer 10 percent off all purchases between 2:00 and 4:30 PM during winter quarter. This promotes a single meal to all four student segments—a vertical cut through the market–product grid.

- *Dinners to night commuters.* The most focussed of all three promotional activities is promoting a single meal to a single student segment. It might consist of a windshield flyer offering a free Frosty with the coupon when the person buys a hamburger and french fries.

Depending on how your promotional activities work, you can repeat, modify, or drop them and design new promotional activities for other segments you feel warrant the effort. This example of promoting your Wendy's restaurant is just a small piece of a complete marketing plan using all the elements of the marketing mix.

Apple's Segmentation Strategy   Steven Jobs and Stephen Wozniak didn't realize they were developing today's multibillion-dollar personal computer (PC) industry when they invented the Apple II in a garage in 1976. Under Jobs's inspirational leadership through the early 1980s, Apple was run with a focus on products and little concern for markets. Apple's control of its brainy, creative young engineers was likened to "Boy Scouts without adult supervision."[14] When IBM entered the PC market in 1981, Apple lost significant market share, and many experts predicted it wouldn't survive.

Enter John Sculley, who in 1983 moved to Apple's presidency from Pepsi-Cola. Sculley, as shown in the accompanying Marketing Action Memo, formalized and gave cohesiveness to Apple's market segmentation strategy and targeted specific Apple machines to particular market segments. The core business is built on Apple's line of Macintosh computers, which it continues to enhance. As in most segmentation situations, a single Apple product does not fit into an exclusive market niche. Rather, there is overlap among products in the

Apple's line of Macintosh computers is targeted at the needs of different market segments.

product line and also among the markets to which they are directed. But a market segmentation strategy enables Apple to offer different products to meet the needs of the different market segments.

By the 1990s Sculley concluded that Apple needed to update its strategy. He explains, "We looked at ourselves in the mirror and wondered if we had a justifiable business strategy for the 1990s."[15] His solution for Apple was to differentiate Apple's line of computers more clearly and to target them at specific niches that were becoming more important. As suggested by the Marketing Action Memo, Sculley and Apple took some creative marketing actions in the early 1990s, such as:

▪ Introducing the Classic line, targeted mainly at small businesses and—secondarily—homes.

▪ Cutting the prices on all Macs by 30 percent, thereby producing a 60 percent increase in the number of units sold.

▪ Introducing the sophisticated Quadra line, targeted at users needing powerful machines, including engineering, scientific, and publishing applications, as well as business ones.

▪ Introducing a revolutionary line of notebook computers (laptops weighing less than six pounds)—the PowerBooks. Cited by *Time, Business Week,* and *Fortune* as a "product of the year," more than a billion dollars worth of PowerBooks were sold in the year after they were introduced.[16]

▪ Making a serious entry into the Japanese market. Apple's initial entry into Japan was a near disaster. Learning a difficult lesson, Apple added far more Japanese-language software to support the Macintosh line, hired a Japanese management team, appointed a local board of directors, and developed a whole new group of motivated distributors. In the process Apple increased its market share more than six times in a four year period.[17]

MARKETING · ACTION · MEMO

How Apple Segments Its Markets

When John Sculley moved from Pepsi-Cola to become president of Apple Computer in 1983, he took over the company that some computer industry wags called "Camp Runamok," because it had no coherent product line that was directed at identifiable market segments.

Sculley took immediate action to avoid potential disaster and set about targeting his firm's computers at specific market segments. Because the market–product grid shifts as a firm's strategy changes, the one shown here is based on the product line that existed in early 1993. Apple's recent market–product strategy has given it computers for small businesses (Performa), travelers (PowerBook), and highly technical users (Quadra). Camp Runamok is back on track.

MARKET		PRODUCT Macintosh					
		Performa	Classic	LC III	Centris	PowerBook/Duo	Quadra
Home		■	■				
School	Students/faculty	■	■	■			
	Administration			■			
College/university	Students/faculty	■	■		■	■	
	Administration			■	■	■	
Small business			■				■
Large corporation	Clerical/manager			■	■	■	
	Technical				■	■	■

Sources: S. Sherman, "How to Prosper in the Value Decade," *Fortune,* November 30, 1992, pp. 90–103; C. Arnst, "PC Makers Head for 'Soho,' " *Business Week,* September 28, 1992, pp. 125–26; and J. Markoff, "Apple to Offer a 2-in-1 Computer," *The New York Times,* October 19, 1992, pp. C1, C4.

▪ Targeting a new family of Macs—the Performas—at the "soho" (small-office, home-office) users and selling them through national retailers like Sears, and national electronics stores like Majestic and Future Shop.[18]

Apple has also made strategic alliances with IBM, Sony, Toshiba, and Sharp that Sculley believes will enable it to be a major player in the consumer electronics and telecommunications revolution he sees on the horizon.[19] Most recently, in an effort to give its customers even greater value, Apple Canada reduced its prices by up to 16 percent on its Macintosh PowerBooks and up to 25 percent on its high-end Quadra 950 computers.[20]

---

1 What are some of the variables used to segment consumer markets?

2 What are some criteria used to decide which segments to choose for targets?

3 Why is usage rate important in segmentation studies?

Concept Check

POSITIONING THE PRODUCT

In Chapter 2, we briefly discussed the importance of having a competitive advantage when targeting a certain segment of the market. As you recall, a firm's competitive advantage is its ability to do, or offer, something better than its competition. The advantage must be of value to the target market. It could be the lowest price, highest quality, best value, or some other advantage desired by the target market. Once the competitive advantage is established, the firm must find a way to translate the advantage into reality for the customer, favourably distinguishing itself from the competition. Having a competitive advantage is meaningless unless the customer understands it and buys into it.

Product positioning refers to the place an offering occupies in the target customers' minds on important attributes relative to competitive offerings. It is how a product is seen through the eyes of the consumer. Through proper positioning, the product's competitive advantage is given life. For example, Duracell believed it had a competitive advantage over its competitors: a battery that had a longer life. A battery that lasted longer was important (valuable) to many consumers who bought batteries. So this was a potentially important competitive advantage for Duracell. Duracell then set out to position the product in the consumer's mind in a meaningful way. It selected a simple positioning theme: "Duracell, the one that lasts" (now, more recently, "No other battery lasts longer"). Duracell successfully occupied that position in the consumers' minds until the Eveready Energizer came along, as we will see later.

Given that positioning is a consumer's *subjective evaluation* of the product, the competitive advantage of a firm or its product can be *real* or just *perceived*. For example, a Lexus automobile doesn't necessarily have to be objectively a better-quality car than the Oldsmobile; the consumer just has to believe that it is. Thus, in many cases, positioning is based on image and not reality. Brewers go to great lengths in positioning their beer brands in the minds of consumers, but in general, most consumers cannot objectively tell the difference in the tastes of various beers, and thus most beer drinkers buy beer on the basis of its perceived image.

APPROACHES TO PRODUCT POSITIONING

There are two broad approaches to positioning a product in the market: head to head in direct competition with other firms, or differentiation of the product, avoiding direct competition. **Head-to-head positioning** means competing directly with competitors on similar product attributes in the same target market. The Duracell versus the Eveready Energizer battery is an example of head-to-head positioning. Dollar Rent-A-Car also uses head-to-head positioning against Avis and Hertz, and Volvo pits its turbocharged cars against Porsche. But head-to-head positioning strategies can raise ethical dilemmas, as described in the Ethics and Social Responsibility Alert.

Differentiation positioning seeks to avoid direct competition by stressing unique aspects of the product. A firm can position its product on a specific attribute, feature, or benefit. BMW calls its car the "ultimate driving machine" to connote superior handling and drivability, which appeals to young drivers. A firm can also position its product for a particular usage situation or problem

ETHICS AND SOCIAL RESPONSIBILITY ALERT

*Can Head-to-Head Positioning of a New Medication
Raise Patients' Costs without Any Benefits?*

The worldwide market for thrombolytics—medicines to break up blood clots in
heart attack victims—is $600 million a year. The pharmaceutical firm that intro-
duced TPA (for tissue plasminogen activator) to compete in the thrombolytics
market used high-pressure marketing and a head-to-head positioning strategy to
convince doctors they should prescribe TPA rather than the traditional strep-
tokinase. The price: $2,500 per treatment for TPA versus $220 for the older
treatment.

Subsequent research showed no difference in the effectiveness of the two
medicines. Researchers say doctors often accept and prescribe the latest drugs
because they are "enamoured" of new technologies, they fear malpractice suits,
and cost is not considered a primary concern. Public health officials, however, are
concerned with this situation and are investigating what *Time* magazine calls these
"overzealous marketing practices in the drug industry." What do you believe
should be done?

Source: Adapted from A. Purris, "Cheaper Can Be Better," *Time,* March 18, 1991, p. 70.

---

solution. Arm & Hammer positioned its baking soda as a refrigerator deodorant;
and Domino's, until recently, had always positioned itself as "the 30-minute
delivery pizza company." Companies also follow a differentiation positioning
strategy among brands within their own product line to try to minimize cannibalization of a brand's sales or shares.

PRODUCT POSITIONING USING PERCEPTUAL MAPS

A key to positioning a product effectively is understanding the perceptions
consumers have of product categories and brands within those categories. In
determining a brand's position and the preferences of consumers, companies
obtain three types of data from consumers:

1 Evaluations of the important attributes for a product class.
2 Judgments of existing brands with the important attributes.
3 Ratings of an "ideal" brand's attributes.

From these data, it is possible to develop a **perceptual map,** a means of
displaying or graphing in two dimensions the locations of products or brands in
the minds of consumers. Marketers can use perceptual maps to see how consumers perceive competing products or brands and then, if necessary, take
actions to try to change the product offering and the image it projects to
consumers. For example, GM interviewed consumers and developed a perceptual map for its automobiles. The two dimensions on the perceptual maps were
low price versus high price and family or conservative versus personal or expressive. GM discovered that most of its cars were perceived as family or

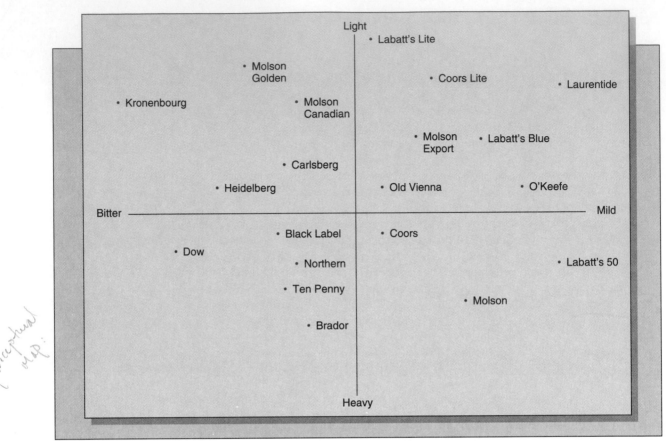

Source: J. E. Brisoux, Université du Québec à Trois-Rivières.

▌*Figure 9–8*
Positioning of brands of beer in Canadian market.

conservative, and few were perceived to be on the low end of the price dimension. Accordingly, GM positioned Saturn as a personal or expressive, low-price vehicle to fill in a glaring gap in its brands.

Figure 9–8 shows a perceptual map of 20 brands of beer sold in the Canadian market. A beer maker can examine this perceptual map to determine its brand's current position, and its closest competition, in terms of consumer perceptions. The beer maker also has to assess the size of the segments looking for a beer with the specific characteristics depicted on the map. For example, Kronenbourg appears to be well separated from its competitors. But the question for the marketers of Kronenbourg is how many beer drinkers want a light, bitter beer. If the segment is too small, Kronenbourg might have to reposition itself in order to become a more viable brand.

REPOSITIONING

In a strict sense, most marketers hope that positioning will be a one-time exercise with a new product or brand. But eventually most firms have to reassess their products' positioning. The trigger might be a recognition that the current position is

Why is Xerox Canada repositioning itself away from its image as a photocopier company? See the text.

eroding as a result of competitive pressures, the position is no longer meaningful to customers, or the performance results are unsatisfactory.[21] When a product is **repositioned,** its place changes in a consumer's mind relative to competitive offerings.

The fast-changing world of office information technology has pressured Xerox Canada to reposition itself in the market. The company that made its name synonymous with photocopiers is repositioning itself as a company with a wider range of options for customers. The company could not afford to be a one-product firm after seeing its market share in the copier segment erode in the face of intense Japanese competition. Xerox's new positioning is as the "document company." In order to execute the repositioning, the company has to also redefine the word *document* in the mind of the customer. In the past, a document was recognized as meaning a physical copy, but today a document could also be in the form of voice or video. The firm is promoting its "other" products and services such as the personal computer, fax machine, laser printer, and computer mouse. This is a big challenge for the billion-dollar company as it moves into the 21st century.[22]

The accompanying Marketing Action Memo shows why and how another Canadian company, Nabob, repositioned itself in the Canadian coffee market.

Sometimes marketers will attempt to reposition a competitor's product and not their own. This is generally referred to as "repositioning the competition."[23] This strategy assumes that if a competitor's product can be repositioned, a new product may be able to move in and take over the position once held by that product in the consumer's mind. As we mentioned earlier, Duracell successfully positioned itself as the "battery that lasts." However, Eveready repositioned Duracell batteries, in the minds of many consumers, through its use of the Energizer bunny and its "still going" positioning theme; and in doing so it took over the position once occupied by Duracell.

M A R K E T I N G · A C T I O N · M E M O

Nabob Repositions Itself to Compete in the 1990s

Nabob, the Vancouver-based company with a 97-year history, has radically transformed itself. It has repositioned itself from a traditional packaged goods company to a coffee company. Product line extensions, packaging design, and marketing and sales focus have all been revamped. The company even changed its name from Nabob Foods to Nabob Coffee Company. Nabob has the number one position in the ground-coffee market in Canada, but that position is being threatened by specialized coffee shops. Young coffee drinkers, especially, are experimenting with gourmet blends and exotic formulas offered by the specialty shops, where they spend up to $2 more for a package of coffee compared with supermarket prices. Nabob feared that these young consumers would bypass the traditional grocery store permanently unless it could capture their interest.

To get the consumer interest, Nabob launched four new products to complement its successful Tra-

dition and Summit blends: African Safari Blend, South Pacific Blend, Milano Espresso Roast, and Full City Dark Roast. Tradition and Summit were also redesigned to fit the new look, and Nabob's sales force were provided with intensive training to make them coffee "experts." Sensitive to consumer reaction to change, and insistent that consumers should know as much about coffee as the company, Nabob launched an aggressive, 52-week in-store media program, using as many as three Infoshelves at once, offering brochures and other materials on coffee. Advertising support in the form of print and television commercials emphasized the company name change, the new products, and the sourcing and roasting process. Nabob hopes that this strategy will help position its products securely in the minds of coffee drinkers.

Source: Adapted from L. Medcalf, "Nabob Brews New, Strictly-Coffee Image," *Marketing*, May 24, 1993, p. 2.

Concept Check

1 What are the two approaches to product positioning?

2 What is repositioning?

3 Why do marketers use perceptual maps in product positioning decisions?

Summary

1 Market segmentation means aggregating prospective buyers into groups that have common needs and will respond similarly to a marketing action.

2 A straightforward approach to segmenting, targeting, and reaching a market involves five steps: (*a*) form prospective buyers into segments, by characteristics such as their needs; (*b*) form products to be sold into groups; (*c*) develop a market–product grid and estimate size of markets; (*d*) select target markets; and (*e*) take marketing actions to reach the target markets.

3 A number of variables are often used to represent customer needs in the market segmentation process. For consumer markets, typical customer variables are region, census metropolitan area, age, income, benefits sought, and usage rate. For industrial markets, comparable variables are geographical location, size of firm, and Standard Industrial Classification (SIC) code.

4 Usage rate is an important factor in a market segmentation study. Users are often divided into heavy, medium, and light users.

5 Nonusers are often divided into prospects and nonprospects. Nonusers of a firm's brand may be important if they are prospects—users of some other brand in the product class that may be convinced to change brands.

6 Criteria used (*a*) to segment markets and (*b*) to choose target segments are related but different. The former include potential to increase profits, similarity of needs of buyers within a segment, difference of needs among segments, and feasibility of a resulting marketing action. The latter include market size, expected growth, the competitive position of the firm's offering in the segment, and the cost of reaching the segment.

7 A market–product grid is a useful way to display what products can be directed at which market segments, but the grid must lead to marketing actions for the segmentation process to be worthwhile.

8 When targeting a certain segment, a company can position its product head to head against the competition or seek a differentiated position. A concern with positioning is often to avoid cannibalization of the existing product line. In positioning, a firm often uses consumer judgments in the form of perceptual maps to locate its product relative to competing ones.

Key Terms and Concepts

market segmentation p. 212   **nonprospects** p. 219
market segments p. 212   **product positioning** p. 228
product differentiation p. 212   **head-to-head positioning** p. 228
market–product grid p. 213   **differentiation positioning** p. 228
usage rate p. 218   **perceptual map** p. 229
80/20 rule p. 219   **repositioning** p. 231
prospects p. 219

Chapter Problems and Applications

1 What variables might be used to segment these consumer markets? (*a*) Lawn mowers, (*b*) frozen dinners, (*c*) dry breakfast cereals, and (*d*) soft drinks.

2 What variables might be used to segment these industrial markets? (*a*) Industrial sweepers, (*b*) photocopiers, (*c*) computerized production control systems, and (*d*) car rental agencies.

3 In Figure 9–7, the dormitory market segment includes students living in college-owned residence halls, sororities, and fraternities. What market needs are common to these students that justify combining them into a single segment in studying the market for your Wendy's restaurant?

4 You may disagree with the estimates of market size given for the rows in the market–product grid in Figure 9–7. Estimate the market size and give a brief justification for these market segments: (*a*) dormitory students, (*b*) day commuters, and (*c*) people who work in the area.

5 Suppose you want to increase revenues from your fast-food restaurant shown in Figure 9–7 even further. What promotion actions might you take to increase revenues from (*a*) dormitory students, (*b*) dinners, and (*c*) after-dinner snacks from night commuters?

6 Savin entered the copier market with a claim that its products were the same as Xerox's, only cheaper. What type of positioning strategy was this?

DRAMA IN REAL LIFE

MIRACLE ON THE FLIGHT DECK

PAGE 58

SECRETS COUPLES DON'T SHARE

PAGE 163

BRYAN ADAMS ON THE RECORD

PAGE 94

March 1993 $2

Reader's Digest

World's Most Widely Read Magazine

More than 28 million copies bought monthly in 17 languages

Relationship Marketing, Information Technology, and Forecasting

AFTER READING THIS CHAPTER YOU SHOULD BE ABLE TO:

- Define and explain the use and importance of relationship marketing.
- Describe how information technology and micromarketing have led to the concept of relationship marketing.
- Describe the factors that have made relationship marketing both necessary and possible.
- Recognize structured and unstructured marketing decisions and their impact on data used in information systems.
- Recognize top-down and buildup approaches to forecasting sales.
- Use the lost-horse and linear extrapolation methods to make a simple forecast.

Relationship Marketing: Reaching Consumers One at a Time—Today and Tomorrow

With a worldwide circulation of 20 million—more than *Time, Newsweek,* and *TV Guide* combined—*Reader's Digest* has the largest circulation in the world. But only 31 percent of the firm's profits come from the magazine, which has editions in more than 30 countries. The Reader's Digest crown jewel, however, is its database which totals 100 million households. *Fortune* magazine calls this database, simply, "the best in the business." If a household buys the book *A Passage to India,* it might receive another book such as, perhaps, *Treasures of China,* or a video about India.[1]

Many companies are able to use very direct and specific marketing actions toward consumers because of giant databases like the one Reader's Digest uses. These databases are filled with information on a household's or an individual's purchase history, anniversary and birth dates, store patronage, and media habits. These databases give major companies the power to almost duplicate the kind of relationship small-town or neighbourhood retailers had with your grandparents. But, as described in the Ethics and Social Responsibility Alert later in this chapter, this closeness raises a number of ethical issues.

Welcome to the era of relationship marketing! In this context, relationship marketing has a far more specific meaning than simply good relationships with customers. Here, the term **relationship marketing** is an organization's effort to develop a long-term, cost-effective link with individual customers for mutual benefit.[2] The president of Reader's Digest says that the database tells the company the likes and dislikes of its many readers and that "our relationship with the reader is the key to the success of this company."[3] Relationship marketing extends the concept of market segmentation described in Chapter 9 to marketing actions undreamed of a decade ago. For example, when using geographic market segmentation, grocery product firms and supermarket chains have found that it isn't good enough to focus on a city or even a postal code area; they are now narrowing the target to a bull's-eye of an individual household or a specific person in that household. Today's databases enable marketers to identify these customers using computer analyses and displays and to reach specific households with very directed and often customized marketing efforts. The result: a revolution in marketing information collection and use that will restructure the links between Canadian and international firms and their customers into the 21st century.

This chapter first describes the strategic role of information and customer relationships in the 1990s and then covers what has made relationship marketing both necessary and possible, how information technology is used in marketing, and sales forecasting.

STRATEGIC ROLE OF INFORMATION AND CUSTOMER RELATIONSHIPS IN THE 1990S

To understand how information is tied to customer relationships today, let us describe three elements of this strategy and discuss information and customer relationships as strategic weapons.

THREE KEY ELEMENTS IN LINKING INFORMATION AND CUSTOMER RELATIONSHIPS

Figure 10–1 shows the three foundation elements in the structure that support continuing, one-to-one relationships between an organization and its customers: information technology, micromarketing, and relationship marketing.

Information Technology   Since the advent of computers after World War II and personal computers in the 1980s, management perceptions of the value and use of information have changed significantly. Even the terms are changing: whereas a decade ago managers talked about manufacturing information systems and marketing information systems, the lines of separation of information among the various departments in a firm are now disappearing. Today, all generally fall under the broader term **information technology,** which involves designing and managing a computer and communication system to satisfy an organization's requirements for information processing and access.

With the existence of today's massive databases, marketing managers are able to query and analyze data almost instantaneously. For example, a product manager for Cheez Whiz at Kraft-General Foods Canada can query a database and discover in which stores the product sells well and in which ones it doesn't.

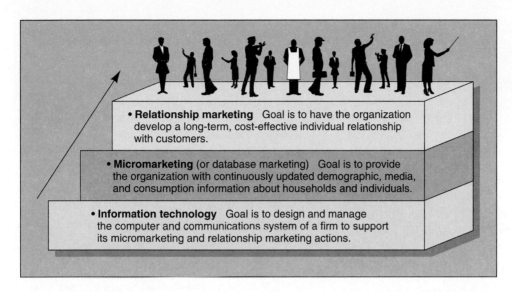

█ *Figure 10–1*
**Relationship marketing
builds on information
technology and
micromarketing to
develop links with
individual customers.**

Micromarketing   The Cheez Whiz example suggests marketing decisions that
can be made at the store level regarding product sales. In the 1990s, many firms
have discovered this is not good enough—they need to target specific households, individuals, or organizational customers. Enter micromarketing, the
middle step in Figure 10–1. **Micromarketing**—also called *database marketing*—is an organization's effort to collect demographic, media, and consumption
profiles of customers in order to target them more effectively. A recent survey
of 500 major Canadian businesses revealed that 93 percent of them already use
database marketing as part of their overall marketing strategy.[4]

As described later in the chapter, traditional media like TV and newspapers
are becoming less and less cost-effective in reaching customers. Micromarketing
has enabled marketers to use direct marketing or direct promotion—such as
direct mail or telemarketing—to reach customers more efficiently.

Relationship Marketing   While micromarketing is a giant step beyond traditional market segmentation, it still falls short of the ideal—a near-personal or
one-to-one continuing interaction between seller and customer, to the mutual
benefit of both. As shown in the top step of Figure 10–1, this leads to today's
focus on relationship marketing—an organization's effort to develop a long-
term, cost-effective link with individual customers for mutual benefit. While
relationship marketing builds on, and needs, both information technology and
micromarketing, the accompanying Marketing Action Memo shows that it goes
a step beyond these in seeking the desired near-personal relationship with
customers when the expected long-term benefits exceed the costs.[5]

Relationship marketing applies to organizations as well as ultimate consumers. For example, an office supply company could track on computer every
order that its customers make. In doing so, it could develop special offers to
particular customers who buy certain products with regularity or target a specific customer who hasn't yet bought a certain product the company feels that
customer might value.

INFORMATION AND CUSTOMER RELATIONSHIPS AS STRATEGIC WEAPONS

Starting in the mid-1980s, business information took on a new dimension. Business strategists became increasingly convinced that information could and would become a strategic weapon by which an innovative firm could attain a sustainable competitive advantage.[6] This gave rise to today's computerized methods of achieving long-run advantage by querying and analyzing on-line databases linking customers and suppliers through remote devices and telecommunications.

Canadian companies are using micromarketing more frequently in order to target customers more effectively.

Information technology can provide a sustainable competitive advantage in a number of ways: building barriers to entry, increasing switching costs (the expense of changing from one supplier to another), and locking customers into essential information and databases. As the electronic and data links among firms get tighter, the likelihood of a sustainable competitive advantage for a firm controlling vital information increases.

Concept Check

1 **What is relationship marketing?**

2 **How do information technology and micromarketing relate to relationship marketing?**

RELATIONSHIP MARKETING: THE REVOLUTION ARRIVES

As shown in Figure 10−2, relationship marketing forces today's marketing manager to be increasingly aware of many complex factors. To comprehend further how relationship marketing has revolutionized today's market segmentation and marketing mix actions, it is necessary to analyze what has made relationship marketing necessary and what has made relationship marketing possible.

WHAT MAKES RELATIONSHIP MARKETING NECESSARY: THE CAUSES

Two sources of marketing problems have helped trigger the rise of relationship marketing: more demanding consumers and excessive business costs.

More Demanding Consumers   As mentioned in Chapter 3, today's consumers are constantly changing. But box 1 in Figure 10−2 notes that one common factor remains: consumers are far more demanding than they were even five years ago. Research studies show that consumers:

- *Want "personalized" offerings.* Consumers increasingly seek the combination of product and services that are tailored to their unique wants and needs. For example, 10 days after specifying their unique wants in a new car order, Japanese consumers buying a Toyota will have their built-to-order car.
- *Desire high quality and value.* Consumers are willing to pay a premium for quality, the characteristics of which they rank from top to bottom as reliability, durability, ease of maintenance, ease of use, a known or trusted brand name, and (last) low price.[7]
- *Require "caring" customer service.* Effective customer service means having the seller's representatives treat customers the way they want to be treated. For IBM this means an electronic customer support system that automatically diagnoses potential trouble to alert IBM service people, who sometimes show up on a customer's doorstep *before* the glitch appears on the customer's IBM equipment.[8]

Figure 10–2
Complex factors influence marketing managers as they develop relationship marketing strategies.

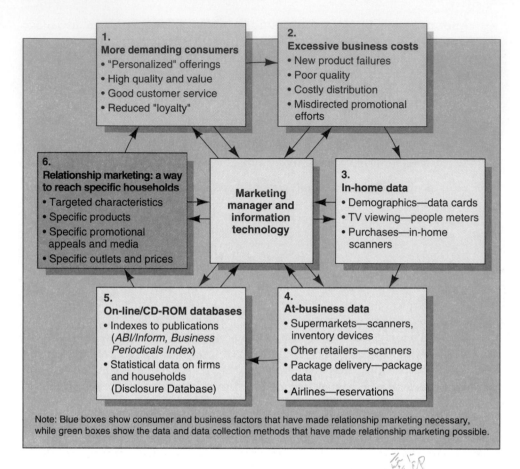

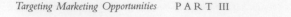

■ *Reduced loyalty to sellers.* For today's consumers, the issue is not that a product, brand, or store served their needs last year but whether it will serve their needs today. Sellers have discovered that defecting customers exact a terrible price in lost revenues, which reemphasizes the importance of the continuing customer links of relationship marketing. Studies show that reducing customer defections by 5 percent increases the future profit stream from 30 percent to 85 percent, depending on the business. IBM estimated that if it could improve satisfaction 1 percent for worldwide customers of its world-class AS/400 minicomputers, it would increase revenues by over $200 million within five years.[9]

Excessive Business Costs   Box 2 in Figure 10–2 identifies some of the key sources of excessive business costs that have driven today's manufacturers and retailers to use relationship marketing. Poor quality can lead directly to new product failures (discussed in greater detail in Chapter 11), customer defections, and billions of dollars in lost revenues and profit. Surveys of top executives show that they feel improving product and service quality is the most critical challenge facing them in the coming years.

Gaining distribution on retailers' shelves is increasingly costly, and as will be discussed in Chapter 11, manufacturers may actually be required to pay for

What may lie in your future: press a touch-sensitive screen at your supermarket checkout counter to receive coupons or recipes while your bill is tallied. The text describes how checkout screens like this are replacing national TV and magazine ads.

retail shelf space for new products. The cost of retail distribution has triggered relationship marketing strategies because both retailers and manufacturers now have computerized records telling them how much revenue retail shelf space should and actually does generate. Products not meeting sales targets are dropped.

In past years, large grocery product manufacturers spent tens or hundreds of millions of dollars annually on radio, TV, and magazine advertisements. Much of this was wasted because consumers have become increasingly blasé about these messages, many of which are no longer penetrating consumers' conscious-ness.[10] The result: these grocery product firms have cut back substantially on national advertising campaigns and instead use micromarketing and relationship marketing strategies to select more cost-effective methods to communicate with specific customers they want to reach. An example is the checkout counter screen at some supermarkets, which gives customers coupons to encourage repeat purchases, buy complementary products (e.g., coupons for baby food to people buying diapers), or even switch to competing brands.

As an indication of the importance of this trend, a study showed that in a single year 275 consumer product firms started building customer databases for more than 500 brands. Most active in this group were Kraft-General Foods, Procter & Gamble, Johnson & Johnson, and Nestlé.[11] Some experts believe that relationship marketing will replace traditional media as the primary marketing tool of the next decade.[12] But many television and radio stations as well as magazines and newspapers are using micromarketing and relationship marketing themselves to attract and keep their advertisers.

For example, *MacLean's* magazine uses Autolink, a database of new car registrations, in this way. *MacLean's* examines how many cars, by make and model, were bought by *MacLean's* subscribers and uses this information to entice auto manufacturers to advertise in the magazine.[13]

There are two potential drawbacks that emerge in developing the huge databases often needed for relationship marketing. One is cost, which is esti-mated to be $1.74 per name for a consumer product.[14] A second factor is potential ethical issues in obtaining consumer names, as described in the ac-companying Ethics and Social Responsibility Alert.

ETHICS AND SOCIAL RESPONSIBILITY ALERT

What Control Should You Have over Your Personal Information?

"We're conducting a survey," reads the letter you open from the XYZ Survey Research Company. The questionnaire asks for your preferences on various consumer products plus personal and demographic information such as name, address, telephone number, occupation, and family income. To encourage you to respond, XYZ offers you free samples of several consumer products.

However, there are several things you are not told. One is that the questionnaire will be sent to 50 million homes this year. Another is that the personal and demographic information will be compiled in databases and sold to other marketers so they can promote their products.

Is this ethical?

Source: Adapted from W. R. Dillon, T. J. Madden, and N. H. Firtle, *Marketing Research in a Marketing Environment,* 2nd ed. (Homewood, IL: Richard D. Irwin, 1990), p. 41.

WHAT MAKES RELATIONSHIP MARKETING POSSIBLE: THE TECHNOLOGY OF INFORMATION

Marketing data have little value by themselves: they are simply facts or numbers. To translate data into information—to put the data into a form in which they can help the marketing manager make decisions leading to marketing actions— the data must be unbiased, timely, pertinent to the problem, accessible, organized, and well presented. This section covers key sources of information that have been revolutionized by technological breakthroughs in collecting, organizing, and presenting marketing data in a consumer's home, in various kinds of business firms, by combining all of these data sources, and through on-line databases.

In-Home Data   To develop relationship marketing strategies (box 3 in Figure 10–2), marketing managers need incredible quantities of raw data about consumers and their households—their demographics and lifestyles, TV viewing habits, use of other promotional media (such as magazines, newspapers, and coupons), and purchases. Historically there have been two especially severe problems in collecting these data: (1) the cost and (2) the potential bias in the data collected. Breakthroughs in technology in the past decade have addressed both issues. Recently invented credit cards now contain detailed data on a consumer's demographics, lifestyle, and household. In-home optical scanners used by services like Arbitron can record purchases not captured by, say, supermarket scanners. Data on TV viewing and use of other promotional media like coupons and direct mail are captured electronically and inexpensively with little intrusion on the consumer's activities. It is important to avoid intruding on a consumer, to avoid having the measurement process alter the consumer's normal marketing behaviour. This concern is the reason Nielsen plans to replace

Apple Newton notepad computer.

today's people meters with "passive people meters." If these work as planned, their image-recognition computerized cameras will automatically record who in the household is watching TV without the intrusion of his having to push buttons to register his TV viewing behaviour.

At-Business Data Business firms themselves (box 4, Figure 10–2) collect huge volumes of detailed data for relationship marketing purposes. All of us have seen our supermarket checkout clerks use electronic optical scanners that "read" the universal product code (UPC) on our purchased items to record on our sales slip. Most supermarkets with annual sales over $2 million now use scanners, the latest versions of which can record data in sufficient detail to enable the supermarket chain and manufacturers to track performance weekly by store, product category, and brand.[15] Other retailers, such as department stores, mass merchandisers, and clothing stores, are increasingly using scanners to track purchases.

Other businesses use electronic tracking of purchases, inventories, and reservations to facilitate their relationship marketing actions. United Parcel Service (UPS) delivery people use hand-held computers that scan a special UPS label and double as data input keyboards, to collect real-time data that permit the location of packages to be identified throughout their trips. And available now at your computer store are "notepad" computers such as Apple's Newton, which enable you to write with a special stylus directly on a screen connected to a personal computer in order to manipulate text and drawings stored in memory. Insurance companies are using these notepad computers so that an auto claims adjuster can outline damaged parts on an exploded-view diagram of a car and let the notepad calculate the cost of the repair.

Single-Source Data: Putting It All Together In the late 1980s, new marketing data services emerged that offered **single-source data,** information provided by a single firm on household demographics and lifestyle, purchases, TV viewing behaviour, and responses to promotions like coupons and free samples.[16] Campbell Soup uses single-source data services to make or adjust its promotional effort. For example, from data it received from a single source supplier, it

Examples of information in on-line databases (indexes, abstracts, and full-text information from journals and periodicals probably available through your college or public library).

NAME	DESCRIPTION
ABI/Inform*	Covers over 800 publications on business and management
CAN/OLE*† (Canadian Business and Current Affairs)	Covers 200 business periodicals and newspapers
CAN/OLE (Statistics Canada Catalogue)	Lists all Statistics Canada publications by industry, topic, product
Infoglobe (Canadian News Index)	Indexes Canadian daily newspapers
Infoglobe (Canadian Periodicals Index)	Covers 350 English- and French-language magazines
CANSIM	Products and services of the latest Canadian census
Dialog (Canadian Key Business Directory and Dun & Bradstreet)	Directory of public and private Canadian companies
Compusearch	Demographic and consumer spending information broken down to six-digit postal code level

*Also available on CD-ROM.
†Canadian Institution for Scientific and Technical Information.

shifted a TV ad campaign for Swanson frozen dinners from a serious to a light theme and increased its sales by 14 percent.[17]

On-Line and CD-ROM Databases   With your own personal computer, a modem, and some communications software, you can access thousands of on-line databases (box 5, Figure 10–2). Hence, on-line databases are no longer restricted to huge corporations and reference libraries. As shown in Figure 10–3, information in on-line databases divides into two general categories: indexes to articles in publications, which are accessed through keyword searches, and statistical and directory data on households, products, and companies. When desired, this information can be transferred to the user's own computer. Because of the cost of the telecommunications link to these on-line databases, many libraries obtain optical CD-ROMs (compact disc, read-only memory) that are read by a laser on special drives attached to microcomputers. Often updated monthly, one CD-ROM can contain the same amount of information as an entire 20-volume encyclopedia.

Concept Check

1 What are the factors that have made relationship marketing (*a*) necessary and (*b*) possible?

2 How do consumer products firms use relationship marketing to reach individual households or consumers?

3 What are single-source data?

USING INFORMATION TECHNOLOGY IN MARKETING

Let's look at when information technology is needed in marketing, key elements in an information system, and an actual information system being used.

WHEN INFORMATION TECHNOLOGY IS NEEDED IN MARKETING

Not every firm needs information technology to help it make marketing decisions. The need for it is largely determined by the value versus the cost of marketing information and the kinds of decisions a marketing manager makes and how they relate to the information included in the information system.

Trade-Offs: Value versus Cost of Marketing Data   Information and data can be valuable commodities, but they can also be very expensive. As mentioned earlier, the facts and figures that make up marketing information have no value by themselves. Their value comes from being organized and interpreted to help the decision maker reach better decisions.

In practice, a marketing manager sets the priority of the data from most valuable to least valuable in solving a problem, assesses the cost of collecting each kind of data, and stops collecting more data on the list when the cost of collection outweighs their value in improving the decisions. Although these are very difficult guidelines to apply, they stress an important issue: the value of the data must be balanced against their cost of collection and use. Great care is needed to ensure that the information technology is user-friendly and that it will assist marketing managers in reaching decisions.

Kinds of Decisions a Marketing Manager Makes   A marketing manager makes two distinctly different kinds of decisions. One type is *structured decisions,* routine and repetitive decisions for which standard solutions exist. A product manager for a grocery products manufacturer may plan dozens of sales promotions (coupons and deals) over a five-year period. For these structured decisions the manager can access the information system to determine what will be the impact on case sales of moving the promotion up two weeks or changing a coupon's price allowance.

In contrast, *unstructured decisions* are complex decisions for which there are no cut-and-dried solutions. For example, a department store manager may ask for an assessment of the impact on sales of changing the department's location within the store. Researchers have found that past experience is especially important for marketing managers in making unstructured decisions such as new products, but not as important for structured decisions such as scheduling consumer promotions.[18]

One-time and special reports don't go into an information system. Only the cost-effective, repetitive information is typically included and becomes the database used, with pertinent models to provide the standardized, periodic reports produced by the information system. To see just how information technology is used in a variety of marketing applications, read the accompanying Marketing Action Memo.

M A R K E T I N G · A C T I O N · M E M O

Information Technology and Marketing

*B*esides streamlining production and inventory, the biggest payoff to new information technology, says Ted Highberger, chief operations officer of Coca-Cola Beverages, Toronto, lies in marketing. Scanners at the checkout counter grab consumer purchase data, information Coke can use to find out who's buying at each store and which products are the big sellers. That's useful information when considering sampling programs, direct marketing campaigns, or new product development. The buzzword used to describe this process of streamlining and improving communications, both with retail customers and shoppers, is *efficient consumer response (ECR)*. And many packaged goods companies and retailers in North America are either taking a hard look at it or are doing something about it right now.

To further their understanding of the marketplace, marketers are also using software programs that take raw demographic and consumer-based data and turn them into information they can use to build marketing programs. Grand & Toy (G&T) is using high-tech to increase consumer responsiveness. The office supply chain can deliver "live" reports on warehouse inventory to each of 114 stores. The information gathered through the high-tech process allows the company to ensure that the proper type and level of inventory is kept in the individual stores and allows G&T to develop highly focussed direct marketing programs. Black's Photo Corporation uses a software program called Conquest/Canada, developed by Toronto-based Compusearch, to make decisions on new store locations. The software combines marketing databases with mapping and topographical software, which allows Black's to break out demographic information by geographic region or store trading area. The program provides information on population, consumer spending, and business activity, including the number of businesses in a potential trading area. Beyond enabling marketers to locate new stores, it also allows them to select areas for direct marketing campaigns.

Source: Adapted from J. Pollock, "Faster, Cheaper, Better," *Marketing*, February 7, 1994, p. 11; and G. Levitch, "Mapping the Market," *Marketing*, February 7, 1994, p. 12.

KEY ELEMENTS IN AN INFORMATION SYSTEM

Today's marketing managers are seeking user-friendly information systems to assist them in their decisions. As shown in Figure 10–4, today's strategic information system that helps a marketing manager develop relationship marketing strategies contains five key elements:

1 *Input devices.* These means of collecting marketing data include in-store and in-home scanners, people meters, and purchase or reservation workstations.
2 *Databases.* The marketing data collected by the input devices are stored in diverse databases containing data on households, products, retailers, media, and promotions.
3 *Models.* The models provide hypotheses about the relationships among the data contained in the databases to enable the decision maker to organize, interpret, and communicate the resulting information in order to reach marketing decisions.
4 *Mainframe or minicomputer.* This is today's main means of collecting, processing, and updating the data coming from the input devices, databases,

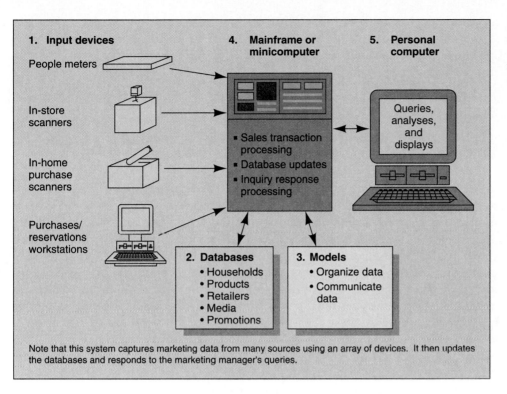

and models. Coming off the drawing boards to replace these older computers are systems of networked microcomputers.[19]

5 *Personal computer.* The PC on the marketing manager's desk serves as an
   input and output device and a means of querying the system to obtain and
   analyze the data it contains.

An information system like this permits a marketing manager to reach decisions
using **sensitivity analysis,** asking "what-if" questions to determine how
changes in a factor like price or advertising affect marketing results like sales
revenues or profits.

---

1 **What is the difference between structured and unstructured decisions for a
   marketing manager?**

2 **What are the five elements in an information system?**

Concept Check

MARKET AND SALES FORECASTING

Forecasting or estimating the actual size of a market is critical both in relationship marketing decisions and more traditional marketing decisions. This is because overestimating the size of a market may mean wasting research and

development, manufacturing, and marketing dollars on new products that fail. Underestimating it may mean missing the chance to introduce successful new products. We will discuss some basic forecasting terms, two major approaches to forecasting, and specific forecasting techniques.

BASIC FORECASTING TERMS

Unfortunately, there are no standard definitions for some forecasting concepts, so it's necessary to take care in defining the terms used.

Market or Industry Potential   The term **market potential,** or **industry potential,** refers to the maximum total sales of a product by all firms to a segment under specified environmental conditions and marketing efforts of the firms. For example, the market potential for cake mix sales to Canadian consumers in 1998 might be 2 million cases—what Pillsbury, Betty Crocker, Duncan Hines, and other cake mix producers would sell to consumers under the assumptions that past patterns of dessert consumption continue and the same level of promotional effort continues relative to other desserts. If one of these assumptions proves false, the estimate of market potential will be wrong. For example, if Canadian consumers suddenly become more concerned about eating refined sugar and shift their dessert preferences from cakes to fresh fruits, the estimate of market potential will be too high.

Sales or Company Forecast   What one firm expects to sell under specified conditions for the uncontrollable and controllable factors that affect sales is the **sales forecast,** or **company forecast.** For example, Duncan Hines might develop its sales forecast of 1 million cases of cake mix for Canadian consumers in 1998, assuming past dessert preferences continue and so does the same relative level of promotional expenditures between it, Pillsbury, and Betty Crocker. If Betty Crocker suddenly cuts its advertising in half, Duncan Hines's old sales forecast will probably be too low.

   With both market potential estimates and sales forecasts, it is necessary to specify some significant details: the product involved (all cake mixes, only white cake mixes, or only Bundt cake mixes); the time period involved (month, quarter, or year); the segment involved (Canadian, western region, upper-income buyer, or single-person households); controllable marketing mix factors (price and level of advertising support); uncontrollable factors (consumer tastes and actions of competitors); and the units of measurement (number of cases sold or total sales revenues).

TWO BASIC APPROACHES TO FORECASTING

A marketing manager rarely wants a single number for an annual forecast, such as 5,000 units or $75 million in sales revenue. Rather, the manager wants this total subdivided into elements she works with, such as sales by product line or sales to a market segment. The two basic approaches to sales forecasting are subdividing the total sales forecast (top-down approach) or building the total sales forecast by summing up the components (buildup approach).

Top-Down Approach   The **top-down approach** to sales forecasting involves subdividing an aggregate estimate into its principal components. A shoe manufacturer can use the top-down approach to estimate the percentage of its total shoe sales in a province and develop province-by-province forecasts for shoe sales for the coming year. *Canadian Markets,* published by the Financial Post, and *Sales and Marketing Management* magazine are sources that are widely used for top-down forecasting information.

For example, using *Canadian Markets* information, one can determine that Ontario has 36.4 percent of the Canadian population, 42.3 percent of the personal income of Canada, and 38.5 percent of Canadian retail sales. If the shoe manufacturer wanted to use a single factor related to expected shoe sales, it would choose the factor that has been closely related to shoe sales historically, in this case the percentage of Canadian retail sales found in Ontario. The top-down forecast would then be that 38.5 percent of the firm's sales would be made in the province of Ontario.

A single factor is rarely a true indicator of sales opportunity in a given market. So, sometimes multiple factors are considered when making forecasts. One of the best-known general-purpose multiple-factor indexes is the Buying Power Index developed by *Sales and Marketing Management* magazine. The BPI for a given market area can be computed as follows:

$$\text{BPI} = (0.2 \times \text{Percent of national population in area})$$
$$+ (0.5 \times \text{Percent of national personal income in area})$$
$$+ (0.3 \times \text{Percent of national retail sales in area})$$

So, given the example of Ontario as a market area, the buying power index would be:

$$0.2(36.4) + 0.5(42.3) + 0.3(38.5) = 39.98$$

Thus, the BPI forecasts that almost 40 percent of the firm's shoe sales should occur in Ontario.

This is slightly higher than if retail sales alone were used for the forecast. The forecast can be converted into dollars by using *Sales and Marketing Management* magazine's "Survey of Buying Power," Part II (in an annual October issue), which gives retail sales of various lines of merchandise such as footwear. Or a marketer could use Statistics Canada information on retail sales or family expenditures.

Buildup Approach   The **buildup approach** sums the sales forecasts of each of the components to arrive at the total forecast. It is a widely used method when there are identifiable components such as products, product lines, or market segments in the forecasting problem.

Figure 10–5 shows how GE's medical technology department uses the buildup approach to develop a sales forecast involving three broad categories of projects or products: work currently under contract that can be forecast precisely, follow-up work that is likely to result from current contracts, and new business that results from GE's proposals for new business, which is difficult to forecast. Each of these three forecasts is the sum of a number of individual products or projects, which for simplicity are not shown. In turn, forecasts for each of the three kinds of business can be summed to give the total sales forecast for the entire department.

Figure 10–5
**Buildup approach to a
2-year sales forecast for
General Electric's
medical technology
department.**

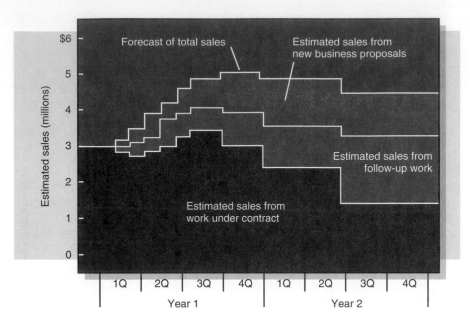

Figure 10–5
**Buildup approach to a
2-year sales forecast for
General Electric's
medical technology
department.**

SPECIFIC SALES FORECASTING TECHNIQUES

Broadly speaking, three main sales forecasting techniques are available that can lead to the forecasts used in the top-down and buildup approaches. Ordered from least costly in terms of both time and money to most costly, these are judgments of the decision maker, surveys of knowledgeable groups, and statistical methods.

Judgments of the Decision Maker   Probably 99.9 percent of all sales forecasts are judgments of the person who must act on the results of the forecast—the individual decision maker. An example is the forecasts of likely sales, and hence the quantity to order, for the 13,000 items stocked in a typical supermarket that must be forecast by the stock clerk or manager. A **direct forecast** involves estimating the value to be forecast without any intervening steps. Examples appear in your daily life: How many quarts of milk should I buy? How much time should I allow to drive to the game? How much money should I get out of the instant cash machine? Your mind may go through some intervening steps but so quickly you're unaware of it.

So in estimating the amount of money to get from the instant cash machine, you probably made some unconscious (or conscious) intervening estimates (such as counting the cash in your billfold or the special events you need cash for) to obtain your direct estimate. Lost-horse forecasting does this in a more structured way. A **lost-horse forecast** involves starting with the last known value of the item being forecast, listing the factors that could affect the forecast, assessing whether they have a positive or a negative impact, and making the final forecast. The technique gets its name from how you'd find a lost horse: go where it was last seen, put yourself in its shoes, consider those factors that could affect where you might go (to the pond if you're thirsty, the hayfield if you're hungry, and so on), and go there. For example, a product manager for Sony portable stereos in 1995 who needed to make a sales forecast through 1998 would start with the known value of 1995 sales and list the positive factors (more teenagers with money, more TV publicity) and the negative ones (competition from other firms) to arrive at the final series of annual sales forecasts.

Surveys of Knowledgeable Groups   If you wonder what your firm's sales will be next year, ask people who are likely to know something about future sales. Four common groups that are surveyed to develop sales forecasts are prospective buyers, the firm's sales force, its executives, and experts.

A **survey of buyers' intentions forecast** involves asking prospective customers whether they are likely to buy the product during some future time period. For industrial products with few prospective buyers who are able and willing to predict their future buying behaviour, this can be effective. For example, there are probably only a few hundred customers in the entire world for Cray Research's supercomputers, so Cray simply surveys these prospects to develop its sales forecasts.

A **sales force survey forecast** involves asking the firm's salespeople to estimate sales during a coming period. Because these people are in contact with customers and are likely to know what customers like and dislike, there is logic to this approach. However, salespeople can be unreliable forecasters—painting too rosy a picture if they are enthusiastic about a new product and too grim a forecast if their sales quota is based on it.

A **jury of executive opinion forecast** involves asking knowledgeable executives inside the firm—such as vice presidents of marketing, research and development, finance, and production—about likely sales during a coming period. Although this approach is fast and includes judgments from diverse functional areas, it can be biased by a dominant executive whose judgments are deferred to by the others.

A **survey of experts forecast** involves asking experts on a topic to make a judgment about some future event. A **Delphi forecast** is an example of a survey of experts and involves polling people knowledgeable about the forecast topic (often by mail) to obtain a sequence of anonymous estimates. The Delphi forecast gets its name from the ancient Greek oracle at Delphi, who was supposed to see into the future. A major advantage of Delphi forecasting is that the anonymous expert does not have to defend his views or feel obliged to agree with a supervisor's estimate.

A **technological forecast** involves estimating when scientific breakthroughs will occur. In 1963, experts used the Delphi method to estimate the year by which a limited degree of weather control would occur. Their estimate: 1990! While this technological forecast looks silly today, the technique is valuable in helping managers make new product development decisions.

Statistical Methods   The best-known statistical method of forecasting is **trend extrapolation,** which involves extending a pattern observed in past data into the future. When the pattern is described with a straight line, it is *linear trend extrapolation.* Suppose that in early 1987 you were a sales forecaster for the Xerox Corporation and had actual sales revenue figures running from 1980 to 1986 (Figure

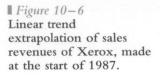

Figure 10-6
Linear trend extrapolation of sales revenues of Xerox, made at the start of 1987.

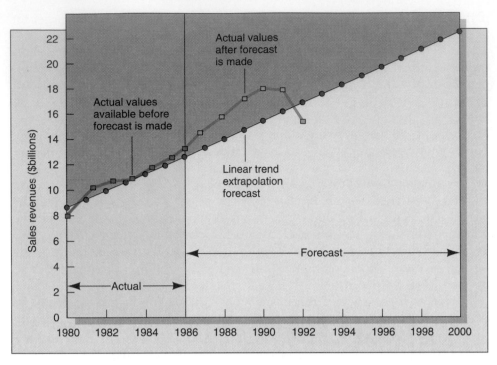

10-6). Using linear trend extrapolation, you draw a line to fit the past data and project it into the future to give the forecast values shown for 1987 to 1998.

If in 1993 you had wanted to compare your forecasts with actual results, you were in for a surprise—illustrating the strength and weakness of trend extrapolation. Trend extrapolation assumes that the underlying relationships in the past will continue into the future, which is the basis of the method's key strength: simplicity. If this assumption proves correct, you have an accurate forecast. However, if this proves wrong, the forecast is likely to be wrong. In this case your forecasts from 1987 through 1991 were too low. Xerox's aggressive new product development and marketing in the 1980s helped alter the factors underlying the linear trend extrapolation and caused the forecast to be too low. However, in 1992 Xerox encountered serious marketing problems and the linear trend forecast was far too high.

In practice, marketing managers often use several of the forecasting techniques to estimate the size of markets important to them. Also, they often do three separate forecasts based on different sets of assumptions: "best case," with optimistic assumptions, "worst case," with pessimistic ones, and "most likely case," with most reasonable assumptions.

Concept Check

1 What is the difference between the top-down and buildup approaches to forecasting sales?

2 How do you make a lost-horse forecast?

3 What is linear trend extrapolation?

Summary

1. Relationship marketing is an organization's effort to develop a long-term, cost-effective link with individual customers for mutual benefit. It represents a revolutionary extension of market segmentation and, more recently, micromarketing.

2. Information and information technology are increasingly seen as a means for a firm to obtain a sustainable competitive advantage.

3. Relationship marketing has been made necessary by more demanding consumers and excessive business and marketing costs. Quality and customer service are essential for Canadian businesses to be competitive in today's international markets.

4. Relationship marketing has been made possible by breakthroughs in the technology of information often collected electronically in home, at business, through single-source data services, and in on-line and CD-ROM databases.

5. Managers generally make two kinds of decisions—structured and unstructured—and must balance the value with the cost of information.

6. Today's strategic information system used for relationship marketing has five key elements: input devices, databases, models, mainframe or minicomputer, and the personal computer on a manager's desk.

7. Two basic approaches to forecasting sales are the top-down and buildup methods. Three forecasting techniques are judgments of individuals, surveys of groups, and statistical methods.

8. Individual judgments are the most widely used forecasting methods. Two common examples are direct and lost-horse forecasts.

9. Asking questions of groups of people who are knowledgeable about likely future sales is another frequently used method of forecasting. Four such groups are prospective buyers, the sales force, executives, and experts.

10. Statistical forecasting methods, such as trend extrapolation, extend a pattern observed in past data into the future.

Key Terms and Concepts

relationship marketing p. 235
information technology p. 236
micromarketing p. 237
single-source data p. 243
sensitivity analysis p. 247
market potential p. 248
industry potential p. 248
sales forecast p. 248
company forecast p. 248
top-down approach p. 249

buildup approach p. 249
direct forecast p. 250
lost-horse forecast p. 250
survey of buyers' intentions forecast p. 251
sales force survey forecast p. 251
jury of executive opinion forecast p. 251
survey of experts forecast p. 251
Delphi forecast p. 251
technological forecast p. 251
trend extrapolation p. 251

Chapter Problems and Applications

1 The chapter described two ways of electronically collecting information on a household's purchases: a scanner at the retailer's sales counter, and an in-home scanner. How do these compare in terms of (*a*) quantity of a household's purchases measured and (*b*) possible bias reflected by consumers' knowing they are being measured?

2 You walk up to the supermarket checkout counter with six cartons of yogourt you want to buy. (*a*) Describe circumstances under which the checkout procedure with electronic scanner (*i*) will measure all six items and (*ii*) could miss the six items. (*b*) What problems do missing sales data cause for relationship marketing?

3 Compare the planned Nielsen passive people meter with the original people meter described in Chapter 8 in terms of (*a*) quality of information on TV viewing and (*b*) ability to get households to participate in the Nielsen TV panel.

4 Aim toothpaste runs an in-store experiment evaluating a coupon promotion along with (*a*) in-store ads in half the stores and (*b*) no in-store ads in the other half of the stores.[20] The results of the Aim experiment are as follows, where a sales index of 100 indicates average store sales in the weeks before the experiment.

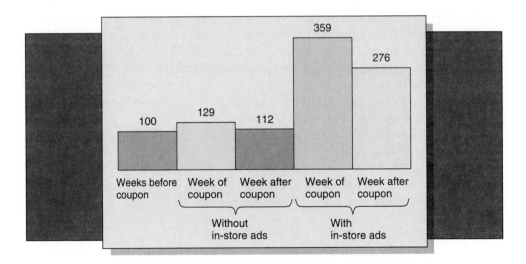

(*a*) What are your conclusions and recommendations? (*b*) How can marketers use experiments like this?

5 Another field experiment with coupons and in-store advertising is run for Wisk detergent. The index of sales is as follows:

	WEEKS BEFORE COUPON	WEEK OF COUPON	WEEK AFTER COUPON
Without in-store ads	100	144	108
With in-store ads	100	268	203

What are your conclusions and recommendations?

6 In designing an information system, the format in which information is presented to a harried marketing manager is often vital. (*a*) If you were a marketing manager and

interrogated your information system, would you rather see the results shown in question 4 or question 5? (*b*) What are one or two strengths and weaknesses of each format?

7 Suppose you are associate dean of your college's business school responsible for scheduling courses for the school year. (*a*) What repetitive information would you include in your information system to help schedule classes? (*b*) What special, one-time information might affect your schedule? (*c*) What standardized output reports do you have to provide? When?

8 Suppose you are to make a sales forecast using a top-down approach to estimate the percentage of a manufacturer's total Canadian sales going to each of the 10 provinces. You plan to use only a single factor—percentage of Canadian population, percentage of effective buying income, or percentage of retail sales. Which of the three factors would you use if your sales forecast were for each of the following manufacturers, and why? (*a*) Sifto salt, (*b*) Christian Dior dresses, and (*c*) Sony compact discs.

9 Which of the following variables would linear trend extrapolation be more accurate for? (*a*) Annual population of Canada or (*b*) annual sales of cars produced in Canada by General Motors. Why?

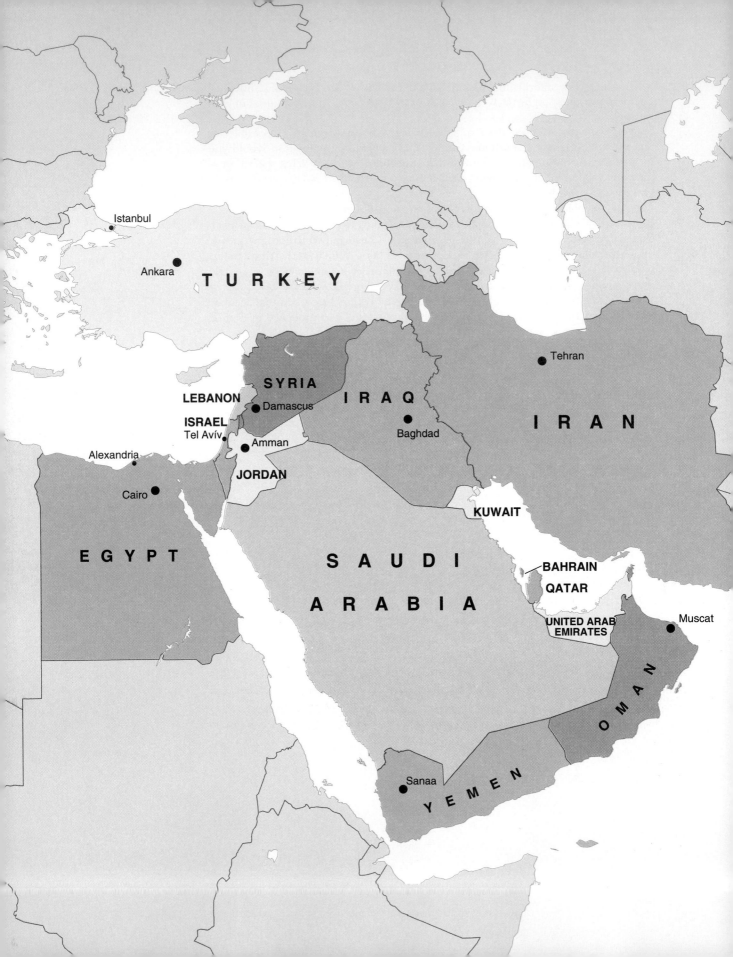

PART IV

Satisfying Marketing Opportunities

*P*art IV covers the unique combination of products, price, place, and promotion that results in an offering for potential customers. How products are developed and managed is the focus of Chapters 11 and 12. Pricing is covered in Chapters 13 and 14 and Appendix A. Chapters 15 through 17 address the place (distribution) element, which includes innovations such as BMW's Vehicle Preparation Centres (VPCs), as well as trends in retail shopping like videotex and teleshopping. Finally, Chapters 18, 19, and 20 cover topics on promotion ranging from the increased use of sales promotion and marketing public relations to global advertising and relationship selling. Overall, these chapters describe the multitude of options available to satisfy marketing opportunities and create customer value.

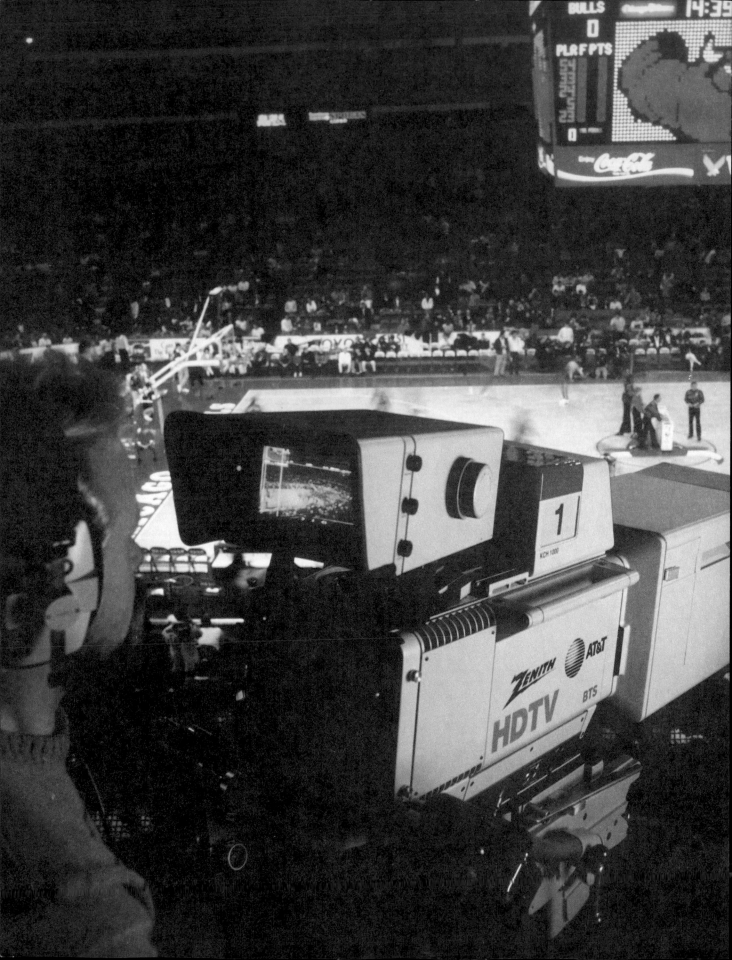

Developing New Products

AFTER READING THIS CHAPTER YOU SHOULD BE ABLE TO:

▸ Understand the ways in which consumer and industrial products can be classified.

▸ Recommend strategies for marketing the different types of consumer products.

▸ Explain the implications of alternative ways of viewing "newness" in new products.

▸ Recognize and understand the purposes of each step of the new product process.

▸ Analyze the factors contributing to a product's success or failure.

$3,500 for This TV! How Many Do You Want?

By 1996, you will probably have the chance to buy a new HDTV—high-definition television—set for $3,500.

But will you actually buy one? That's the question being asked by manufacturers like Zenith and Sony and the TV stations that must send new signals to make the HDTV sets work. And they're not sure about the answer to this multibillion-dollar, new product dice roll.

In case you haven't seen it yourself, most experts believe that HDTV is a knockout. It has richer colours and twice the clarity of your present TV and the sound quality of a compact disc.[1] But broadcast networks, cable systems, and TV stations will all have to make a heavy investment in order to send the HDTV signals. TV stations alone would each need to spend $12 million to $15 million in HDTV equipment.[2] But experts believe consumers will spend billions on HDTV sets in the 10 years following their introduction. (For some interesting facts about HDTV, see the accompanying Marketing Action Memo.)

With this kind of money in the new product sweepstakes, there is little wonder that HDTV is attracting global interest and competition. The HDTV search began in 1986 when Japanese researchers began work on a global standard for television signals. The Japanese invented analogue-technology HDTV signals, but companies in other countries have successfully developed digital HDTV systems. Companies are now competing to have their system named the HDTV standard.

The nagging question still remains: Will consumers pay $3,500 for a better TV? A key issue is whether TV viewing is declining in Canada because of the quality of the TV picture or because of the quality of the programs. The

M A R K E T I N G · A C T I O N · M E M O

The Facts about HDTV

*H*igh-definition television (HDTV) sets are likely to cost $1,000 to $2,000 more than the top-priced large-screen sets of today. Industry officials expect the first HDTV customers to be those "high-end" users. HDTV will provide a wide-angle window on the world with pictures nearly as sharp as real life and sound as precise as a compact disc recording. Ghost images prevalent in today's broadcast pictures will be gone. The scanning lines across the screen that create TV images will be invisible at normal viewing distance. HDTV will probably be phased in over 10 to 15 years, depending on how fast broadcast stations make the investment in the equipment to send HDTV signals and how strong consumer preference is for HDTV.

This means that someday in the 21st century, today's TV sets will be outmoded—unable to receive broadcasts. This will probably not occur until the price of HDTV sets is low enough to make the transition painless for the majority of consumers. New HDTV sets will probably not lead to a huge trash heap of old TV sets. Consumers who have made an investment in videotapes are likely to use those sets to play video games and video movies, unless, of course, they want to invest in an HDTV VCR. Some optimistic television executives hope to have HDTV on the air for the 1996 Summer Olympics. Certainly, the HDTV sets will be available at that time; the question remains whether an HDTV broadcast signal will.

Source: Adapted from "HDTV Coming of Age: How Will It Affect Us?," *Maine Sunday Telegram,* May 30, 1993, p. 7a.

---

question of *Will they buy?* is the ultimate test for any new good or service—from HDTV to your aunt's decision to open that new corner restaurant.

Developing products such as a new, technologically advanced HDTV to meet consumer needs captures the essence of marketing. A **product** is a good, a service, or an idea consisting of a bundle of tangible and intangible attributes that satisfies consumers and is received in exchange for money or some other unit of value. Tangible attributes include physical characteristics such as colour or sweetness, and intangible attributes include becoming healthier or wealthier. Hence, a product includes the breakfast cereal you eat, the accountant who fills out your tax return, or the Canadian Red Cross, which provides you self-satisfaction when you donate your blood. In many instances we exchange money to obtain the product, whereas in other instances we exchange our time and other valuables, such as our blood.

The life of a company often depends on how it conceives, produces, and markets new products. In this chapter we discuss the decisions involved in developing and marketing a new product. Chapter 12 covers the process of managing existing products.

THE VARIATIONS OF PRODUCTS

A product varies in terms of whether it is for consumer or industrial use. For most organizations the product decision is not made in isolation, because companies often offer a range of products. To better appreciate the product decision, let's first define some terms pertaining to products.

10/21

PRODUCT LINE AND PRODUCT MIX

A **product line** is a group of products that are closely related because they satisfy a class of needs, are used together, are sold to the same customer group, are distributed through the same type of outlets, or fall within a given price range.[3] Polaroid has two major product lines consisting of cameras and film; Adidas's product lines are shoes and clothing. Each product line has its own marketing strategy.

Within each product line is the *product item,* a specific product as noted by a unique brand, size, or price. For example, Downy softener for clothes comes in 300 mL and 600 mL sizes; each size is considered a separate item and assigned a distinct ordering code, or *stock-keeping unit (SKU).*

Another way to look at products is by the **product mix,** or the number of product lines offered by a company. Cray Research has a single product line consisting of supercomputers, which are sold mostly to governments and large businesses. Nabisco Brands of Canada, however, has many product lines, consisting of biscuits, cookies, chocolates, candy, cereals, wines, and pet foods, featuring such brands as Ritz and Dr. Ballards.

CLASSIFYING PRODUCTS

Both the federal government and companies classify products, but for different purposes. The government's classification method helps it collect information on industrial activity. Companies classify products to help develop similar marketing strategies for the wide range of products offered. Two major ways to classify products are by degree of product tangibility and type of user.

Degree of Tangibility   Classification by degree of tangibility divides products into one of three categories.[4] First is a *nondurable good,* an item consumed in one or a few uses, such as food products and fuel. A *durable good* is one that usually lasts over an extended number of uses, such as appliances, automobiles, and stereo equipment. *Services* are defined as activities, benefits, or satisfactions offered for sale, such as marketing research, health care, and education. As noted in Chapter 1, services are intangible. According to this classification, government data indicate that Canada is becoming a service economy.

This classification method also provides direction for marketing actions. Nondurable products such as Wrigley's gum are purchased frequently and at relatively low cost. Advertising is important to remind consumers of the item's existence, and wide distribution in retail outlets is essential. A consumer wanting Wrigley's spearmint gum would most likely purchase another brand of spearmint gum if Wrigley's were not available. Durable products, however, generally cost more than nondurable goods and last longer, so consumers usually deliberate longer before purchasing them. Therefore, personal selling is an important component in durable-product marketing because it assists in answering consumer questions and concerns.

Marketing is increasingly being used with services. Services are intangibles, so a major goal in marketing is to make the benefits of purchasing the service real to consumers. Thus, Air Canada shows the fun of a Florida vacation or the joy of seeing grandparents. People who provide the service are often the key to its success in the market because consumers often evaluate the product by the service provider they meet—the Hertz reservation clerk, the receptionist at the university admissions office, or the nurse in the doctor's office.

Type of User   The second major type of product classification is according to the user. **Consumer goods** are products purchased by the ultimate consumer, whereas **industrial goods** are products used in the production of other products for ultimate consumers. In many instances the differences are distinct: Oil of Olay face moisturizer and Bass shoes are clearly consumer products, whereas DEC computers and high-tension steel springs are industrial goods used in producing other products or services.

There are difficulties, however, with this classification because some products can be considered both consumer and industrial items. A Macintosh computer can be sold to consumers as a final product or to industrial firms for office use. Each classification results in different marketing actions. Viewed as a consumer product, the Macintosh would be sold through computer stores. As an industrial product, the Macintosh might be sold by a salesperson offering discounts for multiple purchases. Classifying by the type of user focusses on the market and the user's purchase behaviour, which determine the marketing mix strategy.

CLASSIFYING CONSUMER AND INDUSTRIAL GOODS

Because the buyer is the key to marketing, consumer and industrial product classifications will be broken down further for discussion.

CLASSIFICATION OF CONSUMER GOODS

Convenience, shopping, specialty, and unsought goods are the four types of consumer goods. They differ in terms of effort the consumer spends on the decision, attributes considered in purchase, and frequency of purchase.

Convenience goods are items the consumer purchases frequently, conveniently, and with a minimum of shopping effort. **Shopping goods** are items for which the consumer compares several alternatives on criteria such as price, quality, or style. **Specialty goods** are items, such as Tiffany crystal, that a consumer makes a special effort to search out and buy. **Unsought goods** are items that the consumer either does not know about or knows about but does not initially want. Figure 11–1 shows how the classification of a consumer product into one of these four types results in a stress on different aspects of the marketing mix. Different degrees of brand loyalty and amounts of shopping effort are displayed by the consumer for a product in each of the four classes.

The manner in which a consumer good is classified depends on the individual. One person may view a camera as a shopping good and visit several stores before deciding on a brand, whereas a friend may view cameras as a specialty good and will only buy a Nikon.

The product classification of a consumer good can change and is more likely to do so the longer the product is on the market. When first introduced, the Litton microwave oven was unique, a specialty good. Now there are competing brands on the market, and microwaves are a shopping good for many consumers

BASIS OF COMPARISON	TYPE OF CONSUMER GOOD			
	CONVENIENCE	SHOPPING	SPECIALTY	UNSOUGHT
Product	Toothpaste, cake mix, hand soap, laundry detergent	Cameras, TVs, briefcases, clothing	Rolls-Royce cars, Rolex watches	Burial insurance, thesaurus
Price	Relatively inexpensive	Fairly expensive	Usually very expensive	Varies
Place (distribution)	Widespread; many outlets	Large number of selective outlets	Very limited	Often limited
Promotion	Price, availability, and awareness stressed	Differentiation from competitors stressed	Uniqueness of brand and status stressed	Awareness is essential
Brand loyalty of consumers	Aware of brand, but will accept substitutes	Prefer specific brands, but will accept substitutes	Very brand-loyal; will not accept substitutes	Will accept substitutes
Purchase behaviour of consumers	Frequent purchases; little time and effort spent shopping; routine decision	Infrequent purchases; comparison shopping, use decision time	Infrequent purchases; extensive time spent to decide and get the item	Very infrequent purchases, some comparison shopping

■ *Figure 11–1*
Classification of consumer goods.

CLASSIFICATION OF INDUSTRIAL GOODS

A major characteristic of industrial goods is that their sales are often the result of *derived demand;* that is, sales of industrial products frequently result (or are derived) from the sale of consumer goods. For example, if consumer demand for Ford cars (a consumer product) increases, the company may increase its demand for paint-spraying equipment (an industrial product). Industrial goods are classified not only on the attributes the consumer uses, but also on how the item is to be used. Thus, industrial products may be classified as production or support goods.

Production Goods   Items used in the manufacturing process that become part of the final product are **production goods.** These include raw materials such as grain or lumber, as well as component parts. For example, a company that manufactures door hinges used by GM in its car doors is producing a component part. As noted in Chapter 7, the marketing of production goods is based on factors such as price, quality, delivery, and service. Marketers of these products tend to sell directly to industrial users.

Support Goods   The second class of industrial goods is **support goods,** which are items used to assist in producing other goods and services. Support goods include installations, accessory equipment, supplies, and services.

The Tiffany brand of crystal is an example of a specialty good.

TIFFANY & CO.

- *Installations* consist of buildings and fixed equipment. Because a significant amount of capital is required to purchase installations, the industrial buyer deals directly with construction companies and manufacturers through sales representatives. The pricing of installations is often by competitive bidding.
- *Accessory equipment* includes tools and office equipment and is usually purchased in small-order sizes by buyers. As a result, instead of dealing directly with buyers, sellers of industrial accessories use distributors to contact a large number of buyers.
- *Supplies* are similar to consumer convenience goods and consist of products such as stationery, paper clips, and brooms. These are purchased with little effort, using the straight rebuy decision sequence discussed in Chapter 7. Price and delivery are key factors considered by the buyers of supplies.
- *Services* are intangible activities to assist the industrial buyer. This category can include maintenance and repair services and advisory services such as tax or legal counsel. The reputation of the seller is a major factor in marketing industrial services.

Concept Check

1 Explain the difference between product mix and product line.

2 To which type of good (industrial or consumer) does the term *derived demand* generally apply?

3 A limited problem-solving approach is common to which type of consumer good?

10/21

NEW PRODUCTS AND WHY THEY FAIL

New products are the lifeblood of a company and keep it growing, but the financial risks are large. Before discussing how new products reach the stage of commercialization, at which they are available to the consumer, we'll begin by looking at *what* a new product is.

WHAT IS A NEW PRODUCT? *(4)*

The term *new* is difficult to define. Does changing the colour of a laundry detergent mean it is a new product, as a new hot-air appliance that cooks like a regular oven but with the speed of a microwave would be considered new? There are several ways to view the newness of a product.

Newness Compared with Existing Products   If a product is functionally different from existing offerings, it can be defined as new. The microwave oven and the automobile were once functionally new, but in today's world innovation usually consists of modification of an old product rather than a dramatic functional change.

New in Legal Terms   Consumer and Corporate Affairs Canada (CCAC) has determined that a product can be called "new" only for a limited time. Currently CCAC has indicated that 12 months is the longest period of time a product can be called new.

Newness from the Company Perspective   Successful companies are starting to view newness and innovation in their products at three levels.[5] At the lowest level, which usually involves the least risk, is product line extension. This is an incremental improvement of an exciting or important product for the company, such as Honey Nut Cheerios or Gillette Sensor for women—extensions of the basic Cheerios or men's Sensor product line, respectively. At the next level is a significant new step in the innovation or technology, such as Sony's leap from the micro tape recorder to the Walkman. The third level is true innovation, a truly revolutionary new product, like the first Apple computer in 1976. Some people wonder whether Sony's Data Discman—a portable electronic book using a removable disk, which may lead to novels, textbooks, and encyclopedias on disks—could be such an innovation.[6] Effective new product programs in large firms deal at all three levels.

Newness from the Consumer's Perspective   A fourth way to define new products is in terms of their effects on consumption. This approach classifies new products according to the degree of learning required by the consumer, as shown in Figure 11–2.

With *continuous innovation,* no new behaviour must be learned. Such products require minimal consumer education. Toothpaste in stand-up tubes, ice beer, and the latest game of Nintendo are examples of continuous innovation. Effective marketing of these products depends on generating awareness and having strong distribution in appropriate outlets.

Sony's Data Discman: a revolutionary new product that may replace some books.

	LOW DEGREE OF CHANGE IN BEHAVIOUR AND LEARNING NEEDED BY CONSUMER HIGH		
BASIS OF COMPARISON	**CONTINUOUS INNOVATION**	**DYNAMICALLY CONTINUOUS INNOVATION**	**DISCONTINUOUS INNOVATION**
Definition	Requires no new learning by consumers	Disrupts consumer's normal routine but does not require totally new learning	Establishes new consumption patterns among consumers
Examples	Sensor and New Improved Tide	Electric toothbrush, compact disc player, and automatic flash units for cameras	VCR, microwave oven, and home computer
Marketing emphasis	Generate awareness among consumers and obtain widespread distribution	Advertise benefits to consumers, stressing point of differentiation and consumer advantage	Educate consumers through product trial and personal selling

▌ *Figure 11–2*
Consumption effects define newness.

Microwave cooking: a discontinuous innovation that has revolutionized some consumption patterns.

With *dynamically continuous innovation,* only minor changes in behaviour are required for use. For years, Ron Zarowitz pushed Chrysler to accept the idea of built-in, fold-down child seats in their cars. At the end of six years, the seats appeared as a $200 option in the 1992 Chrysler minivans. Chrysler then started selling them as fast as it could make them.[7] Built-in car seats for children require minor amounts of education and changes in behaviour and so the marketing strategy is to educate prospective buyers about their benefits and advantages.

Discontinuous innovation requires the consumer to learn entirely new consumption patterns in order to use the product. This would be seen in such products as the first television set, personal computer, or microwave oven. Hence, marketing efforts involve not only gaining consumer awareness but also educating consumers on both the benefits and proper use of the innovative product. Personal selling and creative promotion are often needed for discontinuous innovations. Few new products are discontinuous innovations; most are continuous innovations.[8]

WHY PRODUCTS FAIL

Thousands of product failures that occur every year cost Canadian businesses millions of dollars. Some estimates place new product failure rates as high as 80 percent. To learn marketing lessons from these failures, we can analyze why new products fail and then study several failures in detail. As we go through the new product process later in the chapter, we can identify ways such failures might have been avoided—admitting that hindsight is clearer than foresight.

Reasons for New Product Failures   Many factors contribute to new product failures or are symptoms of them: incompatibility with the firm's objectives and capabilities, competition that is too tough, lack of top management support, and lack of money. However, six factors, often present in combination, are far more fundamental:

Read this page find an example

1 *Too small a target market.* The market is too small to warrant the R&D, production, and marketing expenses to reach it. In the early 1990s Kodak discontinued its Ultralife lithium battery. Seen as a major breakthrough because of its 10-year shelf life, the battery was touted as lasting twice as long as an alkaline battery. Yet the product was available only in the 9-volt size, which accounts for less than 10 percent of the batteries sold.[9]

2 *Insignificant point of difference.* Computerized home-banking services have been a technology promoted as the new way to bank, yet consumers see little benefit or need to go home after work and juggle their money between accounts. While the monthly costs of the services have been as low as $10 to $12, consumers have not seen the value.[10]

3 *Poor product quality.* R. J. Reynolds developed the smokeless cigarette at an estimated cost of almost $1 billion. But after five months of test marketing, the product was killed. The reason was best stated by one employee of a 7-Eleven store: "They're terrible. They're nasty. They're beyond nasty."[11]

4 *No access to market.* Manufacturers of potentially better products sometimes can't make prospective buyers aware of them or gain retail shelf space. Dozens of useful computer software programs can't get the attention of prospective buyers or space in computer stores.

5 *Bad timing.* A product is sometimes introduced too soon, too late, or at a time when consumer tastes are shifting dramatically. Campbell Soup thought it had a great idea with its Souper-Combo frozen line: take its soup, add a sandwich, and make them microwavable for busy parents. Launched in 1989, the line was pulled off the market in 1991 because Campbell failed to see the new trend toward healthier food.[12]

6 *Poor execution of the marketing mix.* Coca-Cola thought its Minute Maid Squeeze-Fresh frozen orange juice concentrate in a squeeze bottle was a hit. The idea was that consumers could make one glass of juice at a time and the concentrate would stay fresh in the refrigerator for over a month. After two test markets, the product was finished. Consumers loved the idea, but the product was messy to use, and consumers didn't know how much concentrate to mix.[13]

A Look at Some Failures   Before reading further, study the product failures described in Figure 11-3 and try to identify which of the six reasons is the most likely explanation for their failure. The two examples will be discussed in greater detail.

Del Monte aimed its Barbecue Ketchup at the heavy ketchup-using segment—children and teenagers. The problem is that most consumers in this segment hate onions, so the product's difference—onions mixed with regular ketchup—worked against it. As a result, the target market was too small. The product was subsequently reintroduced as a gourmet sauce for meat cooked on outdoor grills.

Poor execution of the marketing mix hurt Real, Mennen's deodorant. The product was introduced with a $14 million advertising campaign. One problem, though, was that customers found that if they twisted the dispenser too hard, too much cream came out, creating an instant mess. Also, the name

▌*Figure 11–3*
Why did these new products fail?

As explained in detail in the text, new products often fail because of one or a combination of six reasons. Look at the two products described below, and try to identify which reason explains why they failed in the marketplace:

- Del Monte's Barbecue Ketchup, which contained finely chopped onions and was aimed at the heavy ketchup-eating segment.
- Mennen's Real deodorant, a creamlike antiperspirant developed for women that was applied like a roll-on.

Compare your insights with those in the text.

Real gave little indication of the product or its benefits. Where is Real today? It's not completely dead, because it may reappear in an improved version with a new name.[14]

As shown in the accompanying Marketing Action Memo, often a combination of factors separates successful from unsuccessful products. The greatest differences between those products that succeed and those that don't are in *having a real product advantage* and *having a precise protocol*—a statement that identifies a well-defined target market before product development begins; specifies customers' needs, wants, and preferences; and carefully states what the product will be and do. Figure 11–4 shows that many of the factors that are necessary for success involve marketing activities that occur before the product—or hardware—actually undergoes production.[15]

Developing successful new products may sometimes involve luck, but more often it involves having a product that really meets a need and has significant points of difference over competitive products. The likelihood of success is improved by paying attention to the early steps of the new product process described in the next section of the text.

MARKETING · ACTION · MEMO

Winner or Loser: Is New Product Success Just Luck?

What makes some products winners and others losers? Knowing this answer is a key to a new product strategy. Two Canadian professors, R. G. Cooper and E. J. Kleinschmidt, studied 203 new products—winners and losers in the marketplace—to find the answer. Having reviewed previous research in this area, the researchers identified 10 factors reported to lead to success.

To determine whether these factors really differed between winners and losers, they conducted personal interviews with the managers most knowledgeable about 203 products in 125 firms. Figure 11–4 shows the managers' answers about where winners and losers differ. Study the figure. For the conclusions the researchers reached from this information, see the text.

Source: R. G. Cooper and E. J. Kleinschmidt, "New Products—What Separates Winners from Losers?" *Journal of Product Innovation Management,* September 1987, pp. 169–84. Copyright © 1987 by Elsevier Science Publishing Co., Inc.

FACTORS	DIFFERENCE (success-failure)	IMPORTANCE OF DIFFERENCE	MEAN VALUES ON SCALE FROM 0 TO 10		
Existence and quality of "protocol"	2.68	Very important	Failure 5.44 / Success 8.12		
Product advantage	2.32	Very important	F 4.93 / S 7.25		
Effectiveness of pre-hardware activities	1.67	Important	F 3.13 / S 4.80		
Effectiveness of technological activities in new product process	1.51	Important	F 4.06 / S 5.57		
Synergy with firm's marketing strengths	1.30	Important	F 5.00 / S 6.30		
Synergy with firm's technology strengths	1.29	Important	F 5.86 / S 7.15		
Effectiveness of marketing activities in new product process	1.12	Important	F 2.53 / S 3.65		
Top management support	0.92	Important	F 5.37 / S 6.29		
Market potential	0.91	Important	F 5.61 / S 6.52		
Market competitiveness	−0.24	Not important	F 6.44 / S 6.20		

0   2   4   6   8   10
Very unimportant   Very important

1 From a consumer's viewpoint, what kind of innovation would an improved electric toothbrush be? *dynamically continuous ~~favor~~ innovation*

2 What does "insignificant point of difference" mean as a reason for new product failure?

end

(omitted. the rest of the chapter)

THE NEW PRODUCT PROCESS

Most companies, including General Electric, Sony, or Procter & Gamble take a sequence of steps before their products are ready for market. Figure 11–5 shows the seven stages of the **new product process,** the sequence of activities a firm uses to identify business opportunities and convert them to a salable good or service. This sequence begins with new product strategy development and ends with commercialization.[16]

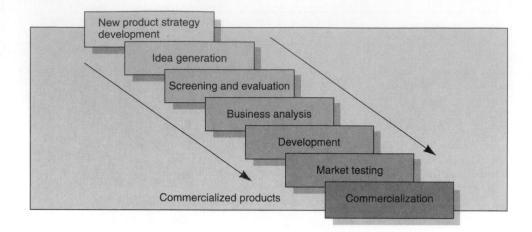

NEW PRODUCT STRATEGY DEVELOPMENT

For companies, **new product strategy development** involves defining the role for a new product in terms of the firm's overall corporate objectives. This step in the new product process has been added by many companies recently to provide a needed focus for ideas and concepts developed in later stages. 3M, for example, has a corporate objective that a quarter of the division's sales must come from products introduced within the past five years.[17]

Objectives: Identify Markets and Strategic Rules   During this step the company uses the environmental scanning process described in Chapter 3 to identify trends that pose either opportunities or threats. Relevant company strengths and weaknesses are also identified. The outcome of new product strategy development is not new product ideas, but markets for which new products will be developed and strategic roles new products might serve—the vital protocol activity shown in Figure 11–4 in connection with the discussion in the Marketing Action Memo on new product winners and losers.

Proactive and Reactive New Product Strategies   New product strategies can generally be classified as either proactive or reactive. Proactive strategies lead to an allocation of resources to identify and seize opportunities. These approaches include future-oriented R&D, consumer research, entrepreneurial development, or acquisition. In a proactive approach to developing new products, many companies scan the international marketplace, and even other industry sectors, to uncover opportunities. Both Molson and Labatt's developed their dry beer on the basis of a new product concept pioneered by leading Japanese brewers. Timex Canada looked to another industry sector for its most recent innovation, the night-light technology in its new IndiGlo watches. Timex discovered the technology, called *electroluminescence,* being widely used to light car and aircraft dashboards. It took Timex 10 years to adapt the technology for the IndiGlo watch, but it believes it now has the first marketable technical breakthrough in the watch industry in the past 15 years. Timex suggests this innovation gives it a marketing edge for about two years before the competition catches up.[18]

Labatt's new Ice Beer.

Reactive strategies involve defensive actions taken in response to a competitor's actions. Many companies often attempt to mirror each other's new products, as in the controversial new beer brand battle between Labatt's Ice Beer and Molson Canadian Ice.[19] A similar situation occurred in the Canadian tea market. Thomas J. Lipton, Toronto, launched its freeze-dried Red Rose instant tea in English Canada and its Salada instant tea in Quebec, where Salada is Lipton's top-selling brand. Tetley responded in kind by marketing its new instant tea. Other firms might take a leapfrog approach. For example, Minolta developed the first autofocus camera, but Canon has extended the technology to improve on Minolta's original product.

Booz, Allen & Hamilton, Inc., an international consulting firm, asked firms what strategic role was served by their most successful recent product. These roles, shown in Figure 11–6, help define the direction of new product development and divide into externally and internally driven factors, which lead to proactive and reactive strategies as just described. For example, Timex developed its IndiGlo watches to help it maintain its one-third share of Canada's maturing watch market, in what would be considered an externally driven move (to defend market share) according to Figure 11–6.[20]

IDEA GENERATION

The development of a pool of concepts for new products, or **idea generation,** must proceed from the results of the previous stages of the new product process. New product ideas are generated by consumers, employees, basic R&D, and competitors.

Customer Suggestions Procter & Gamble surveyed Japanese parents and found that they changed their babies' diapers far more frequently than Canadian or American parents. In response to this market difference, P&G developed

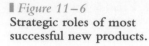

■ *Figure 11–6*
Strategic roles of most
successful new products.

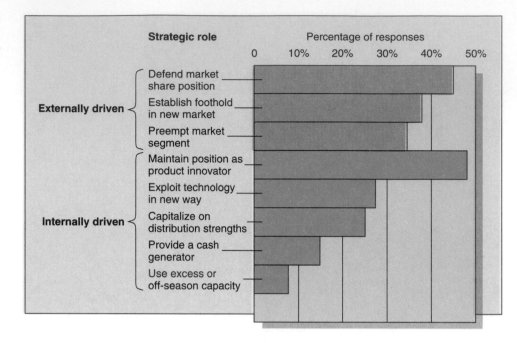

Ultra Pampers, a more absorbent diaper that makes frequent changing less necessary. Today, Ultra Pampers is the market leader in Japan.[21]

Companies often analyze consumer complaints, concerns, or problems to discover new product opportunities. They also pose complaints or concerns to a sample of consumers, who are asked to suggest ways to improve existing products. Bausch & Lomb developed the first alcohol-free mouthwash, Clear Choice, as a result of this kind of research.

Bausch & Lomb, better known for its eye care products, surveyed more than 3,000 consumers to find that the majority didn't realize conventional mouthwash contained up to 21.9 percent alcohol. After making them aware of this fact, Bausch & Lomb asked consumers whether or not it was a concern and if they would be interested in an alcohol-free mouthwash. Many consumers were indeed concerned and did express an interest in an alcohol-free mouthwash product. Clear Choice was developed using purified water-soluble ingredients to perform alcohol's function of binding ingredients. Clear Choice is now vying for a share of Canada's $70 million mouthwash market.[22]

Employee and Co-Worker Suggestions   Employees may be encouraged to suggest new product ideas through suggestion boxes or contests. The idea for General Mills' $250 million-a-year Nature Valley granola bars came when one of its marketing managers observed co-workers bringing granola to work in plastic bags.

Paul Breedlove, a Texas instruments (TI) engineer, discussed with some co-workers an idea for a hand-held calculator that could talk. They just laughed, so he did some work on the idea and eventually sold them on it. The company still refused to fund the idea because it was "too wild," but Breedlove and his believing co-workers got $25,000 from a special fund TI uses to finance

Ultra Pampers: Understanding the needs of Japanese consumers led to a new product success.

long shots. Breedlove's concept came to market as Speak & Spell, a microprocessor that helps children learn to spell. Its success spawned a family of new products such as Speak & Math and Speak & Read, largely because of the commitment by TI to generate a pool of alternative new product ideas.

3M, a leader in product innovation, has a 15 percent rule that allows anyone in the company to spend up to 15 percent of the workweek on anything he wants to. In addition, the company has developed grants of up to $50,000 to carry a concept past the idea stage. This approach allowed one employee,

A family of new products that were thought to be "too wild."

MARKETING · ACTION · MEMO

And in This Corner, the Electronics New Product Champion of the Planet—Sony!

*I*t introduces a barrage of 1,000 new products a year—an average of four each business day. It popularized pocket-sized transistor radios, battery-powered TVs, VCRs, camcorders, compact disc players, and—of course—the Walkman! Its engineers are generally acknowledged to be the most innovative and prolific on planet Earth. It is Sony!

How did Sony reach these heights? Sony founder Masaru Ibuka, who dreamed up most of the Sony products cited above, is revered in Japan. His observation: "The key to success for Sony, and to everything in business science, and technology for that matter, is never to follow the others." He also says, "In Japan we set a clear size and ease-of-use target for a consumer or business product from the very beginning . . . often before we have the technology to achieve it. Current Sony Chairman Akio Morita puts it another way: "Our basic concept has always been this—to give new convenience, or new methods, or new benefits, to the general public with our technology." And he says that while many other firms struggle to create a vision for the coming quarter, Japanese companies have a vision for the coming decade.

Here are some of Sony's recent products:

- *Data Discman.* An electronic book that can hold 100,000 typewritten pages of text and simple graphics stored on a removable disk.
- *Palmtop.* An electronic diary that stores information written on the screen with a special stylus.
- *Mini Disc.* A smaller version of a portable CD player that can both record music and play it back—and keep playing when jarred.

As consumer electronics, computers, entertainment, and telecommunications all go into digital formats, Sony believes it is well poised to compete in the new "digital industry." Sony and many Japanese firms have found ways to create cultures that foster new product innovation. Commenting on these innovation practices, consultant James Swallow observed that Japanese firms "plan like demons, execute brilliantly, and yet are constantly asking how they can do better."

Sources: Adapted from B. R. Schlender, "How Sony Keeps the Magic Going," *Fortune,* February 24, 1992, pp. 76–84; B. Dumaine, "Closing the Innovation Gap," *Fortune,* December 2, 1991, pp. 56–62; and K. Rebello, "Your Digital Future," *Business Week,* September 7, 1992, pp. 56–64.

Sanford Cobb, to develop a lighting technology with a potential for millions of dollars in sales.[23]

Research and Development Breakthroughs   Another source of new products is a firm's basic research, but the costs can be huge. As described in the accompanying Marketing Action Memo, Sony is the acknowledged world leader in new product development in electronics. Its scientists and engineers produce an average of four new products each business day. Sony's research and development breakthroughs have led to innovative products, and its ability to manufacture and market those products has made it a legend in the electronics industry, popularizing VCRs, the Walkman, and—coming into your future?— the Data Discman. Sony believes in cross-fertilization among its departments: its policy of "self-promotion" encourages engineers to seek out interesting projects throughout Sony. If the engineer finds one, she leaves with the boss's blessing. Consultants studying the new product and innovation process say firms need a dual approach to get the most from their R&D: create cultures where new ideas can thrive and have systems that will sift those ideas through the development process and get them to market with lightning speed. Sony seems to have done this for four decades.[24]

Competitive Products   New product ideas can also be found by analyzing the competition. A six-person intelligence team from the Marriott Corporation spent six months travelling around the country staying at economy hotels. The team assessed the competition's strengths and weaknesses on everything from the soundproof qualities of the rooms to the softness of the towels. Marriott then budgeted $500 million for a new economy hotel chain, Fairfield Inns.[25]

SCREENING AND EVALUATION

The third stage of the new product process is **screening and evaluation,** which involves internal and external evaluations of the new product ideas to eliminate those that warrant no further effort.

Internal Approach   Internally, the firm evaluates the technical feasibility of the proposal and whether the idea meets the new product strategy objectives defined in step 1. In 1957 Earl Bakken, founder of Medtronic, built the first external portable heart pacemaker. Working with a team of scientists, Medtronic later built the first implantable pacemaker—a device enabling bedridden people suffering from heart problems to regain their normal, productive lives.

   For internal screening and evaluation in its search for new products, Medtronic has developed the *weighted point system* shown in Figure 11–7, which establishes screening criteria and assigns weights to each one used to evaluate new product ideas. The figure gives a hypothetical evaluation for a new medical device. The 17 specific factors in the figure are grouped into five of the categories cited earlier for new product failures. (The sixth category, poor execution of the marketing mix, enters the new product process later.) Medtronic believes that a score of at least 120 is needed on the "hurdle" in the point system to find a winning new product. Note that in developing state-of-the-art products, technological factors as well as marketing ones carry important weights in the screening criteria.

External Approach   Concept tests are external evaluations that consist of preliminary testing of the new product idea (rather than the actual product) with consumers. Concept tests usually rely on written descriptions of the product but may be augmented with sketches, mock-ups, or promotional literature. Several key questions are asked during concept testing: How does the customer perceive the product? Who would use it? How would it be used?

   Frito-Lay spent a year interviewing 10,000 consumers about the concept of a multigrain snack chip. The company experimented with 50 different shapes before settling on a thin, rectangular chip with ridges and a slightly salty, nutty flavor. The product, called Sun Chips, appeared on the market in 1991.[26]

A year's worth of consumer interviews went into the development of Sun Chips.

GENERAL FACTOR	SPECIFIC FACTOR	SCALE	TOTAL POINTS
Size of target market	Incidence of malady	Undefinable 10,000s 1,000,000s 100,000,000s 0 — 5 — 10 ✓ 15 — 20	12
	Product usage	One per many patients — One per patient 0 — ✓ 5	5
	Cost effective for health care system	No — Yes 0 — 5 ✓ 10	7
	Application of product	Other Spine Brain Brain/Heart Heart 0 ✓ 5 — 10 — 15 — 20	3
Significant point of difference	Treatment evaluation	Similar to existing approaches — Better than existing approaches — Clearly superior to existing approaches 0 — 5 — ✓ 10	10
	Clearness of function	Questioned or uncertain — Direct cause and effect 0 — 5 — ✓ 10	8
Product quality	Restore natural physiology	Partial Total 0 — 5 ✓ 10 — 15 — 20	6
	Restore viability	Partial Full 0 — 5 — 10 — ✓ 15 — 20	13
	Characteristic of product	Capital equipment → External Permanently worn → Implantable Totally implanted 0 — 5 — 10 — 15 — ✓ 20	20
	Mode of operation	Chemical Mechanical Electrical mechanical Electrical 0 — 5 ✓ 10 — 15 — 20	7
	Product development team	Physician only — Engineer only Physician and engineer Physician with engineering training 0 — 5 ✓ 10	6
Access to market	Physician users know Medtronic name?	No — Some (50%) — Yes (all) 0 — 5 — ✓ 10	10
	Inventor's ability, willingness to be champion	Not well known Not willing to promote — Well known Willing to promote 0 — ✓ 5 — 10 — 15 — 20	8
Timing	Technologies in place	No — Partially — Yes 0 — 5 ✓ 10	6
	Entrepreneur in place	No — Partially — Yes 0 — ✓ 5 — 10	4
	Social acceptance	Negative — Positive 0 — 5 — ✓ 10	8
Miscellaneous	Gut feel about success	Uncertain Good chance Positive Highly positive 0 — 5 — ✓ 10 — 15 — 20	12
Total			145

Source: E. Bakken and Medtronic, Inc.

▍*Figure 11–7*
A weighted point system Medtronic uses to try to spot a winning new medical product.

1 What step in the new product process has been added in recent years?

2 What are four sources of new product ideas?

3 What is a weighted point system, as used internally by a firm in the new product process?

BUSINESS ANALYSIS

Business analysis involves specifying the features of the product and the marketing strategy needed to commercialize it and making necessary financial projections. This is the last checkpoint before significant capital is invested in creating a prototype of the product. Economic analysis, marketing strategy review, and legal examination of the proposed product are conducted at this stage. It is at this point that the product is analyzed relative to its existing synergies with the firm's marketing and technological strengths, two criteria noted in Figure 11–4.

The marketing strategy review studies the new product idea in relation to the marketing program to support it. The proposed product is assessed to determine whether it will help or hurt sales of existing products. Likewise, the product is examined to assess whether it can be sold through existing channels or if new outlets will be needed.

After the product's important features are defined, economic considerations focus on several issues, starting with costs of R&D, production, and marketing. For financial projections, the firm must also forecast the possible revenues from future product sales and forecast market shares. Airwick's new product criteria require a product to be both a specialty and a noncommodity household item. The company also wants a new idea to have potential revenues of $30 million to $100 million annually. Investments are expected to be recouped within two years. These requirements have led the company to discard ideas like plant care items, toilet bowl cleaners, and a fire extinguisher—all in the business analysis stage.[27] In this stage the firm also estimates how many units of the product must be sold to cover the costs of production and projects a return on investment to determine the profitability.

As an important aspect of the business analysis, the proposed new product is studied to determine whether it can be protected with a patent. An attractive new product proposal is one in which the technology can be patented or not easily copied.

DEVELOPMENT

Product ideas that survive the business analysis proceed to actual **development,** turning the idea on paper into a prototype. This results in a demonstrable, producible product in hand. Outsiders seldom understand the technical complexities of the development stage, which involves not only manufacturing the product but also performing laboratory and consumer tests to ensure that it meets the standards set. Design of the product becomes an important element.

Liquid Tide, introduced by P&G, looks like a simple modification of its original Tide detergent. However, P&G sees this product as a technological breakthrough: the first detergent without phosphates that cleans as well as existing phosphate detergents.

To achieve this breakthrough, P&G spent 400,000 hours and combined technologies from its laboratories in three countries. The new ingredient in Liquid Tide that helps suspend the dirt in wash water came out of the P&G research lab in Cincinnati. The cleaning agents in the product came from P&G scientists in Japan. Cleaning agent technology is especially advanced in Japan because consumers there wash clothes in colder water (about 70° F) than consumers in Canada (95° F) and Europe (160° F). P&G scientists thought that Liquid Tide also needed water-softening ingredients to make the cleaning agents work better. For this technology it turned to P&G's lab in Belgium, whose experience was based on European water, which has more than twice the mineral content of Canadian wash water.[28]

The prototype product is tested in the laboratory to see if it achieves the physical standards set for it. Prototypes of disposable consumer goods are also subjected to consumer tests, often in-home placements of a product to see if consumers actually perceive it as a better product after they use it. In a blind test, consumers preferred Liquid Tide nine to one over the detergent of their own choice tested in their washers. Often prototypes undergo rigorous field tests. In developing its Air 180 athletic shoe, Nike had runners test the product. They were asked to run a minimum of 75 km a week and tell how the shoes held up.[29]

MARKET TESTING

In the **market testing** stage of the new product process, prospective consumers are exposed to new products under realistic or simulated purchase conditions to see if they will buy. Often a product is developed, tested, refined, and then tested again to get consumer reactions. The testing may be carried out through either test marketing or purchase laboratories.

Test Marketing　Test marketing involves offering a product for sale on a limited basis in a defined area. This test is done to determine whether consumers will actually buy the product and to try different ways of marketing it. Only about a third of the products test-marketed do well enough to go on to the next phase of the new product process. Market tests are usually conducted in cities that are considered representative of Canadian consumers. *Standard markets* are those test sites where companies sell a new product through normal distribution channels and monitor the results. *Selected controlled markets,* sometimes referred to as *forced-distribution markets,* are those in which the total test is conducted by an outside agency. An outside testing service conducts the test by paying retailers for shelf space, thus guaranteeing distribution in the most popular test markets.

In examining the commercial viability of a new product, companies measure sales in the test area, often with store audits that measure the sales in grocery stores and the number of cases ordered by a store from a wholesaler. This gives the company an indication of potential sales volume and market share in the test area. Although test markets have not been able to predict exact future sales or share, they do help a company by giving an idea of relative product performance and the likelihood of having a loser or a winner.

Market tests are also used to check other elements of the marketing mix besides the product itself, such as price, level of promotional support, and distribution. In industrial or business marketing, tests are often used to gain a record of product performance. This experience can then be used as part of the sales presentation when a product is offered elsewhere.

There are difficulties with test marketing, a primary one being how well the results can be projected. The degree to which the test market is representative of the target market for the product is very important. Market tests are also time-consuming and expensive, because production lines as well as promotion and sales programs must be set up. Costs can run over a million dollars, the exact amount depending on the size of the city and the cost of buying media time or space to advertise the product.

Market tests also reveal plans to competitors, sometimes enabling them to get a product into national distribution first or to take actions to disrupt the test markets. When a product can be easily copied by a competitor, test marketing may not be used. Although Hunt-Wesson got its Prima Salsa tomato sauce into the test market first, Chesebrough-Pond's Ragú Extra Thick & Zesty beat it into national introduction. Competitors can also try to sabotage test markets. Pepsi ran Mountain Dew Sports Drink in a test market and Gatorade counterattacked furiously with ads and coupons. Pepsi pulled the product off the market. With such problems, some firms skip test markets completely or use simulated test markets.

Simulated Test Markets   Because of the time, cost, and confidentiality problems of test markets, manufacturers often turn to *simulated* (or *laboratory*) *test markets (STM)*, a technique that simulates a full-scale test market but in a limited fashion. STMs are often run in shopping malls, where consumers are questioned to identify who uses the product class being tested. Willing participants are questioned on usage, reasons for purchase, and important product attributes. Qualified persons are then shown TV commercials or print ads for the test product along with competitors' advertising, and are given money to make a decision to buy or not to buy a package of the product (or the competitors') from a real or simulated store environment. If the test product is not purchased, the consumer may receive it as a free sample. Participants are interviewed later for their reactions and the likelihood of repurchase. On the basis of these reactions, the company may decide to proceed to the last stage of the new product process.[30]

Market testing is a valuable step in the new product process, but not all products can use it. Testing a service beyond the concept level is very difficult because services are intangible and consumers can't see what they are buying. Similarly, market testing of expensive consumer products such as cars or VCRs or costly industrial products like jet engines or computers is impractical.

COMMERCIALIZATION

Finally, the product is brought to the point of **commercialization**—positioning and launching it in full-scale production and sales. Because of the many steps required for developing a new product, bringing a new concept to this stage involves many delays and significant expense. The cost of commercialization has increased for many consumer product companies as retailers have begun to require special payments. Because space is limited in many stores, particularly supermarkets, many retailers require manufacturers to pay a **slotting fee,** a payment a manufacturer makes to place a new item on a retailer's shelf. A recent study in the grocery industry found that manufacturers paid an average of $5.1 million dollars to get a new product on store shelves.[31]

Getting the new product to market does not guarantee success. The cost of failure can be far more than merely sales the new product failed to make. For example, if a new grocery product does not achieve a predetermined sales target, some retailers require a **failure fee,** a penalty payment by a manufacturer to compensate the retailer for sales its valuable shelf space never made.

Lag from Idea to New Product   The time from idea generation to commercialization can be lengthy: 32 years for the heart pacemaker, 55 years for the zipper, 18 years for instant rice. Companies generally proceed carefully because, at this last stage, commercialization, production, and marketing expenses are greatest. To minimize the financial risk of a market failure of a new product introduction, many grocery product manufacturers use *regional rollouts,* introducing the product sequentially into limited geographical areas to allow production levels and marketing activities to build up gradually.

In recent years, companies have begun to recognize that speed is important in bringing a new product to market. A recent study by McKinsey & Company, a management consulting firm, has shown that high-tech products that come to market late but on budget will earn 33 percent less profit over five years. Yet those products that come out on time and 50 percent over budget will earn only 4 percent less profit.[32] IBM, for example, killed several laptop computer prototypes before commercialization because competitors offered better, more advanced machines to the market before IBM. As a result, some companies— such as Sony, NEC, Honda, Fuji, and Hewlett-Packard—have moved away from the development approach that uses the sequence of stages described in this chapter. A new trend, termed *parallel development* (the simultaneous development of both the product and the production process), is being tried. With this approach, multidisciplinary *venture teams* of marketing, manufacturing, and R&D personnel stay with the product from conception to production. The results are significant. Honda has cut car development from five years to three, while Hewlett-Packard has reduced the development time for computer printers from 54 months to 22.[33] Early reports indicate that involving these multidisciplinary teams early in the product development process also leads to increased success rates for the new products introduced.[34]

How the New Product Process Reduces Failures   Figure 11−8 identifies the purpose of each stage of the new product process and the kinds of marketing

STAGE OF PROCESS	PURPOSE OF STAGE	MARKETING INFORMATION AND METHODS USED
New product strategy development	Identify new product niches to reach in light of company objectives	Company objectives; assessment of firm's current strengths and weaknesses in terms of market and product
Idea generation	Develop concepts for possible products	Ideas from employees and co-workers, consumers, R&D, and competitors; methods of brainstorming and focus groups
Screening and evaluation	Separate good product ideas from bad ones inexpensively	Screening criteria, concept tests, and weighted point systems
Business analysis	Identify the product's features and its marketing strategy, and make financial projections	Product's key features, anticipated marketing mix strategy; economic, marketing, production, legal, and profitability analyses
Development	Create the prototype product, and test it in the laboratory and on consumers	Laboratory and consumer tests on product prototypes
Market testing	Test product and marketing strategy in the marketplace on a limited scale	Test markets, simulated test markets (STMs)
Commercialization	Position and offer product in the marketplace	Perceptual maps, product positioning, regional rollouts

▮ *Figure 11–8*
Marketing information and methods used in the new product process.

information and methods used. Firms that follow the seven stages in the new product process reduce risks and have a better chance of averting new product failures. A look at Figure 11–8 suggests information that might help avoid some new product failures. Although using the new product process does not guarantee successful products, it does increase a firm's success rate. (See the accompanying Ethics and Social Responsibility Alert.)

New techniques to reduce product failure are being experimented with at this time. One emerging technique is the use of virtual reality (VR), or envisioning laboratories. VR is the creation of simulated environments by way of sophisticated computer animation software. VR can create simulations of new products with which the consumer can often interface via a headset or helmet. Consumers can provide feedback concerning what they like or do not like about the product concept, without the need for actual expensive prototypes. Changes can be made within minutes and consumers can evaluate the changes on the spot. Some architectural firms are already using VR. Simulated building designs are created, and customers can provide instant feedback about the direction the design is heading. Xerox is also using a form of VR to test the designs of new office workstations.

In the near future, VR may spawn a host of new products or services itself, such as fantasy trips and the ability to create and manage one's own simulated environment.

ETHICS AND SOCIAL RESPONSIBILITY ALERT
The Cost of New Product Failure

Between 15,000 and 20,000 new products are launched annually in Canada and the United States. Yet very few survive. Most research indicates that new product success is the exception and not the rule. Still, millions and millions of dollars are spent to develop and support new products. But who pays the costs when products fail? First, many companies simply go out of business as a result of new product failure, costing jobs and creating hardship in affected communities. Other companies may survive new product failures but often have to reduce their number of personnel in order to offset the costs of the failure. Very often, prices on a company's existing products go up when new products fail, and the consumer pays the price. Finally, resources—natural, labour, and monetary—are lost forever as a result of failure.

While new products are often the lifeblood of a corporation, many question the expenditures on new products especially when the likelihood of success is low. Money that might go to improving the quality of employees' work life, or to new measures to protect the environment, may be siphoned away for new product development. On one hand, companies look to innovation and product improvement to stay ahead of the competition. Consumers are also demanding new and improved products, and we know that older products must eventually be replaced by new ones as societal needs change. But what are the ethical and social responsibility issues involved in spending scarce resources on new products that may do little to improve society in general? Moreover, and more important, should the total costs of failure to the business, employee, consumer, and society be carefully considered in deciding whether to develop new products?

VR technology may help reduce new product failure.

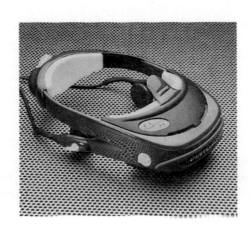

1 How does the development stage of the new product process involve testing the product inside and outside the firm?

2 What is a test market?

3 What is commercialization of a new product?

Summary

1 A product is a good, a service, or an idea consisting of a bundle of tangible and intangible attributes that satisfies consumers and is received in exchange for money or some other unit of value. A company's product decisions involve the product item, product line, and range of its product mix.

2 Products can be classified by tangibility and by user. By degree of tangibility, products divide into nondurable goods, durable goods, and services. By user, the major distinctions are consumer or industrial goods. Consumer goods consist of convenience, shopping, specialty, and unsought products. Industrial goods are for either production or support.

3 There are several ways to define *new product,* such as the degree of distinction from existing products, a time base specified by Consumer and Corporate Affairs Canada, a company perspective, or effect on a consumer's usage pattern.

4 In terms of its effect on a consumer's use of a product, a discontinuous innovation represents the greatest change and a continuous innovation the least. A dynamically continuous innovation is disruptive but not totally new.

5 The failure of a new product is usually attributable to one of six reasons: too small a target market, insignificant point of difference, poor product quality, no access to market, poor timing, and poor execution of the marketing mix.

6 The new product process consists of seven stages. Objectives for new products are determined in the first stage, new product strategy development; this is followed by idea generation, screening and evaluation, business analysis, development, market testing, and commercialization.

7 Ideas for new products come from several sources, including consumers, employees, R&D laboratories, and competitors.

8 Screening and evaluation are done internally, using a weighted point system, or externally, using concept tests.

9 Business analysis involves defining the features of the new product, a marketing strategy to introduce it, and a financial forecast.

10 Development involves not only producing a prototype product but also testing it in the lab and on consumers to see that it meets the standards set for it.

11 In market-testing new products, companies often rely on test markets to see that consumers will actually buy the product when it's offered for sale and that other marketing mix factors are working. Products surviving this stage are commercialized—taken to market.

Key Terms and Concepts

product p. 260

product line p. 261

product mix p. 261

consumer goods p. 262

industrial goods p. 262

convenience goods p. 262

shopping goods p. 262

specialty goods p. 262

unsought goods p. 262

production goods p. 263

support goods p. 263

new product process p. 269

new product strategy development p. 270

idea generation p. 271

screening and evaluation p. 275

business analysis p. 277

development p. 277

market testing p. 278

commercialization p. 280

slotting fee p. 280

failure fee p. 280

Chapter Problems and Applications

1 Products can be classified as either consumer or industrial goods. How would you classify the following products? (*a*) Johnson's baby shampoo, (*b*) a Black & Decker two-speed drill, and (*c*) an arc welder.

2 Are products like Nature Valley granola bars and Eddie Bauer hiking boots convenience, shopping, specialty, or unsought goods?

3 On the basis of your answer to problem 2, how would the marketing actions differ for each product and the classification to which you assigned it?

4 In terms of the behavioural effect on consumers, how would a PC, such as a Macintosh or an IBM PS/2, be classified? In light of this classification, what actions would you suggest to the manufacturers of these products to increase their sales in the market?

5 Several alternative definitions were presented for a new product. How would a company's marketing strategy be affected if it used (*a*) the legal definition or (*b*) a behavioural definition?

6 In terms of the weighted point system used to screen new product ideas at Medtronic (Figure 11–7), what is the significance of the following factors: incidence of malady, treatment evaluation, restoration of natural physiology, and physicians' knowledge of Medtronic name? What are the advantages and disadvantages of such a system?

7 Test marketing and purchase laboratories are two approaches for assessing the potential commercial success of a new product. On the basis of the strengths and weaknesses of each approach, what methods would you suggest for the following

items? (*a*) A new, improved ketchup, (*b*) a three-dimensional television system that took the company 10 years to develop, and (*c*) a new children's toy on which the company holds a patent.

8 Look back at Figure 11–6, which outlines the roles for new products. If a company's new product was designed to defend market share, what type of positioning strategy might be implemented?

9 Concept testing is an important step in the new product process. Outline the concept tests for (*a*) an electrically powered car and (*b*) a new loan payment system for automobiles that is based on a variable interest rate. What are the differences in developing concept tests for products as opposed to services?

Managing the Product

AFTER READING THIS CHAPTER YOU SHOULD BE ABLE TO:

▸ Explain the product life cycle concept and relate a marketing strategy to each stage.

▸ Recognize the differences in product life cycles for various products and their implications for marketing decisions.

▸ Understand alternative approaches to managing a product's life cycle.

▸ Identify the attributes of a successful brand name.

▸ Explain the rationale for alternative brand name strategies employed by companies.

▸ Understand the benefits of packaging and warranties in the marketing of a product.

Managing the Clearly Canadian Brand in a Growing Alternative Beverage Category

Clearly Canadian Beverages, a Vancouver-based company, brought its fruit-flavoured sparkling water drinks to the top of the alternative beverage or new-age drink category in just five years. The alternative beverage segment is a catchall that includes almost anything that doesn't contain alcohol and isn't a soda or soft drink. In general, the category includes "healthful" carbonated or noncarbonated flavoured waters and other beverages sold as an alternative to soft drinks. This market, which started out as a niche market, has become more mainstream and has reached market maturity. Thus, the competition in its category is fierce, with about 50 competitors and with about 20 that are Clearly Canadian knockoffs. New entries into the new-age market include Snapple Beverages and Seagram's, with its two-calorie Quest beverage.

The major soft drink producers, who were losing some of their diet soda market to these new beverages, are also marketing their own new-age beverages. Pepsi, for example, has joined with Lipton, and Coke has hooked up with Nestlé, to market ready-to-drink tea lines. With aggressive new entries, Clearly Canadian has to use its resources to meet this increasing competition.

Beverage World, the industry journal, suggests that Clearly Canadian did not invent the alternative beverage or new-age drink category, but through its pricing, packaging, distribution, positioning, formulating, and financing it may have perfected it. An entrepreneurial corporate culture and a lean internal operation allow Clearly Canadian to respond quickly to changing market conditions. The company is also committed to education of management and staff so that the organization can have the skills to plan and execute effective marketing strategies. New flavours such as Summer Strawberry; product line extensions such as 23-ounce multiserving bottles and four-packs; comprehensive promotional activities including advertising, sampling, merchandising, and incentive programs for the 7,500 salespeople—these all help keep Clearly Canadian in its market leadership position.

Canada is home to one-fifth of all the world's freshwater, and it enjoys a worldwide reputation for its pure, clean, crystalline water. Clearly Canadian has been able to leverage that reputation as the basis for its competitive advantage, achieving sales in excess of $155 million in 1993. In further efforts to keep ahead of the competition, Clearly Canadian has expanded into Mexico, the Caribbean, England, and Ireland and has a licensing arrangement in Japan with Asahi Breweries Ltd., Asia's third-largest beverage company.[1]

The marketing of Clearly Canadian beverages since 1989 illustrates the effective management of a product in the marketplace. This chapter shows how the actions taken by Clearly Canadian are typical of those made by successful marketers in managing products and brands.

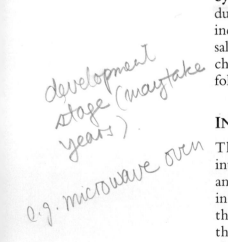

PRODUCT LIFE CYCLE

Products, like people, have been viewed as having a life cycle. The **product life cycle** consists of the stages a product goes through in the marketplace: introduction, growth, maturity, and decline. Figure 12–1 shows two curves—total industry sales revenue, and total industry profit—which represent the sum of sales revenue and profit of all firms producing the product.[2] The reasons for the changes in each curve and the marketing decisions involved are discussed in the following pages.

INTRODUCTION STAGE

The introduction stage of the product life cycle occurs when a product is first introduced to its intended target market. During this period, sales grow slowly and profit is minimal. The lack of profit is often a result of large investment costs in product development, such as the $200 million spent by Gillette to develop the Sensor razor shaving system. The marketing objective for the company at this stage is to create consumer awareness and stimulate trial—the initial purchase of a product by a consumer.

Companies often spend heavily on advertising and other promotional tools to build awareness among consumers in the introduction stage.[3] For example, Frito-Lay reportedly spent $30 million to promote its Sun Chips multigrain snacks to consumers and retailers, and Gillette spent $35 million in advertising alone to introduce the Sensor razor to consumers.[4] These expenditures are often made to stimulate *primary demand,* or desire, for the product class (such as in-line skates or multigrain snack chips) rather than for a specific brand, since there are

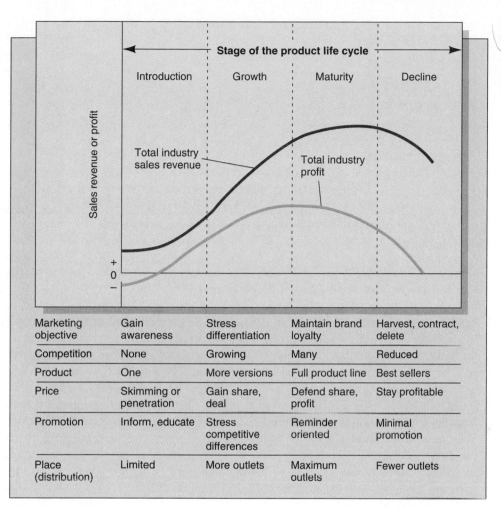

How stages of the product life cycle relate to a firm's marketing objectives and marketing mix actions.

Stage of the product life cycle			
Introduction	**Growth**	**Maturity**	**Decline**
Marketing objective	Gain awareness	Stress differentiation	Maintain brand loyalty	Harvest, contract, delete
Competition	None	Growing	Many	Reduced
Product	One	More versions	Full product line	Best sellers
Price	Skimming or penetration	Gain share, deal	Defend share, profit	Stay profitable
Promotion	Inform, educate	Stress competitive differences	Reminder oriented	Minimal promotion
Place (distribution)	Limited	More outlets	Maximum outlets	Fewer outlets

no competitors with the same product. As competitors introduce their own products and the product progresses along its life cycle, company attention is focussed on creating *selective demand,* or demand for a specific brand.

Other marketing mix variables are also important at this stage. Gaining distribution is often a challenge because channel intermediaries may be hesitant to carry a new product. Moreover, in this stage a company often restricts the number of variations of the product to ensure control of product quality. For example, Clearly Canadian originally came in only a few flavours, and Gillette originally offered only a single version of the Sensor razor.

During introduction, pricing can be either high or low. A high initial price may be used as part of a *skimming* strategy to help the company recover the costs of development, as well as capitalize on the price insensitivity of early buyers. 3M is a master of this strategy. According to a 3M manager, "We hit fast, price high, and get the heck out when the me-too products pour in."[5] High prices also tend to attract competitors more eager to enter the market because they see the opportunity for profit. To discourage competitive entry, a company can price low, or use *penetration pricing.* This pricing strategy also helps build unit

▌ *Figure 12–2*
Product life cycle for the stand-alone fax machine for business use, 1970–1995.

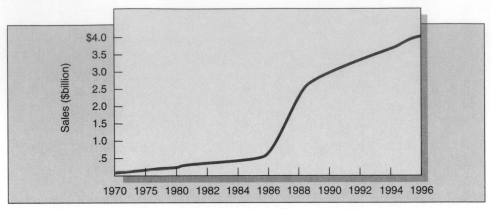

Source: Chart drawn from Dataquest, Inc., statistics and projections. Used with permission.

volume, but a company must closely monitor costs. These and other pricing techniques are covered in depth in Chapter 14.

Figure 12–2 charts the stand-alone fax machine product life cycle for business use from the early 1970s through 1995.[6] As shown, sales grew slowly in the 1970s and early 1980s after Xerox pioneered the first lightweight portable fax machine that sent and received documents. Fax machines were originally sold direct to businesses through company salespeople, and were premium-priced. The average price for a fax machine in 1980 was $12,700. By today's standards, those fax machines were primitive. They contained mechanical parts, not electronic circuitry, and offered few of the features seen in today's models.

Several product classes are poised to enter the introductory stage of the product life cycle or have been only recently commercialized. These include high-definition television (HDTV, described in Chapter 11), electronic-imaging cameras, and electric cars.

GROWTH STAGE

The second stage of the product life cycle, growth, is characterized by rapid increases in sales. It is in this stage that competitors appear. For example, Figure 12–2 shows the dramatic increase in sales of fax machines from 1985 to 1990. The number of companies selling fax machines was also increasing, from one in the early 1970s to four in the late 1970s to seven manufacturers in 1983, which sold nine brands. By 1990 there were some 25 manufacturers and 60 possible brands from which to choose.

The result of more competitors and more aggressive pricing is that profit usually peaks during the growth stage. For instance, the average price for a fax machine declined from $3,300 in 1985 to $1,500 in 1990, to as low as $300 in 1995. At this point the emphasis of advertising shifts to selective demand, in which product benefits are compared with those of competitors' offerings.

Product sales in the growth stage grow at an increasing rate because of new people trying or using the product and a growing proportion of *repeat purchasers*—people who tried the product, were satisfied, and bought again. As a product moves through the life cycle, the ratio of repeat to trial purchasers

grows. Failure to achieve substantial repeat purchasers usually means an early death for a product. Alberto-Culver introduced Mr. Culver's Sparklers, which were solid air fresheners that looked like stained glass. The product moved quickly from the introduction to the growth stage, but then sales plummeted. The problem was there were almost no repeat purchasers because buyers treated the product like cheap window decorations, left the fresheners in place, and didn't buy new ones. Durable fax machines meant that replacement purchases were rare; however, it was common for more than one machine to populate a business as use became more widespread.

Changes start to appear in the product during the growth stage. To help differentiate a company's brand from those of its competitors, an improved version or new features are added to the original design and product proliferation occurs. Changes in fax machines included models with built-in telephones, models that used plain, rather than thermal, paper for copies, models that integrated telex for electronic mail purposes, and models that allowed for secure (confidential) transmissions. For Clearly Canadian and Sun Chips, new flavours and package sizes were added during the growth stage. Gillette introduced a modified design of its Sensor razor for women.

In the growth stage it is important to gain as much distribution for the product as possible. In the retail store, for example, this often means that competing companies fight for display and shelf space. Expanded distribution in the fax industry is an example. In 1986, early in the growth stage, only 11 percent of office machine dealers carried this equipment. By the early 1990s, more than 60 percent of these dealers carried fax equipment, distribution was expanded to other stores selling electronic equipment, and the fight continues for which brands will be displayed.

Numerous product classes or industries are in the growth stage of the product life cycle. Examples include disposable 35-mm cameras, nonalcoholic beer, and laptop computers. Cellular telephones are in the growth stage in Canada but are appearing to enter the maturity stage in Great Britain.

MATURITY STAGE

The third stage, maturity, is characterized by a gradual levelling off of total industry sales or product class revenue. Also, marginal competitors begin to leave the market. Most consumers who would buy the product are either repeat purchasers of the item or have tried and abandoned it. Sales increase at a decreasing rate in the maturity stage, as few new buyers enter the market. Profit declines because there is fierce price competition among many sellers and the cost of gaining each new buyer at this stage is greater than the resulting revenue.

Marketing expenses in the maturity stage are often directed toward holding market share through further product differentiation, and price competition continues through rebates and price discounting. Companies also focus on retaining distribution outlets. A major factor in a company's strategy is to reduce overall marketing costs by improving its promotional and distribution efficiency.

Stand-alone fax machines for business use entered the maturity stage in late 1990. Sixty-five percent of industry sales were captured by five products at this time (Sharp, Murata, Canon Panasonic, and Ricoh), reflecting the departure of many marginal competitors. Industry sales growth had slowed, compared with triple-digit average annual dollar increases in the four previous years.

Numerous product classes and industries are in the maturity stage of their product life cycle. These include carbonated soft drinks, personal computers, automobiles, and TVs.

DECLINE STAGE

The decline stage occurs when sales and profits begin to drop. Frequently, a product enters this stage not because of any wrong strategy on the part of the company, but because of environmental changes. New technology led to video cameras, which pushed 8-mm movie cameras into decline. Similarly, the merging of personal computer and facsimile technology began to replace the stand-alone fax machine in 1993. The decline stage for stand-alone fax machines for business use is projected for the year 2000. Wine coolers, popular in the late 1980s, are now in the decline stage as drinking preferences have changed. Advertising and promotional support for a product in this stage diminish, as does investment in major product development. Products in the decline stage tend to consume a disproportionate share of management time and financial resources relative to their potential future worth. To handle a declining product, a company follows one of three strategies: deletion, harvesting, or contracting.

Deletion   Product deletion, or dropping the product from the company's product line, is the most drastic strategy. Since a residual core of consumers still

consume or use a product even in the decline stage, product elimination decisions are not taken lightly. When Coca-Cola decided to drop what is now
known as Classic Coke, consumer objection was so intense that the company
brought the product back.

Harvesting   In a second strategy, harvesting, a company retains the product but
reduces marketing support costs.[7] The product continues to be offered, but salespeople do not allocate time in selling, nor are advertising dollars spent. The purpose
of harvesting is to maintain the ability to meet customer requests. For example,
IBM continues to sell typewriters in the era of word-processing equipment.

Contracting   Some companies operate on a scale that makes it financially
unwise for them to carry a product after sales decline below a certain level.
However, this same sales level might be profitable for a smaller company, and
the larger firm may contract with a smaller company to manufacture the product. In this way its production budget is freed for more profitable items, but the
item is still available to customers. An alternative to contracting manufacturing
is to contract the marketing: manufacturing efficiencies may allow a company
to continue producing a product, but marketing costs may require other companies to sell it.

SOME DIMENSIONS OF THE PRODUCT LIFE CYCLE

Some important aspects of product life cycles are their length, the shapes of their
curves, and how they vary with different levels of the products.

Length of the Product Life Cycle   There is no exact time that a product takes
to move through its life cycle. As a rule, consumer products have shorter life
cycles than industrial products.[8] For example, many new consumer food products move from the introduction stage to maturity in 18 months. The availability of mass communication vehicles informs consumers faster and shortens
life cycles. Also, the rate of technological change tends to shorten product life
cycles as new product innovation replaces existing products.

The Shape of the Product Life Cycle   The product life cycle curve shown in
Figure 12–1 might be referred to as a *generalized life cycle,* but not all products
have the same shape to their curves. In fact, there are several different life cycle
curves, each type suggesting different marketing strategies. Figure 12–3 shows
the shape of life cycle curves for four different types of products: high learning,
low learning, fashion, and fad products.[9]
    A *high learning product* is one for which significant education of the cus-
tomer is required and there is an extended introductory period (Figure 12–3A).
Products such as home computers have had this type of life cycle curve because
consumers have to understand the benefits of purchasing the product or be
educated in a new way of performing a familiar task. Convection ovens, for
example, necessitate that the consumer learn a new way of cooking and alter
familiar recipes.
    In contrast, for a *low learning product* sales begin immediately because little
learning is required by the consumer and the benefits of purchase are readily

Figure 12–3
Alternative product life cycles.

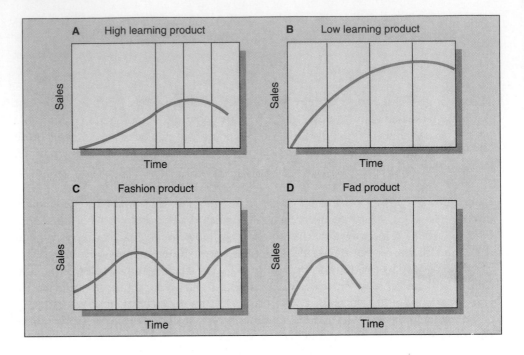

understood (Figure 12–3B). This product often can be easily imitated by competitors, so the marketing strategy is to broaden distribution quickly. In this way, as competitors rapidly enter, most retail outlets already have the innovator's product. It is also important to have the manufacturing capacity to meet demand. A recent example of a successful low learning product is Frito-Lay's Sun Chips, discussed earlier. Sun Chips achieved $100 million in sales the first year it was introduced.

A *fashion product* (Figure 12–3C), such as hemline lengths on skirts or lapel widths on sports jackets, is introduced, declines, and then seems to return. Life cycles for fashion products most often appear in women's and men's clothing styles. The length of the cycles may be years or decades.

A *fad,* such as wall walkers or toe socks, experiences rapid sales on introduction and then an equally rapid decline (Figure 12–3D). One entrepreneur, hoping to create a worldwide fad, has paid for exclusive rights to the Great Wall of China. He plans to sell rubble from the wall mounted on a little wooden base. Some companies make fads their primary business. For example, the promoter of Teenage Mutant Ninja Turtles has come up with what he hopes is a new fad: C.O.W.-Boys of Moo Mesa, featuring Marshall Moo Montana, Geronimoo, Saddle Sore, Col. Cudster, Buffalo Bull, and Sheriff Terrorbull. Will C.O.W.-Boys catch on? They debuted on Saturday morning TV in late 1992, toys based on the characters appeared in early 1993, and you can expect to see live costumed-character appearances, video games, books, songs, shampoos, and soaps soon.[10]

The Product Level: Class, Form, and Brand   In managing a product it is important to often distinguish among the multiple life cycles (industry, class, and form) that may exist. **Product class** refers to the entire product category or

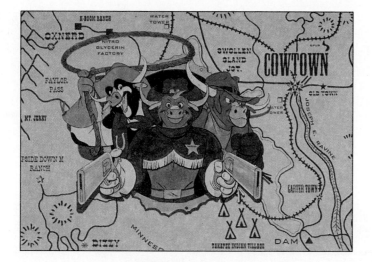

A new consumer fad?

industry, such as the total cigarette industry. **Product form** pertains to variations within the class. For example, in the cigarette industry there are filter and nonfilter product forms. A final type of life cycle curve can represent the brand. The entire product class of cigarettes is in the late maturity or decline stage of its life cycle, with filter cigarettes (product form) dominating over nonfilters. Most brands of cigarettes, except new brands, are in the mature or decline stage of their life cycle.

The Life Cycle and Consumers   The life cycle of a product depends on sales to consumers. Not all consumers rush to buy a product in the introductory stage, and the shapes of the life cycle curves indicate that most sales occur after the product has been on the market for some time. In essence, a product diffuses, or spreads, through the population, a concept called the *diffusion of innovation.*[11]

Some people are attracted to a product early, while others buy it only after they see their friends with the item. Figure 12–4 shows the consumer population divided into five categories of product adopters based on when they adopt a new product. Brief profiles accompany each category. For any product to be successful, it must be purchased by innovators and early adopters. This is why manufacturers of new pharmaceuticals try to gain adoption by leading hospitals, clinics, and physicians who are widely respected in the medical field. Once accepted by innovators and early adopters, new products move on to adoption by the early majority, late majority, and laggard categories.

Several factors affect whether a consumer will adopt a new product or not. Common reasons for resisting a product in the introduction stage are usage barriers (the product is not compatible with existing habits); value barriers (the product provides no incentive to change); risk barriers, which can be physical, economic, or social; and psychological barriers, such as cultural differences or image.[12]

Companies attempt to overcome these barriers in numerous ways, such as offering consumers samples, or money-back guarantees. When Lever Brothers introduced its Lever 2000 triple-threat skin soap bar that moisturizes, deodor-

■ *Figure 12–4*
**Five categories and
profiles of product
adopters.**

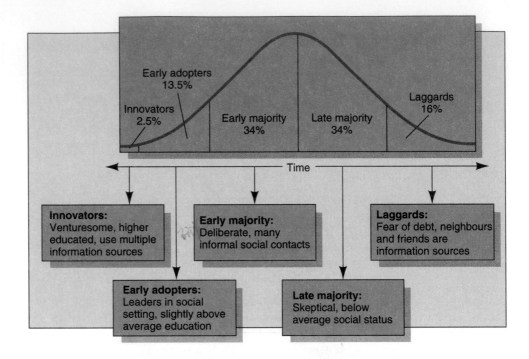

izes, and kills bacteria, it had to give consumers an incentive to change from
their current soap. How? The company sent samples of the new product to
millions of households and recorded sales of $27.6 million.[13]

Concept Check

1 Advertising plays a major role in the _____ stage of the product
   life cycle, and _____ plays a major role in maturity.

2 How do high learning and low learning products differ?

3 What does the life cycle for a fashion product look like?

MANAGING THE PRODUCT LIFE CYCLE

An important task for a firm is to manage its products through the successive
stages of their life cycles. This section discusses the role of the product manager,
who is usually responsible for this, and analyzes three ways to manage a product
through its life cycle: modifying the product, modifying the market, and repositioning the product.

ROLE OF A PRODUCT MANAGER

The product manager (sometimes called *brand manager*) manages the marketing
efforts for a close-knit family of products or brands. Introduced by P&G in
1927, the product manager style of marketing organization is used by consumer

Effective sampling of Lever 2000 helped launch this successful product.

goods firms such as Kraft-General Foods and Frito-Lay and by industrial firms such as Intel and Hewlett-Packard. All product managers are responsible for managing existing products through the stages of the life cycle, and some are also responsible for developing new products. Product managers' marketing responsibilities include developing and executing a marketing plan for the product line including approving ad copy, media selection, and package design. The role of product managers in planning, implementing, and controlling marketing strategy is covered in depth in Chapters 21 and 22.

MODIFYING THE PRODUCT

Product modification involves altering a product's characteristic, such as its quality, performance, or appearance, to try to increase and extend the product's sales. Johnson Controls, Inc., a battery manufacturer for companies like Sears, has developed a backup battery. Backup batteries are similar to traditional car batteries, except that they have been modified to have reserve power. If you find a battery of this kind dead because you left the lights on, you simply switch a lever on the battery and initiate its backup power.[14] Another kind of product modification is illustrated in Black & Decker's changing the angle on its Phillips screwdriver to prevent the tip from slipping out of the screw.[15]

New features, packages, or scents can be used to change a product's characteristics and give the sense of a revised product. Procter & Gamble revamped Pert shampoo with a new formula that combined a shampoo and hair conditioner in one application. Prior to the modification, Pert was in the decline stage of the life cycle with only 2 percent of the market. After reformulation, Pert Plus became the top-selling shampoo in an industry with over 1,000 competitors.[16]

A modified shampoo led to a market leader.

But some marketers are not turning to new features or packages; instead, they are turning to the past to extend the life of their products. Capitalizing on growing adult nostalgia for the past, companies are retromarketing their products. **Retromarketing** is product differentiation based on consumer nostalgia for brands and packages of yesterday. Old-style packaging and old-fashioned advertising themes are being used to prop up maturing products. Maxwell House coffee used Norman Rockwellesque advertising and a redesign of a 1950s package to revive its brand. Coca-Cola Canada is now using an updated version of its universally recognized contour design bottle for single-serve Coca-Cola Classic and Diet Coke, hoping to appeal to adults who will remember the trademark bottle from their childhood.[17]

MODIFYING THE MARKET

With **market modification strategies,** a company tries to increase a product's use among existing customers, create new use situations, or find new customers.

Increasing Use   Promoting more frequent usage has been a strategy of Woolite, a laundry soap. Originally intended for the hand washing of woolen material, Woolite now promotes itself for use with all fine clothing items. The Florida Orange Growers Association advocates drinking orange juice throughout the day rather than for breakfast only.

Creating New Use Situation   Finding new uses for an existing product has been the major strategy in extending the life of Arm & Hammer baking soda. This product, originally intended as a baking ingredient, is now being promoted as a toothpaste; a deodorizer for cat litter, carpeting, and refrigerators; and a fire extinguisher.

Finding New Users   To prevent sales declines in wall-to-wall carpeting, carpet manufacturers found new user groups such as schools and hospitals. To expand company sales, Nautilus, a manufacturer of fitness equipment for gyms, recently entered the home market. Commercial accounts represented 95 percent of the company's sales, but the home market has a $1 to $5 billion sales potential. Sales of home video games plummeted from $3 billion in 1982 to $100 million in 1985. But sales rebounded to $3.5 billion in 1992 when Nintendo and Sega targeted two new segments: 8- to 14-year olds, most of whom can't remember the old games, and adults who want more sophisticated games.[18]

REPOSITIONING THE PRODUCT

Often a company decides to reposition its product or product line in an attempt to prevent sales decline. As we saw in Chapter 9, *product repositioning* is changing the place a product occupies in a consumer's mind relative to competitive products. A firm can reposition a product by changing one or more of the four marketing mix elements. Four factors that trigger a repositioning action are discussed in the following.

Reacting to a Competitor's Position   One reason to reposition a product is because a competitor's entrenched position is adversely affecting sales and market share. Procter & Gamble recently repositioned its venerable Ivory soap bar in response to the success of Lever 2000, sold by Lever Brothers. Lever 2000, a bar soap that moisturizes, deodorizes, and kills bacteria, eroded P&G's dominance of the bar soap market. P&G responded with its own triple-threat soap called New Ivory Ultra Safe Skin Care Soap. The problem? The new Ivory doesn't float![19]

Reaching a New Market   Dannon introduced Yop, a liquid yogourt, in France. The product flopped because the French were not interested in another dairy product. When Dannon repositioned Yop as a soft drink for the health-conscious French consumer, sales soared.[20]

Repositioning can involve more than merely changing advertising copy. The New Balance Company changed its product's position as a running shoe for the serious runner to a shoe for the mass market. The distribution strategy was altered from selling only through specialty running stores to selling through discount and department stores as well.

Catching a Rising Trend   Changing consumer trends can also lead to repositioning. From 1980 to 1991 annual per capita consumption of beef fell almost 5 kgs., while consumption of poultry rose by almost 12 kgs. For many years pork producers positioned their product as similar to beef. Noticing the trend toward poultry, a dramatic repositioning campaign was implemented, changing the focus from beef to poultry with the campaign tag line "pork: the other white meat" and a nutritional message. Consumer demand for pork rose 2 to 3 percent in 1991 and again in 1992.[21]

Changing the Value Offered   In repositioning a product, a company can decide to change the value it offers buyers and trade up or down. **Trading up** involves adding value to the product (or line) through additional features of higher-quality materials. Japanese automakers built their reputations with reliable and affordable cars. Many have since traded up, as evidenced by Honda's Acura, Toyota's Lexus, and Nissan's Infiniti, to compete in the luxury sedan market historically occupied by Mercedes-Benz and Cadillac. Dog food manufacturers also have traded up by offering super premium foods based on "life-stage nutrition." Mass merchandisers can trade up by adding a designer clothes section to their store, as shown by recent actions by K mart, Sears, and The Bay.

Trading down involves reducing the number of features, quality, or price. For example, airlines have added more seats, thus reducing leg room, and eliminated extras, such as snack service and food portions. Trading down often exists when companies engage in **downsizing**—reducing the content of packages without changing package size and maintaining or increasing the package price. For instance, Fabergé's Brut antiperspirant deodorant spray comes in its regular-size can at the same price, but the content has been reduced by 28 grams.[22] Firms have been criticized for this practice, as described in the accompanying Ethics and Social Responsibility Alert.

ETHICS AND SOCIAL RESPONSIBILITY ALERT

Consumers Are Paying More for Less in Downsized Packages

For more than 30 years, Starkist put 6.5 ounces of tuna into its regular-sized can. Today, Starkist puts 6.125 ounces of tuna into its can but charges the same price. Colgate-Palmolive's Ajax king-size laundry detergent package has remained the same size, but the contents have been cut from 61 ounces to 55 ounces and the package price increased from $2.59 to $2.79. Procter & Gamble has cut the number of Pampers disposable diapers in its packages while leaving the price the same. The price of Mennen Speed Stick deodorant has not changed, but it now comes in a larger package with 2.25 ounces of deodorant versus 2.5 ounces in the previous, smaller package. Other companies such as Quaker Oats, Hershey Foods, Gerber Products, and Ragú Foods have allegedly engaged in similar practices.

Consumer advocates charge that "downsizing" packages while maintaining or increasing prices is a subtle and unannounced way of taking advantage of consumers' buying habits. Manufacturers argue that this practice is a way of keeping prices from rising beyond psychological barriers for their products.

Is downsizing an unethical practice if manufacturers do not inform consumers that the package contents are less than they were previously?

Sources: Based on "It's the Pits," *Consumer Reports,* February 1992, p. 203; J. B. Hinge, "Critics Call Cuts in Package Size Deceptive Move," *The Wall Street Journal,* February 5, 1991, pp. B1, B8; and J. Dagnoli, "State AGs Attack Downsized Brand," *Advertising Age,* February 18, 1991, pp. 1, 46.

Concept Check

1 How does a product manager help manage a product's life cycle?

2 What does "creating new use situations" mean in managing a product's life cycle?

3 Explain the difference between trading up and trading down in repositioning.

BRANDING

A basic decision in marketing products is **branding,** in which an organization uses a name, a phrase, a design, symbols, or a combination of these to identify its products and distinguish them from those of competitors. A **brand name** is any word, "device" (design, sound, shape, or colour), or combination of these used to distinguish a seller's goods or services. Some brand names can be spoken, such as Clearly Canadian. Other brand names cannot be spoken, such as the rainbow-coloured apple (the *logotype,* or *logo*) that Apple Computer puts

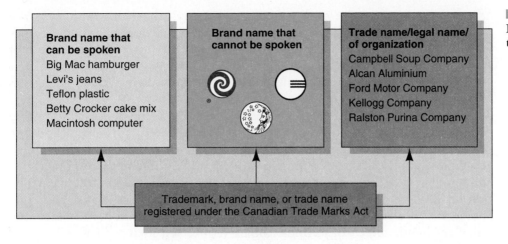

Examples of well-known trademarks.

on its machines and in its ads. A **trade name** is a commercial, legal name under which a company does business. The Campbell Soup Company is the trade name of that firm.

A **trademark** identifies that a firm has legally registered its brand name or trade name so the firm has its exclusive use, thereby preventing others from using it. In Canada, trademarks are registered under the Trade Marks Act with Consumer and Corporate Affairs Canada. A well-known trademark can help a company advertise its offerings to customers and develop their brand loyalty. Figure 12-5 shows examples of well-known trademarks.

Because a good trademark can help sell a product, *product counterfeiting,* or manufacture of low-cost copies of popular brands by someone other than the original producer, has been a growing problem. Counterfeit products can steal sales from the original manufacturer or hurt the company's reputation.

Trademark protection is a significant issue in global marketing. For instance, the transformation of the Soviet Union into individual countries has meant that many firms, such as Xerox, have had to reregister trademarks in each of the republics to prohibit misuse and generic use ("xeroxing") of their trademarks.[23]

THE VALUE OF BRANDING

Branding policy is important not only for manufacturers but also for retailers and consumers. Retailers value branding because consumers shop at stores that carry their desired brands. Some retailers have created their own store brands to further enhance loyalty from their customers. Sears exclusively offers the Kenmore brand for its appliance line and Craftsman as the brand for tools. Canadian Tire offers its Motormaster brand on a variety of its automotive and home care products.

A good brand name is of such importance to a company that it has led to a concept called **brand equity,** an added value a brand name gives to a product beyond the functional benefits provided.[24] This value consists of two distinct advantages. First, brand equity provides a competitive advantage: for example, the Sunkist label implies quality fruit, and Clearly Canadian is known as the leader in the alternative beverage category. A second advantage of brand equity is its ability to endure environmental changes. Globalization of markets and freer trade means many more brands will be brought to the consciousness of consumers. One brand that will continue to be popular despite these changes is Coca-Cola, the world's best-known brand.[25]

Consumers, however, may benefit most from branding. Recognizing competing products by distinct trademarks or names allows them to be more efficient shoppers. Consumers can recognize and avoid products with which they are dissatisfied, while becoming loyal to other, more satisfying brands. As discussed in Chapter 6, brand loyalty often eases consumers' decision making by eliminating the need for an external search. Also, the expense of establishing a brand in the marketplace means that some brands are reintroduced years after they apparently died. For example, Buick resurrected its Roadmaster brand in 1993 after the name had been discontinued for about 20 years.

LICENSING

Brand equity is evident in the strategy of licensing. **Licensing** is a contractual agreement whereby a company allows another firm to use its brand name, patent, trade secret, or other property for a royalty or a fee. Licensing can be very profitable to a licensor and a licensee. The National Hockey League (NHL) has 245 licensees providing over 1,000 products and receives a percentage of the wholesale price of the products sold. Licensed products for the NHL

Licensed products are an important part of the NHL's marketing activities.

Ruffles and Chee-tos are in Israel now, and more PepsiCo snack foods may follow.

brought in more than $600 million in 1993, and the NHL expects licensing to hit the $1 billion mark by the end of 1995.[26]

Licensing also assists companies in entering global markets with minimal risk. As mentioned in the chapter opener, Clearly Canadian has entered the Japanese market through a licensing agreement with Asahi Breweries.[27] PepsiCo International licensed Elite Foods in Israel to produce and market Frito-Lay's Ruffles potato chips and Chee-tos cheese-flavoured corn puffs. These brands now capture 15 percent of the salty-snack market in Israel.[28]

PICKING A GOOD BRAND NAME

We take brand names such as Dial, Sony, Coke, BMW, and Porsche for granted, but it is often a difficult and expensive process to pick a good name. Five criteria are mentioned most often in selecting a good brand name.[29]

The name should suggest the product's benefits. For example, Accutron (watches), Easy-Off (oven cleaner), Glass Plus (glass cleaner), Cling Free (anti-static cloth for drying clothes), and Tidy Bowl (toilet bowl cleaner) all clearly describe the benefits of purchasing the product.

The name should be memorable, distinctive, and positive. In the auto industry, when a competitor has a memorable name, others quickly imitate. When Ford named a car the Mustang, Pinto, Colt, Maverick, and Bronco soon followed. The Thunderbird stimulated the Phoenix, Eagle, Sunbird, and Firebird.

The name should fit the company or product image. Sharp is a name that can apply to audio and video equipment. Excedrin is a scientific-sounding name, good for an analgesic. However, naming a personal computer PCjr, as

IBM did with its first computer for home use, neither fit the company nor the product. PCjr sounded too much like a toy and stalled IBM's initial entry into the home use market.

The name should have no legal or regulatory restrictions. Legal restrictions produce trademark infringement suits, and regulatory restrictions arise through improper use of words.

Finally, the name should be simple (such as Bold laundry detergent, Sure deodorant, and Bic pens), and should be emotional (such as Joy and My Sin perfumes). In the development of names for international use, having a non-meaningful brand name has been considered a benefit. A name such as Exxon does not have any prior impressions or undesirable images among a diverse world population of different languages and cultures.[30]

BRANDING STRATEGIES

In deciding to brand a product, companies have several possible strategies, including manufacturer branding, reseller branding, or mixed branding approaches.

Manufacturer Branding   With **manufacturer branding,** the producer dictates the brand name using either a multiproduct or a multibrand approach. **Multiproduct branding** is the use of one name for all a company's products. This approach is often referred to as a *blanket* or *family* branding strategy (Figure 12−6).

There are several advantages to multiproduct branding. Capitalizing again on brand equity, consumers who have a good experience with the product will transfer this favourable attitude to other items in the product class with the same

▌*Figure 12−6*
Alternative branding strategies.

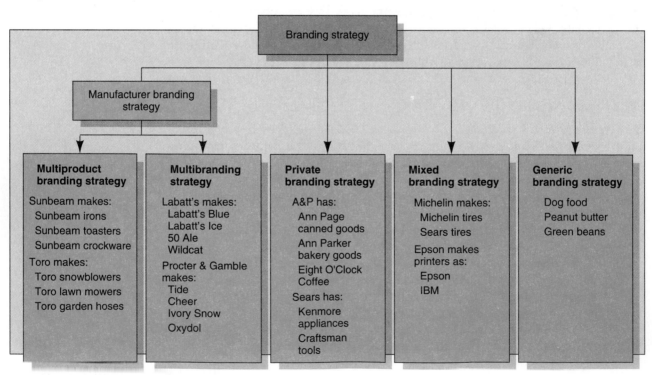

Branding strategy

Manufacturer branding strategy

Multiproduct branding strategy	Multibranding strategy	Private branding strategy	Mixed branding strategy	Generic branding strategy

Sunbeam makes:
  Sunbeam irons
  Sunbeam toasters
  Sunbeam crockware
Toro makes:
  Toro snowblowers
  Toro lawn mowers
  Toro garden hoses
	Labatt's makes:
	  Labatt's Blue
	  Labatt's Ice
	  50 Ale
	  Wildcat
	Procter & Gamble makes:
	  Tide
	  Cheer
	  Ivory Snow
	  Oxydol
		A&P has:
		  Ann Page
		  canned goods
		  Ann Parker
		  bakery goods
		  Eight O'Clock
		  Coffee
		Sears has:
		  Kenmore
		  appliances
		  Craftsman
		  tools
			Michelin makes:
			  Michelin tires
			  Sears tires
			Epson makes
			printers as:
			  Epson
			  IBM
				Dog food
				Peanut butter
				Green beans

name. Therefore, this brand strategy makes possible *line extensions,* the practice of using a current brand name to enter a new market segment in its product class. Campbell Soup Company effectively employs a multiproduct branding strategy with soup line extensions. It offers regular Campbell soup, home-cooking style, chunky, and "healthy request" varieties and more than 100 soup flavours.[31] This strategy can also result in lower advertising and promotion costs because the same name is used on all products, thus raising the level of brand awareness.

A strong brand equity also allows for *brand extension,* the practice of using a current brand name to enter a completely different product class.[32] For instance, the equity in the Tylenol name as a trusted pain reliever allowed Johnson & Johnson to successfully extend this name to Tylenol Cold & Flu and Tylenol PM, a sleep aid. Fisher-Price, an established name in children's toys, was able to extend this name to children's shampoo and conditioners and baby bath and lotion products.[33]

However, there are some risks to the multiproduct branding approach. Poor performance of one item may have a negative impact on similarly named items in the line. Also, too many uses for one brand name can dilute the image of a product line.

An alternative manufacturer's branding strategy, **multibranding,** involves giving each product a distinct name. Multibranding is a useful strategy when each brand is intended for a different marketing segment. P&G makes Camay soap for those concerned with soft skin, Safeguard for those who want deodor-ant protection, and Lava for those who desire a strong cleaner. Competing internationally, P&G even uses multiple brand names for the same product. Pert Plus Shampoo is sold as Rejoice in Hong Kong, Pert Plus in the Middle East, and Vidal Sassoon in the United Kingdom. However, international branding strategies do differ. In Japan, where corporate names are important, P&G markets the company's name prominently with the brand name of the product.

Compared with the multiproduct approach, promotional costs tend to be higher with multibranding. The company must generate awareness among consumers and retailers for each new brand name without the benefit of any previous impressions. The advantages of this approach are that each brand is unique to each market segment and there is no risk that a product failure will affect other products in the line.

The multibranding approach in Europe is slowly being replaced by **euro-branding,** the strategy of using the same brand name for the same product across all countries in the 12-nation European Community. This strategy has many of the benefits linked with multiproduct branding in addition to making pan-European advertising and promotion programs possible. But this strategy is not always easily implemented, especially for firms that have been successful using a European multibranding strategy. Changing to a euro-brand strategy takes time and money—and a little reeducating of the consumer, who must look for a once-familiar product with a new name. Growth in North American branding will also be inevitable under NAFTA. Moreover, with globalization of world markets and growing homogenization of consumer needs, the prospects of successful *global* branding increase. A **global brand** would have the same name, personality, and positioning in worldwide markets.[34] Coca-Cola is an example of a successful global brand.

Strong brand equity enabled Fisher–Price to extend its brand name to other children's products.

Private Branding   A company uses **private branding,** often called *private labelling* or *reseller branding,* when it manufactures products but sells them under the brand name of a wholesaler or retailer. Radio Shack, Loblaws, and Canadian Tire are large retailers that have their own brand names. Some research suggests that consumers switch to private labels to save money because of the recessionary times we live in. As the economy recovers, it is believed, people may switch back to national brands. Still, many companies, including almost all supermarket chains in Canada, offer private labels. Most consumers have come to expect them to, in part because of aggressive marketing for President's Choice, Loblaws' successful private-label brand, which may have legitimized the private label category in Canada.[35]

Matsushita of Japan manufactures VCRs for Magnavox, GE, Sylvania, Philco, and some major reseller or retail brands. The advantage to the manufacturer is that promotional costs are shifted to the retailer or other company, and the manufacturer can often sell more units through others than by itself. There is a risk, though, because the manufacturer's sales depend heavily on the efforts of others.

Mixed Branding   A compromise between manufacturer and private branding is **mixed branding,** in which a firm markets products under its own name and that of a reseller because the segment attracted to the reseller is different from the manufacturer's own market. Sanyo and Toshiba manufacture television sets for Sears, as well as for themselves. This process is similar to that used by

Michelin, which manufactures tires for Sears as well as under its own name. A new development in mixed branding strategy has been explored by Polaroid. It is allowing Minolta, a competing camera company, to sell the Spectra Pro instant camera as the Minolta Instant Pro. Minolta has a very strong brand name in cameras, and Polaroid believes the Minolta name will lend positive identification to the high-end camera market.[36]

Generic Branding   An alternative branding approach is the **generic brand,** which is a no-brand product such as dog food, peanut butter, or green beans. There is no identification other than a description of the contents. The major appeal is that the price is up to one-third less than that of branded items. Generic brands account for less than one percent of total grocery sales.[37] The limited appeal of generics has been attributed to the popularity of private brands and greater promotional efforts for manufacturer brand-name items. Consumers who use generics see these products as being as good as brand-name items, and in light of what they expect, users of these products are relatively pleased with their purchases.

PACKAGING

The **packaging** component of a product refers to any container in which it is offered for sale and on which information is communicated. To a great extent, the customer's first exposure to a product is the package, and it is an expensive and important part of the marketing strategy. A grocery product package is especially important because packaging designers using eye cameras have discovered that a typical consumer's eye sweep of a grocery shelf is a mere few seconds. Today's packaging costs run in the billions of dollars, and these costs are inevitably passed on to the Canadian consumer.

CREATING CUSTOMER VALUE THROUGH PACKAGING

Despite the cost, packaging is essential because packages provide important benefits for the manufacturer, retailer, and ultimate consumer.

Communication Benefits   A major benefit of packaging is the information on it conveyed to the consumer, such as directions on how to use the product and the composition of the product, which is needed to satisfy legal requirements of product disclosure. Other information consists of seals and symbols, either government-required or commercial seals of approval (such as the Good House-keeping seal, or CSA approved).

Functional Benefits   Packaging often plays an important functional role, such as convenience, protection, or storage. Quaker State has changed its oil containers to eliminate the need for a separate spout, and Borden has changed the shape of its Elmer's Wonder Bond adhesive to prevent clogging of the spout.

The convenience dimension of packaging is becoming increasingly important. For example, microwave popcorn has been a major market success.

New packaging for
traditional products.

Consumer protection has become an important function of packaging, including the development of tamper-resistant containers. Today, companies commonly use safety seals or pop-tops that reveal previous opening. Nevertheless, no package is truly tamper resistant.

Another functional value of packaging is in extending storage and *shelf life* (the time a product can be stored before it spoils). New technology allows products requiring refrigeration to be packaged in paper-sealed containers, which dramatically increase their shelf life.

Perceptual Benefits   A third component of packaging is the perception created in the consumer's mind. Procter & Gamble changes the packaging for Clearasil every year, to give the appearance of a new cream, which is important to the target market of teenagers who purchase the product.[38]

A package can connote status, economy, or even product quality. Equally fresh potato chips were wrapped in two different types of bags: wax paper and polyvinyl. Consumers rated the chips in the polyvinyl as crisper and even tastier, even though the chips were identical.[39]

In the past, the colour of packages was selected subjectively. For example, the famous Campbell's soup can was the inspiration of a company executive who liked Cornell University's red-and-white football uniforms. Today, there is greater recognition that colour affects consumers' perceptions. Owens-Corning judged the pink colour of its fibre insulation to be so important that the colour was given trademark status by the courts.[40]

Functional and perceptual aspects of packaging consume an enormous amount of time and research dollars among manufacturers.

GLOBAL TRENDS IN PACKAGING

Companies worldwide are seeing packaging as a way to increase sales of existing brands.[41] Valvoline Motor Oil Company tested 40 variations on its packaging of motor oil before deciding to increase the size and add more colour to the label.

MARKETING · ACTION · MEMO

Package Designs in the 1990s

Marketplace forces, rather than design trends, will drive packaging design in the 1990s and beyond. Smart companies are recognizing the value of strategically relevant packaging which addresses their marketing objectives and business realities instead of aesthetic preferences. The competitive environment, in particular, will have companies focussing on the package designs that can create shelf impact. The emphasis will be on package elements that will get consumers' attention in those few precious seconds when they make that important choice at the point of purchase. Environmental concerns over excessive packaging will also continue to impact on package design. New legislation will require packaged goods companies to undertake packaging audits and draft new ways to further reduce packaging.

Fundamental shifts in consumer behaviour will impact on package design in specific industries. For example, with the shift from consumer fitness to wellness, consumer health care products will require packaging that is more informative. For example, consumers wanting to self-medicate will look for products with packages that communicate efficacy without being intimidating.

Greater consumer acceptance of private-label brands will continue to create a challenge for national brands, particularly in the food industry. National brands will develop packaging solutions that cannot be easily mimicked by private-label brands, or designs that can be legally protected. This will involve not only the use of graphics on packaging but also packaging structures and materials. In the future, package designs will have to do much more than simply look pretty. They must communicate and inspire and motivate the consumer in a highly competitive visual arena. The package design must also be ownable in the sense that Kellogg's Corn Flakes owns the rooster and McDonald's owns the golden arches. The design must become so much a part of the brand identity that imitation becomes either noncredible or simply insulting.

Source: Adapted from R. Budish, "Designing for the '90s," *Marketing,* January 1, 1994, p. 12; and T. Pigeon, "Packages I Wish I'd Done," *Marketing,* January 31, 1994, p. 12.

But redesigns are not without expense—some packaging changes can cost upwards of $300,000, because of alterations in production equipment. There can also be other risks, such as confusing the consumer.

There are two different trends in packaging. One trend involves environmental sensitivity. Because of the growing concern about solid-waste disposal, packaging is receiving a great deal of attention. Lever Brothers is trying to address these concerns with a test of a "bag-in-box" package for Wisk laundry detergent. Procter & Gamble uses recycled cardboard in 70 percent of its paper packaging, and is packaging Tide and Cheer detergents in jugs that contain 25 percent recycled plastic. Spic and Span liquid cleaner is packaged in 100 percent recycled material, and a similar approach is used by Heinz for its ketchup bottle.

European countries have strict packaging guidelines pertaining to environmental sensitivity. Many of these now exist in the provisions governing trade within the 12-nation European Community.[42] In Germany, for instance, 80 percent of packaging material must be collected, and 80 percent of this amount must be recycled or reused to reduce solid waste in landfills. North American firms marketing in Europe have responded to these guidelines, and ultimately benefited North American consumers. The history of Procter & Gamble's

Downy Refill liquid fabric softener is an example.[43] The product's plastic bottle is reusable, and the refill carton uses 75 percent less packaging material. First introduced in Germany in 1987, the product moved to Canada in 1989, and then to the United States in late 1990. Downey Refill now accounts for 40 percent of Downy sales.

A second trend involves the health and safety concerns of packaging materials. Studies suggest that microwave heating of some packages can lead to potentially cancer-causing agents seeping into food products. The major concern relates to packaging that contains heat susceptors—thin, metallized plastic-film strips that help brown microwavable food. Companies like Du Pont and 3M are working to develop alternatives in anticipation of regulatory changes regarding packaging.[44]

The accompanying Marketing Action Memo discusses the future of package designs and the marketing role the package will play in the 1990s and beyond.

PRODUCT WARRANTY

A final component for product consideration is the **warranty,** which is a statement indicating the liability of the manufacturer for product deficiencies. There are various degrees of product warranties with different implications for manufacturers and customers.

THE VARIATONS OF A WARRANTY

Some companies offer *express warranties,* which are written statements of liabilities. In recent years the government has required greater disclosure on express warranties to indicate whether the warranty is a limited-coverage or a full-coverage alternative. A *limited-coverage warranty* specifically states the bounds of coverage and, more important, areas of noncoverage, whereas a *full warranty* has no limits of noncoverage. Peugeot is a company that boldly touts its warranty coverage.

With greater frequency, manufacturers are being held to *implied warranties,* which assign responsibility for product deficiencies to the manufacturer. Studies show that warranties are important and affect a consumer's product evaluation. Brands that have limited warranties tend to receive less positive evaluations than full-warranty items.[45]

Consumer and Corporate Affairs Canada is responsible for protecting consumer rights with regard to warranties.

THE GROWING IMPORTANCE OF WARRANTIES

Warranties are important in light of increasing product liability claims. In the early part of the 20th century the courts protected companies, but the trend now is toward "strict liability" rulings, where a manufacturer is liable for any product defect, whether it followed reasonable research standards or not. This issue is hotly contested between companies and consumer advocates.

Warranties represent much more than just protection of the buyer from negative consequences—they can hold a significant marketing advantage for the producer. Sears has built a strong reputation for its Craftsman tool line with a simple warranty: if you break a tool, it's replaced with no questions asked. Zippo has an equally simple guarantee: "If it ever fails, we'll fix it free."

---

1 How does a generic brand differ from a private brand?

2 Explain the role of packaging in terms of perception.

3 What is the difference between an expressed and an implied warranty?

Summary

1 Products have a finite life cycle consisting of four stages: introduction, growth, maturity, and decline. The marketing objectives for each stage differ.

2 In the introductory stage the need is to establish primary demand, whereas the growth stage requires selective demand strategies. In the maturity stage the need is to maintain market share; the decline stage necessitates a deleting, harvesting, or contracting strategy.

3 There are various shapes to the product life cycle. High learning products have a long introductory period, and low learning products rapidly enter the growth stage. There are also different curves for fashions and fads. Different product life cycle curves can exist for the product class, product form, and brand.

4 In managing a product's life cycle, changes can be made in the product itself or in the target market. Product modification approaches include changes in the quality, performance, or appearance. Market modification approaches entail increasing a product's use among existing customers, creating new use situations, or finding new users.

5 Product repositioning can be done by modifying the product, as well as through changes in advertising, pricing, or distribution.

6 Branding enables a firm to distinguish its product in the marketplace from those of its competitors. A good brand name should suggest the product's benefits, be memorable, fit the company or product image, be free of legal restrictions, and be simple and emotional. In international marketing, nonmeaningful brand names avoid cultural problems and undesirable images.

7 Licensing of a brand name is being used by many companies. The company allows the name to be used without having to manufacture the product.

8 Manufacturers can follow one of three branding strategies: a manufacturer's brand, a reseller brand, or a mixed brand approach. With a manufac-

turer's branding approach, the company can use the same brand name for all products in the line (multiproduct, or family, branding) or can give products different brands (multibranding). With global markets and freer trade, global branding, euro-branding, and North American branding will grow.

9 A reseller, or private, brand is used when a firm manufactures a product but sells it under the brand name of a wholesaler or retailer. A generic brand is a product with no identification of manufacturer or reseller that is offered on the basis of price appeal.

10 Packaging provides communication, functional, and perceptual benefits. The two emerging trends in packaging are greater concerns regarding the environmental impact and the safety of packaging materials.

11 The warranty, a statement of a manufacturer's liability for product deficiencies, is an important aspect of a manufacturer's product strategy.

Key Terms and Concepts

product life cycle p. 288
product class p. 294
product form p. 295
product modification p. 297
retromarketing p. 298
market modification strategies p. 298
trading up p. 299
trading down p. 299
downsizing p. 299
branding p. 300
brand name p. 300
trade name p. 301
trademark p. 301

brand equity p. 301
licensing p. 302
manufacturer branding p. 304
multiproduct branding p. 304
multibranding p. 305
euro-branding p. 305
global branding p. 305
private branding p. 306
mixed branding p. 306
generic brand p. 307
packaging p. 307
warranty p. 310

Chapter Problems and Applications

1 Several years ago, Apple Computer was one of the first to mass-market PCs. IBM, the giant, had no competing product, but within a short time it announced its PC model. Steven Jobs, the founder of Apple, is said to have exclaimed "We're glad to see IBM is entering the market." According to the product life cycle, is there any rationale for this statement?

2 Listed are three different products in various stages of the product life cycle. What marketing strategies would you suggest to these companies? (*a*) Cantel cellular tele-

phone company—growth stage; (*b*) Water Doctor tap-water purifying systems—introductory stage; and (*c*) hand-held manual can openers—decline stage.

3 In many communities the birthrate has dropped substantially, adversely affecting hospitals' pediatric medicine departments. Although pediatrics as a specialty is declining, hospitals still need a complete service mix. As the chief executive of a hospital, what decline strategies would you suggest?

4 It has been suggested that products are intentionally made to break down or wear out. Is this strategy a planned product modification approach?

5 The product manager of GE is reviewing the penetration of trash compactors in Canadian homes. After more than a decade in existence, this product is in relatively few homes. What problems account for this poor acceptance? What is the shape of the trash compactor life cycle?

6 For several years Ferrari has been known as the manufacturer of expensive luxury automobiles. The company plans to attract the major segment of the car-buying market who purchase medium-priced automobiles. As Ferrari considers this trading-down strategy, what branding strategy would you recommend? What are the trade-offs to consider with your strategy?

7 The nature of product warranties has changed as the government reassesses the meaning of warranties. How does the regulatory trend toward warranties affect product development?

Pricing: Relating Objectives to Revenues and Costs

AFTER READING THIS CHAPTER YOU SHOULD BE ABLE TO:

▸ Identify the elements that make up a price.

▸ Recognize the constraints on a firm's pricing latitude and the objectives a firm has in setting prices.

▸ Explain what a demand curve is and how it affects a firm's total and marginal revenue.

▸ Recognize what price elasticity of demand means to a manager facing a pricing decision.

▸ Explain the role of costs in pricing decisions.

▸ Calculate a break-even point for various combinations of price, fixed cost, and variable cost.

fundamental micro-economic

Economics 101: Potato Chip Style

As vice president of Frito-Lay, the world's premier marketer of snack chips, you are faced with a dilemma. A recent drought causes a potato shortage and a rise in raw potato prices. Fewer potatoes at a higher cost spell trouble for you. Consumers will still want to have their potato chips, but higher potato costs will pinch your profit margin, and fewer potatoes will mean a limited supply of chips to sell. What should you do?

Discussion among company executives results in a two-pronged response. First, the bag price of the potato chips would increase 10 cents to cover higher potato costs and provide an acceptable profit margin on fewer bags sold. Second, potato chip promotional activities would be reduced.

According to Dwight Riskey, vice president of marketing research and new business at Frito-Lay, in this situation "we attempt to manage demand for potato chips using price and other tools at our disposal." Frito-Lay did experience such a situation, and its response did work. The company was able to synchronize demand and supply during the shortage. Once the shortage passed, Frito-Lay resumed its promotion for potato chips and reduced the bag price by a dime to the original.[1] This was Potato Chip Economics 101.

This chapter and Chapter 14 cover important factors organizations use in developing prices. The role of price in marketing strategy and a step-by-step procedure organizations use to set prices for products and services are discussed.

Relevant concepts from economics and accounting show how each assists the marketing executive in developing the price component in the marketing mix.

NATURE AND IMPORTANCE OF PRICE

The price paid for goods and services goes by many names. You pay *tuition* for your education, *rent* for an apartment, *interest* on a bank credit card, and a *premium* for car insurance. Your dentist or physician charges you a *fee,* a professional or social organization charges *dues,* and transportation companies charge a *fare.* In business, a consultant may require a *retainer* for services rendered, an executive is given a *salary,* a salesperson receives a *commission,* and a worker is paid a *wage.* Of course, what you pay for clothes or a haircut is termed a *price.*

WHAT IS A PRICE?

These examples highlight the many varied ways that price plays a part in our daily lives. From a marketing viewpoint, **price** is the money or other considerations (including other goods and services) exchanged for the ownership or use of a good or service. For example, Shell Oil recently exchanged 1 million pest control devices for sugar from a Caribbean country, and Wilkinson Sword exchanged some of its knives for advertising used to promote its razor blades. This practice of exchanging goods and services for other goods and services

▌*Figure 13–1*
The price of four different purchases.

ITEM PURCHASED	PRICE EQUATION					
	PRICE	=	LIST PRICE	−	DISCOUNTS AND ALLOWANCES	+ EXTRA FEES
New car bought by an individual	Final price	=	List price	−	Quantity discount Cash discount Trade-ins	+ Financing charges Special accessories
Term in college bought by a student	Tuition	=	Published tuition	−	Scholarship Other financial aid Discounts for number of credits taken	+ Special activity fees
Bank loan obtained by a small business	Principal and interest	=	Amount of loan sought	−	Allowance for collateral	+ Premium for uncertain creditworthiness
Merchandise bought from a wholesaler by a retailer	Invoice price	=	List price	−	Quantity discount Cash discount Season discount Functional or trade discount	+ Penalty for late payment

rather than for money is called **barter.** These and similar transactions account for $5 billion annually in domestic and international trade.[2]

For most products and services, money is exchanged, although the amount is not always the same as the list or quoted price. Suppose you decide to buy two identical Dodge Viper two-seat sports cars sold by Chrysler.[3] The Dodge Viper is powered by an 8-litre aluminum V-10 engine and accelerates from 0 to 100 and returns to a dead stop in just 14.5 seconds. The list price is $55,630 for each. As a quantity discount for buying two Dodge Vipers, you get $7,000 off the list price for each. You agree to pay half down and the other half when the cars are delivered, which results in a financing fee of $3,000 per car. You are allowed $1,000 for your only trade—your 1982 Honda—amounting to $500 off the price of each car.

Applying the **price equation** (as shown in Figure 13–1) to your purchase, your price per car is:

Price = List price − Discounts and allowances + Extra fees
     = $55,630 − ($7,000 + $500) + $3,000
     = $51,130

Are you still interested? Perhaps you might look at the Porsche 959 or Ferrari F40 to compare prices. Figure 13–1 also illustrates how the price equation applies to a variety of different products and services.

PRICE AS AN INDICATOR OF VALUE

From a consumer's standpoint, price is often used to indicate value when it is paired with the perceived benefits of a product or service. Specifically, **value** can be defined as the ratio of perceived benefits to price (value = perceived benefits/price).[4] This relationship shows that for a given price, as perceived benefits increase, value increases. Also, for a given price, value decreases when perceived benefits decrease. Creative marketers engage in **value-based pricing,** the practice of simultaneously increasing product and service benefits and maintaining or decreasing price.[5]

For some products, price influences the perception of overall quality, and ultimately value, to consumers.[6] For example, in a survey of home furnishing buyers, 84 percent agreed with the statement "The higher the price, the higher the quality." For computer software it has been shown that consumers believe a low price implies poor quality.[7]

Consumer value assessments are often comparative. Here value involves the judgment by a consumer of the worth and desirability of a product or service relative to substitutes that satisfy the same need.[8] In this instance a "reference value" emerges, which involves comparing the costs and benefits of substitute items. For example, although Equal, a sugar substitute with NutraSweet, might be more expensive than sugar, some consumers "value" it more highly than sugar because Equal contains no calories.

How consumers make value assessments is not fully understood. Nevertheless, innovative companies now recognize that value is more than a low price, as detailed in the accompanying Marketing Action Memo.

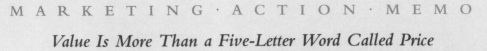

MARKETING · ACTION · MEMO

Value Is More Than a Five-Letter Word Called Price

Providing "value" for consumers has become a global challenge, because Canadian consumers are not alone in demanding greater satisfaction for their money. A recent survey of consumers in France, Germany, and the United Kingdom indicates that value was the single most important factor in making a purchase decision, followed by the perceived quality of a product or brand.

Deciphering the value = perceived benefits/price equation has become a full-time job for marketers. For Pizza Hut, value means adding 25 percent more toppings on its Lover's line of pizzas without increasing the price. At Procter & Gamble, a company spokesperson notes, "Value is not just price but also is linked to the performance and meeting expectations and needs of consumers." For Kohler Company, value is created from innovative product design. The company's recent introduction of a walk-in bathtub that is safe for children and the elderly is one example. Even though a walk-in bathtub is priced higher than conventional step-in bathtubs, it has proven to be a great marketing success.

Savvy marketers know that value is more than a low price. It arises from imaginative ways companies satisfy the needs of customers.

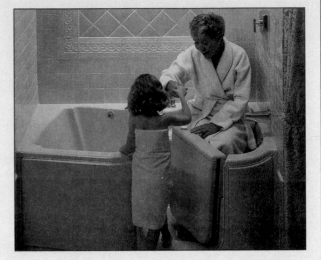

Sources: Based on N. Giges, "Europeans Buy Outside Goods, but Like Local Ads," *Advertising Age*, April 27, 1992, pp. I-2, I-26; "Pizza Hut to Hold Prices While Adding 25% More Toppings," *The Wall Street Journal*, May 6, 1992, p. B8; "What Works for One Works for All," *Business Week*, April 20, 1992, pp. 112–13; J. Lawrence, "Laundry Soap Marketers See the Value of 'Value!' " *Advertising Age*, September 21, 1992, pp. 3, 56; and S. Sherman, "How to Prosper in the Value Decade," *Fortune*, November 30, 1992, pp. 90–91ff.

PRICE IN THE MARKETING MIX

Pricing is also a critical decision made by a marketing executive, because price has a direct effect on a firm's profits. This is apparent from a firm's **profit equation:**

Profit = Total revenue − Total cost

or

Profit = (Unit price × Quantity sold) − Total cost

What makes this relationship even more important is that price affects the quantity sold, as illustrated with demand curves later in this chapter. Furthermore, since the quantity sold sometimes affects a firm's costs because of efficiency of production, price also indirectly affects costs. So pricing decisions influence both total revenue and total cost, which makes pricing one of the most important decisions marketing executives face.[9]

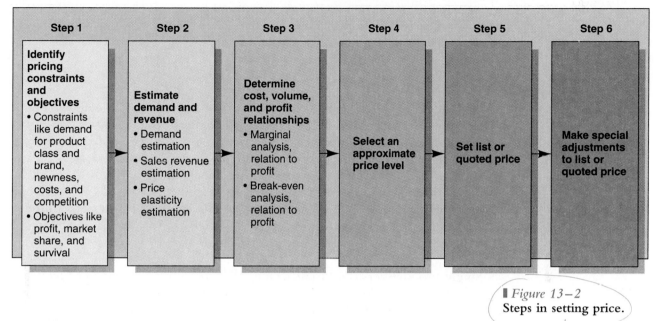

■ *Figure 13–2*
Steps in setting price.

10/28 ✳

The importance of price in the marketing mix necessitates an understanding of six major steps involved in the process organizations go through in setting prices (Figure 13–2):

- Identify pricing constraints and objectives.
- Estimate demand and revenue.
- Determine cost, volume, and profit relationships.
- Select an approximate price level.
- Set list or quoted price.
- Make special adjustments to list or quoted price.

The first three steps are covered in this chapter and the last three in Chapter 14.

STEP 1: IDENTIFYING PRICING CONSTRAINTS AND OBJECTIVES

Let's first review pricing constraints so that we can better understand the nature of pricing alternatives. We will then discuss the variety of pricing objectives that may be set by organizations.

IDENTIFYING PRICING CONSTRAINTS

Factors that limit the latitude of prices a firm may set are **pricing constraints.** Consumer demand for the product clearly affects the price that can be charged. Other constraints on price are set by factors within the organization: newness of the product, whether it is part of a product line, and cost of and flexibility in changing a price. Competitive factors such as the nature of competition and prices set by competitors also restrict the latitude of an organization's ability to set price. Legal and regulatory constraints on pricing are discussed in Chapter 14.

primary/secondary
demand:

Demand for the Product Class, Product, and Brand   The number of potential buyers for the product class (cars), product (sports cars), and brand (Dodge Viper) clearly affects the price a seller can charge. So does whether the item is a luxury, like a Dodge Viper, or a necessity, like bread and a roof over one's head. The nature of demand is discussed later in the chapter.

Newness of the Product: Stage in the Product Life Cycle   The newer a product and the earlier it is in its life cycle, the higher is the price that can usually be charged. When NutraSweet was introduced in 1983, it was the only non-artificial sugar substitute that was safe to use, contained few calories, and was sweeter than sugar. The newness of the product coupled with patent protection meant that a premium price of $92 per pound could be charged. However, once its patent expired in December 1992, rivals emerged (such as Johnson & Johnson's sweetener Sucralose), which affected the pricing latitude for NutraSweet. NutraSweet's price per pound in January 1993 was $52.[10]

Single Product versus a Product Line   When Sony introduced its CD player, not only was it unique and in the introductory stage of its product life cycle but also it was the *only* CD player Sony sold, so the firm had great latitude in setting a price. Now, with a line of CD player products, the price of individual models has to be consistent with the others based on features provided and meaningful price differentials that communicate value to consumers.

Cost of Producing and Marketing the Product   In the long run, a firm's price must cover all the costs of producing and marketing a product. If the price doesn't cover the cost, the firm will fail, so in the long run a firm's costs set a floor under its price.

Cost of Changing Prices and Time Period They Apply   If Air Canada asks Pratt & Whitney (P&W) to provide spare jet engines to power the Boeing 747 airplanes in its fleet, P&W can easily set a new price for the engines to reflect its latest information, since only one buyer has to be informed. But if Sears Canada decides that sweater prices are too low in its winter catalogues after thousands of catalogues have been mailed to customers, it has a big problem. It can't easily inform thousands of potential buyers that the price has changed, so Sears Canada must consider the cost of changing prices and the time period for which they apply in developing the price list for its catalogue items. In actual practice, research indicates that most firms change the price for their major products once a year.[11]

Type of Competitive Markets   The seller's price is constrained by the type of market in which it competes. Economists generally delineate four types of competitive markets: pure monopoly, oligopoly, monopolistic competition, and pure competition. Figure 13–3 shows that the type of competition dramatically influences the latitude of price competition and in turn the nature of product differentiation and extent of advertising. A firm must recognize the general type of competitive market it is in to understand the latitude of both its price and nonprice strategies. For example:

STRATEGIES AVAILABLE	TYPE OF COMPETITIVE MARKET			
	PURE MONOPOLY (One seller who sets the price for a unique product)	OLIGOPOLY (Few sellers who are sensitive to each other's prices)	MONOPOLISTIC COMPETITION (Many sellers who compete on nonprice factors)	PURE COMPETITION (Many sellers who follow the market price for identical, commodity products)
Price competition	None: sole seller sets price	Some: price leader or follower of competitors	Some: compete over range of prices	Almost none: market sets price
Product differentiation	None: no other producers	Various: depends on industry	Some: differentiate products from competitors'	None: products are identical
Extent of advertising	Little: purpose is to increase demand for product class	Some: purpose is to inform but avoid price competition	Much: purpose is to differentiate firm's products from competitors'	Little: purpose is to inform prospects that seller's products are available

Handwritten annotations: "Regurcable TV." under Pure Monopoly; "Esso/Shell" under Oligopoly; "butter" under Monopolistic Competition; "corn" under Pure Competition.

▌ Figure 13–3

Pricing, product, and advertising strategies available to firms in four types of competitive markets.

▪ *Pure monopoly:* Ontario Hydro, an electric power company, receives approval from the public utility commission for the rates it can charge Ontario consumers. In most areas of the province, it is the only source of electricity for consumers and runs public-service ads to show them how to conserve electricity.

▪ *Oligopoly:* The few sellers of aluminum (Alcan or Alcoa) or gasoline (Esso or Shell), try to avoid price competition because it can lead to disastrous price wars in which all lose money. Yet firms in such industries stay aware of a competitor's price cuts or increases and may follow suit. The products can be undifferentiated (aluminum) or differentiated (grade of gasoline); informative advertising that avoids head-to-head price competition is used.

Handwritten annotation: "Big players"

▪ *Monopolistic competition:* Regional or private brands of peanut butter compete with national brands like Skippy and Jif. Both price competition (regional, private brands being lower-priced than national brands) and nonprice competition (product features and advertising) exist.

▪ *Pure competition:* Hundreds of local grain elevators sell corn, whose price per bushel is set by the marketplace. Within strains, the corn is identical, so advertising only informs buyers that the seller's corn is available.

Handwritten annotation: "players are small & no power in the mkt"

Competitors' Prices A firm must know or anticipate what specific price its present and potential competitors now charge or will charge. When the NutraSweet Company planned the market introduction of Simplesse® all-natural fat substitute, it had to consider the price of fat replacements already available as well as potential competitors including Procter & Gamble's Olestra. The desire to know competitor prices can result in sharing price information among competitors. But competitors cannot use such information to price fix (to agree to set prices and thus reduce competition), a practice illegal under the Competition Act.

objectives may be changed over-time.

IDENTIFYING PRICING OBJECTIVES

Goals that specify the role of price in an organization's marketing and strategic plans are known as **pricing objectives.** To the extent possible, organizational pricing objectives are also carried to lower levels in the organization, such as in setting objectives for marketing managers responsible for an individual brand.[12] H. J. Heinz, for example, has specific pricing objectives for its Heinz ketchup brand that vary by country (see the accompanying Marketing Action Memo). Chapter 2 discussed several objectives that an organization may pursue at the organizational or marketing level, which can tie in directly with the organization's pricing policies.

Profit   Three different objectives relate to a firm's profit, usually measured in terms of return on investment (ROI) or return on assets. One objective is *managing for long-run profits,* which is followed by many Japanese firms that are willing to forgo immediate profit in cars, TV sets, or computers to develop quality products that can penetrate competitive markets in the future. A *maximizing current profit* objective, such as during the present quarter or year, is common in many firms because the targets can be set and performance measured quickly. Canadian firms are sometimes criticized for this short-run orientation. A *target return* objective involves a firm like Clearly Canadian or Esso setting a goal (such as 20 percent) for pretax ROI. These three profit objectives have different implications for a firm's pricing objectives.

Sales   Given that a firm's profit is high enough for it to remain in business, its objectives may be to increase sales revenue. The hope is that the increase in sales revenue will in turn lead to increases in market share and profit. Cutting price on one product in a firm's line may increase that product's sales revenue but reduce that of related products. Objectives related to sales revenue or unit sales have the advantage of being translated easily into meaningful targets for marketing managers responsible for a product line or brand—far more easily than objectives connected with an ROI target, for example.

Market Share   Market share is the ratio of a firm's sales revenues or unit sales to those of the industry (competitors plus the firm itself). Companies often pursue a market share objective when industry sales are flat or declining and they want to get a larger share. In their battle for market share, Pepsi and Coke often use price specials or discounts. However, while increased market share is a primary goal of some firms, others see it as a means to other ends: increasing sales and profits.

Unit Volume   Many firms use unit volume, the quantity produced or sold, as a pricing objective. These firms often sell multiple products at very different prices and are sensitive to matching production capacity with unit volume. Using unit volume as an objective, however, can sometimes be misleading from a profit standpoint. Volume can be increased by employing sales incentives (such as lowering prices, giving rebates, or offering lower interest rates). By doing this the company chooses to lower profits in the short run to quickly sell its product.

H. J. Heinz Pricing Objectives Vary in the Global Ketchup Marketplace

H.J. Heinz Company has been making and marketing ketchup for more than a century. Heinz ketchup, the firm's flagship brand, holds more than 50 percent of the North American ketchup market. About one-half of all ketchup consumed in the world is sold by Heinz.

This seasoned global marketer sells ketchup in over 200 countries. Like other global marketers, Heinz pursues different pricing objectives for its ketchup in different countries. For instance, in those countries where competition is intense and Heinz is not the market leader, the company tends to price its ketchup aggressively with the objectives of building dollar sales, unit volume, and market share. In Japan, Heinz has focussed its pricing objective on protecting its profitability. Thus, its ketchup prices are higher than competitors'.

Sources: Based on J. P. Jeannet and H. D. Hennessey, *Global Marketing Strategies,* 2nd ed. (Boston: Houghton Mifflin Company, 1992), p. 430; "Ketchup War Will Be Fought to the Last Drop," *Financial Times,* February 21, 1990, p. 18; "Counting Costs of Dual Pricing in the Run-Up to 1992," *Financial Times,* July 9, 1990, p. 4; and G. Hoover, A. Campbell, and P. J. Spain, eds., *Hoover's Handbook—1991: Profiles of Over 500 Major Corporations* (Austin, TX: The Reference Press, 1991), p. 283.

This happened recently when Fiat offered $1,600 rebates and zero-interest financing in Italy on its $10,000 Uno compact car.[13]

Customer Value Providing customer value may be an important organizational or marketing objective. To provide it, many firms will engage in value-based pricing, increasing product or service benefits while maintaining or lowering prices. Others offer "everyday low prices" or specific values, like Wendy's "value menu."

Fiat used rebates and zero-interest financing to stimulate unit sales of its Uno compact car in Italy.

Survival In some instances, profits, sales, and market share are less important objectives of the firm than mere survival. Continental Airlines has struggled to attract passengers with low fares, no-penalty advance-booking policies, and aggressive promotions to improve the firm's cash flow. This pricing objective has helped Continental to stay alive in the competitive airline industry.

Social Responsibility A firm may forgo higher profit on sales and follow a pricing objective that recognizes its obligations to customers and society in general. Medtronics followed this pricing policy when it introduced the world's first heart pacemaker. Gerber supplies a specially formulated product free of charge to children who cannot tolerate foods based on cow's milk.[14] Government agencies, which set many prices for services they offer, use social responsibility as a primary pricing objective.

Concept Check

1 What do you have to do to the list price to determine the final price?

2 How does the type of competitive market a firm is in affect its latitude in setting price?

STEP 2: ESTIMATING DEMAND AND REVENUE

Basic to setting a product's price is the extent of customer demand for it. Understanding demand requires a look at how economists and businesspeople view it.

FUNDAMENTALS IN ESTIMATING DEMAND AND REVENUE

Newsweek conducted a pricing experiment in 11 cities.[15] In one city, newsstand buyers paid $2.25. In five cities, newsstand buyers paid the regular $2.00. In another city, the price was $1.50, and in four other cities it was only $1.00. By comparison, the regular newsstand price for *Time* was $1.95. Why did *Newsweek* conduct the experiment? According to a *Newsweek* executive at that time, "We want to figure out what the demand curve for our magazine at the newsstand is." And you thought that demand curves only existed to confuse you on a test in basic economics!

The Demand Curve   A **demand curve** shows a maximum number of products consumers will buy at a given price. Demand curve D_1 in Figure 13–4 shows the newsstand demand for *Newsweek* under present conditions. Note that as price falls, more people buy. But price is not the complete story in estimating demand. Economists stress three other key factors:

1 *Consumer tastes.* As we saw in Chapter 3, these depend on many factors such as demographics, culture, and technology. Because consumer tastes can change quickly, up-to-date marketing research is essential.
2 *Price and availability of other products.* As the price of close substitute products falls (*Time* for *Newsweek*) and their availability increases, the demand for a product declines.
3 *Consumer income.* In general, as real consumer income (allowing for inflation) increases, demand for a product also increases.

The first of these two factors influences what consumers *want* to buy, and the third affects what they *can* buy. Along with price, these are often called **demand factors,** or factors that determine consumers' willingness and ability to pay for goods and services.

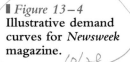

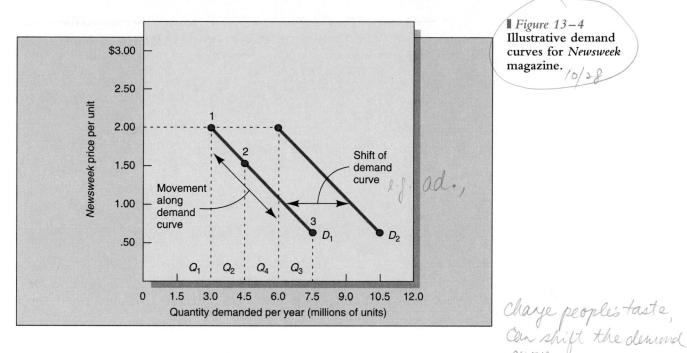

*Chage people's taste,
Can shift the demand
curve.*

Movement along versus Shift of a Demand Curve   Demand curve D_1 in
Figure 13–4 shows that as the price is lowered from $2 to $1.50, the quantity
demanded increases from 3 million to 4.5 million units per year. This is an
example of a movement along a demand curve and assumes that other factors
(consumer tastes, price and availability of substitutes, and consumer income)
remain unchanged.

What if some of these factors change? For example, if advertising causes
more people to want *Newsweek,* newsstand distribution is increased, and consumer incomes double, then the demand increases. This is shown in Figure
13–4 as a shift of the demand curve to the right, from D_1 to D_2. This means
that more *Newsweek* magazines are wanted for a given price: at a price of $2, the
demand is 6 million units per year (Q_4) on D_2 rather than 3 million units per
year (Q_1) on D_1.

FUNDAMENTALS IN ESTIMATING REVENUE

While economists may talk about demand curves, marketing executives are
more likely to speak in terms of revenues generated. Demand curves lead
directly to three related revenue concepts critical to pricing decisions: **total
revenue, average revenue,** and **marginal revenue** (Figure 13–5).

Demand Curves and Revenue   Figure 13–6A again shows the demand curve
for *Newsweek,* but it is now extended to intersect both the price and quantity
axes. The demand curve shows that as price is reduced, the quantity of *Newsweek* magazines sold increases. This relationship holds whether the price is
reduced from $3 to $2.50 on the demand curve or is reduced from $1 to $0 on
the curve. In the former case the market demands no *Newsweek* magazines,
whereas in the latter case 9 million could be given away at $0 per unit.

Total revenue (TR) is the total money received from the sale of a product. If:

TR = Total revenue
 P = Unit price of the product
 Q = Quantity of the product sold

then:

  TR = $P \times Q$

Average revenue (AR) is the average amount of money received for selling one unit of the product, or simply the price of that unit. Average revenue is the total revenue divided by the quantity sold:

$$AR = \frac{TR}{Q} = P$$

Marginal revenue (MR) is the change in total revenue obtained by selling one additional unit:

$$MR = \frac{\text{Change in TR}}{\text{1 unit increase in } Q} = \frac{\Delta TR}{\Delta Q}$$

It is likely that if *Newsweek* were given away, more than 9 million would be demanded. This fact illustrates two important points. First, it can be dangerous to extend a demand curve beyond the range of prices for which it really applies. Second, most demand curves are rounded (or convex) to the origin, thereby avoiding an unrealistic picture of what demand looks like when a straight-line curve intersects either the price axis or the quantity axis.

Figure 13–6B shows the total revenue curve for *Newsweek* calculated from the demand curve shown in Figure 13–6A. The total revenue curve is developed by simply multiplying the unit price times the quantity for each of the points on the demand curve. Total revenue starts at $0 (point *A*), reaches a maximum of $6,750,000 at point *D,* and returns to $0 at point *G*. This shows that as price is reduced in the *A*-to-*D* segment of the curve, total revenues are increased. However, cutting price in the *D*-to-*G* segment results in a decline in total revenue.

Marginal revenue, which is the slope of the total revenue curve, is positive but decreasing when the price lies in the range from $3 to above $1.50 per unit. But below $1.50 per unit, marginal revenue is actually negative, so the extra quantity of magazines sold is more than offset by the decrease in the price per unit.

For any downward–sloping straight-line demand curve, the marginal revenue curve always falls at a rate twice as fast as the demand curve. As shown in Figure 13–6A, the marginal revenue becomes $0 per unit at a quantity sold of 4.5 million units—the very point at which total revenue is maximum (see Figure 13–6B). Because a rational marketing manager would never operate in the region of the demand curve in which marginal revenue is negative, only the positive portion is shown in typical graphs of demand curves.

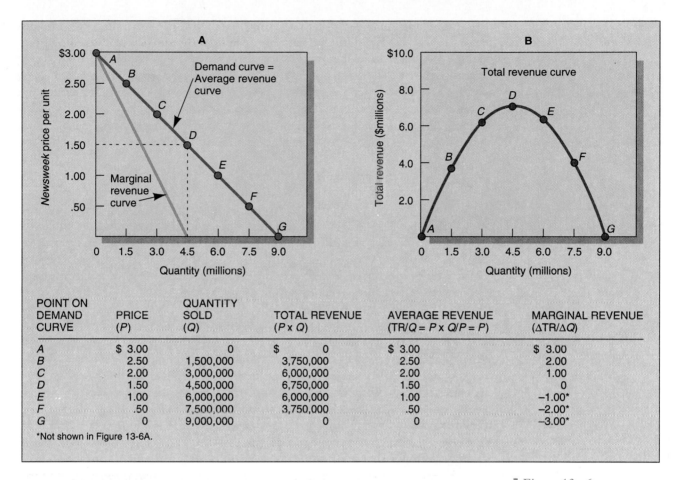

POINT ON DEMAND CURVE	PRICE (P)	QUANTITY SOLD (Q)	TOTAL REVENUE (P x Q)	AVERAGE REVENUE (TR/Q = P x Q/P = P)	MARGINAL REVENUE (ΔTR/ΔQ)
A	$ 3.00	0	$ 0	$ 3.00	$ 3.00
B	2.50	1,500,000	3,750,000	2.50	2.00
C	2.00	3,000,000	6,000,000	2.00	1.00
D	1.50	4,500,000	6,750,000	1.50	0
E	1.00	6,000,000	6,000,000	1.00	−1.00*
F	.50	7,500,000	3,750,000	.50	−2.00*
G	0	9,000,000	0	0	−3.00*

*Not shown in Figure 13-6A.

Figure 13–6
How a downward-sloping demand curve affects total, average, and marginal revenue.

What price did *Newsweek* select after conducting its experiment? They kept the price at $2.00. However, through expanded newsstand distribution and more aggressive advertising, *Newsweek* was later able to shift its demand curve to the right and charge a price of $2.50 without affecting its newsstand volume.

Price Elasticity of Demand With a downward-sloping demand curve, we have been concerned with the responsiveness of demand to price changes. This can be conveniently measured by **price elasticity of demand,** or the percentage change in quantity demanded relative to a percentage change in price. Price elasticity of demand (*E*) is expressed as follows:

$$E = \frac{\text{Percentage change in quantity demanded}}{\text{Percentage change in price}}$$

Because quantity demanded usually decreases as price increases, price elasticity of demand is usually a negative number. However, for the sake of simplicity and by convention, elasticity figures are shown as positive numbers.

Price elasticity of demand assumes three forms: elastic demand, inelastic demand, and unitary demand elasticity. *Elastic demand* exists when a small percentage decrease in price produces a larger percentage increase in quantity demanded. Price elasticity is greater than 1 with elastic demand. *Inelastic demand* exists when a small percentage decrease in price produces a smaller percentage increase in quantity demanded. With inelastic demand, price elasticity is less than 1. *Unitary demand* exists when the percentage change in price is identical to the percentage change in quantity demanded. In this instance, price elasticity is equal to 1.

Price elasticity of demand is determined by a number of factors. First, the more substitutes a product or service has, the more likely it is to be price elastic. For example, butter has many possible substitutes in a meal and is price elastic, but gasoline has almost no substitutes and is price inelastic. Second, products and services considered to be necessities are price inelastic. For example, open-heart surgery is price inelastic, whereas airline tickets for a vacation are price elastic. Third, items that require a large cash outlay compared with a person's disposable income are price elastic. Accordingly, cars and yachts are price elastic; books and movie tickets tend to be price inelastic.

Price elasticity is important to marketing managers because of its relationship to total revenue. For example, with elastic demand, total revenue increases when price decreases, but decreases when price increases. With inelastic demand, total revenue increases when price increases and decreases when price decreases. Finally, with unitary demand, total revenue is unaffected by a slight price change. Because of this relationship between price elasticity and a firm's total revenue, it is important that marketing managers recognize that price elasticity of demand is not the same over all possible prices of a product. Figure 13–6B illustrates this point using the *Newsweek* demand curve shown in Figure 13–6A. As the price decreases from $2.50 to $2, total revenue increases, indicating an elastic demand. However, when the price decreases from $1 to 50 cents, total revenue declines, indicating an inelastic demand. Unitary demand elasticity exists at $1.50.

Price Elasticities for Brands and Product Classes   Marketing executives also recognize that the price elasticity of demand is not always the same for product classes (such as stereo receivers) or brands within a product class (such as Sony and Teac). For example, marketing experiments on brands of cola, coffee, and snack and specialty foods generally show elasticities of 1.5 to 2.5, indicating they are price elastic. By comparison, entire product classes of fruits and vegetables have elasticities of about 0.8—they are price inelastic.[16]

The price elasticity of demand for cigarettes has become a hotly debated public health issue and a matter of corporate ethics and social responsibility (see the Ethics and Social Responsibility Alert). Recently, several Canadian provinces have decreased the amount of taxes on cigarettes, creating lower prices. However, the price of cigarettes in Canada is still much higher than in many parts of the United States. Ironically, while prices for cigarettes are dropping in some provinces, the United States is introducing higher excise taxes on cigarettes, for two reasons. First, US health care reform will cost money, and the US

ETHICS AND SOCIAL RESPONSIBILITY ALERT

The Pricing of Cigarettes

A key public health policy issue in Canada is how to get smokers to curtail their smoking behaviour and how to prevent nonsmokers from becoming smokers. One of the more notable considerations in the fight against smoking is the use of economic disincentives such as high cigarette prices. In Canada, cigarette prices have increased substantially over the past two decades, mainly because of high excise taxes placed on the product. The price elasticity of cigarettes is not only relevant to the marketers of cigarettes, but also important for public policymakers examining the effect of high prices on demand for cigarettes. For example, cigarette producers can increase prices substantially and some people will continue to smoke, perhaps even giving up purchasing other products so they can afford to buy cigarettes. What are the ethics involved in raising prices, knowing that some people will continue to buy the product, even if they cannot afford to buy?

Some Canadian provinces have recently reduced the amount of taxes on cigarettes, thus lowering the prices at the retail level. Some suggest this move was to reduce the amount of cigarette smuggling, or illegally bringing in cheaper cigarettes, from the United States, which, in effect, reduces tax revenues for the provinces. Should the government, on one hand, advocate a smoke-free society while, on the other, showing concern for maintaining tax revenues that come from the product? While some experts believe education is the key to preventing and reducing the incidence of smoking, the pricing of cigarettes and the matter of price elasticity will continue to play a role in the debate over cigarette smoking. What ethical and social responsibility do the government and cigarette producers have in connection with the issue of cigarette pricing?

government will use the taxes on cigarettes to partially offset the new health care costs. Second, the US government believes that higher prices will curtail smoking and lessen the incidences of smoking-related diseases, which are a burden on the health care system. However, research generally shows that cigarettes are price inelastic. But price elasticity does differ depending on the age of the smoker. Younger smokers (under 25 years of age) are price elastic, while those over 25 years of age are price inelastic. It is hoped that higher cigarette prices will at least prevent smoking initiation by teenagers and lessen it for others.[17]

Concept Check

1 What is the difference between a movement along and a shift of a demand curve?

2 What does it mean if a product has a price elasticity of demand that is greater than 1?

STEP 3: DETERMINING COST, VOLUME, AND PROFIT RELATIONSHIPS

The profit equation described earlier in this chapter showed that profit = total revenue − total cost. Therefore, understanding the role and behaviour of costs is critical for all marketing decisions, particularly pricing decisions. Four cost concepts are important in pricing decisions: **total cost, fixed cost, variable cost,** and **marginal cost** (Figure 13−7).

MARGINAL ANALYSIS AND PROFIT MAXIMIZATION

A basic idea in business, economics, and indeed everyday life is marginal analysis. In personal terms, marginal analysis means that people will continue to do something as long as the incremental return exceeds the incremental cost. This same idea holds true in marketing and pricing decisions. In this setting, **marginal analysis** means studying whether revenue received from the sale of an additional product (marginal revenue) is greater than the additional cost of producing and selling it (marginal cost); if it is greater, a firm can reasonably expand its output of that product.[18]

Marginal analysis is central to the concept of maximizing profits. In Figure 13−8A, marginal revenue and marginal cost are graphed. Marginal cost starts out high at lower quantity levels, decreases to a minimum through production and marketing efficiencies, and then rises again as a result of the inefficiencies of overworked labour and equipment. Marginal revenue follows a downward slope. In Figure 13−8B, total cost and total revenue curves corresponding to the marginal cost and marginal revenue curves are graphed. Total cost initially rises

▍*Figure 13−7*
Fundamental cost concepts.

Total cost (TC) is the total expense incurred by a firm in producing and marketing a product. Total cost is the sum of fixed cost and variable cost.

Fixed cost (FC) is the sum of the expenses of a firm that are stable and do not change with the quantity of product that is produced and sold. Examples of fixed costs are rent on a building, executive salaries, and insurance.

Variable cost (VC) is the sum of the expenses of a firm that vary directly with the quantity of product that is produced and sold. For example, as the quantity sold doubles, the variable cost doubles. Examples are the direct labour and direct materials used in producing a product and the sales commissions that are tied directly to the quantity sold. As mentioned above:

TC = FC + VC

Variable cost expressed on a per unit basis is called *unit variable cost (UVC).*
Marginal cost (MC) is the change in total cost that results from producing and marketing one additional unit:

$$MC = \frac{\text{Change in TC}}{\text{1 unit increase in Q}} = \frac{\Delta TC}{\Delta Q}$$

as quantity increases but increases at the slowest rate at the quantity where marginal cost is lowest. The total revenue curve increases to a maximum and then starts to decline, as shown in Figure 13–8B.

The message of marginal analysis, then, is to operate up to the quantity and price level where marginal revenue equals marginal cost (MR = MC). Up to the output quantity at which MR = MC, each increase in total revenue resulting from selling one additional unit exceeds the increase in the total cost of producing and marketing that unit. Beyond the point at which MR = MC, however, the increase in total revenue from selling one more unit is less than the cost of producing and marketing that unit. At the quantity at which MR = MC, the total revenue curve lies farthest above the total cost curve and they are parallel.

BREAK-EVEN ANALYSIS *(review for next lesson)*

Marketing managers often employ a simpler approach for looking at cost, volume, and profit relationships, which is also based on the profit equation.[19] **Break-even analysis** is a technique that analyzes the relationship between total revenue and total cost to determine profitability at various levels of output. The **break-even point** (BEP) is the quantity at which total revenue and total cost are equal and beyond which profit occurs. In terms of the definitions in Figure 13–7:

$$BEP_{Quantity} = \frac{Fixed\ cost}{Unit\ price - Unit\ variable\ cost}$$

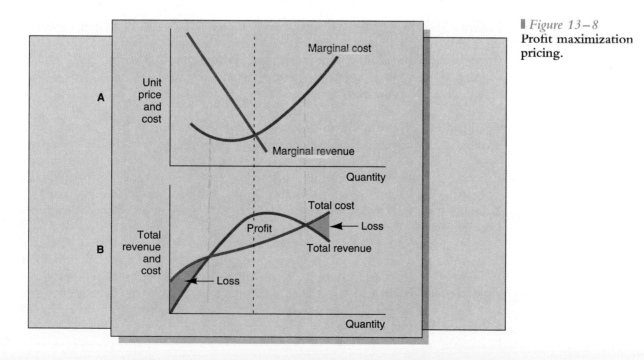

▌ *Figure 13–8*
Profit maximization pricing.

QUANTITY SOLD(Q)	PRICE PER BUSHEL (P)	TOTAL REVENUE (TR) (P × Q)	UNIT VARIABLE COST (UVC)	TOTAL VARIABLE COSTS (TVC) (UVC × Q)	FIXED COST (FC)	TOTAL COST (TC) (TVC + FC)	PROFIT (TR − TC)
0	$2	$ 0	$1	$ 0	$2,000	$2,000	$−2,000
1,000	2	2,000	1	1,000	2,000	3,000	−1,000
2,000	2	4,000	1	2,000	2,000	4,000	0
3,000	2	6,000	1	3,000	2,000	5,000	1,000
4,000	2	8,000	1	4,000	2,000	6,000	2,000
5,000	2	10,000	1	5,000	2,000	7,000	3,000
6,000	2	12,000	1	6,000	2,000	8,000	4,000

▌*Figure 13−9*
**Calculating a break-even
point.**

Calculating a Break-Even Point   Consider, for example, a corn farmer who wishes to identify how many bushels of corn he must sell to cover his fixed cost at a given price. Suppose the farmer had a fixed cost (FC) of $2,000 (for real estate taxes, interest on a bank loan, and other fixed expenses) and a unit variable cost (UVC) of $1 per bushel (for labour, corn seed, herbicides, and pesticides). If the price (P) is $2 per bushel, his break-even quantity is 2,000 bushels:

$$\text{BEP}_{\text{Quantity}} = \frac{\text{FC}}{P - \text{UVC}} = \frac{\$2,000}{\$2 - \$1} = 2,000 \text{ bushels}$$

Figure 13−9 shows that the break-even quantity at a price of $2 per bushel is 2,000 bushels, since at this quantity total revenue equals total cost. At less than 2,000 bushels, the farmer incurs a loss; and at more than 2,000 bushels, he makes a profit. Figure 13−10 shows a graphic presentation of the break-even analysis, called a **break-even chart.**

Applications of Break-Even Analysis   Because of its simplicity, break-even analysis is used extensively in marketing, most frequently to study the impact on profit of changes in price, fixed cost, and variable cost. The mechanics of break-even analysis are the basis of the widely used electronic spreadsheets offered by computer programs such as Lotus 1-2-3® that permit managers to answer "what-if," questions about the effect of changes in price and cost on their profit.

Although use of electronic spreadsheets in pricing is covered in Chapter 14, an example here will show the power of break-even analysis. As described in Figure 13−11, if an electronic calculator manufacturer automates its production, thereby increasing fixed cost and reducing variable cost by substituting machines for workers, this increases the break-even point from 333,333 to 500,000 units per year.

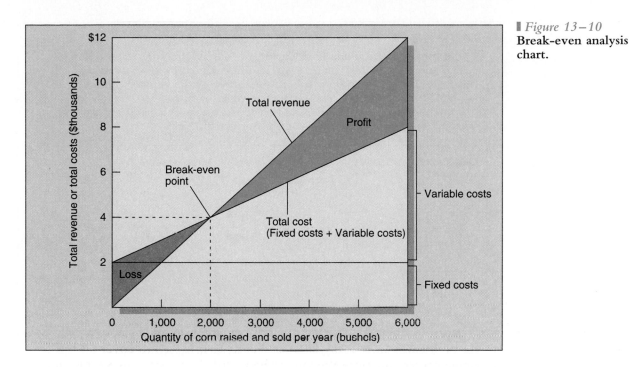

But what about the impact of the higher level of fixed cost on profit? Remember, profit at any output quantity is given by:

Profit = Total revenue − Total cost

$$= (P \times Q) - [FC + (UVC \times Q)]$$

So profit at 1 million units of sales before automation is:

Profit = $(P \times Q) - [FC + (UVC \times Q)]$
$= (\$10 \times 1,000,000) - [\$1,000,000 + (\$7 \times 1,000,000)]$
$= \$10,000,000 - \$8,000,000$
$= \$2,000,000$

After automation, profit is:

Profit = $(P \times Q) - [FC + (UVC \times Q)]$
$= (\$10 \times 1,000,000) - [\$4,000,000 + (\$2 \times 1,000,000)]$
$= \$10,000,000 - \$6,000,000$
$= \$4,000,000$

Automation, by adding to fixed cost, increases profit by $2 million at 1 million units of sales. Thus, as the quantity sold increases for the automated plant, the potential increase or leverage on profit is tremendous. This is why with large production and sales volumes, automated plants for GM cars or Texas Instruments calculators produce large profits. Also, firms in other industries, such as airline, railroad, and hotel and motel industries, that require a high fixed cost can reap large profits when they go even slightly beyond the break-even point.

Executives in virtually every mass production industry—from locomotives and cars
to electronic calculators and breakfast cereals—are searching for ways to increase
quality and reduce production costs to remain competitive in world markets. Increasingly they are substituting robots, automation, and computer-controlled
manufacturing systems for blue- and white-collar workers.

To understand the implications of this on the break-even point and profit, consider this example of an electronic calculator manufacturer:

BEFORE AUTOMATION			AFTER AUTOMATION		
P	$=$	\$10 per unit	P	$=$	\$10 per unit
FC	$=$	\$1,000,000	FC	$=$	\$4,000,000
UVC	$=$	\$7 per unit	UVC	$=$	\$2 per unit
$BEP_{Quantity}$	$=$	$\dfrac{FC}{P - UVC}$	$BEP_{Quantity}$	$=$	$\dfrac{FC}{P - UVC}$
	$=$	$\dfrac{\$1,000,000}{\$10 - \$7}$		$=$	$\dfrac{\$4,000,000}{\$10 - \$2}$
	$=$	333,333 units		$=$	500,000 units

The automation increases the fixed cost and increases the break-even quantity
from 333,333 to 500,000 units per year. So if annual sales fall within this range,
the calculator manufacturer will incur a loss with the automated plant, whereas it
would have made a profit if it had not automated.

But what about its potential profit if it sells 1 million units a year? Look carefully
at the two break-even charts below and see the text to check your conclusions:

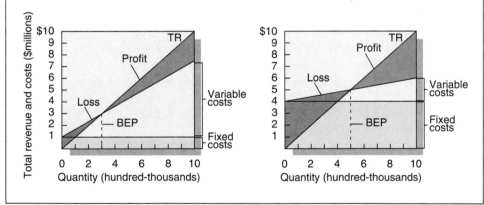

1 **What is the difference between fixed cost and variable cost?**

2 **What is a break-even point?**

Summary

1 Price is the money or other considerations exchanged for the ownership or use of a product or service. Although price typically includes money, the amount exchanged is often different from the list or quoted price because of allowances and extra fees.

2 Consumers use price as an indicator of value when it is paired with the perceived benefits of a good or service. Sometimes price influences consumer perceptions of quality itself and at other times consumers make value assessments by comparing the costs and benefits of substitute items.

3 Pricing constraints such as demand, product newness, costs, competitors, other products sold by the firm, and the type of competitive market restrict a firm's pricing latitude.

4 Pricing objectives, which specify the role of price in a firm's marketing strategy, may include pricing for profit, sales revenue, market share, unit sales, customer value, survival, or some socially responsible price level.

5 A demand curve shows the maximum number of products consumers will buy at a given price and for a given set of *(a)* consumer tastes, *(b)* price and availability of other products, and *(c)* consumer income. When any of these change, there is a shift of the demand curve.

6 Price elasticity of demand measures the sensitivity of units sold to a change in price. When demand is elastic, a reduction in price is more than offset by an increase in units sold, so that total revenue increases.

7 It is necessary to consider cost behaviour when making pricing decisions. Important cost concepts include total cost, variable cost, fixed cost, and marginal cost.

8 Break-even analysis shows the relationship between total revenue and total cost at various quantities of output for given conditions of price, fixed cost, and variable cost. The break-even point is where total revenue and total cost are equal.

Key Terms and Concepts

price p. 316
barter p. 317
price equation p. 317
value p. 317
value-based pricing p. 317
profit equation p. 318
pricing constraints p. 319
pricing objectives p. 322

demand curve p. 324
demand factors p. 324
total revenue p. 325
average revenue p. 325
marginal revenue p. 325
price elasticity of demand p. 327
total cost p. 330
fixed cost p. 330

Chapter Problems and Applications

1 How would the price equation apply to the purchase price of *(a)* gasoline, *(b)* an airline ticket, and *(c)* a checking account?

2 What would be your response to the statement "Profit maximization is the only legitimate pricing objective for the firm?"

3 How is a downward-sloping demand curve related to total revenue and marginal revenue?

4 A marketing executive once said, "If the price elasticity of demand for your product is inelastic, then your price is probably too low." What is this executive saying in terms of the economic principles discussed in this chapter?

5 A marketing manager reduced the price on a brand of cereal by 10 percent and observed a 25 percent increase in quantity sold. The manager then thought that if the price were reduced by another 20 percent, a 50 percent increase in quantity sold would occur. What would be your response to the marketing manager's reasoning?

6 A student theatre group at a university has developed a demand schedule that shows the relationship between ticket prices and demand based on a student survey, as follows:

TICKET PRICE	NUMBER OF STUDENTS WHO WOULD BUY
$1	300
2	250
3	200
4	150
5	100

a Graph the demand curve and the total revenue curve based on these data. What ticket price might be set based on this analysis?

b What other factors should be considered before the final price is set?

7 Touché Toiletries, Inc., has developed an addition to its Lizardman Cologne line tentatively branded Ode d'Toade Cologne. Unit variable costs are 45 cents for a 3-ounce bottle, and heavy advertising expenditures in the first year would result in total fixed costs of $900,000. Ode d'Toade Cologne is priced at $7.50 for a 3-ounce bottle. How many bottles of Ode d'Toade must be sold to break even?

8 Suppose that marketing executives for Touché Toiletries reduced the price to $6.50 for a 3-ounce bottle of Ode d'Toade and the fixed costs were $1,100,000. Suppose further that the unit variable cost remained at 45 cents for a 3-ounce bottle. *(a)* How many bottles must be sold to break even? *(b)* What dollar profit level would Ode d'Toade achieve if 200,000 bottles were sold?

9 Executives of Random Recordings, Inc., produced an album entitled *Sunshine/ Moonshine* by the Starshine Sisters Band. The cost and price information was as follows:

Album cover	$	1.00 per album
Songwriter's royalties		0.30 per album
Recording artists' royalties		0.70 per album
Direct material and labour costs to produce the album		1.00 per album
Fixed cost of producing an album (advertsing, studio fee, etc.)		100,000.00
Selling price		7.00 per album

a Prepare a chart like that in Figure 13−10 showing total cost, fixed cost, and total revenue for album quantity sold levels starting at 10,000 albums through 100,000 albums at 10,000 album intervals, that is, 10,000, 20,000, 30,000, and so on.

b What is the break-even point for the album?

SONIC

THE HEDGEHOG

2

©S

Pricing: Arriving at the Final Price

AFTER READING THIS CHAPTER YOU SHOULD BE ABLE TO:

▸ Understand how to establish the initial "approximate price level" using demand-based, cost-based, profit-based, and competition-based methods.

▸ Identify the major factors considered in deriving a final list or quoted price from the approximate price level.

▸ Describe adjustments made to the approximate price level based on geography, discounts, and allowances.

▸ Prepare basic financial analyses useful in evaluating alternative prices and arriving at the final sales price.

▸ Describe the principal laws and regulations affecting pricing practices.

Twice the Fun, Half the Price: Super Mario versus Sonic in a Clash of Electronic Titans

Who could ever replace Nintendo's Super Mario Brothers 3 and The Legend of Zelda? Sega Enterprises Ltd. hopes that Sonic, its jaunty little intergalactic hedgehog, is up to the task.

The estimated $6 billion home video game industry has experienced a battle as ferocious as any of its high-tech games. The aim? Capturing the hearts and pocketbooks of video-crazed young people.

Armed with new electronic muscle powered by 16-bit microchips, the Super Nintendo Entertainment System and Sega's Genesis offer greater computing power for game users, improved colour, and better animation to heighten game play. Even better news for buyers is that all this is available at half the price! Nintendo and Sega have been engaged in a price war that has slashed prices for video game systems from $200 to $89. Why? An increasingly saturated market where many households already have a video game system, the entrance of Sega to challenge Nintendo's dominance of this market, and manufacturing economies in producing games have all contributed to the pricing of new systems.

The new generation of video game systems featuring CD-ROM (compact disc read-only memory) technology presents an equally challenging pricing problem for Nintendo and Sega. Initially priced at $300, CD-ROM video game systems supplied by Nintendo and Sega will have to demonstrate that the thrill of playing the game justifies the price.[1]

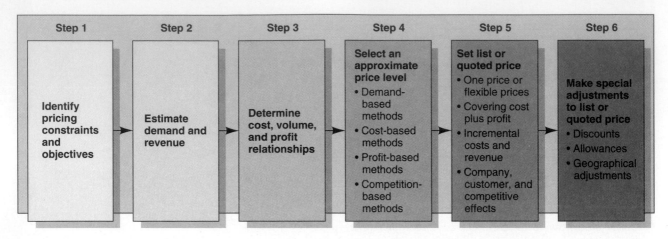

Figure 14–1
Steps in setting price.

Pricing of video game systems illustrates how factors related to demand, cost, and competition affect prices for a single firm and an entire industry. The Nintendo and Sega battle will continue to focus on the imaginative application of technology at price points that create value for the consumer.

This chapter describes how companies select an appropriate price level, highlights important considerations in setting a list or quoted price, and identifies various price adjustments that can be made to prices set by the firm—the last three steps an organization uses in setting price (Figure 14–1). In addition, an overview of legal and regulatory aspects of pricing is provided.

STEP 4: SELECT AN APPROXIMATE PRICE LEVEL

A key to a marketing manager's setting a final price for a product is to find an "approximate price level" to use as a reasonable starting point. Four common approaches to helping find this approximate price level are demand-based, cost-based, profit-based, and competition-based methods (Figure 14–2). Although these methods are discussed separately, some of them overlap, and an effective marketing manager will consider several in searching for an approximate price level.

DEMAND-BASED METHODS

Demand-based methods of finding a price level weigh factors underlying expected customer tastes and preferences more heavily than such factors as cost, profit, and competition.

Skimming Pricing   A firm introducing a new or innovative product can use **skimming pricing,** setting the highest initial price that customers really desiring the product are willing to pay. These customers are not very price sensitive, because they weigh the new product's price, quality, and ability to satisfy their needs against the same characteristics of substitutes. As the demand

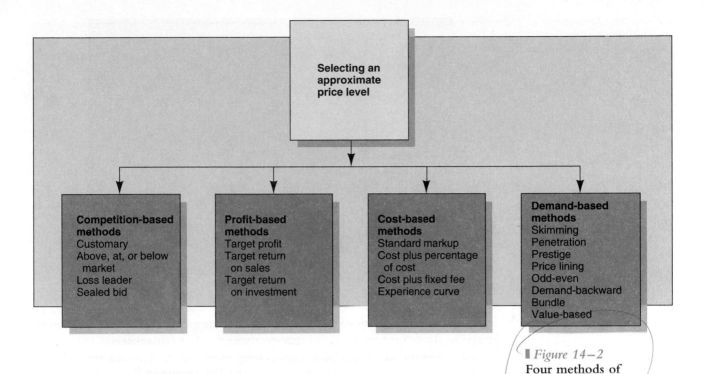

Selecting an approximate price level

Competition-based methods
Customary
Above, at, or below
 market
Loss leader
Sealed bid

Profit-based methods
Target profit
Target return
 on sales
Target return
 on investment

Cost-based methods
Standard markup
Cost plus percentage
 of cost
Cost plus fixed fee
Experience curve

Demand-based methods
Skimming
Penetration
Prestige
Price lining
Odd-even
Demand-backward
Bundle
Value-based

I *Figure 14–2*
Four methods of selecting an approximate price level.

of these customers is satisfied, the firm lowers the price to attract another, more price-sensitive segment. Thus, skimming pricing gets its name from skimming successive layers of "cream," or customer segments, as prices are lowered in a series of steps.

The initial pricing of VCRs at more than $1,500 and the Trivial Pursuit game at $39.95 are examples of skimming pricing. Within three years after their introductions, both products were often priced at less than half their initial prices. Sometimes minor modifications are made in the product when it is offered at a lower price to a new segment; publishing hardback bestselling novels in paperback is an example. Skimming pricing is an effective strategy when (1) enough prospective customers are willing to buy the product immediately at the high initial price to make these sales profitable, (2) the high initial price will not attract competitors, (3) lowering price has only a minor effect on increasing the sales volume and reducing the unit costs, and (4) customers interpret the high price as signifying high quality. These four conditions are most likely to exist when the new product is protected by patents or copyrights or its uniqueness is understood and appreciated by customers. Skimming will probably be used on the first HDTV sets, and Nintendo and Sega are using this strategy for their CD-ROM video game systems, priced at $300.

Penetration Pricing   Setting a low initial price on a new product to appeal immediately to the mass market is **penetration pricing,** the exact opposite of skimming pricing. IBM consciously chose a penetration strategy when it introduced a line of high-powered personal computers for business and scientific purposes. Pricing the computers at roughly half of what competitors were charging, a company spokesperson said, "We've priced these things to go."[2]

CD-ROM video game systems were introduced with skimming pricing.

The conditions favouring penetration pricing are the reverse of those supporting skimming pricing: (1) many segments of the market are price sensitive, (2) a low initial price discourages competitors from entering the market, and (3) unit production and marketing costs fall dramatically as production volumes increase. These conditions exist in the European personal computer market today. A firm using penetration pricing may maintain the initial price for a time to gain profit from its low introductory level or lower the price further, counting on the new volume to generate the necessary profit.

In some situations penetration pricing may follow skimming pricing. A company might initially price a product high to attract price-insensitive consumers and recoup initial research and development costs and introductory promotional expenditures. Once this is done, penetration pricing is used to appeal to a broader segment of the population and increase market share.[3] Apple Computer and Digital Equipment did this in Japan recently when each cut its personal computer prices to increase its market share.[4]

Prestige Pricing   As noted in Chapter 13, consumers may use price as a measure of the quality or prestige of an item so that as price is lowered beyond some point, demand for the item actually falls. **Prestige pricing** involves setting a high price so that status-conscious consumers will be attracted to the product and buy it (Figure 14–3A). The demand curve slopes downward and to the right between points *A* and *B* but turns back to the left between points *B* and *C,* since demand is actually reduced between points *B* and *C*. From *A* to *B* buyers see the lowering of price as a bargain and buy more; from *B* to *C* they become dubious about the quality and prestige and buy less. A marketing manager's pricing strategy here is to stay above price P_0 (the initial price). Heublein, Inc., successfully repositioned its Popov brand of vodka to make it a prestige brand. It increased price by 8 percent, which led to a 1 percent decline in market share but a whopping 30 percent increase in profit.[5]

price = quality

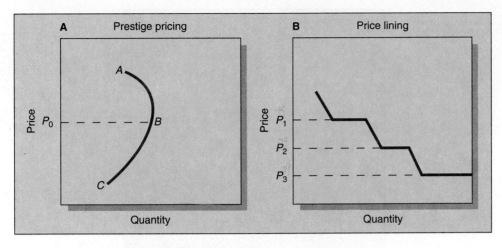

Figure 14–3
Demand curves for two
types of demand-based
methods.

Rolls-Royce cars, diamonds, perfumes, fine china, and crystal have an element of prestige pricing appeal in them and may sell worse at lower prices than at higher ones.

Price Lining   Often a firm that is selling not just a single product but a line of products may price them at a number of different specific pricing points, in a practice called **price lining.** For example, a department store manager may price a line of women's dresses at $59, $79, and $99. As shown in Figure 14–3B, this assumes that demand is elastic at each of these price points but inelastic between them. In some instances all the items might be purchased for the same cost and then marked up at different percentages to achieve these price points based on colour, style, and expected demand. In other instances manufacturers design products for different price points and retailers apply approximately the same markup percentages to achieve the three or four different price points offered to consumers. Sellers often feel that a limited number of (such as three or four) price points is preferable to 8 or 10 different ones, which may only confuse prospective buyers.[6]

Odd–Even Pricing   Sears offers a Craftsman radial saw for $499.99; Leon's prices a five-piece living room set at $2,499; and Kmart has Windex glass cleaner on sale for 99 cents. Why not simply price these items at $500, $2,500, and $1, respectively? These retailers are using **odd–even pricing,** which involves setting prices a few dollars or cents under an even number. The presumption is that consumers see the Sears radial saw as priced at "something over $400" rather than "about $500." In theory, demand increases if the price drops from $500 to $499.99. There is some evidence to suggest this does happen. However, consumers may interpret these odd-ending prices as meaning lower quality.[7]

Demand-Backward Pricing   Manufacturers sometimes estimate the price that consumers would be willing to pay for a relatively expensive item, such as a

Waterford uses prestige pricing for its crystal.

shopping good. They then work backward through the margins that may have to be paid to retailers and wholesalers to determine what price they can charge wholesalers for the product. This **demand-backward pricing** results in the manufacturer's deliberately adjusting the quality of the component parts in the product to achieve the target price. Global Upholstery of Ontario found that if it could produce a budget stenographer's chair to retail at $50, it would be able to obtain a sizable share of the low end of the steno chair market. Global brought together engineers, designers, and outside resource people in order to determine how to do it. They figured out what each component should cost and how to design and tool it in order to arrive at the $50 retail price.[8] This is an example of a successful use of demand-backward pricing.

Bundle Pricing   A frequently used demand-oriented pricing practice is **bundle pricing**—the marketing of two or more products in a single "package" price. For example, Air Canada offers vacation packages that include airfare, car rental, and lodging. Apple Computer sells hardware, software, and maintenance contracts together. Bundle pricing is based on the idea that consumers value the package more than the individual items. This is due to benefits received from not having to make separate purchases and enhanced satisfaction from one item given the presence of another. Moreover, bundle pricing often provides a lower total cost to buyers and lower marketing costs to sellers.[9]

Value-Based Pricing   With the growing number of value-conscious consumers, many marketers are using value-based pricing to appeal to this group. As we saw in Chapter 13, **value-based pricing** involves increasing product or service benefits while maintaining or decreasing prices or simply lowering prices on standard items consumers buy with regularity such as grocery items or standard fare at fast-food restaurants. It can also take the form of an "everyday low-price" (EDLP) retail strategy. But value-based pricing is also being adopted by manufacturers of larger-ticket items. In 1994, General Motors of Canada began promoting its value-based pricing strategy for about 80 percent of its vehicles sold in Canada.

Concept Check

1 **What are the circumstances in pricing a new product that might support skimming or penetration pricing?**

2 **What is odd–even pricing?**

COST-BASED METHODS

In cost-based methods the price setter stresses the supply or cost side of the pricing problem, not the demand side. Price is set by looking at the production and marketing costs and then adding enough to cover direct expenses, overhead, and profit.

Standard Markup Pricing   Managers of supermarkets and other retail stores have such a large number of products that estimating the demand for each product as a means of setting price is impossible. Therefore, they use **standard markup pricing,** which entails adding a fixed percentage to the cost of all items in a specific product class. This percentage markup varies depending on the type of retail store (such as furniture, clothing, or grocery) and on the product involved. High-volume products usually have smaller markups than do low-volume products. Supermarkets such as Loblaws, Safeway, IGA, and A&P have different markups for staple items and discretionary items. The markup on staple items like sugar, flour, and dairy products varies from 10 percent to 23 percent, whereas markups on discretionary items like snack foods and candy range from 27 percent to 47 percent. These markups must cover all expenses of the store, pay for overhead costs, and contribute something to profits. For supermarkets, these markups, which may appear very large, result in only a 1 percent profit on sales revenue if the store is operating efficiently. By comparison, consider the markups on snacks and beverages purchased at your local movie theatre. Markups for these products can be as large as 87 percent! An explanation of how to compute a markup, along with operating statement data and other ratios, is given in Appendix A following this chapter.

Figure 14–4 shows the way standard markups combine to establish the selling price of the manufacturer to the wholesaler, the wholesaler to the retailer, and the retailer to the ultimate consumer. For example, the markups on a home appliance (for simplicity, sold to consumers for exactly $100) can increase as the product gets closer to the ultimate consumers; that is, the manufacturer has a 15 percent markup on its selling price, the wholesaler 20 percent, and the retailer 40 percent.

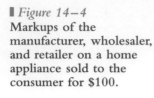

Figure 14–4
Markups of the manufacturer, wholesaler, and retailer on a home appliance sold to the consumer for $100.

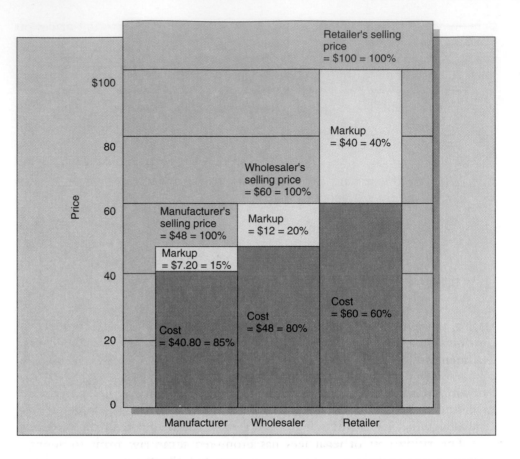

These larger markups later in the channel reflect the fact that as the product gets closer to the ultimate consumer, the seller has a smaller volume of the product and must provide a greater number of services or amount of individual attention to the buyer. The manufacturer gets $48 for selling the appliance to the wholesaler, who gets $60 from the retailer, who gets $100 from the ultimate consumer. As noted in the discussion of demand-backward pricing, if the manufacturer targets the price to the ultimate consumer at $100, it must verify that this includes adequate markups for the retailer, the wholesaler, and itself.

Cost plus Percentage-of-Cost Pricing   Some manufacturing, architectural, and construction firms use a variation of standard markup pricing. In **cost plus percentage-of-cost pricing,** they add a fixed percentage to the production or construction cost. This is often used to price one- or few-of-a-kind items, as when an architectural firm charges a fee of 13 percent of the construction costs of a house. Thus, for a house whose construction cost was $100,000 and the architect's fee was 13 percent of construction cost, or $13,000, the final price would be $113,000.

Experience curve pricing is often used to set prices for electronic products.

Cost plus Fixed-Fee Pricing   In buying highly technical, few-of-a-kind products such as aircraft or space satellites, the government has found that its contractors are reluctant to specify a formal, fixed price for the procurement. Therefore it uses **cost plus fixed-fee pricing,** which means that a supplier is reimbursed for all costs, regardless of what they turn out to be, but is allowed only a fixed fee as profit that is independent of the final cost of the project.

The rising cost of legal fees has prompted some law firms to adopt a version of this pricing method. Rather than bill clients on an hourly basis, lawyers and their clients agree on a fixed fee based on expected costs plus a profit for the law firm.[10]

Experience Curve Pricing   The method of **experience curve pricing** is based on the learning effect, which holds that the unit cost of many products and services declines by 10 percent to 30 percent each time a firm's experience at producing and selling them doubles.[11] This reduction is regular or predictable enough that the average cost per unit can be mathematically estimated. For example, if the firm estimates that costs will fall by 15 percent each time volume doubles, then the cost of the 100th unit produced and sold will be about 85 percent of the cost of the 50th unit, and the 200th unit will be 85 percent of the 100th unit. Therefore, if the cost of the 50th unit is $100, the 100th unit would cost $85, the 200th unit would be $72.25, and so on. Since prices often follow costs with experience curve pricing, a rapid decline in price is possible. Japanese and Canadian firms often adopt this pricing method. This cost-based pricing method complements the demand-based pricing strategy of skimming followed by penetration pricing. For example, CD player prices have decreased from $900 to less than $200, fax machine prices have declined from $1,000 to under $300, and cellular telephones that sold for $4,000 are now priced as low as $99.

PROFIT-BASED METHODS

A price setter may choose to balance both revenues and costs to set price using profit-based methods. These might either involve a target of a specific dollar volume of profit or express this target profit as a percentage of sales or investment.

Target Profit Pricing   A firm may set an annual target of a specific dollar volume of profit, which is called **target profit pricing.** Suppose a picture framing store owner wishes to use target profit pricing to establish a price for a typical framed picture and assumes:

- Variable cost is a constant $22 per unit.
- Fixed cost is a constant $26,000.
- Demand is insensitive to price up to $60 per unit.
- A target profit of $7,000 is sought at an annual volume of 1,000 units (framed pictures).

The price can be calculated as follows:

$$\text{Profit} = \text{Total revenue} - \text{Total cost}$$
$$\text{Profit} = (P \times Q) - [\text{FC} + (\text{UVC} \times Q)]$$
$$\$7,000 = (P \times 1,000) - [\$26,000 + (\$22 \times 1,000)]$$
$$\$7,000 = 1,000P - (\$26,000 + \$22,000)$$
$$1,000P = \$7,000 + \$48,000$$
$$P = \$55$$

Note that a critical assumption is that this higher average price of a framed picture will not cause the demand to fall.

Target Return-on-Sales Pricing   A difficulty with target profit pricing is that although it is simple and the target involves only a specific dollar volume, there is no benchmark of sales or investment used to show how much of the firm's effort is needed to achieve the target. Firms like supermarket chains often use **target return-on-sales pricing** to set typical prices that will give the firm a profit that is a specified percentage—say, 1 percent—of the sales volume. Suppose the owner decides to use target return-on-sales pricing for the frame shop and makes the same first three assumptions shown previously. The owner now sets a target of 20 percent return on sales at an annual volume of 1,250 units. This gives:

$$\text{Target return on sales} = \frac{\text{Target profit}}{\text{Total revenue}}$$
$$20\% = \frac{\text{TR} - \text{TC}}{\text{TR}}$$
$$0.20 = \frac{P \times Q - [\text{FC} + \text{UVC} \times Q]}{\text{TR}}$$
$$0.20 = \frac{P \times 1,250 - [\$26,000 + (\$22 \times 1,250)]}{P \times 1,250}$$
$$P = \$53.50$$

			SIMULATION			
ASSUMPTIONS OR RESULTS	FINANCIAL ELEMENT	LAST YEAR	A	B	C	D
Assumptions	Price per unit (*P*)	$50	$54	$54	$58	$58
	Units sold (*Q*)	1,000	1,200	1,100	1,100	1,000
	Change in unit variable cost (UVC)	0%	+10%	+10%	+20%	+20%
	Unit variable cost	$22.00	$24.20	$24.20	$26.40	$26.40
	Total expenses	$8,000	Same	Same	Same	Same
	Owner's salary	$18,000	Same	Same	Same	Same
	Investment	$20,000	Same	Same	Same	Same
	State and federal taxes	50%	Same	Same	Same	Same
Spreadsheet simulation results	Net sales (*P* × *Q*)	$50,000	$64,800	$59,400	$63,800	$58,000
	Less: COGS★ (*Q* × UVC)	22,000	29,040	26,620	29,040	26,400
	Gross margin	$28,000	$35,760	$32,780	$34,760	$31,600
	Less: total expenses	8,000	8,000	8,000	8,000	8,000
	Less: owner's salary	18,000	18,000	18,000	18,000	18,000
	Net profit before taxes	$ 2,000	$ 9,760	$ 6,780	$ 8,760	$ 5,600
	Less: taxes	1,000	4,880	3,390	4,380	2,800
	Net profit after taxes	$ 1,000	$ 4,880	$ 3,390	$ 4,380	$ 2,800
	Investment	$20,000	$20,000	$20,000	$20,000	$20,000
	Return on investment	5.0%	24.4%	17.0%	21.9%	14.0%

★Cost of goods sold.

So at a price of $53.50 per unit and an annual quantity of 1,250 frames:

$$\text{TR} = P \times Q = \$53.50 \times 1,250 = \$66,875$$
$$\text{TC} = \text{FC} \times (\text{UVC} \times Q) = 26,000 + (22 \times 1,250) = \$53,500$$
$$\text{Profit} = \text{TR} - \text{TC} = \$66,875 - \$53,500 = \$13,375$$

As a check:

$$\text{Target return on sales} = \frac{\text{Target profit}}{\text{Total revenue}} = \frac{\$13,375}{\$66,875} = 20\%$$

Figure 14–5
Results of computer spreadsheet simulation to select price to achieve a target return on investment.

Target profit objective

Target Return-on-Investment Pricing   Firms like GM and many public utilities set annual return–on-investment (ROI) targets such as ROI of 20 percent. **Target return-on-investment pricing** is a method of setting prices to achieve this target.

Suppose the store owner sets a target ROI of 10 percent, which is twice that achieved the previous year. She considers raising the average price of a framed picture to $54 or $58—up from last year's average of $50. To do this, she might improve product quality by offering better frames and higher-quality matting, which will increase the cost but also probably will offset the decreased revenue from the lower number of units that can be sold next year.

To handle this wide variety of assumptions, today's managers use computerized spreadsheets to project operating statements based on a diverse set of assumptions. Figure 14–5 shows the results of computerized spreadsheet simulation, with assumptions shown at the top and the projected results at the bottom. A previous year's operating statement results are shown in the column headed "Last year," and the assumptions and spreadsheet results for four different sets of assumptions are shown in columns A, B, C, and D.

In choosing a price or another action using spreadsheet results, the decision maker must (1) study the results of the computer simulation projections and (2) assess the realism of the assumptions underlying each set of projections. For example, the store owner sees from the bottom row of Figure 14–5 that all four spreadsheet simulations exceed the after-tax target ROI of 10 percent. But after more thought she judges it to be more realistic to set an average price of $58 per unit, allow the unit variable cost to increase by 20 percent to account for more expensive framing and matting, and settle for the same unit sales as the 1,000 units sold last year. She selects simulation D in this computerized spreadsheet approach to target ROI pricing and has a goal of 14 percent after-tax ROI. Of course, these same calculations can be done by hand, but this is far more time-consuming.

COMPETITION-BASED METHODS

Rather than emphasize demand, cost, or profit factors, a price setter can stress what competitors or "the market" is doing.

Customary Pricing   For some products where tradition, a standardized channel of distribution, or other competitive factors dictate the price, **customary pricing** is used. For example, candy bars offered through standard vending machines have a customary price of 50 cents, and a significant departure from this price may result in a loss of sales for the manufacturer. Hershey typically has changed the amount of chocolate in its candy bars depending on the price of raw chocolate rather than vary its customary retail price, so it can continue selling through vending machines.

Above-, At-, or Below-Market Pricing   For most products it is difficult to identify a specific market price for a product or product class. Still, marketing managers often have a subjective feel for the competitors' price or market price. Using this benchmark, they then may deliberately choose a strategy of **above-, at-, or below-market pricing.**

Among watch manufacturers, Rolex takes pride in emphasizing that it makes one of the most expensive watches you can buy—a clear example of above-market pricing. Manufacturers of national brands of clothing such as Alfred Sung and retailers like Holt Renfrew deliberately set premium prices for their products.

Large mass-merchandise chains such as Sears and The Bay generally use at-market pricing. These chains often establish the going market price in the minds of their competitors. Similarly, Revlon generally prices its products "at market." Such a manufacturer also provides a reference price for competitors that use above- and below-market pricing.

In contrast, a number of firms such as Zellers use a strategy of below-market pricing. Manufacturers of all generic products and retailers who offer their own private brands of products ranging from peanut butter to shampoo deliberately set prices for these products about 8 percent to 10 percent below the prices of nationally branded competitive products such as Skippy peanut butter, Vidal Sassoon shampoo, or Crest toothpaste. Many firms that price below market use a value-based slogan to promote their lower prices, such as Suave shampoo (why pay more?) or ABC detergent (gets clothes clean; why pay more?).

Loss-Leader Pricing   For a special promotion many retail stores deliberately sell a product below its customary price to attract attention to it. For example, grocery stores will often use produce or paper goods (e.g., bathroom tissue) as loss leaders. The purpose of **loss-leader pricing** is not to increase sales of the particular product but to attract customers in hopes they will buy other products as well, particularly the discretionary items carrying large markups.

Sealed-Bid Pricing   When the Federal Department of Supply and Services wants to buy a million number 2 wooden pencils for the army, it would probably use **sealed-bid pricing.** The buying agency widely publicizes specifications for the items to inform prospective manufacturers, who are invited to submit a bid that includes a specific price for the quantity ordered. The bid must be submitted by a specific time to a specific buying agency at a specific location. Several days later the bids are opened in public and read aloud, and the lowest qualified bidder is awarded the contract.

---

1 **What is standard markup pricing?**

2 **What profit-based pricing method should a manager use in order to reflect the percentage of the firm's resources used in obtaining the profit?**

3 **What is the purpose of loss-leader pricing when used by a retail firm?**

Concept Check

STEP 5: SET THE LIST OR QUOTED PRICE

The first four steps in setting price covered in Chapter 13 and this chapter result in an approximate price level for the product that appears reasonable. But it still remains for the manager to set a specific list or quoted price in light of all relevant factors.

ONE-PRICE VERSUS FLEXIBLE-PRICE POLICY

A seller must decide whether to follow a one-price or a flexible-price policy. A **one-price policy** is setting the same price for similar customers who buy the same product and quantities under the same conditions. In contrast, a **flexible-price policy** is offering the same product and quantities to similar customers, but at different prices. However, flexible pricing carried to the extreme could be a form of price discrimination, a practice prohibited under the Competition Act.

Prices paid by an ultimate consumer illustrate the differences in these two policies, although the same principles apply to manufacturers and wholesalers as well. When you buy a Coca-Cola for 75 cents from a vending machine or a Wilson Sting tennis racket from a discount store, you are offered the product at a single price. You can buy it or not, but there is no variation in the price under the seller's one-price policy. But with a house, the seller generally uses a flexible-price policy, and you might negotiate a purchase at a price that lies within a range of prices. Flexible prices give sellers greater discretion in setting the final price in light of demand, cost, and competitive factors.

Car dealers have traditionally used flexible pricing based on buyer–seller negotiations to agree on a final sale price. However, as detailed in the accompanying Marketing Action Memo, experiments with a one-price policy have shown that it can create greater customer satisfaction and improved value perceptions.

PRICING TO COVER COST PLUS PROFIT

Unless you are the federal government or some other nonprofit organization, in the long run prices you set must cover all costs and contribute some profit or you'll go out of business. This may not be true in the short run or may not even apply to prices of specific products in a product line. Prices of rib steak, as loss leaders in a supermarket, don't cover costs but are used because customers buy other high-margin products to offset this loss. Gillette safety razors and Barbie dolls may be priced below cost to stimulate sales of Gillette blades and Barbie's clothes, on which highly profitable margins exist. Many firms no longer exist because in the long run their revenues couldn't cover their costs and provide adequate profit.

Only <u>one</u> store has the lowest price as the law... guaranteed! If you see advertised a lower, current Canadian retail store price on any item we have in stock, find that item at ZELLERS and bring it, with our competitor's ad, to the check-out and we'll be glad to beat their price!

Zellers

because... the lowest price is the law!

Some retailers like Zellers use below-market pricing and guarantee that pricing policy to consumers.

BALANCING INCREMENTAL COSTS AND REVENUES

When a price is changed or new advertising or selling programs are planned, their effect on the quantity sold must be considered. This assessment, called *marginal analysis* (Chapter 13), involves a continuing, concise trade-off of incremental costs against incremental revenues.

Do marketing and business managers really use marginal analysis? Yes, they do, but they often don't use phrases like *marginal revenue, marginal cost,* and *elasticity of demand.*

Think about these managerial questions:

- How many extra units do we have to sell to pay for that $1,000 advertisement?
- How much savings on unit variable cost do we have to get to keep the break-even point the same if we invest in a $10,000 labour-saving machine?
- Should we hire three more salespeople or not?

All these questions are a form of managerial or incremental analysis, even though these exact words are not used.

Figure 14–6 shows the power—and some limitations—of marginal analysis applied to a marketing decision. Note that the frame store owner must either conclude that a simple advertising campaign will more than pay for itself in additional sales or not undertake the campaign. The decision could also have been made to increase the average price of a framed picture to cover the cost of the campaign, but the principle still applies: expected incremental revenues from pricing and other marketing actions must more than offset incremental costs.

Suppose the owner of a picture framing store is considering buying a series of magazine ads to reach her upscale target market. The cost of the ads is $1,000, the average price of a framed picture is $50, and the unit variable cost (materials plus labour) is $30.

This is a direct application of marginal analysis that an astute manager uses to estimate the incremental revenue or incremental number of units that must be obtained to at least cover the incremental cost. In this example, the number of extra picture frames that must be sold is obtained as follows:

$$\text{Incremental number of frames} = \frac{\text{Extra fixed cost}}{\text{Price} - \text{Unit variable cost}}$$
$$= \frac{\$1,000 \text{ of advertising}}{\$50 - \$30}$$
$$= 50 \text{ frames}$$

So unless there are some other benefits of the ads, such as long-term goodwill, she should buy the ads only if she expects they will increase picture frame sales by at least 50 units.

The example in Figure 14–6 shows both the main advantage and the main difficulty of marginal analysis. The advantage is its common sense usefulness, and the difficulty is obtaining the necessary data to make decisions. The owner can measure the cost quite easily, but the incremental revenue generated by the ads is difficult to measure. She could partly solve this problem by offering $2 off the purchase price with use of a coupon printed in the ad to see which sales resulted from the ad.

COMPANY, CUSTOMER, AND COMPETITIVE EFFECTS

As the final list or quoted price is set, the effects on the company, customers, and competitors must be assessed.

Company Effects   For a firm with several products, a decision on the price of a single product must also consider the impact on the demand for other products in the line. IBM has an enviable record of assessing the impact of a price change in a mainframe computer on the substitutes (its other mainframe computers) and complements (its peripheral equipment) in its product line. In contrast, IBM has often struggled in its attempts to position its personal computers by price points as new models are added to its line.[12]

Customer Effects   In setting price, retailers weigh factors heavily that satisfy the perceptions or expectations of ultimate consumers, such as the customary prices for a variety of consumer products. Retailers have found that they should not price their store brands 20 to 25 percent below manufacturers' brands. When they do, consumers often view the lower price as signalling lower quality and don't buy.[13] Manufacturers and wholesalers must choose prices that result in profit for resellers in the channel to gain their cooperation and support. Toro failed to do this on its lines of lawn mowers and snow throwers. It decided to augment its traditional hardware outlet distribution by also selling through big discounters such as Kmart. To do so, it set prices for the discounters substantially

ETHICS AND SOCIAL RESPONSIBILITY ALERT

Putting a Value on Life

What price should be charged for a product that will treat acquired immunodeficiency syndrome (AIDS)? Executives at Burroughs Wellcome Company had to make this determination when the company received approval from the government to market Retrovir®, a drug found to be effective in the treatment of AIDS.

The initial cost for a one-year patient supply of Retrovir® was $8,000. According to a company official, the high price was due to the "uncertain market for the drug, the possible advent of new therapies, and profit margins customarily generated by new medicines." (The estimated research and development cost of the drug was between $80 and $100 million.) A critic countered, saying, "Burroughs Wellcome has an obligation to give up a significant amount of money to allow people to get access."

What ethical and social responsibility does Burroughs Wellcome have in connection with the pricing of Retrovir®?

Sources: Based on "Drugs: Is the Price Right?" *Newsweek,* March 8, 1993, p. 38; "AIDS Activists Press Boycotts of Drug Firms," *The Wall Street Journal,* March 8, 1991, pp. B1, B4; and B. O'Reilly, "The Inside Story of the AIDS Drug," *Fortune,* November 5, 1990, pp. 112–29.

below those for its traditional hardware outlets. Many unhappy hardware stores abandoned Toro products in favour of mowers and snow throwers from other manufacturers.

Consideration of the customer can sometimes have serious ethical overtones, particularly in the pharmaceutical industry (see the Ethics and Social Responsibility Alert).

Competitive Effects   A manager's pricing decision is immediately apparent to most competitors, who may retaliate with price changes of their own. Therefore, a manager who sets a final list or quoted price must anticipate potential price responses from competitors. Regardless of whether a firm is a price leader or follower, it wants to avoid cutthroat price wars in which no firm in the industry makes a satisfactory profit. Gasoline companies generally avoid price wars since they can be disastrous for all players.

STEP 6: MAKE SPECIAL ADJUSTMENTS TO THE LIST OR QUOTED PRICE

When you pay 50 cents for a bag of M&M's candy in a vending machine or receive a quoted price of $5,000 from a contractor to build a new kitchen, the pricing sequence ends with the last step just described: setting the list or quoted price. But when you are a manufacturer of M&M's candies or gas grills and sell your product to dozens or hundreds of wholesalers and retailers in your channel

▌ *Figure 14–7*
**Three special
adjustments to list or
quoted price.**

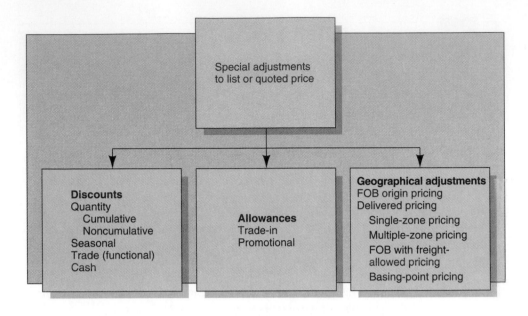

▌ *Figure 14–7*
**Three special
adjustments to list or
quoted price.**

of distribution, you may need to make a variety of special adjustments to the list or quoted price. Wholesalers also must adjust list or quoted prices they set for retailers. Three special adjustments to the list or quoted price are discounts, allowances, and geographical adjustments (Figure 14–7).

DISCOUNTS

Discounts are reductions from list price that a seller gives a buyer as a reward for some activity of the buyer that is favourable to the seller. Four kinds of discounts are especially important in marketing strategy: quantity, seasonal, trade (functional), and cash discounts.

Quantity Discounts   To encourage customers to buy larger quantities of a product, firms at all levels in the channel of distribution offer **quantity discounts,** which are reductions in unit costs for a larger order.[14] For example, an instant photocopying service might set a price of 10 cents a copy for copies 1 to 25, 9 cents a copy for 26 to 100, and 8 cents a copy for 101 or more. Because the photocopying service gets more of the buyer's business and has longer production runs that reduce its order-handling costs, it is willing to pass on some of the cost savings in the form of quantity discounts to the buyer.

Quantity discounts are of two general kinds: noncumulative and cumulative. *Noncumulative quantity discounts* are based on the size of an individual purchase order. They encourage large individual purchase orders, not a series of orders. This discount is used by Federal Express to encourage companies to ship a large number of packages at one time. *Cumulative quantity discounts* apply to the accumulation of purchases of a product over a given time period, typically a year. Cumulative quantity discounts encourage repeat buying by a single customer to a far greater degree than do noncumulative quantity discounts. A

Toro uses seasonal discounts to stimulate consumer demand.

recent decision by Burger King to replace Pepsi-Cola with Coca-Cola in its outlets was based on the cumulative quantity discounts offered by Coca-Cola on its syrup.[15]

Seasonal Discounts To encourage buyers to stock inventory earlier than their normal demand would require, manufacturers often use seasonal discounts. A firm like Toro that manufactures lawn mowers and snow throwers offers seasonal discounts to encourage wholesalers and retailers to stock up on lawn mowers in January and February and on snow throwers in July and August—five or six months before the seasonal demand by ultimate consumers. This enables Toro to smooth out seasonal manufacturing peaks and troughs, thereby contributing to more efficient production. It also rewards wholesalers and retailers for the risk they accept in assuming increased inventory carrying costs and having supplies in stock at the time they are wanted by customers.

Trade (Functional) Discounts To reward wholesalers and retailers for marketing functions they will perform in the future, a manufacturer often gives trade, or functional, discounts. These reductions off the list or base price are offered to resellers in the channel of distribution on the basis of (1) where they are in the channel and (2) the marketing activities they are expected to perform in the future.

Suppose a manufacturer quotes price in the following form: list price—$100 less 30/10/5. The first number in the percentage sequence always refers to the retail end of the channel, and the last number always refers to the wholesaler

Terms	List price less 30/10/5	
	Manufacturer's suggested retail price	$100.00
Subtract	Retail discount, 30 percent of manufacturer's suggested retail price	30.00
Yields	Retail cost or wholesale sales price	$ 70.00
Subtract	Wholesaler discount, 10 percent of wholesale sales price	7.00
Yields	Wholesaler cost or jobber sales price	$ 63.00
Subtract	Jobber discount, 5 percent of jobber sales price	3.15
Yields	Jobber cost, or manufacturer's sales price	$ 59.85

or jobber closest to the manufacturer in the channel. The trade discounts are simply subtracted one at a time. This price quote shows $100 as the manufacturer's suggested retail price; 30 percent of the suggested retail price is available to the retailer to cover costs and provide a profit of $30 ($100 × 0.3 = $30); wholesalers closest to the retailer in the channel get 10 percent of their selling price ($70 × 0.1 = $7); and the final group of wholesalers in the channel (probably jobbers) that are closest to the manufacturer get 5 percent of their selling price ($63 × 0.05 = $3.15). Thus, starting with the manufacturer's retail price and subtracting the three trade discounts shows that the manufacturer's selling price to the wholesaler or jobber closest to it is $59.85 (Figure 14–8).

Traditional trade discounts have been established in various product lines such as hardware, food, and pharmaceutical items. Although the manufacturer may suggest the trade discounts shown in the example just cited, the sellers are free to alter the discount schedule depending on their competitive situation.

Cash Discounts   To encourage retailers to pay their bills quickly, manufacturers offer them cash discounts. Suppose a retailer receives a bill quoted at $1,000, 2/10 net 30. This means that the bill for the product is $1,000, but the retailer can take a 2 percent discount ($1,000 × 0.02 = $20) if payment is made within 10 days and send a check for $980. If the payment cannot be made within 10 days, the total amount of $1,000 is due within 30 days. It is usually understood by the buyer that an interest charge will be added after the first 30 days of free credit.

Naive buyers may think that the 2 percent discount offered is not substantial. What this means is that the buyer pays 2 percent on the total amount to be able to use that amount an extra 20 days—from day 11 to day 30. In a 360-day business year, this is an effective annual interest rate of 36 percent (2% × 360/20 = 36%). Because the effective interest rate is so high, firms that cannot take advantage of a 2/10 net 30 cash discount often try to borrow money from their local banks at rates far lower than the 36 percent they must pay by not taking advantage of the cash discount.

Retailers provide cash discounts to consumers as well to eliminate the cost of credit granted to consumers.[16] These discounts take the form of discount-for-cash policies. For example, Canadian Tire probably has one of the oldest discounts-for-cash concepts in Canada. They offer 3 percent off for cash purchases in the form of cash-bonus coupons that consumers use against their next purchases.

Canadian Tire's cash bonus coupon.

ALLOWANCES

Allowances—like discounts—are reductions from list or quoted prices to buyers for performing some activity.

Trade-In Allowances   A new car dealer can offer a substantial reduction in the list price of that new Ford Taurus by offering you a trade-in allowance of $500 for your 1980 Chevrolet. A trade-in allowance is a price reduction given when a used product is part of the payment on a new product. Trade-ins are an effective way to lower the price a buyer has to pay without formally reducing the list price.

Promotional Allowances   Sellers in the channel of distribution can qualify for **promotional allowances** for undertaking certain advertising or selling activities to promote a product. Various types of allowances include an actual cash payment or an extra amount of "free goods" (such as a free case of pizzas to a retailer for every dozen cases purchased). Frequently, a portion of these savings is passed on to the consumer.[17]

Some companies, like Procter & Gamble, have chosen to reduce promotional allowances to retailers by using an everyday low-pricing policy (EDLP). P&G saves on promotional allowance expenditures by offering these lower manufacturer list prices to the retailers. The manufacturer's EDLP policy often plays a direct role in the retailer's ability to offer its customers everyday low prices.[18]

GEOGRAPHICAL ADJUSTMENTS

Geographical adjustments are made by manufacturers or even wholesalers to list or quoted prices to reflect the cost of transportation of the products from seller to buyer. The two general methods for quoting prices related to transportation costs are FOB origin pricing and uniform delivered pricing.

FOB Origin Pricing   *FOB* means "free on board" some vehicle at some location, which means the seller pays the cost of loading the product onto the vehicle that is used (such as a barge, railroad car, or truck). **FOB origin pricing** usually involves the seller's naming the location of this loading as the seller's factory or warehouse (such as "FOB Toronto" or "FOB factory"). The title to the goods passes to the buyer at the point of loading, so the buyer becomes responsible for picking the specific mode of transportation, for all the transportation costs, and for subsequent handling of the product. Buyers farthest from the seller face the big disadvantage of paying the higher transportation costs.

Uniform Delivered Pricing   When a **uniform delivered pricing** method is used, the price the seller quotes includes all transportation costs. It is quoted in a contract as "FOB buyer's location," and the seller selects the mode of transportation, pays the freight charges, and is responsible for any damage that may occur, since the seller retains title to the goods until delivered to the buyer. Although they go by various names, four kinds of delivered pricing methods are single-zone pricing, multiple-zone pricing, FOB with freight-allowed pricing, and basing-point pricing.

In *single-zone pricing* all buyers pay the same delivered price for the products, regardless of their distance from the seller. So although a store offering free delivery in a metropolitan area has lower transportation costs for goods shipped to customers nearer the store than for those shipped to distant ones, customers pay the same delivered price.

In *multiple-zone pricing* a firm divides its selling territory into geographic areas, or zones. The delivered price to all buyers within any one zone is the same, but prices across zones vary depending on the transportation cost to the zone and the level of competition and demand within the zone. This system is used in setting prices on long-distance phone calls.

With *FOB with freight-allowed pricing,* also called *freight absorption pricing,* the price is quoted by the seller as "FOB plant—freight allowed." The buyer is allowed to deduct freight expenses from the list price of the goods, so the seller agrees to pay, or "absorbs," the transportation costs.

Basing-point pricing involves selecting one or more geographical locations (basing points) from which the list price for products plus freight expenses are charged to the buyer. For example, a company might designate Montreal as the basing point and charge all buyers a list price of $100 plus freight from Montreal to their location. Basing-point pricing methods have been used in the steel, cement, and lumber industries, where freight expenses are a significant part of the total cost to the buyer and products are largely undifferentiated.

LEGAL AND REGULATORY ASPECTS OF PRICING

Arriving at a final price is clearly a complex process. The task is further complicated by legal and regulatory restrictions. Chapter 3 described the regulatory environment of companies. Here we elaborate on the specific laws and regulations affecting pricing decisions. Five pricing practices have received the most scrutiny: price-fixing, price discrimination, deceptive pricing, predatory pricing and delivered pricing.

Price-Fixing   A conspiracy among firms to set prices for a product is termed **price-fixing.** Price-fixing is illegal per se under the Competition Act (*per se* means in and of itself). When two or more competitors explicitly or implicitly set prices, this practice is called *horizontal price-fixing.*

- *Bait and switch.* A deceptive practice exists when a firm offers a very low price on a product (the bait) to attract customers to a store. Once in the store, the customer is persuaded to purchase a higher-priced item (the switch) by means of a variety of tricks, including downgrading the promoted item and not having the item in stock or refusing to take orders for the item.
- *Bargains conditional on other purchases.* This practice may exist when a buyer is offered "1-cent sales," "buy 1, get 1 free," and "Get 2 for the price of 1." Such pricing is legal only if the first items are sold at the regular price, not a price inflated for the offer. Substituting lower-quality items on either the first or second purchase is also considered deceptive.
- *Comparable value comparisons.* Advertising such as "retail value $100, our price $85" is deceptive if a verified and substantial number of stores in the market area did not price the item at $100.
- *Comparisons with suggested prices.* A claim that a price is below a manufacturer's suggested or list price may be deceptive if few or no sales occur at that price in a retailer's market area.
- *Former price comparison.* When a seller represents a price as reduced, the item must have been offered "in good faith" at a higher price for a substantial previous period. Setting a high price for the purpose of establishing a reference for a price reduction is deceptive.

Vertical price-fixing involves controlling agreements between independent buyers and sellers (a manufacturer and a retailer) whereby sellers are required not to sell products below a minimum retail price. This practice, called *resale price maintenance,* is also illegal under provisions of the Competition Act.

It is important to recognize that a manufacturer's "suggested retail price" is not illegal per se. The issue of legality arises only when manufacturers enforce such a practice by coercion. Furthermore, there appears to be a movement toward a "rule of reason" in pricing cases. This rule holds that circumstances surrounding a practice must be considered before making a judgment about its legality. The "rule of reason" perspective is the direct opposite of the per se rule, which holds that a practice is illegal in and of itself.

Price Discrimination The Competition Act prohibits **price discrimination**—the practice of charging different prices to different buyers for goods of like grade and quality. However, it is not easy to prove that price discrimination has actually taken place. The Competition Act also covers promotional allowances. To legally offer promotional allowances to buyers, the seller must do so on a proportionally equal basis to all buyers distributing the seller's products. In general, this rule of reason applies frequently in price discrimination cases and is often applied to cases involving flexible pricing practices of firms.

Deceptive Pricing Price deals that mislead consumers fall into the category of deceptive pricing. Deceptive pricing is outlawed by the Competition Act. Consumer and Corporate Affairs Canada monitors such practices. The five most common deceptive pricing practices are described in Figure 14—9. As you read, it should be clear that laws cannot be passed and enforced to protect consumers and competitors against all of these practices. So it is essential to rely on the ethical standards of those making and publicizing pricing decisions.

Predatory Pricing   **Predatory pricing** is the practice of charging a very low price for a product with the intent of driving competitors out of business. Once competitors have been driven out, the firm raises its prices. This practice is illegal under the Competition Act. Proving the presence of this practice has been difficult and expensive because it must be shown that the predator explicitly attempted to destroy a competitor and the predatory price was below the defendant's average cost.

Delivered Pricing   **Delivered pricing** is the practice of refusing a customer delivery of an article on the same trade terms as other customers in the same location. It is a noncriminal offense, but the Competition Tribunal can prohibit suppliers from engaging in such a practice.

Concept Check	1 Why would a seller choose a flexible-price policy over a one-price policy?
	2 If a firm wished to encourage repeat purchases by a buyer throughout a year, would a cumulative or a noncumulative quantity discount be a better strategy?

Summary

1 Four general methods of finding an approximate price level for a product or service are demand-based, cost-based, profit-based, and competition-based pricing methods.

2 Demand-based pricing methods stress consumer demand and revenue implications of pricing and include eight types: skimming, penetration, prestige, price lining, odd–even, demand-backward pricing, bundle pricing, and value-based pricing.

3 Cost-based pricing methods emphasize the cost aspects of pricing and include four types: standard markup, cost plus percentage-of-cost, cost plus fixed-fee, and experience curve pricing.

4 Profit-based pricing methods focus on a balance between revenues and costs to set a price and include three types: target profit, target return-on-sales, and target return-on-investment pricing.

5 Competition-based pricing methods stress what competitors or the marketplace is doing and include four types: customary; above-, at-, or below-market; loss-leader; and sealed-bid pricing.

6 Given an approximate price level for a product, a manager must set a list or quoted price by considering factors such as a one-price versus a flexible-price policy; pricing to cover cost plus profit in the long run; balancing incremental costs and revenues; and the effects of the proposed price on the company, customer, and competitors.

7 List or quoted price is often modified through discounts, allowances, and geographical adjustments.

8 Legal and regulatory issues in pricing focus on price-fixing, price discrimination, deceptive pricing, predatory pricing, and delivered pricing.

Key Terms and Concepts

skimming pricing p. 340
penetration pricing p. 341
prestige pricing p. 342
price lining p. 343
odd–even pricing p. 343
demand-backward pricing p. 344
bundle pricing p. 344
value-based pricing p. 344
standard markup pricing p. 345
cost plus percentage-of-cost pricing p. 346
cost plus fixed-fee pricing p. 347
experience curve pricing p. 347
target profit pricing p. 348
target return-on-sales pricing p. 348
target return-on-investment pricing p. 349
customary pricing p. 350

above-, at-, or below-market
  pricing p. 350
loss-leader pricing p. 351
sealed-bid pricing p. 351
one-price policy p. 351
flexible-price policy p. 351
quantity discounts p. 356
promotional allowances p. 359
FOB origin pricing p. 359
uniform delivered
  pricing p. 360
basing-point pricing p. 360
price-fixing p. 360
price discrimination p. 361
predatory pricing p. 362
delivered pricing p. 362

Chapter Problems and Applications

1 Under what conditions would a camera manufacturer adopt a skimming price approach for a new product? A penetration approach?

2 What are some similarities and differences between skimming pricing, prestige pricing, and above-market pricing?

3 A producer of microwave ovens has adopted an experience curve pricing approach for its new model. The firm believes it can reduce the cost of producing the model by 20 percent each time volume doubles. The cost to produce the first unit was $1,000. What would be the approximate cost of the 4,096th unit?

4 The Hesper Corporation is a leading manufacturer of high-quality upholstered sofas. Current plans call for an increase of $600,000 in the advertising budget. If the firm sells its sofas for an average price of $850 and the unit variable costs are $550, then what dollar sales increase will be necessary to cover the additional advertising?

5 Suppose executives estimate that the unit variable cost for their VCR is $100, the fixed cost related to the product is $10 million annually, and the target volume for next year is 100,000 recorders. What sales price will be necessary to achieve a target profit of $1 million?

6 A manufacturer of motor oil has a trade discount policy whereby the manufacturer's suggested retail price is $30 per case with the terms of 40/20/10. The manufacturer sells its products through jobbers, who sell to wholesalers, who sell to gasoline stations. What will the manufacturer's sale price be?

7 What are the effective annual interest rates for the following cash discount terms? (*a*) 1/10 net 30, (*b*) 2/10 net 30, and (*c*) 2/10 net 60.

8 Suppose a manufacturer of exercise equipment sets a suggested price to the consumer of $395 for a particular piece of equipment to be competitive with similar equipment. The manufacturer sells its equipment to a sporting goods wholesaler, who receives a 25 percent markup, and a retailer, who receives a 50 percent markup. What demand-based pricing method is being used, and at what price will the manufacturer sell the equipment to the wholesaler?

Financial Aspects of Marketing

Basic concepts from accounting and finance provide valuable tools for marketing executives. This appendix describes an actual company's use of accounting and financial concepts and illustrates how they assist the owner in making marketing decisions.

THE CAPLOW COMPANY

An accomplished artist and calligrapher, Jane Westerlund, decided to apply some of her experience to the picture framing business. She bought an existing retail frame store, The Caplow Company, from a friend who owned the business and wanted to retire. She avoided the do-it-yourself end of the framing business and chose two kinds of business activities: (1) cutting the frame, mats, and glass for customers who brought in their own pictures or prints to be framed and (2) selling prints and posters that she had purchased from wholesalers.

To understand how accounting, finance, and marketing relate to each other, let's analyze the operating statement for her frame shop, some general ratios of interest that are derived from the operating statement, and some ratios that pertain specifically to her pricing decisions.

THE OPERATING STATEMENT

The operating statement (also called an *income statement* or *profit-and-loss statement*) summarizes the profitability of a business firm for a specific time period, usually a month, quarter, or year. The title of the operating statement for The Caplow Company shows it is for a one-year period (Figure A–1). The purpose of an operating statement is to show the profit of the firm and the revenues and expenses that led to that profit. This information tells the owner or manager what has happened in the past and suggests actions to improve future profitability.

The left side of Figure A–1 shows that there are three key elements to all operating statements: sales of the firm's goods and services, costs incurred in making and selling the goods and services, and profit or loss, which is the difference between sales and costs.

Sales Elements The sales element of Figure A–1 has four terms that need explanation:

- *Gross sales* are the total amount billed to customers. Dissatisfied customers or errors may reduce the gross sales through returns or allowances.

Figure A–1
Example of an operating statement.

	THE CAPLOW COMPANY OPERATING STATEMENT FOR THE YEAR ENDING DECEMBER 31, 1995		
Sales	Gross Sales		$80,500
	Less: Returns and allowances		500
	Net sales		80,000
Costs	Cost of goods sold:		
	Beginning inventory at cost	$ 6,000	
	Purchases at billed cost	$21,000	
	Less: Purchase discounts	300	
	Purchases at net cost	20,700	
	Plus freight-in	100	
	Net cost of delivered purchases	20,800	
	Direct labour (framing)	14,200	
	Cost of goods available for sale	41,000	
	Less: Ending inventory at cost	5,000	
	Cost of goods sold		36,000
	Gross margin (gross profit)		44,000
	Expenses:		
	Selling expenses:		
	Sales salaries	2,000	
	Advertising expense	3,000	
	Total selling expense	5,000	
	Administrative expenses:		
	Owner's salary	18,000	
	Bookkeeper's salary	1,200	
	Office supplies	300	
	Total administrative expense	19,500	
	General expenses:		
	Depreciation expense	1,000	
	Interest expense	500	
	Rent expense	2,100	
	Utility expenses (heat, electricity)	3,000	
	Repairs and maintenance	2,300	
	Insurance	2,000	
	Social insurance and Canada Pension	2,200	
	Total general expense	13,100	
	Total expenses		37,600
Profit or loss	Profit before taxes		6,400

- *Returns* occur when a customer gives the item purchased back to the seller, who either refunds the purchase price or allows the customer a credit on subsequent purchases. In any event, the seller now owns the item again.
- *Allowances* are given when a customer is dissatisfied with the item purchased and the seller reduces the original purchase price. Unlike returns, in the case of allowances the buyer owns the item.
- *Net sales* are simply gross sales minus returns and allowances.

The operating statement for The Caplow Company shows:

Gross sales	$80,500
Less: Returns and allowances	500
Net sales	$80,000

The low level of returns and allowances shows the shop generally has done a good job in satisfying customers, which is essential in building the repeat business necessary for success.

Cost Elements   The *cost of goods sold* is the total cost of the products sold during the period. This item varies according to the kind of business. A retail store purchases finished goods and resells them to customers without reworking them in any way. In contrast, a manufacturing firm combines raw and semifinished materials and parts, uses labour and overhead to rework these into finished goods, and then sells them to customers. All these activities are reflected in the cost of goods sold item on a manufacturer's operating statement. Note that the frame shop has some features of a pure retailer (prints and posters it buys that are resold without alteration) and a pure manufacturer (assembling the raw materials of moulding, matting, and glass to form a completed frame).

Some terms that relate to cost of goods sold need clarification:

- *Inventory* is the physical material that is purchased from suppliers, may or may not be reworked, and is available for sale to customers. In the frame shop, inventory includes moulding, matting, glass, prints, and posters.
- *Purchase discounts* are reductions in the original billed price for reasons like prompt payment of the bill or the quantity bought.
- *Direct labour* is the cost of the labour used in producing the finished product. For the frame shop, this is the cost of producing the completed frames from the moulding, matting, and glass.
- *Gross margin* (*gross profit*) is the money remaining to manage the business, sell the products or services, and give some profit. Gross margin is net sales minus cost of goods sold.

The two right-hand columns in Figure A–1 between "Net sales" and "Gross margin" calculate the cost of goods sold:

Net sales		$80,000
Cost of goods sold		
Beginning inventory at cost	$ 6,000	
Net cost of delivered purchases	20,800	
Direct labour (framing)	14,200	
Cost of goods available for sale	41,000	
Less: ending inventory at cost	5,000	
Cost of goods sold		36,000
Gross margin (*gross profit*)		$44,000

This section considers the beginning and ending inventories, the net cost of purchases delivered during the year, and the cost of the direct labour going into making the frames. Subtracting the $36,000 cost of goods sold from the $80,000 net sales gives the $44,000 gross margin.

Three major categories of expenses are shown in Figure A–1 below the gross margin.

- *Selling expenses* are the costs of selling the product or service produced by the firm. For The Caplow Company there are two such selling expenses: sales salaries of part-time employees waiting on customers, and the advertising expense of simple newspaper ads and direct-mail ads sent to customers.
- *Administrative expenses* are the costs of managing the business, and, for The Caplow Company, include three expenses: the owner's salary, a part-time bookkeeper's salary, and office supplies expense.
- *General expenses* are miscellaneous costs not covered elsewhere; for the frame shop these include seven items: depreciation expense (on equipment), interest expense, rent expense, utility expenses, repairs and maintenance expense, insurance expense, and social insurance and Canada Pension.

As shown in Figure A–1, selling, administrative, and general expenses total $37,600 for The Caplow Company.

Profit Element   What the company has earned, the *profit before taxes,* is found by subtracting cost of goods sold and expenses from net sales. For The Caplow Company, Figure A–1 shows that profit before taxes is $6,400.

GENERAL OPERATING RATIOS TO ANALYZE OPERATIONS

Looking only at the elements of Caplow's operating statement that extend to the right-hand column highlights the firm's performance on some important dimensions. Using operating ratios such as *expense-to-sales ratios* for expressing basic expense or profit elements as a percentage of net sales gives further insights:

ELEMENT IN OPERATING STATEMENT	DOLLAR VALUE	PERCENTAGE OF NET SALES
Gross sales	$80,500	
Less: Returns and allowances	500	
Net sales	80,000	100%
Less: Cost of goods sold	36,000	45
Gross margin	44,000	55
Less: Total expenses	37,600	47
Profit (or loss) before taxes	6,400	8%

Westerlund can use this information to compare her firm's performance from one time period to the next. To do so, it is especially important that she keep the same definitions for each element of her operating statement, also a significant factor in using the electronic spreadsheets discussed in Chapter 14. Performance comparisons between periods are more difficult if she changes definitions for the accounting elements in the operating statement.

She can use either the dollar values or the operating ratios (the value of the element of the operating statement divided by net sales) to analyze the firm's performance. However, the operating ratios are more valuable than the dollar values for two reasons: the simplicity of working with percentages rather than dollars and the availability of operating ratios of typical firms in the same industry, which are published by Dun & Bradstreet and trade associations. Thus,

Westerlund can compare her firm's performance not only with that of *other* frame shops but also with that of *small* frame shops that have annual net sales, for example, of under $100,000. In this way she can identify where her operations are better or worse than other, similar firms'. For example, if trade association data showed a typical frame shop of her size had a ratio of cost of goods sold to net sales of 37 percent, compared with her 45 percent, she might consider steps to reduce this cost through purchase discounts, reducing inbound freight charges, finding lower-cost suppliers, and so on.

RATIOS TO USE IN SETTING AND EVALUATING PRICE

Using The Caplow Company as an example, we can study four ratios that relate closely to setting a price: (1) markup, (2) markdown, (3) stockturns, and (4) return on investment. These terms are defined in Figure A–2 and explained in the following.

Markup   Both markup and gross margin refer to the amount added to the cost of goods sold to arrive at the selling price, and they may be expressed either in dollar or percentage terms. However, the term *markup* is more commonly used in setting retail prices. Suppose the average price Westerlund charges for a framed picture is $80. Then in terms of the first two definitions in Figure A–2 and the earlier information from the operating statement:

▎*Figure A–2*
How to calculate selling price, markup, markdown, stockturn, and return on investment.

ELEMENT OF PRICE	DOLLAR VALUE
Cost of goods sold	$36
Markup (or gross margin)	44
Selling price	$80

NAME OF FINANCIAL ELEMENT OR RATIO	WHAT IT MEASURES	EQUATION
Selling price ($)	Price customer sees	Cost of goods sold (COGS) + Markup
Markup ($)	Dollars added to COGS to arrive at selling price	Selling price − COGS
Markup on selling price (%)	Relates markup to selling price	$\dfrac{\text{Markup}}{\text{Selling price}}\times 100 = \dfrac{\text{Selling price} - \text{COGS}}{\text{Selling price}}\times 100$
Markup on cost (%)	Relates markup to cost	$\dfrac{\text{Markup}}{\text{COGS}}\times 100 = \dfrac{\text{Selling price} - \text{COGS}}{\text{COGS}}$
Markdown (%)	Ability of firm to sell its products at initial selling price	$\dfrac{\text{Markdowns}}{\text{Net sales}}\times 100$
Stockturn rate	Ability of firm to move its inventory quickly	$\dfrac{\text{COGS}}{\text{Average inventory at cost}}$ or $\dfrac{\text{Net sales}}{\text{Average inventory at selling price}}$
Return on investment (%)	Profit performance of firm compared with money invested in it	$\dfrac{\text{Net profit after taxes}}{\text{Investment}}\times 100$

The third definition in Figure A–2 gives the percentage markup on selling price:

$$\text{Markup on selling price (\%)} = \frac{\text{Markup}}{\text{Selling price}} \times 100$$

$$= \frac{44}{80} \times 100 = 55\%$$

and the percentage markup on cost is obtained as follows:

$$\text{Markup on cost (\%)} = \frac{\text{Markup}}{\text{Cost of goods sold}} \times 100$$

$$= \frac{44}{36} \times 100 = 122.2\%$$

Inexperienced retail clerks sometimes fail to distinguish between the two definitions of markup, which (as the preceding calculations show) can represent a tremendous difference, so it is essential to know whether the base is cost or selling price. Marketers generally use selling price as the base for talking about "markups" unless they specifically state they are using cost as a base.

Retailers and wholesalers that rely heavily on markup pricing (discussed in Chapter 14) often use standardized tables that convert markup on selling price to markup on cost, and vice versa. The next two equations show how to convert one to the other:

$$\text{Markup on selling price (\%)} = \frac{\text{Markup on cost (\%)}}{100\% + \text{Markup on cost (\%)}} \times 100$$

$$\text{Markup on cost (\%)} = \frac{\text{Markup on selling price (\%)}}{100\% - \text{Markup on selling price (\%)}} \times 100$$

Using the data from The Caplow Company gives:

$$\text{Markup on selling price (\%)} = \frac{\text{Markup on cost (\%)}}{100\% + \text{Markup on cost (\%)}} \times 100$$

$$= \frac{122.2}{100 + 122.2} \times 100 = 55\%$$

$$\text{Markup on cost (\%)} = \frac{\text{Markup on selling price (\%)}}{100\% - \text{Markup on selling price (\%)}} \times 100$$

$$= \frac{55}{100 - 55} \times 100 = 122.2\%$$

The use of an incorrect markup base is shown in Westerlund's business. A markup of 122.2 percent on her cost of goods sold for a typical frame she sells gives 122.2% × \$36 = \$44 of markup. Added to the \$36 cost of goods sold, this gives her selling price of \$80 for the framed picture. However, a new clerk working for her who erroneously priced the framed picture at 55 percent of cost of goods sold set the final price at \$55.80 (\$36 of cost of goods sold plus 55% × \$36 = \$19.80). The error, if repeated, can be disastrous: frames would be accidentally sold at \$55.80, or \$24.20 below the intended selling price of \$80.

Markdown   A markdown is a reduction in a retail price that is necessary if the item will not sell at the full selling price to which it has been marked up. The item might not sell for a variety of reasons: the selling price was set too high or the item is out of style or has become soiled or damaged. The seller "takes a markdown" by lowering the price to sell it, thereby converting it to cash to buy future inventory that will sell faster.

The markdown percentage cannot be calculated directly from the operating statement. As shown in the fifth item of Figure A–2, the numerator of the markdown percentage is the total dollar markdowns. Markdowns are reductions in the prices of goods that are purchased by customers. The denominator is net sales.

Suppose The Caplow Company had a total of $700 in markdowns on the prints and posters that are stocked and available for sale. Since the frames are custom made for individual customers, there is little reason for a markdown there. Caplow's markdown percent is then:

$$\text{Markdown (\%)} = \frac{\text{Markdowns}}{\text{Net sales}} \times 100$$

$$= \frac{\$700}{\$80,000} \times 100$$

$$= 0.875\%$$

Other kinds of retailers often have markdown ratios several times this amount. For example, women's dress stores have markdowns of about 25 percent, and menswear stores have markdowns of about 2 percent.

Stockturn Rate   A business firm is anxious to have its inventory move quickly, or "turn over." Stockturn rate, or simply stockturns, measures this inventory movement. For a retailer a slow stockturn rate may show it is buying merchandise customers don't want, so this is a critical measure of performance. When a firm sells only a single product, one convenient way to measure stockturn rate is simply to divide its cost of goods sold by average inventory at cost. The sixth item in Figure A–2 shows how to calculate stockturn rate using information in the operating statement:

$$\text{Stockturn rate} = \frac{\text{Cost of goods sold}}{\text{Average inventory at cost}}$$

The dollar amount of average inventory at cost is calculated by adding the beginning and ending inventories for the year and dividing by 2 to get the average. From Caplow's operating statement, we have:

$$\text{Stockturn rate} = \frac{\text{Cost of goods sold}}{\text{Average inventory at cost}}$$

$$= \frac{\text{Cost of goods sold}}{\dfrac{\text{Beginning inventory} + \text{Ending inventory}}{2}}$$

$$= \frac{\$36,000}{\dfrac{\$6,000 + \$5,000}{2}}$$

$$= \frac{\$36,000}{\$5,500}$$

$$= 6.5 \text{ stockturns per year}$$

What is considered a "good" stockturn varies by the kind of industry. For example, supermarkets have limited shelf space for thousands of new products from manufacturers each year, so they watch stockturn carefully by product line. The stockturn rate in supermarkets for breakfast foods is about 17 times per year, for pet food is about 22 times, and for paper products is about 25 times per year.

Return on Investment   A better measure of the performance of a firm than the amount of profit it makes in a year is its ROI, which is the ratio of net income to the investment used to earn that net income. To calculate ROI, it is necessary to subtract income taxes from profit before taxes to obtain net income, then divide this figure by the investment that can be found on a firm's balance sheet (another accounting statement that shows the firm's assets, liabilities, and net worth). While financial and accounting experts have many definitions for "investment," an often-used definition is "total assets."

For our purposes, let's assume that Westerlund has total assets (investment) of $20,000 in The Caplow Company, which covers inventory, store fixtures, and framing equipment. If she pays $1,000 in income taxes, her store's net income is $5,400, so her ROI is given by the seventh item in Figure A–2:

Return on investment = Net income/investment × 100
= $5,400/$20,000 × 100
= 27%

If Westerlund wants to improve her ROI next year, the strategies she might take are found in this alternative equation for ROI:

ROI = Net sales/investment × Net income/net sales
= Investment turnover × Profit margin

This equation suggests that The Caplow Company's ROI can be improved by raising turnover or increasing profit margin. Increasing stockturns will accomplish the former, whereas lowering cost of goods sold to net sales will cause the latter.

Marketing Channels and Wholesaling

AFTER READING THIS CHAPTER YOU SHOULD BE ABLE TO:

▼ Explain what is meant by a marketing channel of distribution and why intermediaries are needed.

▼ Recognize differences between marketing channels for consumer and industrial products and services.

▼ Describe the types of functions of firms that perform wholesaling activities.

▼ Distinguish among traditional marketing channels and different types of vertical marketing systems.

▼ Describe factors considered by marketing executives when selecting and managing a marketing channel.

Whatever Happened to the Corner Computer Store?

Thinking about buying a new personal computer or replacing your old one? Not only do you have a bewildering choice of brands, but your options of where to buy are almost limitless.

The PC industry is driven by technological advances and distribution innovation. A decade ago, 90 percent of PCs were purchased from computer stores, many of which were owner-operated. Today, you can buy PCs from department stores, discount electronics stores, superstores like CompUSA, mass merchandisers, and even retail catalogue showroom stores like Consumers Distributing. You can order one through the mail from Dell Computer, Inc., pick one out at a travelling computer show, or visit a value-added reseller such as Micro Age, which will add software to your PC.

The distribution revolution in PC marketing has also caught on in Western Europe, where the corner computer stores are struggling to compete against superstores and mail-order firms.[1] Distribution is critical not only to PCs but also for the marketing success of such diverse products as magazines, automobiles, snack foods, beverages, health care products, and cosmetics. Similarly, distribution is so important in marketing private and business airplanes that Cessna Aircraft considers its dealers to be the firm's greatest asset.

This chapter focusses on marketing channels of distribution and their importance as a component in the marketing mix. It then shows how such channels benefit consumers and what sequence of firms makes-up a marketing channel. Finally, it describes factors that influence the choice and management of marketing channels, including channel conflict and legal restrictions.

NATURE AND IMPORTANCE OF MARKETING CHANNELS

Reaching prospective buyers, either directly or indirectly, is a prerequisite for successful marketing. At the same time, buyers benefit from distribution systems used by firms.

DEFINING MARKETING CHANNELS OF DISTRIBUTION

You see the results of distribution every day. You may have purchased Lay's potato chips at the 7-Eleven store, your lunch at McDonald's, and Levi's jeans at Sears. Each of these items was brought to you by a marketing channel of distribution, or simply a **marketing channel,** which consists of individuals and firms involved in the process of making a product or service available for use or consumption by consumers or industrial users.

Marketing channels can be compared to a pipeline through which water flows from source to terminus. Marketing channels make possible the flow of goods from a producer, through intermediaries, to a buyer. Intermediaries go by various names (Figure 15–1) and perform various functions. Some intermediaries actually purchase items from the seller, store them, and resell them to buyers. For example, Nabisco produces cookies and sells them to food wholesalers. The wholesalers then sell the cookies to supermarkets and grocery stores, which in turn sell them to consumers. Other intermediaries such as brokers and agents represent sellers but do not actually take title to products—their role is to bring a seller and a buyer together. Century 21 real estate agents are examples of this type of intermediary. The importance of intermediaries is made even clearer when we consider the functions they perform and the value they create for buyers.

▌ *Figure 15–1*
Terms used for marketing intermediaries.

TERM	MEANING
Middleman	Any intermediary between manufacturer and end user markets
Agent or broker	Any intermediary with legal authority to act on behalf of the manufacturer
Wholesaler	An intermediary who sells to other intermediaries, usually to retailers; usually applies to consumer markets
Retailer	An intermediary who sells to consumers
Distributer	An imprecise term, usually used to describe intermediaries who perform a variety of distribution functions, including selling, maintaining inventories, extending credit, and so on; a more common term in industrial markets, but may also be used to refer to wholesalers
Dealer	An even more imprecise term that can mean the same as distributor, retailer, wholesaler, and so forth

Source: Adapted from F. E. Webster, Jr., *Marketing for Managers* (New York: Harper & Row, 1974), p. 191. Copyright © 1974 by F. E. Webster, Jr. Reprinted by permission of HarperCollins Publishers.

RATIONALE FOR INTERMEDIARIES

Few consumers appreciate the value created by intermediaries; however, producers recognize that intermediaries make selling goods and services more efficient because they minimize the number of sales contacts necessary to reach a target market. Figure 15–2 shows a simple example of how this comes about in the personal computer industry. Without a retail intermediary (such as Computerland), IBM, Apple, Compaq, and Epson would each have to make four contacts to reach the four buyers shown who are in the target market. However, each producer has to make only one contact when Computerland acts as an intermediary. Equally important from a macromarketing perspective, the total number of industry transactions is reduced from 16 to 8, which reduces producer cost and hence benefits the consumer. This simple example also illustrates why computer manufacturers constantly compete with each other to gain access to computer retailers such as Computerland and Micro Age.

Functions Performed by Intermediaries   Intermediaries make possible the flow of products from producers to buyers by performing three basic functions (Figure 15–3). Most prominently, intermediaries perform a transactional function that involves buying, selling, and risk taking because they stock merchandise in anticipation of sales. Intermediaries perform a logistical function evident in the gathering, storing, and dispersing of products (see Chapter 16, on physical distribution). Finally, intermediaries perform facilitating functions, which assist producers in making goods and services more attractive to buyers.

All three groups of functions must be performed in a marketing channel, even though each channel member may not participate in all three. Channel members often negotiate about which specific functions they will perform. Sometimes conflict results and a breakdown in relationships among channel

▌ *Figure 15–2*
How intermediaries minimize transactions.

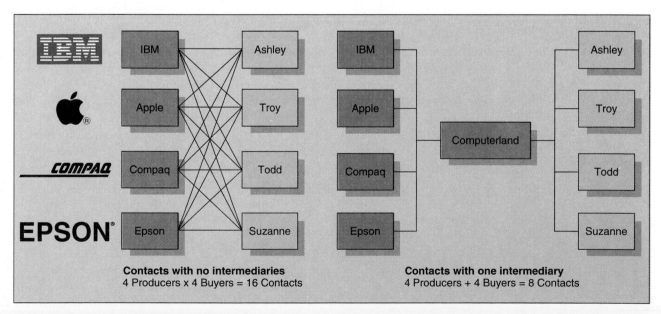

| Figure 15–3
Marketing channel functions performed by intermediaries.

TYPE OF FUNCTION	DESCRIPTION
Transactional functions	*Buying.* Purchasing products for resale or as an agent for supply of a product
Selling. Contacting potential customers, promoting products, and soliciting orders
Risk taking. Assuming business risks in the ownership of inventory that can become obsolete or deteriorate
Logistical functions	*Assorting.* Creating product assortments from several sources to serve customers
Storing. Assembling and protecting products at a convenient location to offer better customer service
Sorting. Purchasing in large quantities and breaking into smaller amounts desired by customers
Transporting. Physically moving a product to customers
Facilitating functions	*Financing.* Extending credit to customers
Grading. Inspecting, testing, or judging products and assigning them quality grades
Marketing information and research. Providing information to customers and suppliers, including competitive conditions and trends

Source: Based on F. E. Webster, Jr., *Industrial Marketing Strategy* (New York: John Wiley & Sons, 1979), pp. 162–63.

members occurs. This happened recently when PepsiCo, Inc., terminated its marketing and distribution arrangement with its bottler in France, citing poor performance. However, because all channel functions had to be performed, PepsiCo could eliminate this intermediary but not the functions it performed. So PepsiCo either had to find another bottler (which it did) or set up its own bottling operation to perform the channel functions.[2]

Value Created by Intermediaries   Consumers also benefit from intermediaries. Having the goods and services you want, when you want them, where you want them, and in the form you want them is the ideal result of marketing channels. In more specific terms, marketing channels help create value for consumers through the four utilities described in Chapter 1: time, place, form, and possession. Time utility refers to having a product or service when you want it. For example, Federal Express provides next-morning delivery. Place utility means having a product or service available where consumers want it, such as having an Esso gas station located on a long stretch of lonely highway. Form utility involves enhancing a product or service to make it more appealing to buyers, for example, tailoring services provided by Bretton's clothing store. Possession utility entails efforts by intermediaries to help buyers take possession of a product or service, such as having airline tickets delivered by a travel agency.

Concept Check

1 What is meant by a marketing channel?

2 What are the three basic functions performed by intermediaries?

CHANNEL STRUCTURE AND ORGANIZATION

A product can take many routes on its journey from a producer to buyers, and marketers search for the most efficient route from the many alternatives available.

MARKETING CHANNELS FOR CONSUMER GOODS AND SERVICES

Figure 15−4 shows the four most common marketing channels for consumer goods and services. It also shows the number of levels in each marketing channel, as evidenced by the number of intermediaries between a producer and ultimate buyers. As the number of intermediaries between producer and buyer increases, the channel is viewed as increasing in length. Thus the producer → wholesaler → retailer → consumer channel is longer than the producer → consumer channel.

Channel A represents a **direct channel,** because a producer and ultimate consumers deal directly with each other. Many products and services are distributed this way. A number of insurance companies sell their financial services using a direct channel and branch sales offices, and World Book Educational Products sells its encyclopedias door-to-door. Because there are no intermediaries in a direct channel, the producer must perform all channel functions.

The remaining three channel forms are **indirect channels,** because intermediaries are inserted between the producer and consumers and perform numerous channel functions.

Channel B, with a retailer added, is most common when a retailer is large and can buy in large quantities from a producer or when the cost of inventory

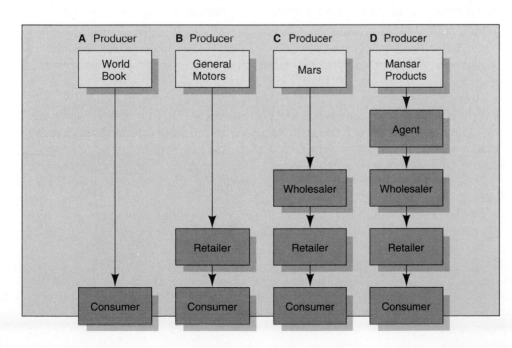

▌ *Figure 15−4*
Common marketing channels for consumer goods and services.

makes it too expensive to use a wholesaler. Manufacturers such as GM, Ford, and Chrysler use this channel, and a local car dealer acts as a retailer. Why is there no wholesaler? So many variations exist in the product that it would be impossible for a wholesaler to stock all the models required to satisfy buyers; in addition, the cost of maintaining an inventory would be too high. However, large retailers such as Zellers, 7-Eleven, Safeway, and The Bay buy in sufficient quantities to make it cost-effective for a producer to deal with only a retail intermediary.

Adding a wholesaler as in channel C is most common for low-cost, low-unit value items that are frequently purchased by consumers, such as candy, confectionary items, and magazines. For example, Mars sells its line of candies to wholesalers in case quantities; then they can break down (sort) the cases so that individual retailers can order in boxes or much smaller quantities.

Channel D, the most indirect channel, is employed when there are many small manufacturers and many small retailers. An agent is used to help coordinate a large supply of the product. Mansar Products, Ltd., is a Belgian producer of specialty jewellery that uses agents to sell to wholesalers which then sell to many small retailers.

MARKETING CHANNELS FOR INDUSTRIAL GOODS AND SERVICES

The four most common channels for industrial goods and services are shown in Figure 15–5.[3] In contrast with channels for consumer products, industrial channels typically are shorter and rely on one intermediary or none at all because industrial users are fewer in number, tend to be more concentrated geographically, and buy in larger quantities (see Chapter 7).

Channel A, represented by IBM's large, mainframe computer business, is a direct channel. Firms using this channel maintain their own sales force and are responsible for all channel functions. This channel arrangement is employed

▌ *Figure 15–5*
Common marketing channels for industrial goods and services.

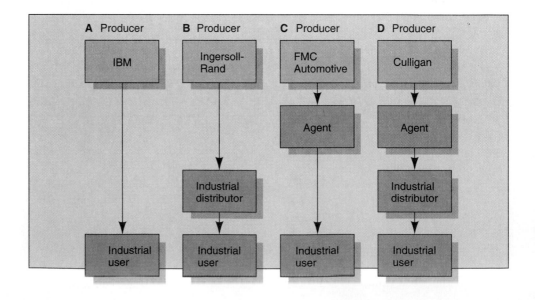

when buyers are large and well defined, the sales effort requires extensive negotiations, and the products are of high unit value and require hands-on expertise for installation or use.[4]

Channels B, C, and D are indirect channels with one or more intermediaries to reach industrial users. In Channel B an **industrial distributor** performs a variety of marketing channel functions, including selling, stocking, and delivering a full product assortment and financing.[5] In many ways, industrial distributors are like wholesalers in consumer channels. Ingersoll-Rand, for example, uses industrial distributors to sell its line of pneumatic tools.

Channel C introduces a second intermediary, an *agent,* who serves primarily as the independent selling arm of producers and represents a producer to industrial users. For example, FMC Automotive, a producer of auto parts, has an agent call on industrial users rather than employ its own sales force.

Channel D is the longest channel and includes both agents and distributors. For instance, Culligan, a producer of water treatment equipment, uses agents to call on distributors, who sell to industrial users.

MULTIPLE CHANNELS AND STRATEGIC ALLIANCES

In some situations producers use **dual distribution,** an arrangement whereby a firm reaches different buyers by employing two or more different types of channels for the same basic product.[6] For example, GE sells its large appliances directly to home and apartment builders but uses retail stores to sell to consumers. In some instances, firms use multiple channels when a multibrand strategy is employed (see Chapter 12). Hallmark sells its Hallmark greeting cards through Hallmark stores and select department stores, and its Ambassador brand cards through discount and drugstore chains. In other instances, a firm will distribute modified products through different channels.

A recent innovation in marketing channels is the use of **strategic channel alliances,** whereby one firm's marketing channel is used to sell another firm's products. An alliance between Pepsi-Cola and Thomas J. Lipton Company is a case in point. Lipton relies upon Pepsi-Cola's extensive bottling network to distribute Lipton Original, a ready-to-drink iced tea sold only in bottles.[7] Strategic alliances are very popular in global marketing, where the creation of marketing channel relationships is expensive and time-consuming.[8] For example, General Motors distributes the Swedish Saab through its dealers in Canada. And Kraft General Foods uses the distribution system of Ajinomoto, a major Japanese food company, to market its Maxwell House coffee in Japan.

These examples illustrate the creative routes to the marketplace available through dual distribution and strategic channel alliances. They also show how innovative firms can reach more buyers and increase sales volume. Read the accompanying Market Action Memo so you won't be surprised when you are served Nestlé (not General Mills) Cheerios in Europe, Mexico, and parts of Asia.

DIRECT MARKETING CHANNELS

Many firms use a direct marketing channel to reach buyers. Direct marketing channels are the simplest channel type; the people who produce the goods and

MARKETING · ACTION · MEMO

Nestlé and General Mills: Cereal Partners Worldwide

Can you say Nestlé Cheerios *miel amandes*? Millions of French start their day with this European equivalent of General Mills' Honey Nut Cheerios, made possible by Cereal Partners Worldwide (CPW). CPW is the food industry's first strategic alliance designed to be a global business; it joined the cereal manufacturing and marketing capability of General Mills with the worldwide distribution clout of Swiss-based Nestlé.

From its headquarters near Lake Geneva, Switzerland, CPW first launched General Mills cereals under the Nestlé label in France, the United Kingdom, Spain, Portugal, and Italy in 1991, and recorded sales of $250 million. In 1992, distribution moved to include Mexico and Germany. Asia—particularly the Philippines—was targeted in 1993, and by 2000, CPW expects to achieve its goal of $1 billion in sales. The General Mills–Nestlé strategic alliance is also likely to increase the ready-to-eat worldwide market share of these companies, which are already rated as the two best-managed firms in the world.

Sources: Based on D. Mussey, "Cereal Partners Target Kellogg in Germany," *Advertising Age,* October 26, 1992, pp. I-1, I-23; "Cafe au Lait, a Croissant—and Trix," *Business Week,* August 24, 1992, pp. 50–51; and C. Knowlton, "Europe Cooks Up a Cereal Brawl," *Fortune,* June 5, 1991, pp. 175–79.

services interact directly with the customer. However, at this point you should be made aware that while the term *direct marketing* can refer to a direct channel of *distribution,* it can also be used to describe a channel of *communication* or promotion activity. Many marketers use direct marketing to both distribute products and communicate with their customers. Those who use direct channels of distribution obviously rely heavily on direct marketing communications, sometimes called direct *promotion* (e.g., direct mail), to reach their customers. But they can and often do use indirect communication (promotion) via traditional media (e.g., TV advertising) to support their direct marketing efforts. Some traditional direct marketers like L.L. Bean (apparel) and Avon (cosmetics and gifts) and Dell Computer (computer software) use television, magazine, or newspaper advertising to communicate with customers and prospects but still directly distribute to those customers. So, just because a firm uses a direct marketing channel, it does not restrict the possibility of using various forms of communications to reach the customer, both direct and indirect.[9]

Many firms that use indirect channels of distribution have recognized the value of communicating directly with their customers and are increasingly using direct marketing communications techniques to enhance and support the traditional media they use. Manufacturers such as Nestlé and Sunkist, in addition to using indirect channels composed of wholesalers and retailers, employ direct marketing techniques such as catalogues and telemarketing to reach more buyers. At the same time, retailers such as Sears Canada use catalogues to augment conventional store merchandising activities.

Direct marketing, as a channel of distribution and communications function, includes such activities as direct selling (face-to-face or personal selling, to be covered in Chapter 20), mail-order selling, direct mail sales, catalogue sales, telemarketing, videotex, and television home shopping (for example, the Canadian Home Shopping Network).[10] The development and availability of databases (Chapter 10) on customers and prospects have created opportunities for many firms, those using direct and/or those using indirect channels, to use a variety of direct marketing methods.

Direct marketing is covered again in Chapter 17, as both a channel of distribution and a means of communication for nonstore retailers. It is also discussed in Chapter 18 as an increasingly important part of a firm's overall promotional mix.

A Closer Look at Wholesaling Intermediaries

Channel structures for consumer and industrial products assume various forms based on the number and type of intermediaries. Knowledge of the roles played by these intermediaries is important for understanding how channels operate in practice.

The terms *wholesaler, agent,* and *retailer* have been used in a general fashion consistent with the meanings given in Figure 15–1. However, on closer inspection a variety of specific types of intermediaries emerges. Figure 15–6 shows a common classification of intermediaries that engage in wholesaling activities—those activities involved in selling products and services to those who are buying for the purpose of resale or business use. Intermediaries engaged in retailing activities are discussed in detail in Chapter 17. Figure 15–7 describes the functions performed by major types of independent wholesalers.[11]

Merchant Wholesalers   Merchant wholesalers are independently owned firms that take title to the merchandise they handle. They go by various names, including industrial distributor (described earlier). About 80 percent of the firms engaged in wholesaling activities are merchant wholesalers.

Merchant wholesalers are classified as either full-service or limited-service wholesalers, depending on the number of functions performed. Two major types of full-service wholesalers exist. **General merchandise** (or full-line) **wholesalers** carry a broad assortment of merchandise and perform all channel functions. This type of wholesaler is most prevalent in the hardware, drug, and clothing industries. However, these wholesalers do not maintain much depth or assortment within specific product lines. **Specialty merchandise** (or limited-line) **wholesalers** offer a relatively narrow range of products but have an extensive assortment within the product lines carried. They perform all channel functions and are found in the health foods, automotive parts, and seafood industries.

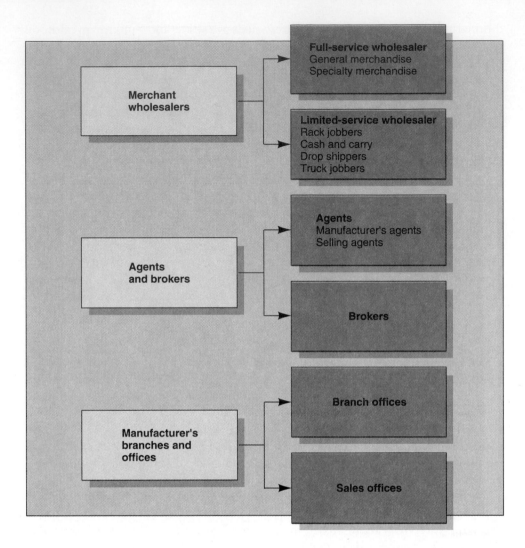

Four major types of limited-service wholesalers exist. **Rack jobbers** furnish the racks or shelves that display merchandise in retail stores, perform all channel functions, and sell on consignment to retailers, which means they retain the title to the products displayed and bill retailers only for the merchandise sold. Familiar products such as hosiery, toys, housewares, and health and beauty aids are sold by rack jobbers. **Cash-and-carry wholesalers** take title to merchandise but sell only to buyers who call on them, pay cash for merchandise, and furnish their own transportation for merchandise. They carry a limited product assortment and do not make deliveries, extend credit, or supply market information. This wholesaler is common in electric supplies, office supplies, hardware products, and groceries. **Drop shippers,** or *desk jobbers,* are wholesalers who own the merchandise they sell but do not physically handle, stock, or deliver it. They simply solicit orders from retailers and other wholesalers and have the merchandise shipped directly from a producer to a buyer. Drop shippers are used for bulky products such as coal, lumber, and chemicals, which are

| FUNCTIONS PERFORMED | MERCHANT WHOLESALERS | | | | | | AGENTS AND BROKERS | | |
| | FULL SERVICE | | LIMITED SERVICE | | | | | | |
	GENERAL MERCHANDISE	SPECIALTY MERCHANDISE	RACK JOBBERS	CASH AND CARRY	DROP SHIPPERS	TRUCK JOBBERS	MANUFACTURER'S AGENTS	SELLING AGENTS	BROKERS
TRANSACTIONAL FUNCTIONS									
Buying	●	●	●	●	●	●	○	○	○
Sales calls on customers	●	●	●	○	●	●	●	●	●
Risk taking (taking title to products)	●	●	●	●	●	●	○	○	○
LOGISTICAL FUNCTIONS									
Creates product assortments	●	●	●	●	○	●	◐	○	●
Stores products (maintains inventory)	●	●	●	●	○	●	○	○	◐
Sorts products	●	●	●	●	●	●	○	○	○
Transports products	●	●	●	○	○	●	◐	○	○
FACILITATING FUNCTIONS									
Provides financing (credit)	●	●	●	○	●	○	○	◐	○
Provides market information and research	●	●	◐	○	◐	○	◐	◐	●
Grading	●	●	◐	○	◐	○	○	◐	●

★ Key: ● , Yes; ◐ , sometimes; ○ , no.

Figure 15–7
Functions performed by independent wholesaler types.

sold in extremely large quantities. **Truck jobbers** are small wholesalers who have a small warehouse from which they stock their trucks for distribution to retailers. They usually handle limited assortments of fast-moving or perishable items that are sold for cash directly from trucks in their original packages. Truck jobbers handle products like bakery items, dairy products, meat, and tobacco.

Agents and Brokers Unlike merchant wholesalers, agents and brokers do not take title to merchandise and typically provide fewer channel functions. They make their profit from commissions or fees paid for their services, whereas merchant wholesalers make their profit from the sale of the merchandise they own.[12]

M A R K E T I N G · A C T I O N · M E M O

Mr. Coffee + Agents + Brokers = Customer Value

Vincent Marotta hated the way coffee tasted, but he was convinced that the poor taste was not a quality of the coffee itself but of the machines that brewed it. In 1972, he developed the prototype for what is now known as Mr. Coffee, the first electric-drip coffeemaker. By 1992 over 50 million Mr. Coffees had been sold, as well as billions of coffee filters. Was Mr. Coffee's success only a result of a high-quality product that satisfied a need, and of effective advertising using Joe DiMaggio as its spokesperson? Not quite. Distribution played an integral role in creating value for customers.

Mr. Coffee and its filters were sold by manufacturer's agents who called on appliance and mass merchandise stores. In time, however, it became apparent that Mr. Coffee users found it inconvenient to visit appliance and mass merchandise stores to buy replacement filters. These customers would benefit by having filters in the stores where they bought their coffee, namely, in thousands of retail food outlets. Therefore, a national network of food brokers was hired to sell Mr. Coffee filters to supermarkets and grocery stores. The result? It is estimated that about 75 percent of Mr. Coffee's filter sales come from retail food outlets.

When the company introduced the Ice Tea Pot by Mr. Coffee, it used its network of manufacturer's agents to call on appliance and mass merchandise stores. Filters were sold by food brokers to retail food outlets, and another success was brewed.

Sources: Based on an interview with Mr. James Yurak, executive vice president, Mr. Coffee, June 1, 1990; "After a Little Reheating, Mr. Coffee Is Just Fine," *Business Week*, August 20, 1990, p. 77; "The Yankee Clipper Returns to 'Pitch' in Mr. Coffee Lineup," *The Wall Street Journal*, August 22, 1990, p. B3; and "DiMaggio a Sure Bet in Day of Pete Rose," *Dallas Times Herald*, August 30, 1990, p. A19

Manufacturer's agents and selling agents are the two major types of agents used by producers. **Manufacturer's agents,** or *manufacturer's representatives,* work for several producers and carry noncompetitive, complementary merchandise in an exclusive territory.[13] Manufacturer's agents act as a producer's sales arm in a territory and are principally responsible for the transactional channel functions, primarily selling. They are used extensively in the automotive supply, footwear, and fabricated steel industries. However, Japanese computer firms and Apple have used manufacturer's agents as well. By comparison, **selling agents** represent a single producer and are responsible for the entire marketing function of that producer. They design promotional plans, set prices, determine distribution policies, and make recommendations on product strategy. Selling agents are used by small producers in the textile, apparel, food, and home furnishing industries.

Brokers are independent firms or individuals whose principal function is to bring buyers and sellers together to make sales. Brokers, unlike agents, usually have no continuous relationship with the buyer or seller but negotiate a contract between two parties and then move on to another task. Brokers are used extensively by producers of seasonal products (such as fruits and vegetables) and in the real estate industry.

A unique broker that acts in many ways like a manufacturer's agent is a food broker, representing buyers and sellers in the grocery industry. Food brokers differ from conventional brokers because they act on behalf of producers on a permanent basis and receive a commission for their services. For example, Nabisco uses food brokers to sell its candies, margarine, and Planters peanuts, but it sells its line of cookies and crackers directly to retail stores. Do agents and brokers create value for customers? The accompanying Marketing Action Memo describes how Mr. Coffee used both manufacturer's agents and brokers to become a leader in the electric-drip coffeemaker market.

Manufacturer's Branches and Offices   Unlike merchant wholesalers, agents, and brokers, manufacturer's branches and offices are wholly owned extensions of the producer that perform wholesaling activities. Producers will assume wholesaling functions when there are no intermediaries to perform these activities, customers are few in number and geographically concentrated, or orders are large or require significant attention. Wholesaling activities performed by producers are conducted by means of a branch office or sales office. A *manufacturer's branch office* carries a producer's inventory, performs the functions of a full-service wholesaler, and is an alternative to a merchant wholesaler. A *manufacturer's sales office* does not carry inventory, typically performs only a sales function, and serves as an alternative to agents and brokers.

VERTICAL MARKETING SYSTEMS

The traditional marketing channels described so far represent a loosely knit network of independent producers and intermediaries brought together to distribute goods and services. However, new channel arrangements are emerging to improve efficiency in performing channel functions and achieving greater marketing impact. For example, **vertical marketing systems** are professionally managed and centrally coordinated marketing channels designed to achieve channel economies and maximum marketing impact.[14] Figure 15–8 depicts the major types of vertical marketing systems: corporate, contractual, and administered.

Corporate Systems   The combination of successive stages of production and distribution under a single ownership is a *corporate vertical marketing system*. For example, a producer might own the intermediary at the next level down in the channel. This practice, called *forward integration,* is exemplified by Polo/Ralph Lauren, which manufactures clothing and also owns apparel shops.[15] Other examples of forward integration include Goodyear and Singer. Alternatively, a retailer might own a manufacturing operation, a practice called *backward integration.* For example, Safeway supermarkets operate their own bakeries.

Contractual Systems   Under a *contractual vertical marketing system,* independent production and distribution firms integrate their efforts on a contractual basis to

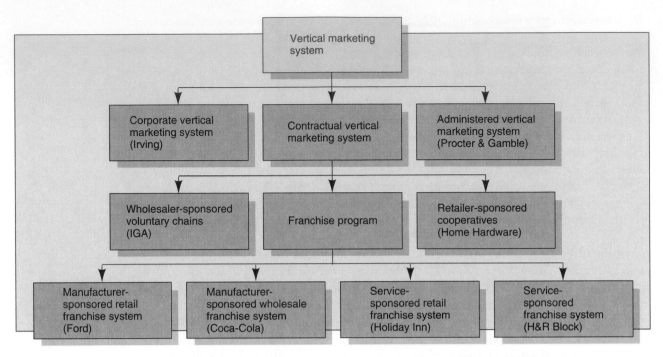

▌*Figure 15–8*
Types of vertical marketing systems.

obtain greater functional economies and marketing impact than they could achieve alone. Contractual systems are the most popular among the three types of vertical marketing systems and are estimated to account for about 40 percent of all retail sales.

Three variations of contractual systems exist. *Wholesaler-sponsored voluntary chains* involve a wholesaler that develops a contractual relationship with small, independent retailers to standardize and coordinate buying practices, merchandising programs, and inventory management efforts. With the organization of a large number of independent retailers, economies of scale and volume discounts can be achieved to compete with chain stores. IGA stores represent wholesaler-sponsored voluntary chains. *Retailer-sponsored cooperatives* exist when small, independent retailers form an organization that operates a wholesale facility cooperatively. Member retailers then concentrate their buying power through the wholesaler and plan collaborative promotional and pricing activities. An example of a retailer-sponsored cooperative is Home Hardware.

The most visible variation of contractual systems is **franchising,** a contractual arrangement between a parent company (a franchisor) and an individual or a firm (a franchisee) that allows a certain type of business to be operated under an established name and according to specific rules. Four types of franchise arrangements are most popular. Manufacturer-sponsored retail franchise systems are most prominent in the automobile industry, where a manufacturer such as Ford licenses dealers to sell its cars subject to various sales and service conditions. Manufacturer-sponsored wholesale systems are evident in the soft drink industry, where Pepsi-Cola licenses wholesalers (bottlers), who purchase concentrate from Pepsi-Cola and then carbonate, bottle, promote, and distribute its products to supermarkets and restaurants. Service-sponsored retail franchise systems are provided by firms that have designed a unique approach for

H&R Block represents a successful service franchise system.

performing a service and wish to profit by selling the franchise to others. Holiday Inn, Avis, and McDonald's represent this franchising approach. Service-sponsored franchise systems exist when franchisors license individuals or firms to dispense a service under a trade name and specific guidelines. An example is H&R Block. Service-sponsored franchise arrangements are expected to be the fastest-growing type of franchise in the 1990s. Franchising is discussed further in Chapter 17.

Administered Systems   In comparison, *administered vertical marketing systems* achieve coordination at successive stages of production and distribution by the size and influence of one channel member rather than through ownership. P&G, given its broad product assortment ranging from disposable diapers to detergents, is able to obtain excellent cooperation from supermarkets in displaying, promoting, and pricing its products. Sears gains numerous concessions from manufacturers in terms of product specifications, price levels, and promotional support.

---

1 What is the difference between a direct and an indirect channel?

2 Why are channels for industrial products typically shorter than channels for consumer products?

3 What is the principal distinction between a corporate vertical marketing system and an administered vertical marketing system?

Concept Check

CHANNEL CHOICE AND MANAGEMENT

Marketing channels not only link a producer to its buyers, but also provide the means through which a firm implements various elements of its marketing strategy.[16] Therefore, choosing a marketing channel is a critical decision.

FACTORS AFFECTING CHANNEL CHOICE AND MANAGEMENT

The final choice of a marketing channel by a producer depends on a number of factors that often interact with each other. Some of these factors are shown in Figure 15–9 and will now be discussed.

Environmental Factors   The changing environment described in Chapter 3 has an important effect on the choice and management of a marketing channel. For example, the Fuller Brush Company and Avon, names synonymous with door-to-door selling, now use catalogues and telemarketing to reach customers.[17] Rising employment among women, resulting in fewer women at home during working hours, prompted this action. Advances in the technology of growing, transporting, and storing perishable cut flowers have allowed some retailers to eliminate flower wholesalers and buy direct from flower growers around the world. Technological advances have also made it possible to market personal computers that require less training for users, thus enabling the broadened distribution of these products.

Consumer Factors   Consumer characteristics have a direct bearing on the choice and management of a marketing channel. Determining which channel is most appropriate is based on answers to fundamental questions such as: Who are potential customers? Where do they buy? When do they buy? How do they buy? What do they buy? These answers also indicate the type of intermediary best suited to reaching target buyers. For example, Ricoh Company, Ltd., studied the serious (as opposed to recreational) camera user and concluded that a change in marketing channels was necessary. The company terminated its contract with a wholesaler who sold to mass merchandise stores and began using manufacturer's agents who sold to photo specialty stores. These stores agreed to stock and display Ricoh's full line and promote it prominently, and sales volume

▌ *Figure 15–9*
Many factors affect channel choice.

ENVIRONMENTAL FACTORS	PRODUCT FACTORS
▪ Economic	▪ Perishability
▪ Regulatory	▪ Value
▪ Technological	▪ Size
	▪ Life Cycle
CONSUMER FACTORS	**COMPANY FACTORS**
▪ Location	▪ Resources
▪ Buying behaviour	▪ Product mix

tripled within 18 months.[18] Similarly, user sophistication and unique needs have spurred changes in the personal computer marketing channel over time. Consumers looking for convenient locations and lower prices have led to the distribution of computers through mass merchandise and warehouse style retailers all across Canada.[19]

Product Factors   In general, highly sophisticated products such as large scientific computers, unstandardized products such as custom-built machinery, and products of high unit value are distributed directly to buyers. Unsophisticated, standardized products with low unit value, such as table salt, are typically distributed through indirect channels. A product's stage in the life cycle also affects marketing channels. Figure 15–10 shows the dominant retail marketing channel for personal computers since their introduction in the 1970s.[20]

Company Factors   A firm's financial, human, or technological capabilities affect channel choice. For example, firms that are unable to employ a sales force might use manufacturer's agents or selling agents to reach wholesalers or buyers. If a firm has multiple products for a particular target market, it might use a direct channel, whereas firms with a limited product line might use intermediaries of various types to reach buyers. The role of company factors is evident in the distribution of correctable typewriter ribbons.[21] IBM distributes its ribbons directly through its own sales force, which sells and services IBM office products. However, Burroughs, Liquid Paper, and General Ribbon use indirect channels in part because of more limited resources and a narrower product line. They reach buyers through wholesalers, office supply dealers, and typewriter machine dealers.

Company factors also apply to intermediaries. For example, personal computer hardware and software producers wishing to reach business users might

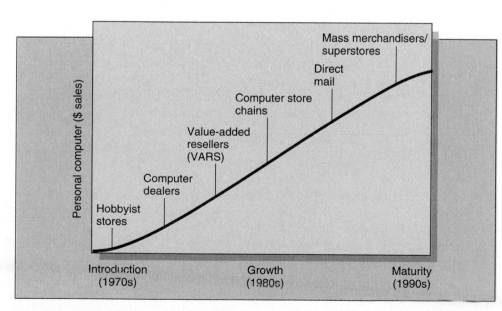

I *Figure 15–10*
Dominant retail marketing channel for personal computers over the PC life cycle.

look to value-added resellers such as Micro Age, which has its own sales force and service staff that calls on businesses.

CHANNEL DESIGN CONSIDERATIONS

Recognizing that numerous routes to buyers exist and also recognizing the factors just described, marketing executives typically consider three questions when choosing a marketing channel and intermediaries:

1 Which channel and intermediaries will provide the best coverage of the target market?
2 Which channel and intermediaries will best satisfy the buying requirements of the target market?
3 Which channel and intermediaries will be the most profitable?

Target Market Coverage   Achieving the best coverage of the target market requires attention to the density and type of intermediaries to be used at the retail level of distribution. Three degrees of distribution density exist: intensive, exclusive, and selective. **Intensive distribution** means that a firm tries to place its products and services in as many outlets as possible. Intensive distribution is usually chosen for convenience products or services; for example, chewing gum, automatic teller machines, and cigarettes.

Exclusive distribution is the extreme opposite of intensive distribution, because only one retail outlet in a specified geographical area carries the firm's product. Exclusive distribution is typically chosen for specialty products or services; for example, automobiles, some women's fragrances, men's suits, and yachts. Sometimes manufacturers sign exclusive distribution agreements with retail chain stores.

Selective distribution lies between these two extremes and means that a firm selects a few retail outlets in a specific area to carry its products. This is the most common form of distribution intensity and is usually associated with shopping goods or services such as Rolex watches.

The type or availability of a retail outlet will also influence whether a target market is reached. For example, GM, Toyota, Nissan, and Honda have established new dealers for their new cars to reach different target markets. The L'eggs division of the Hanes Corporation distributes fashionable white pantyhose to nurses through catalogues because supermarkets and department stores do not typically carry these items.[22]

Satisfying Buyer Requirements   A second consideration in channel design is gaining access to channels and intermediaries that satisfy at least some of the interests buyers might want fulfilled when they purchase a firm's products or services. These interests fall into four categories: information, convenience, variety, and attendant services.

Information is an important requirement when buyers have limited knowledge or desire specific data about a product or service. Properly chosen intermediaries communicate with buyers through in-store displays, demonstrations, and personal selling. Computer stores originally grew in popularity as a source for small computers because they provided such information. Similarly, direct sales firms such as Amway, Avon, and Tupperware have been able to identify the unique information needs of Japanese women and successfully communicate the benefits of their products and method of selling. Amway is one of the fastest-growing firms in Japan, and Avon records almost $350 million in Japanese sales each year through direct selling.[23]

Convenience has multiple meanings for buyers, such as proximity or driving time to a retail outlet. For example, 7-Eleven stores, with hundreds of outlets nationwide, satisfy this interest for buyers, and candy, tobacco, and snack food firms benefit by gaining display space in these stores. For other consumers, convenience means a minimum of time and hassle. The rapid growth of Jiffy Lube, which promises to change engine oil and filters in less than 10 minutes, appeals to this aspect of convenience.[24]

Variety reflects buyers' interest in having numerous competing and complementary items to choose from. Variety is evident in both the breadth and depth of products and brands carried by intermediaries, which enhances their attraction to buyers. Thus, a manufacturer of men's ties would seek distribution through stores that offer a full line of men's clothing.

Attendant services provided by intermediaries are an important buying requirement for products such as appliances that require delivery, installation, and credit. Therefore, Whirlpool seeks dealers that provide such services.

Consumer desire to reduce time and hassle has prompted growth of Jiffy Lube.

Profitability   The third consideration in designing a channel is profitability, which is determined by the margins earned (revenues minus cost) for each channel member and for the channel as a whole. Channel cost is the critical dimension of profitability. Costs include distribution, advertising, and selling expenses associated with different types of marketing channels. The extent to which channel members share these costs determines the margins received by each member and by the channel as a whole.

GLOBAL DIMENSIONS OF MARKETING CHANNELS

Marketing channels around the world reflect traditions, customs, geography, and the economic history of individual countries and societies. Even so, the basic marketing channel functions must be performed. But differences do exist, and these are illustrated by highlighting marketing channels in Japan.

Intermediaries outside Western Europe and North America tend to be small, numerous, and often owner-operated. Japanese marketing channels tend to include many intermediaries based on tradition and lack of storage space. As many as five intermediaries are involved in the distribution of soap in Japan, compared with one or two in North America (see Figure 15–11).[25]

Understanding marketing channels in global markets is often a prerequisite to successful marketing. For example, Gillette attempted to sell its razors and blades through company salespeople in Japan as it does in North America, thus eliminating wholesalers traditionally involved in marketing toiletries. Warner-Lambert Company sold its Schick razors and blades through the traditional Japanese channel involving wholesalers. The result? Gillette holds 10 percent of the Japanese razor and blade market and Schick holds 62 percent.[26]

Channel relationships must also be considered. In Japan, the distribution *keiretsu* (translated as "alignments") bonds producers and intermediaries to-

For the answer to how Schick became the razor and blade market share leader in Japan read the text.

Figure 15–11
Marketing channel for soap in Japan.

gether.[27] The bond, through vertical integration and social and economic ties, ensures that each channel member benefits from the distribution alignment. The dominant member of the distribution *keiretsu,* which is typically a producer, has considerable influence over channel member behaviour, including which competing products are sold by other channel members. Well-known Japanese companies such as Matsushita (electronics), Nissan and Toyota (automotive products), Nippon Gakki (musical instruments), and Kirin (and other brewers and distillers) employ the distribution *keiretsu* extensively. Shisedo and Kanebo, for instance, influence the distribution of cosmetics through Japanese department stores.

CHANNEL RELATIONSHIPS: CONFLICT, COOPERATION, AND LAW

Unfortunately, because channels consist of independent individuals and firms, there is always potential for disagreements concerning who performs which channel functions, how profits are allocated, which products and services will be provided by whom, and who makes critical channel-related decisions. These channel conflicts necessitate measures for dealing with them. Sometimes they result in legal action.

Conflict in Marketing Channels   Channel conflict arises when one channel member believes another channel member is engaged in behaviour that prevents it from achieving its goals.[28] Two types of conflict occur in marketing channels: vertical conflict and horizontal conflict.

Vertical conflict occurs between different levels in a marketing channel; for example, between a manufacturer and a wholesaler or retailer or between a wholesaler and a retailer. Three sources of vertical conflict are most common. First, conflict arises when a channel member bypasses another member and sells or buys products direct. Second, disagreements over how profit margins are distributed among channel members produce conflict. A third conflict situation arises when manufacturers believe wholesalers or retailers are not giving their products adequate attention. For example, H. J. Heinz Company found itself in a conflict situation with its supermarkets in Great Britain when supermarkets promoted and displayed private brands at the expense of Heinz brands.[29]

Horizontal conflict occurs between intermediaries at the same level in a marketing channel, such as between two or more retailers (Zellers and Kmart) or two or more wholesalers that handle the same manufacturer's brands. Two sources of horizontal conflict are most common. First, horizontal conflict arises when a manufacturer increases its distribution coverage in a geographical area. For example, a franchised Cadillac dealer in Toronto might complain to GM that another franchised Cadillac dealer has located too close to its dealership.

Second, dual distribution causes conflict when different types of retailers carry the same brands. For instance, Revlon's Charlie perfume can be found in drug stores, department stores, and discount stores, which may lead to complaints by any one of the retailers.

Securing Cooperation in Marketing Channels   Conflict can have destructive effects on the workings of a marketing channel, so it is necessary to secure cooperation among channel members. One means is through a **channel captain,** a channel member that coordinates, directs, and supports other channel members. Channel captains can be producers, wholesalers, or retailers. P&G assumes this role because it has a strong consumer following in brands such as Crest, Tide, and Pampers. Therefore it can set policies or terms that supermarkets will follow. Sears and Kmart are retail channel captains because of their strong consumer image, number of outlets, and purchasing volume.

A firm becomes a channel captain because it is typically the channel member with the greatest power to influence the behaviour of other members.[30] Power can take four forms. First, economic power arises from the ability of a firm to reward or influence other members given its strong financial position or customer franchise. IBM and Sears have such economic power. Expertise is a second source of power over other channel members. Third, identification with a particular channel member may also create power for that channel member. For instance, retailers may compete to carry the Ralph Lauren line, or clothing manufacturers may compete to be carried by Eaton's or The Bay. In both instances the desire to be associated with a channel member gives that firm power over others. Finally, power can arise from the legitimate right of one channel member to dictate the behaviour of other members. This situation would occur under contractual vertical marketing systems where a franchisor could legitimately direct how a franchisee behaves. Other means for securing cooperation in marketing channels rest in the different variations of vertical marketing systems.

Channel power can be used to gain concessions from other channel members. Some manufacturers are expected to pay supermarket chains allowances, in the form of cash or free goods, to stock and display products. Some manufacturers call these allowances "extortion," as described in the Ethics and Social Responsibility Alert.

Legal Considerations   Conflict in marketing channels is typically resolved through negotiation or the exercise of power by channel members. Sometimes conflict produces legal action. Therefore knowledge of legal restrictions affecting channel strategies and practices is important. Some restrictions were described in Chapter 14, namely, price-fixing and price discrimination. However, other legal considerations unique to marketing channels warrant attention.

In general, suppliers do have the right to choose the intermediaries who carry or represent their products. However, suppliers can run into legal difficulty over *refusing to deal* with customers who can meet the usual trade terms offered by the supplier. The Competition Act looks seriously at cases where a supplier withholds or withdraws products from a customer if such behaviour will adversely affect that customer.

ETHICS AND SOCIAL RESPONSIBILITY ALERT

The Ethics and Responsibility of Channel Power

How firms acquire and use power in marketing channels has often prompted legal restrictions. Nevertheless, power gained through the economic strength, expertise, identification with others, and legitimate rights of channel members can be used in numerous ways.

Recently, some supermarket chains have demanded slotting allowances from manufacturers, paid in the form of money or free goods, to stock and display products. The allowances, which can range from $100 for a single store to upwards of $25,000 for a supermarket chain, have been labelled "ransom" and "extortional allowances." Supermarket operators see these allowances as a reasonable cost of handling business for manufacturers.

Is the practice of charging slotting allowances unethical behaviour?

Sources: Based on J. A. Siguaw and K. Douglas Hoffman, "The Role of Slotting Allowances in Retail Channel Relationships: Review and Propositions," *American Marketing Association Educators' Proceedings* (Chicago: American Marketing Association, 1992), pp. 494–95; L. Therrien, "Want Shelf Space at Supermarkets? Ante Up," *Business Week,* August 7, 1989, pp. 60–61; and C. Donahue, "Conflict in the Aisles," *Adweek's Marketing Week,* September 4, 1989, pp. 20–21.

Dual distribution is a situation where a manufacturer distributes through its own vertically integrated channel in direct competition with wholesalers and retailers that also sell its products. If the manufacturer's behaviour is viewed as an attempt to unduly lessen competition by eliminating wholesalers or retailers, then such action may violate the Competition Act and would be examined by the Bureau of Competition Policy.

Vertical integration is viewed in a similar light. Like dual distribution, it is not illegal, but the practice could be subject to legal action if such integration were designed to eliminate or lessen competition unduly.

Exclusive dealing and tied selling are prohibited under the Competition Act if they are found to unduly lessen competition or create monopolies. *Exclusive dealing* exists when a supplier requires channel members to sell only its products or restricts distributors from selling directly competitive products. Tied selling occurs when a supplier requires a distributor purchasing some products to buy others from the supplier. These arrangements often arise in franchising. Tied selling would be investigated by the Bureau of Competition Policy if the tied products could be purchased at fair market value from other suppliers at desired standards of the franchisor and if the arrangements were seen as restricting competition. Full-line forcing is a special kind of tied selling. This is a supplier's requiring that a channel member carry its full line of products to sell a specific item in the supplier's line.

Resale or market restrictions refer to a supplier's attempt to stipulate to whom distributors may resell the supplier's products and in what specific geographic areas or territories they may be sold. These practices could be subject to review under the Competition Act if such restrictions were deemed to be restraining or lessening competition.

1 What are the three degrees of distribution density?

2 What are the three questions marketing executives consider when choosing a marketing channel and intermediaries?

3 What is meant by exclusive dealing?

Summary

1 A marketing channel consists of individuals and firms involved in the process of making a product or service available for use by consumers or industrial users.

2 Intermediaries make possible the flow of products and services from producers to buyers by performing transactional, logistical, and facilitating functions. At the same time, intermediaries create time, place, form, and possession utility for consumers.

3 Channel structure describes the route taken by products and services from producers to buyers. Direct channels represent the shortest route because producers interact directly with buyers. Indirect channels include intermediaries between producers and buyers.

4 In general, marketing channels for consumer products and services contain more intermediaries than do channels for industrial products and services. In some situations, producers use multiple channels and strategic channel alliances for reaching buyers.

5 Numerous types of wholesalers can exist within a marketing channel. The principal distinction between the various types of wholesalers lies in whether they take title to the items they sell and the channel functions they perform.

6 Vertical marketing systems are professionally managed and centrally coordinated marketing channels designed to achieve channel function economies and marketing impact. A vertical marketing system may be one of three types: corporate, administered, or contractual.

7 Marketing managers consider environmental, consumer, product, and company factors when choosing and managing marketing channels.

8 Channel design considerations are based on the target market coverage sought by producers, the buyer requirements to be satisfied, and the profitability of the channel. Target market coverage comes about through one of three levels of distribution density: intensive, exclusive, and selective distribution. Buyer requirements are evident in the amount of information, convenience, variety, and service sought by consumers. Profit-

ability relates to the margins obtained by each channel member and the channel as a whole.

9 Marketing channels in the global marketplace reflect traditions, customs, geography, and the economic history of individual countries and societies. These factors influence channel structure and relationships among channel members.

10 Conflicts in marketing channels are inevitable. Vertical conflict occurs between different levels in a channel. Horizontal conflict occurs between intermediaries at the same level in the channel.

11 Legal issues in the management of marketing channels typically arise from six practices: dual distribution, vertical integration, exclusive dealing, tied selling, refusal to deal, and resale restrictions.

Key Terms and Concepts

marketing channel p. 374	drop shippers p. 382
direct channel p. 377	truck jobbers p. 383
indirect channels p. 377	manufacturer's agents p. 384
industrial distributor p. 379	selling agents p. 384
dual distribution p. 379	brokers p. 384
strategic channel alliances p. 379	vertical marketing systems p. 385
direct marketing p. 381	franchising p. 386
general merchandise wholesalers p. 381	intensive distribution p. 390
specialty merchandise wholesalers p. 381	exclusive distribution p. 390
rack jobbers p. 382	selective distribution p. 390
cash-and-carry wholesalers p. 382	channel captain p. 393

Chapter Problems and Applications

1 A distributor for Celanese Chemical Company stores large quantities of chemicals, blends these chemicals to satisfy requests of customers, and delivers the blends to a customer's warehouse within 24 hours of receiving an order. What utilities does this distributor provide?

2 Suppose the president of a carpet manufacturing firm has asked you to look into the possibility of bypassing the firm's wholesalers (who sell to carpet, department, and furniture stores) and selling direct to these stores. What caution would you voice on this matter, and what type of information would you gather before making this decision?

3 What type of channel conflict is likely to be caused by dual distribution, and what type of conflict can be reduced by direct distribution? Why?

4 How does the channel captain idea differ among corporate, administered, and contractual vertical marketing systems with particular reference to the use of the different forms of power available to firms?

5 Suppose 10 firms in an industry wished to reach 10,000 potential customers by selling to them direct. How many sales contacts would be required in this industry if each firm called on each customer? How many sales contacts would be required if an intermediary were placed between the firms and potential customers?

6 Comment on this statement: The only distinction among merchant wholesalers and agents and brokers is that merchant wholesalers take title to the products they sell.

7 How do specialty, shopping, and convenience goods generally relate to intensive, selective, and exclusive distribution? Give a brand name that is an example of each goods-distribution matchup.

CHAPTER 16

Physical Distribution and Logistics Management

▸ Explain what physical distribution and logistics management are and how they relate to the marketing mix.

▸ Understand the nature of logistics trade-offs among transportation, inventory, and other logistics elements.

▸ Understand how managers trade off different "logistics costs" relative to customer service in order to reach a logistics decision.

▸ Recognize the growing importance of customer service in successful marketing.

▸ Describe the major logistics functions of transportation, warehousing and materials handling, order processing, and inventory management.

Distribution: Often the Key to a Satisfied Customer

Congratulations! You just won $3 million in Lotto 6/49. You decide it's time to trade in your tired '68 Volkswagen beetle and get a "Beamer." With check in hand you head for the nearest BMW dealer, assuming your new 325i convertible will be waiting for you. You reason that it's a simple challenge—make a car in a German factory 6,000 miles away and transport it over land, an ocean, and land again using train, ship, and truck to get it to a showroom. One other thing. It had better not have any dents, scratches, or signs of wear. You're not about to put $50,000 on the table for a banged-up car.

In order to ensure that your BMW arrives in the showroom on time and without any dings in transit, BMW tracks each car by computer every step of the way until final destination at the showroom. BMW invested over $40 million to build Vehicle Preparation Centres (VPCs) in order to thoroughly check every single car imported to North America. The company believes VPCs are an important link in ensuring BMW quality.[1]

Retail products that aren't in the right place at the right time and in the proper condition for sale to consumers who may have already decided to buy them illustrate the critical nature of the movement and storage of products in a firm's marketing plan. The best-laid product and promotional strategies of a firm may be destroyed by poor distribution of the products it wishes to sell. This chapter examines the physical distribution process, which moves products from producer to consumer, and how a firm balances distribution costs against the need for effective customer service.

SIGNIFICANCE OF PHYSICAL DISTRIBUTION AND LOGISTICS MANAGEMENT

We often hear the term *physical distribution,* but may rarely hear the term *logistics.* In this section we shall contrast the two concepts, describe the increasing importance of logistics and how these activities vary among firms, and relate logistics to marketing strategy decisions.

RELATING PHYSICAL SUPPLY, PHYSICAL DISTRIBUTION, AND LOGISTICS

Generally, marketing managers use **physical distribution management** to mean organizing the movement and storage of a finished product until it reaches the customer. Logistics implies a broader view and attempts to coordinate both the inbound flow of raw materials *and* the outbound flow of finished product. Because these two flows are not simply mirror images of each other, we prefer to discuss the broader term of logistics, or *logistics management,* in this chapter. **Logistics management** is organizing the cost-effective *flow* of raw materials, in-process inventory, finished goods, and related information from point of origin to point of consumption to satisfy *customer requirements.*[2]

Three elements of this definition deserves emphasis. First, logistics deals with decisions needed to move a product from the source of raw materials to consumption, or the *flow* of the product. Second, those decisions have to be made in a *cost-effective* manner. While it is important to drive down the costs of a firm's logistics system, there is a limit—the third point of emphasis. A firm needs to drive down logistics costs as long as it can deliver expected *customer service,* which means satisfying customer requirements. In other words, customer needs determine the outputs of the logistics system, and hence the role of management is to see that those needs are satisfied in the most cost-effective manner.

Figure 16–1 demonstrates the relation of physical supply, physical distribution, and logistics to the operations of a manufacturing firm. This chart shows how the firm receives its physical supply in the form of raw materials and parts from its suppliers, converts these to finished products, and then engages in the

▌ *Figure 16–1*
Relation of physical supply, physical distribution, and logistics to a manufacturing firm's operations.

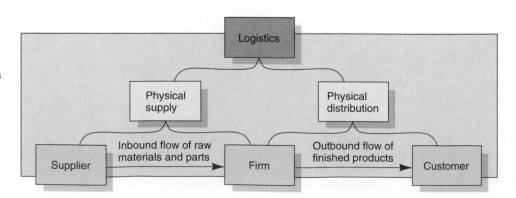

distribution of these products to its customers. Note that these concepts also apply to nonmanufacturing firms, such as retailers and wholesalers, for which the inbound activities include the finished goods that are resold to customers without physical modification.

INCREASING IMPORTANCE OF LOGISTICS SYSTEMS

Several factors account for the trend of increased emphasis on logistics systems. There has been a large growth in the differentiation of products in order to respond to consumer demands. The effect of this increased product differentiation is that inventory control has become more complex, and thus there are many more things to keep track of. Consider, for example, that L. L. Bean currently carries approximately 5,000 different products. However, when each product is divided by size, colour, or other distinguishing features, L. L. Bean must track 54,000 separate items.[3] In today's environment, the increasing costs of carrying inventory make it clear that inventories cannot grow unchecked. Thus, while firms are under pressure to provide high levels of customer service by having many items available, they need to control the cost of such service.

Dramatic savings in inventory are possible when efficient transportation systems and information technology can be substituted for inventory. For example, continuously upgraded computer and information technology has permitted efficient tracking of the thousands of items manufacturers produce. The emergence of such technologies as hand-held computers, scanning, and bar coding has had a profound impact on the ability of firms to control the flow of their products.

Hand-held computers and bar coding have reduced delayed and lost shipments and improved customer service significantly.

HOW MOVEMENT AND STORAGE ACTIVITIES VARY AMONG FIRMS

For firms that don't physically move or store many items, logistics costs will be minor. For example, insurance companies and banks distribute mainly paperwork, and most of their inbound materials are supplies. At the other end of the spectrum are firms that produce many products from diverse raw materials at widely separated plants and which, in turn, distribute products to widely dispersed markets. For large consumer products companies that compete both nationally and internationally, such as Procter & Gamble, the range of logistics problems can be enormous. For example, P&G produces approximately 80 different brands, all of which require a different mix of raw materials. The logistics system has to move all the raw materials to the appropriate manufacturing plant and then distribute the finished products (brands) to the marketplace. This involves moving products to thousands of wholesalers and retailers around the world. In addition, P&G's logistics managers must also control a number of information flows, including how much inventory is where, the order-processing system for customers, the reordering process from the factories, and the level of customer service that the logistics system is delivering. Because of the scope of P&G's logistics problems, it has learned to simplify matters by working closely with its major distributors or customers.

The relative importance of logistics to a firm can be evaluated on a number of key factors:

- Number, weight, volume, and perishability of raw materials and final products.
- Number of material supply points.
- Number of material processing points.
- Number of product consumption points.

As the number of any of these factors increases, the complexity and cost of the logistics system increase as well.

Information is available through an annual survey of members of the Council of Logistics Management that focusses on distribution costs but does not include the cost of inbound raw materials.[4] As a percentage of sales, the average for all firms (including manufacturers, wholesalers, and retailers) was 7.93 percent. In other words, for every dollar of sales, almost 8 cents was spent on distribution costs (see Figure 16–2).

RELATION OF LOGISTICS TO MARKETING STRATEGY

Recalling your own shopping experiences can show the critical relationship between marketing and logistics. Consider your disappointment after travelling to a store—in response to an advertised sale—only to find that the items were out of stock or had been lost or damaged in transit. Imagine how the manufacturer may have reacted upon learning that the product was not on the shelf, after spending huge sums on its extensive promotional campaign. The bottom line is that poorly executed logistics can do serious damage to an otherwise excellent marketing strategy. To demonstrate the importance of logistics' rela-

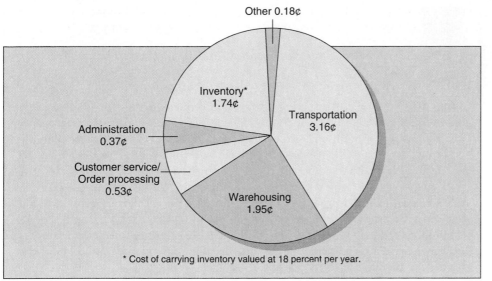

Source: Council of Logistics Management.

■ *Figure 16–2*
Breakdown of the 7.93 cents of each sales dollar used for physical distribution of manufactured goods.

tionship to marketing, consider how logistics impacts the four Ps—product factors, pricing factors, promotional factors, and place factors.

Product Factors   The physical characteristics of the product, as well as its raw materials, will often dictate what kinds of transportation can be used, the length of time inventory can be accumulated, and whether markets can be served from one or many locations. One physical characteristic that has important logistics implications is the perishability of the product, or its *shelf life*. For example, the distribution of fresh foods requires timely transportation and low inventories in order to minimize spoilage. Time-dated food materials must be kept fresh on the store shelves and not be allowed to spoil in the warehouse. These products may require specialized transport and storage facilities, such as refrigerated vehicles. Other products have a very short time frame in which to retain their freshness, such as fresh-cut flowers, fresh seafoods, or out-of-town newspapers. These require premium transportation, such as air freight, and in some cases they can only be distributed to a regional market. For example, newspapers such as *The Globe & Mail* are printed in a number of cities around the country for regional distribution the same day.

   One of the most important links between a product's physical characteristics and logistics is the product package. On the one hand, the marketer views the package as an important point-of-purchase promotional device. On the other hand, there are many logistical implications associated with the packaging decision. Does the protective packaging reduce the density of the product so that less product can be loaded into the transport vehicle or warehouse? If so, logistics costs will increase. Does the product's package require it to be placed in an exterior package or carton? In this case, additional handling will be required at the retail level in order to prepare the product for sale. As described in the accompanying Ethics and Social Responsibility Alert, package features

ETHICS AND SOCIAL RESPONSIBILITY ALERT
What Are the Social Costs of Packaging?

Some experts believe that the logistics systems of many firms depend too heavily on packaging. While efficient packaging materials allow a firm to use cheaper modes of transportation or less specialized warehouse services, these benefits are offset by costs imposed on society in general. Specifically, what should society do with the excessive packaging that comes with the product? In many cases, the packaging material is difficult to dispose of or is quickly filling landfills. Further, the focus on recycled products is a complicated issue and has its own costs and benefits. For example, Procter & Gamble has introduced a plastic bottle for its Ultra Downy fabric softener that is made of 100 percent recycled plastic. However, because P&G will colour the bottle as part of its marketing program, the bottle will be difficult to recycle once it is used.

What are the benefits and costs to society of such packaging trends? What should communities do to counter the trend of overpackaging? What are the responsibilities of global citizens to counteract the trend of overpackaging?

Source: J. Holusha, "P&G Downy Bottles Use Recycled Plastic," *The New York Times,* January 14, 1993, p. C5; B. Van Voorst, "The Recycling Bottleneck," *Time,* September 14, 1992, p. 52; and P. Elmer-Dewitt, "Summit to Save the Earth," *Time,* June 1, 1992, pp. 42–58.

can make handling, stacking, filling, or disposing of the package more difficult, and once again logistics costs will increase.

Pricing Factors   Pricing interacts with logistics in several ways. As mentioned in the discussion of geographical pricing adjustments in Chapter 14, price quotations such as FOB origin assign responsibility for arranging and paying for transportation services to the buyer. Logistics costs are also important for determining quantity discounts. Transportation rate structures generally contain a quantity discount provided by the carrier such that lower rates per unit are available for larger shipments. These incentives often form the basis of a firm's quantity discount program.

Promotional Factors   Promotion interacts with logistics in the areas of advertising, sales promotion, and personal selling. Advertising and promotional campaigns must be planned and coordinated with the logistics system to ensure product availability at the appropriate time. Suppose Procter & Gamble attempts to boost trial of its Crest tartar-control toothpaste using a massive coupon campaign. If consumers attempting to redeem the coupons find the product out of stock, it is doubtful whether they would save them and redeem them later. Worse yet, they may try a competitor's brand instead. Thus, distribution must be synchronized to ensure timely and efficient handling of orders. Also, the logistics function must be prepared for the peaks of activity that are caused by various trade promotions, contests, or other incentives that may occur during the year.

A logistics manager's nightmare: how to get this dual pack on a retailer's shelf while balancing logistics and marketing benefits and costs.

Place Factors   It is the responsibility of logistics to get the product to the right place at the right time in usable condition. Logistics also plays an important part in determining where a firm locates its plants and distribution centres relative to markets. Such decisions must consider transportation costs as well as the ability of the product to be transported long distances and be stored for long periods of time.

Concept Check

1 What are the three important characteristics of the logistics concept?

2 Why is logistics more important to a consumer goods manufacturer than to a bank?

3 How does logistics interact with the product element of the marketing mix?

OBJECTIVES OF THE LOGISTICS SYSTEM

The objective of a logistics system is to minimize relevant logistics costs while delivering maximum customer service. Recently, firms have begun to realize that logistics costs are also dependent on their relationship with suppliers, carriers, and customers. This has led to the practice of forming strategic alliances between buyers, sellers, and the transportation system that connects them. Alliances create cooperation between the parties. Suppliers and carriers, for example, can set up special procedures allowing more frequent deliveries of smaller shipments at scheduled times. Shipments can be arranged and labelled in a specific way so they can be moved through a distribution centre with a minimum of rehandling. In some cases shipments may be delivered directly to the retail store, bypassing the distribution centre.

These strategic alliances are often supported by sophisticated information systems that involve shared databases of customer information and **electronic data interchange (EDI),** computers linked in two different firms to transmit documents such as purchase orders, bills of lading, and invoices. As we saw in Chapter 2, Canadian Tire uses EDI to track inventory and to communicate with suppliers. This ensures product availability and facilitates planning shipments to lower distribution costs.[5]

TOTAL LOGISTICS COST CONCEPT

For our purposes, **total logistics cost** includes expenses associated with transportation, materials handling and warehousing, inventory, stockouts (being out of inventory), and order processing. A more complete list of decisions that are associated with the flow of product and make up total logistics cost includes:

- Traffic and transportation.
- Warehousing and storage.
- Packaging.
- Materials handling.
- Inventory control.

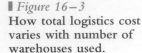

Figure 16–3
How total logistics cost
varies with number of
warehouses used.

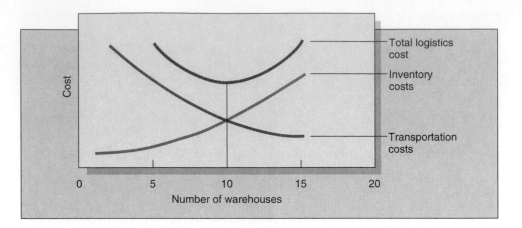

- Order processing.
- Customer service level.
- Plant and wholesale site location.
- Return goods handling.

Note that many of these costs are interrelated so that changes in one will impact the others. For example, as a firm attempts to minimize its transportation costs by shipping in larger quantities, it will also experience an increase in inventory levels. Larger inventory levels will increase inventory costs but should also reduce stockouts. It is important, therefore, to study the impact on all of the logistics decision areas when considering a change in one.

Figure 16–3 provides a graphic example. An oft-used logistics strategy is for a firm to have a number of warehouses, which receive shipments in large quantities and then redistribute smaller shipments to local customers. As the number of warehouses increases, inventory costs rise and transportation costs fall. That is, more inventory is warehoused, but it is transported in volume closer to customers. In Figure 16–3, having 10 warehouses will create the net effect of minimizing the total costs of the logistics system. This means the total cost curve is minimized at a point where neither of the two individual cost elements is at a minimum but the overall system is.

The dynamic changes in today's transportation services provided IBM the opportunity to lower its total logistics costs. IBM has begun closing 120 parts warehouses because Federal Express (the overnight air service) now inventories high-priced parts for IBM's computer workstations. The inventories kept at Fed-Ex's sorting hubs mean that high-cost overnight transportation is being substituted for IBM's higher-cost parts warehouses scattered across Canada and the United States. The result: better service for IBM customers at a lower total cost.[6] Many distribution and logistics experts believe that this IBM–Federal Express relationship will be more common in the future as manufacturers (like IBM) use third-party logistics firms (like Federal Express) to serve customers more efficiently.[7]

CUSTOMER SERVICE CONCEPT

If logistics is a *flow,* the end of it—or *output*—is the service delivered to customers. However, service can be expensive. One firm found that to increase

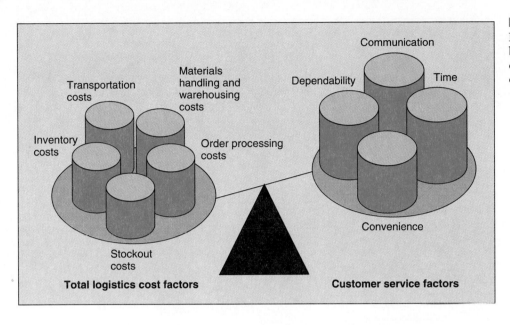

❚ *Figure 16–4*
**Logistics managers
balance total logistics
cost factors against
customer service factors.**

on-time delivery from a 95 percent rate to a 100 percent rate tripled total logistics costs. Higher levels of service require tactics such as more inventory to reduce stockouts, more expensive transportation to improve speed and lessen damage, and double or triple checking of orders to ensure correctness. A firm's goal should be to provide adequate customer service while controlling logistics costs. Customer service is now seen not merely as an expense, but as a strategic tool for increasing customer satisfaction and sales. For example, in 1990 3M completed a survey about customer service among 18,000 European customers in 16 countries. The survey revealed surprising agreement in all countries about the importance of customer service and stressed factors like condition of product delivered, on-time delivery, quick delivery after order placement, and effective handling of problems.[8]

Within the context of logistics, **customer service** is the ability of a logistics system to satisfy users in terms of time, dependability, communications, and convenience.[9] As suggested by Figure 16–4, a logistics manager's key task is to balance these four customer service factors against total logistics cost factors.

Time   In a logistics setting, time refers to **lead time** for an item, which means the lag from ordering an item until it is received and ready for use. This is also referred to as **order cycle time** or **replenishment time** and may be more important to retailers or wholesalers than consumers. The various elements that make up the typical order cycle include recognition of the need to order, order transmittal, order processing, documentation, and transportation. A current emphasis in logistics is to reduce lead time so that the inventory levels of customers may be minimized. Another emphasis is to make the process of reordering and receiving products as simple as possible, often through electronic data interchange and other computer-based ordering and inventory systems. The order processing portion of lead time will be discussed later in this chapter.

CN works closely with Christie Brown & Co. to get Mr. Christie's cookies delivered on time and in damage-free condition to your local store.

Dependability   Dependability is the consistency of replenishment. This is important to both intermediaries and consumers. It can be broken into three elements: consistent lead time, safe delivery, and complete delivery. Studies indicate that dependability is a key element in customer service.[10] Consistent service allows planning (such as appropriate inventory levels), whereas inconsistencies create surprises. Intermediaries may be willing to accept longer lead times if they know about them in advance and can thus make plans. While surprise delays may shut down a production line, early deliveries will be almost as troublesome because of the problems of storing the extra inventory.

Communication   Communication is a two-way link between buyer and seller that helps in monitoring service and anticipating future needs. Status reports on orders are a typical example of improved communication between buyer and seller. The increased communication capability of transportation carriers has enhanced the accuracy of such tracing information and improved the ability of buyers to schedule shipments. Note, however, that such information is still reactive and is not a substitute for consistent on-time deliveries. In contrast, some firms have established strategic alliances with vendors and customers in an effort to institutionalize a more proactive flow of useful information.

Convenience   The concept of convenience for a logistics manager means that there should be a minimum of effort on the part of the buyer in doing business with the seller. Is it easy for the customer to order? Are the products available from many outlets? Does the buyer have to buy huge quantities of the product? Will the seller arrange all necessary details, such as transportation? The seller must concentrate on removing unnecessary barriers to customer convenience.

TYPE OF FIRM	CUSTOMER SERVICE STANDARD
Wholesaler	At least 98% of orders filled accurately
Manufacturer	Order cycle time of no more than 5 days
Retailer	Returns accepted within 30 days
Airline	At least 90% arrivals on time
Trucker	A maximum of 5% loss and damage per year
Restaurant	Lunch served within 5 minutes of order

▌*Figure 16–5*
Examples of customer service standards.

CUSTOMER SERVICE STANDARDS

Firms that operate effective logistics systems usually develop a set of written customer service standards. These serve as objectives and provide a benchmark against which results can be measured for control purposes. In developing these standards, information is collected on customers' needs. It is also necessary to know what competitors offer as well as the willingness of customers to pay a bit more for better service. After these and similar questions are answered, realistic standards are set and an ongoing monitoring program is established. Note that the examples in Figure 16–5 suggest that customer service standards will differ by type of firm.

Concept Check

1 What is a current strategy adopted by firms attempting to squeeze costs from their logistics system while delivering customer service?

2 In what ways do key customer service factors differ between a manufacturer and a retailer?

3 What is the relationship between transportation costs and volume shipped? What impact does it have on the pricing system of the firm?

MAJOR LOGISTICS FUNCTIONS

Four key elements in a logistics system include transportation, warehousing and materials handling, order processing, and inventory management. These are described in more detail in the following sections.

TRANSPORTATION

Transportation provides the movement of goods necessary in a logistics system. There are five basic modes of transportation: railroads, motor carriers, air carriers, pipelines, and water carriers. The following discussion will focus only on railroads, motor and air carriers, and modal combinations involving two or more modes, such as highway trailers on a rail flatcar.

▌*Figure 16–6*
Advantages and disadvantages of five modes of transportation.

MODE	RELATIVE ADVANTAGES	RELATIVE DISADVANTAGES
Rail	Full capability Extensive routes Low cost	Some reliability, damage problems Not always complete pickup and delivery Sometimes slow
Truck	Complete pickup and delivery Extensive routes Fairly fast	Size and weight restrictions Higher cost More weather-sensitive
Air	Fast Low damage Frequent departures	High cost Limited capabilities
Pipeline	Low cost Very reliable	Limited routes (accessibility) Slow
Water	Low cost Huge capacities	Slow Limited routes and schedules More weather-sensitive

All modes can be evaluated on six basic service criteria:

- *Cost.* Charges for transportation.
- *Time.* Speed of transit.
- *Capability.* What can be realistically carried with this mode.
- *Dependability.* Reliability of service regarding time, loss, and damage.
- *Accessibility.* Convenience of the mode's routes (such as pipeline availability).
- *Frequency.* Scheduling.

Figure 16–6 summarizes service advantages and disadvantages of five of the modes of transportation available.

Railroads   Railroads carry heavy, bulky items over long distances. Of the commodities tracked by the rail industry, coal, farm products, chemicals, and nonmetallic minerals represent the majority of the total tonnage. Railroads have the ability to carry larger shipments than trucks (in terms of total weight per vehicle), but their routes are less extensive. Service innovations include unit trains and intermodal service. A *unit train* is dedicated to one commodity (often coal), using permanently coupled cars that run a continuous loop from a single origin to a single destination and back. Even though the train returns empty, the process captures enough operating efficiencies to make it one of the lowest-cost transportation alternatives available. Unit trains are held to a specific schedule so that the customers can plan on reliable delivery, and usually carry products that can be loaded and unloaded quickly and automatically.

Railroads have been able to apply the unit train concept to **intermodal transportation,** the combining of different transportation modes in order to get the best features of each. The result is a service that attracts high-valued freight, which would normally go by truck. The most popular combination is

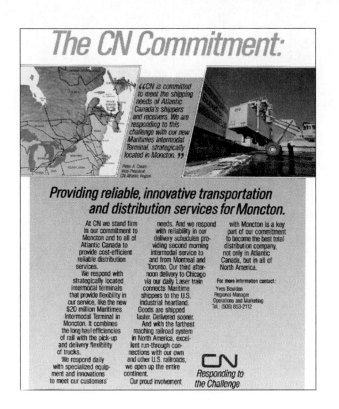

CN offers intermodal transportation to its customers.

truck–rail, also referred to as *piggyback* or *trailer on flatcar (TOFC)*. The other popular use of an intermodal combination is associated with export–import traffic and uses containers in place of trailers. These containers can be loaded on ships, trains, and truck trailers, so in terms of the on-land segment of international shipments, a container is handled the same way as a trailer. Containers are used in international trade because they take up less space on oceangoing vessels.

Motor Carriers   In contrast to the railroad industry, the for-hire motor carrier industry is composed of many small firms. There are hundreds of motor trucking companies in Canada. In addition, there are many independent truckers and firms that own their own trucks for transporting their own products.

The greatest advantage of motor carriers is complete door-to-door service. Trucks can go almost anywhere there is a road, and with the design of specialized equipment they can carry most commodities. Their physical limitations are size and weight restrictions enforced by the provinces. Trucks have a reputation for maintaining a better record than rail for loss and damage and providing faster, more reliable service, especially for shorter distances. As a result, trucks carry higher-valued goods that are time-sensitive and expensive to carry in inventory. The trade-off is that truck rates are higher than rail rates.

Air Carriers and Express Companies   Air freight is costly, but its speed may create savings in lower inventory. The items that can be carried are limited by

If speed is important,
then shipping by air is
appropriate.

Source: Canadian Air Cargo.

space constraints and are usually valuable, time-sensitive, and light in weight, such as perishable flowers, clothing, and electronic parts. Products moved in containers are especially amenable to this mode of shipment. Specialized firms provide ground support by collecting shipments and delivering them to the air terminal. When air freight is handled by the major airlines—such as Canadian Airlines or Air Canada—it is often carried as cargo in the luggage space of scheduled passenger flights. This strategy allows the airline to utilize excess capacity that would otherwise be lost.

Freight Forwarders   **Freight forwarders** are firms that accumulate small shipments into larger lots and then hire a carrier to move them, usually at reduced rates. Recall that transportation companies provide rate incentives for larger quantities. Forwarders collect many small shipments consigned to a common destination and pay the carrier the lower rate based on larger volume. They often turn less-than-truckload (LTL) shipments into full truckloads, thereby qualifying for better shipping rates from the carrier. The forwarder passes along some of the savings to the individual shippers in the form of a discount off the small-quantity rate. The difference is the forwarder's margin. In general, the shipment receives improved service at lower cost. While forwarders may specialize in a particular mode—such as air freight—they are available for all modes of transportation. International freight forwarders play an equally important role in the export–import trades.

MARKETING · ACTION · MEMO

Fly-by-Night Idea—Customer Service + KISS = Federal Express

*A*rmed with one of his college term papers, which got a C− grade, Frederick W. Smith didn't build a better mousetrap and wait for the world to beat a path to his door. Instead, he set out to show the world that with his simple new innovation *he* could beat a path to everybody else's door.

He gave the name *Federal Express* to his door-to-door flying parcel service that uses garish orange, white, and purple jets. And he advertised "absolutely, positively overnight" delivery for his small-parcel service—limited to 70 pounds, the weight one person can carry. "I figured we had to be enormously reliable," says Smith, "since our service is frequently used for expensive spare parts, live organs, or other emergency shipments."

But Federal Express isn't your typical fly-by-night outfit. After all, Smith *did* write his term paper at Yale, and he *did* use a family trust of $4 million to get started—and Federal Express *did* lose $29 million in its first 26 months of operation.

What Smith had was a good idea, a good understanding of customer service, and the tenacity and resources to stick with it. First, Smith reasoned, he had to own his own jet aircraft so *all* parcels could be picked up early in the evening, flown to a single sorting center (Memphis), and rerouted to their final destination before dawn. That's part of Fred Smith's KISS ("Keep it simple, stupid") principle.

Always looking for a better idea, in 1989 Federal Express started a new, lower-priced delivery service called FedEx Standard Overnight. The new overnight service offers delivery of documents and packages by the following afternoon at a price lower than that charged for the current service that promises delivery by 10:30 A.M. This offering further segments the overnight delivery market by providing—you guessed it—a customer service at lower price to those customers who don't need morning delivery.

Sources: Based on B. M. Iwamoto, "Night Moves," *Express Magazine*, Winter 1990, pp. 21–23; R. Christie, "When It Doesn't Have to Be There Fast," *The Wall Street Journal*, June 28, 1989, p. B1; and R. Rowan, "Business Triumphs of the Seventies," *Fortune*, December 1979, p. 34.

As an example of specialization in one transportation mode, airlines will in some cases subcontract excess space to *air freight forwarders,* or *express companies,* which are firms that market air express services to the general public. Where markets are large enough, major airlines have responded with pure air freight service between specific airports—often involving international destinations. Federal Express is an example of a company responding to the need for widely available overnight air freight service, as described in the accompanying Marketing Action Memo.

1 What are some new kinds of train service offered by railroads to compete more effectively with other modes of transportation?

2 What is intermodal transportation?

3 What are the inherent advantages of truck transportation?

WAREHOUSING AND MATERIALS HANDLING

Warehouses may be classified in one of two ways: storage warehouses and distribution centres. In *storage warehouses* the goods are intended to come to rest for some period of time, as in the aging of products or in storing household goods. *Distribution centres,* on the other hand, are designed to facilitate the timely movement of goods and represent a very important part of the logistics system. Distribution centres are the focus of the following discussion and represent the second most significant cost for logistics systems.

Distribution centres not only allow firms to hold their stock in decentralized locations but are also used to facilitate sorting and consolidating products from different plants or different suppliers. Some physical transformation can also take place in distribution centres such as mixing or blending different ingredients, labelling, and repackaging. They may also serve as sales offices and order processing centres. The success of many retailing chains such as Wal-Mart and Zellers is due to sophisticated distribution centres that serve their retail outlets.[11]

Materials handling, which involves moving goods over short distances into, within, and out of warehouses and manufacturing plants, is a key part of warehouse operations. The two major problems with this activity are high

Storage warehouses often stock a large, stable volume of goods.

Materials handling
through automation.

labour costs and high rates of loss and damage. Every time an item is handled, there is a chance for loss or damage. Common materials handling equipment includes forklifts, cranes, and conveyors. Recently, materials handling in warehouses has been automated by using computers and robots to reduce the cost of holding, moving, and recording the inventories of stores.

ORDER PROCESSING

There are several stages in the processing of an order, and a failure at any one of them can cause a problem with the customer. The process starts with transmitting the order by a variety of means such as computer or electronic data interchange (EDI). This is followed by entering the order in the appropriate databases and sending the information to those needing it. For example, a regional warehouse is notified to prepare an order. After checking inventory, a new quantity may need to be reordered from the production line, or purchasing may be requested to reorder from a vendor. If the item is currently out of stock, a back order is created and the whole process of keeping track of a small part of the original order must be managed. In addition, credit may have to be checked for some customers, all paperwork associated with the order must be prepared, transportation must be arranged, and a confirmation of the order must be sent. Order processing systems are generally evaluated in terms of speed and accuracy.

INVENTORY MANAGEMENT

Inventory management is one of the primary responsibilities of the logistics manager. The major problem is maintaining the delicate balance between too little and too much. Too little inventory may result in poor service, stockouts, brand switching, and loss of market share; too much leads to higher costs because of the money tied up in inventory and the chance that the inventory may become obsolete. Note that the management of a firm's inventory level often depends on the performance of vendors such as the reliability of transportation carriers or the order cycle of suppliers.

Reasons for Inventory   Traditionally, carrying inventory has been justified on several grounds: to offer a buffer against variations in supply and demand, often caused by uncertainty in forecasting demand, to provide better service for those customers who wish to be served on demand, to promote production efficiencies, to provide a hedge against price increases by suppliers, to promote purchasing and transportation discounts, and to protect the firm from contingencies such as strikes and shortages.

Inventory Costs   Specific inventory costs are often hard to detect because they are difficult to measure and occur in many different parts of the firm. A classification of inventory costs includes:

- *Capital costs.* The opportunity costs resulting from tying up funds in inventory instead of using them in other, more profitable investments. These are related to interest rates.
- *Inventory service costs.* Items such as insurance and taxes that are present in many provinces.
- *Storage costs.* Warehousing space and materials handling.
- *Risk costs.* Possible loss, damage, pilferage, perishability, and obsolescence.

Storage costs, risk costs, and some service costs vary according to the characteristics of the item inventoried. For example, perishable products or highly seasonal items have higher risk costs than a commodity-type product such as lumber. Capital costs are always present and are proportional to the *values* of the item and prevailing interest rates. The costs of carrying inventory vary with the particular circumstances but quite easily could range from 10 to 35 percent for different firms.

Newer Inventory Strategies   Conventional wisdom during the 1970s and 1980s was that a firm should protect itself against uncertainty by maintaining a reserve inventory at each of its production and stocking points. This has been described as a "just-in-case" philosophy of inventory management and led to unnecessary high levels of inventory. In contrast is the **just-in-time (JIT) concept,** a supply system that operates with very low inventories and requires fast, on-time delivery. When parts are needed for production, they arrive from suppliers "just in time," which means neither before nor after they are needed. Note that JIT is used in situations where demand forecasting is reliable, such as when supplying a production line, and is not suitable for inventories that are to be stored over significant periods of time. JIT exploits new communications technologies such as EDI that hook customers' computers to suppliers' computers.

Proponents cite several advantages to JIT. First, there are the financial advantages that come from lower inventory levels and faster turnover. Second, the Japanese experience suggests JIT yields better reliability in production scheduling and product quality. For JIT to work properly, however, suppliers must be able to provide fast, reliable deliveries or there will be failures relative to customer service. Consequently, with JIT the supplier assumes more responsibility and risk for inventory, quality products, and on-time delivery than ever before. Ideally, to reduce these risks suppliers move closer to the user. This is easier in a smaller country like Japan, but more difficult in a country like Canada, the largest country in the world. But some supply companies are able to locate near their major buyers. For example, automotive parts suppliers often locate close to the automobile manufacturers in order to exploit JIT. If suppliers cannot locate near their customers, then reliable transportation is critical for JIT to be effective. Canadian Tire uses its private truck fleet and Canadian National Railroad to move its over 40,000 product items to its 400 Canadian Tire stores nationwide on a timely basis.

Some experts believe that JIT should be understood as more than a system designed to merely reduce inventory costs. JIT must be viewed as an outgrowth of quality control or quality improvement programs that seek zero inventory with 100 percent product quality. As such, JIT can serve as a source of competitive advantage in terms of rapid response and quality assurance.[12]

Concept Check

1 What the basic trade-offs between the modes of transportation?

2 What type of inventory should use storage warehouses and which type should use distribution centres?

3 What are the strengths and weaknesses of a just-in-time system?

Summary

1 A comprehensive definition of physical distribution activities, called *business logistics,* includes the coordination of both inbound and outbound activities, an emphasis on cost-effective flows, and customer service.

2 The importance of logistical activities varies among firms. The complexity of the system increases with the width of the product line, number of supply points, and number of geographic markets served.

3 Although some marketers may pay little attention to logistics, they do so at their own peril. Logistics directly affects the success of the marketing program and all areas of the marketing mix.

4 The total logistics cost concept suggests that a system of interrelated costs is present such as transportation, materials handling and warehousing, inventory, and stockout costs.

5 Minimizing total logistics cost is irrelevant without specifying an acceptable customer service level that must be maintained. The importance of customer service varies among industries.

6 Although key customer service factors depend on the situation, important elements of the customer service program are likely to be time-related dependability, communications, and convenience.

7 The modes of transportation (e.g., railroads, motor carriers, air carriers, and trucks) offer shippers different service benefits. Better service often costs more, although it should result in savings in other areas of the logistics system.

8 The function of warehousing in a logistics system is to facilitate storage and movement of goods. Distribution centres provide flexibility and facilitate sorting and consolidating products from different plants or different suppliers.

9 Inventory management is critical, since too much inventory greatly increases costs and too little may result in stockouts. Various methods are available to manage inventory. A currently popular approach is the just-in-time concept, which attempts to minimize inventory in the system while improving quality control.

10 Some buyers and sellers have developed strategic alliances designed to make the logistics transaction as efficient as possible.

Key Terms and Concepts

physical distribution management p. 400
logistics management p. 400
electronic data interchange (EDI) p. 405
total logistics cost p. 405
customer service p. 407
lead time p. 407

order cycle time p. 407
replenishment time p. 407
intermodal transportation p. 410
freight forwarders p. 412
materials handling p. 414
just-in-time (JIT) concept p. 416

Chapter Problems and Applications

1 List several companies to which logistical activities are unimportant. Also list several whose focus is only on the inbound or outbound side.

2 Give an example of how logistical activities might affect trade promotion strategies.

3 What are some types of businesses in which order processing may be among the paramount success factors?

4 What behavioural problems might arise to negate the logistics concept within the firm?

5 List the customer service factors that would be vital to buyers in the following types of companies: *(a)* manufacturing, *(b)* retailing, *(c)* hospitals, and *(d)* construction.

6 Name some cases when extremely high service levels (e.g., 99 percent) would be warranted.

7 Name the mode of transportation that would be the best for the following products: *(a)* farm machinery, *(b)* cut flowers, *(c)* frozen meat, and *(d)* coal.

8 The auto industry is a heavy user of the just-in-time concept. Why? What other industries would be good candidates for its application? What do they have in common?

Retailing

AFTER READING THIS CHAPTER YOU SHOULD BE ABLE TO:

▼ Identify retailers in terms of the utilities they provide.

▼ Explain the alternative ways to classify retail outlets.

▼ Develop retailing mix strategies over the life cycle of a retail store.

▼ Explain the impact of computers on retail methods and store operations.

The Many Faces of Retailing

Retailing has many faces and takes place in various types of ways. Retailing occurs when the Mary Kay Cosmetics representative delivers the products you ordered to your door. It occurs when you walk into a department store and buy that pair of Levi's. It happens when you and your friends stop for a hamburger at Burger King. Retailing takes place when you get a Coke before class from the vending machine. It occurs when you call that 800 number you saw on your television screen and order a new CD, and retailing takes place when you pick up a box of Rice Krispies at the grocery store.

One trend in retailing is the growth in the nonstore concept. For example, Dell Computer Corporation has taken the retail concept beyond the confines of a physical location by marketing Dellware, its new catalogue service. It offers over 1,000 software packages and hardware peripherals from name-brand suppliers. Dellware offers telephone ordering and fast delivery. In this way, Dellware will compete with store-based computer suppliers like ComputerLand.[1] Dellware is just one of many companies in Canada involved in the various forms of retailing, the most highly visible component of the marketing distribution channel.

This chapter will outline some of the variety and range of decisions required in retailing. Where do your customers shop? If you're selling books, cosmetics, or auto accessories, what retail outlet should carry your product? If you're thinking of opening a store, what type should it be? Do consumers expect direct marketing through catalogues, or the telephone? How much will you charge for products you plan to sell?

These are difficult and important questions that are an integral part of retailing. In the channel of distribution, retailing is where the customer meets the product. It is through retailing that exchange (a central aspect of marketing) occurs. **Retailing** includes all activities involved in selling, renting, and providing goods and services to ultimate customers for personal, family, or household use.

THE VALUE OF RETAILING

Retailing is an important marketing activity. Not only do producers and consumers meet through retailing actions, but retailing also creates customer value and has a significant impact on the economy. To consumers, the value of retailing is in the form of utilities provided. Retailing's economic value is represented by the people employed in retailing, as well as by the total amount of money exchanged in retail sales.

CONSUMER UTILITIES OFFERED BY RETAILING

The utilities provided by retailers are of major value to consumers. Time, place, possession, and form utilities are offered by most retailers in varying degrees, but one utility is often stressed more than the others. Look at Figure 17–1 to see how well you can match the retailer with the utility being stressed in the description.

Having 15,000 representatives across Canada, as Mary Kay Cosmetics does, puts the company's products close to the customer, providing place utility. By providing financing or leasing and taking used cars as trade-ins, Saturn makes the purchase easier and provides possession utility. Form utility—production or alteration of a product—is offered by As You Like It. The company custommakes your sandwich on site to your specifications. Finding toy shelves stocked

Figure 17–1
Which company best represents which utilities?

Mary Kay Cosmetics	A company that has 15,000 Canadian representatives who sell skin care and beauty products to men and women across Canada. Mary Kay products are not sold in stores.
Saturn	Saturn dealers have adopted a one-price strategy that eliminates the need for negotiating. Instead, all customers are offered the same price. Test drives, financing, trade-ins, leasing are all offered to encourage customers to feel comfortable with their purchase.
As You Like It	A popular eating establishment in Halifax, largely known for custom-made sandwiches tailored specifically to the customer's needs.
Toys " Я " Us	A distinctive toy store with a backward *R*, this company is what every kid dreams about. Walking into a Toys " Я " Us store is like living under the Christmas tree. Unlike most stores, which reduce their space allotted to toys after the Christmas season, everything is always available at Toys " Я " Us.

MATCH THEM UP

Time	Place	Possession	Form
_____	_____	_____	_____

in May is the time utility dreamed about by every child (and many parents) who enters Toys " Я " Us. Many retailers offer a combination of the four basic utilities. Some supermarkets, for example, offer convenient locations (place utility) and are open 24 hours (time utility). In addition, consumers may seek additional utilities such as entertainment, recreation, or information.[2]

THE ECONOMIC IMPACT OF RETAILING

Retailing provides value to the individual consumer and is important to the economy as a whole. Retail sales in Canada are estimated to reach $300 billion in 1996. The retail sector also employs over 1.8 million people in Canada, or approximately 15 percent of the total employed labour force.[3] Just three major retail categories—food stores, motor vehicle dealers, and clothing and shoe stores—represent 55 percent of the total retail trade in Canada. Figure 17–2 shows the percentage of total retail trade by major retail categories. These six categories represent over 75 percent of the total retail trade, making them significant contributors to the Canadian economy.

The magnitude of retail sales is hard to imagine. Some of Canada's top retailers such as the Hudson's Bay Company, Sears Canada, and Canadian Tire each had sales in the billions in 1994. Their sales levels surpass even the GNP of several small nation–states.

The Value of Cross-Border Retailing   There is much debate over the relative impact that cross-border shopping has on the Canadian economy. Some believe the value of retail trade is declining in Canada as a result of Canadians' shopping in the United States. However, estimates show that only about 2 percent of total Canadian retail trade is lost to cross-border shopping. Moreover, some experts believe that cross-border shopping has actually improved the scope and nature of retailing in Canada. Canadian retailers, in an effort to keep customers on this side of the border, have become more efficient and better able to offer increased value to their customers.[4]

The cross-border concept involves more than just customers crossing the Canadian–US border. Retailers on both sides are crossing the border looking for market opportunities. White Spot restaurants of British Columbia has recently expanded into Washington state hoping to attract cross-border shoppers and residents of northern Washington by capitalizing on the spillover of radio and TV advertising that airs on southwestern British Columbia stations. At the same time, some American retailers are heading north. Major US chains such as Toys " Я " Us and The Gap have set up shop in Canada. Michaels Stores, a Texas arts

Food stores	25.0%
Motor vehicle dealers	21.0%
Clothing and shoe stores	9.0%
Service stations	8.7%
Department stores	8.0%
Furniture and appliance stores	4.0%

▌*Figure 17–2*
Percentage of total Canadian retail trade by major retail categories.

Source: *Canadian Markets* (Toronto: The Financial Post, 1993).

and crafts retailer, has also opened 20,000-square-foot outlets in Ontario and plans to go Canada-wide with its large-format store concept.[5] But one of the biggest cross-border moves in recent history has been the entry of Wal-Mart into the Canadian market. The $55- to $60-billion-a-year retail juggernaut moved north by acquiring 120 Woolco stores in 1994. Undoubtedly the arrival of US firms in Canada will create some market disruption for domestic companies. But consumers benefit from such cross-border retail expansions by having increased store and product choices, and possible new employment opportunities.

The Value of Global Retailing   Retailing also adds value to the world economy. A study on global retailing found that the top 100 retailers in the world took in more than $1 trillion (US). These global retail companies operate almost 185,000 stores and have their head offices based in 15 countries. The top 100 global retailers had average sales of approximately $10 billion, profits of $240 million, and more than 1,900 outlets. Just the top 10, including US-based Wal-Mart and Kmart, as well as Swiss-based Metro/Kaufhof International, had total sales of over $271 billion, close to the annual total of all retail sales in Canada.[6]

Concept Check	1 **When a Mary Kay representative brings products into a potential buyer's home, what utility is provided?**
	2 **Two measures of the importance of retailing in the Canadian economy are _____ and _____ .**

CLASSIFYING RETAIL OUTLETS

For manufacturers, consumers, and the economy, retailing is an important component of marketing that has several variations. Because of the wide number of alternative forms of retailing, it is easier to understand the differences among retail institutions by recognizing that outlets can be classified in several ways:

- **Form of ownership.** Who owns the outlet.
- **Level of service.** The degree of service provided to the customer.
- **Merchandise line.** How many different types of products a store carries and in what assortment.
- **Method of operation.** The manner in which services are provided—how and where the customer purchases products.

Within each method of classification there are several alternative types of outlets, as shown in Figure 17–3 and explained in the following pages.

FORM OF OWNERSHIP

Independent Retailer   One of the most common forms of retail ownership is the independent business, owned by an individual. The neighbourhood dry

METHOD OF CLASSIFICATION	DESCRIPTION OF RETAIL OUTLET
Form of ownerhship	Independent retailer
	Corporate chain
	Contractual system
	▪ Retailer-sponsored cooperative
	▪ Wholesaler-sponsored voluntary chain
	▪ Franchise
Level of service	Self-service
	Limited service
	Full service
Merchandise line	Depth
	▪ Single line
	▪ Limited line
	Breadth
	▪ General merchandise
	▪ Scrambled merchandising
Method of operation	Store retailing
	Nonstore

cleaner or florist is often an independent retailer. The advantage of this form of ownership for the owner is that she can be her own boss. For customers the independent store often provides a high level of personal service.

Corporate Chain   A second form of ownership, the corporate chain, involves multiple outlets under common ownership. If you've ever shopped at The Bay, Zellers, Eaton's, or Loblaws, you've shopped at a chain outlet.

In a chain operation, centralization in decision making and purchasing is common. Chain stores have advantages in dealing with manufacturers, particularly as the size of the chain grows. A large chain can bargain with a manufacturer to obtain good service or volume discounts on orders. Consumers also benefit in dealing with chains because there are multiple outlets with similar merchandise and consistent management policies.

But many chains are feeling greater competitive pressure from various types of retailers. Sears Canada, for example, must compete against higher-end specialty retailers on the one hand, and warehouse clubs and other discounters on the other. Sears Canada lost over $90 million in 1992 and introduced cost-cutting measures on every front. But the Canadian operation is doing somewhat better than the US parent, Sears, Roebuck & Co., which closed down its catalogue division and laid off 50,000 people.

Sears Canada is using a value-added strategy both in its stores and through its catalogue in order to retain existing customers and attract new ones. Sears recently launched a coupon book insert in its catalogue, which is distributed to over 3.5 million Canadian households. By adding value to the catalogue, Sears Canada hopes to increase profits. Sears Canada will also be using database marketing in order to develop and target certain markets and customers. In the near future, specialized versions of catalogues may be developed and distributed to customers on the basis of their past buying behaviour.[7]

The Woolworth chain, on the other hand, unable to stay competitive, was forced to close its 123 Canadian stores in 1993. Twenty-two will remain closed, and the remaining 101 stores will be converted to The Bargain! Shop. Woolco stores, another chain owned by F. W. Woolworth, also found the Canadian market too crowded and too competitive and, as mentioned previously in the chapter, sold out to the US Wal-Mart chain. With Wal-Mart's entry into Canada, Sears Canada will feel even more competitive pressure.

Contractual System   Under contractual systems, independently owned stores band together to act like a chain. The three kinds described in Chapter 15 are retailer-sponsored cooperatives, wholesaler-sponsored voluntary chains, and franchises. One retailer-sponsored cooperative is Guardian Drugs or Uniprix, which consists of neighbourhood pharmacies that all agree with several other independent pharmacies to buy their products from the same wholesaler. In this way, members can take advantage of volume discounts commonly available to chains and also give the impression of being a large chain, which may be viewed more favourably by some consumers. Wholesaler-sponsored voluntary chains such as Independent Grocers' Alliance (IGA) try to achieve similar benefits.

As noted in Chapter 15, in a franchise system an individual or a firm (the franchisee) contracts with a parent company (the franchisor) to set up a business or retail outlet. McDonald's, Holiday Inn, and H&R Block all involve some level of franchising. The franchisor usually assists in setting up the store, selecting the store location, advertising, and training personnel. The franchisee pays a one-time franchise fee and an annual royalty, usually tied to the store's sales. Although this might be seen as a relatively new phenomenon, this ownership approach has been used with gas stations since the early 1900s. Franchising is attractive because of the opportunity for people to enter a well-known, established business where managerial advice is provided. Also, the franchise fee may be less than the cost of setting up an independent business. The International Franchise Association recently reported that franchising is one of the strongest segments of the economy and the source of over 160,000 new jobs each year.[8]

Franchise fees paid to the franchisor can range from as little as $3,000 for a Domino's Pizza franchise to $50,000 for a TGI Friday restaurant franchise.[9] When the fees are combined with other costs such as real estate and equipment, however, the total investment can be substantial. Figure 17–4 shows some businesses that can be entered through franchise along with the total costs of

Many independent stores, such as neighbourhood grocery stores, form alliances in the form of retailer-sponsored cooperatives.

▌*Figure 17–4*
The possibilities and costs of franchising.

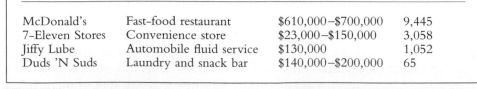

FRANCHISE	LINE OF BUSINESS	TOTAL START-UP COST	NUMBER OF FRANCHISES
McDonald's	Fast-food restaurant	$610,000–$700,000	9,445
7-Eleven Stores	Convenience store	$23,000–$150,000	3,058
Jiffy Lube	Automobile fluid service	$130,000	1,052
Duds 'N Suds	Laundry and snack bar	$140,000–$200,000	65

Sources: S. Caminiti, "Look Who Likes Franchising Now." *Fortune,* September 21, 1991, pp. 125–28; R. E. Bond and C. E. Bond, *The Source Book of Franchising Opportunities* (Homewood, IL: Dow Jones-Irwin, 1991).

becoming a franchisee. By selling franchises, an organization reduces the cost of expansion but loses some control. A good franchisor, however, will maintain strong control of the outlets in terms of delivery and presentation of merchandise.

LEVEL OF SERVICE

Even though most customers perceive little variation in retail outlets by form of ownership, differences among retailers are more obvious in terms of level of service. In some department stores, individual dressing room stalls are not provided; rather, all the customers try on clothes in a large, enclosed area. Some grocery stores have customers bag the food in sacks brought from home. Other outlets provide a wide range of customer services from gift wrapping to wardrobe consultation.

Self-Service   Self-service is at the extreme end of the level-of-service continuum, because the customer performs many functions and little is provided by the outlet. Home building supply outlets, discount stores, and catalogue showrooms are often self-service. Warehouse stores, usually in buildings several times larger than a conventional store, are self-service with all nonessential customer services eliminated. Price Club/Costco Warehouse Club is an example of the no-frills, self-service approach.

Limited Service   Limited-service outlets provide some services, such as credit, merchandise return, and telephone ordering, but not others, such as custom making of clothes. Department stores are typically considered limited-service outlets.

Full Service   The full-service retailer provides a complete list of services to cater to its customers. Specialty stores are among the few stores in this category. Nordstrom, a US-based retail chain, has set the standard for full service among North American department stores. The store typically has 50 percent more salespeople on the floor than similar-sized stores. Salespeople often write customers thank-you notes, or deliver purchases to customers' homes.

MERCHANDISE LINE

Retail outlets also vary by their merchandise lines, the key distinction being the breadth and depth of the items offered to customers (Figure 17–5). **Breadth of product line** refers to the variety of different items a store carries. **Depth of product line** refers to the assortment of each item a store carries—for a shoe store, for instance, running shoes, dress shoes, and children's shoes.

Depth of Line   Stores that carry a considerable assortment (depth) of a related line of items are limited-line stores. Sports Experts stores carry considerable depth in sports equipment ranging from weight-lifting accessories to running shoes. Stores that carry tremendous depth in one primary line of merchandise are single-line stores. Victoria's Secret carries great depth in women's lingerie.

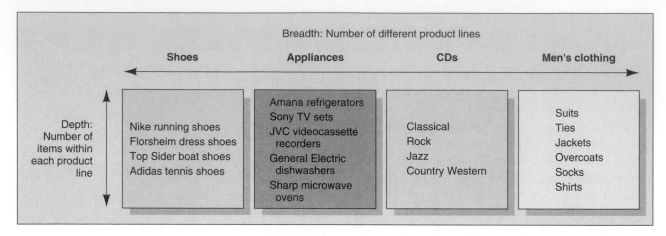

Both limited- and single-line stores are often referred to as *specialty outlets*. Specialty store growth is strong in Canada, including specialty clothing, gift, and coffee stores, such as Starbucks. These specialty outlets usually provide consumers with knowledgeable staff and personal attention.[10]

Specialty discount outlets focus on one type of product, like electronics, business supplies, or party goods, at very competitive prices. These outlets are referred to in the trade as *category killers* because they often dominate the market. Toys " Я " Us, for example, controls 20 percent of the toy market.

Breadth of Line   Stores that carry a broad product line, with limited depth, are referred to as *general merchandise stores*. For example, a large department store carries a wide range of different types of products, but not unusual sizes. The breadth and depth of merchandise lines are important decisions for a retailer. Traditionally, outlets carried related lines of goods. Today, however, **scrambled merchandising,** offering several unrelated product lines in a single store, is common. The modern drugstore, such as Shoppers Drug Mart, carries food, camera equipment, magazines, paper products, toys, small hardware items, and pharmaceuticals. Department stores repair automobiles, provide travel planning, and sell insurance.

Scrambled merchandising is convenient for consumers because it eliminates the number of stops required on a shopping trip. However, for the retailer this merchandising policy means there is competition between very dissimilar types of retail outlets, or **intertype competition.** A local bakery may compete with a department store, a discount outlet, or even a local gas station. Scrambled merchandising and intertype competition make it more difficult to be a retailer.

A form of scrambled merchandising, the **hypermarket,** has been successful in Europe since the late 1960s. Hypermarkets are large stores (over 200,000 square feet) offering a mix of 40 percent food products and 60 percent general merchandise. Prices are typically 5 to 20 percent below discount store prices.

The general concept behind the stores is simple: "one-stop" shopping. Hypermarkets have not been popular in North America. Only a few outlets have been opened, and none have met with much success. Consumers find the stores too big. The competitive environment is also too tough; wholesale clubs beat hypermarkets on price, category killers beat them on selection, and discounters beat them on location.

Searching for a better concept, some retailers have opened superstores which combine a typical merchandise store with a full-size grocery outlet. Superstores run about 100,000 to 150,000 square feet, about half the size of a hypermarket.

In addition to superstores, there are also oversized (large-format) store concepts opening in Canada, including large-format specialty outlets. IDOMO Furniture, for example, opened a 120,000-square-foot store offering a wider and more upper-market range of furniture than its major competitor, IKEA. IDOMO's new store provides a supervised video room for kids, atriums, showroom galleries, and a restaurant that cooks gourmet pizza in a wood-burning stove. Loomis & Toles, a commercial art supplies retailer, has opened a large-format (20,000-square-foot) outlet in Downsview, Ontario, in order to provide expanded merchandise selection, including do-it-yourself supplies.[11]

METHOD OF OPERATION

Retail outlets have begun to vary widely in the way their products are provided, and in their method of operation. Classifying retail outlets by method of operation means dividing these outlets into store and nonstore retailing.

Store Retailing   Traditionally, retailing meant that the consumer went to the store and purchased a product—which is store retailing. Most of the retailing examples discussed earlier in the chapter, such as corporate chains, department stores, and limited- and single-line specialty stores, involve store retailing.

Nonstore Retailing   Viewing retailing as an activity limited to sales in a store is too narrow an approach. Nonstore retailing occurs outside a retail outlet, through a direct channel and direct marketing approach such as mail order, vending machines, teleshopping, and in-home retailing.

Few areas of retailing have grown as rapidly during the past decade as mail-order retailing. Mail-order retailing is attractive because it eliminates the cost of a store and clerks. Mail-order retailing with catalogues is big business in Canada. Over 800 Canadian catalogue companies brought in $2.2 billion in sales.[12] A Canadian study shows that close to 60 percent of adult Canadians make a catalogue mail-order purchase in a given year.[13] The Canadian market has already attracted some US catalogue retailers such as L.L. Bean. Now, Lands' End is boosting its circulation in Canada using an aggressive advertising campaign and offering products specific to the Canadian market. For a profile of the catalogue shopper, read the accompanying Marketing Action Memo.

As the growth in mail-order retailing begins to slow, two trends will emerge. One is specialization, or niche catalogues, which reduce postage costs and increase response rates by focussing on a very narrow line of products. L.L. Bean has already developed individual catalogues for fly fishing devotees and hunters. Lands' End continually develops specialized catalogues as it looks for new market niches. The second trend is toward selling through or opening retail

M A R K E T I N G · A C T I O N · M E M O

Who Are the Catalogue Shoppers?

Catalogue retailers often compete with traditional store-based retailers. But what type of consumer do catalogues attract? The distinctions between the consumers who buy through catalogues and those who do not are quite sharp. Demographically, catalogue shoppers are better educated, are more likely to work in professional or managerial capacities, and earn more money, on average, than noncatalogue shoppers. More women than men shop through catalogues (58 percent versus 42 percent). Catalogue shoppers are more likely to be married, and more likely to have larger households (three or more people), than noncatalogue shoppers.

Lifestyle research reveals that catalogue shoppers are more comfortable with modern technology—the use of home computers, VCRs, and answering machines. They tend to lead more active lifestyles including travel. They tend to shop more often than noncatalogue users and are more likely to buy familiar brands than those who don't buy through catalogues. While both groups rank five determinants for choice of retailer (selection, price, quality, location, and service) in much the same order, quality is more important to the catalogue shopper. Catalogue shoppers are also more likely to buy higher-price goods.

Source: Adapted from J. Pollock, "Catalogue Study Revealed," *Marketing,* April 18, 1994, p. 3; and J. Marney, "Consumers Now Driven by Need, Not Want," *Marketing,* March 1, 1993, p. 7.

---

stores. Traditional catalogue retailers are now moving into store retailing in an effort to reach noncatalogue shoppers. There are some threats to the continued success of mail-order retailers. One concern is market saturation. Another is the rising cost of postage, which reduces the profitability of this form of retailing.

Nonstore retailing also includes vending machines, which make it possible to serve customers when and where stores cannot. Vending machine sales in Canada are estimated at over $450 million.[14] Maintenance and operating costs are high, so product prices in vending machines tend to be higher than those in stores. Typically, small convenience products are available in vending machines. Two trends, however, signal likely continued growth for vending sales. First, improved technology will soon allow vending machines to accept credit cards. This change will permit more expensive items to be sold through this form of retailing.[15] Second, there is a movement toward smaller vending units that can be installed in the workplace. Coca-Cola has developed a small desktop vending unit, while Pepsi-Cola has invented its own version.[16] In the future, few locations will be immune to vending machine deployment. As the accompanying Ethics and Social Responsibility Alert points out, our schools may become the new vending machine battleground.

Another form of nonstore retailing is computer-assisted retailing (sometimes called *videotex*). It allows customers to view products on their TV screen or computer and then order the desired item from their terminal. Several companies have entered this form of retailing in recent years. One of the largest is Prodigy, where for $9.95 per month a customer can have access to a computerized database of products. Prodigy has merchandise from stores like Sears, catalogue retailers, and manufacturers such as Xerox and Sony. Travel reserva-

ETHICS AND SOCIAL RESPONSIBILITY ALERT

A Big Vending Deal in the Toronto School System

The Toronto Board of Education recently signed a deal with Pepsi-Cola Canada that gives the bottler sole vending machine access to the city's public schools in exchange for a $1.14 million payment. Many have no problems with Pepsi making the deal. Pepsi was presented with a marketing opportunity to reach close to 90,000 students, its primary market, and it outhustled its competitors to clinch the deal. The controversy centres on whether or not there should have been a deal in the first place. Some argue that our schools should be exempt from the marketing battleground. Some suggested that boards of education should not be initiating deals to give marketers even higher profiles than they already have in our hypercommercialized society.

However, some ask, What's the problem with the deal? Kids are already exposed to thousands of ads daily. Most of the kids wear brand images on their clothing and shoes, so what is one more message? And besides, it raises a little extra money to help cash-poor schools. But others suggest there is a principle at stake. Students should not be treated as a target market bartered off to the biggest bidder, especially by those who are supposed to safeguard them. The Board of Education argues that the vending rights were contracted out in the same way as any other product that is purchased by the board. But others argue that this product is not the same as bulk toilet paper, chalk, or auto shop equipment. Offering a marketer a long-term exclusive right to expose its product to a captive audience is different. Is the board, in essence, renting access to the minds of its students? Faced with economic hard times, should boards of education sign deals like this as an option over closing cafeterias or laying off teachers? Should our schools become a vending battleground?

Source: Adapted from an editorial by W. Gooding, "Pop Goes the Principles," *Marketing,* January 31, 1994, p. 23.

tions, stock transactions, and encyclopedia searches can also be made via this system. Prodigy charges retailers up to $25,000 to sign up for the service, and there is an ongoing fee of approximately one-third of the retailer's gross margin.[17] Southam Inc. of Ontario recently developed a Canadian version of Prodigy, available to Canadian consumers starting in 1994.

Another form of nonstore retailing is television home shopping (teleshopping), in which the consumer sits at home and tunes in to a television show on which products are displayed. This form of nonstore shopping has experienced rapid growth during the late 1980s and early 1990s. The United States has two major networks, the Home Shopping Network and QVC, while Canada has one major network, the Canadian Home Shopping Network, which reaches over 6 million Canadian households, 24 hours a day, seven days a week.

The limitation of teleshopping in the past has been the lack of buyer-seller interaction and the fact that consumers cannot control the items they see. But

Modems allow computer users access to many types of information and services.

two new technologies—fibre optics and digital compression—will soon allow consumers to interact with the TV set and choose from as many as 500 channels. Consumers will be able to travel this so-called information highway picking and choosing from menus and deciding when and what to watch. Experts anticipate that these advances will reach as many as half of all cable subscribers by 1998.[18]

The development of computer-assisted retailing and teleshopping has varied from one country to another. For example, based on the progress of telecommunications systems and television networks, forecasts in Germany predict that by the end of 1995 home shopping will account for 3.5 percent of total retail sales, while the prediction in France is 25 percent.[19]

Concept Check

1 Centralized decision making and purchasing are an advantage of _____ ownership.

2 Would a shop for big men's clothes carrying pants in sizes 40 to 60 have a broad or a deep product line?

3 What are some examples of nonstore retailing?

RETAILING STRATEGY

This section identifies how a retail store may position itself and describes specific actions the store can take to develop a retailing strategy.

POSITIONING A RETAIL STORE

The four classification alternatives presented in the previous section help determine one store's position relative to its competitors.

Retail Positioning Matrix   The **retail positioning matrix** is a matrix developed by the MAC Group, Inc., a management consulting firm.[20] This matrix positions retail outlets on two dimensions: breadth of product line and value added. As defined previously, breadth of product line is the range of products sold through each outlet. The second dimension, *value added,* includes elements such as location (as with 7-Eleven stores), product reliability (as with Holiday Inn or McDonald's), or prestige (as with Brooks Brothers).

The retail positioning matrix in Figure 17–6 shows four possible positions. An organization can be successful in any position, but unique strategies are required within each quadrant. Consider the four stores shown in the matrix:

1   Eaton's tends to have high value added and broad product line. Retailers in this quadrant pay great attention to store design and product lines. Merchandise often has a high margin of profit and is of high quality. The stores in this position typically provide high levels of service.

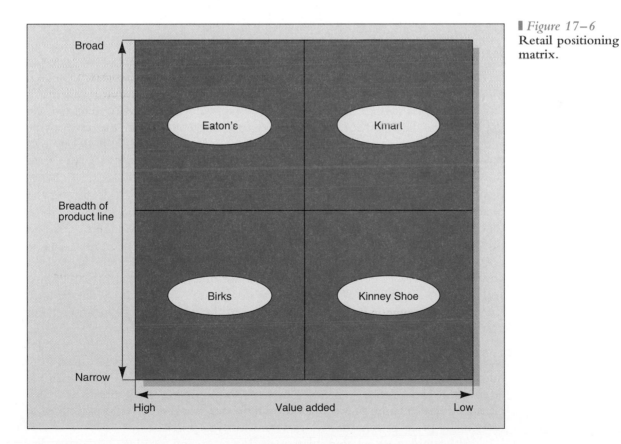

Figure 17–6
Retail positioning matrix.

2 Kmart has low value added and a broad line. Kmart and similar firms typically trade a lower price for increased volume in sales. Retailers in this position focus on price with low service levels and an image of being a place for good buys.

3 Birks has high value added and a narrow line. Retailers of this type typically sell a very restricted range of products that are of high status quality. Customers are also provided with high levels of service.

4 Kinney has low value added and a narrow line. Such retailers are specialty mass merchandisers. Kinney, for example, carries attractively priced shoes for the entire family. These outlets appeal to value-conscious consumers. Economies of scale are achieved through centralized advertising, merchandising, buying, and distribution. Stores are usually the same in design, layout, and merchandise; hence they are often referred to as "cookie-cutter" stores.

Keys to Positioning   To successfully position a store, it must have an identity that has some advantages over the competitors yet is recognized by consumers. A company can have outlets in several positions on the matrix, but this approach is usually done with different store names. Hudson's Bay Company, for example, owns Simpsons and The Bay department stores (with high value added and a broad line) and Zellers stores (low value added and a broad line). Shifting from one box in the retail positioning matrix to another is also possible, but all elements of retailing strategy must be reexamined.

RETAILING MIX

In developing retailing strategy, managers work with the **retailing mix,** which includes the goods and services, physical distribution, and communications tactics chosen by a store (Figure 17–7).[21] Decisions relating to the mix focus on the consumer. Each of the areas shown is important, but we will cover only three basic areas: pricing, store location, and image and atmosphere. The communications and promotion components are discussed in Chapters 18 through 20.

Retail Pricing   In setting prices for merchandise, retailers must decide on the markup, markdown, and timing for markdowns. As mentioned in Appendix A following Chapter 14, *markup* refers to how much should be added to the cost the retailer paid for a product to reach the final selling price. Retailers decide on the *original markup,* but by the time the product is sold, they end up with a *maintained markup.* The original markup is the difference between retailer cost and initial selling price. When products do not sell as quickly as anticipated, their price is reduced. The difference between the final selling price and retailer cost is the maintained markup, which is also called the *gross margin.*

Discounting a product, or taking a *markdown,* occurs when the product does not sell at the original price and an adjustment is necessary. Often new models or styles force the price of existing models to be marked down. Discounts may also be used to increase demand for complementary products.[22] For example, retailers might take a markdown on stereos to increase sales of CDs, or reduce the price of cake mix to generate frosting purchases.

Although most retailers plan markdowns, many retailers use price discounting as part of their regular merchandising policy, with some now using an

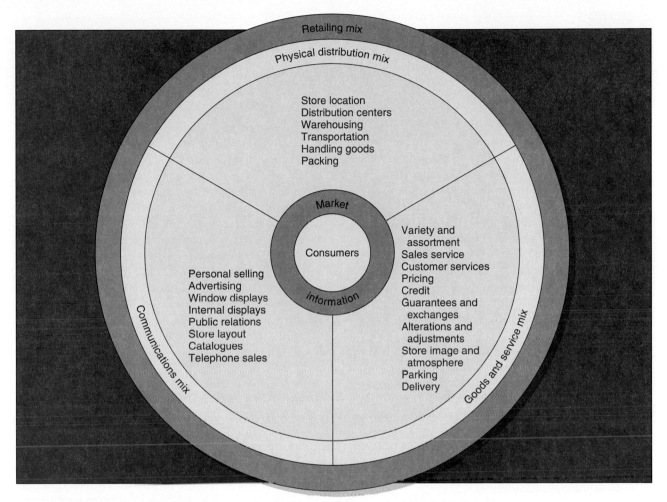

Source: Adapted from W. Lazer and E. J. Kelley, "The Retailing Mix: Planning and Management," *Journal of Retailing,* vol. 37, Spring 1961, pp. 34–41. By permission of The American Marketing Association.

▌ *Figure 17–7*
The retailing mix.

everyday low pricing (EDLP) strategy. Emphasizing consistently low prices and eliminating markdowns or sales has been a successful strategy for some retailers, including Home Depot. Because consumers often use price as an indicator of product quality, however, the brand name of the product and the image of the store become important decision factors in these situations.[23]

A final issue, timing, involves deciding when to discount the merchandise. Many retailers take a markdown as soon as sales fall off to free up valuable selling space and cash. However, other stores delay markdowns to discourage bargain hunters and maintain an image of quality. There is no clear answer, but retailers must consider how the timing might affect future sales.

Off-Price Retailing   Off-price retailing is a retail pricing practice that is most commonly found in clothing sales. **Off-price retailing** is the selling of brand-name merchandise at lower-than-regular prices.

There is a difference between the off-price retailer and a discount store. Off-price merchandise is bought by the retailer from manufacturers with excess

M A R K E T I N G · A C T I O N · M E M O

Warehouse Clubs in Canada

Warehouse clubs in Canada are giving traditional retailers a run for their money, according to Nielsen Marketing Research, Toronto. According to Nielsen, the city with the greatest growth potential for warehouse clubs is Toronto, because there are fewer clubs serving that city than either Montreal or Calgary. In Montreal, the clubs represent 6.9 percent of all grocery purchases; in Calgary the figure is 4.4 percent; and in Toronto, 1 percent. Penetration of warehouse clubs is highest in Montreal—where 27 percent of shoppers visited a club in a 32-week period—followed by Calgary, where 25 percent of the population shopped at a club during that same period. Penetration was lowest in Toronto, with only 5 percent of the population purchasing goods from the two clubs in the area during the time of the study.

Montreal and Calgary consumers also shop at clubs more frequently—every 7 and 8 weeks, respectively—than Toronto shoppers, who visit them once every 14 weeks. Club shoppers spend marginally less in traditional grocery supermarkets than do others. But their total food purchases, including dollars spent at the clubs, are considerably greater than those of shoppers who buy food only at supermarkets. Though there are regional differences, the most popular items bought at club stores are similar across all three markets. Popular categories include bread and bakery products, ready-to-eat cereals, detergents, snack foods, frozen dinners, bulk cheeses, and produce. The most frequently purchased food items account for about 28 percent of all club purchases. Health and beauty items are also strong, with more than 60 percent of all shoppers buying those products.

Source: Adapted from J. Pollock, "Warehouse Clubs Still Growing in Canadian Markets," *Marketing*, June 14, 1993, p. 8.

---

inventory at prices below wholesale prices, while the discounter buys at full wholesale price but takes less of a markup than do traditional department stores. Because of this difference in the way merchandise is purchased by the retailer, selection at an off-price retailer is unpredictable, and consumers must be willing to search or hunt for what they want at different off-price retailers or at different times. However, savings to the consumer at off-price retailers are reported as high as 70 percent off the prices of a traditional department store.

There are two growing variations of off-price retailing. One is warehouse clubs. These large stores, often larger than 100,000 square feet, began as rather stark outlets with no elaborate displays, customer service, or home delivery. They require an annual membership fee (usually $25) for the privilege of shopping there.

While a typical Kmart store stocks 100,000 items, warehouse clubs carry about 3,500 items and usually stock just one brand name of appliance or food product. Service is minimal, and customers usually must pay by cash or cheque. However, the extremely competitive pricing of merchandise makes warehouse clubs attractive.[24] The most popular warehouse clubs include Sam's Wholesale Club and Price Club/Costco Warehouse Club. To get an idea about the presence of warehouse clubs in Canada, read the accompanying Marketing Action Memo.

A second variation of off-price retailing is the factory outlet store. These outlets include companies that market clothing and shoes, such as Bass shoes, Ralph Lauren, and Levi's. Consumers can save up to 50 percent off suggested retail prices. Manufacturers use the stores to clear merchandise and to reach consumers who focus on value shopping. Even some department stores have their own factory outlet stores. Some experts expect the next trend to combine outlet stores, off-price retailers, and department store clearance centres in "value-retail centres."[25]

Store Location   A second aspect of the retailing mix involves deciding where to locate the store and how many stores to have. Department stores, which started downtown in most cities, have followed customers to the suburbs, and in recent years more stores have been opened in large regional malls. Most stores today are near several others in one of five settings: the central business district, the regional centre, the community shopping centre, the strip, or the power centre.

The **central business district** is the oldest retail setting, the community's downtown area. Until the regional outflow to suburbs, it was the major shopping area, but the suburban population has grown at the expense of the downtown shopping area.

Regional shopping centres are the suburban malls of today, containing up to 100 stores or more. The typical drawing distance of a regional centre is over 5 to 10 miles from the mall, and could be as high as 50 miles. These largest shopping areas often contain one or two *anchor stores,* which are well-known national or regional stores such as Sears, Eaton's, or the The Bay. The largest variation of a regional centre is the West Edmonton Mall in Alberta. The shopping centre is a conglomerate of 600 stores, six amusement centres, 110 restaurants, and a 355-room Fantasyland Hotel.[26]

A more limited approach to retail location is the **community shopping centre,** which typically has one primary store (usually a department store outlet) and often about 20 to 40 outlets. Generally, these centres serve a population of about 100,000.

Not every suburban store is located in a shopping mall. Many neighbourhoods have clusters of stores, referred to as a **strip location,** to serve people who are within a 5- to 10-minute drive and live in a population base of under 30,000. Gas station, hardware, laundry, and grocery outlets are commonly found in a strip location. Unlike the larger shopping centres, the composition of these stores is usually unplanned.

A new variation of the strip shopping location is called the **power centre,** which is a huge shopping strip with multiple anchor (or national) stores. Power centres are seen as having the convenient location found in many strip centres and the additional power of national stores. These large strips often have two to five anchor stores and often contain a supermarket, which brings the shopper to the power centre on a weekly basis.[27]

Retail Image and Atmosphere   Deciding on the image of a retail outlet is an important retailing mix factor that has been widely recognized and studied since the late 1950s. Pierre Martineau described image as "the way in which the store is defined in the shopper's mind, partly by its functional qualities and partly by the aura of psychological attributes."[28] In this definition, *functional* refers to the mix elements such as price ranges, store layouts, and breadth and depth of merchandise lines. The psychological attributes are the intangibles, such as a sense of belonging, excitement, style, or warmth. Image has been found to include impressions of the corporation that operates the stores, the category or type of store, the product categories in the store, the brands in each category, and the marketing activities of the store.[29]

Closely related to the concept of image is the store's atmosphere, or ambiance. Many retailers believe that sales are affected by layout, colour, lighting, and music in the store, as well as by how crowded it is. In addition, the physical surroundings that influence customers may affect the store's employees.[30] In creating the right image and atmosphere, a retail store tries to identify its target audience and what the target audience seeks from a buying experience so the store will fortify the beliefs and emotional reactions buyers are seeking.[31]

Many stores are spending considerable time and money to create the right image and atmosphere for their customers. For example, Southland Canada, operator of 7-Eleven stores across the country, is sprucing up its image. In addition to remodelling its stores, 7-Eleven is offering customers a 100 percent satisfaction guarantee.[32] The Hudson's Bay Company spent $40 million to open 13 new stores in British Columbia and Alberta and to convert the former Woodward's department store chain, which it took over in 1993. In constructing the new stores and renovating the former Woodward's stores, the company wanted to project the image of being "Canada's fashion department store," with marketing emphasis placed on soft lines such as personal and home fashions.[33]

The West Edmonton Mall.

1 What are the two dimensions of the retail positioning matrix?

2 How does original markup differ from maintained markup?

3 An area with two anchor stores and up to 100 other stores is a(n) _____ centre.

THE CHANGING NATURE OF RETAILING

Retailing is the most dynamic aspect of the channel of distribution. Stores like factory outlets show that new retailers are always entering the market, searching for a new position that will attract customers. The reason for this continual change is explained by two concepts: the wheel of retailing and the retail life cycle.

THE WHEEL OF RETAILING

The **wheel of retailing** is a diagram of the forms retail outlets pass through once they enter the market.[34] Usually they enter as low-status, low-margin stores such as a drive-in hamburger stand with no indoor seating and a limited menu (Figure 17–8, box 1). Gradually these outlets add fixtures and more embellishments to their stores (in-store seating, plants, and chicken sandwiches

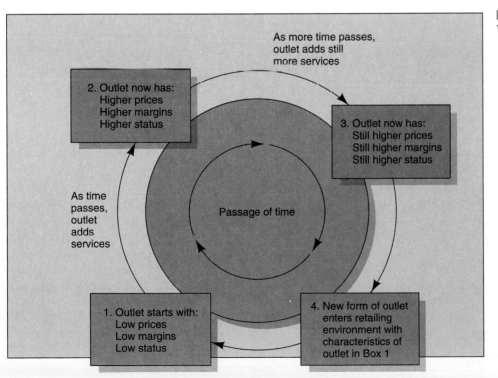

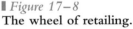
Figure 17–8
The wheel of retailing.

■ *Figure 17–9*
The retail life cycle.

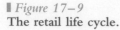

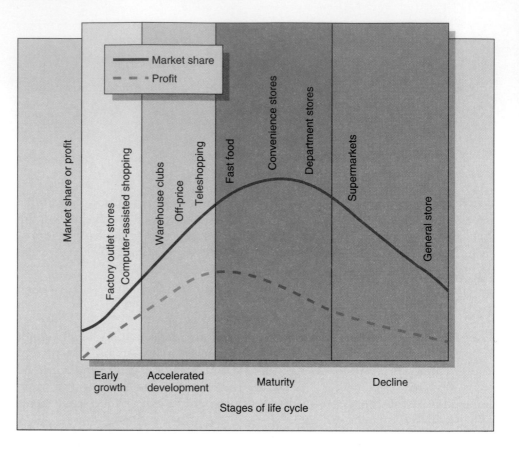

Figure 17–9
The retail life cycle.

as well as hamburgers) to increase their attractiveness for customers. With these additions, prices and status rise (box 2 in Figure 17–8). As time passes, these outlets add still more services and their prices and status increase even further (box 3). These retail outlets then face some new form of retail outlet that appears as a low-status, low-margin operator (box 4), and the wheel of retailing turns as the cycle starts to repeat itself.

In the 1950s, McDonald's and Burger King had very limited menus of hamburgers and french fries. Most stores had no inside seating for customers. Over time, the wheel of retailing for fast-food restaurants has turned. These chains have changed by altering their stores and expanding their menus. As the wheel turns today, McDonald's has new products such as pizza and lasagna, as well as new formats and new décor options.

Discount stores were a major new retailing form in the 1960s and priced their products below those of department stores. In the 1980s, as prices in discount stores rose, they found themselves overpriced compared with a new form of retail outlet—the warehouse retailer. Today, off-price retailers and factory outlets are offering prices even lower than the warehouses'!

THE RETAIL LIFE CYCLE

The process of growth and decline that retail outlets, like products, experience is described by the **retail life cycle**.[35] Figure 17–9 shows the retail life cycle

INSTITUTIONAL TYPE	PERIOD OF FASTEST GROWTH	PERIOD FROM INCEPTION TO MATURITY (YEARS)	STAGE OF LIFE CYCLE
General store	1800–1840	100	Declining
Single-line store	1820–1840	100	Mature
Department store	1860–1940	80	Mature
Variety store	1870–1930	50	Declining
Corporate chain	1920–1930	50	Mature
Discount store	1955–1975	20	Mature
Conventional supermarket	1935–1965	35	Mature/declining
Shopping centre	1950–1965	40	Mature
Gasoline station	1930–1950	45	Mature
Convenience store	1965–1975	20	Mature
Home improvement centre	1965–1980	15	Late growth
Superspecialists	1975–1985	10	Mature
Warehouse clubs	1990–?	5 (projected)	Late growth
Computer-assisted retailing	1990–?	7 (projected)	Early growth
Hypermarkets	1990–1992	3	Mature/declining
Factory outlets	1990–?	5 (projected)	Early growth

Source: Adapted from J. B. Mason and M. L. Mayer, *Modern Retailing: Theory and Practice,* 5th ed. (Homewood, IL: Business Publications/Richard D. Irwin, 1990), p. 25.

▌ *Figure 17–10*
The evolution of today's retail institutions.

and the position of various current forms of retail outlets on it. Early growth is the stage of emergence of a retail outlet, with a sharp departure from existing competition. Market share rises gradually, although profits may be low because of start-up costs. In the next stage, accelerated development, both market share and profit achieve their greatest growth rates. Usually multiple outlets are established as companies focus on the distribution element of the retailing mix. In this stage some later competitors may enter. Wendy's, for example, appeared on the hamburger chain scene almost 20 years after McDonald's had begun operation. The key goal for the retailer in this stage is to establish a dominant position in the fight for market share.

The battle for market share is usually fought before the maturity phase, and some competitors drop out of the market. New retail forms enter in the maturity phase, stores try to maintain their market share, and price discounting occurs. In the early 1990s, the major fast-food chains like Wendy's and McDonald's began to aggressively discount their prices. McDonald's introduced its "value menu" by offering 69¢ cheeseburgers and $1.99 Happy Meals, while Wendy's followed with a kid's Value Menu.[36]

The challenge facing retailers is to delay entering the decline stage in which market share and profit fall rapidly. In 1991 specialty apparel retailers, which include The Gap, Limited, and Benetton, noticed a decline in market share for the first time after a decade of growth. To prevent further decline, these retailers will need to find ways of discouraging their customers from moving to low-margin, mass-volume outlets or high-price, high-service boutiques.[37]

Figure 17–10 shows how many of today's retail institutions evolved. It shows the difficult challenge facing today's retailers: the time retail forms take to move from early growth to maturity is decreasing, so there is less time for a retailer to achieve profitability. Department stores took 100 years to reach maturity, whereas warehouse clubs are expected to reach maturity in five years. As a result, retailers must continually modify their mix to avoid early decline.

FUTURE CHALLENGES IN RETAILING

The challenges facing retailers come from many directions, including the advent of computerization, the cost of shrinkage, and the retailing of services. Because services marketing has become a dominant trend in recent years, Chapter 24 covers this topic. The following sections address the former two issues.

COMPUTERIZATION OF THE RETAIL STORE

Computers are in use today in most medium to large stores in the form of computerized checkouts (or scanning systems) that read a code of information about the items being purchased. They are rapidly replacing traditional cash registers. One survey found that 77 percent of all medium-sized retailers ($50 million to $500 million in sales) and 82 percent of large retailers (over $500 million in sales) are committed to scanning technology.

    To record the items being purchased, scanning systems use the **universal product code (UPC),** which is a number assigned to identify each product. It is represented by a series of bars with varying widths. The scanner converts this UPC symbol, identifies the product, and accesses the price stored in the firm's computer. The advantages of scanners for retailers and consumers include faster checkouts, fewer errors, and better control of inventory. In addition, scanner data can be used to track current and new product sales, to monitor the impact of price changes and coupons, and to assess the effectiveness of promotional activities.[38] Technology has also affected the way retail operations order merchandise. Many retailers now place orders and communicate with vendors using EDI (electronic data interchange).

THE SHRINKAGE PROBLEM

A long-standing, growing problem in retailing is **shrinkage,** or theft of merchandise by customers and employees. Some research suggests that internal theft by employees is much more of a problem than theft by customers. Either way, shrinkage ends up costing Canadian retailers hundreds of millions of dollars annually. This cost is ultimately passed on to consumers in the form of higher prices. Retailers have begun to use a variety of approaches to combat this problem. Guards and detectives, employee awareness programs, locked cases, and magnetic detectors on merchandise are a few of the approaches.[39] These are but a few examples of how retailers are battling a significant problem that affects their profits and consumers' prices.

1 According to the wheel of retailing, when a new retail form appears, how would you characterize its image?

2 Market share is usually fought out before the _____ stage of the retail life cycle.

3 What is shrinkage?

Summary

1 Retailing provides a number of values to the customer in the form of various utilities: time, place, possession, and form. Economically, retailing is important in terms of the people employed and the money exchanged in retail sales.

2 Retailing outlets can be classified along several dimensions: the form of ownership, level of service, merchandise line, or method of operation.

3 There are several forms of ownership: independent, chain, trade cooperative, or franchise.

4 Stores vary in the level of service, being self-service, limited service, or full service.

5 Retail outlets vary in terms of the breadth and depth of their merchandise lines. Breadth refers to the number of different items carried, and depth refers to the assortment of each item offered.

6 In terms of method of operation, retailing includes store and nonstore retailing. Nonstore retailing includes mail order, vending machines, computer-assisted shopping, teleshopping, and in-home retailing.

7 A retail store positions itself on two dimensions: breadth of product line and value added, which includes elements such as location, reliability, and prestige.

8 Retailing strategy is based on the retailing mix, consisting of goods and services, physical distribution, and communications.

9 In retail pricing, retailers must decide on the markup, markdown, and timing for the markdown. Off-price retailers offer brand-name merchandise at lower-than-regular prices. This retailing form is most common in the clothing industry.

10 Retail store location is an important retail mix decision. The common alternatives are the central business district, a regional shopping centre, a community shopping centre, or a strip location. A relatively new development is the power centre, which is a strip location with multiple national anchor stores and a supermarket.

11 Retail image and atmosphere help retailers create the appropriate buying experience for their target market.

12 New retailing forms are explained by the wheel of retailing. Stores enter as low-status, low-margin outlets. Over time, they add services and raise margins, thus preparing the entry of a new form of low-status, low-margin retailing outlet.

13 Like products, retail outlets have a life cycle consisting of four stages: early growth, accelerated development, maturity, and decline. Over the past 100 years the time it takes for each new retailing form to reach maturity has declined.

14 Computerized scanning systems are playing a major role in retail store operations. Scanners read the UPC symbol for each item and provide timely sales and inventory data. Interactive technology such as EDI allows networking between retailers and their suppliers.

Key Terms and Concepts

retailing p. 421

form of ownership p. 424

level of service p. 424

merchandise line p. 424

method of operation p. 424

breadth of product line p. 427

depth of product line p. 427

scrambled merchandising p. 428

intertype competition p. 428

hypermarket p. 428

retail positioning matrix p. 433

retailing mix p. 434

off-price retailing p. 435

central business district p. 437

regional shopping centres p. 437

community shopping centre p. 437

strip location p. 437

power centre p. 437

wheel of retailing p. 439

retail life cycle p. 440

universal product code (UPC) p. 442

shrinkage p. 442

Chapter Problems and Applications

1 Discuss the impact of the growing number of dual-income households on *(a)* non-store retailing and *(b)* the retail mix.

2 How does value added affect a store's competitive position?

3 In retail pricing, retailers often have a maintained markup. Explain how this maintained markup differs from original markup and why it is so important.

4 What are the similarities and differences between the product and retail life cycles?

5 How would you classify Kmart in terms of its position on the wheel of retailing versus that of an off-price retailer?

6 Develop a chart to highlight the role of each of the three main elements of the retailing mix across the four stages of the retail life cycle.

7 In Figure 17–6 Kinney Shoes was placed on the retail positioning matrix. What strategies should Kinney follow to move itself into the same position as Birks?

8 Breadth and depth are two important components in distinguishing among types of retailers. Discuss the breadth and depth implications of the following retailers discussed in this chapter: *(a)* Mary Kay Cosmetics, *(b)* Dell Computer, and *(c)* Lands' End.

9 According to the wheel of retailing and the retail life cycle, what will happen to factory outlet stores?

10 The text discusses the development of teleshopping and computer-assisted retailing in Canada. How does the development of each of these retailing forms agree with the implications of the retail life cycle?

Promotional Process, Sales Promotion, and Public Relations

AFTER READING THIS CHAPTER YOU SHOULD BE ABLE TO:

▸ Explain the communications process and its elements.

▸ Understand the need for an integrated approach to promotion, sometimes called integrated marketing communications.

▸ Select the promotional approach appropriate to a product's life cycle stage and characteristics.

▸ Differentiate between the advantages of push and pull strategies.

▸ Understand the alternative strengths and weaknesses of consumer-oriented and trade-oriented sales promotions.

▸ Appreciate the value of marketing public relations (MPR).

▸ Understand the concept of direct marketing (direct promotion).

Promotion Gets Personal at P&G

Business for marketers such as Procter & Gamble (P&G) used to be much simpler. Utilitarian products such as Crest, Tide, and Ivory were designed for a large, homogeneous market. Promotion techniques consisted of network television and radio advertising, as well as couponing. Distribution was through supermarkets, which had an abundance of shelf space.

P&G, one of Canada's largest advertisers, spends $100 million in a typical year on traditional media in an attempt to reach its customers. But today's marketplace has fractured into smaller and smaller segments requiring new promotion techniques to help business communicate with consumers on a more personal level. P&G, in addition to its traditional advertising, is now using the walls of dentists' offices, videocassettes, and supermarket shopping carts to spread its messages. Other promotions, designed to encourage comparisons with competitors' products, such as product samples or in-store trials, are also being used by P&G.[1]

To help encourage a long-term relationship with its customers, P&G is testing a checkout system called Visions and a frequent-shopper program called Vision Value Club. To participate, customers insert an electronic card into the checkout register, and as each product is scanned the price and other information are shown on a colour monitor. Each product purchased provides the customer with "points," which can be accumulated and exchanged for merchandise—much like a frequent-flyer program on an airline.[2]

As new techniques are added to P&G's promotional efforts, funds are also being redistributed among the traditional methods. Coupons are likely to receive less attention in the future, while cable television and specialized magazines are likely to be popular alternatives. These changes are part of P&G's marketing strategy, which is designed to make it a leader in each of its 39 product categories. As a pioneer of consumer marketing techniques and the current leader in 22 product categories, P&G is leading the way to a new era of marketing and promotion.[3]

Promotion represents the fourth element in the marketing mix. The promotional element comprises a mix of tools available for the marketer, sometimes called the promotional or marketing communications mix: advertising, personal selling, sales promotion, marketing public relations (MPR), and direct marketing (direct promotion). All of these elements can be used to inform prospective buyers about the benefits of the product, persuade them to try it, and remind them later about the benefits they enjoyed by using the product. This chapter first gives an overview of the communications process and then introduces the concept of integrated marketing communications, briefly discusses all the elements of the promotional mix, and provides some details on sales promotion, marketing public relations (MPR), and direct marketing. Chapter 19 covers advertising, and Chapter 20 discusses personal selling.

THE COMMUNICATION PROCESS

Communication is the sharing of meaning and requires five elements: a source, a message, a receiver, and the processes of encoding and decoding[4] (Figure 18–1). The **source** may be a company or a person who has information to convey. The information sent by a source, such as a description of a new weight reduction drink, forms the **message.** Consumers who read, hear, or see the message are the **receivers.** The message is communicated by means of a channel—television, radio, or a salesperson standing outside the door.

▌ *Figure 18–1*
The communication process.

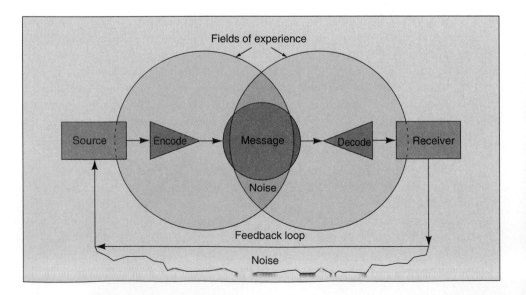

A source and a message.

ENCODING AND DECODING

Encoding and decoding are essential to communication. **Encoding** is the process of having the sender transform an abstract idea into a set of symbols. **Decoding** is the reverse, or the process of having the receiver take a set of symbols, the message, and transform them back to an abstract idea. Look at the accompanying automobile advertisement: who is the source, and what is the message?

Decoding is performed by the receivers according to their own frame of reference: their attitudes, values, and beliefs.[5] In the ad, Lexus is the source and the message is this advertisement, which appeared in *Forbes* magazine (the channel). How would you interpret (decode) this advertisement? The picture and text in the advertisement show that the source's intention is to introduce a unique product and to position Lexus as a company in "the relentless pursuit of perfection"—a position the source believes will appeal to the upper-income readers of the magazine.

The process of communication is not always a successful one. Errors in communication can happen in several ways. The source may not adequately transform the abstract idea into an effective set of symbols, a properly encoded message may be sent through the wrong channel and never make it to the receiver, the receiver may not properly transform the set of symbols into the correct abstract idea, or finally, feedback may be so delayed or distorted that it is of no use to the sender. Although communication appears easy to perform, truly effective communication can be very difficult.

For the message to be communicated effectively, the sender and receiver must have a shared **field of experience**—similar understanding and knowledge. Figure 18−1 shows two circles representing the fields of experience of the sender and receiver, which overlap in the message. Some of the better-known communication problems have occurred when Canadian and U.S. companies have taken their messages to cultures with different fields of experience. Many misinterpretations are merely the result of bad translations. For example, General Motors made a mistake when its "body by Fisher" claim was translated into Flemish as "corpse by Fisher."[6]

FEEDBACK

Figure 18−1 shows a line labelled feedback loop. **Feedback** is the communication flow from the receiver back to the sender and indicates whether the message was decoded and understood as intended. Chapter 19 reviews approaches called *pretesting* that ensure that advertisements are decoded properly.

NOISE

Noise includes extraneous factors that can work against effective communication by distorting a message or the feedback received (Figure 18−1). Noise can be a simple error, such as a printing mistake that affects the meaning of a newspaper advertisement, or using words or pictures that fail to communicate the message clearly. Noise can also occur when a salesperson's message is mistaken by the buyer, such as when a buyer concentrates on not liking the salesperson's smoking rather than hearing the sales message.

Concept Check

1 What are the five elements required for communication to occur?

2 A difficulty for Canadian companies advertising in international markets is that the audience does not share the same _____.

3 A misprint in a newspaper ad is an example of _____.

AN INTEGRATED COMMUNICATIONS APPROACH

Almost every marketing technique and approach used over the years is essentially some form of communication. A product's design sends a message. The same is true of a product's package. Distribution channels are a form of communication: a product sold in a discount store may communicate a different message from a similar product sold in an upscale department store. The same can be said about price: the price of a product also sends a message. Marketers are now recognizing the need to integrate all forms of communication reaching the target audience so that consistency in the message is achieved.

Integrated marketing communications (IMC) is a new way of looking to the whole, where marketers once saw only parts such as advertising, public relations, sales promotion, direct marketing, packaging, and so forth.[7] In other words, integrated marketing communications is about solving the problem of communicating with customers or prospects. It does not come down to "do advertising," or "do public relations" or "do direct marketing." IMC means selecting the correct communications vehicle or channel, whatever works best in solving the communications problem.

Don Schultz, one of the pioneer thinkers on the concept, defines **integrated marketing communications** as:

> the process of developing and implementing various forms of persuasive communications programs with customers and prospects over time. The goal is to influence or directly affect the behaviour of the selected communications audience. IMC considers all sources of brand or company contacts which a customer or prospect has with the product or service as potential delivery channels for future messages. Further, IMC makes use of all forms of communications which are relevant to the customer and prospects, and to which they might be receptive. In sum, the IMC process starts with the customer or prospect and then works back to determine and define forms and methods through which persuasive communications programs should be developed.

But why has integrated marketing communications become so important today? Schultz explains:

> During the 1950s to the 1970s almost everyone in Canada and the United States could, and often did, see and perhaps hear the same marketing messages. An almost homogeneous mass media and mass marketing culture had developed. Marketing organizations created broadly demanded products for these mass markets. Retail distribution systems developed to sell to and through these markets. And marketing communications professionals developed plans, programs, and systems to communicate to these mass markets. These marketing systems worked like well-oiled machines through the mid-1980s. Then technology collided with society and human wants and needs. Suddenly consumers, who now had more information than ever before, began to demand specialized products, distribution systems, and communication. What once had been a mass market splintered into hundreds if not thousands of separate, individual markets driven by lifestyle, ethnic background, income, geography, education, gender, and all other things that make one person different from another.[8]

In essence, a "demassification" of the marketplace had occurred. Enter the need for a new communications approach. And it is occurring. As the chapter opener illustrated, companies are integrating a variety of communications or promotional techniques in order to effectively reach consumers with clear, consistent communications. While we will deal with several of the elements of the communications or promotional mix separately, and in detail, you should remember that these elements should be combined through an integrated marketing communications approach in order to achieve maximum effectiveness in today's marketplace.

THE PROMOTIONAL MIX

To communicate effectively with consumers, a company may have to rely on a variety of techniques. A company can use any combination of the five major promotional or marketing communications alternatives: advertising, personal selling, sales promotion, public relations, and direct marketing (promotion). A firm's **promotional mix** (marketing communications mix) is the combination of the elements it chooses to use. Figure 18–2 summarizes the distinctions among the five elements. Three of these elements—advertising, sales promotion, and public relations—are considered *mass forms of communication,* because

PROMOTIONAL ELEMENT	MASS VERSUS PERSONAL	PAYMENT	STRENGTHS	WEAKNESSES
Advertising	Mass	Fees paid for space or time	• Efficient means for reaching large numbers of people	• High absolute costs • Difficult to receive good feedback
Personal selling	Personal	Fees paid to salespeople as either salaries or commissions	• Immediate feedback • Very persuasive • Can select audience • Can give complex information	• Extremely expensive per exposure
Sales promotion	Mass	Wide range of fees paid, depending on promotion selected	• Effective at changing behaviour in short run • Very flexible	• Easily abused • Can lead to promotion wars • Easily duplicated
Public relations	Mass	No direct payment to media	• Often most credible source in the consumer's mind	• Difficult to get media cooperation
Direct marketing	Mass or personal	Wide range of costs or fees, depending on technique used	• Precision targeting, if databases are used • Reaches people not reached by traditional media • Generates leads for salespeople	• Cannot be used for all products • Some consumers reluctant to buy through direct marketing

■ *Figure 18–2*
The promotional mix.

they reach groups of prospective buyers. In contrast, personal selling is a *personal form of communication,* because the seller usually talks person to person with the individual prospective buyer. Direct marketing is a communications approach (mass or personal) in which messages are delivered directly to individual consumers, who are asked to respond by phone, mail, or personal visit. It can involve the use of a variety of techniques such as telemarketing, direct mail, or direct-response television advertising (e.g., ads with "800" numbers).

ADVERTISING

Advertising is any directly paid form of mass communication about an organization, good, service, or idea by an identified sponsor. The *paid* aspect of this definition is important, because the space for the advertising message normally must be bought. An occasional exception is the public-service announcement, where the advertising time or space is donated. A full-page, four-colour ad in *Châteline,* for example, costs about $30,000. The *mass* component of advertising is also important. Advertising involves mass media (such as TV, radio, magazines, and newspapers), which are impersonal and do not have, in general, an immediate feedback loop as does personal selling. We say "in general" because some advertising, direct-response advertising (Chapter 19), can provide some quick feedback: people can call an advertised telephone number and communicate with a company representative.

Before the advertising message is sent, marketing research plays a valuable role; for example, it determines that the message is understood by the target market and that the target market will actually see the medium chosen.

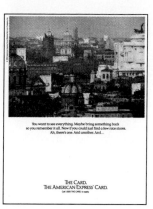

There are several advantages to a firm's using advertising in its promotional mix. It can be attention-getting—as is the accompanying American Express ad—and also communicate specific product benefits to prospective buyers. By paying for the advertising space, a company can control *what* it wants to say and, to some extent, to *whom* the message is sent. If a stereo company wants college students to receive its message about CD players, advertising space can be purchased in a college campus newspaper. Advertising also allows the company to decide *when* to send its message, which includes how often. The mass aspect of advertising also has its advantages. Once the message is created, the same message is sent to all receivers in a market segment. If the message is properly pretested, the company can trust that the same message will be decoded by all receivers in the market segment.

Advertising has some disadvantages. As shown in Figure 18–2 and discussed in depth in Chapter 19, the costs to produce and place a message are significant, and the lack of direct feedback, with most ads, makes it difficult to know how well the message was received.

PERSONAL SELLING

The second major element of the promotional mix is **personal selling,** defined as the two-way flow of communication between buyer and seller, designed to influence a person's or a group's purchase decision. Unlike advertising, personal selling is usually face-to-face communication between the sender and receiver (although, as discussed in Chapter 20, use of telephone sales, or telemarketing, is growing). Why do companies use personal selling?

There are important advantages to personal selling, as summarized in Figure 18–2. A salesperson can control to *whom* the presentation is made. Although some control is available in advertising by choosing the medium, some people may read the college newspaper, for example, who are not in the target audience for CD players. For the CD-player manufacturer, those readers outside the target audience are *wasted coverage.* Wasted coverage can be reduced with personal selling. The personal component of selling has another advantage over advertising in that the seller can see or hear the potential buyer's reaction to the message. If the feedback is unfavourable, the salesperson can modify the message.

The flexibility of personal selling can also be a disadvantage. Different salespeople can change the message so that no consistent communication is given to all customers. The high cost of personal selling is probably its major disadvantage. On a cost-per-contract basis, it is generally the most expensive of the five elements of the promotional mix.

SALES PROMOTION

A third promotional element is **sales promotion,** a short-term inducement of value offered to arouse interest in buying a good or service. Used in conjunction with advertising or personal selling, sales promotions are offered to intermediaries (trade promotions) as well as to ultimate consumers (consumer promotions). Coupons, rebates, samples, and sweepstakes are just a few examples of consumer sales promotions discussed later in this chapter. Trade promotions such as allowances and discounts and cooperative advertising will also be discussed later.

The advantage of sales promotions is that the short-term nature of these programs, such as coupons or sweepstakes with an expiration date, often stimulates sales for the duration. Offering value to the consumer in terms of a cents-off coupon or rebate provides an incentive to buy.

But sales promotions do have their drawbacks. Sales gains are often temporary, with sales dropping off when the deal ends.[9] Also, if sales promotions are conducted continually, they lose their effectiveness. Customers begin to delay purchase until a coupon is offered, or they question the product's value. Some aspects of sales promotions are also regulated by the federal and many provincial governments. These issues are reviewed later in this chapter. In essence, sales promotions should be used when necessary and in conjunction with other promotional elements as part of a company's integrated effort to attract and retain customers.[10]

PUBLIC RELATIONS

A type of mass communication consisting of an organization's indirectly paid presentations regarding its activities, products, or services is termed **public relations (PR).** There are costs involved with the PR function (e.g., staff), but the organization does not directly *pay* for space in a mass medium. The primary objective of PR is to influence the perceptions, opinions, and attitudes that relevant publics have toward an organization. These publics could include customers, prospects, shareholders, and government. Public relations becomes **marketing public relations (MPR)** when its focus is to help solve marketing problems specifically and it becomes well integrated into a company's overall marketing and promotional strategies. While public relations may deal with an organization's image in general, MPR is designed to deal with the marketing image of the organization and its brands of products. Some MPR tools include publicity (e.g., news releases), special events sponsorships, and public-service activities. *Publicity* is often used synonymously with *public relations,* but publicity is just one of many tactics that can be part of the MPR function.

An advantage that many MPR techniques have is credibility. For example, a positive review of a company's product in a newspaper or magazine article is not perceived by the reader as a form of advertising, and thus it is more believable than an advertisement. In addition to more credibility, many MPR techniques can often deliver more information about an organization or a product than paid advertising. The high cost of media advertising limits the amount of detail an organization can provide in broadcast or print media.

There is a disadvantage to some MPR activities, notably publicity. Since there is no contractual agreement between the organization and the media, the organization may have little control over how a message may be presented or whether it is presented at all. We will discuss publicity as one of many marketing public relations tools later in this chapter.

DIRECT MARKETING (DIRECT PROMOTION)

Direct marketing is the fifth element of the promotional mix. In this context, **direct marketing** is defined as an approach in which promotional communications are delivered *directly* to individual consumers, who are asked to *respond* by phone, mail, or personal visit. It can involve the use of personal selling, often in the form of telemarketing, using specific databases on customers or prospects. Direct mail efforts, again using databases, are one of the most common forms of direct marketing. Or direct marketing can utilize mass media, provided that the customer or prospect has a means to respond directly to the marketer, as in direct-response advertising (see Chapter 19). Since the term *direct marketing* may also be used to refer to a type of distribution channel (direct channels; see Chapter 15), some people prefer to use the term *direct promotion,* or *direct-response communication.* Many marketers, whether using direct or indirect channels of distribution, engage in a variety of direct marketing or promotion activities. While direct marketing can use a variety of communications channels, mass or personal, the direct response between marketer and customer is what differentiates it from most of the other forms of promotion. The growth of database marketing, or micromarketing (Chapter 10), has enabled marketers to use a variety of direct marketing techniques.

While conventional mass media such as print and broadcast can be used to deliver direct promotion messages, the marketer loses some precision in targeting. With the advent of accurate and comprehensive databases on customers and prospects, more finely tuned direct marketing, or direct promotion, is possible. Moreover, as explained in Chapter 10, these databases allow the marketers to build a relationship with their customers (relationship marketing). To work best, direct marketing must integrate previously separated marketing mix elements like targeting (databases), distribution, and personalized communications.

There are several advantages in using direct marketing as part of an integrated marketing communications effort. Direct marketing offers more precision in targeting messages, thus minimizing wasted coverage on nonprospects. If a database is used, the communications used can be customized or personalized for each targeted individual.

Many elements of a direct marketing program such as the creative or the specific offer can be tested on a small scale. Response levels can be measured and compared with other promotional activities used. Over time, ongoing fine tuning can occur based on the measured response rates. Direct marketing also offers a way to reach customers or prospects not easily reached through traditional media. Direct marketing techniques such as direct mail can complement personal selling efforts by generating leads for salespeople. However, direct marketing has some disadvantages. Some products do not lend themselves to selling through certain forms of direct marketing. For example, the cost of using direct marketing for low-priced convenience products would probably be too high. Products the consumer would like to inspect first before buying may not sell well through direct marketing; a presentation by a salesperson may be more effective in that case. Unless the company is known to the customer, there may be reluctance to buy via direct marketing. A phone call or a direct mail offer may not be enough in this case to get a positive customer response.

Concept Check

1 Explain the difference between advertising and public relations when both use television.

2 Which promotional element should be offered only on a short-term basis?

3 Cost per contract is high with the _____ element of the promotional mix.

SELECTING PROMOTIONAL TOOLS

In putting together the appropriate promotional or marketing communications mix, a marketer must consider the balance of elements to use. Should advertising be emphasized more than personal selling? When should a promotional rebate be offered? Should a direct marketing technique like personalized direct mail be used? Several factors affect such decisions: the target audience for the promotion,[11] the stage of the product's life cycle, characteristics of the product, decision stage of the buyer, and even the channel of distribution.

THE TARGET AUDIENCE

Promotional efforts can be directed to the ultimate consumer, to an intermediary (retailer, wholesaler, or industrial distributor), or to both. Promotional efforts designed to reach buyers of consumer products often rely on mass media. Geographic dispersion and a large number of potential buyers are the primary reasons for a mass approach. Personal selling is used at the place of purchase, generally the retail store.

Promotion directed to industrial buyers often involves advertising in selected trade publications, such as *Fence* magazine for buyers of fencing material. Because industrial buyers often have specialized needs or technical questions, personal selling is particularly important. The salesperson can provide information and the necessary support after sales.

Intermediaries are often the focus of promotional efforts. As with industrial buyers, personal selling is a major promotional element. The salespeople inform retailers about future advertising efforts to ultimate users, for example, and they assist retailers in making a profit. Intermediaries' questions often pertain to the allowed markup, merchandising support, and return policies, which are best handled by a salesperson.

THE PRODUCT LIFE CYCLE

All products have a product life cycle (see Chapter 12), and the composition of the promotional mix changes over the four life cycle stages, as shown for Purina Puppy Chow in Figure 18–3.

Introduction Stage   Informing consumers in an effort to increase their level of awareness is the primary promotional objective in the introduction stage of the product life cycle. In general, all the promotional mix elements are used at this

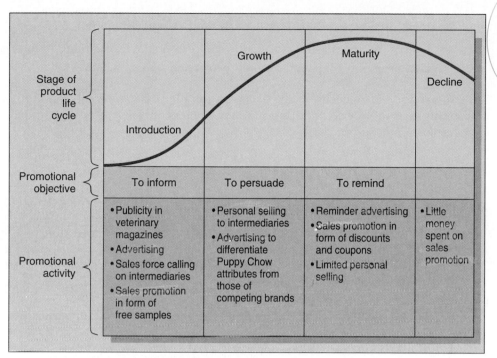

	Growth	Maturity	
Stage of product life cycle			Decline
Introduction			

Promotional objective	To inform	To persuade	To remind	
Promotional activity	• Publicity in veterinary magazines • Advertising • Sales force calling on intermediaries • Sales promotion in form of free samples	• Personal selling to intermediaries • Advertising to differentiate Puppy Chow attributes from those of competing brands	• Reminder advertising • Sales promotion in form of discounts and coupons • Limited personal selling	• Little money spent on sales promotion

▌ *Figure 18–3*
Promotional tools used over the product life cycle of Purina Puppy Chow.

time, although the use of specific mix elements during any stage depends on the product and situation. Stories on Purina's new nutritional food are placed in *Dog World* magazine, trial samples are sent to registered dog owners in 10 major cities, advertisements are placed during reruns of the TV show "Lassie," and the sales force (personal selling and direct marketing) begins to approach supermarkets to get orders. Advertising is particularly important as a means of reaching as many people as possible to build up awareness and interest. Public relations activities may even begin slightly before the product is commercially available.

Growth Stage   The primary promotional objective of the growth stage is to persuade the consumer to buy the product—Purina Puppy Chow—rather than substitutes, so the marketing manager seeks to gain brand preference and solidify distribution. Sales promotion assumes less importance in this stage, and public relations is not a factor because it depends on novelty of the product. The primary promotional element is advertising, which stresses brand differences. Personal selling is used to solidify the channel of distribution. For consumer products such as dog food, the sales force calls on the wholesalers and retailers in hopes of increasing inventory levels and gaining shelf space. For industrial products, the sales force often tries to get contractual arrangements to be the sole source of supply for the buyer.

Maturity Stage   In the maturity stage, the need is to maintain existing buyers, and advertising's role is to remind buyers of the product's existence. Sales promotion, in the form of discounts and coupons offered to both ultimate consumers and intermediaries, is important in maintaining loyal buyers. In a test of one mature consumer product, it was found that 80 percent of the product's

Purina Puppy Chow: a product in the maturity stage of its life cycle.

sales at this stage resulted from sales promotions.[12] Price cuts and discounts can also significantly increase a mature brand's sales. The sales force at this stage seeks to satisfy intermediaries. An unsatisfied customer who switches brands is hard to replace.

Decline Stage   The decline stage of the product life cycle is usually a period of phaseout for the product, and little money is spent in the promotional mix—especially in sales promotions.

PRODUCT CHARACTERISTICS

The proper blend of elements in the promotional mix also depends on the type of product. Three specific characteristics should be considered: complexity, risk, and ancillary services. *Complexity* refers to the technical sophistication of the product and hence the amount of understanding required to use it. It's hard to provide much information in a one-page magazine ad or 30-second television ad, so the more complex the product, the greater the emphasis on personal selling.

A second element is the degree of *risk* represented by the product's purchase. Risk for the buyer is a cost in financial terms (such as $2,750 spent for an IBM ThinkPad 700 portable computer), or social or physical terms. A hair transplant procedure might represent all three risks—it may be expensive, people can see and evaluate the purchase, and there may be a chance of physical harm. Although advertising helps, the greater the risk, the greater the need for personal selling.

The level of *ancillary services*—service or support after the sale—required by a product also affects the promotional strategy. This consideration is common to many industrial products and consumer purchases. Who will repair your auto-

Some products represent a financial risk for consumers.

mobile or VCR? Advertising's role is to establish the seller's reputation. However, personal selling is essential to build buyer confidence and provide evidence of customer service.

STAGES OF THE BUYING DECISION

Knowing the customer's stage of decision making can also affect the promotional mix. Figure 18–4 shows how the importance of four directly paid promotional elements varies with the three stages in a consumer's purchase decision.

Prepurchase Stage   In the prepurchase stage advertising is more helpful than personal selling, because advertising informs the potential customer of the existence of the product and the seller. Sales promotion in the form of free samples can also play an important role to gain low-risk trial. When the salesperson calls on the customer after heavy advertising, there is some recognition of what the salesperson represents. This is particularly important in industrial settings, in which sampling of the product is usually not possible. Direct marketing techniques, such as direct mail or direct-response TV ads, could be used to encourage prospects to phone for more information on the product, or to mail a request for a sample. Telemarketing may also be used.

Purchase Stage   At the purchase stage the importance of personal selling is highest, whereas the impact of advertising is lowest. Sales promotion in the form of coupons, deals, point-of-purchase displays, and rebates can be very helpful in encouraging demand. Direct marketing techniques, such as direct mail, encouraging direct response are also useful at this stage.

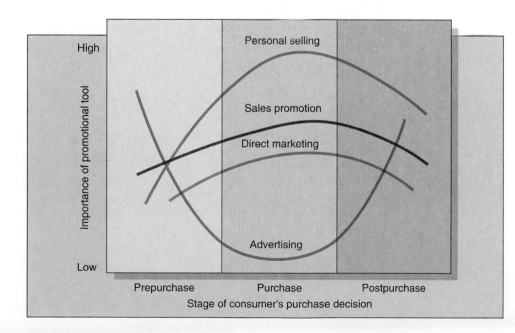

▌ *Figure 18–4*
How the importance of four promotional elements varies during the consumer's purchase decision.

Postpurchase Stage In the postpurchase stage, the salesperson is still important. In fact, the more personal contact after the sale, the more the buyer is satisfied. Advertising is also important to assure the buyer that the right purchase was made. Advertising and personal selling help reduce the buyer's postpurchase anxiety.[13] Sales promotion in the form of coupons can help encourage repeat purchases from satisfied first-time triers.

CHANNEL STRATEGIES

Chapter 15 discussed the channel flow from producer to intermediaries to consumer. Achieving control of the channel is often difficult for the manufacturer, and promotional strategies can assist in moving a product through the channel of distribution. This is where a manufacturer has to make an important decision whether to use a push strategy, a pull strategy, or both in its channel of distribution.[14]

Push Strategy Figure 18–5A shows how a manufacturer uses a **push strategy,** directing the promotional mix to channel members to gain their cooperation in ordering and stocking the product. In this approach, personal selling and trade promotions play major roles. Salespeople call on wholesalers to encourage orders and provide sales assistance. Trade promotions, such as case discount allowances (20 percent off the regular case price), are offered to stimulate demand. By pushing the product through the channel, the goal is to get channel members to push it to their customers.

Many Canadian companies spend a significant amount of their marketing resources on trade promotions. According to a recent Canadian study, the average marketer spends 50 to 60 percent of its marketing budget on trade allowances, such as fees paid to retailers to gain regular shelf displays or special

Figure 18–5
A comparison of push and pull promotional strategies.

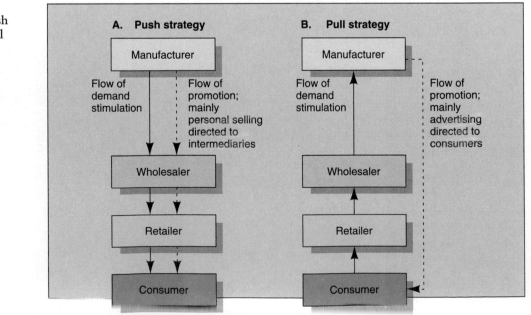

BASIS OF COMPARISON	HEAVIER RELIANCE ON . . .	
	ADVERTISING	PERSONAL SELLING
Target audience	Ultimate consumers	Resellers and industrial buyers
Risk in purchase	Low	High
Size of decision-making unit	Small	Large
Complexity of product	Simple	Complex
Level of ancillary services	Low	High
Stage of purchase decision	Prepurchase	Purchase
Channel strategy	Pull	Push
Geographical dispersion of customers	Great	Little

▌ *Figure 18–6*
When to emphasize advertising or personal selling.

end-of-aisle displays for promotions and new product listings. The rest of the spending is split between consumer promotion, direct mail, advertising, and public relations activities.[15]

Pull Strategy In some instances manufacturers face resistance from channel members who do not want to order a new product or increase inventory levels of an existing brand. As shown in Figure 18–5B, a manufacturer may then elect to implement a **pull strategy** by directing its promotional mix at ultimate consumers to encourage them to ask the retailer for the product. Seeing demand from ultimate consumers, retailers order the product from wholesalers and thus the item is pulled through the intermediaries. Pharmaceutical companies, for example, historically marketed only to doctors. Now they typically spend millions to advertise prescription drugs directly to consumers. The strategy is designed to encourage consumers to ask their physicians for a specific drug by name—pulling it through the channel. Successful advertising strategies, such as Nicoderm's "Ask your doctor" campaign, can have dramatic effects on the sales of a product.[16]

WHEN TO STRESS ADVERTISING AND PERSONAL SELLING

In the promotional mix, public relations and sales promotions are supportive and rarely the key elements in a firm's strategy. Often a firm must make a trade-off between emphasizing advertising or personal selling. Figure 18–6 summarizes the major factors that lead to an emphasis on either approach.

1 **For consumer products, why is advertising emphasized more than personal selling?**

2 **At what stage of the product life cycle is public relations an important promotional activity?**

3 **Explain the differences between a push and a pull strategy.**

Concept Check

MARKETING · ACTION · MEMO

Sales Promotion Goes Global

*A*round the world, the interest in sales promotion activities has increased dramatically. This is particularly true in countries with powerful channel intermediaries or limited electronic media advertising. At Nestlé, analysis of the importance of promotion in the marketing mix showed significant differences between countries. The accompanying table illustrates the promotional differences of one packaged good in five countries.

	US	JAPAN	UK	CANADA	MEXICO
Promotion expenditures (% of sales)	27%	33%	26%	27%	1%
Advertising	12	39	42	19	68
Consumer promotion	26	25	25	15	11
Trade promotion	62	36	33	66	22

Examples of some of the sales promotion differences found in other countries include:

- In the United Kingdom, marketers have noticed a very high rate of coupon misredemption. One reason is that UK consumers have only recently begun to use coupons and are unfamiliar with the rules, often turning in coupons for products they have not purchased.
- In Canada, contests must include a skill-testing question and there must be a means of entry that does not require a purchase.

- In Lima, Peru, where inflation has reached 400 percent, consumers are very responsive to promotions that reduce their cost or provide premiums. One department store attracted 200,000 new customers with a trading stamp program.

As international sales promotion use increases, brands will require attention from an international sales promotion coordinator who will:

- Facilitate transfer of successful promotion ideas.
- Suggest modifications based on differences in permitted promotional techniques.
- Develop and present sales promotion training programs.
- Gather performance data on promotions run in multiple countries.

Local and regional brands will logically require unique sales promotion programs that address differences in economic development, market maturity, perceptions, regulations, and trade structure in each country.

Sources: G. Guido, "What U.S. Marketers Should Consider in Planning a Pan-European Approach," *Journal of Consumer Marketing,* Spring 1992, pp. 29–33; V. Watkins, "Promotions in Canada Have Special Legal Requirements," *Marketing News,* December 7, 1992, p. 14; "Misredemption on the Rise Overseas," *Promo,* May 1992, pp. 56–57; and K. Kashani and J. A. Quelch, "Can Sales Promotion Go Global?" *Business Horizons,* May–June 1990, pp. 37–43. Copyright 1990 by The Foundation for the School of Business at Indiana University. Used with permission.

SALES PROMOTION

THE IMPORTANCE OF SALES PROMOTION

Sales promotion is sometimes considered a supplemental ingredient of the promotional mix and is not as visible as advertising, but billions are spent annually on it. As shown in Figure 18–7, during the 1980s there was a major shift of dollars from media advertising to trade and consumer promotion.[17] As the use of sales promotion has increased, marketers have developed methods for selecting and assessing the impact of the various techniques. These methods require a good understanding of the advantages and disadvantages of each kind of sales

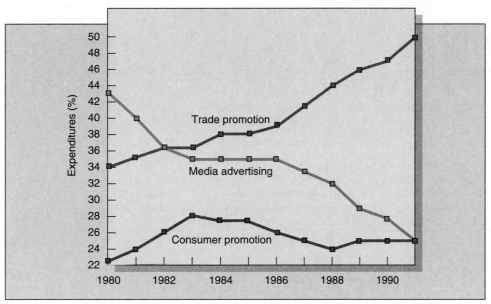

Source: "Where the Promotion Dollar Goes." *Adweek's Marketing Week,* June 19, 1990, p. 10. Reprinted with permission of *Adweek's Marketing Week.* See also "Category Management: Marketing for the '90s," *Marketing News,* September 14, 1992, pp. 12–13.

❚ *Figure 18–7*
Trends in expenditures for media advertising, trade promotion, and consumer promotion.

promotion.[18] In addition, if the sales promotions are used in other countries, some of the issues described in the accompanying Marketing Action Memo must be considered.

CONSUMER-ORIENTED SALES PROMOTIONS

Directed to ultimate consumers, **consumer-oriented sales promotions,** or simply consumer promotions, are sales tools used to support a company's advertising and personal selling. The alternative consumer-oriented sales promotion tools are shown in Figure 18–8.

A study of consumer-oriented sales promotions showed that the following types are most frequently used.[19]

TYPE OF PROMOTION	FREQUENCY OF USE
Coupons (direct to consumer)	100%
Cents-off promotions	87
Refunds	77
Premiums	70
Coupons (in retailers' ads)	66
Samples (new products)	64
Sweepstakes	64

Coupons   A coupon is a sales promotion technique that usually offers a discounted price on a product to the consumer to encourage trial. Billions of coupons are distributed in Canada every year. In 1993, Canadians redeemed over 327 million coupons (an overall redemption rate of 1.5 percent) having an

KIND OF SALES PROMOTION	OBJECTIVES	ADVANTAGES	DISADVANTAGES
Coupons	Stimulate demand	Encourage retailer support	Consumers delay purchases
Deals	Increase trial; retaliate against competitor's actions	Reduce consumer risk	Consumers delay purchases; perceived product value reduced
Premiums	Build goodwill	Attract consumers with free or reduced-price merchandise	Consumers buy for premium, not product
Contests	Increase consumer purchases; build business inventory	Encourage consumer involvement with product	Require creative or analytical thinking
Sweepstakes	Encourage present customers to buy more; minimize brand switching	Get customer to use product and store more often	Sales drop after sweepstakes
Samples	Encourage new product trial	Low risk for consumer	High cost for company
Continuity programs	Encourage repeat purchases	Help create loyalty	High cost for company
Point-of-purchase displays	Increase product trial; provide in-store support for other promotions	Provide good product visibility	Hard to get retailer to allocate high-traffic space
Rebates	Encourage customers to purchase; stop sales decline	Effective at stimulating demand	Easily copied; steal sales from future; reduce perceived product value

▌ *Figure 18–8*
Sales promotion alternatives.

average face value of 65 cents. This means Canadians saved over $200 million dollars on products as a result of using coupons.[20]

Studies show that when coupons are used, a company's market share does increase during the period immediately after they are distributed.[21] There are indications, however, that couponing can reduce gross revenues by lowering the price paid by already-loyal consumers.[22] Therefore, manufacturers and retailers are particularly interested in coupon programs directed at potential first-time buyers. Marketers also have to be concerned with the overall cost of couponing. Coupons are far more expensive than just the face value of the coupon; a 25-cent coupon can cost three times that after paying for the advertisement to deliver and support the coupon, dealer handling, clearing-house costs, and redemption. In addition, misredemption, or paying the face value of the coupon even though the product was not purchased, also adds to the costs of couponing.

Two of the fastest-growing forms of couponing in Canada are the retailer in-ad coupon and electronic couponing, designed to replace retailer in-ad couponing in the future. Retailer in-ad coupons appear in retailers' regular weekly newspaper or flyer advertisements. However, redemption rates on retailer in-ad

coupons are lower (less than 1 percent) than on regular coupons, mainly because they are valid for only a few days and redeemable only at the issuing retailer.

Electronic couponing is the 1990s version of the paper coupon, but it is faster, more convenient, and controversial. Instead of clipping coupons from newspapers or grocery-chain flyers, consumers can get special discount cards from the chains in exchange for basic customer information (for database marketing purposes). All shoppers have to do is present their discount cards to the cashier, who puts them through the checkout scanner. The store's computer automatically deducts all eligible discounts from the shoppers' bills. Electronic couponing is currently being used in big food store chains like Loblaws, A&P, Miracle Food Mart, and Dominion. This is because these chains have the necessary scanning equipment. These retailers like electronic couponing because it reduces the handling costs of couponing, and it allows them to collect valuable information on their customers.

Manufacturers, however, complain that electronic couponing can be a poor motivator for consumers to switch brands compared with regular coupons. Consumers can get the discount even if they don't know that the couponed product is on sale. Others complain that electronic coupons have comparatively low face values, as little as half that of regular coupons, and thus may not trigger any conscious switching behaviour. Still, manufacturers expect redemption rates to be much higher on electronic couponing, since consumers will automatically get the discount in store. But these higher redemption rates will mean higher costs to the manufacturer without the possibility of obtaining new customers on an ongoing basis.[23]

Deals   Deals are short-term price reductions, commonly used to increase trial among potential customers or to retaliate against a competitor's actions. For example, if a rival manufacturer introduces a new cake mix, the company responds with a "two packages for the price of one" deal. This short-term price reduction builds up the stock on the kitchen shelves of cake mix buyers and makes the competitor's introduction more difficult.

Premiums   A promotional tool often used with consumers is the premium, which consists of merchandise offered free or at a significant savings over retail. This latter type of premium is called *self-liquidating,* because the cost charged to the consumer covers the cost of the item. Burger King, for example, offered watches based on the movie *The Nightmare before Christmas* for about $2.00 with a purchase of one of its meals. By offering a premium at a low price, companies encourage customers to return frequently or to use more of a product.

Contests   In the fourth sales promotion in Figure 18–8, the contest, consumers apply their analytical or creative thinking to try to win a prize. For example, Pepsi ran a contest called the "You Got the Right One Baby Uh Huh Challenge" by inviting people to perform their own renditions of the popular Ray Charles jingle. Thousands of people took part in the challenge, and Pepsi increased its sales during the contest.[24]

Sweepstakes   *Reader's Digest* and Publisher's Clearing House are two of the better-promoted sweepstakes. These sales promotions require participants to submit some kind of entry form but are purely games of chance requiring no analytical or creative effort by the consumer. Canada has federal and provincial regulations covering sweepstakes, contests, and games regarding their fairness, to ensure that the chance of winning is represented honestly and to guarantee that the prizes are actually awarded.

Samples   Another common consumer sales promotion is sampling, or offering the product free or at a greatly reduced price. Often used for new products, sampling puts the product in the consumer's hands. A trial size is generally offered that is smaller than the regular package size. If consumers like the sample, it is hoped they will remember and buy the product. Kimberly-Clark used sampling to promote its UltraTrim diapers. It undertook a personally addressed sample mailing to 235,000 Canadian households using a database of

mothers provided primarily by Welcome Wagon. The sampling program was backed up by TV advertising developed specifically for the Canadian market, as well as newspaper and magazine ads with coupons.[25]

Sampling is also used to support established products. Pepsi, for example, has used sampling in the hope of converting Coca-Cola drinkers. Pepsi also used free samples to attract new customers.

Continuity Programs   Continuity programs are a sales promotion tool used to encourage and reward repeat purchases by acknowledging each purchase made by a consumer and offering a premium as purchases accumulate. Trading stamps, which were first used by supermarkets and gas stations in the 1960s and 1970s, are an example. More recently airlines and hotels have used frequent-flyer and frequent-traveler programs to reward loyal customers. Even GM has a continuity program—a credit card that allows consumers to accumulate up to $3,500 in "points" toward the purchase of a new Chevrolet, Pontiac, Oldsmobile, Buick, or Cadillac.[26]

Point-of-Purchase Displays   In a store aisle, you often encounter a sales promotion called a *point-of-purchase display*. These product displays take the form of advertising signs, which sometimes actually hold or display the product, and are often located in high-traffic areas near the cash register or the end of an aisle. The accompanying picture shows gravity-feed bins that Nabisco uses for its animal crackers; it helps ensure product freshness, provides storage, and captures the consumer's attention as an end-of-aisle, point-of-purchase display.[27] A recent survey of retailers found that 87 percent plan to use more point-of-purchase materials in the future, particularly for products that can be purchased on impulse.[28]

Some studies estimate that two-thirds of a consumer's buying decisions are made in the store. This means that grocery product manufacturers want to get their message to you at the instant you are next to their brand in your supermarket aisle—perhaps through a point-of-purchase display. At many supermarkets this may be done through the VideOcart. Sitting on the handlebar of your supermarket shopping cart, the VideOcart's liquid crystal display (LCD) screen

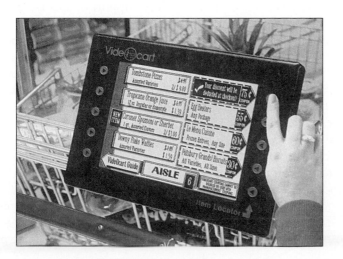

The VideOcart: gentle video reminders on your shopping trip through your supermarket.

A gravity-feed bin that doubles as a point-of-purchase display.

will remind you twice per aisle about products next to your cart that you might consider buying. The displays on your screen are triggered by transmitters on the store shelves and can be updated by satellite connections with the manufacturer. Other in-store promotions such as interactive kiosks are also becoming popular.[29]

Rebates   A final consumer sales promotion in Figure 18–8, the cash rebate, offers the return of money based on proof of purchase. This tool has been used heavily by car manufacturers facing increased competition. Computer companies like Apple have also used it effectively in selling PCs to ultimate consumers. When the rebate is offered on lower-priced items such as detergent or dog food, the time and trouble of mailing in a proof-of-purchase to get the rebate check means that many buyers—attracted by the rebate offer—never take advantage of it. However, this "slippage" is less likely to occur with frequent users of rebate promotions.[30] In fact, a firm now offers a 900 number for consumers to call for information about rebates and for personalized rebate certificates.[31]

TRADE-ORIENTED SALES PROMOTIONS

Trade-oriented sales promotions, or simply trade promotions, are sales tools used to support a company's advertising and personal selling directed to wholesalers, retailers, or distributors. Some of the sales promotions just reviewed are used for this purpose, but there are three other common approaches targeted uniquely to these intermediaries: allowances and discounts, cooperative advertising, and training of distributors' sales forces.

Allowances and Discounts   Trade promotions often focus on maintaining or increasing inventory levels in the channel of distribution. An effective method for encouraging such increased purchases by intermediaries is the use of allowances and discounts. However, overuse of these "price reductions" can lead to retailers' changing their ordering patterns in the expectation of such offerings. Although there are many variations that manufacturers can use with discounts and allowances, three common approaches include the merchandise allowance, the case allowance, and the finance allowance.[32]

Reimbursing a retailer for extra in-store support or special featuring of the brand is a *merchandise allowance.* Performance contracts between the manufacturer and trade member usually specify the activity to be performed, such as a picture of the product in a newspaper with a coupon good at only one store. The merchandise allowance then consists of a percentage deduction from the list case price ordered during the promotional period. Allowances are not paid by the manufacturer until it sees proof of performance (such as a copy of the ad placed by the retailer in the local newspaper).

A second common trade promotion, a *case allowance,* is a discount on each case ordered during a specific time period. Such an allowance is usually deducted from the invoice. A variation of the case allowance is the "free goods" approach, whereby retailers receive some amount of the product free based on the amount ordered, such as one case free for every ten cases ordered.[33]

A final trade promotion, the *finance allowance,* involves paying retailers for financing costs or financial losses associated with consumer sales promotions.

MARKETING · ACTION · MEMO

The Benefits of Trade and Consumer Sales Promotions

Clearly Canadian Beverage Corporation of Vancouver has taken 25 percent of the nearly $2 billion alternative or New Age beverage market with its flavoured sparkling-water drinks. Its success, according to the company, can be attributed to both trade and consumer sales promotion. A large portion of Clearly's $45 million integrated promotion budget is spent on sales promotions including two major summer promotions, one for consumers and one for its salespeople. The Clearly Climbing incentive program offers prizes to any of the 12,000 salespeople who meet or exceed their distribution and product presence goals. The consumer promotion, called Kick Back for Summer, involves the use of point-of-purchase sweepstakes in which the consumer can win Clearly merchandise. The company is also heavily involved in sampling either at mall locations or at air shows, where it participates as a corporate sponsor.

Weston Bakeries of Quebec is also a firm believer in sales promotion, especially to support brand advertising. One of the things Weston does that few others do is to tie promotions to popular television shows. For example, Weston sponsors a youth-oriented TV program called Club 100 Watts, launched a bread called Weston 100 Watts, and conducted other sales promotion activities tied in directly to the show.

Sources: Adapted from B. Mackin, Jr., "Promotion Marketing," *Marketing*, May 24, 1993, p. 14; G. Chiasson, "Promotion Marketing," *Marketing*, May 24, 1993, p. 14.

This trade promotion is regularly used and has several variations. One type is the floor stock protection program—manufacturers give retailers a case allowance price for products in their warehouse, which prevents shelf stock from running down during the promotional period. Also common are freight allowances, which compensate retailers that transport orders from the manufacturer's warehouse.

Cooperative Advertising   Resellers often perform the important function of promoting the manufacturer's products at the local level. One common sales promotional activity is to encourage both better quality and greater quantity in the local advertising efforts of resellers through **cooperative advertising.** This is a program by which a manufacturer pays a percentage of the retailer's local advertising expense for advertising the manufacturer's products.

Usually the manufacturer pays a percentage, often 50 percent, of the cost of advertising up to a certain dollar limit, which is based on the amount of the purchases the retailer makes of the manufacturer's products. In addition to paying for the advertising, the manufacturer often furnishes the retailer with a selection of different ad executions, sometimes suited for several different media. A manufacturer may provide, for example, several different print layouts as well as a few broadcast ads for the retailer to adapt and use.[34]

Training and Motivation of Distributors' Sales Forces   One of the many functions the intermediaries perform is customer contact and selling for the producers they represent. A manufacturer's success often rests on the ability and motivation of the reseller's sales force to represent its products.

Thus it is in the best interest of the manufacturer to help train and motivate the reseller's sales force. Because the reseller's sales force is often less sophisticated and knowledgeable about the products than the manufacturer might like, training can increase sales performance. Training activities include producing manuals and brochures to educate the reseller's sales force. The sales force then uses these aids in selling situations. Other activities include national sales meetings sponsored by the manufacturer and field visits to the reseller's location to inform and motivate the salesperson to sell the products. Increasingly, manufacturers are developing comprehensive incentive and recognition programs to motivate resellers' salespeople to sell their products. The integration of training and motivational programs for resellers' salespeople into an overall promotional or marketing communications mix is important for marketers. Such activities ensure that the outcome of the meeting between customer and salesperson is positive and produces results.[35] The accompanying Marketing Action Memo shows how Canadian companies benefit from both trade and consumer sales promotions.

Concept Check

1 Which sales promotional tool is most common for new products?

2 What is the difference between a coupon and a deal?

3 Which trade promotion is used on an ongoing basis?

PUBLIC RELATIONS

As noted earlier, a type of mass communication consisting of an organization's indirectly paid presentation regarding its activities, products, or services is termed *public relations (PR)*. PR attempts to influence the perceptions, opinions, and attitudes that relevant publics have toward an organization. Marketing public relations (MPR) consists of public relations efforts designed to solve marketing problems specifically, especially when well integrated into overall marketing and promotional strategies. As indicated earlier in the chapter, while public relations may deal with an organization's image in general, MPR is designed to deal with the marketing image of the organization and its brands of products.

MARKETING PUBLIC RELATIONS: TOOLS AND TACTICS

Marketing public relations can be used in a variety of situations to support other promotional or marketing initiatives. MPR can be used to obtain news coverage about new products, or about new uses for existing products. MPR can be used to counter negative coverage resulting from product recalls, product tamperings, and other crisis communications situations. Finally, MPR can be used to create or enhance the favourable image of a corporation. Specifically, MPR can involve the use of any of the following tools and tactics.[36]

Publicity   Publicity is the creation and dissemination of information about a company or product in order to obtain favourable media coverage. Publicity

ETHICS AND SOCIAL RESPONSIBILITY ALERT
Use or Misuse of Publicity?

Publicity campaigns, including boycott threats by Greenpeace, have recently prompted two major paper producers to cancel forest product contracts with Mac-Millan Bloedal. Kimberly-Clark of Dallas and Scott of London, United Kingdom cancelled contracts worth $2.5 million and $5 million, respectively. The cancellations are major victories for Greenpeace, which has been using publicity campaigns designed to end clear-cutting in Clayoquot Sound on the west coast of Vancouver Island. Jeff Domansky, public relations director at Scali McCabe Sloves, Vancouver, says Greenpeace appeared to be winning the war of public opinion in British Columbia until the spectre of boycotts—hence, the possibility of layoffs—became apparent. A national poll conducted by Angus Reid found 67 percent of respondents were opposed to logging. However, a British Columbia–only Angus Reid poll found 60 percent of respondents supported logging in Clayoquot Sound.

Dennis Fitzgerald, MacBlo's manager of environmental communications, says the company has dispatched a team to meet with customers in Europe. According to Fitzgerald, "They're trying to put to bed a lot of misconceptions that Greenpeace is planting. When you look at the information that Greenpeace is promoting in Europe, there's just outrageous distortions there. It's so flagrantly misleading that Europeans come over here and are surprised to see trees still standing anywhere." At home, MacBlo has placed ads in daily newspapers lambasting Greenpeace for threatening its customers with boycotts. MacBlo recognizes that Greenpeace is a formidable opponent in such a battle to gain public opinion. Fitzgerald says, "We don't have the same toys and tactics available to us as they do, nor do we wish to. But certainly their agility in some of these stunts does gather media attention." Fitzgerald wonders if Greenpeace's tactics will be useful in the long run in terms of affecting public opinion, but, he says, "They certainly can capture press attention."

Should the debate over logging be fought using publicity? Are there dangers when organizations use publicity to promote certain causes or to promote their positions on the issue?

Source: Adapted from B. Mackin, Jr., "$7.5 Million in Lost Contracts Prompts MacBlo Ad Action," *Marketing,* March 28, 1994, p. 4.

---

usually takes the form of news releases, news conferences, press kits, or informational documents. The goal is to have the media tell the company's story. Publicity is used in positive situations such as new product launches, as well as in negative marketing situations such as product failure cases. Nonprofit organizations rely heavily on publicity to spread their messages; PSAs (public-service announcements), in which free space or time is donated by the media, is a common use of publicity for these organizations. However, concerns are often expressed about the possible misuse of publicity by organizations when promoting their ideas or causes (see the accompanying Ethics and Social Responsibility Alert).

Special events sponsorship   A growing area of marketing public relations is the creation, or support, and publicizing of company-sponsored seminars, conferences, sports competitions, entertainment events, or other celebrations. The goal of events sponsorship is to create a forum to disseminate company information or to create brand identification among members of the target audience. College sports events such as the CIAU hockey and football championships are sponsored by Coca-Cola and General Motors. Labatt's, General Motors, Reebok, and Canon were among the sponsors of the 1994 Commonwealth Games in Victoria. Volvo sponsors professional men's tennis and leverages that activity by sponsoring club-level, grassroots tournaments. Volvo has found that for every dollar it spends on sponsoring an event, it gets back seven times as much in equivalent media time.[37]

Public-service activities   Public-service activities include establishing or supporting community-based initiatives that benefit the well-being of society. Ciba-Geigy Canada sponsors Health & Welfare Canada's Quit 4 Life Program, which encourages teens to quit smoking. Labatt's and Molson breweries both sponsor responsible-use-of-alcohol initiatives.

Cause-related marketing (CRM) is another way for a company to get involved in public-service activities. CRM is a company's way of making charitable contributions to a worthy cause or nonprofit organization from the sales of one or more of its products. Bank of Montreal's Project Sunshine is designed to raise funds for children's hospitals through the sale of a calendar produced by the bank. CRM activities often generate positive publicity for the company involved.

Promotional materials   Annual reports, brochures, newsletters, or video presentations about a company and its products are also MPR tools. These materials provide information to target publics and often generate publicity. Newsletters, for example, have been found to build company and brand awareness.[38]

Good marketing public relations activities should be planned and integrated into an overall promotional or marketing communications plan. For example, when an organization sponsors an event, it does not rely solely on the publicity that may evolve from that sponsorship. Rather, it often takes out paid advertising and/or executes a sales promotion program before, during, and/or after the event as part of an integrated strategy. Marks and Spencer (Canada) effectively used a variety of MPR activities to improve consumer awareness of and attitudes toward its operations. When it closed 25 of its stores and redesigned most of the remaining 42, MPR was used to inform customers and the business community about what was happening to the stores.

Marks and Spencer relied almost exclusively on MPR to spread its marketing message. It used press releases, contacts with food and fashion publications, fashion shows, and other in-store events as part of its MPR strategy. These activities were coordinated with its traditional advertising and in-store personal selling efforts.[39]

DIRECT MARKETING

Earlier, we defined direct marketing as promotional communications that are delivered directly to individual consumers, who are asked to respond by phone, mail, or personal visit. Direct marketing includes telemarketing or, most commonly, direct mail activities, often using specific databases on customers or prospects.

Direct marketing can utilize mass media, provided that the customer or prospect has a means to respond directly to the marketer, such as direct-response advertising (to be discussed in Chapter 19). This direct response between marketer and customer is what differentiates direct marketing from most of the other forms of promotion. The Canadian Direct Marketing Association estimates that direct marketing spending (all forms) in Canada is about $8.5 billion and is growing at a rate of 8 percent per year. We will focus here on the most dominant form of direct marketing in the Canadian marketplace, direct mail. Many marketers classify direct mail as a form of advertising medium, and it is usually discussed as one of several advertising alternatives. However, while direct mail is certainly a communications vehicle, it is also the principal form of direct marketing used in Canada today.

DIRECT MAIL

For many years, **direct mail** has been the foundation of the direct marketing industry. While new forms of direct marketing such as telemarketing, fax marketing, computer shopping, and teleshopping have now developed, direct mail is still expected to be the primary direct marketing tool into the next decade.

Many firms rely solely on direct mail as both their communications and distribution channel. Many others use it as a supplemental communications and marketing tool. Consumer product companies such as book and record clubs, publishers, and insurance companies typically rely on direct mail. Direct mail is also being used in the consumer health care industry. MediTrust, Pharmex, and Rx Direct are three Canadian direct mail pharmacies that deliver prescription drugs to customers by overnight courier. Many business-to-business marketers also use direct mail, such as IBM, Xerox, and commercial bankers. As we saw in Chapter 17, many nonstore retailers depend exclusively on direct mail, while others—such as Sears Canada—that operate retail store outlets use direct mail (catalogues) to augment their store marketing efforts.

To be effective in using direct mail, marketers must begin with appropriately selected targets, both customers and prospects. Many marketers work from their own in-house databases, which contain lists and profiles of their customers. Others buy or rent lists from companies that are known as list brokers. Many of

these brokerage firms will custom-develop a list based on the type of customer being sought by the direct mail firm. These brokerage firms will often have information on customers who have bought from other direct marketers and use this information to screen potential targets. The so-called compiled lists can be expensive, however, and many firms will instead buy or rent lists of names and addresses of potential customers selected from magazine subscription or organizational directory lists. In doing so, they risk losing some targeting precision.

The direct mail firm may combine the in-house lists of customers and various purchased or rented lists to develop a comprehensive mailing list. In most cases, the firm will use computers to merge the lists and delete any repeated names through a purging process. The direct mail marketer must then develop an offer and determine how to present it to the customer whether through a catalogue or another format such as brochure or personalized letter. In general, the firm will test the offer and the format of the direct mail piece using either focus groups or a small test mailing. On the basis of the response, the firm will either make changes or go with the tested piece.

The next important step in the direct mail process is to promptly deal with the customer or prospect responses. The company must have inventory, order-filling, shipping, and billing capabilities. Customers must receive what they ordered at the price they ordered it and within a reasonable time frame. Finally, the company must be prepared to deal with customer complaints, make adjustments, deal with returns, and ensure customer satisfaction. Most direct mail companies value their customers and maintain ongoing relationships with them (relationship marketing). Current and comprehensive databases allow companies to build such one-to-one relationships with their customers.

PROMOTION AND SELF-REGULATION

Unfortunately, over the years many consumers have been misled—or even deceived—by some form of promotional activity. Examples include sweepstakes in which gifts were not awarded, rebate offers that were a terrible inconvenience, and advertisements whose promises were great until the buyer read the small print.

Promotional efforts targeted at special groups such as children and the elderly also raise ethical concerns. For example, providing free product samples to children in elementary schools, or linking product lines to TV programs and movies, has led to questions about the need for various restrictions on promotional activities. Although there are federal and provincial rules and regulations governing promotional practices in Canada, some observers believe more regulation is needed.

More formal regulation of promotional activities would be very expensive to police and enforce. As a result, there are increasing efforts by advertising agencies, trade associations, and marketing organizations at *self-regulation*. As we saw in Chapter 3, major Canadian advertising agencies who are members of the Canadian Advertising Foundation must adhere to the code of conduct (Canadian Code of Advertising Standards) established by the Advertising Standards Council, its self-regulatory body. The Canadian Direct Marketing Association, whose member companies represent 80 percent of direct marketing sales in Canada, also has a code of practice which is mandatory for all its members to follow. Under its code, for example, all CDMA members must comply with the consumer's right to privacy and honour consumers' requests to have their names removed from direct mail and telemarketing lists. Still, the federal government and many provincial governments are considering new regulations, particularly as they pertain to privacy (e.g., the brokering of names and addresses of consumers for direct marketing purposes), as well as the enforcement of "do not call" and "do not mail" requests made by consumers.

By imposing standards that reflect the values of society on their promotional activities, marketers can facilitate the development of new promotional methods, minimize regulatory constraints and restrictions, and help consumers gain confidence in the communications efforts used to influence their purchases. As organizations strive for effective self-regulation, marketing executives will need to make sound ethical judgments about the use of existing and new promotional practices.

Concept Check

1 **What is publicity?**

2 **What is the major medium used for direct marketing in Canada?**

Summary

1 Communication is the sharing of meaning and requires a source, a message, a receiver, and the processes of encoding and decoding.

2 For effective communication to occur, the sender and receiver must have a shared field of experience. Feedback from receiver to sender helps determine whether decoding has occurred or noise has distorted the message.

3 Integrated marketing communications is the process of developing and implementing various forms of persuasive communications programs with customers and prospects over time. The goal is to influence or affect the behaviour of the selected audience.

4 The promotional or marketing communications mix consists of advertising, personal selling, sales promotion, public relations, and direct marketing. These tools vary according to whether they are personal, can be identified with a sponsor, and can be controlled regarding to whom, where, and how often the message is sent.

5 In selecting the appropriate promotional mix, marketers must consider the target audience, the stage of the product's life cycle, characteristics of the product, decision stage of the buyer, and the channel of distribution.

6 The target for promotional activities can be the ultimate consumer, an intermediary, or both. Promotional activities directed to ultimate con-

sumers rely more on advertising, whereas personal selling is more important in reaching industrial buyers and intermediaries.

7 The emphasis on the promotional tools varies with a product's life. In introduction, awareness is important. During growth, creating brand preference is essential. Advertising is more important in the former stage and personal selling in the latter. Sales promotion helps maintain buyers in the maturity stage. Direct marketing activities such as direct-response advertising and direct mail can be used in the introduction, growth, and maturity stages.

8 The appropriate promotional mix depends on the complexity of the product, the degree of risk associated with its purchase, and the need for ancillary services.

9 In the prepurchase stage of a customer's purchase decision, advertising is emphasized; at the purchase stage, personal selling is most important; and during the postpurchase stage, advertising, personal selling, and sales promotion are used to reduce postpurchase anxiety. Direct marketing techniques such as direct-response advertising or direct mail can be used in both the prepurchase and purchase stages, and to a lesser extent in the postpurchase stage.

10 When a push strategy is used, personal selling and sales promotions directed to intermediaries play major roles. In a pull strategy, advertising and sales promotions directed to ultimate consumers are important.

11 More money is being shifted to sales promotion activities, away from advertising. Selecting sales promotions requires a good understanding of the advantages and disadvantages of each sales promotion option.

12 There is a wide range of consumer-oriented sales promotions: coupons, deals, premiums, contests, sweepstakes, samples, continuity programs, point-of-purchase displays, and rebates.

13 Trade-oriented promotions consist of allowances and discounts, cooperative advertising, and training and motivation programs for distributors' sales forces. These are used at all levels of the channel.

14 Public relations (PR) is a type of mass communication consisting of an organization's indirectly paid presentation regarding its activities, products, or services. Marketing public relations (MPR) consists of PR efforts designed to solve marketing problems. Basic MPR tools include publicity, special events sponsorship, public-service activities, and promotional materials such as annual reports and newsletters.

15 Direct marketing involves promotional communications that are delivered directly to individual consumers, who are asked to respond by phone, mail, or personal visit. It includes telemarketing, or, most commonly, direct mail activities, often using specific databases on customers or prospects. It can utilize mass media, provided that the customer or prospect has a means to respond directly to the marketer, such as direct-response advertising.

16 By imposing self-regulation standards that reflect the values of society on their promotional activities, marketers can facilitate the development of new promotional methods, minimize regulatory constraints, and help consumers gain confidence in the communications used to influence their purchases.

Key Terms and Concepts

communication p. 448	advertising p. 452
source p. 448	personal selling p. 453
message p. 448	sales promotion p. 453
receivers p. 448	public relations (PR) p. 454
encoding p. 449	marketing public relations (MPR) p. 454
decoding p. 449	direct marketing p. 455
field of experience p. 449	push strategy p. 460
feedback p. 450	pull strategy p. 461
noise p. 450	consumer-oriented sales promotions p. 463
integrated marketing communications p. 451	trade-oriented sales promotions p. 468
	cooperative advertising p. 469
promotional mix p. 451	direct mail p. 473

Chapter Problems and Applications

1 After listening to a recent sales presentation, Mary Smith signed up for membership at the local health club. On arriving at the facility, she learned there was an additional fee for racquetball court rentals. "I don't remember that in the sales talk; I thought they said all facilities were included with the membership fee," complained Mary. Describe the problem in terms of the communication process.

2 Develop a matrix to compare the five elements of the promotional mix on three criteria—to *whom* you deliver the message, *what* you say, and *when* you say it.

3 Explain how the promotional tools used by an airline would differ if the target audience were *(a)* consumers who travel for pleasure and *(b)* corporate travel departments that select the airlines to be used by company employees.

4 Suppose you introduced a new consumer food product and invested heavily both in national advertising (pull strategy) and in training and motivating your field sales force to sell the product to food stores (push strategy). What kinds of feedback would you receive from both the advertising and your sales force? How could you increase both the quality and quantity of each?

5 Fisher-Price Company, long known as a manufacturer of children's toys, has introduced a line of clothing for children. Outline a promotional plan to get this product introduced in the marketplace.

6 Many insurance companies sell health insurance plans to companies. In these companies the employees pick the plan, but the set of offered plans is determined by the company. Recently Blue Cross, a health insurance company, ran a television ad stating, "If your employer doesn't offer you Blue Cross coverage, ask why." Explain the promotional strategy behind the advertisement.

7 Identify the sales promotion tools that might be useful for *(a)* Tastee Yogourt—a new brand introduction, *(b)* 3M self-sticking Post-it notes, and *(c)* Wrigley's spearmint gum.

8 If you were planning to use a direct marketing technique to promote or sell a new ski jacket you had developed, what approach would you use (e.g., direct mail, telemarketing)? How would you go about executing the plan?

COSMOPOLITAN IS A UNIVERSAL LANGUAGE.

In more than 80 countries, in 12 languages and 28 editions. Whether you need to tell your story universally or locally, from Sydney to Siena to Stuttgart to Seattle, there is no better way to reach young women than Cosmopolitan. Call Seth Hoyt at (212) 649-3282.

COSMOPOLITAN. THE LARGEST SELLING YOUNG WOMEN'S MAGAZINE IN THE WORLD.

Advertising

AFTER READING THIS CHAPTER YOU SHOULD BE ABLE TO:

▸ Explain the differences between product advertising and institutional advertising and the variations within each type.

▸ Understand the steps to develop, execute, and evaluate an advertising program.

▸ Understand alternative ways to set an advertising budget.

▸ Explain the advantages and disadvantages of alternative advertising media.

Advertising around the World

In 1989, Young & Rubicam, a major international advertising agency, opened an office in Moscow. In 1992, Campbell Soup introduced a single ad campaign for France, Germany, Belgium, and the Netherlands. Today, China and Mexico are investing in their television networks to increase advertising and programming revenues. Overall, the world of advertising—for advertising agencies, advertisers, and the media—is changing dramatically in order to make room for worldwide advertising.[1]

But why are companies advertising on a global basis? First, because new markets such as China and the republics of the former Soviet Union are opening up to world trade. In addition, groups of countries are creating larger markets such as the European Community (EC) and eliminating trade barriers with pacts such as the North American Free Trade Agreement (NAFTA). Second, print media and TV now provide easy access to hundreds of countries. *Cosmopolitan,* for example, is sold in more than 80 countries, 12 languages, and 28 editions. It has a circulation of close to 200,000 in Canada alone. CNN reaches 92 million households in 130 countries. Finally, companies are eager to attract new customers: Unilever and Procter & Gamble each spent over $1 billion on advertising outside North America as they attempt to build awareness and brand loyalty for their products throughout the world.[2]

How to advertise around the world is not without some controversy, however. Many companies are developing campaigns based on a single theme, image, or brand name for multiple countries (global branding), while other companies are convinced that each country requires a unique campaign customized to the specific interests of local consumers.

In either case, successful advertising is a challenge. Advertising typically has only a few seconds to communicate its message. It is also the most visible and highly criticized element of the promotional mix.

Chapter 18 described **advertising** as any directly *paid* form of *mass* communication about an organization, good, service, or idea by an identified sponsor. Two terms are highlighted: directly *paid* distinguishes advertising from public relations where there is no direct payment to media, and *mass* separates it from personal selling.

TYPES OF ADVERTISEMENTS

As you look through any magazine, the number of advertisements and the varying themes can be overwhelming. Advertisements are prepared for different purposes, but they basically consist of two types: product and institutional. These two types can be further classified on the basis of whether they are designed to get the consumer to take immediate action (direct response) or to influence future purchases or actions by the consumer (delayed response).

PRODUCT ADVERTISEMENTS

Focussing on selling a good or service, **product advertisements** take three forms: pioneer (or informational), competitive (or persuasive), and reminder.

Used in the introductory stage of the life cycle, *pioneering advertisements* tell people what a product is, what it can do, and where it can be found. The key objective of a pioneering ad, such as that for the Sony MiniDisc recorder/player, is to inform the target market. Properly developed informative ads have been found to be interesting, convincing, and effective, according to consumer judgment.[3]

Advertising that promotes a specific brand's features and benefits is *competitive* advertising. The objective of such a message is to persuade the target market to select the firm's brand rather than that of a competitor. An increas-

Example of a pioneering ad.

ingly common form of competitive advertising is comparative advertising, which shows one brand's strengths relative to those of competitors.[4] Some research suggests that one-third of all television commercials are comparative ads.[5] Firms that use comparative advertising must be able to support their claims in order to meet government as well as self-regulatory requirements established by the Canadian Code of Advertising Standards.

Reminder advertising is used to reinforce previous knowledge of a product. Reminder advertising is good for products that have achieved a well-recognized position and are in the mature phase of their product life cycle. Another type of reminder ad, reinforcement, is used to assure current users they made the right choice. One example: "Aren't you glad you use Dial. Don't you wish everybody did?"

INSTITUTIONAL ADVERTISEMENTS

The objective of **institutional advertisements,** sometimes called *corporate advertising,* is to build goodwill or an image for an organization, rather than promote a specific good or service. Institutional advertising has been used by Bank of Montreal, General Motors, and Molson to build confidence in the company name. Often this form of advertising is used to support public relations activities.[6] Four alternative forms of institutional advertisements are often used:

1 *Advocacy* advertisements state the position of a company on an issue. As we have seen earlier, Molson runs an extensive advertising campaign encouraging the responsible use of alcohol.

2 *Pioneering institutional* advertisements, like the pioneering ad category for products discussed earlier, are used for a new announcement about what a company is, what it can do, or where it is located. Canada Trust uses a pioneering institutional ad campaign to better position itself in the personal banking market in Canada using the theme "thinking like a customer," as shown in the accompanying ad.

3 *Competitive institutional* advertisements promote the advantages of one product class over another and are used in markets where different product

An example of a
pioneering institutional
ad.

classes compete for the same buyers. The Dairy Bureau of Canada runs its
"You Drink Milk and it Shows" ads with the objective of increasing
demand for milk as it competes against other beverage types.

4 *Reminder institutional* advertisements, like the corresponding product ads,
   simply bring the company's name to the attention of the target market
   again.

DIRECT-RESPONSE VERSUS DELAYED-RESPONSE ADVERTISING

While advertising is classified as product or institutional, both types can be
further classified as either direct-response or delayed-response advertising.
Direct-response advertising (product or institutional) seeks to motivate the
customer to take immediate action. A television ad wanting you to call an 800
number and order a product now is a direct-response ad. A newspaper ad with
a coupon, redeemable on a product only if bought by the next day is a direct-
response ad.

Delayed-response advertising, on the other hand, presents images
and/or information designed to influence the consumer in the near future when
making purchases or when taking other actions. Most national automobile
advertising, for example, is delayed-response in nature; advertisers do not expect
you to drop everything and run to your car dealer immediately to buy a car.
However, a local car dealer ad announcing a special sale for 24 hours only is a
direct-response ad.

Unitel, a new player in the Canadian long-distance telephone market, used a direct-response television ad campaign very successfully. Its ad agency, Ogilvy & Mather of Toronto, ran a television ad with a toll-free phone number and the message "If you want to save money, make this call." Unitel will not divulge just how many inquiries it received as a result of the campaign but claims the response rate was good. Moreover, Unitel does suggest it has already garnered 2 percent of Canada's $7.5 billion long-distance market. Direct-response advertising is growing as companies are looking for more immediate return on their advertising and a measured response in terms of advertising effectiveness. Direct-response advertising is also increasing as a result of the growth in the direct marketing industry. Still, most advertising, product or institutional, is considered delayed-response advertising; the advertiser is simply planting a seed hoping to cultivate sales in the future.

Concept Check

1 What is the difference between pioneering and competitive ads?

2 What is the purpose of institutional advertising?

3 What is direct-response advertising?

DEVELOPING THE ADVERTISING PROGRAM

Because media costs are high, advertising decisions must be made carefully, using a systematic approach. Paralleling the planning, implementation, and control steps described in the strategic marketing process (Chapter 2), the advertising decision process is divided into developing, executing, and evaluating the advertising program (Figure 19–1). Development of the advertising program focusses on the four *W*s:

- *Who* is the target audience?
- *What* are the advertising objectives, the amounts of money that can be budgeted for the advertising program, and the kind of message to use?
- *When* should the advertisements be run?
- *Where* should the advertisements be run?

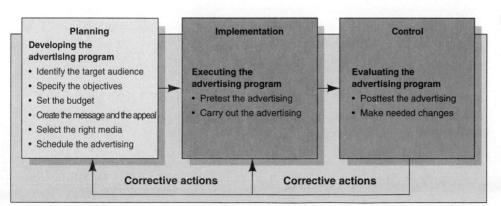

▌*Figure 19–1*
The advertising decision process.

IDENTIFYING THE TARGET AUDIENCE

The first decision in developing the advertising program is identifying the *target audience,* the group of prospective buyers toward which an advertising program is directed. To the extent that time and money permit, the target audience for the advertising program is the target market for the firm's product, which is identified from marketing research and market segmentation studies. The more a firm knows about its target audience's profile—including their lifestyles, attitudes, and values—the easier it is to develop an advertising program. If a firm wanted to reach you with its ads, it would need to know what TV shows you watch and what magazines you read.

SPECIFYING ADVERTISING OBJECTIVES

After the target audience is identified, a decision must be reached on what the advertising should accomplish. Consumers can be said to respond through a **hierarchy of effects,** which is the sequence of stages a prospective buyer goes through from initial awareness of a product to eventual action (either trial or adoption of the product).[7]

- *Awareness.* The consumer's ability to recognize and remember the product or brand name.
- *Interest.* An increase in the consumer's desire to learn about some of the features of the product or brand.
- *Evaluation.* The consumer's appraisal of the product or brand on important attributes.
- *Trial.* The consumer's actual first purchase and use of the product or brand.
- *Adoption.* Through a favourable experience on the first trial, the consumer's repeated purchase and use of the product or brand.

For a totally new product, the sequence applies to the entire product category, but for a new brand competing in an established product category it applies to the brand itself. These steps can serve as guidelines for developing advertising objectives.

Although sometimes an objective for an advertising program involves several steps in the hierarchy of effects, it often focusses on a single stage. No matter what the specific objective might be, from building awareness to increasing repeat purchases, advertising objectives should possess three important qualities: they should be designed for a well-defined target audience, be measurable, and cover a specified time period.

SETTING THE ADVERTISING BUDGET

After setting the advertising objectives, a company must decide how much to spend. From Figure 19–2 (top 15 Canadian advertisers), it is clear that some companies invest heavily in advertising expenditures in order to reach Canadian households. General Motors was Canada's biggest advertiser in 1993, spending over $113 million. Determining the ideal amount for an ad budget is difficult

RANK	COMPANY	AD EXPENDITURES (THOUSANDS)
1	General Motors of Canada	$113,048.4
2	Procter & Gamble	84,499.5
3	The Thomson Group	70,159.3
4	BCE	53,972.9
5	John Labatt Ltd.	50,036.0
6	Eaton's of Canada	47,135.1
7	Sears Canada	46,582.1
8	Government of Canada	43,928.7
9	The Molson Companies	42,873.6
10	Chrysler Canada	41,171.5
11	Paramount Communications	36,476.8
12	Kraft General Foods Group	36,293.5
13	Imasco	35,625.2
14	McDonald's Restaurants of Canada	35,475.8
15	UL Canada	35,198.9

Source: *Marketing,* May 2, 1994, p. 21.

▌ *Figure 19–2*
Ad expenditures by Canadian organizations in 1993.

because there is no precise way to measure the exact results of spending advertising dollars. However, there are several methods used to set the advertising budget.

Percentage of Sales   In the **percentage of sales budgeting** approach, funds are allocated to advertising as a percentage of past or anticipated sales, in terms of either dollars or units sold. A common budgeting method,[8] this approach is often stated in terms such as, "Our ad budget for this year is 3 percent of last year's gross sales." The advantage of this approach is obvious: it's simple and provides a financial safeguard by tying the advertising budget to sales. However, there is a major fallacy in this approach, which implies that sales cause advertising. Using this method, a company may reduce its advertising budget because of a downturn in past sales or an anticipated downturn in future sales—situations where it may need advertising the most.

Competitive Parity   A second common approach to set ad budgets, **competitive parity budgeting,** matches competitors' absolute level of spending or the proportion per point of market share. This approach has also been referred to as *matching competitors* or *share of market*. It is important to consider the competition in budgeting.[9] Consumer responses to ads are affected by competing ads, so if a competitor runs 30 radio ads each week, it may be difficult for a firm to get its message across with only 5 messages.[10] The competitor's budget level, however, should not be the only determinant in setting a company's budget. The competition might have very different advertising objectives, which require a different level of advertising expenditures.

All You Can Afford   Common to many small businesses is **all you can afford budgeting,** in which money is allocated to advertising only after all other budget items are covered. As one company executive said in reference to this budgeting process, "Why, it's simple. First I go upstairs to the controller and ask how much they can afford to give this year. He says a million and a half. Later, the boss comes to me and asks how much we should spend, and I say 'Oh, about a million and a half.' Then we have our advertising appropriation."[11]

Fiscally conservative, this approach has little else to offer. Using this budgeting philosophy, a company acts as though it doesn't know anything about an advertising–sales relationship or what its advertising objectives are.

Objective and Task   The best approach to budgeting is **objective and task budgeting,** whereby the company determines its advertising objectives, outlines the tasks to accomplish these objectives, and determines the advertising cost of performing these tasks.[12]

This method takes into account what the company wants to accomplish and requires that the objectives be specified.[13] Strengths of the other budgeting methods are integrated into this approach because each previous method's strength is tied to the objectives. For example, if the costs are beyond what the company can afford, objectives are reworked and the tasks revised. The difficulty with this method is the judgment required to determine the tasks needed to accomplish objectives. Would two insertions or four in *Time* magazine be needed to achieve a specific awareness level? Figure 19–3 shows a sample media plan with objectives, tasks, and budget outlined. The total amount to be budgeted is $314,000. If the company can afford only $200,000, the objectives must be reworked, tasks redefined, and the total budget recalculated.

CREATING THE MESSAGE AND THE APPEAL

The central element of an advertising program is designing the message that the intended audience will see (as in magazines, newspapers, and TV) or hear (as in radio and TV) and the message's basic appeal. The message content and basic appeal are largely driven by the basic positioning strategy determined by the company. As we saw in Chapter 9, it is through positioning that a firm's

▌*Figure 19–3*
The objective and task approach.

OBJECTIVE	
To increase awareness among college students for the new CD-player cleaning kit. Awareness at the end of one semester should be 20 percent of all students, up from the existing 0 percent today.	
TASKS	**COSTS**
Advertisements once a week for a semester in 500 college papers	$280,000
Advertisements weekly for a semester on the nationally syndicated "Rockline" radio show	25,000
Three monthly, full-page ads in *Audio* magazine	9,000
Total budget	$314,000

competitive advantage is translated into reality for the consumer. Thus, the message and appeal are designed to execute the desired positioning. The specific message content and the type of appeal used must emphasize the product dimensions important to the consumer as determined through research and established by the positioning strategy.

Message Content   Every advertising message is made up of both informational and persuasive elements. These two elements, in fact, are so intertwined that it is sometimes difficult to tell them apart. For example, basic information in many ads such as the product name, benefits, features, and price are presented in a way that tries to attract attention and encourage purchase. On the other hand, even the most persuasive advertisements have to contain at least some basic information to be successful. Importantly, the message content must stress the product's ability to deliver on benefits deemed important to a prospective buyer.

Message Appeal   Once advertisers determine message content, or what will be said, they must then determine how it will be said, or the message appeal. Information and persuasive content must be combined in the form of an appeal to provide the basic reason for the consumer to act. Although the marketer can use many different types of appeals, common advertising appeals include fear appeals, sex appeals, and humorous appeals.

Fear appeals suggest to the consumer that he can avoid some negative experience through the purchase and use of a product, or through a change in behaviour. Insurance companies often try to show the negative effects of premature death on the relatives of those who don't carry enough life or mortgage insurance. Food producers encourage the purchase of low-fat, high-fibre products as a means of reducing cholesterol levels and the possibility of a heart attack.[14] When using fear appeals, the advertiser must be sure that the appeal is strong enough to get the audience's attention and concern, but not so strong that it will lead them to "tune out" the message.

In contrast, *sex appeals* suggest to the audience that the product will increase the attractiveness of the user. Sex appeals can be found in almost any product category, from automobiles to toothpaste. Unfortunately, many commercials that use sex appeals are only successful at gaining the attention of the audience; they may have little impact on how consumers think, feel, or act. Some advertising experts even argue that such appeals get in the way of successful communication by distracting the audience from the purpose of the ad.

Humorous appeals imply either directly or more subtly that the product is more fun or exciting than competitors' offerings. Like fear and sex appeals, humour appeals are widely used in advertising and can be found in many product categories. Yokohama just recently used humour to market its snow tires in Quebec and the Maritimes. This is considered a departure from the traditional "serious approach" used by most tire manufacturers. Unfortunately for the advertiser, humour tends to wear out quickly, thus boring the consumer. Eveready ads, featuring the Energizer battery bunny, frequently change to avoid this advertising "wear-out."

A creative advertisement with "honesty" for Subaru.

Creating the Right Ad   The "creative people" in the company doing the advertising, or its advertising agency, have the responsibility to create attention-getting, believable advertising. The creative efforts involve determining specific message content and the use of an appropriate appeal.

In recent years, advertisers have become more concerned over the effectiveness of advertising. The debate over reasons for the success or failure of advertising programs usually comes down to a discussion of the ad itself or the media (e.g., television or radio) used. Recent Canadian research has found that only one in five new advertising campaigns are successful. Of those that fail, poorly designed ads account for almost 80 percent of the failures while media problems account for only 20 percent. Tandemar Advertising Research, of Montreal and Toronto, tracked 350 campaigns in 50 different categories over a four-year period, using a system called Adgraph Continuous Tracking.

Poor campaigns, according to Adgraph, usually involve one or more of the following problems: failure to make brand linkage (the association of the creative idea with the brand), lack of persuasive communication, inappropriate strategy, or poor use of media.

Better-performing ads tended to use mnemonic or brand linkage, relevance or consistency to historic image, uniqueness in a category, newsworthiness, and humour. What didn't appear to affect ad performance was energy level, use of music, use of animals, plot involvement, or soft versus hard sell. The study suggests that poor ad quality cannot be offset with heavy media buying. In other words, if the advertising is bad, advertisers cannot spend double in the media to make it better.[15]

Thus, the production quality of the ads is often just as important as the ad message itself. But, creating quality advertisements is a complex process. Producing artwork, layout, and production can be costly and time-consuming. A high-quality 30-second TV commercial typically costs about $150,000 to produce. Some can be much more expensive; two 15-second Rolaids commercials cost $500,000 and involved 75 people over a six-month period to produce. Typically, many "takes" are necessary to get things "right."[16]

In an attempt to ensure that the "right ads" are created, some advertising agencies are taking what they call a more "honest" approach. Growing consumer scepticism over advertising claims is one reason why advertisers feel this straightforward option is advisable. One agency that produces commercials for Subaru and Nike suggests that honesty in advertising can be startling and refreshing to the consumer, given the number of ads that are based on hype or exaggeration. The agency, Wieden & Kennedy, believes the success of the Subaru "what to drive" and Nike "just do it" ads is based on their honest, straightforward approach.[17]

Concept Check

1 **What are the characteristics of good advertising objectives?**

2 **What is the weakness of the percentage of sales budgeting approach?**

SELECTING THE RIGHT MEDIA

In addition to determining the right message and appeal, every advertiser must select the right media to place its advertisements. The *advertising media,* or the means by which the message is communicated to the target audience, include newspapers, magazines, radio, and TV, as well as other options. The "media selection" decision should be made on the basis of the target audience, type of product, nature of the message, campaign objectives, available budget, and costs of the alternative media. Figure 19–4 shows the net advertising revenues by major medium in Canada from 1986 to 1991. It shows that net advertising revenue grew, overall, from 1986 to 1990 but fell off in 1991 to $8.3 billion. This was the first drop in ad revenues in Canada in decades. The major cause of this decline, and of the predicted slow future growth for the major advertising media, is a shift in communications budgets to other elements of the promotional mix such as sales promotion and direct marketing.

Choosing a Medium and a Vehicle within That Medium   In deciding where to place advertisements, a company has several media to choose from and a number of alternatives, or vehicles, within each medium. Often advertisers use a mix of media forms and vehicles to maximize the exposure of the message to the target audience while at the same time minimizing costs. These two conflicting goals of maximizing exposure and minimizing costs are of central importance to media planning.

Basic Terms   Media buyers speak a language of their own, so all advertisers involved in selecting the right media for their campaigns must be familiar with

Figure 19-4

Net advertising revenues by medium in Canada (in thousands of dollars).

MEDIUM	1986	%	1987	%	1988	%	1989	%	1990	%	1991	%
Radio*	611,540	9.3	648,486	9.1	705,850	9.6	751,037	9.3	761,687	9.0	741,397	8.9
Television†	1,108,000	16.8	1,215,000	17.0	1,368,000	18.5	1,504,000	18.7	1,616,000	19.1	1,633,000	19.6
Dailies	1,203,570	18.3	1,278,000	17.8	1,447,939	19.6	1,472,788	18.3	1,521,925	18.0	1,441,462	17.3
Weekend supplements	31,058	0.5	28,800	0.4	26,292	0.4	24,110	0.3	21,723	0.3	20,573	0.3
Weeklies (semi, tri, etc.), including controlled distribution	459,048	7.0	520,000	7.3	604,656	8.2	656,052	8.1	690,823	8.2	654,200	7.9
Magazines, general	225,941	3.4	223,681	3.1	241,668	3.3	264,545	3.3	269,042	3.2	260,432	3.1
Business papers	157,544	2.4	165,100	2.3	154,067	2.1	194,339	2.4	207,943	2.5	155,953	1.9
Farm papers	21,102	0.3	20,200	0.3	22,878	0.3	23,821	0.3	25,488	0.3	19,116	0.2
Religious, school and other	43,409	0.7	44,299	0.6	40,971	0.5	42,213	0.5	46,012	0.5	52,914	0.6
Other print	1,587,884	24.1	1,700,049	23.8	1,450,900	19.6	1,588,800	19.7	1,604,700	19.0	1,680,100	20.2
Yellow pages‡	588,500	8.9	700,600	9.8	667,298	9.0	745,090	9.2	832,203	9.8	837,635	10.1
Outdoor§	545,000	8.3	610,000	8.5	658,800	8.9	796,489	9.9	855,429	10.1	828,050	9.9
Total, all media	6,582,596	100.0	7,154,215	100.0	7,389,319	100.0	8,063,284	100.0	8,452,975	100.0	8,324,832	100.0

*Includes estimated revenue from CBC.

†All figures revised to include revenue from specialty stations.

‡1986 and 1987 include revenue from city and phone directories; effective 1988 only revenues for yellow pages are included.

§Includes factory shipments of advertising signs and displays as well as firms in other outdoor advertising business (renting space, putting up billboards or other displays, placing advertising matter on streetcars, buses, and other transmit systems, and advertising revenue of other producers, show card writers, sign painters, etc.).

Source: Canadian Media Directors' Council, *Media Digest*, 1993–94, p. 6.

TERM	WHAT IT MEANS
Reach	The number of different people exposed to an advertisement.
Rating	The percentage of households in a market that are tuned to a particular TV show or radio station.
Frequency	The average number of times an individual is exposed to an advertisement.
Gross rating points (GRPs)	Reach multiplied by frequency.
Cost per thousand (CPM)	The cost of advertising divided by the number of thousands of individuals or households that are exposed.

▌*Figure 19–5*
The language of the media buyer.

some common terms used in the advertising industry. Figure 19–5 shows the most common terms used in media decisions.

Because advertisers try to maximize the number of individuals in the target market exposed to the message, they must be concerned with reach. **Reach** is the number of different people exposed to an advertisement.

The exact definition of reach sometimes varies among alternative media. Newspapers often use reach to describe their total circulation or the number of different households that buy the paper. Television and radio stations, in contrast, describe their audience using the term **rating**—the percentage of households in a market that are tuned to a particular TV show or radio station. In general, advertisers try to maximize reach in their target market at the lowest cost.

Although reach is important, advertisers are also interested in exposing their target audience to a message more than once. This is because consumers often do not pay close attention to advertising messages, some of which contain large amounts of relatively complex information. When advertisers want to reach the same audience more than once, they are concerned with **frequency,** the average number of times a person in the target audience is exposed to a message or an advertisement. Greater frequency is desirable, like greater reach.

When reach is multiplied by frequency, an advertiser will obtain a commonly used reference number called **gross rating points** (GRPs). To obtain the appropriate number of GRPs to achieve an advertising campaign's objectives, the media planner must balance reach and frequency. For example, a firm could have one ad plan that will reach 30 percent of Canadian households 5 times (on average) for a total of 150 GRPs, or it could have another plan that reaches 50 percent of Canadian households 3 times (on average) for a total of 150 GRPS. Which is better? While the reach is the same in both games, one plan gives greater frequency. If the costs are the same, the plan with the greater frequency would be more desirable. But often costs are not the same, so media planners must consider the comparative costs of various ad plans, usually on a cost per thousand basis. **Cost per thousand** (CPM) refers to the cost of reaching 1,000 individuals or households wtih an advertising message in a given medium (M is the Roman numeral for 1,000).

Advertisers with a finite ad budget cannot maximize both reach and frequency. With a fixed budget, reach and frequency are inversely related. If one goes up, the other goes down. In such situations, it is becoming more common for companies to trade some reach for greater frequency. In other words, advertisers will consciously decide to reach fewer customers but to communicate with them more frequently. Striking a balance between reach and frequency is important, but so is the overall weight (GRPs) of a campaign. Canadian research shows that ad campaigns with fewer than 100 GRPs per week media weight are far less effective than those between 100 and 125 GRPs.[18]

DIFFERENT MEDIA ALTERNATIVES

Figure 19–6 summarizes the advantages and disadvantages of the important advertising media. All, except direct mail, will be described in more detail. We have already examined direct mail in detail in Chapter 17 as a dominant direct marketing tool. However, you should remember that it is an advertising medium and is often used by companies that are not direct marketers.

Television   Television is a valuable medium because it communicates through both sight and sound. Print advertisements alone could never give you the sense of a sports car cornering at high speed or communicate Ford's excitement about its new Probe. In addition, television is the only medium that can reach 99

▌*Figure 19–6*
Advantages and disadvantages of major advertising media.

MEDIUM	ADVANTAGES	DISADVANTAGES
Television	Reaches extremely large audience; uses picture, print, sound, and motion for effect; can target specific audiences.	High cost to prepare and run ads; short exposure time and perishable message; difficult to convey complex information.
Radio	Low cost; can target specific audiences; ads can be placed quickly; can use sound, humour, and intimacy effectively.	No visual excitement; short exposure time and perishable message; difficult to convey complex information.
Magazines	Can target specific audiences; high-quality colour; long life of ad; ads can be clipped and saved; can convey complex information.	Long time needed to place ad; limited control of ad position; relatively high cost; competes for attention with other magazine features.
Newspapers	Excellent coverage of local markets; ads can be placed and changed quickly; ads can be saved; quick consumer response; low cost.	Ads compete for attention with other newspaper features; can't control ad position on page; short life span; can't target specific audiences.
Direct mail	Best for targeting specific audiences; very flexible (3D, pop-up ads); ad can be saved; measurable; no competition with editorial matter.	Relatively high cost; audience often sees it as "junk mail."
Outdoor	Low cost; local market focus; high visibility; opportunity for repeat exposures.	Message must be short and simple; low selectivity of audience; criticized as traffic hazard, eyesore.

Sources: C. L. Bovée and W. F. Arens, *Contemporary Advertising,* 4th ed. (Homewood, IL: Richard D. Irwin, 1992), pp. 437–44; and W. G. Nickels, J. M. McHugh, and S. M. McHugh, *Understanding Business,* 3rd ed. (Homewood, IL: Richard D. Irwin, 1993), p. 332.

percent of the homes in Canada.[19] On average, Canadian adults watch about 25 hours of TV a week.

Television's major disadvantage is cost: the price of a 30-second commercial on CTV, during prime time, can be as high as $28,000.[20] Because of these high charges, some advertisers have reduced the length of their commercials from 30 seconds to 15 seconds. This practice, referred to as *splitting 30s,* reduces costs but severely restricts the amount of information and emotion that can be conveyed.[21] All televison networks will accept 15-second commercials from advertisers, but the 30-second ad represents 75 percent of all TV commercials shown in Canada.[22] Another problem with television is the likelihood of wasted coverage—having people outside the market for the product see the advertisement. In recent years, the cost and wasted coverage problems of TV have been reduced through the introduction of cable TV. Advertising time is often less expensive on cable channels than the major networks. In addition, cable TV offers many specialty channels with very narrowly defined audiences such as MuchMusic, TSN, YTV, CBC Newsworld, and Chinavision, the first national Chinese-language pay television network in Canada.

The television networks are also working closer with advertisers to ensure the effectiveness of their TV advertising. For example, custom copywriting of a commercial to fit the program or program genre during which it airs has become popular. Eastern Bakeries of New Brunswick was one of the first Canadian advertisers to do a TV pool of commercials, custom-written for particular programs. For example, ad spots seen during "Dinosaurs" included references directly tied to the show such as a tongue-in-cheek recipe for "triceratops on toast."[23] It is hoped that this concept will provide greater advertising effectiveness, since the message is created and targeted for a specific TV show's audience.

Advertisers are also using direct-response television ads in order to better gauge the effectiveness of their advertisements. Some marketers suggest that an advertiser can tell whether a direct-response ad is effective or not because 90 percent of all responses to such ads will likely be received within 15 minutes after the ads' running.[24]

The newest development in television advertising is the **infomercial.** Originally, these program-length commercials (usually 30 minutes) were seen only on late-night television and often featured get-rich-quick schemes. Most of the infomercials were done in a direct-response format, with on-going requests for consumers to call a toll-free number for information or to order a product or service. But infomercials have become more mainstream and are being used to promote many of the top brands in the marketplace. Volvo and Saturn automobiles, for example, have used infomercials successfully. Many advertisers see the infomercial as a powerful advertising, sales promotion, and direct-response communications tool.

Radio   There are close to 700 radio stations broadcasting in Canada; about 52 percent are AM stations, and 48 percent are FM. Combined, these stations reach 95 percent of all people age 12 and over.[25] The major advantage of radio is that it is a segmented medium. There are many different stations with different programming formats designed to attract certain market segments (e.g., country

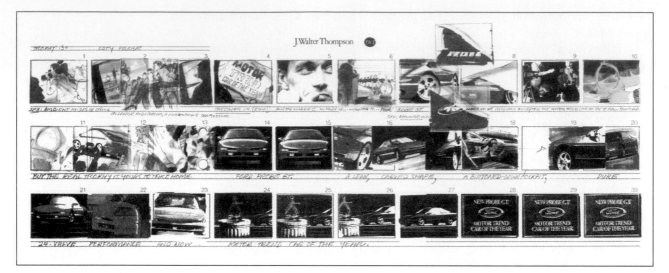

TV storyboards lead to commercials, which communicate with sight and sound.

stations, hard rock stations). The average adult in Canada, aged 18 or over, tunes in to radio about 23 hours per week. Radio is also a portable medium with good out-of-home reach, particularly during drive time.

The disadvantage of radio is that it has limited use for products that must be seen. Another problem is the ease with which consumers can tune out a commercial by switching stations. Radio is also a medium that must compete for people's attention as they engage in other activities such as driving, working, or relaxing. Peak listening time for radio in Canada is between 6 A.M. and 9 A.M.

Magazines   There are over 500 consumer magazines in Canada, as well as several important general business magazines.[26] The marketing advantage of this medium is the great number of special-interest publications that appeal to narrowly defined segments. Skiers read *Ski Canada* magazine, craftspeople subscribe to *Crafts Plus,* pet owners buy *Pets* magazine, and gardeners peruse *Canadian Gardening*. Each magazine's readers often represent a unique customer profile. *The Hockey News* has a distinctively male, sports-oriented audience, so a hockey equipment manufacturer that places an ad in *The Hockey News* knows it is reaching the desired target audience. In addition to the distinct audience profiles of magazines, good colour production is an advantage that allows magazines to create strong images.[27]

The cost of advertising in national magazines is a disadvantage. The cost of a full-page, four-colour ad in *Maclean's* is over $26,000. But many national publications publish regional editions (*Maclean's* publishes 13), which reduce absolute cost and wasted coverage. In addition to cost, a limitation of magazines is their infrequency. At best, magazines are printed on a weekly basis, with many specialized publications appearing only monthly or less often.

High technology is arriving in magazine ads. Cardboard pop-up ads have been used by Dodge trucks, for example. Revlon offered actual samples of eye shadow in fashion magazines, and if you read *Architectural Digest* you could even

smell a Rolls-Royce interior using a special scent strip. And for something new? Interactive disk ad inserts! Recently, Apple Canada inserted a DOS-formatted 3.5-inch diskette into 28,000 subscriber and newsstand copies of *Profit* magazine. The disk provides users a sample of Apple's graphical user interface. The interactive element of the diskette allows readers to explore Apple technology.[28] *Canadian Business* magazine plans to offer Corporate 500 data on a diskette insert, around which ad space will be available.

Newspapers Newspapers are an important local medium with excellent reach potential. There are over 100 daily newspapers and over 1,000 community newspapers in Canada. The average paid circulation for the dailies is over 5 million copies, and the average weekly circulation for the weeklies is over 14 million. Household penetration of the dailies is 63 percent. About 62 percent of Canadians read a weekly paper.[29] Dailies allow advertisements to focus on specific current events, such as a 24-hour sale. Community newspapers can be used by local retailers and other businesses with a good degree of certainty of reaching customers in their trade area. Local retailers often use newspapers as their primary advertising medium.

Newspapers are rarely saved by the purchaser, so companies are generally limited to ads that call for immediate customer action, or direct response (although customers can clip and save ads they want). Companies also cannot depend on newspapers for colour reproduction as good as that in most magazines.

National advertising campaigns rarely include this medium except in conjunction with local distributors of their products. In these instances both parties often share the advertising cost, using a cooperative advertising program, as described in Chapter 18.

Outdoor A very effective medium for reminding consumers about your product is outdoor advertising. The most common form of outdoor advertising,

called *billboards,* often results in good reach and frequency and has been shown to increase purchase rates.[30] The visibility of this medium is good supplemental reinforcement for well-known products, and it is a relatively low-cost, flexible media alternative. A company can buy space just in the desired geographic market. A disadvantage to billboards, however, is that no opportunity exists for lengthy advertising copy. Also, a good billboard depends on traffic patterns and sight lines. In many areas, environmental laws have limited the use of this medium. To overcome some of the problems faced by street-level billboards, mall posters are available at 400 shopping centres across Canada and are designed to reach pedestrian traffic coming to and leaving the malls. Transit shelter advertising is also available in many markets.

If you ever lived in a metropolitan area, chances are you might have seen another form of outdoor advertising, transit advertising (not be to confused with transit shelter ads). This medium includes messages on the interiors and exteriors of buses, subway cars, and taxis. As the use of mass transit grows, transit advertising may become increasingly important. Selectivity is available to advertisers, who can buy space by neighbourhood or bus route. Total-paint buses are also available, buses that may be totally painted on the outside to carry an advertising message. One disadvantage to this medium is that the heavy travel times, when audiences are the largest, are not conducive to reading advertising copy. People are standing shoulder to shoulder on the subway, hoping not to miss their stop, and little attention is paid to the advertising.

Other Media   As traditional media have become more expensive and cluttered, advertisers have been attracted to a variety of nontraditional advertising options, called *place-based media.* Messages are placed in locations that attract a specific target audience such as airports, doctors' offices, health clubs, bars, theatres (where ads are played on the screen before the movies are shown),[31] elevators, the Jumbotron at SkyDome, and even public bathroom stalls. Other new media options include *product placement*—paying to have a brand-name product used in a movie—or even placing an ad in video games (see the accompanying Marketing Action Memo), as well as *electronic advertising* such as automatic dialing systems to deliver prerecorded messages to telephone users.

MARKETING·ACTION·MEMO

Product Placement in Video Games: A New Advertising Medium

According to Microtime Media, a London-based agency, video and computer games are destined to be the next big thing in advertising. The agency says the popularity of interactive entertainment makes it ideal for product placement. In just over 10 years, the industry has grown into a business worth $8 billion dominated by Japan's Sega and Nintendo. Now, leading advertisers such as PepsiCo International, Coca-Cola, snack-food giant McVities, and the Professional Golf Association are selling their wares via the games.

Microtime, pioneer of this emerging advertising medium, says the video and computer games guarantee a captive audience. According to Daniel Bobroff, the agency's managing director, "With interactive entertainment, your audience's attention is heightened. They can't disappear to make a cup of tea during a commercial break." Advertisers were initially sceptical, questioning the effectiveness of the medium, but now they cannot deny its popularity. In the United Kingdom, 87 percent of 5 to 19-year-olds play interactive games regularly, and according to other research, household penetration by the hardware is about 30 percent in the United Kingdom, 20 percent in Germany, and 18 percent in France.

And now that compact discs can store television-quality graphics, advertisers can no longer ignore the games' potential. Microtime, which is seeking to expand across Europe, has already sold space on 20 titles, including space on the best-selling James Pond II–Codename Robocod for McVities Penguin biscuits. Volvo and Canon will sponsor the newly released PGA European Tour game, targeted at golf enthusiasts. Bobroff says that advertising benefits the consumer by reducing the cost of the games' technology and hence the price. As we saw in the opening vignette in Chapter 14, video game companies have been looking at ways to offer their technology to consumers at price points that create value. With product placement, they may have found a unique way to do so.

Source: Adapted from J. Koranteng, "Now, a Product Placement from Our Sponsor," *Marketing*, April 4, 1994, p. 10.

Selection Criteria   Choosing among these alternative media is difficult and hinges on several factors. First, knowing the media habits of the target audience is essential to deciding among the alternatives. Second, product attributes occasionally necessitate that certain media be used. For example, if colour is a major aspect of the product appeal, radio is excluded. Newspapers allow advertising for quick action to confront competitors, and magazines are more appropriate for complicated messages because the reader can spend more time reading the message. The final factor in selecting a medium is cost. When possible, alternative media are compared using a common denominator that reflects both reach and cost—a measure such as CPM.

SCHEDULING THE ADVERTISING

There is no correct schedule to advertise a product, but three factors must be considered. First is the issue of *buyer turnover,* which is how often new buyers enter the market to buy the product. The higher the buyer turnover, the greater

An ad to stimulate
seasonal demand.

is the amount of advertising required. A second issue in scheduling is the *purchase frequency;* the more frequently the product is purchased, the less repetition is required. Finally, companies must consider the *forgetting rate,* the speed with which buyers forget the brand if advertising is not seen.

Setting schedules requires an understanding of how the market behaves. Most companies tend to follow one of three basic approaches:

1 *Steady ("drip") schedule.* When seasonal factors are unimportant, advertising is run at a steady or regular schedule throughout the year.
2 *Flighting ("intermittent") schedule.* Periods of advertising are scheduled between periods of no advertising to reflect seasonal demand.
3 *Pulse ("burst") schedule.* A flighting schedule is combined with a steady schedule because of increases in demand, heavy periods of promotion, or introduction of a new product.

For example, products such as dry breakfast cereals have a stable demand throughout the year and would typically use a steady schedule of advertising. In contrast, products such as snow skis and suntan lotions have seasonal demands and receive flighting-schedule advertising during the seasonal demand period. Some products such as toys or automobiles require pulse-schedule advertising to facilitate sales throughout the year and during special periods of increased demand (such as holidays or new car introductions). Some evidence suggests that pulsing schedules are superior to other advertising strategies.[32]

Concept Check

1 You see the same ad in *Time* and *Maclean's* magazines and on billboards and TV. Is this an example of reach or frequency?

2 What is the most selective medium available?

3 What factors must be considered when choosing among alternative media?

EXECUTING THE ADVERTISING PROGRAM

As shown earlier in Figure 19–1, executing the advertising program involves pretesting the advertising message and actually carrying out the advertising program. John Wanamaker once remarked, "I know half my advertising is wasted, but I don't know what half." By evaluating advertising efforts, marketers can try to ensure that their advertising expenditures are not wasted.[33] Evaluation is usually done at two separate times: before and after the advertisements are run in the actual campaign. Several methods used in the evaluation process at the stages of idea formulation and message development will be discussed here. Posttesting methods are reviewed in the section on evaluation.

PRETESTING ADVERTISING

To determine whether the advertisement communicates the intended message or to select among alternative versions of the advertisement, **pretests** are conducted before the advertisements are placed in any medium.

Portfolio Tests Portfolio tests are used to test message alternatives. The test ad is placed in a portfolio with several other ads and stories, and consumers are asked to read through the portfolio. Afterward subjects are asked for their impressions of the ads on several evaluative scales, such as from "very informative" to "not very informative."

Jury Tests Jury tests involve showing the ad to a panel of consumers and having them rate how they liked it, how much it drew their attention, and how attractive they thought it was. This approach is similar to the portfolio test in that consumer reactions are obtained. However, unlike the portfolio test, a test advertisement is not hidden within other ads.

Theatre Tests Theatre testing is the most sophisticated form of pretesting. Consumers are invited to view new television shows or movies in which test commercials are also shown. Viewers register their feelings about the advertisements either on hand-held electronic recording devices used during the viewing or on questionnaires afterward.

CARRYING OUT THE ADVERTISING PROGRAM

The responsibility for actually carrying out the advertising program can be handled in one of three ways, as shown in Figure 19–7. The **full-service agency** provides the most complete range of services, including market research, media selection, message development, artwork, and production. Agencies that assist a client by both developing and placing advertisements are usually compensated by receiving 15 percent of media costs. However, many advertising agencies are now charging a straight fee for service, since the commission-based system has come under attack by advertisers. The credibility of the agency's advice to increase advertising expenditures is often called into question when the agency gains additional compensation as the ad budget increases. Many advertising agencies are aware of this problem. Some have even started to offer a money-back guarantee if the advertising doesn't produce results (see the accompanying Marketing Action Memo).

    Limited-service agencies specialize in one aspect of the advertising process such as providing creative services to develop the advertising copy or buying previously unpurchased media space. Limited-service agencies that deal in creative work are compensated by a contractual agreement for the services

TYPE OF AGENCY	SERVICES PROVIDED
Full-service agency	Does research, selects media, develops message, and produces artwork
Limited-service agency	Specializes in one aspect of creative process; usually provides creative production work; buys previously unpurchased media space
In-house agency	Provides range of services, depending on company needs

▌ *Figure 19–7*
Alternative structures of advertising agencies used to carry out the advertising program.

MARKETING · ACTION · MEMO

A Money-Back Guarantee from an Ad Agency?

Richards & Company has challenged Labatt Breweries president Hugo Powell to put his money where his mouth is. Powell, who lashed out at agencies' lack of accountability in a speech to the Canadian Congress of Advertising, was one of 30 corporate presidents who received a direct mail piece from Toronto-based R&C promoting its money-back guarantee, under which upper and lower performance targets are set. If final results fall below the lowest target, Richards would only receive its per-hour cost rate, making no profit. But if results exceed the target, its profit margin will rise accordingly on a prorated basis.

Agency founder Brian Richards said he will not guarantee sales, because of the many influences outside agency control, but he will guarantee such things as awareness building, trial and retrial, coupon redemption, and store traffic building. Although the agency has been offering the guarantee since 1980, the Upper Canada Brewing Company recently became the first to accept it. Richards said he has $120,000 riding on the guarantee of trial and regular-use targets, but is not "losing any sleep" over the possible outcome, because the brewery's market share has "already increased substantially."

The days of subjective decision making on strategic and creative issues are coming to an end, Richards said, and in today's business climate companies "would be wise to examine one of their largest 'unaudited' expenditures and insist on accountability." Richards said that while his direct mail piece resulted in five good leads, he is not optimistic the industry will soon see the changes that Powell calls for. Richards puts the blame on traditional agencies, which promote creative work that wins awards but not sales results. He also said clients suffer from "a Canadian disease—they don't trust [the guarantee]. They would rather stay with their own agency [which] has no responsibility for anything, no accountability. If I tried this in the U.S., I would have no problem. But here the entrenched thinking is frightening." Even Powell, Richards said, has not replied to his offer.

Source: Adapted from L. Medcalf, "Ad Agency Offers a Money-Back Guarantee," *Marketing,* March 22, 1993, p. 3.

performed. Finally, **in-house agencies** made up of the company's own advertising staff may provide full services or a limited range of services.

EVALUATING THE ADVERTISING PROGRAM

The advertising decision process does not stop with executing the advertising program. The advertisements must be posttested to determine whether they are achieving their intended objectives, and results may indicate that changes must be made in the advertising program.

POSTTESTING ADVERTISING

An advertisement may go through **posttests** after it has been shown to the target audience to determine whether it accomplished its intended purpose. Five approaches common in posttesting are:[34]

Starch scores an
advertisement.

Aided Recall (Recognition–Readership)   After being shown an ad, respondents are asked whether their previous exposure to it was through reading,
viewing, or listening. The Starch test, shown in the accompanying photo, uses
aided recall to determine the percentage who remember seeing a specific magazine ad (*noted*), who saw or read any part of the ad identifying the product or
brand (*seen–associated*), and who read at least half of the ad (*read most*). Elements
of the ad are then tagged with the results, as shown in the picture.

Unaided Recall   A question such as, "What ads do you remember seeing
yesterday?" is asked of respondents without any prompting to determine
whether they saw or heard advertising messages.

Attitude Tests   Respondents are asked questions to measure changes in their
attitudes after an advertising campaign, such as whether they have a more
favourable attitude toward the product advertised.[35]

Inquiry Tests   Additional product information, product samples, or premiums
are offered to an ad's readers or viewers. Ads generating the most inquiries are
presumed to be the most effective.

Sales Tests   Sales tests involve studies such as controlled experiments (e.g.,
using radio ads in one market and newspaper ads in another and comparing the
results) and consumer purchase tests (measuring retail sales that result from a
given advertising campaign). The most sophisticated experimental methods
today allow a manufacturer, a distributor, or an advertising agency to manipulate
an advertising variable (such as schedule or message) through cable systems and
observe subsequent sales effects by monitoring data collected from checkout
scanners in supermarkets.[36]

MAKING NEEDED CHANGES

Results of posttesting the advertising copy are used to reach decisions about changes in the advertising program. If the posttest results show that an advertisement is doing poorly in terms of awareness or cost efficiency, it may be dropped and other ads run in its place in the future. On the other hand, sometimes an advertisement may be so successful it is run repeatedly or used as the basis of a larger advertising program. The Chevy truck ad campaign "like a rock" is a good example.

IMPORTANT CHANGES IN ADVERTISING AND SOCIETY

Advertising has been attacked by critics with accusations that it is often misleading, manipulates children, debases language, creates materialism, and perpetuates stereotyping of women and minorities. Canadian research shows that consumers do have some negative feelings toward advertising. In particular, most Canadians believe it does manipulate children and that it is often misleading. One study found that almost 70 percent of consumers surveyed wanted more regulation on advertising; over 40 percent wanted alcohol advertising banned, and 30 percent wanted all children's advertising banned.[37] The Canadian government banned the use of commercial advertising by tobacco companies over five years ago, but the Ethics and Social Responsibility Alert shows how some tobacco companies are skirting the ban.

ETHICS AND SOCIAL RESPONSIBILITY ALERT

The Ethics of Tobacco Companies That Skirt the Ad Ban

Apparently, the five-year-old tobacco ad ban in Canada is not preventing cigarette companies from reaching their target markets, including the young adult, according to a report by the Canadian Council on Smoking and Health. The study suggests that people in the Ottawa–Hull area are exposed to tobacco company communications through the use of "sponsorhip ads." The study estimates that consumers are exposed at least 295 million times per year to such ads. The council says this form of advertising is extremely visible to children, despite the industry's claim that its marketing does not target the young. The report criticized Imperial Tobacco of Montreal's use of transit advertising to promote the Matinee Ltd. Fashion Foundation, noting that 100,000 students ride Ottawa's OC Transpo buses daily. The council is calling for the federal government either to ban tobacco sponsorship advertising or require that tobacco products be sold in plain packages to break the link between the packages and the sponsorship ads.

What do you think about this situation? While the tobacco companies are within the legal guidelines set by the Canadian government, is this form of advertising ethical?

Source: Adapted from "Tobacco Sponsorships Skirt Ad Ban," *Marketing*, January 31, 1994, p. 1.

Several aspects of advertising are changing given the interests and concerns of society. The first is advertising to children. There are both tighter government regulations and self-regulatory guidelines set by advertising organizations to control advertising directed toward children. For instance, Quebec does not allow any advertising directed toward children. The Canadian Code of Advertising Standards sets specific guidelines for advertisers who do advertise to children outside Quebec. YTV, a youth specialty channel in Canada, does not accept commercials between Monday and Friday, 9:00 AM to 3:30 PM, prime viewing times for preschoolers. In addition, there are no commercial messages allowed during any program for children under five years of age.

The second change involves a move toward more realistic advertising. This includes the realistic depiction of women and minorities and the use of situations that reflect reality (e.g., divorce and death). Realistic portrayals of women and minorities are not only desirable but fundamental in a modern marketplace. While one Canadian study found that women believe they are not realistically depicted in advertising and are offended by existing depictions,[38] other research shows that Canadian advertisers are moving to improve the situation.[39] Such initiatives are socially desirable and can only help improve the consumer's image of advertising in the long run.

The use of advertising by professionals (e.g., lawyers, dentists, accountants) is another area where change is occurring. Many professional bodies are relaxing their restrictions on the use of advertising. Most professionals and consumers appear to want such liberalization of professional services advertising.[40]

Concept Check

1 Explain the difference between pretesting and posttesting of advertising messages.

2 What is the difference between aided- and unaided-recall posttests?

Summary

1 Advertising may be classified as either product or institutional, and can be further classified in terms of whether it is seeking a direct-response or delayed-response from the consumer. Product advertising can take three forms: pioneering, competitive, or reminder. Institutional ads are of these three types plus one more: advocacy.

2 The advertising decision process involves developing, executing, and evaluating the advertising program. Developing the advertising program focusses on determining who is the target audience, what to say, when to say it, and where the message should be said.

3 Setting advertising objectives is based on the hierarchy of effects. Objectives should be measurable, have a specified time period, and state the target audience.

4 Budgeting methods often used are percentage of sales, competitive parity, and the all you can afford approaches. The best budgeting approach is based on the objectives set and tasks required.

5 The ad message and appeal must execute the firms's desired product positioning, stressing the key benefits of a product to the target audience. Common appeals include fear, sex, and humour.

6 In selecting the right medium, there are distinct trade-offs among television, radio, magazine, newspaper, outdoor, and other media. The decision is based on media habits of the target audience, product characteristics, message requirements, and media costs.

7 In determining advertising schedules, a balance must be made between reach and frequency. Scheduling must take into account buyer turnover, purchase frequency, and the rate at which consumers forget.

8 Advertising is evaluated before and after the ad is run. Pretesting can be done with portfolio, jury, or theatre tests. Posttesting is done on the basis of aided recall, unaided recall, attitude tests, inquiry tests, and sales tests.

9 To execute an advertising program, companies can use several types of advertising agencies. These firms can provide a full range of services or specialize in creative or placement activities. Some firms use their own in-house agency.

Key Terms and Concepts

advertising p. 480
product advertisements p. 480
institutional advertisements p. 481
direct-response advertising p. 482
delayed-response advertising p. 482
hierarchy of effects p. 484
percentage of sales budgeting p. 485
competitive parity budgeting p. 485
all you can afford budgeting p. 485
objective and task budgeting p. 486
reach p. 491

rating p. 491
frequency p. 491
gross rating points p. 491
cost per thousand p. 491
infomercial p. 493
pretests p. 498
full-service agency p. 499
limited-service agencies p. 499
in-house agencies p. 500
posttests p. 500

Chapter Problems and Applications

1 How does competitive product advertising differ from competitive institutional advertising?

2 Suppose you are the advertising manager for a new line of children's fragrances. Which form of media would you use for this new product?

3 You have recently been promoted to be director of advertising for the Timkin Tool Company. In your first meeting with Mr. Timkin, he says, "Advertising is a waste! We've been advertising for six months now and sales haven't increased. Tell me why we should continue." Give your answer to Mr. Timkin.

4 A large life insurance company has decided to switch from using a strong fear appeal to a humorous approach. What are the strengths and weaknesses of such a change in message strategy?

5 Some national advertisers have found that they can have more impact with their advertising by running a large number of ads for a period and then running no ads at all for a period. Why might such a flighting schedule be more effective than a steady schedule?

6 Which medium has the lowest cost per thousand?

MEDIUM	COST	AUDIENCE
TV show	$5,000	25,000
Magazine	2,200	6,000
Newspaper	4,800	7,200
FM radio	420	1,600

7 Suppose a Canadian bank has just developed two versions of an advertisement to encourage senior citizens to direct-deposit their old-age pension checks with the bank. Direct deposit means the government sends the funds directly to the bank, so that the consumer does not have to go and deposit the check. Suggest how the bank can evaluate the two ads.

8 The Toro Company has a broad product line. What timing approach would you recommend for the advertising of (*a*) the lawn mower line and (*b*) the new line of lawn and garden furniture?

9 What are two advantages and two disadvantages of the advertising posttests described in the chapter?

10 What advantages does direct-response advertising have over delayed-response advertising? Why isn't all advertising designed to be direct response?

CHAPTER 20

Personal Selling and Sales Management

AFTER READING THIS CHAPTER YOU SHOULD BE ABLE TO:

▸ Recognize different types of personal selling.

▸ Describe the stages in the personal selling process.

▸ Specify the functions and tasks in the sales management process.

▸ Determine whether a firm should use manufacturer's representatives or a company sales force.

▸ Calculate the number of people needed in a company's sales force.

▸ Understand how firms recruit, select, train, motivate, compensate, and evaluate salespeople.

The Sales Professional

For many people, the word *salesperson* conjures up an image of a fast-talking, yarn-spinning individual in loud clothes who travels a lot and is only interested in peddling his products, even if the customer doesn't need or want them. This stereotypical image of a salesperson still exists in the minds of many people and is actually perpetuated in movies, television, and the press. Yet, the modern professional salesperson is nothing like that. Over 1 million Canadians work in sales, and most recognize the important role they play in their organizations.[1] Today's sales professionals are the vital link between the customer and the organization. They are often highly trained, are given freedom to act, and receive financial rewards associated with attracting customers and cultivating satisfying relationships with them over time.

Many successful salespeople often become an important part of an organization's management team. A sales manager, for example, is responsible for recruiting, selecting, training, managing, and compensating salespeople. Many leading executives in Canadian corporations started their careers in sales. Most of them believe that selling allowed them to learn about the business from the ground up. Most important, understanding the needs of customers enabled them to become effective decision makers in their new executive roles. Many college students—perhaps yourself—either have a negative image of the sales profession or are at least aware of the perceived negativity associated with this career. Unfortunately, this mind-set often serves as a barrier in attracting capable individuals into a profession that can offer valuable rewards, including financial and personal growth.

Success as a professional salesperson requires really understanding customers' needs, sound knowledge of the company's products, effective communications skills, and a desire to ensure customer satisfaction after the sale. It has been said many times that nothing happens in business until a product is sold. The professional salesperson is often the catalyst in making business happen. This chapter examines the scope and significance of personal selling and sales management in marketing. It highlights the many forms of personal selling and outlines the selling process. Finally, the functions of sales management are described.

SCOPE AND SIGNIFICANCE OF PERSONAL SELLING AND SALES MANAGEMENT

Chapter 18 described personal selling and management of the sales effort as part of a firm's promotional mix. Although it is important to recognize that personal selling is a useful vehicle for communicating with present and potential buyers, it is much more. Take a moment to answer the questions in the personal selling and sales management quiz in Figure 20–1. As you read on, compare your answers with those in the text.

NATURE OF PERSONAL SELLING AND SALES MANAGEMENT

Personal selling requires a two-way flow of communication between a buyer and a seller—often in a face-to-face encounter—designed to influence a person's or group's purchase decision. However, with advances in telecommunications, personal selling also takes place over the telephone, through teleconferencing and interactive computer links between buyers and sellers.

Personal selling remains a highly human-intensive activity despite the use of technology. Accordingly, the salepeople must be managed. **Sales management** consists of planning the selling program and implementing and controlling the personal selling effort of the firm. Numerous tasks are involved in managing personal selling, including setting objectives; organizing the sales

▌*Figure 20–1*
Personal selling and sales management quiz.

1 About how much does it cost for a consumer product salesperson to make a single sales call? (check one)

$100 _____ $150 _____ $200 _____
$125 _____ $175 _____ $225 _____

2 "A salesperson's job is finished when a sale is made." True or false? (circle one)
True   False

3 On average, sales training programs devote about what percentage of time to sales techniques? (check one)

20% _____   40% _____   60% _____
30% _____   50% _____   70% _____

force; recruiting, selecting, training, and compensating salespeople; and evaluating the performance of individual salespeople.

PERVASIVENESS OF SELLING

"Everyone lives by selling something," wrote the author Robert Louis Stevenson a century ago. His observation still holds true today. In reality, every occupation that involves customer contact has an element of personal selling. For example, lawyers, accountants, bankers, and company personnel recruiters perform sales-related activities, whether or not they acknowledge it.

The over 1 million people classified as salespeople in Canada work in a variety of sales positions. They work as manufacturing sales personnel, real estate brokers, stockbrokers, or salesclerks in retail stores.

Many executives in major companies have held sales positions at some time in their careers. For example, Victor Kiam, the flamboyant president and chief executive officer of Remington Products, Inc., previously held a sales position at Lever Brothers. It might be said that today Kiam is Remington's most visible salesperson. Many key executives in major Canadian companies have significant sales and marketing experience in their work history. Thus, selling often serves as a stepping-stone to top management, as well as being a career path in itself.

PERSONAL SELLING IN MARKETING

Personal selling serves three major roles in a firm's overall marketing effort. First, salespeople are the critical link between the firm and its customers. This role requires that salespeople match company interests with customer needs to satisfy both parties in the exchange process. Second, salespeople *are* the company in a consumer's eyes. They represent what a company is or attempts to be and are often the only personal contact a customer has with the company. For example, the "look" projected by salespeople for Avon Products, Inc., is an important factor in communicating the benefits of the company's cosmetic line.

Third, personal selling may play a dominant role in a firm's promotional efforts. This situation typically arises when a firm uses a push strategy, described

Victor Kiam, president and CEO of Remington Products, Inc., is also Remington's "principal salesperson."

in Chapter 18. Avon, for example, pays almost 40 percent of its total sales dollars for selling expenses.[2] Pharmaceutical firms and office and educational equipment manufacturers also rely heavily on personal selling in the promotion of their products.

CREATING CUSTOMER VALUE THROUGH SALESPEOPLE

As the critical link between the firm and its customers, salespeople can create customer value in many ways. For instance, by being close to the customer, salespeople can identify creative solutions to customer problems. Salespeople can create value by easing the customer buying process, offering instructions and advice. Customer value is also created by salespeople who follow through after the sale to ensure that customers are satisfied and to find out whether they need any further assistance.

Customer value creation is made possible by **relationship selling,** the practice of building ties to customers through a salesperson's attention and commitment to customer needs over time. Relationship selling involves mutual respect and trust among buyers and sellers. It focusses on creating long-term customers, not a one-time sale.[3]

Concept Check	1 **What is personal selling?**
	2 **What is involved in sales management?**

THE MANY FORMS OF PERSONAL SELLING

Personal selling assumes many forms based on the amount of selling done and the amount of creativity required to perform the sales task. Broadly speaking, three types of personal selling exist: order taking, order getting, and sales support activities.[4] While some firms use only one of these types of personal selling, others use a combination of all three. Figure 20–2 compares order getters and order takers to illustrate some important differences between them.

ORDER TAKING

Typically, an **order taker** processes routine orders or reorders for products that were already sold by the company. The primary responsibility of order takers is to preserve an ongoing relationship with existing customers and maintain sales. Two types of order takers exist. *Outside order takers* visit customers and replenish inventory stocks of resellers, such as retailers or wholesalers. For example, Frito-Lay salespeople call on supermarkets, neighbourhood grocery stores, and other establishments to ensure that the company's line of snack products (such as Doritos and Tostitos) is in adequate supply. In addition, outside order takers typically provide assistance in arranging displays. *Inside order takers,* also called *order clerks* or *salesclerks,* typically answer simple questions, take orders, and

▌ *Figure 20–2*
Comparing order takers and order getters.

BASIS OF COMPARISON	ORDER TAKERS	ORDER GETTERS
Objective	Handle routine product orders or reorders	Identify new customers and sales opportunities
Purchase situation	Focus on straight rebuy purchase situations	Focus on new buy and modified rebuy purchase situations
Activity	Perform order processing functions	Act as creative problem solvers
Training	Require significant clerical training	Require significant sales training
Source of sales	Maintain sales volume	Create new sales volume

complete transactions with customers. Many retail clerks are inside order takers, as are people who take orders from buyers by telephone. In industrial settings, order taking arises in straight rebuy situations. Order takers, for the most part, do little selling in a conventional sense and engage in little problem solving with customers. They often represent simple products that have few options, such as confectionery items, magazine subscriptions, and highly standardized industrial products.

ORDER GETTING

An **order getter** sells in a conventional sense and identifies prospective customers, provides customers with information, persuades customers to buy, closes sales, and follows up on customers' use of a product or service. Like order takers, order getters can be inside (an automobile salesperson) or outside (an IBM salesperson). Order getting involves a high degree of creativity and customer empathy and typically is required for selling complex or technical products with many options, so considerable product knowledge and sales training are necessary. In modified rebuy or new buy purchase situations in industrial selling, an order getter acts as a problem solver who identifies how a particular product may satisfy a customer's need. Similarly, in the purchase of a service, such as insurance, an insurance agent can provide a mix of plans to satisfy a buyer's needs depending on income, stage of the family's life cycle, and investment objectives.

Order getting is an expensive process.[5] It is estimated that the median direct cost of a single sales call for an industrial product is $198.67; for a consumer product, $210.43; and for a service, $193.58. (What amount did you check for question 1 in Figure 20–1?) The direct annual cost for a "typical" salesperson, with compensation and field expenses (including travel, entertainment, food, and lodging), is $52,594 for industrial products, $48,659 for consumer products, and $48,461 for services. These costs illustrate why telephone selling (telemarketing), with a significantly lower cost per call (in the range of $20 to $25) and little or no field expense, is so popular today.

A Xerox Corporation advertisement featuring team selling.

SALES SUPPORT PERSONNEL

Sales support personnel augment the selling effort of order getters by performing a variety of services. For example, **missionary salespeople** do not directly solicit orders but rather concentrate on performing promotional activities and introducing new products. They are used extensively in the pharmaceutical industry, where they persuade physicians to prescribe a firm's product. Actual sales are made through wholesalers or directly to pharmacists who fill prescriptions. A **sales engineer** is a salesperson who specializes in identifying, analyzing, and solving customer problems and brings know-how and technical expertise to the selling situation, but often does not actually sell products and services. Sales engineers are popular in selling industrial products such as chemicals and heavy equipment.

In many situations, firms engage in **team selling,** the practice of using an entire team of professionals in selling to and servicing major customers.[6] Team selling is used when specialized knowledge is needed to satisfy the different interests of individuals in a customer's buying centre. For example, a selling team might consist of a salesperson, a sales engineer, a service representative, and a financial executive, each of whom would deal with a counterpart in the customer's firm. Team selling takes different forms. In **conference selling,** a salesperson and other company resource people meet with buyers to discuss problems and opportunities. In **seminar selling,** a company team conducts an educational program for a customer's technical staff, describing state-of-the-art developments. IBM and Xerox Corporation pioneered team selling in working with prospective buyers. Other firms have embraced this practice and created value for their customers, as described in the accompanying Marketing Action Memo.

MARKETING · ACTION · MEMO

Creating Customer Value through Team Selling

The day of the lone salesperson calling on a customer is rapidly becoming history. Many companies today are using teams of professionals to work with customers to improve relationships, find better ways of doing things, and, of course, create and sustain value for their customers.

Xerox and IBM pioneered team selling, but other firms were quick to follow as they spotted the potential to create and sustain value for their customers. Recognizing that corn growers needed a herbicide they could apply less often, a Du Pont team of chemists, sales and marketing executives, and regulatory specialists created just the right product that recorded sales of $57 million in its first year. Procter & Gamble uses teams of marketing, sales, advertising, computer systems, and distribution personnel to work with its major retailers to identify ways to develop, promote, and deliver products. Pitney Bowes, Inc., which produces sophisticated computer systems that weigh,

rate, and track packages for firms like UPS and Federal Express, also uses sales teams to meet customer needs. These teams consist of sales personnel, "carrier management specialists," and engineering and administrative executives who continually find ways to improve the technology of shipping goods across town and around the world.

Efforts to create and sustain customer value through team selling will become more popular as customers also seek greater value for their money. According to the vice president for procurement of a Fortune 500 company, "Today, it's not just getting the best price but getting the best value—and there are a lot of pieces to value."

Sources: Based on "Smart Selling," *Business Week,* August 3, 1992, pp. 16–50; S. Caminiti, "Finding New Ways to Sell More," *Fortune,* July 27, 1992, pp. 100–103; and T. Murray, "Team Selling: What's the Incentive?" *Sales & Marketing Management,* June 1991, pp. 89–92.

Concept Check

1 **What is the principal difference between an order taker and an order getter?**

2 **What is team selling?**

THE PERSONAL SELLING PROCESS: BUILDING RELATIONSHIPS

Selling, and particularly order getting, is a complicated activity that involves building buyer–seller relationships. Although the salesperson–customer interaction is essential to personal selling, much of a salesperson's work occurs before this meeting and continues after the sale itself. The **personal selling process** consists of six stages: prospecting, preapproach, approach, presentation, close, and follow-up (Figure 20–3).

PROSPECTING

Personal selling begins with *prospecting*—the search for and qualification of potential customers.[7] For some products that are one-time purchases such as

Figure 20–3
Stages and objectives of the personal selling process.

STAGE	OBJECTIVE	COMMENTS
Prospecting	Search for and qualify prospects	Start of the selling process; prospects produced through advertising, referrals, and cold canvassing.
Preapproach	Gather information and decide how to approach the prospect	Information sources include personal observation, other customers, and own salespeople.
Approach	Gain prospect's attention, stimulate interest, and make transition to the presentation	First impression is critical; gain attention and interest through reference to common acquaintances, a referral, or product demonstration.
Presentation	Begin converting a prospect into a customer by creating a desire for the product or service	Different presentation formats are possible; however, involving the customer in the product or service through attention to particular needs is critical; important to deal professionally and ethically with prospect scepticism, indifference, or objections.
Close	Obtain a purchase commitment from the prospect and create a customer	Salesperson asks for the purchase; different approaches include the trial close and assumptive close.
Follow-up	Ensure that the customer is satisfied with the product or service	Resolve any problems faced by the customer to ensure customer satisfaction and future sales possibilities.

encyclopedias, continual prospecting is necessary to maintain sales. There are three types of prospects. A *lead* is the name of a person who may be a possible customer. A *prospect* is a customer who wants or needs the product. If an individual wants the product, can afford to buy it, and is the decision maker, this individual is a *qualified prospect*.

Leads and prospects are generated using several sources. For example, advertising may contain a coupon or a toll-free number to generate leads, as shown in the accompanying 3M advertisement. Some companies use exhibits at trade fairs, professional meetings, and conferences to generate leads or prospects. Staffed by salespeople, these exhibits are used to attract the attention of prospective buyers and disseminate information. Another approach for generating leads is through *cold canvassing* in person or by telephone. This approach simply means that a salesperson may open a telephone directory, pick a name, and visit or call that individual. Although the refusal rate is high with cold canvassing, this approach can be successful.

Because of the development and growth in database marketing, prospecting has become a little easier, and often the response rates are much higher since the databases allow for greater precision when targeting. But cold canvassing is often criticized by consumers as an intrusion on their privacy. As we saw in Chapter 18, many trade associations have codes of ethics for dealing with this issue, such as adhering to consumer's "do not call," "do not mail," or "do not visit" requests. Also, greater government regulation of such practices is being considered. For example, under proposed CRTC regulations, telemarketers will be required to inform consumers that they have the right to say no to such solicitations.[8]

PREAPPROACH

Once a salesperson has identified a qualified prospect, preparation for the sale begins with the preapproach. The *preapproach* stage involves obtaining further information on the prospect and deciding on the best method of approach. Activities in this stage include finding information on who the prospect is, how the prospect prefers to be approached, and what the prospect is looking for in a product or service. For example, a stockbroker will need information on a prospect's discretionary income, investment objectives, and preference for discussing brokerage services over the telephone or in person. For industrial products the preapproach involves identifying the buying role of a prospect (for example, influencer or decision maker), important buying criteria, and the prospect's receptivity to a formal or informal presentation. Identifying the best time to contact a prospect is also important.

APPROACH

The *approach* stage involves the initial meeting between the salesperson and prospect, where the objectives are to gain the prospect's attention, stimulate interest, and build the foundation for the sales presentation itself and the basis for a working relationship.[9] The first impression is critical at this stage, and it is common for salespeople to begin the conversation with a reference to common acquaintances, a referral, or even the product or service itself. Which tactic is taken will depend on the information obtained in the prospecting and preapproach stages.

The approach stage is very important in international settings. In many societies outside Canada, considerable time is devoted to nonbusiness talk designed to establish a rapport between buyers and sellers. For instance, it is common that two or three meetings occur before business matters are discussed in the Middle East and Asia.

PRESENTATION

The *presentation* is at the core of the order-getting selling process, and its objective is to convert a prospect into a customer by creating a desire for the

A 3M prospecting advertisement for its Post-it brand notes.

product or service. Three major presentation formats exist: stimulus–response format, formula selling format, and need-satisfaction format.

Stimulus–Response Format   The **stimulus–response presentation** format assumes that given the appropriate stimulus by a salesperson, the prospect will buy. With this format the salesperson tries one appeal after another, hoping to "hit the right button." A counter clerk at McDonald's is using this approach when she asks whether you'd like an order of french fries or a dessert with your meal. The counter clerk is engaging in what is called *suggestive selling*. Although useful in this setting, the stimulus–response format is not always appropriate, and for many products a more formalized format is necessary.

Formula Selling Format   A more formalized presentation, the **formula selling presentation** format, is based on the view that a presentation consists of information that must be provided in an accurate, thorough, and step-by-step manner to inform the prospect. A popular version of this format is the *canned sales presentation,* which is a memorized, standardized message conveyed to every prospect.[10] Used frequently by firms in telephone and door-to-door selling of consumer products (for example, Fuller Brush Company and Encyclopaedia Britannica), this approach treats every prospect the same, regardless of differences in needs or preference for certain kinds of information. Canned sales presentations can be advantageous when the differences between prospects are unknown or with novice salespeople who are less knowledgeable about the product and selling process than experienced salespeople. Although it guarantees a thorough presentation, it often lacks flexibility and spontaneity and, more important, does not provide for feedback from the prospective buyer—a critical component in the communication process and the start of a relationship.

Need-Satisfaction Format The stimulus–response and formula selling formats share a common characteristic: the salesperson dominates the conversation. By comparison, the **need-satisfaction presentation** format emphasizes probing and listening by the salesperson to identify needs and interests of prospective buyers. Once these are identified, the salesperson tailors the presentation to the prospect and highlights product benefits that may be valued by the prospect. The need-satisfaction format, which emphasizes problem solving, is the most consistent with the marketing concept. Two selling styles are associated with this format. **Adaptive selling** involves adjusting the presentation to fit the selling situation, such as knowing when to offer solutions and when to ask for more information. **Consultative selling** focusses on problem identification, where the salesperson serves as an expert on problem recognition and resolution.[11] Both styles are used for industrial products such as computers and heavy equipment. Many consumer service firms such as brokerage and insurance firms and consumer product firms like Xerox Canada and Gillette also subscribe to these selling styles.

Handling Objections A critical concern in the presentation stage is handling objections. *Objections* are excuses for not making a purchase commitment or decision. Some objections are valid and are based on the characteristics of the product or service or price. However, many objections reflect prospect scepticism or indifference. Whether valid or not, experienced salespeople know that objections do not put an end to the presentation. Rather, techniques can be used to deal with objections in a courteous, ethical, and professional manner. The following six techniques are the most common.[12]

1 *Acknowledge and convert the objection.* This technique involves using the objection as a reason for buying. For example, a prospect might say, "The price is too high." The reply: "Yes, the price is high because we use the finest materials. Let me show you . . ."

2 *Postpone.* The postpone technique is used when the objection will be dealt with later in the presentation: "I'm going to address that point shortly. I think my answer would make better sense then."

3 *Agree and neutralize.* Here a salesperson agrees with the objection, then shows that it is unimportant. A salesperson would say, "That's true and others have said the same. However, they concluded that issue was outweighed by the other benefits."

4 *Accept the objection.* Sometimes the objection is valid. Let the prospect express such views, probe for the reason behind it, and attempt to stimulate further discussion on the objection.

5 *Denial.* When a prospect's objection is based on misinformation and clearly untrue, it is wise to meet the objection head on with a firm denial.

6 *Ignore the objection.* This technique is used when it appears that the objection is a stalling mechanism or is clearly not important to the prospect.

Each of these techniques requires a calm, professional interaction with the prospect, and is most effective when objections are anticipated in the preapproach stage. Handling objections is a skill requiring a sense of timing, appreciation for the prospect's state of mind, and adeptness in communication. Objections should also be handled ethically. Lying and misrepresenting product or service features are grossly unethical practices.

CLOSE

The *closing* stage in the selling process is when a purchase commitment is obtained from the prospect. This stage is the most important and the most difficult because the salesperson must determine when the prospect is ready to buy. Telltale signals indicating a readiness to buy include body language (prospect reexamines the product or contract closely), statements ("This equipment should reduce our maintenance costs"), and questions ("When could we expect delivery?"). The close itself can take several forms. Three closing techniques are used when a salesperson believes a buyer is about ready to make a purchase: trial close, assumptive close, and urgency close. In a *trial close,* the prospect is asked to make a decision on some aspect of the purchase: "Would you prefer the blue or the grey model?" An *assumptive close* entails asking the prospect to make choices concerning delivery, warranty, or financing terms under the assumption that a sale has been finalized. An *urgency close* is used to commit the prospect quickly by making reference to the timeliness of the purchase: "The low-interest financing ends next week," or, "That is the last unit we have in stock." Of course, these statements should be used only if they accurately reflect the situation; otherwise, such claims would be unethical. When a prospect is clearly ready to buy, the final close is used and a salesperson asks for the order.[13]

Knowing when the prospect is ready to buy becomes even more difficult in cross-cultural buyer–seller negotiations where societal customs and language play a large role. Read the accompanying Marketing Action Memo to understand the multiple meanings of *yes* in Japan and other societies in the Far East.

FOLLOW-UP

The selling process does not end with the closing of a sale; rather, professional selling requires customer follow-up. One marketing authority equated the follow-up with courtship and marriage,[14] by observing, "the sale merely consummates the courtship. Then the marriage begins. How good the marriage is depends on how well the relationship is managed." The *follow-up* stage includes making certain the customer's purchase has been properly delivered and installed and difficulties experienced with the use of the item are addressed. Attention to this stage of the selling process solidifies the buyer–seller relationship. Moreover, research shows that the cost and effort to obtain repeat sales from a satisfied customer is roughly half of that necessary to gain a sale from a new customer.[15] In short, today's satisfied customers become tomorrow's qualified prospects or referrals. (What was your answer to question 2 in the quiz?)

M A R K E T I N G · A C T I O N · M E M O

Honing Your Cultural Ear for Global Sales Negotiations

*B*y the year 2000, the economy of East Asia— spanning from Japan to Indonesia—will almost equal that of North America and total about four-fifths of the European Community economy. The marketing opportunities in East Asia are great, but effective selling in these countries will require a keen cultural ear. Seasoned global marketers know that in many Asian societies it is impolite to say no, and *yes* has multiple meanings.

Yes in Asian societies can have at least four meanings. It can mean that listeners are simply acknowledging that a speaker is talking to them even though they don't understand what is being said, or it can mean that a speaker's words are understood but not

agreed with. A third meaning of *yes* conveys that a presentation is understood but other people must be consulted before any commitment is possible. Finally, *yes* can also mean that a proposal is understood and accepted. However, experienced negotiators also note that this *yes* is subject to change if the situation is changed.

This one example illustrates why savvy salespeople are sensitive to cultural underpinnings when engaged in cross-cultural sales negotiations.

Sources: Based on P. R. Cateora, *International Marketing,* 8th ed. (Homewood, IL: Richard D. Irwin, 1993), p. 145; L. Kraar, "Asia 2000," *Fortune,* October 5, 1992, pp. 111–42; C. R. Ruthstrom and K. Matejka, "The Meanings of 'Yes' in the Far East," *Industrial Marketing Management,* vol. 19, 1990, pp. 191–92; and S. Frank, "Global Negotiating," *Sales & Marketing Management,* May 1992, pp. 64–69.

---

1 What are the six stages in the personal selling process?

2 What is the distinction between a lead and a qualified prospect?

3 Which presentation format is most consistent with the marketing concept? Why?

Concept Check

THE SALES MANAGEMENT PROCESS

Selling must be managed if it is going to contribute to a firm's overall objectives. Although firms differ in the specifics of how salespeople and the selling effort are managed, the sales management process is similar across firms. Sales management consists of three interrelated functions: sales plan formulation, sales plan implementation, and evaluation and control of the sales force (Figure 20–4).

SALES PLAN FORMULATION

Formulating the sales plan is the most basic of the three sales management functions. The **sales plan** is a statement describing what is to be achieved and where and how the selling effort of salespeople is to be deployed. Formulating

■ *Figure 20–4*
The sales management
process.

Source: Based on G. A. Churchill, Jr., N. M. Ford, and O. C. Walker, Jr., *Sales Force Management,* 4th ed. (Homewood, IL: Richard D. Irwin, 1993), pp. 11–12.

the sales plan involves three tasks: setting objectives, organizing the sales force, and developing account management policies.

Setting Objectives   Setting objectives is central to sales management because this task specifies what is to be achieved. In practice, objectives are set for the total sales force and for each salesperson. Selling objectives can be output-related and focus on dollar or unit sales volume, number of new customers added, and profit. Alternatively, they can be input-related and emphasize the number of sales calls and selling expenses. Output- and input-related objectives are used for the sales force as a whole and for each salesperson. A third type of objective that is behaviourally related is typically specific for each salesperson and includes her product knowledge, customer service, and selling and communication skills. Increasingly, firms are also emphasizing knowledge of competition as an objective, since salespeople are calling on customers and should see what competitors are doing.[16] But should salespeople explicitly ask their customers for information about competitors? Read the accompanying Ethics and Social Responsibility Alert to see how salespeople view this practice.

Whatever objectives are set, they should be precise and measurable and specify the time period over which they are to be achieved. Once established, these objectives serve as performance standards for the evaluation of the sales force—the third function of sales management.

Organizing the Sales Force   Establishing a selling organization is the second task in formulating the sales plan. Three questions are related to organization. First, should the company use its own sales force, or should it use independent agents such as manufacturer's representatives? Second, if the decision is made to employ company salespeople, then should they be organized according to geography, customer type, or product or service? Third, how many company salespeople should be employed?

The decision to use company salespeople or independent agents is made infrequently.[17] However, Apple Computer recently switched from using agents to its own sales force, and Coca-Cola's food division replaced its sales force with independent agents (food brokers). The optoelectronics division of Honeywell, Inc., has switched back and forth between agents and its own sales force over the last 25 years. The decision is based on an analysis of economic and behav-

ETHICS AND SOCIAL RESPONSIBILITY ALERT

The Ethics of Asking Customers about Competitors

Salespeople are a valuable source of information about what is happening in the marketplace. By working closely with customers and asking good questions, salespeople often have firsthand knowledge of customer problems and wants. They are also able to spot the activities of competitors. However, should salespeople explicitly ask customers about competitor strategies such as pricing and promotion programs?

Gaining knowledge about competitors by asking customers for information is a ticklish ethical issue. Research indicates that 25 percent of North American salespeople engaged in business-to-business selling consider this practice unethical and their companies have explicit guidelines for this practice. It is also noteworthy that a greater percentage of Japanese salespeople consider this practice to be unethical.

Do you believe that asking customers about competitor practices is unethical? Why or why not?

Sources: Based on B. A. Weitz, S. B. Castleberry, and J. F. Tanner, Jr., *Selling: Building Partnerships* (Homewood, IL: Richard D. Irwin, 1992), pp. 7–8; A. J. Dubinsky, M. A. Jolson, R. E. Michaels, M. Kotobe, and C. U. Lim, "Ethical Perceptions of Field Sales Personnel: An Empirical Assessment," *Journal of Personal Selling & Sales Management,* Fall 1992, pp. 9–21; and A. J. Dubinsky, M. A. Jolson, M. Kotobe, and C. U. Lim, "A Cross-National Investigation of Industrial Salespeople's Ethical Perceptions," *Journal of International Business Studies,* Fourth Quarter 1991, pp. 651–70.

ioural factors. An economic analysis examines the costs of using both types of salespeople and is a form of break-even analysis.

Consider a situation in which independent agents would receive a 5 percent commission on sales and company salespeople would receive a 3 percent commission, salaries, and benefits. In addition, with company salespeople, sales administration costs would be incurred for a total fixed cost of $500,000 per year. At what sales level would independent or company salespeople be less costly? This question can be answered by setting the costs of the two options equal to each other and solving for the sales level amount, as shown in the following equation:

$$\underset{0.03(X) + \$500,000}{\text{Total cost of company sales people}} = \underset{0.05(X)}{\text{Total cost of independent agents}}$$

where X = sales volume. Solving for X, sales volume equals $25 million, indicating that below $25 million in sales independent agents would be cheaper, but above $25 million a company sales force would be cheaper.

Economics alone does not answer this question, however. A behavioural analysis is also necessary and should focus on issues related to the control, flexibility, effort, and availability of independent and company salespeople.[18] Figure 20–5 shows the common behavioural arguments for independent agents

CRITERIA	CASE FOR COMPANY SALES FORCE	CASE FOR INDEPENDENT AGENTS
Control	Company selects, trains, supervises, and can use multiple rewards to direct salespeople.	Agents are equally well selected, trained, and supervised by the representative organization.
Flexibility	Company can transfer salespeople, change customer selling practices, and otherwise direct its own sales force.	Little fixed cost is present with agents; mostly there are variable costs; therefore, firm is not burdened with overhead.
Effort	Sales effort is enhanced because salespeople represent one firm, not several; firm loyalty is present; there is better customer service because salespeople receive salary as well as commission.	Agents might work harder than salespeople because compensation is based solely on commissions; customer service is good, since it builds repeat business.
Availability	Knowledgeable agents might not be available where and when needed.	Entrepreneurial spirit of agents will make them available where a marketing opportunity exists.

versus a company sales force. An individual firm must weigh the pros and cons of the economic and behavioural considerations before making this decision.

If a company elects to employ its own salespeople, then it must choose an organizational structure based on geography, customer, or product (Figure 20–6). A geographical structure is the simplest organization, where Canada, or indeed the globe, is first divided into regions and each region is divided into districts or territories. Salespeople are assigned to each district with defined geographical boundaries and call on all customers and represent all products sold by the company. The principal advantage of this structure is that it can minimize travel time, expenses, and duplication of selling effort. However, if a firm's products or customers require specialized knowledge, then a geographical structure is not suitable.

When different types of buyers have different needs, a customer sales organizational structure is used. In practice this means that a different sales force calls on each separate type of buyer. For example, Firestone Tire & Rubber has one sales force that calls on its own dealers and another that calls on independent dealers, such as gasoline stations. The rationale for this approach is that more effective, specialized customer support and knowledge is provided to buyers. However, this structure often leads to higher administrative costs and some duplication of selling effort, since two separate sales forces are used to represent the same products.

A variation of the customer organizational structure is **major account management,** the practice of using team selling to focus on important customers so as to build mutually beneficial, long-term, cooperative relationships.[19]

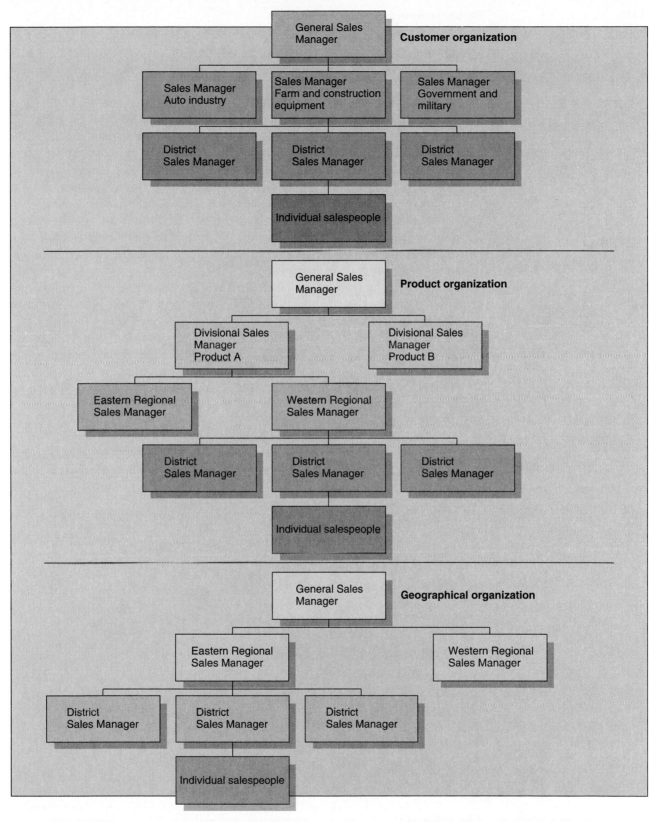

Customer organization

General Sales Manager

Sales Manager Auto industry | Sales Manager Farm and construction equipment | Sales Manager Government and military

District Sales Manager | District Sales Manager | District Sales Manager

Individual salespeople

Product organization

General Sales Manager

Divisional Sales Manager Product A | Divisional Sales Manager Product B

Eastern Regional Sales Manager | Western Regional Sales Manager

District Sales Manager | District Sales Manager | District Sales Manager

Individual salespeople

Geographical organization

General Sales Manager

Eastern Regional Sales Manager | Western Regional Sales Manager

District Sales Manager | District Sales Manager | District Sales Manager

Individual salespeople

▌ *Figure 20−6*
Organizing the sales force by customer, product, and geography.

Major account management involves teams of sales, service, and often technical personnel who work with purchasing, manufacturing, engineering, logistics, and financial executives in customer organizations. This recent innovation, which often assigns company personnel to a customer account, results in "customer specialists" who can provide exceptional service. At the same time, it suffers from the same disadvantages of the typical customer sales organization.

When specific knowledge is required to sell certain types of products, then a product sales organization is used. For example, Procter & Gamble has a sales force that sells household cleaning products and another that sells food products. The primary advantage of this structure is that salespeople can develop expertise with technical characteristics, applications, and selling methods associated with a particular product or family of products. However, this structure also produces high administrative costs and duplication of selling effort, since two company salespeople call on the same customer.

In short, there is no one best sales organization for all companies in all situations. Rather, the organization of the sales force should reflect the marketing strategy of the firm.

The third question related to sales force organization involves determining the size of the sales force. For example, why does Frito-Lay have about 10,000 salespeople who call on supermarkets and grocery stores to sell snack foods? The answer lies in the number of accounts (customers) served, the frequency of calls on accounts, the length of an average call, and the amount of time a salesperson can devote to selling.

A common approach for determining the size of a sales force is the **workload method.**[20] This formula-based method integrates the number of customers served, call frequency, call length, and available selling time to arrive at a figure for the sales force size. For example, Frito-Lay needs about 10,000 salespeople according to the workload method formula:

$$NS = \frac{NC \times CF \times CL}{AST}$$

where

NS = Number of salespeople

NC = Number of customers

CF = Call frequency necessary to service a customer each year

CL = Length of an average call

AST = Average amount of selling time available per year

Frito-Lay sells its products to 400,000 supermarkets, grocery stores, and other establishments. Salespeople should call on these accounts at least once a week, or 52 times a year. The average sales call lasts 43 minutes (0.72 hour). An average salesperson works 2,000 hours a year (50 weeks × 40 hours a week), but 10 hours a week are devoted to nonselling activities such as travel, leaving 1,500 hours a year. Using these guidelines, Frito-Lay would need:

$$NS = \frac{315,000 \times 52 \times 0.72}{1,500} = 9,984 \text{ salespeople}$$

The value of this formula is apparent in its flexibility, since a change in any one of the variables will affect the number of salespeople needed. Changes are determined, in part, by the firm's account management policies

Developing Account Management Policies   The third task in formulating a sales plan is to develop **account management policies** specifying whom salespeople should contact, what kinds of selling and customer service activities should be engaged in, and how these activities should be carried out.[21] These policies might state which individuals in a buying organization should be contacted, the amount of sales and service effort that different customers should receive, and the kinds of information salespeople should collect before or during a sales call.

An example of an account management policy in Figure 20–7 shows how different accounts or customers can be grouped according to level of opportunity and the firm's competitive sales position. When specific account names are placed in each cell, salespeople clearly see which accounts should be contacted, with what level of selling and service activity, and how to deal with them. Accounts in cells 1 and 2 might have high frequencies of sales calls and increased time spent on a call. Cell 3 accounts will have lower call frequencies, and cell 4 accounts might be contacted by telephone or direct mail rather than in person.

SALES PLAN IMPLEMENTATION

The sales plan is implemented through several specific tasks. Whereas sales plan formulation focusses on "doing the right things," implementation emphasizes "doing things right." The three major tasks involved in implementing a sales plan are sales force recruitment and selection, sales force training, and sales force motivation and compensation.

▌*Figure 20–7*
Account management policy grid.

		COMPETITIVE POSITION OF SALES ORGANIZATION	
		HIGH	LOW
ACCOUNT OPPORTUNITY	High	1 *Attractiveness.* Accounts offer good opportunity, since they have high potential and sales organization has a strong position. *Account management policy.* Accounts should receive high level of sales calls and service to retain and possibly build accounts.	3 *Attractiveness.* Accounts may offer good opportunity if sales organization can overcome its weak position. *Account management policy.* A heavy sales and service effort should be emphasized to build sales organization position or shift resources to other accounts if a stronger sales organization position is impossible.
	Low	2 *Attractiveness.* Accounts are somewhat attractive, since sales organization has a strong position, but future opportunity is limited. *Account management policy.* Accounts should receive moderate levels of sales and service to maintain current position of sales organization.	4 *Attractiveness.* Accounts offer little or no opportunity, and sales organization position is weak. *Account management policy.* Accounts should receive minimal level of sales and service effort by replacing personal calls with telephone sales or direct mail. Consider dropping account.

Sales Force Recruitment and Selection   Effective recruitment and selection of salespeople is one of the most crucial tasks of sales management. It entails finding people who match the type of sales position required by a firm. Recruitment and selection practices would differ greatly between order-taking and order-getting sales positions, given the differences in the demands of these two jobs. Therefore, recruitment and selection begin with a carefully crafted job analysis.

A **job analysis** is a written description of what a salesperson is expected to do, and therefore it differs among firms.[22] Figure 20–8 shows a job analysis for building materials salespeople—an order-getting sales position. This analysis identifies eight major job factors and describes important activities associated with each. Note particularly the frequent mention of customer service functions and relationship building and the specific reference to personal integrity and selling ethics.

Firms use a variety of methods for evaluating prospective salespeople. Personal interviews, reference checks, and background information provided on application blanks are the most frequently used methods.[23]

▌ *Figure 20–8*
Job analysis for an order-getting salesperson.

JOB FACTOR	ACTIVITIES
Assisting and working with district management	Assisting district sales management in market surveys, new product evaluations, etc. Preparing reports on territorial sales expenses Managing a sales territory within the sales expense budget Using district management to make joint sales calls on customers
Customer service	Arranging credit adjustments on incorrect invoicing, shipping, and order shortages Informing customers of supply conditions on company products Assisting customers and prospects in providing credit information to the company
Personal integrity and selling ethics	Representing company products at their true value Working within the merchandising plans and policies established by the company Investigating and reporting customer complaints
Direct selling	Knowing correct applications and installations of company products Making sales presentations that communicate product benefits Handling sales presentations
Developing relationships with customers	Maintaining a friendly, personal relationship with customers Using equipment to strengthen the business relationship with customers Providing customers with technical information on company products
Keeping abreast of market conditions	Keeping customers informed of market conditions that affect their businesses Keeping the company informed of market conditions
Meeting sales objectives	Identifying the person with authority to make the purchasing decision Closing the sale and obtaining the order Selling company products at a volume that meets or exceeds expectations
Maintaining complete customer records	Maintaining customer records that are complete and up to date Checking customers' inventory and recommending orders

L. M. Lamont and W. J. Lundstrom, "Defining Industrial Sales Behavior: A Factor Analytic Study," *1974 Combined Proceedings* (Chicago: American Marketing Association, 1974), pp. 493–98; by permission of the American Marketing Association.

Sales Force Training   Whereas recruitment and selection of salespeople is a one-time event, sales force training is an ongoing process that affects both new and seasoned salespeople. For example, new IBM salespeople train for two years, and experienced IBM salespeople are expected to spend 15 percent of their time each year in additional training. Sales training covers much more than selling practices. On average, training programs devote 35 percent of time to product information, 30 percent to sales techniques, 25 percent to market and company information, and 10 percent to other topics, including ethical practices.[24] (What was your answer to question 3 on the quiz?)

Training salespeople is an expensive and time-consuming process.[25] The direct cost of training a new industrial product salesperson (excluding salary) is $22,236 and training takes eight months. Training a new consumer product salesperson costs $11,616 and takes five months, and training new salespeople in service industries costs $14,501 and takes seven months. On-the-job training is the most popular type of training, followed by individual instruction by experienced salespeople. Formal classes and seminars taught by sales trainers are also growing in popularity.

Sales Force Motivation and Compensation   A sales plan cannot be successfully implemented without motivated salespeople. Research on salesperson motivation suggests that (1) a clear job description, (2) effective sales management practices, (3) a sense of achievement, and (4) proper incentives or rewards will produce a motivated salesperson.[26] A study on the attractiveness of different rewards given to salespeople by companies indicates that more pay was most preferred, followed in order by opportunities for personal growth, a personal sense of accomplishment, promotion, liking and respect for peers, job security, and recognition.[27]

The importance of more pay as a motivating factor means that close attention must be given to how salespeople are financially rewarded for their efforts. Salespeople are paid using one of three plans: straight salary, straight commission, or a combination of salary and commission. Under a *straight salary compensation plan* a salesperson is paid a fixed fee per week, month, or year. With a *straight commission compensation plan* a salesperson's earnings are directly tied to the sales or profit generated. For example, an insurance agent might receive a 2 percent commission of $2,000 for selling a $100,000 life insurance policy. A *combination compensation plan* contains a specified salary plus a commission on sales or profit generated. Obviously each plan has its advantages and disadvantages and is particularly suited to certain situations (Figure 20–9).

Of course, nonmonetary rewards are also given to salespeople for meeting or exceeding objectives. These rewards include trips, honour societies, distinguished salesperson awards, and letters of commendations.[28] Some unconventional rewards include the new pink Cadillacs, fur coats, and jewellery given by Mary Kay Cosmetics to outstanding salespeople.

Effective recruitment, selection, training, motivation, and compensation programs combine to create a productive sales force. Ineffective practices often lead to costly sales force turnover. US and Canadian firms experience an annual 27 percent turnover rate, which means that about one of every four salespeople is replaced each year. The expense of replacing and training a new salesperson,

Mary Kay recognizes a top salesperson.

	STRAIGHT SALARY	STRAIGHT COMMISSION	COMBINATION
Frequency of use	12%	5%	83%
Especially useful	When compensating new salespeople; when a firm moves into new sales territories that require developmental work; when salespeople need to perform many nonselling activities	When highly aggressive selling is required; when nonselling tasks are minimized; when company cannot closely control sales force activities	When sales territories have relatively similar sales potentials; when firm wishes to provide incentive but still control sales force activities
Advantages	Provides salesperson with maximum amount of security; gives sales manager large amount of control over salespeople; easy to administer; yields more predictable selling expenses	Provides maximum amount of incentive; by increasing commission rate, sales managers can encourage salespeople to sell certain items; selling expenses relate directly to sales resources	Provides certain level of financial security; provides some incentive; selling expenses fluctuate with sales revenue; sales manager has some control over salesperson's nonselling activities
Disadvantages	Provides no incentive; necessitates closer supervision of salespeople's activities; during sales declines, selling expenses remain at same level	Salespeople have little financial security; sales manager has minimum control over sales force; may cause salespeople to provide inadequate service to smaller accounts; selling costs less predictable	Selling expenses less predictable; may be difficult to administer

Source: Adapted from G. A. Churchill, Jr., N. M. Ford, and O. C. Walker, Jr., *Sales Force Management: Planning, Implementation, and Control,* 4th ed. (Homewood, IL: Richard D. Irwin, 1993), p. 591.

▌ *Figure 20–9*
Comparison of different compensation plans.

including the cost of lost sales, can be as high as $75,000.[29] Moreover, new recruits are often less productive than established salespeople.

SALES FORCE EVALUATION AND CONTROL

The final function in the sales management process is evaluating and controlling the sales force. It is at this point that salespeople are assessed as to whether sales objectives were met and account management policies were followed. Both quantitative and behavioural measures are used.

Quantitative Assessments   Quantitative assessments are based on input- and output-related objectives set forth in the sales plan. Input-related measures focus on the actual activities performed by salespeople such as those involving sales calls, selling expenses, and account management policies. The number of sales calls made, selling expense related to sales made, and the number of reports submitted to superiors are the most frequently used input measures.

Output measures focus on the results obtained and include sales produced, accounts generated, profit achieved, and orders produced compared with calls made. Dollar sales volume, last year/current year sales ratio, the number of new accounts, and sales of specific products are the most frequently used measures when evaluating salesperson output.[30]

Behavioural Evaluation Less quantitative behavioural measures are also used to evaluate salespeople. These include subjective and often informal assessments of a salesperson's attitude, product knowledge, selling and communication skills, appearance, and demeanour. Even though these assessments are highly subjective, they are frequently considered, and in fact inevitable, in salesperson evaluation.[31] Moreover, these factors are often important determinants of quantitative outcomes.

Concept Check

1 What are the three types of selling objectives?

2 What three factors are used to structure sales organizations?

3 Sales training typically focusses on what two sales-related issues?

Summary

1 Personal selling requires a two-way flow of communication between a buyer and a seller, often in a face-to-face encounter, designed to influence a person's or group's purchase decision. Sales management consists of planning the sales program and implementing and controlling the personal selling effort of the firm.

2 Personal selling is pervasive in the Canadian economy, since virtually every occupation that involves customer contact has an element of selling attached to it.

3 Personal selling plays a major role in a firm's marketing effort. Salespeople occupy a boundary position between buyers and sellers. They *are* the company to many buyers and account for a major cost of marketing in a variety of industries; and they can create value for customers

4 Three types of personal selling exist: order-taking, order-getting, and sales support activities. Each type differs from the others in terms of actual selling done and the amount of creativity required to perform the job.

5 The personal selling process, particularly for order getters, is a complex activity involving six stages: prospecting, preapproach, approach, presentation, close, and follow-up.

6 The sales management process consists of three interrelated functions: sales plan formulation, sales plan implementations, and evaluation of the sales force.

7 A sales plan is a statement describing what is to be achieved and where and how the selling effort of salespeople is to be deployed. Sales planning involves setting objectives, organizing the sales force, and developing account management policies.

8 Effective sales force recruitment and selection efforts, sales training that emphasizes selling skills and product knowledge, and motivation and compensation practices are necessary to successfully implement a sales plan.

9 Salespeople are evaluated using quantitative and behavioural measures that are linked to selling objectives and account management policies.

Key Terms and Concepts

personal selling p. 508
sales management p. 508
relationship selling p. 510
order taker p. 510
order getter p. 511
missionary salespeople p. 512
sales engineer p. 512
team selling p. 512
conference selling p. 512
seminar selling p. 512
personal selling process p. 513

stimulus–response presentation p. 516
formula selling presentation p. 516
need-satisfaction presentation p. 517
adaptive selling p. 517
consultative selling p. 517
sales plan p. 519
major account management p. 522
workload method p. 524
account management policies p. 525
job analysis p. 526

Chapter Problems and Applications

1 Jane Dawson is a new sales representative for the Charles Schwab brokerage firm. In searching for clients, Jane purchased a mailing list of subscribers to the *Financial Post* and called them all regarding their interest in discount brokerage services. She asked if they had any stocks and if they had a regular broker. Those people without a regular broker were asked their investment needs. Two days later Jane called back with investment advice and asked if they would like to open an account. Identify each of Jane Dawson's actions in terms of the steps of selling.

2 For the first 50 years of business the Johnson Carpet Company produced carpets for residential use. The sales force was structured geographically. In the past five years a large percentage of carpet sales has been to industrial users, hospitals, schools, and architects. The company has also broadened its product line to include area rugs, Oriental carpets, and wall-to-wall carpeting. Is the present sales force structure appropriate, or would you recommend an alternative?

3 Where would you place each of the following sales jobs on the order taker/order getter continuum shown below? *(a)* Burger King counter clerk, *(b)* automobile insurance salesperson, *(c)* IBM computer salesperson, *(d)* life insurance salesperson, and *(e)* shoe salesperson.

Order taker   **Order getter**

4 For each of the following firms, which compensation plan would you recommend, and what reasons would you give for your recommendations? *(a)* A newly formed company that sells lawn care equipment on a door-to-door basis directly to consumers, *(b)* the Nabisco Company, which sells heavily advertised products in supermarkets by having the sales force call on these stores and arrange shelves, set up displays, and make presentations to store buying committees, and *(c)* the Wang word-processing division, which makes word-processing system presentations to company buying committees consisting of purchasing agents and future users.

5 The TDK tape company services 1,000 audio stores throughout Canada. Each store is called on 12 times a year, and the average sales call lasts 30 minutes. Assuming a salesperson works 40 hours a week, 50 weeks a year, and devotes 75 percent of the time to actual selling, how many salespeople does TDK need?

6 A furniture manufacturer is currently using manufacturer's representatives to sell its line of living room furniture. These representatives receive an 8 percent commission. The company is considering hiring its own salespeople and has estimated that the fixed cost of managing and paying their salaries would be $1 million annually. The salespeople would also receive a 4 percent commission on sales. The company has sales of $25 million, and sales are expected to grow by 15 percent next year. Would you recommend that the company switch to its own sales force? Why or why not?

7 Suppose someone said to you, "The only real measure of a salesperson is the amount of sales produced." How might you respond?

8 Which type of personal selling—order getting, order taking, or support—is the most likely to be taken over by interactive computer links between buyers and sellers? Why?

Managing the Marketing Process

*P*art V explains the phases of the strategic marketing process: planning, implementation, and control. In Chapter 21, key aspects of the marketing planning process are discussed, including alternative marketing strategies and the concept of sustainable competitive advantage. The chapter illustrates how firms like Alcan, Procter & Gamble, Johnson & Johnson, and others have made successful strategic marketing decisions. In Chapter 22, ways in which companies can improve implementation and better control marketing plans are discussed. Also in this chapter, the outstanding implementation and control activities of Domino's Pizza are described.

Leopard *(Felis pardus)* resting in the Masai Mara Game Reserve, Kenya. Photo: Jean-Guy Thibault.

AFRICAN SAFARI. ALCAN ALUMINUM.

Alcan is a Canadian company. Yet when photographers go to Africa to shoot big game, most use Nikon, Canon, Minolta and Konica cameras made with precision tooled aluminum from our Japanese partners.

Aluminum is being used increasingly in the precise engineering and manufacture of camera bodies, lenses, meters and tripods. Indeed, it is replacing heavier metals in practically every component of advanced professional photo equipment.

Alcan aluminum has been at home in the wilds of Africa and around the world for decades in many types of 4WD vehicles as well, including the venerable Land Rover and its swank sister, the Range Rover.

In fact, aluminum gear has become the new norm on all kinds of expeditions, from mountaineering, to undersea, to NASA space exploration.

In photography, exploration, automotive, aerospace, marine, research, recycling and corporate citizenship, Alcan is aluminum to the world.

ALCAN IS ALUMINUM

CHAPTER 21

The Strategic Marketing Process: The Planning Phase

AFTER READING THIS CHAPTER YOU SHOULD BE ABLE TO:

▸ Understand the role of the strategic marketing process.

▸ Recognize the steps in the planning phase of the strategic marketing process.

▸ List the alternative marketing strategies and cost-reduction strategies available to increase profit.

▸ Understand the concept of sustainable competitive advantage.

▸ Explain how marketing managers can use sales response functions, the growth–share matrix, and the market–product grid to help plan strategy.

▸ Recognize what must be included in a strategic marketing plan.

Alcan . . . A Strategy That Worked

More than a decade ago, in the midst of a recession, Alcan Aluminium Limited reaffirmed its commitment to the aluminum business. At that time, some of Alcan's competitors decided to broaden their asset bases and reduce their dependence on aluminum, a metal which experts believed was entering the maturity stage of the product life cycle. Alcan also recognized that worldwide consumption of aluminum was growing at a slow rate. But Alcan believed there were still opportunities in the industry and set out to develop new strategies to exploit those opportunities.

One major opportunity Alcan identified was to become a fabricator of finished aluminum products, rather than remain simply a supplier of raw ingots or sheets. It was manufactured products, Alcan believed, that could provide increased profitability. The company committed itself to a multibillion-dollar program to modernize and expand its facilities to become an innovative aluminum manufacturer.

Alcan enhanced existing, and developed new, resources and skills in order to develop a sustainable competitive advantage in the markets in which it intended to compete. Among those resources and skills were a broad manufacturing base, an advanced technology network, research and development expertise, and, very important, low-cost energy.

Alcan possessed hydroelectric facilities that generated electricity for two-thirds of its total smelting capacity worldwide. This enabled Alcan to become one of the lowest-cost primary producers of aluminum in the world. This was a key sustainable competitive advantage for a company competing in an industry that uses vast amounts of energy in the manufacturing process. But Alcan didn't stop with its low-cost advantage. The company devoted time and money to R&D in order to develop new manufacturing processes and new product applications.

The strategy worked. The company not only remained one of the world's largest producers of primary aluminum, it also became one of the biggest producers of fabricated aluminum products. As a result, Alcan was consistently one of the most profitable companies in Canada during the mid-1980s and early 1990s.[1] But by 1993-1994, Alcan faced new challenges. The increasing volumes of aluminum exports from the former Soviet Union caused world inventories of aluminum to rise and prices for ingot and fabricated products to fall. So, despite record production volumes, Alcan's revenues declined. However, as Alcan did in the early 1980s, it is developing new strategies in response to, and in anticipation of, evolving market conditions. The company believes it can plan and execute the strategies necessary to prosper in the growing, but lower-priced, aluminum market of the 1990s.

This chapter covers the planning phase of the strategic marketing process. It discusses the importance of marketing planning and frameworks to improve the planning process. In Chapter 22, the implementation and control phases of the strategic marketing process are discussed.

THE PURPOSE OF THE STRATEGIC MARKETING PROCESS

The exact nature of the strategic marketing process can vary from organization to organization, but its purpose is the same. As we saw in Chapter 2, the **strategic marketing process** involves steps taken at the product and market levels to allocate resources to viable marketing opportunities; and involves phases of planning, implementation, and control. How to effectively and efficiently allocate the resources to capitalize on various opportunities is discussed later in this chapter.

The essential output of the strategic marketing process is a plan of action (the marketing plan) that will realize or achieve specified marketing objectives. Although the actual format, design, and structure will vary, in Chapter 2 you saw a format for a strategic marketing plan (Figure 2–3) that could be used by almost any organization. It is reproduced in Figure 21–1 for review.

Marketing plans can fall into two categories. **Annual marketing plans** deal with the marketing objectives and strategies for the company for a single year, whereas **long-range marketing plans** extend two to five years into the future. Except for firms in industries like autos, steel, or forest products, marketing plans rarely go beyond five years into the future, because the tremendous number of uncertainties present make the benefits of planning less than the effort expended. To allow adjustments for the increasing uncertainties in the marketplace, many firms are even trying to develop a process that allows strategic thinking more frequently than just once a year.[2]

```
    I  SITUATION ANALYSIS
       Internal assessment
       External assessment

   II  SWOT (INTERNAL STRENGTHS AND WEAKNESSES, AND EXTERNAL
       OPPORTUNITIES AND THREATS)

  III  MARKETING OBJECTIVES

   IV  MARKETING STRATEGY
       Generic strategy options
       Target market (market segment)
       Sustainable competitive advantage and positioning

    V  MARKETING MIX
       Product
       Price
       Place (distribution)
       Promotion (integrated marketing communications)

   VI  BUDGET
       Forecasts

  VII  MARKETING ORGANIZATION

 VIII  CONTROL AND EVALUATION
```

Figure 21–1
Format for a strategic marketing plan.

The steps a consumer packaged goods firm, such as food or health and beauty products, takes in developing its annual marketing plan are shown in Figure 21–2. This annual planning cycle starts with a detailed marketing research study of present users and ends after 48 weeks with the approval of the plan by the division general manager—10 weeks before the fiscal year starts. Between these points there are continuing efforts to uncover new ideas through brainstorming and key-issues sessions with specialists both inside and outside the firm. The plan is fine-tuned through a series of often excruciating reviews by several layers of management, which leave few surprises and little to chance.

THE PLANNING PHASE OF THE STRATEGIC MARKETING PROCESS

Figure 21–3 summarizes the strategic marketing process and its three phases: planning, implementation, and control. We will deal with many of the aspects of each phase of the process in this chapter and Chapter 22. The critical steps in the planning phase of the strategic marketing process are: conduct a situation analysis; determine SWOT; set marketing objectives; determine marketing strategy, including a sustainable competitive advantage; develop the marketing mix; and set the marketing budget. We will briefly discuss the situation analysis,

❙ *Figure 21–2*

Steps a large consumer packaged goods firm takes in developing its annual marketing plan.

STEPS IN ANNUAL MARKETING PLANNING PROCESS	WEEKS BEFORE APPROVAL OF PLAN					
	50	40	30	20	10	0
1. Obtain up-to-date marketing information from marketing research study of product users.	▲					
2. Brainstorm alternatives to consider in next year's plan with own marketing research and outside advertising agency personnel.	▲					
3. Meet with internal media specialists to set long-run guidelines in purchase of media.		▲				
4. Obtain sales and profit results from last fiscal year, which ended 16 weeks earlier.			▲			
5. Identify key-issues (problems and opportunities) to address in next year's plan by talks with marketing researchers, advertising agency, and other personnel.				▲		
6. Hold key-issues meeting with marketing director; form task force of line managers if significant product, package, or size change is considered.				▲		
7. Write and circulate key-issues memo; initiate necessary marketing research to reduce uncertainty.				◣▲		
8. Review marketing mix elements and competitors' behaviour with key managers, keeping marketing director informed.					▰▲	
9. Draft marketing plan, review with marketing director, and revise as necessary.					▰▲	
10. Present plan to marketing director, advertising agency, division controller, and heads of responsible line departments (product, packaging, sales, etc.) and make necessary changes.					▲	
11. Present marketing plan to division general manager for approval, 10 weeks before start of fiscal year.						▲
KEY: ▲ Planned period of work, △ Planned completion date						

Source: Adapted from S. F. Stasch and P. Langtree, "Can Your Marketing Planning Procedures Be Improved?" *Journal of Marketing,* Summer 1980, p. 82; by permission of the American Marketing Association.

SWOT, and marketing objectives and then focus on planning marketing strategy, including the alternative strategies available to the marketer as well as the concept of sustainable competitive advantage. Frameworks to improve marketing planning will also be discussed.

SITUATION ANALYSIS

As discussed in Chapter 2, a situation analysis involves an internal assessment of the firm and an external assessment of the market or industry as well as the overall environment in which the firm competes in order to identify where the firm has been, where it is now, and where it is headed. The situation analysis also involves identifying and interpreting potential trends in the environment (an

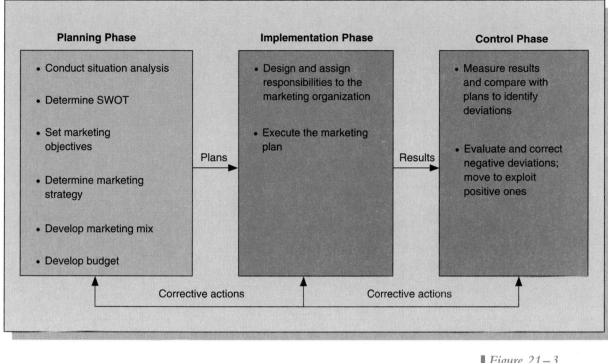

■ *Figure 21–3*
The phases of the
strategic marketing
process.

environmental scan; see Chapter 3). To find where a firm has been, is now, and is heading requires very detailed information (see Chapter 2, Figure 2–4).

A survey of 176 product managers shows the actual information they use in developing their marketing plans (Figure 21–4). At least 70 percent of the product managers made forecasts of their own product's sales, direct costs, and direct contribution (gross margin). At least half also used forecasts of industry sales, projections of their own market share, and projected profitability statements of their own product. Shaded rows in Figure 21–4 show data used by more than half of those surveyed.

Of these six kinds of information, only one deals with something other than the product manager's own product: forecasts of industry sales. In most situation analyses, two principal ingredients are the size of the industry market now and its growth rate in the near future. This tells the product manager what the size of the total pie is and the amount by which it is growing annually, and enables the manager to assess the size of the slice (the product's market share) obtained now and likely to be obtained in the future. Figure 21–4 doesn't show explicitly how the forecasts are made. But you should be aware that they are derived on the basis of not only past history of the firm and industry, but also an assessment of other external factors such as future social trends that can impact on the growth rate of the industry and the firm.

KIND OF DATA	PLANNING ACTIVITY	PLANNING DATA	PERCENTAGE USING
Basic forecast data	Sales forecasts	Three-year forecasts of "own" product sales	72%
		Three-year forecasts of industry sales	59
		"Own" product sales forecasts by segments	39
		Industry sales forecasts by segments	22
	Market share forecasts	Three-year projections of "own" product's share	52
		Projections of "own" product's share by segments	44
		Three-year projections of competing products' shares	34
		Projections of competing products' shares by segments	30
	Product contribution forecasts	Estimate of product's direct costs	71
		Three-year projection of product's direct contribution	70
		Estimates of product's direct contribution by segments	17
Strategy analysis data	Relative market share forecasts	Absolute market share converted to relative share*	49
		Three-year projections of product's relative share	38
		Estimates of product's relative share by segments	33
	Value of market share forecasts	Value of market share computed	28
		Three-year projections of product's relative share	15
		Estimates of market share by segments	11
Financial data	Profit and financial forecasts	Product profitability statements for three or more years	52
		Present value of income streams for market share alternatives	25

*Relative market share, defined later in the chapter for strategic business units, in this case is sales of the firm's product divided by sales of the leading product in the industry.

Source: Adapted from T. J. Cosse and J. E. Swan, "Strategic Marketing Planning by Product Managers—Room for Improvement?" *Journal of Marketing,* Summer 1983, pp. 92–102; by permission of the American Marketing Association.

▌ *Figure 21–4*
Information that product managers use for their marketing plans (shaded planning data were used by more than half of the product managers surveyed).

SWOT

While the situation analysis deals with many factors that can affect a firm and the industry in which it competes, the most important output of such analysis is the determination of a SWOT (internal strengths and weaknesses and external opportunities and threats).

The SWOT sets out the critical factors that can have a major effect on the firm in its future. With a SWOT, the firm can build on vital strengths, correct weaknesses, exploit significant opportunities, and avoid any threats to its survival and growth. The situation analysis and the SWOT allow the firm to set realistic marketing objectives, and to determine appropriate strategy alternatives to achieve those objectives.

MARKETING OBJECTIVES

Marketing objectives tie in directly with corporate objectives set by the organization and should be quantified both in terms of how much (such as an increase in unit sales from 375,000 to 500,000) and when (such as "by the end of fiscal year 1996"). Arriving at these objectives requires involvement not only of the product managers but also of senior management and other personnel

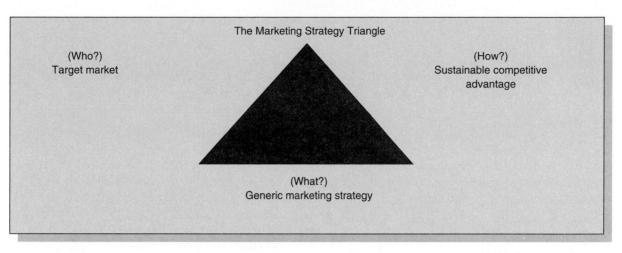

The Marketing Strategy Triangle

(Who?)
Target market

(How?)
Sustainable competitive
advantage

(What?)
Generic marketing strategy

▌ *Figure 21–5*
**The marketing strategy
triangle.**

inside and outside the firm. Involving senior management is essential throughout the planning process so the company can alter objectives and strategies if
they are too far off the mark.

Involvement of middle-level and lower-level cross-functional personnel
inside and outside the firm is needed for the creative ideas they bring to the
planning and objective-setting process. It also gives them personal "ownership"
in the objectives when they are called on to carry out the plans or even to
discover new ideas that may lead to new business.[3] As shown in the accompanying Marketing Action Memo, 3M publicizes its corporate objectives to its
employees and encourages them to convert their ideas into products that can
lead to the start of entirely new divisions. This is probably the ultimate success
in tying personal and corporate objectives together to the benefit of both
employee and employer.

MARKETING STRATEGY

A marketing strategy is the means by which marketing objectives are to be
achieved. One of the most crucial aspects of the planning phase of the strategic
marketing process is selecting the best marketing strategy to use given the
various alternatives available to the firm.

As we saw in Chapter 2, marketing strategy is characterized by determining *what* to do (generic marketing strategy), *who* will be the focus of the strategy
(target market or market segment), and *how* to do it (sustainable competitive
advantage and positioning). The marketing strategy triangle from Chapter 2 is
reintroduced here in Figure 21–5. One aspect of the marketing strategy triangle, the target market, was discussed in detail in Chapter 9. It will be discussed
later, in brief, when the market–product grid is introduced as a framework for
improving marketing planning. The focus in this section will be on generic
marketing strategies and the concept of sustainable competitive advantage.

Generic Strategies to Increase Profit   If a business wants to increase its profits,
it can attempt to increase revenues, decrease expenses, or do both (Figure 21–6).

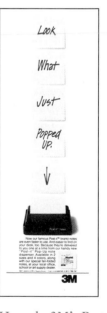

How do 3M's Post-it
notes reflect the
company's corporate
goals? See the
accompanying Marketing
Action Memo for the
answer.

MARKETING · ACTION · MEMO

3M's "Divide and Grow" Process: Achieving Personal Ownership of Corporate Goals

Someone has estimated that each day close to half the *world's* population benefits in some way from 3M products. Whether the estimate is correct or not, each day billions of people are exposed to some of 3M's 60,000 products, including:

- Scotch brand antistatic videotape.
- Scotchlite reflective road signs.
- Translucent dental braces.
- Synthetic ligaments for damaged knees.
- Optical fibre splices.

The bonds that tie together 45 major product lines utilizing 85 distinct technologies in more than 101 international factories are four specific corporate goals:

- 10 percent or better annual growth in earnings per share.
- 27 percent return on capital employed.
- 20 to 25 percent return on equity.
- 25 percent of a division's sales coming from products or services introduced within the past five years.

3M has succeeded in building what it calls "a company of entrepreneurs" through a process of "divide and grow." This means that each of 3M's 89,000 employees is encouraged to take an idea—even when others lose faith in it—and run with it. If the idea succeeds, the employee has a chance to manage the product as though it were his own business. That single product may spin off enough related products to become an entire 3M division. This is one reason 3M encourages its technical researchers to "bootleg" 15 percent of their time pursuing whatever they think is best for 3M.

As customers have become concerned about the economy and value, 3M employees have focussed on developing products that can be marketed as cost-saving devices. They are also working on ideas to bring new products to emerging markets such as Poland, the Czech Republic, and the former Soviet Union. In addition, 3M has reduced the length of its product development cycle—in some cases by 50 percent.

This divide and grow process gives employees a personal stake in the four 3M corporate goals. It has given the world thousands of products—from exotic medical devices to low-tech Post-it notes—and is producing more than 200 new products annually.

Sources: S. Blount, "It's Just a Matter of Time," *Sales and Marketing Management,* March 1992, pp. 33–43; K. Kelly, "3M Run Scared? Forget about It," *Business Week,* September 16, 1991, pp. 59–62; R. Mitchell, "Masters of Innovation: How 3M Keeps Its New Products Coming," *Business Week,* April 10, 1989, pp. 58–63; C. Knowlton, "What America Makes Best," *Fortune,* March 28, 1988, p. 45; and S. Feyder, "3M Changes Some Elements of Its Style," *Minneapolis Star Tribune,* May 23, 1988, pp. 1D, 9D.

Such strategies can be adopted by any firm, regardless of the product or industry involved.

Generic Marketing Strategies to Increase Revenues   The generic strategy of increasing revenue can be achieved only by using one or a combination of four generic marketing strategies (Figure 21–6): market penetration, product development, market development, and diversification; these were described in Chapter 2. However, in order to effectively execute any of these strategies, a firm requires a sustainable competitive advantage, which will be discussed later.

Procter & Gamble has followed a successful strategy of market penetration (present markets, present products) by concentrating its efforts on becoming the

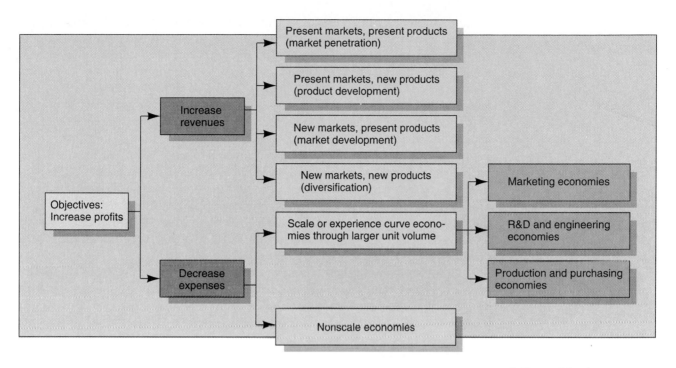

▌ *Figure 21–6*
**Alternative generic
marketing strategies and
cost-reduction strategies
for increasing a firm's
profits.**

market leader in each of its 39 product categories. It is currently first in 22 categories, up from 17 several years ago.[4] As we will see later, to obtain market leadership in each product category, P&G required a sustainable competitive advantage.

Johnson & Johnson has succeeded with a product development strategy—finding new products for its existing markets—to complement its popular brands such as Tylenol pain reliever and Accuvue contact lenses. Johnson & Johnson developed Tylenol PM, a combination painkiller and sleeping pill; and Surevue, a long-lasting disposable contact lens.[5]

Walt Disney Company has pursued a market development strategy (new market, present product) since the success of the original Disneyland in Anaheim, California. The first market expansion was to Orlando, Florida, followed by theme parks in Tokyo and Paris.[6] Disney has also pursued a diversification strategy by entering into the motion picture business with the development of Touchstone Pictures and by buying an NHL franchise, the Mighty Ducks.

Generic Strategies to Decrease Expenses   In addition to marketing strategies to increase revenue, a firm can consider strategies to decrease expenses in order to increase profitability (see Figure 21–6). These strategies fall into two broad categories. One is relying on scale economies or experience curve benefits from an increased volume of production to drive unit costs down and gross margins up. Scale economies may occur in marketing, as well as in R&D, engineering, production, and purchasing.

The other generic strategy to decrease expenses is simply finding other ways to reduce costs, such as cutting the number of managers, increasing the effectiveness of the sales force through training, or reducing product rejects

through better quality control. Many firms, including Xerox Canada, have reduced costs through work force reductions and quality improvement programs. As we will see later, cost reduction efforts can assist a firm in developing a sustainable competitive advantage as a low-cost producer or value provider.

Sustainable Competitive Advantage   Regardless of the generic marketing strategies selected by an organization, the success of those strategies is highly dependent on the unique resources and special skills of the organization. As we stated in Chapter 2, it is these resources and skills that "drive," or form the basis for, the development of a firm's sustainable competitive advantage (SCA): a strength, relative to competitors, to be used in the markets a firm serves or the products it offers. In essence, it is the organization's resources and skills that give the business the potential to provide *value* to the customer either at a lower cost (as low-cost provider) or in a way that leads to noncost differentiation (e.g., product superiority).[7]

In other words, these resources and skills do not automatically give a business a sustainable competitive advantage; they are only something that can be leveraged to achieve cost and/or noncost differentiation advantages. Resource-based "drivers" include abilities to achieve economies of scale, brand equity, and reputation, while skill-based drivers include such things as quality product design and innovativeness.

A true sustainable competitive advantage must resist erosion by competitive actions and reactions (i.e., it must be sustainable). Most important, while the SCA must be tough for competitors to imitate or copy, it must also be valuable to the customer.[8]

Cost leadership entails performing most activities at a lower cost than competitors while offering a product of equal or better quality. The chapter opener illustrated that Alcan's SCA of being a low-cost producer was achieved as a result of low-cost power, infrastructure improvement and modernization, and a series of cost-cutting measures. Alcan could not have achieved its successful market penetration without this sustainable competitive advantage.

An SCA achieved through differentiation (noncost) appears to be increasingly sought by marketers. Leveraging resources and skills can result in an SCA on the product dimension (product quality, branding, reputation, ongoing innovation), distribution (locational convenience and responsiveness), promotion (better use of media, creation of the perception of value through promotion), or customer service.[9] Lexus, for example, leveraged its resources and skills (e.g., capital for R&D, as well as skills in product design and engineering) to produce a quality luxury automobile.

P&G is a company with both the resources (capital) and skills (R&D, product innovation) that have enabled it to dominate many of the product categories in which it competes. P&G's market penetration strategy for its products could not have been successful without an SCA. The SCA for many of its brands is largely a result of building brand equity (the added value the brand name gives the product beyond its functional benefits). In fact, the success of Tide, Crisco, and Crest has just as much to do with their brand equity and reputation (e.g., awareness, perceived quality, and loyalty) as it has with their actual performance characteristics. In other words, these products may indeed offer superior performance compared with the competitors', but it is the brand equity and reputation of the products built by P&G's creative marketing and promotion that have been integral to their success.

More recently, the use of information technology (IT) resources and skills has become another way to achieve a sustainable competitive advantage. IT can allow a company to do things faster, better, and less expensively, or to get closer to the customer in order to build a relationship.[10]

As we saw in Chapter 9, once a firm determines its sustainable competitive advantage it must *position* itself in the mind of the consumer on that competitive dimension. In other words, the consumer must see the firm or its product or brand as "better" in some way compared with the competition. For example, Lexus uses its theme "the relentless pursuit of perfection" to position itself in the mind of the consumer as a quality luxury automobile. Maintaining a sustainable competitive advantage and proper positioning requires an ongoing commitment and investment by the firm in order to prevent erosion due to competitive efforts to duplicate or copy the advantage.

---

1 **Why is industry growth important to a product manager?**

2 **What are four generic marketing strategies to increase revenue?**

3 **What is sustainable competitive advantage?**

Concept Check

FRAMEWORKS TO IMPROVE MARKETING PLANNING

Marketing planning for a firm with many products competing in many markets—a multiproduct, multimarket firm—is a complex process. Three techniques that are useful in helping marketing executives in such a firm make important marketing strategy and resource allocation decisions are sales response functions, the growth–share matrix, and the market–product grid. Each of these techniques is discussed in terms of how it is used in marketing planning, and its strengths and weaknesses.

SALES RESPONSE FUNCTIONS

A **sales response function** relates the expense of marketing effort to the marketing results obtained.[11] For simplicity in the examples that follow, only the effect of annual marketing effort on annual sales revenue will be analyzed, but the concept applies as well to other measures of marketing success, such as profit, units sold, or levels of awareness.

Maximizing Incremental Revenue minus Incremental Costs   Economists give marketing managers a specific guideline for optimal resource allocation: allocate the firm's marketing, production, and financial resources to the markets and products where the excess of incremental revenue over incremental costs is greatest. This parallels the marginal revenue–marginal cost analysis of Chapter 13.

■ *Figure 21–7*
Sales response function
showing the situation for
two different years.

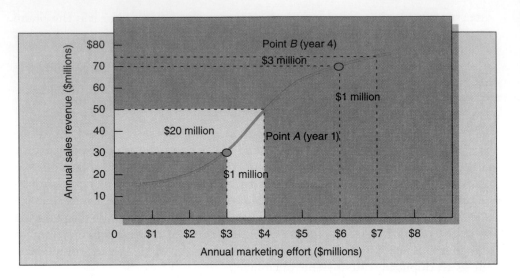

Figure 21–7 illustrates this resource allocation principle. The firm's annual marketing effort, such as sales and advertising expenses, is plotted on the horizontal axis. As this annual marketing effort increases, so does the resulting annual sales revenue. The relationship is assumed to be S-shaped, showing that an additional $1 million of marketing effort results in far greater increases in sales revenues in the mid-range (such as $4 million) than at either end (such as $2 million or $7 million).

A Numerical Example of Resource Allocation   Suppose Figure 21–7 shows the situation for a new General Mills product such as Yoplait fat-free yogourt. Also assume that the sales revenue response function doesn't change through time. Point *A* shows the position of the firm in year 1, and point *B* shows it three years later in year 4. Marketing effort in the form of advertising and other promotions has increased from $3 million to $6 million a year, while sales revenue has increased from $30 million to $70 million a year.

Let's look at the major resource allocation question: what are the probable increases in sales revenue in years 1 and 4 for an extra $1 million of marketing effort? As Figure 21–7 reveals:

Year 1
  Increase in marketing effort from $3 million to $4 million = $1 million
  Increase in sales revenue from $30 million to $50 million = $20 million
  Ratio of incremental sales revenue to effort = $20,000,000:$1,000,000 = 20:1
Year 4
  Increase in marketing effort from $6 million to $7 million = $1 million
  Increase in sales revenue from $70 million to $73 million = $3 million
  Ratio of incremental sales revenue to effort = $3,000,000:$1,000,000 = 3:1

Thus, in year 1, a dollar of extra marketing effort returned $20 in sales revenue, whereas in year 4 it returned only $3. If no other expenses are incurred, it might make sense to spend $1 million in year 4 to gain $3 million in incremental sales revenue. However, it may be far wiser for General Mills to invest the money in one of its other businesses. In essence, the sales response function shows a firm where to put incremental resources so that the incremental returns will be greatest over the foreseeable future.

ALLOCATING MARKETING RESOURCES IN PRACTICE

General Mills, like many firms in packaged goods businesses, does extensive analysis using **share points,** or percentage points of market share, as the common basis of comparison to allocate marketing resources effectively. This allows it to seek answers to the question, How much is it worth to us to try to increase our market share by another 1 [or 2, or 5, or 10] percentage point?

This also enables higher-level managers to make resource allocation trade-offs among different kinds of businesses owned by the company, such as between Pop Secret popcorn and Red Lobster restaurants. To make these resource allocation decisions, marketing managers must estimate the market share for the product, the revenues associated with each point of market share (it may be $50 million for popcorn and $10 million for seafood restaurants), and the contribution to overhead and profit (or gross margin) of each share point.

Sales response functions have helped General Mills make marketing strategy and resource allocation decisions. For example, General Mills expanded its production capacity to produce more Squeezit fruit drinks; developed an improved flour product, Bisquick Reduced Fat; introduced a brand extension, Multi-Grain Cheerios; created a new snack product called Gushers; and accelerated expansion of Red Lobster restaurants while shifting promotional efforts from price to limited-time menu events.

These decisions indicate the wide variety of established product improvements, new products and markets, and increased marketing support options that General Mills can utilize to meet company growth and profit targets. Occasionally, another strategy—acquisition—represents the best allocation of resources. For example, Kraft General Foods (KGF) acquired Nabisco's ready-to-eat cereals division in Canada for $450 million. This acquisition represented the most cost-effective method of increasing KGF's Canadian market share in the cereal category. Specifically, it gives KGF the number 2 selling cereal in Canada (Shreddies) and basically doubled its market share of the $700 million Canadian ready-to-eat cereal market overnight.[12]

Strengths and Weaknesses Sales response functions provide an important guideline for making strategic decisions, specifically as they pertain to resource allocation. It allows the firm to make assessments of where resources would be better spent. However, a good information base is required to make these judgments and may not always be available. Data deficiencies concerning absolute market size, share point data, and growth rates of the industry can affect the usefulness of sales response functions. Moreover, the impact of increased marketing efforts on sales revenues can be offset or enhanced depending on competitors' planned efforts, efforts which the firm may not be able to quantify.

BCG's GROWTH–SHARE MATRIX

Many large firms address their complex strategy and resource allocation decisions by breaking their organization into decentralized profit centres, often called **strategic business units** (SBUs), each of which is treated as though it were a separate, independent business. Ideally, an SBU has several distinct characteristics: it is a single business that can be planned independently of other businesses, has its own competitors, and has one manager with profit responsibility.[13] Planning is done first at the SBU level, then SBUs are combined into groups, and finally groups are combined into a complete picture of the entire company.

Information Needed   An internationally known management consulting firm, the Boston Consulting Group (BCG), has developed one of the most recognized approaches to **business portfolio analysis,** analyzing a firm's SBUs as though they were a collection of separate investments. BCG advises its clients to locate the position of each of its SBUs on a growth–share matrix (Figure 21–8). The vertical axis is the **market growth rate,** which is the annual rate of growth of the specific market or industry in which a given SBU is competing. This axis in the figure runs from 0 to 20 percent, although in practice it might run even higher. The axis has arbitrarily been divided at 10 percent into high-growth and low-growth areas.

　　The horizontal axis is the **relative market share,** defined as the sales of the SBU divided by the sales of the largest firm in the industry. A relative market share of 10× (at the left end of the scale) means that the SBU has 10 times the share of its largest competitor, whereas a share of 0.1× (at the right end of the scale) means it has only 10 percent of the sales of its largest competitor. The scale is logarithmic and is arbitrarily divided into high and low relative market shares at a value of 1×.

▌*Figure 21–8*
Boston Consulting Group growth–share matrix for a strong, diversified firm showing some strategic plans.

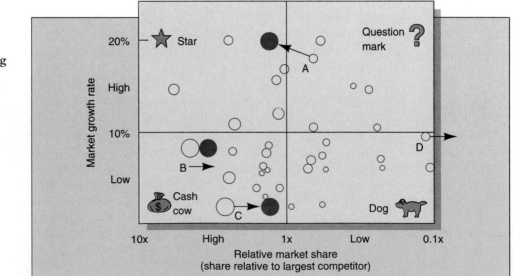

Source: Adapted from "The Experience Curve Reviewed, IV. The Growth Share Matrix of the Product Portfolio," © 1973, The Boston Consulting Group.

BCG has given specific names and descriptions to the four resulting quadrants in its growth–share matrix based on the amount of cash they generate for or require from the firm:

- Cash cows (lower left quadrant) are SBUs that typically generate large amounts of cash, far more than they can invest profitably in their own product line. They have a dominant share of a slow-growth market and provide cash to pay large amounts of company overhead and to invest in other SBUs.
- Stars (upper left quadrant) are SBUs with a high share of high-growth markets that may not generate enough cash to support their own demanding needs for future growth. When their growth slows, they are likely to become cash cows.
- Question marks or problem children (upper right quadrant) are SBUs with a low share of high-growth markets. They require large injections of cash just to maintain their market share, much less increase it. Their name implies management's dilemma for these SBUs: choosing the right ones to invest in and phasing out the rest.
- Dogs (lower right quadrant) are SBUs with a low share of low-growth markets. Although they may generate enough cash to sustain themselves, they do not hold the promise of ever becoming real winners for the firm. Dropping SBUs in this quadrant from a business portfolio is generally advocated except when relationships with other SBUs, competitive considerations, or potential strategic alliances exist.[14]

The hollow circles in Figure 21–8 show the location of the SBUs in a strong, diversified firm. The area of each hollow circle is proportional to the corresponding SBU's annual sales revenue.

Use in Marketing Planning   The portfolio in Figure 21–8 is a strong and diversified one because over half the SBUs have high relative market shares, there are many stars, the cash cows are strong and numerous enough to feed the needs of the question marks, and even most of the question marks and dogs have high market shares. Most firms are unable to influence the market growth rate—the factor shown on the vertical axis; an exception is a firm whose product is strong enough to stimulate primary demand for the entire product class. If a firm cannot affect market growth, its main planning alternative using business portfolio analysis is to try to change the relative market share, the factor on the horizontal axis. This is done mainly through a conscious management decision to either inject cash into or withdraw cash from a specific SBU.

A firm must determine what role to assign each SBU in trying to assemble its ideal future portfolio.[15] BCG identifies four alternative objectives for an SBU. Ranked from most to least cash infused into an SBU, these four alternatives are described here with reference to Figure 21–8.

1 *Build.* Increase the SBU's market share through injections of cash, even forgoing short-term profits to do so. This is often an appropriate strategy for question marks that need large amounts of cash to become stars. By injecting cash into SBU A in Figure 21–8, a firm hopes to move it from its present question mark position to a star (solid circle). Once, Intel was rapidly losing its

memory chip business to low-cost international competitors. In response, it poured billions of dollars into R&D—$2.5 billion in 1993 alone—and focussed on improving its new product development procedures. Today Intel is the world's largest chip maker, fending off competitors with new products (such as the Pentium™ processor) every two to three years.[16]

2 *Hold.* Maintain the SBU's market share, without appreciably altering the cash it uses. SBU B is typical of a holding strategy often applied to cash cows that are generating large amounts of cash and are intended to retain that same position in the future. The Eaton's retail chain is using a holding strategy for its department stores that are in a slow-growth segment of the retail market.

3 *Harvest.* Increase the SBU's short-term cash output, even if this results in a loss of market share. This strategy can be used with question marks, dogs, or cash cows; an example of the latter is shown as SBU C. The resulting cash can then be pumped into stars or question marks. When General Mills marketing research showed that the décor in Red Lobster restaurants was losing customer appeal, it diverted cash from its profitable consumer food divisions to remodel 125 units in 1993 and 100 units in 1994 at a cost of $200,000 per restaurant.

4 *Divest.* Sell the SBU to put its cash, physical, and human resources to use elsewhere in the firm. Question marks and dogs (such as SBU D) that require too much cash are candidates for divestiture. General Electric sold its small-appliance division to Black & Decker to raise cash for other GE businesses.

Just as most products have life cycles, so do most SBUs. An SBU often starts out as a question mark and then moves counterclockwise around the growth–share matrix—question mark to star to cash cow to dog—as industry competition increases. This means a firm's portfolio of SBUs and their positions are changing continuously, and the firm must always be on the lookout for new products and business opportunities to become the stars and cash cows in its future portfolio.

Strengths and Weaknesses   Primary strengths of business portfolio analysis include forcing a firm to assess each of its SBUs in terms of its relative market share and industry market growth rate, which in turn requires the firm to forecast which SBUs will be cash producers and cash needers in the future. Weaknesses are that it is often difficult to get the information needed to locate each SBU on the growth–share matrix, there are other important factors missing from the analysis such as possible synergies among the SBUs when they use the same sales force or research and development facilities, and there are problems in motivating people in an SBU that has been labelled a dog or even a cash cow and is unlikely to get new resources from the firm to grow and provide opportunities for promotion.[17] In addition, planners have had difficulty incorporating information on competitors into portfolio analysis.[18]

Underlying the BCG analysis is the assumption about the importance of the firm's absolute market share and, in turn, relative market share. Many early analyses suggested that if a firm could gain an increase in market share, then a sizable increase in ROI would automatically follow, a conclusion about which there is increasing debate.[19]

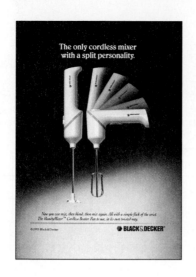

GE's "divest" strategy
was the start of Black &
Decker's small-appliance
line.

MARKET–PRODUCT GRID

A marketing manager responsible for an individual SBU can use the market–
product grid to identify specific product opportunities or market niches that
might be pursued. 寻求   面富.

Information Needed   As summarized in Chapter 9, the process of segmenting
a market first necessitates finding characteristics to form market segments and
then product clusters. Displaying these in a table forms a market–product grid.
The use of this grid in the strategic marketing process is based on detailed
information such as: past, current, and projected data on (1) revenues, expenses,
and profits, (2) for the entire industry and the firm's own products, (3) in total
and by individual market segments and product clusters.

Use in Marketing Planning   The market–product grid facilitates trade-offs in
the strategic marketing process. Suppose you are a product manager for Great
Lawns Corporation's line of nonpowered lawn mowers sold to the consumer
market. You are looking for new product and new market opportunities to
increase your revenues and profits.

    You conduct a market segmentation study and develop a market–product
grid to analyze future opportunities. You identify three major segments in the
consumer market based on geography: city, suburban, and rural areas. These
segments relate to the size of lawn a consumer must mow. The product clusters *Groups*
are nonpowered, powered walking, and powered riding mowers.

    Five alternative marketing strategies are shown in market–product grids in
Figure 21–9.[20]

   ■ *Market–product concentration.* Great Lawns' initial strategy focussed its efforts
on one market segment (city households with small lawns) with a single product
line (nonpowered mowers). Most large markets evolve from initial market-
product concentration strategies.[21] At the same time, large firms are focussing on
smaller and smaller target markets.[22]

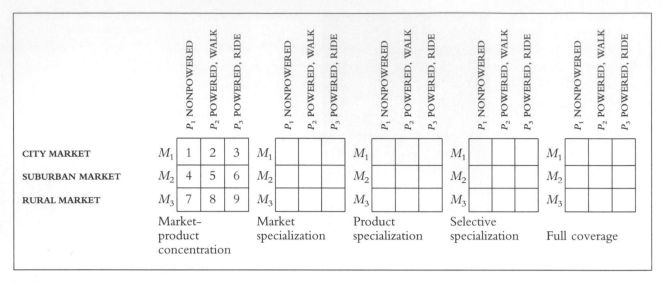

■ *Figure 21–9*
Market–product grid of alternative strategies for a lawn mower manufacturer.

■ *Market specialization.* This entails retaining the focus on a single market segment (city households) but adding two new product lines (powered walking and powered riding mowers). The strategic problem is developing and manufacturing two product lines new to Great Lawns.

■ *Product specialization.* This involves retaining Great Lawns' focus on a single product line (nonpowered mowers) but marketing it to two unknown markets (suburban and rural households). The potential danger is entering two markets in which a producer may have no marketing experience or distribution outlets.

■ *Selective specialization.* This involves targeting separate product lines for separate segments: nonpowered mowers for city households and powered walking mowers for suburban dwellers. The difficulty is the lack of scale economies available in the two previous strategies.

■ *Full coverage.* With this strategy, Great Lawns will offer all three product lines in all three market segments.

The five grids in Figure 21–9 highlight some trade-offs that marketing managers face in designing strategies. For example, marketing economies of scale run horizontally across the rows: adding new products for a given market segment represents few new marketing expenses but sizable new R&D and production expenses. The reverse is true for R&D and production economies of scale: these run vertically down a column. This often means balancing marketing economies of scale available from expanding across the rows against R&D and production economies available by expanding vertically down the columns.

As a firm expands under a product specialization strategy, it usually gains additional revenue by entering new markets with its existing line of products. Thus, Great Lawns can expect new revenues by selling nonpowered mowers to suburban and rural households. However, this is often not the case in expanding by selling new products to an existing market segment under a market specialization strategy. Great Lawns, which now offers only nonpowered mowers, may gain new sales revenue by offering powered mowers to city households but with the potential danger of merely stealing the new sales from city customers formerly buying nonpowered mowers. This product cannibalism can present real revenue problems for a firm. For example, when General Foods introduced its freeze-dried Maxim brand, it stole sales from the company's Maxwell House brand.[23]

The market–product grid also clarifies trade-offs described in Chapter 2. For example, the first grid in Figure 21–9 suggests four opportunities to a Great Lawns mower product manager:

- *Increase market penetration (present markets, present products).* Gain more sales in cell 1.
- *Undertake market development (new markets, present products).* Take the nonpowered mower into the new markets in cells 4 and 7.
- *Undertake product development (present markets, new products).* Produce new powered walking and riding mowers for the existing market, which means obtaining revenues from cells 2 and 3.
- *Undertake diversification (new markets, new products).* Produce new powered walking and riding mowers for new suburban and rural markets, which means obtaining revenues from cells 5, 6, 8, and 9.

Market development or product development strategies pose fewer dangers for Great Lawns than diversification because each involves solving only one new unknown—either new market challenges for the marketing department or new product challenges for the R&D and manufacturing departments. Diversification causes difficulties for the firm in *both* marketing and R&D and manufacturing. A diversification strategy can be dangerous because it may result in a firm's acquiring a business it can't run, a violation of the dictum "Stick to your knitting."[24] In undertaking moves into new markets or new products, a firm must be aware of barriers or gateways to entry such as technology, patents, and strong existing production or distribution systems.[25]

Strengths and Weaknesses   The market–product grid benefits marketing managers in the strategic marketing process by identifying potential opportunities to fill market niches or product gaps for the firm, highlighting potential economies of scale in either marketing or R&D and manufacturing that result from entering new markets or offering new products, and showing potential revenue losses caused by product cannibalism. The disadvantages include the time and effort needed to form meaningful market segments, to form useful product clusters, and to develop revenue and profit estimates for the cells in the grid.

Concept Check

1 What is the difference between a star and a cash cow in BCG's growth–share matrix?

2 If Great Lawns chose to take its nonpowered mower into suburban and rural markets, would the economies of scale accrue to marketing or R&D and production?

SOME PLANNING AND STRATEGY LESSONS

Applying these frameworks is not automatic but requires a great deal of managerial judgment. Commonsense requirements of an effective marketing plan are discussed below, followed by problems that can arise.

REQUIREMENTS OF AN EFFECTIVE MARKETING PLAN

Dwight D. Eisenhower, when he commanded Allied armies in World War II, made his classic observation, "Plans are nothing; planning is everything." It is the process of careful planning that focusses an organization's efforts and leads to success. The plans themselves, which change with events, are often secondary. Effective planning and plans are inevitably characterized by identifiable objectives, specific strategies or courses of action, and the means to execute them.

Measurable, Achievable Goals   Ideally, objectives should be measurable in terms of *what* is to be accomplished and by *when*. This means, where possible, goals should be quantified: "Increase market share from 18 percent to 22 percent by December 31, 1997" is preferable to "Maximize market share given our available resources." As noted previously, these measurable goals also provide a benchmark with which to compare results to determine when corrective action is required.

   To motivate the people in an organization whose job it is to reach the goals, the goals must be achievable. Unrealistically difficult goals will not motivate marketing personnel.

A Base of Facts and Valid Assumptions   The more a marketing plan is based on facts and valid assumptions, rather than guesses, the less uncertainty and risk are associated with executing it. Using marketing research to verify some assumptions increases the chance of successfully implementing a plan.

Simple but Clear and Specific Plans   Effective execution of plans requires that the doers understand what, when, and how they are to accomplish their tasks. Superfluous elements in a plan should be dropped so that the remaining ones are as straightforward as possible, thereby preventing misunderstandings.

Complete and Feasible Plans   Marketing plans must be complete in the sense that a marketing program has been designed that has considered all the marketing mix factors and incorporated the key ones in the marketing plan. Marketing resources must be adequate to make the plan feasible.

Controllable and Flexible Plans   Few plans are carried to completion without a hitch. Results of marketing actions are compared with the measurable, targeted goals to discern problem areas and trigger new, corrective actions. Marketing plans must provide for this control, which in turn allows replanning—the flexibility to update the original plans.

PROBLEMS IN MARKETING PLANNING AND STRATEGY

From postmortems on company plans that did work and on those that did not, a picture emerges as to where problems occur in the planning phase of a firm's strategic marketing process.[26] The following list explores these problems:

1 Corporate plans may be based on very poor assumptions about environmental factors, especially changing economic conditions and competitors' actions.

2 Planners and their plans may have lost sight of their customers' needs. Schwinn failed to see the changing preferences of its consumers, from 10-speed bicycles to mountain bikes. But Figure 21–10 shows that Whirlpool and

▌ *Figure 21–10*
Results of strategic marketing plans.

FIRM	STRATEGY	RESULT
PLANS THAT DID WORK		
Burger King	Introduce a new MTV-like advertising campaign designed to bring 18- to 34-year-olds to dinner.	The jumpy, jiggly music video-style ads are attracting people of all ages. Dinner sales are up 20 percent, and market share has increased from 15.9 percent to 17 percent.
Whirlpool	Use market research to design new products; each year the company surveys 180,000 households.	Since 1982 Whirlpool has tripled in size. Based on its research it introduced the industry's first pan-European advertising campaign—increasing international sales from 0 percent five years ago to 40 percent today.
Merck	Develop important drugs (such as cholesterol-reducing Mevacor, and a powerful antibiotic, Primaxin); hire research scientists with world-class reputations.	Ranked number one on the *Fortune* 1993 list of most admired corporations for the seventh straight year.
PLANS THAT DIDN'T WORK		
Oldsmobile	Create a new image for Oldsmobile that makes it distinct from other GM lines (such as Buick) with the "This is not your father's Oldsmobile" and "The power of intelligent engineering" campaigns.	Oldsmobile sales declined 60 percent over a five-year period. The company put its advertising account up for review for the first time since 1934.
Schwinn Bicycle Company	Focus on production cost reduction and distribution of 10-speed bicycles. Utilize strong brand name and powerful retail distribution network.	Missed the market shift to mountain bikes and specialty bikes. Market share dropped from 25 percent to 5 percent.

Sources: G. Morgenson, "Look Who's Coming to Dinner," *Forbes,* March 1, 1993, pp. 104–5; S. Solo, "How to Listen to Consumers," *Fortune,* January 11, 1993, pp. 77–78; J. Reese, "America's Most Admired Corporations," *Fortune,* February 8, 1993, pp. 44–47; M. Landler, "How Leo Burnett Kept Olds in Its Garage," *Business Week,* February 22, 1993, pp. 60–65; S. Makridakis, "What Can We Learn from Corporate Failure?" *Long Range Planning,* August 1991, pp. 115–26; and A. Tanzer, "Bury Thy Teacher," *Forbes,* December 21, 1992, pp. 90–95.

ETHICS AND SOCIAL RESPONSIBILITY ALERT

How to Add New Values to Strategic Marketing Plans

How can companies change their strategic marketing process to reflect the interests of the many constituents (e.g., the community, customers, employees, shareholders, and suppliers) they serve? Although many approaches have had success, several actions are critical:

1 Identify, define, and prioritize critical values.
2 Measure employee perceptions of the values.
3 Assess customer perceptions of the degree to which company actions conform to these values.
4 Audit current management practices and modify them to reflect values.
5 Use a reward system that reinforces values.

Using these guidelines can help companies develop appropriate value-driven strategies. For example, when Johnson & Johnson (J&J) was faced with the cyanide crisis for its Tylenol brand, it used its primary value—trust of the doctors, nurses, patients, and others who use J&J products—to guide the company's response: complete cooperation with the media and total recall of the product. Similarly, Ford Motor Company recently specified three values—people, products, and profits—to guide its attempts to become more competitive. Why are people first? "Because people are our most important asset. Everything that we are and can accomplish can only be done by people," says Ford chairman and CEO Donald Peterson. Ford's strategies now focus first on employees and their work environment.

What values would you specify for Ford? For your current employer?

Sources: L. Ginsburg and N. Miller, "Value-Driven Management," *Business Horizons,* May–June 1992, pp. 23–27; R. L. Osborn, "Core Value Statements: The Corporate Compass," *Business Horizons,* September–October 1991), pp. 28–34; and C. E. Watson, "Managing with Integrity: Social Responsibilities of Business as Seen by America's CEOs, *Business Horizons,* (July–August 1991), pp. 99–109.

Merck had marketing strategies that succeeded because of customer-oriented products.

3 Too much time and effort may be spent on collection and analysis of data required for the plans. The result is that line managers have their focus diverted from developing and implementing creative strategies. Westinghouse has cut its planning instructions for operating units "that looked like an auto repair manual" to five or six pages.

4 Responsibility for planning and strategy development may be assigned to the planners so that line operating managers feel no sense of ownership in implementing the plans. Andy Grove, CEO of Intel, observed, "We had the very ridiculous system . . . of delegating strategic planning to strategic planners. The strategies these [planners] prepared had no bearing on anything we actually did."[27] The solution is to assign more planning activities to line operating managers.

BALANCING VALUE AND VALUES IN STRATEGIC MARKETING PLANS

The focus of this chapter is on using the strategic marketing process to compete with products offered by other businesses. However, several important trends are likely to influence the strategic marketing process in the future. The first, value-based planning, combines marketing planning ideas and financial planning techniques to assess how much a division or an SBU contributes to the price of a company's stock (or shareholder wealth). Value is created when the financial return of a strategic activity exceeds the cost of the resources allocated to the activity.[28]

The second trend is the increasing interest in value-driven strategies, which incorporate concerns for ethics, integrity, employee health and safety, and environmental safeguards with more common corporate values such as growth, profitability, customer service, and quality. Some experts have observed that although many corporations cite broad corporate values in advertisements, press releases, and company newsletters, they have not yet changed their strategic plans to reflect the stated values. Because plans depend on goals, the next step will require that organizations learn to specify value-based objectives.[29] See the accompanying Ethics and Social Responsibility Alert for guidelines that help add new values to the planning process.

1   What is the significance of the S shape of the sales response function in Figure 21–7?

2   What are two techniques, besides sales response functions, that can be used to improve marketing planning?

3   Why is it important to include line operating managers in the planning process?

Concept Check

Summary

1   The strategic marketing process involves steps taken at the product and market levels to allocate resources to viable marketing opportunities, and involves phases of planning, implementation, and control.
2   The essential output of the strategic marketing process is the marketing plan—an annual or a long-range plan.
3   Critical steps in the planning phase of the strategic marketing process are conducting a situation analysis; determining SWOT; setting marketing objectives; determining a marketing strategy including a sustainable competitive advantage; developing the marketing mix; and setting the marketing budget.

4   With so much at risk from bad decisions, the planning phase of the strategic marketing process requires an enormous amount of detailed information. This information is obtained through a situation analysis.

5   Generic strategies for a firm to increase profits are (*a*) increasing revenues, (*b*) decreasing expenses, and (*c*) a combination of both.

6   Generic marketing strategies to increase revenue include (*a*) market penetration, (*b*) product development, (*c*) market development, and (*d*) diversification. A marketer can pursue one or more at the same time.

7   Three techniques that are useful in helping marketing executives in a large firm make important marketing strategy and resource allocation decisions are (*a*) sales response functions, (*b*) the growth–share matrix, and (*c*) the market–product grid.

8   Sales response functions help marketers assess what the market's response to additional marketing effort will be.

9   Boston Consulting Group's (BCG's) growth–share matrix enables a firm to position its strategic business units (SBUs) on a two-dimensional graph whose axes are (*a*) annual market (industry) growth rate and (*b*) the SBU's relative market share (firm's sales divided by those of the largest competitor).

10 The market–product grid displays an SBU's market segments and product clusters in a table to identify opportunities to fill market niches; assess economies of scale in marketing, R&D, and production; and project possible lost revenues if new products steal sales from existing products.

11 An effective marketing plan has measurable, achievable objectives; uses facts and valid assumptions; is simple, clear, and specific; is complete and feasible; and is controllable and flexible.

Key Terms and Concepts

strategic marketing process p. 536
annual marketing plans p. 536
long-range marketing plans p. 536
sales response function p. 545
share points p. 547

strategic business units p. 548
business portfolio analysis p. 548
market growth rate p. 548
relative market share p. 548

Chapter Problems and Applications

1   Campbell Soup now has 60 percent of the canned soup business. Write a specific marketing objective for Campbell Soup.

2   In 1996, General Mills plans to invest $700 million in expanding its cereal and restaurant businesses. To allocate this money between these two businesses, what information would General Mills like to have?

3 Which of the four generic marketing strategies used to increase revenue is probably easiest for an established firm to pursue? Of the four, which one has the most risk?

4 Is it possible for a firm to develop more than one specific competitive advantage which it can use to compete in a specific product market?

5 Assume a firm faces an S-shaped sales response function. What happens to the ratio of incremental sales revenue to incremental marketing effort at the (*a*) bottom, (*b*) middle, and (*c*) top of this curve?

6 What happens to the ratio of incremental sales revenue to incremental marketing effort when the sales response function is an upward-sloping straight line?

7 Explain why a product often starts out as a question mark and then moves counterclockwise around BCG's growth–share matrix.

8 Suppose Apple Computer wants to increase its profits by increasing its revenues. Use its market–product grid shown in a Marketing Action Memo in Chapter 9 ("How Apple Segments Its Markets") to identify an action it might take for each of the four generic marketing strategies for increasing revenues.

9 In Figure 21–10, which generic marketing strategies for increasing revenues seem to have been followed by (*a*) Burger King, (*b*) Whirlpool, and (*c*) Merck?

10 Experts suggest it is not necessary to have a "real" competitive advantage; it is only necessary that the consumer "perceive" that you do. What does this mean? Is it possible?

•

CHAPTER 22

The Strategic Marketing Process: Implementation and Control Phases

AFTER READING THIS CHAPTER YOU SHOULD BE ABLE TO:

▸ Understand the implementation and control phases of the strategic marketing process.

▸ Describe the alternatives for organizing marketing activities and the role of a product manager in a marketing department.

▸ List the key activities needed to ensure that a marketing plan is implemented effectively.

▸ Schedule a series of tasks to meet a deadline using a Gantt chart.

▸ Understand how sales and profitability analyses and marketing audits are used to evaluate and control marketing plans.

How to Implement a Plan—in 30 Minutes!

In 1960, Thomas S. Monaghan bought a tiny Italian restaurant for $500. His objective was to make enough money to finance his architecture degree. His plan for accomplishing this was to deliver tasty, hot, custom-made pizzas to customers who placed their order by telephone. Although Monaghan's plan was simple and focussed, it would take him years to master the implementation and control phases of the idea, which would eventually become a very successful home-delivered meal business.

Monaghan began by "staking out a business niche—free delivery—and doing it better and faster than anyone else."[1] That simple concept led to important business practices. For example, although the cheese is half the cost of a pizza, Monaghan insisted on using expensive, 100 percent real cheese to ensure that his pizza was better than competitors' products. In addition, he developed a unique appeal: delivery of a hot pizza to a customer's house within 30 minutes of the phone order. To ensure wide market coverage, Monaghan began franchising the concept. He called his firm Domino's Pizza, Inc., and by 1980 it had 398 outlets.

The rapid growth of Domino's also required highly motivated employees. The big carrot for good performance as a driver and in the store is—surprise—a Domino's Pizza franchise. Today, Domino's has over 5,500 outlets across the United States and Canada and the average delivery time is 23 minutes. The company has sales in excess of $2.6 billion.

Domino's is Canada's largest national pizza delivery operation and the third-largest national pizza player after sit-down establishments McDonald's and Pizza Hut. But the competition has increased substantially in the past few years. McDonald's entry into the pizza business instantly made it the biggest player. Little Caesar's, one of Domino's primary competitors, has become more aggressive in Canada and the United States with major media campaigns, focussing on its two-for-one pizza concept. Many regional pizza makers are also chasing value-conscious consumers by providing heavy discounts or two-for-one offers. Many others offer fast and free delivery, copying one of Domino's strengths.

Domino's is also concerned about other fast-food competitors who are encroaching on its business. Kentucky Fried Chicken, for example, is now in the delivery business, and McDonald's Canada is testing the home delivery concept. Domino's is responding in various ways to these competitive threats. It has altered its menu to include new items such as garlic breadsticks, salads, and pan pizzas. Domino's has undertaken direct marketing efforts involving millions of flyers in neighbourhoods surrounding its 155 Canadian franchises. Sponsorship of NHL hockey is another element in Domino's strategy, as is a new national TV campaign featuring celebrity spokesperson Wayne Gretzky. The message: "Only the great ones deliver." Donny Domino, the company's first animated character since the Noid, has also been introduced. There is also a new emphasis on local tie-ins and free giveaways using a "Something for Nothing" slogan.[2]

Figure 22–1
The phases of the strategic marketing process.

As we saw in Chapter 21, a company must be willing to invest in order to maintain its sustainable competitive advantage in the face of competitive pres-

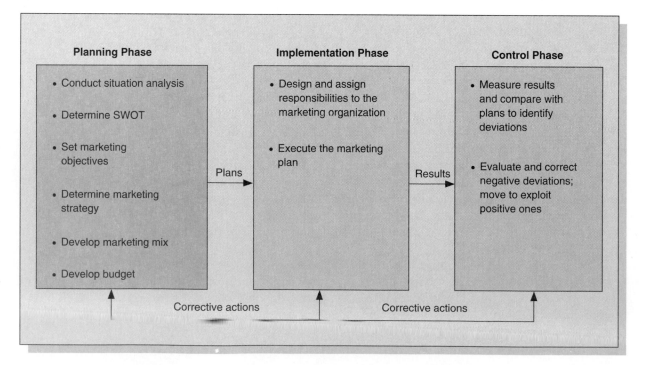

Planning Phase	Implementation Phase	Control Phase
• Conduct situation analysis	• Design and assign responsibilities to the marketing organization	• Measure results and compare with plans to identify deviations
• Determine SWOT		
• Set marketing objectives	• Execute the marketing plan	• Evaluate and correct negative deviations; move to exploit positive ones
• Determine marketing strategy		
• Develop marketing mix		
• Develop budget		

Plans → Results →

Corrective actions   Corrective actions

sures. Monaghan is doing just that. To ensure the success of his marketing plan, precise, effective actions are taken. There is also a willingness to be flexible and to respond to the changing marketplace and uncontrollable or unforeseen events. For example, Domino's recently had to pay millions of dollars in damages to a person involved in an accident with one of Domino's delivery vehicles. Because of this, Domino's has dropped the 30-minute guarantee on delivery, which was an integral part of its positioning strategy. However, the company is still promising free and prompt delivery.

The original idea for Domino's Pizza was clear and simple, but implementation and control are not so simple. But with constant evaluation of important performance measures, such as average delivery time, and attention to detail, Monaghan is proving that the implementation and control phases of the strategic marketing process can be accomplished effectively. This chapter focusses on these two phases of the strategic marketing process (Figure 22–1).

THE IMPLEMENTATION PHASE OF THE STRATEGIC MARKETING PROCESS

The Monday morning diagnosis of a losing football coach often runs something like, "We had an excellent game plan; we just didn't execute it."

IS PLANNING OR IMPLEMENTATION THE PROBLEM?

The planning versus execution issue applies to the strategic marketing process as well: a difficulty when a marketing plan fails is determining whether the failure is due to a poor plan or poor implementation.

Figure 22–2 shows the outcomes of good and bad marketing planning and good and bad marketing implementation. Good planning and good implemen-

MARKETING IMPLEMENTATION	MARKETING PLANNING AND STRATEGY	
	GOOD (APPROPRIATE)	BAD (INAPPROPRIATE)
Good (effective)	1 *Success:* Marketing plan achieves its objectives.	2 *Trouble:* Solution lies in recognizing that only the strategy is at fault and correcting it.
Bad (ineffective)	3 *Trouble:* Solution lies in recognizing that only implementation is at fault and correcting it.	4 *Failure:* Marketing plan flounders and fails to achieve its objectives.

Figure 22–2
Results of good and bad marketing planning and implementation.

tation in cell 1 spell success, as with the Swiss Corporation for Microelectronics and Watchmaking (SMH), which combined a strong product—its Swatch brand watches—with excellent promotion, distribution, and pricing.

NeXT Computer, Inc., fell into the "bad–bad" cell 4, with its NeXT workstation, which used a proprietary hardware strategy that discouraged many potential customers. In addition, efforts at implementing marketing functions, such as the sales force, were "just too small and strapped for cash to reach many prospects," said the former NeXT vice president of marketing, Michael Slade.[3] Four years after its introduction, NeXT, Inc., closed its computer factory to focus on its software business.

Cells 2 and 3 indicate trouble because either the marketing planning or the marketing implementation—not both—is bad. A firm or product does not stay permanently in cell 2 or 3. If the problem is solved, the result can be success (cell 1); if not, it is failure (cell 4).[4] Toyota used good implementation on a bad strategy (cell 2) when it applied its superior automobile marketing skills to the introduction of its T100 pickup truck. Consumer response was well below forecasts, because the truck was too big to compete with smaller "compact" pickups and too small and underpowered to compete with full-size options.[5]

Goodyear Tire & Rubber Co. found itself in cell 3 after it successfully developed all-season radial tires but created problems with its dealer distribution network by raising wholesale prices. The poor implementation led to a 2-point decline in market share—a drop of 3 million tires.[6]

INCREASED EMPHASIS ON MARKETING IMPLEMENTATION

In the 1990s, the implementation phase of the strategic marketing process has emerged as a key factor to success. In the past, organizations imposed plans designed by corporate staff on line managers, who were responsible for implementation. The predictable result was near disaster for many firms as line operating personnel ignored the plans in which they had no ownership.

Many companies responded to the problem by reorganizing. For example, GE reduced the size of its corporate strategic planning staff from 350 to approximately 20. Like many organizations, GE also reduced the number of layers of middle managers and pushed decision-making authority lower in the organization, involving line managers in the planning process. Although these steps have been helpful, some experts argue that they are not enough, that "boundaryless organizations" in which technology, information, managers, and managerial practices are shared across traditional organizational structures will be necessary in the future.[7] See the accompanying Marketing Action Memo for a description of important implementation characteristics of tomorrow's organizations.

IMPROVING IMPLEMENTATION OF MARKETING PLANS

No magic formula exists to guarantee effective implementation of marketing plans. In fact, the answer seems to be equal parts of good management skills and practices. Managerial skills that contribute to successful implementation include an ability to interact with people inside and outside the company; a capacity to

MARKETING · ACTION · MEMO

Implementation in the Organization of Tomorrow

*I*n today's global marketplace, corporations struggle to reduce their response time to windows of opportunity. One of the reasons is that few companies have the complete expertise necessary to quickly launch new products in diverse and changing markets. To excel at implementation of marketing strategies, the organization of tomorrow will emphasize adaptability by taking advantage of information technology and acting, as Peter Drucker suggests, like a symphony orchestra.

Frank Ostroff and Doug Smith at the consulting firm McKinsey & Co. have suggestions for firms making the transition, including:

1 Organize around process, not task.
2 Flatten the hierarchy.
3 Give leaders responsibility for process performance.
4 Link performance to customer satisfaction.
5 Create teams that have managerial and nonmanagerial responsibilities.
6 Reward team performance.

In addition, companies will need to utilize networks of suppliers, customers, and even competitors to create *strategic alliances*.

These developments are described by many terms today, including the *boundaryless company,* the *virtual corporation,* and *capabilities-based* competition, but regardless of the terminology, you can bet that the future will bring exciting changes in the way marketing plans are implemented. Organizations as diverse as GE, Hallmark Cards, Eastman Kodak, and even the Zoological Society of San Diego are already trying many of these ideas!

Sources: J. Byrne, R. Brandt, and O. Port, "The Virtual Corporation," *Business Week,* February 8, 1993, pp. 98–103; H. Hinterhuber and W. Popp, "Are You a Strategist or Just a Manager?" *Harvard Business Review,* January–February 1992, pp. 105–13; T. Steward, "The Search for the Organization of Tomorrow," *Fortune,* May 18, 1992, pp. 92–98; and G. Stalf, P. Evans, and L. Shulman, "Competing on Capabilities: The New Rules of Corporate Strategy," *Harvard Business Review,* March–April 1992, pp. 57–69.

budget time, people, and money; an ability to track or monitor marketing activities; and an affinity for creating communication networks within the organizational structure.[8] Important management practices include moving decisions as far down the organization as possible, setting deadlines, and rewarding individuals for successful implementation. Combining these skills and practices suggests some guidelines for improving plan implementation.

Communicate Goals and the Means of Achieving Them   Those called on to implement plans need to understand both the goals sought and how they are to be accomplished. Everyone in Domino's Pizza—from Tom Monaghan to telephone order takers, make-line people, and drivers—is clear on what the firm's goal is: to deliver tasty, hot pizzas without delay to homes of customers who order them by telephone. All Domino's personnel are trained in detail to perform their respective jobs to help achieve that goal. The goals must be consistent with organizational capabilities and they should be modified as capabilities change.[9]

A popular mechanism for helping members of any organization achieve its goals today is the use of teams. A *team* is a small number of people with complementary skills who are mutually accountable to a common set of performance goals. Motorola, Inc., for example, used teams to develop hand–held cellular phones that were superior to competitive products manufactured in Japan. Successful teams typically have fewer than 10 members, a common purpose and focus, and a mix of skills—including technical expertise, problem-solving abilities, and interpersonal skills.[10]

TIME MAGAZINE CALLS THE DODGE VIPER "THE MOST SOUGHT-AFTER SPORTS CAR IN YEARS."

Have a Responsible Champion Willing to Act   Successful high-technology plans such as the plans for Sony's MiniDisc, Chrysler's Dodge Viper, and Cray Computer's supercomputers, almost always have a **product or plan champion** who is able and willing to cut red tape and move forward.[11] Such people often have the uncanny ability to move back and forth between big-picture strategy questions and specific details when the situation calls for it. This champion idea applies to the successful implementation of marketing plans, but the title varies with the firm and position. For Domino's Pizza this person in day-to-day operations is the franchise owner who is running the restaurant, whereas for Sara Lee Corporation it might be the product manager responsible for Chef Pierre pies. Diffused responsibility in marketing plans at best can mean important delays and at worst can result in disaster when team members don't know who is responsible for decisions.

Reward Successful Plan Implementation   When an individual or a team is rewarded for achieving the organization's goal, it has maximum incentive to see a plan implemented successfully because it has personal ownership and a stake in that success. At a General Electric surge protector plant, employees receive a bonus each quarter in which the facility meets plantwide performance goals. This also means employees are more willing to jump into critical situations and perform tasks that are "below" them or not in their job descriptions. Drivers delivering Domino's pizza take their job seriously—because it may lead directly to their owning a franchise in a few years.

Take Action and Avoid "Paralysis by Analysis"   In their book *In Search of Excellence*, Thomas J. Peters and Robert H. Waterman, Jr., warn against paralysis by analysis, the tendency to excessively analyze a problem instead of taking action. To overcome this pitfall, they call for a "bias for action" and recommend a "do it, fix it, try it" approach.[12] They conclude that perfectionists finish last, so getting 90 percent perfection and letting the marketplace help in the fine tuning makes good sense in implementation.

Lockheed Aircraft's Skunk Works got its name from the comic strip "Li'l Abner" and its legendary reputation from achieving superhuman technical feats with a low budget, ridiculously short deadlines, and only 7 percent to 25 percent of the people used in comparable aircraft industry programs. Under the leadership of Kelly Johnson, in 35 years the Skunk Works has turned out the first jet airplane (the P-80), the highest-flying reconnaissance plane (the U-2), and aviation's fastest jet (the SR-71). Called out of retirement to work on the nation's most **untrackable** aircraft (the F-117 Stealth fighter), Johnson restated two of his basic tenets: make decisions promptly and avoid paralysis by analysis. Chris Haney and Scott Abbott, the Canadian inventors of Trivial Pursuit, took only 45 minutes to develop their basic concept. Then, they quickly developed the prototype and test-marketed the product. By making prompt decisions and avoiding paralysis by analysis, these entrepreneurs created the biggest-selling adult game in Canada.[13]

Sometimes, plan champions are notoriously brash in overcoming organizational hurdles. The US Navy's Admiral Grace Murray Hopper not only gave the world the COBOL computer language but also the word *bug*—meaning any glitch in a computer or computer program. Probably more important is this plan champion's famous advice for moving decisions to actions by cutting through an organization's red tape: "Better to ask forgiveness than permission." Using this strategy, 3M's Art Fry championed Post-it notes to success, an idea he got when looking for a simple way to mark his hymnal while singing in his church choir.

Foster Open Communication to Surface the Problems   Bugs and glitches aren't limited to computer programs—both technical and marketing plans have them too—but success often lies in fostering a work environment that is open enough so doers are willing to speak out when they see problems without fear of recrimination. The focus is placed on trying to solve the problem as a group rather than finding someone to blame. Solutions are solicited from anyone who has a creative idea to suggest—from the janitor to the president—without regard to status or rank in the organization.

Two more Kelly Johnson axioms from Lockheed's Skunk Works apply here: when trouble develops, surface the problem immediately; and get help—don't keep the problem to yourself. This latter point is important even if it means getting ideas from competitors.

Saturn is GM's attempt to create a new company where participatory management and improved communications led to a successful product. The goal is to sell 80 percent of its cars to drivers who otherwise would have purchased a Honda or a Toyota. To accomplish this, GM has invested $5 billion

For the unusual way GM developed its Saturn, see the text.

in the project, and has tried to avoid some of the common communication problems of large organizations. To encourage discussion of possible cost reductions, each employee receives 100 to 750 hours of training, including balance sheet analysis. As a result, even a $30 error in a telephone bill was detected by employees. To avoid the "NIH syndrome"—the reluctance to accept ideas "not invented here" or not originated inside one's own firm—Saturn engineers bought 70 import cars to study for product design ideas, and selected options that would most appeal to their target market. Finally, to create a management–labour partnership all decisions are reached by consensus, including the selection of suppliers, the advertising agency, and dealers.[14]

The consumer response to Saturn has been phenomenal. Some dealers have waiting lists of nearly 300 people who want to buy the car. In its second year of production, the Saturn was rated third in new-car buyer satisfaction, behind only Lexus and Infiniti. Now, Saturn has the difficult task of increasing production to meet demand, reducing costs to become profitable (the company lost $700 million in 1992), and maintaining the company's innovative communication practices that made Saturn what *Advertising Age* called "one of the most successful new brands in marketing history." [15]

Schedule Precise Tasks, Responsibilities, and Deadlines   Successful implementation requires that people know the tasks for which they are responsible and the deadline for completing them. For Domino's Pizza's drivers, the task (deliver a hot pizza) and deadline (within a reasonable amount of time after the telephone order) are very clear.

To implement the tasks required to carry out its marketing plans, the Royal Canadian Mint prepares **action item lists** that have three columns: the task, the name of the person responsible for accomplishing that task, and the date by which the task is to be finished. Action item lists are forward looking, clarify the targets, and put strong pressure on people to achieve their designated tasks by the deadline.

Related to action item lists are formal *plan schedules,* which show the relationships through time of the various plan tasks. Starting with the design of the Polaris submarines in the 1950s, computer-based scheduling techniques such as PERT (Program Evaluation and Review Technique) developed in defence programs became very complex. However, simplified software programs based on these techniques are now available for PCs.

Scheduling an action plan involves identifying the main tasks, determining the time required to complete each, arranging the activities to meet the deadline, and assigning responsibilities to complete each task.

Suppose, for example, that you and two friends are asked to do a term project on the problem, How can the college increase attendance at its performing arts concerts?[16] And suppose further that the instructor limits the project in the following ways:

1 The project must involve a mail survey of the attitudes of a sample of students.
2 The term paper with the survey results must be submitted by the end of the 11-week quarter.

To begin the assignment, you need to identify all the project tasks and then estimate the time you can reasonably allocate to each one. As shown in Figure 22−3, it would take 15 weeks to complete the project if you did all the tasks sequentially; so to complete it in 11 weeks, your team must work on different parts at the same time, and some activities must be independent enough to overlap. This requires specialization and cooperation. Suppose that of the three of you (A, B, and C), only student C can type. Then you (student A) might assume the task of constructing the questionnaire and selecting samples, and student B might tabulate the data. This division of labor allows each student to concentrate on and become expert in one area, but you should also cooperate. Student C might help A and B in the beginning, and A and B might help C later on.

You must also figure out which activities can be done concurrently to save time. In Figure 22−3 you can see that task 2 must be completed before task 4. However, task 3 might easily be done before, at the same time as, or after task 2. Task 3 is independent of task 2.

Scheduling production and marketing activities—from a term project to a new product rollout to a space shuttle launch—can be done efficiently with Gantt charts. Figure 22−4 shows one variation of a Gantt chart used to schedule the class project, demonstrating how the concurrent work on several tasks enables the students to finish the project on time. Developed by Henry L. Gantt, this method is the basis for the scheduling techniques used today, including elaborate computerized methods. The key to all scheduling techniques is to distinguish tasks that *must* be done sequentially from those that *can* be done concurrently. As in the case of the term project, scheduling tasks concurrently often reduces the total time required for a project.

Source: Adapted from W. Rudelius and W. B. Erickson, *An Introduction to Contemporary Business*, 4th ed. (New York: Harcourt Brace Jovanovich, 1985), p. 94. Copyright © 1985 by Harcourt Brace Jovanovich, Inc. Reprinted by permission of the publisher.

| Figure 22−3
Tasks in completing a term project.

Shown below are the tasks you might face as a member of a student team to complete a marketing research study using a mail questionnaire. Elapsed time to complete all the tasks is 15 weeks. How do you finish the project in an 11-week quarter? For an answer, see the text.

TASK	TIME (WEEKS)
1 Construct a rough-draft questionnaire and test it for clarity (in person, not by mail) on friends.	2
2 Type and mimeograph a final questionnaire.	2
3 Randomly select the names of 200 students from the school directory.	1
4 Address and stamp envelopes; mail questionnaires.	1
5 Collect returned questionnaires.	3
6 Tabulate and analyze data from returned questionnaires.	2
7 Write final report.	3
8 Type and submit final report.	1
Total time necessary to complete all activities.	15

❙ *Figure 22–4*
**Gantt chart for
scheduling the term
project.**

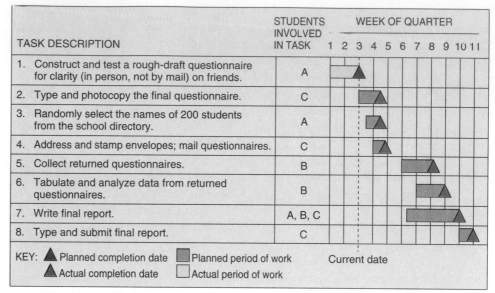

TASK DESCRIPTION	STUDENTS INVOLVED IN TASK	WEEK OF QUARTER 1 2 3 4 5 6 7 8 9 10 11
1. Construct and test a rough-draft questionnaire for clarity (in person, not by mail) on friends.	A	
2. Type and photocopy the final questionnaire.	C	
3. Randomly select the names of 200 students from the school directory.	A	
4. Address and stamp envelopes; mail questionnaires.	C	
5. Collect returned questionnaires.	B	
6. Tabulate and analyze data from returned questionnaires.	B	
7. Write final report.	A, B, C	
8. Type and submit final report.	C	

KEY: ▲ Planned completion date   ▢ Planned period of work   Current date
       ◮ Actual completion date   ▢ Actual period of work

Source: Adapted from W. Rudelius and W. B. Erickson, *An Introduction to Contemporary Business*, 4th ed. (New York: Harcourt Brace Jovanovich, 1985), p. 95.

Scheduling any action plan translates plans into specific, understandable tasks, forces planners to distinguish sequential from concurrent tasks, reducing the time to implement the plan, and forces people to take responsibility for specific tasks and allot time to them. Otherwise, they tend to concentrate on the tasks they prefer and neglect the others.

Concept Check

1 How have organizations changed as the importance of implementation has increased?

2 What is the meaning and importance of a product or plan champion?

3 Explain the difference between sequential and concurrent tasks in a Gantt chart.

ORGANIZING FOR MARKETING

A marketing organization is needed to implement the firm's marketing plans. Basic issues in today's marketing organizations include understanding how line versus staff positions and divisional groupings interrelate to form a cohesive marketing organization and the role of the product manager.

Line versus Staff and Divisional Groupings   Although simplified, Figure 22–5 shows the organization of Pillsbury's Prepared Dough Products business unit in detail and highlights the distinction between line and staff positions in marketing. People in **line positions,** such as group marketing managers, have the authority and responsibility to issue orders to the people who report to them,

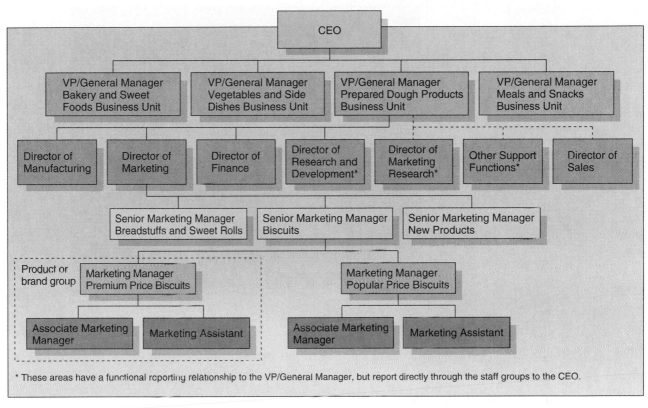

* These areas have a functional reporting relationship to the VP/General Manager, but report directly through the staff groups to the CEO.

▌ *Figure 22–5*
**Organization of the
Pillsbury Company.**

such as marketing managers. In this organizational chart, line positions are connected with solid lines. Those in **staff positions** (shown by dotted lines) have the authority and responsibility to advise people in line positions but cannot issue direct orders to them. For example, the directors of R&D, marketing research, and sales advise the vice president/general manager of the Prepared Dough Products business unit but do not report directly to him. Instead, they report directly to other vice presidents (not shown in this organizational chart) who issue them orders.

Most marketing organizations use divisional groupings—such as product line, functional, geographical, and market-based—to implement plans and achieve their organizational objectives. Three of these appear in some form in Pillsbury's organizational chart in Figure 22–5. At the top of its organization, Pillsbury organizes by **product line groupings,** in which a unit is responsible for specific product offerings. For example, Pillsbury has four main product lines: bakery and sweet foods, vegetables and side dishes, prepared dough products, and meals and snacks. These product line groupings reflect a Pillsbury reorganization that grouped products by the way consumers think about them, rather than by the distribution systems they use (dry grocery, frozen, and refrigerated foods).

The Prepared Dough Products business unit is organized by **functional groupings** such as manufacturing, marketing, and finance, which are the different business activities within a firm.

Products from Pillsbury's
line of prepared dough
products.

Pillsbury uses **geographical groupings** for its more than 500 field sales representatives. Each director of sales has several regional sales managers reporting to her, such as western, eastern, and so on. These, in turn, have district managers reporting to them (although for simplicity these are not shown in the chart).

A fourth method of organizing a company is to use **market-based groupings,** which assign responsibility for a specific type of customer to a unit. When this method of organizing is combined with product groupings, the result is a *matrix organization*. Xerox, for example, "turned the traditional vertically organized company on its side" and focussed on specific product and market combinations.[17]

A relatively new position in consumer products firms is the *category manager* (senior marketing manager in Figure 22–5). Category managers have profit-and-loss responsibility for an entire product line—all biscuit brands, for example. They attempt to reduce the possibility of one brand's actions hurting another brand in the same category. The popularity of category management among packaged goods manufacturers has increased rapidly as supermarket buyers have become responsible for purchasing, merchandising, and promoting entire categories.[18]

Role of the Product Manager   The key person in the product or brand group shown in Figure 22–5 is the manager who heads it. As mentioned in Chapter 12, this person is often called the *product manager* or *brand manager,* but in Pillsbury he carries the title *marketing manager.* This person and the assistants in the product group are the basic building blocks in the marketing department of most consumer and industrial product firms. The function of a product manager is to plan, implement, and control the annual and long-range plans for the

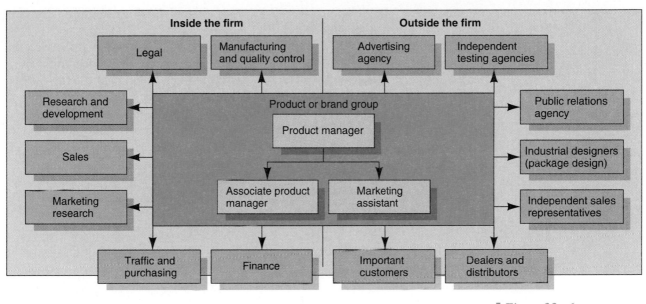

▌ *Figure 22–6*
Units with which the product manager and product group work.

products for which he is responsible. This responsibility includes six primary tasks:[19]

1   Developing long-range competitive strategies for the product that will achieve sales, profit, and market share objectives.
2   Preparing annual marketing plans, sales forecasts, and budgets.
3   Working with outside agencies to develop promotion plans and campaigns.
4   Developing support for the product from the firm's sales force and distributors.
5   Gathering continuous marketing research information on customers, noncustomers, dealers, competitors, the product's performance, and new opportunities and problems.
6   Finding ways to improve the existing products and create new ones.

Although these six functions are common to both consumer product and industrial product managers, some important differences exist. Consumer product managers are typically responsible for fewer products and spend more time working with marketing people inside their firm (marketing research, packaging design, and sales) and outside it (advertising agencies and distributors). In contrast, industrial product managers like those in Intel who are responsible for integrated circuit chips usually have more products and spend more time working with technical personnel in the firm's engineering, production, and R&D departments and talking directly to sales representatives and important customers.[20]

There are both benefits and dangers to the product manager system used by many consumer product and industrial product companies. On the positive side, product managers become strong advocates for the assigned products. This means they can react quickly to problems or changes in the marketplace and cut red tape to work with people in various functions both inside and outside the organization (Figure 22–6); can orchestrate and balance both marketing and nonmarketing activities; and can assume profit-and-loss responsibility for the performance of the product line.

Balanced against these benefits are some potential dangers that all relate to one factor: even though product managers have major responsibilities, they have relatively little direct authority. Product managers, responsible for one or more products, typically have two people reporting to them at most—often only one person in industrial product manager positions. However, all the other groups and functions shown in Figure 22–6 must be coordinated and used to meet the product's goals.[21] To successfully coordinate the many functions, managers must use persuasion rather than orders. Further, because promotions or transfers to other products may take place after only a few years on the job, product managers often become concerned with immediate results rather than long-term performance of their products.[22]

Concept Check

1 **What is the difference between a line and a staff position in a marketing organization?**

2 **What are four groupings used within a typical marketing organization?**

THE CONTROL PHASE OF THE STRATEGIC MARKETING PROCESS

The essence of control, the final phase of the strategic marketing process, is comparing results with planned goals for the marketing plan and taking necessary actions.

THE MARKETING CONTROL PROCESS

Ideally, quantified goals from the marketing plans developed in the planning phase have been accomplished by the marketing actions taken in the implementation phase (Figure 22–7) and measured as results in the control phase. A marketing manager then uses *management by exception,* which means identifying results that deviate from plans to diagnose their causes and take new actions. Often, results fall short of plans and a corrective action is needed. For example, after 50 years of profits Caterpillar accumulated losses of $1 billion. To correct the problem, Caterpillar focussed its marketing efforts on core products and reduced its manufacturing costs.[23] At other times the comparison shows that performance is far better than anticipated, in which case the marketing manager tries to identify the reason and move quickly to exploit the unexpected opportunity.

Marketing control is an especially difficult and important problem in today's corporations, with many divisions carrying diverse products and services among which scarce resources must be deployed. David Johnson faced such a situation when he recently took over as CEO of Campbell Soup Company. Through a control process Johnson began to focus on products related to two

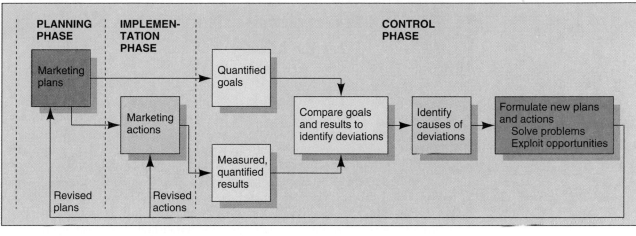

❙ *Figure 22–7*
The control phase of the strategic marketing process.

technologies—heat processing and frozen processing—and reduced the resources allocated to businesses such as salmon farming and meal delivery and products like fresh salads and the Souper Combo (a frozen soup-and-sandwich package). Investments are now directed at the well-known soup brand and competitive offerings such as the Swanson frozen dinner line.[24]

Measuring Results   Without some quantitative goal, no benchmark exists with which to compare actual results. Manufacturers of both consumer and industrial products are increasingly trying to develop marketing plans that have not only specific objectives but also specific procedures for monitoring and measuring them. See the accompanying Ethics and Social Responsibility Alert for a discussion about the difficulty associated with selecting appropriate performance measures.

Taking Marketing Actions   When results deviate significantly from plans, some kind of action is essential. Deviations can be the result of the process used to specify objectives, or can be due to changes in the marketplace.[25] Timex Canada was losing market share because it didn't have the strategies or the people in place to keep pace with a quickly changing industry. To stop the decline, Timex completely rethought its strategies, product lines, and executions. A massive corporate restructuring and the implementation of a multibrand strategy promoting fashion and sports and activity styles were the keys to their revitalization and maintenance of their number-one position in the industry.[26]

SALES ANALYSIS

For controlling marketing plans, **sales analysis**—using the firm's sales records to compare actual results with sales goals and identify areas of strength and weakness—is critical. All the variables that might be used in market segmentation may be used in **sales component analysis** (also called *microsales analysis*), which traces sales revenues to their sources, such as specific products, sales territories, or customers. Common breakdowns include:

ETHICS AND SOCIAL RESPONSIBILITY ALERT

What You Measure Is What You Get

The control phase of the strategic marketing process requires that results of marketing actions be measured and quantified. Traditional measures have included sales revenue, return on investment, and earnings per share. Organizations that focus on these financial figures, however, tend to encourage strategies that ignore important marketing goals. In today's competitive environment, performance measures such as customer satisfaction, new product development cycle time, order response time, market share, and sales force motivation deserve consideration as marketing actions are evaluated. Part of the difficulty of using multiple performance measures is that improvement along one dimension might lead to a decline on another dimension. Dell Computer, for example, has been able to increase sales and maintain customer service levels, but profit margins are declining.

How would you deal with this problem? When should financial goals have a lower priority than other performance dimensions?

Sources: R. Kaplan and D. Norton, "The Balanced Scorecard—Measures That Drive Performance," *Harvard Business Review,* January–February 1992, pp. 71–79; and R. Eccles, "The Performance Measurement Manifests," *Harvard Business Review,* January–February 1991, pp. 131–39.

- Customer characteristics: demographics, Standard Industrial Classification, size, reason for purchase, and type of reseller (retailer or wholesaler).
- Product characteristics: model, package size, and colour.
- Geographical region: sales territory, city, province, and region.
- Order size.
- Price or discount class.
- Commission to the sales representative.

Today's computers can easily produce these breakdowns, provided the input data contain these classifications. Therefore it is critical that marketing managers request the breakdowns they require from accounting and information systems departments. The danger is that marketing managers or chief executive officers are so overwhelmed by the volume of computerized reports that they can't spot the key performance numbers in the report needed for control and subsequent action.

PROFITABILITY ANALYSIS

To their surprise, marketing managers often discover the 80/20 principle (see Chapter 9) the hard way, on the job. **Profitability analysis** enables the manager to measure the profitability of the firm's products, customer groups, sales territories, channels of distribution, and even order sizes. This leads to decisions to expand, maintain, reduce, or eliminate specific products, customer groups, or channels.[27]

For example, following the 80/20 principle, a marketing manager will try to find the common characteristics among the 20 percent of the customers (or products, brands, sales districts, salespeople, or kinds of orders) that are generating 80 percent (or the bulk) of revenues and profits to find more like them to exploit competitive advantages. Conversely, the 80 percent of customers, products, brands, and so on that are generating few revenues and profits may need to be reduced or even dropped entirely unless a way is found to make them profitable.

Profitability analysis provides the basis for such decisions. The type of profitability analysis discussed here is **contribution margin analysis,** which monitors controllable costs and indicates the contribution to profit of specific marketing factors. To obtain cost information for this type of analysis, companies such as Hewlett-Packard are developing new accounting systems based on input from marketing, manufacturing, product design, and accounting.[28]

Figure 22−8 is an example of a contribution margin analysis of the sales performance of three sales representatives who make up a sales district. The report, provided by a spreadsheet program, breaks the sales revenue, contribution margin, and personal selling costs down by sales territory to show the net contribution of each sales representative.

▌ *Figure 22−8*
Comparative income statement for three sales representatives and the total sales district.

	E. MARTIN		J. TAYLOR		W. JONES		DISTRICT TOTALS	
	DOLLARS (Thousands)	PER-CENTAGE	DOLLARS (Thousands)	PER-CENTAGE	DOLLARS (Thousands)	PER-CENTAGE	DOLLARS (Thousands)	PER-CENTAGE
Sales	$2,200	100.00%	$2,500	100.00%	$2,000	100.00%	$6,700	100.00%
Cost of goods sold	1,721	78.23	1,887	75.48	1,543	77.15	5,151	76.88
Contribution margin	479	21.77	613	24.52	457	22.85	1,549	23.12
Account costs								
Freight	63	2.86	65	2.60	60	3.00	188	2.80
Inventory	44	2.00	30	1.20	39	1.95	113	1.69
Accounts receivable	64	2.91	75	3.00	59	2.95	198	2.96
Technical services	18	0.82	18	0.72	17	0.85	53	0.79
Advertising and promotion	21	0.96	35	1.40	18	0.90	74	1.10
Total customer costs	$210	9.55%	$223	8.92%	$193	9.65%	$626	9.34%
Personal selling costs								
Compensation	$31.50	1.43%	$33.00	1.32%	$29.90	1.50%	$94.40	1.41%
Transportation	6.00	0.27	5.00	0.20	7.00	0.35	18.00	0.27
Lodging, meals	3.50	0.16	3.50	0.14	4.00	0.20	11.00	0.16
Telephone	1.35	0.06	1.70	0.07	1.20	0.06	4.25	0.06
Entertainment	3.00	0.14	1.00	0.04	2.50	0.12	6.50	0.10
Samples, brochures	2.00	0.09	2.00	0.08	1.50	0.07	5.50	0.08
Miscellaneous	0.50	0.02	0.50	0.02	0.30	0.02	1.30	0.02
Total personal selling costs	$ 47.85	2.17%	$46.70	1.87%	$46.40	2.32%	$140.95	2.10%
Net territory contribution	$221.15	10.05%	$343.30	13.73%	$217.60	10.88%	$782.05	11.67%

Figure 22-9 Marketing audit questions.

PRODUCTS/SERVICES: THE REASON FOR EXISTENCE

1 Is the product/service free from deadwood?
2 What is the life cycle stage?
3 How will user demands or trends affect you?
4 Are you a leader in new product innovation?
5 Are inexpensive methods used to estimate new product potentials before considerable amounts are spent on R&D and market introduction?
6 Do you have different quality levels for different markets?
7 Are packages/brochures effective salespeople for the products/services they present?
8 Do you present products/services in the most appealing colours (formats) for markets being served?
9 Are there features or benefits to exploit?
10 Is the level of customer service adequate?
11 How are quality and reliability viewed by customers?

CUSTOMER: USER PROFILES

1 Who are the current and the potential customer?
2 Are there geographic aspects of use: regional, rural, urban?
3 Why do people buy the product/service; what motivates their preferences?
4 Who makes buying decisions; when, where?
5 What is the frequency and quantity of use?

MARKETS: WHERE PRODUCTS/SERVICES ARE SOLD

1 Have you identified and measured major segments?
2 Are small, potential market segments overlooked in trying to satisfy the majority?
3 Are the markets for the products/services expanding or declining?
4 Should different segments be developed; are there gaps in penetration?

COMPETITORS: THEIR INFLUENCE

1 Who are the principal competitors, how are they positioned, and where are they headed?
2 What are their market shares?
3 What features of competitors' products/services stand out?
4 Is the market easily entered or dominated?

PRICING: PROFITABILITY PLANNING

1 What are the objectives of current pricing policy: acquiring, defending, or expanding?
2 Are price policies set to produce volume or profit?
3 How does pricing compare with competition in similar levels of quality?
4 Does cost information show profitability of each item?

5 What is the history of price deals, discounts, and promotions?
6 Are intermediaries making money from the line?
7 Can the product/service support advertising or promotion programs?
8 Will the manufacturing process require more volume?

MARKETING CHANNELS: SELLING PATHS

1 Does the system offer the best access to all target markets?
2 Do product/service characteristics require specials?
3 What is the most profitable type of presentation for each market: direct versus reps, master distributors or dealers, etc?
4 What are the trends in distribution methods?

SALES ADMINISTRATION: SELLING EFFICIENCY

1 Are customers getting coverage in proportion to their potential?
2 Are sales costs planned and controlled?
3 Does the compensation plan provide optimum incentive and security at reasonable cost?
4 Is performance measured against potential?
5 Are selling expenses proportionate to results and potentials within markets or territories?
6 Are there deficiencies in recruitment, selection, training, motivation, supervision, performance, promotion, or compensation?
7 Are effective selling aids and sales tools provided?

ADVERTISING: MEDIA PROGRAM

1 Are media objectives and strategies linked to the marketing plan?
2 What are the objectives of the ad program?
3 How is media effectiveness measured?
4 Is advertising integrated with promotion and sales activity?
5 Is the ad agency's effectiveness periodically evaluated?
6 Do you dictate copy theme and content to the agency?
7 Are you spending realistically, in relation to budget?

SALES PROMOTION: SALES INDUCEMENT

1 Does the sales promotion support a marketing objective?
2 Is it integrated with advertising and selling activity?
3 How is it measured for results?
4 Are slogans, trademarks, logos, and brands being used effectively?
5 Is point-of-sale material cost-effective?
6 Are you effectively using couponing, tie-ins, incentives, sampling, stuffers, or combination offers?
7 How do you evaluate trade shows for effectiveness?

Source: Adapted from H. W. Goetsch, "Conduct a Comprehensive Marketing Audit to Improve Marketing Planning," *Marketing News*, March 18, 1983, p. 14; by permission of the American Marketing Association.

The specific costs for each sales representative are expressed as a percentage of sales revenue, or an **expense-to-sales ratio.** This ratio reveals important deviations from the average for the total district. For example, sales representative Taylor's personal selling costs are 1.87 percent of sales revenues, while the district average is 2.10 percent, because Taylor's costs in such areas as transportation, lodging, and entertainment are lower than those of the other representatives.[29]

THE MARKETING AUDIT

Both sales and profitability analyses like those just discussed have great value in the control phase of the strategic marketing process, but the focus of such analyses is usually quite narrow, such as monthly, quarterly, or annual deviations that address a specific product, customer segment, sales territory, or order size.

Often a broader marketing perspective is needed, one that covers a longer time horizon and relates the marketing mix factors to environmental, consumer, competitive, and industry variables. This is the role of a **marketing audit,** which is a comprehensive, unbiased, periodic review of the strategic marketing process of a firm or strategic business unit (SBU). The purpose of the marketing audit, which serves as both a planning and a control technique, is to identify new problems and opportunities that warrant an action plan to improve performance.[30]

Most firms undertaking a marketing audit use a checklist such as that shown in Figure 22–9. Before deciding where the firm or SBU should go (the objective-setting step in the planning phase), the firm must determine where it is now through a situation analysis. The checklist used covers factors ranging from the marketing mix factors and customer profiles to markets and competitors.

For a meaningful, comprehensive marketing audit, the individual or team conducting the audit must have free rein to talk to managers, employees, salespeople, distributors, and customers, as well as have access to all pertinent internal and external reports and memoranda. The audit needs to involve top management and the doers in the process to ensure that resulting action recommendations have their support.

Concept Check

1 **What two components of the strategic marketing process are compared to control a marketing plan?**

2 **What is the difference between a sales analysis and a profitability analysis?**

3 **What is a marketing audit?**

Summary

1 The implementation phase of the strategic marketing process is concerned with executing the marketing plan developed in the planning phase. Successful marketing plans require both effective planning and effective implementation.

2 As implementation has increased in importance, many companies have reorganized and reduced the size of their corporate planning staff to improve their implementation efforts.

3 Keys to successful marketing implementation include communicating both goals and means of achieving them; finding a product or plan champion; rewarding successful implementation; acting rather than overanalyzing; fostering open communications to surface problems; and scheduling precise tasks, responsibilities, and deadlines.

4 Essential to good scheduling is separating tasks that can be done concurrently from those that must be done sequentially. Gantt charts are a simple, effective means of scheduling.

5 Organizing marketing activities necessitates recognition of two different aspects of an organization: *(a)* line and staff positions and *(b)* product line, functional, geographical, and market-based groupings.

6 The product manager performs a vital marketing role in both consumer and industrial product firms, interacting with numerous people and groups both inside and outside the firm.

7 In many consumer product organizations the product manager heads up a product or brand group. A product manager has important responsibilities in being an advocate for the product line but often suffers from a lack of direct authority to get things done.

8 The control phase of the strategic marketing process involves measuring the results of the actions from the implementation phase and comparing them with goals set in the planning phase. Deviations are identified, and actions are taken to correct deficiencies and exploit opportunities.

9 Sales analyses, profitability analyses, and marketing audits are used to control marketing plans.

Key Terms and Concepts

product or plan champion p. 566
action item list p. 568
line positions p. 570
staff positions p. 571
product line groupings p. 571
functional groupings p. 571
geographical groupings p. 572

market-based groupings p. 572
sales analysis p. 575
sales component analysis p. 575
profitability analysis p. 576
contribution margin analysis p. 577
expense-to-sales ratio p. 579
marketing audit p. 579

Chapter Problems and Applications

1 Tom Monaghan's first Domino's Pizza restaurant was near a college campus. What implementation problems are *(a)* similar and *(b)* different for restaurants near a college campus versus a military base?

2 What is the "offering" to a Domino's Pizza customer? What needs to be measured to determine if the offering is satisfactory to customers?

3 If General Electric decides to use teams to implement its plans and achieve its goals, what characteristics will improve their likelihood of success?

4 A common theme among managers who succeed repeatedly in plan implementation is fostering open communication. Why is this so important?

5 Parts of tasks 6 and 7 in Figure 22–4 are done *both* concurrently and sequentially. How can this be? How does it help the students meet the term paper deadline?

6 In Pillsbury's organizational chart in Figure 22–5, where do product line, functional, and geographical groupings occur?

7 In what way can a product manager in a grocery products firm have *both (a)* significant responsibility and *(b)* limited authority?

8 Why are quantified objectives in the planning phase of the strategic marketing process important for the control phase?

9 In Figures 22–8, which sales representative makes the least net territory contribution to the sales district? Why?

PART VI

Expanding Marketing Settings

*M*arketing *has become an imported activity in many new settings. The traditional focus on packaged goods in the Canadian market has now expanded to include goods and services in the global marketplace. Chapter 23 describes the concept of international marketing and explains how the marketing concepts discussed in previous chapters can be applied to compete in an international arena. Chapter 23 also identifies key multinational trade groups, such as the rapidly growing Pacific Rim countries, that will shape world trade in the future. In Chapter 24, examples from various services companies provide insight about the role of marketing as the Canadian and global economies become increasingly service-based. Part VI emphasizes that applying marketing to international markets and services represents some of today's most exciting opportunities for marketing managers and for consumers.*

International Marketing

AFTER READING THIS CHAPTER YOU SHOULD BE ABLE TO:

▸ Describe why Canadian firms are undertaking international marketing.

▸ Contrast global, customized, and "glocalized" approaches to international marketing.

▸ Understand the importance of environmental factors (economic, political, and cultural) in successful international marketing.

▸ Identify alternative modes of entering international marketing operations.

▸ Explain how and why Canadian firms may have to adapt their marketing mix when entering the international arena.

Reaching the Biggest One-Nation Middle-Class Market on the Globe

Quick! What country has the largest middle-class market in the world? China or Russia? No. United States or Japan? No. The answer: India. India has 100 million upper middle-class and 200 million lower middle-class consumers. Indian upper middle-class consumers have incomes exceeding the equivalent of $1,750 Canadian. Whoa! Does that income qualify as middle class? As discussed later in the chapter, Canadian firms considering entering new global markets look at what incomes in a nation can actually buy, as well as their Canadian dollar equivalent.[1]

A look at India's attractions and drawbacks for firms considering entering global markets gives an idea of the dilemmas they face. On the plus side is the size of the consumer market. For example, 200 million lower middle-class consumers with annual household incomes of between $850 and $1,750 buy more than 75 percent of the country's unit sales of radios and more than 60 percent of laundry detergents. With the income disparities in India, every firm is targeting a different market. Gillette's subsidiary Indian Shaving Products targets the 240 million city dwellers, and it sells more than 2.7 billion blades in India—more than Gillette sells in any other country. Also, India's technical workforce is the third largest in the world, and India has a huge pool of English-speaking managers. In contrast to the former Soviet bloc, India has a history of private businesses working alongside state-owned operations.

On the minus side are the political and economic uncertainties that firms entering the Indian market face. A key is India's recent actions to dismantle parts of its central planning bureaucracy to encourage foreign investment. India is now simplifying its spider's web of regulations known as the license *raj*—Hindi for "rule"—to allow foreign firms to participate in up to 51 percent of joint ventures and take dividends out of the country. When Pepsi-Cola sought the opportunity to invest in India in 1986, the proposal encountered 20 parliamentary debates, 15 committee reviews, and 5,000 press articles—many of them unfavourable. Firms entering the Indian marketplace hope that these hurdles are now gone, and they are counting on pressure from India's growing middle class to force the government to open the country to global marketers.[2]

Something must be going right for foreign investment in India. In a recent 15-month period, the government approved $1.3 billion in investments by international firms including IBM, Kellogg, BMW, Fujitsu, DuPont, and Coca-Cola.

After defining exactly what international marketing is and why firms such as these assume great risks to do it, this chapter discusses the importance of environmental factors in successful international marketing, describes alternative means of entering the international market, and explains how successful marketing plans in Canada often have to be modified for use abroad.

THE SCOPE OF INTERNATIONAL MARKETING

Why would successful Canadian firms like Alcan, Bombardier, and Northern Telecom want to enter international markets when domestic marketing seems so much easier? Indeed, with the potential problems of foreign languages, different currencies, volatile political and legal arenas, and different consumer needs and expectations, why get involved in international marketing at all? Let us try to answer these questions.

WHAT INTERNATIONAL MARKETING IS

Stated simply, **international marketing** is marketing across national boundaries. Since the end of World War II, improved travel, communications, and technology have fostered a 10-fold increase in trade among nations.

As mentioned briefly in Chapter 5, the General Agreement on Tariffs and Trade (GATT) is an international agreement established in 1948 that seeks to "liberalize world trade and place it on a secure basis, thereby contributing to economic growth and development and to the welfare of the world's peoples."[3] It assists in reducing trade barriers around the world and in creating more favourable conditions for world trade. Since GATT was established, this agreement has helped build world trade from $60 billion to $4 trillion annually. However, GATT negotiations "to liberalize world trade" can bog down and extend for years because of the desire of countries to protect jobs in their domestic industries.

BENEFITS AND DIFFICULTIES OF INTERNATIONAL MARKETING

A company choosing to enter international markets can achieve many benefits, but it can also encounter many difficulties.

Benefits of International Marketing The main reason for companies to do international marketing is to exploit a better business opportunity in terms of increased sales and profits. Either firms are limited in their home country or their opportunities are great in the foreign countries. Some firms get a large portion of their sales revenues from international operations, such as MacMillan Bloedal (57 percent), Chrysler Canada (60 percent), and the Royal Canadian Mint (80 percent).[4]

Many companies find themselves with little room for growth in their domestic market. Competition may increase and leave a smaller portion of the pie to enjoy, or demand may shift to a newer, better product. The economic environment in the home country may be undesirable because of higher taxes or a recession. It would seem logical to turn to other markets in any of these cases. For example, Japan's Yaohan Department Store Company—faced with a recession at home—is now constructing the world's largest department store in Shanghai and expects to build 1,000 supermarkets in China by the year 2000.

Hence foreign markets may offer an opportunity for growth. A product that is mature and facing dwindling sales at home may be new and exciting in other countries. For example, France's Sodima, whose Yoplait yogourt was in a mature phase of its product life cycle at home, was happy to license its product to General Mills for sale in North America, where yogourt sales were growing rapidly. Similarly, McDonald's Canada is encouraged by its sales in Russia, where the hamburger market is in the early stage of the product life cycle and competition is less intense than in Canada. Volvo cannot sell enough cars in its own domestic Swedish market, so it must achieve global sales to achieve necessary production and marketing economies of scale. Figure 23–1 summarizes the main reasons why Canadian companies consider entering international markets. (Also see the accompanying Marketing Action Memo.)

Why do firms "go international," and why must Volvo seek markets outside its domestic Swedish market? For the answers, see the text.

Difficulties of International Marketing Is international marketing easy? Not in the least. For Canadian and US firms anxious to enter the Japanese market and make profits quickly, strategy consultant Kenichi Ohmae reminds them it took perhaps 50 years to build their firm and 15 years to develop their European business. So he asks these firms to recognize that in entering the Japanese market—one of the toughest markets in the world—it may take at least 25 years to achieve the same success found in Canada, the United States, or Europe.[5] As we saw in Chapter 5, one of Canada's famous chocolate makers, Ganong Brothers, found that entering the Japanese market does take time and patience.

---

1 To counter adverse economic factors in the home market.
2 To extend a product's life cycle.
3 To reduce or avoid competition.
4 To enhance economies of scale in production and marketing.
5 To spread fixed costs over more units sold.
6 To dispose of inventories.
7 To export (and import) new technology.
8 To increase profits or shareholder economic well-being.

▌ *Figure 23–1*
Key reasons Canadian firms "go international."

MARKETING · ACTION · MEMO

Sico Goes International

Faced with a flat market on its home turf, paint producer Sico is beefing up its marketing and making ambitious plans to expand across North America and into Asia. Sico's success at penetrating international markets depends on its sense of reality, its financial capacity, and its marketing expertise, according to Roger Samson, vice president of Sico. Growth may have to come through acquisitions, so the company can maintain quality levels, which Samson says Sico has the financial capacity to make. But Sico must get to know the markets and adapt its marketing to the realities of the international market.

Sico has six plants in Canada, four in Quebec, and boasts sales of $145 million. Its two main brands, Sico and Crown Diamond, hold well over 50 percent of Quebec's $205 million paint market, where Sico's products are bought four times more often than those

of its nearest competitor, CIL. Its strength in Quebec makes Sico the second-largest player in the $1.5 billion national consumer market—with an 11 percent share of market—even though to date it hardly has a presence outside of Quebec. Sico plans to expand first into neighbouring provinces such as Ontario, although its industrial products are already available in British Columbia and Mexico. Sico is looking at countries such as Vietnam and China as new markets to penetrate. But while international markets are an important priority, Sico is also making moves to ensure it protects its domestic markets from new private-label paints and against new competition provided by stores such as Wal-Mart and Aikenhead.

Source: Adapted from G. Chiasson, "Sico Paints Global Plan," *Marketing,* March 28, 1994, p. 4.

Although international marketing involves the same principles of domestic marketing discussed throughout the book, those principles must be applied with care. Campbell Soup, the company with a 60 percent market share in the North American wet soups category, lost $30 million in Great Britain. The problem was that Campbell's didn't clearly communicate that the soup was condensed, and consumers saw it as a poor value compared with the larger cans stocked next to it. Canadians recognize the brand names of foreign products that have been introduced successfully here: Honda and BMW cars, Sony TV sets, Nestlé candy bars, and Shell gasoline products. Although this chapter will describe foreign successes in Canada, it will also identify how Canadian firms can overcome difficulties in marketing their products abroad.

THE IMPORTANCE AND FOCUS OF INTERNATIONAL MARKETING

To understand the role of international marketing among today's global firms, it is necessary to analyze both its importance and the focus of firms competing in world markets.

Importance of International Marketing   As we saw in Chapter 5, the dollar value of world trade is expected to exceed $4 trillion in 1996. Canada is a trading nation, exporting 25 percent of its gross domestic product, or about

MARKETING · ACTION · MEMO

Canada's Competitiveness in an International Context

Since 1990, Kodak Canada has provided financial support for a publication on Canada's business competitiveness in the international arena. The publication, *Scorecard on Canada's International Competitiveness*, written by Joseph D'Cruz and Alan Rugman, of the University of Toronto, provides some insight into where Canada fits in terms of international competitiveness. The data on Canada are taken from the *World Competitiveness Report* published annually by the International Institute of Management Development and the World Economic Forum, both based in Switzerland. They measure the business competitiveness of 22 industrialized nations and 15 newly industrialized countries. The scoring is based on 371 criteria that cover everything from natural resources through labour productivity to environmental concerns. Countries are ranked overall, and then ranked in terms of specific areas of economic and business performance.

Overall, the results show Canada is at best a middling player on the world stage. Canada ranked 11th, overall, among 22 industrialized countries, and about 15th if you also take into account the newly industrialized nations. But if one looks beyond the overall ranking to Canada's ranking on key factors of competitiveness, our country ranked third in terms of strength in the financial sector, and fifth in terms of infrastructure. However, we ranked 12th in terms of economic strength, 14th on quality of management, 16th on use of science and technology, and 20th with respect to involvement in world trade. The report by D'Cruz and Rugman raises questions about Canada's present and future ability to compete effectively in the international arena.

Source: J. D'Cruz and A. Rugman, *Scorecard on Canada's International Competitiveness* (Kodak Canada, 1993); and "Where in the World is Canada Heading," *Marketing*, February 21, 1994, p. 35.

$180 billion worth of goods and services. Not only are international markets important for the firms themselves that compete in them, but Canadian foreign policy often focusses on achieving fair treatment for Canadian firms in global competition, because of consumer welfare and the thousands of jobs that are at stake. In fact, Canada is often in the forefront of advocating an international economy that is based on fairness.[6] However, as the accompanying Marketing Action Memo points out, there is some concern over Canada's ability to compete in the international arena. This is an important issue, since as a practical matter, all major manufacturing firms throughout the world must now compete in the "triad" markets of North America, Western Europe, and the Far East. And increasingly these firms are looking for opportunities in Latin America, Eastern Europe and the former Soviet bloc, India, China, and other locales as well. A central question is whether or not Canada, as a country, has effectively prepared itself to compete effectively in this new international context.

Focus of Global Corporations   A **global corporation** is a business firm that looks at the entire world as one market and conducts research and development, manufacturing, financing, and marketing activities wherever they can best be done. Such firms have a truly global focus—national boundaries and regulations are largely irrelevant, and the best people available are placed in key positions regardless of national origin. The phrase *global corporation* is replacing *multinational corporation* because the latter has developed an unpleasant, predatory connotation. A global corporation runs its business and makes its decisions on the basis of all the possible choices in the world, not simply favouring domestic options because they are convenient.

GLOBAL VERSUS CUSTOMIZED PRODUCTS, OR A HYBRID?

As international marketing grows, firms selling both consumer and industrial products in foreign countries face a dilemma: should they use a global or a customized strategy in the products they sell, or a strategy in between?

✓ A **global approach** is an international marketing strategy that assumes that the way the product is used and the needs it satisfies are universal. Therefore, the marketing mix need not be adjusted for each country. In contrast, a **customized approach** (or *local approach*) is an international marketing strategy that assumes that the way the product is used and the needs it satisfies are unique to each country. This, then, requires a marketing mix tailored to the needs, values, customs, languages, and purchasing power of the target country. The global approach is less common but has been successful for some firms.

Many firms, as discussed later, have often encountered problems when they simply took existing products and marketing plans into foreign countries with almost no change (a global approach). Other firms watched these errors and shifted to a customized strategy. An example is Kodak's European launch of its Ektaprint copier–duplication line. It had watched Xerox take a successful North American copier into Great Britain only to discover that the equipment didn't fit through narrower British doorways. When Kodak introduced its European copier into Europe, the design included a narrower width than its North American models, language keys on the control panel that are tailored to

These ads are identical except one is in English and the other Italian. This illustrates a "global strategy," whose advantages and dangers are covered in the text.

individual countries, and a variable reduction capability for different page sizes, since there is no standard paper size in Europe comparable to the North American 8½ × 11 inch.

Some global strategists, however, argue that a firm can overreact and carry customized marketing too far in trying to respond to wants of consumers, and that a global strategy is needed.[7] When a global strategy succeeds, huge savings are possible in manufacturing, packaging, and advertising costs. For example, when Colgate-Palmolive introduced its Colgate tartar-control toothpaste in over 40 countries, its marketing executives in these countries received only two TV ads from which to choose. The ads were translated into the local language and were a success. Colgate-Palmolive estimates that it saved up to $2 million in TV production costs for each country that ran the same TV ad.[8] The Strenesse magazine ads, shown here in English and Italian, illustrate this global strategy.

But when a globalization strategy doesn't work, it can be a disaster. Parker Pen, Ltd., is an example. In 1982, it was making about 500 styles of pens and letting local marketing managers in about 150 countries create their own ads and packaging. Using a globalization strategy, by 1984 it had reduced the number of styles of pens to about 100 and offered only a single ad campaign— one that could be translated into local languages. The strategy backfired because local marketing managers resented the standardization of ads and advertising agencies. The company almost went bankrupt until it returned to its customized strategy and let each country develop its own ads.[9]

McDonald's—the undisputed world hamburger ruler—seems to have achieved the ideal hybrid between a global and a customized strategy. Although it has standardized much of its menu, it gives a degree of flexibility to franchisees to allow for local customer preferences in their countries. Experts have coined

Does McDonald's use a global or a customized strategy overseas—or something in between? For McDonald's very successful strategy, see the text.

Assess environmental factors in international markets	Evaluate alternatives for international operations	Tailor marketing plan to the country
Political conditions	Exporting	Select the country
Economic conditions	Licensing	Establish the marketing organization
Cultural conditions	Joint venture	Design and implement the marketing plan
	Direct ownership	

the term **glocalization** to describe the McDonald's approach, which is an international marketing strategy that allows the local organization to tailor a firm's global umbrella strategy to the needs, customs, values, and lifestyles of the local market.

McDonald's in Germany and France has beer on its menu, and its restaurants in Japan offer saki. In the Philippines, where noodle houses are popular, its customers can find—what else?—McSpaghetti! After 14 years of negotiations, McDonald's first Moscow restaurant opened in early 1990 with an awesome size: 700 seats, 27 cash registers, and the ability to serve 40,000 customers per day. But McDonald's had to train these customers how to eat their Russian "Big Mak," because Russians weren't used to eating finger food and initial customers disassembled their Big Maks and ate them one layer at a time.[10] McDonald's has successfully opened two more restaurants in Moscow, and has plans for 20 in that city.

Companies such as Kodak, Colgate-Palmolive, and McDonald's had to make a series of decisions when they entered international markets. These decisions, outlined in Figure 23–2, are discussed in more detail throughout the remainder of the chapter.

Concept Check

1 Given the risks involved, what are several reasons why a firm might undertake international marketing?

2 What is a global corporation?

3 How does glocalization combine two international marketing strategies?

ASSESSING ENVIRONMENTAL FACTORS

Global firms conduct continuing environmental scans of the five sets of environmental forces summarized earlier in Figure 3–1 (social, economic, technological, competitive, and regulatory). This section will focus on three kinds of uncontrollable environmental variables—political, economic, and cultural conditions—that affect international marketing in strikingly different ways from those in domestic markets. This is why many global firms considering marketing efforts in a new country undertake serious on site marketing research—ranging from using published data to interviews with end users and distributors in the country.[11]

Traditional marketing research methods used in Canada often need to be modified in surveying foreign consumers. For example, telephone surveys in former republics of the Soviet Union would not give a representative sample of consumers, because only 28 percent of city families and 9 percent of farm families in these countries have their own telephone.

POLITICAL CONDITIONS

The difficulties in assessing the political conditions of a country lie not only in identifying the current conditions but also in estimating exactly how long those conditions will last. Some global companies use analyses ranging from computer projections to intuition and lost-horse forecasts (see Chapter 10) to assess a country's condition. The dimensions being evaluated include political stability, trade barriers, trade incentives, and multination and trade groups.

Political Stability Billions of dollars have been lost in the Middle East as a result of war and changes in governments. Holiday Inn has been badly hurt during the war in Lebanon. Petroleum firms have lost vast sums throughout the Iran–Iraq and Gulf wars. Losses like these encourage careful selection of stable countries not likely to be suddenly at war.

When instability is suspected, companies do everything they can to protect themselves against losses. Companies will limit their trade to exporting products into the country, minimizing investments in new plants in the foreign economy. Currency will be converted as soon as possible. Many global firms are now reluctant to expand operations in Hong Kong, currently a British crown colony, because of uncertainties about what will happen after 1997, when it reverts to China. Similarly, billions of dollars of investment are on hold by Western firms waiting to see what kind of political stability is in store for countries in Eastern Europe, the former Soviet Union, and Latin America.

Trade Barriers Even stable, friendly countries can change their policies toward international marketing and initiate various kinds of trade barriers. Quotas can be revised or set; currency can be blocked; duties, tariffs, and boycotts can be imposed; and in extreme cases companies can be expropriated. A **quota** is a legal limit placed on the amount of a product allowed to enter or leave a country. **Blocked currency** means that a government will not allow its currency to be converted into other currencies. A **duty** is a special tax on imports or exports. A **tariff** is an official schedule of the duties imposed by a government on imports or exports. A **boycott** is the refusal by the government of one country to have dealings with another country, often to express disapproval for past actions. **Expropriation** is a host country's taking over a foreign company or its assets.

One way to measure a country's attitude toward international trade is to examine the restraints the country puts on it. If tariffs, quotas, and government bureaucracy are plentiful and restrictive, chances are the country is not very receptive to foreign involvement in its economy. Most Canadians see Canada as actively encouraging international trade.

Trade Incentives   Just as countries can discourage international trade through trade barriers, they can also encourage it through offering investment incentives, helping in site location, and providing other services. Hungary is currently offering a five-year "tax holiday"—a period during which no corporate taxes will be assessed—to encourage foreign firms to develop manufacturing facilities there. In addition, a country or group of countries can establish equitable standards to enable foreign products to compete fairly in their domestic markets, the topic discussed next.

Multination Trade Groups   One of the current contrasts in international activities is that while many parts of the former Soviet bloc have been broken apart politically and economically (the former countries of Czechoslovakia, Yugoslavia, and the USSR), many countries in the West have formed stronger economic ties through multination trade groups. The two largest are NAFTA (the North American Free Trade Agreement) and the EC (European Community), which were discussed earlier, in Chapter 5.

A brief look at the NAFTA and EC situations illustrates both the potential upside and downside of such multination agreements. The collective importance of these two groups is huge, as shown by the percentage of the world total for various measures of economic activity:

	PERCENTAGE OF WORLD TOTAL	
MEASURE	NAFTA	EC
Population	7	6
Gross national product	27	28
Total exports	16	38
Grain production	19	9

On the upside, NAFTA negotiations will roll back 20,000 separate tariffs over the next 10 to 15 years and reduce dairy and textile quotas, thereby making many imported and domestic products cheaper to Canadian consumers. NAFTA will also increase jobs in industries like telecommunications, banking, and high technology. But with Mexican wage rates about one-sixth of those in Canada and the United States, and with much less stringent employment and environmental rules, some economists suggest that Canada and the United States will lose many manufacturing jobs in industries like cars and appliances to Mexico over the next decade.[12] Figure 23–3 shows the imports and exports among Canada, Mexico, and the United States, the three members of NAFTA.

On December 31, 1992, the 12 European Community nations reduced most of the barriers to the free flow of goods, services, capital, and labour across their national borders. These countries hope this will be a first step to a giant economic leap forward for their peoples and businesses. But nationalism and protectionism in areas such as oilseed production, banking, and insurance are hurting the EC's goal of a single currency and total elimination of trade barriers.[13]

As shown in Figure 23–4, the collective economic size of the 12 nations that make up the European Community gives it great international significance. The size of the EC market is one reason many global firms are increasing their activity in EC countries. A second reason is that even huge corporations in large

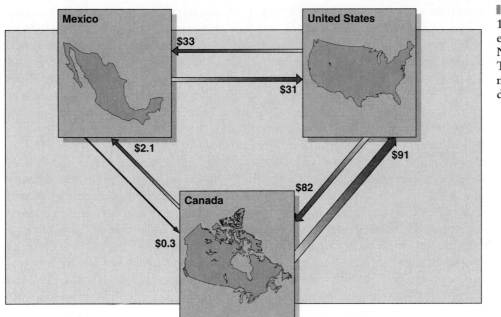

Figure 23–3
1991 imports and exports among the three North American Free Trade Agreement nations, in billions of dollars.

Sources: "The Barriers Come Tumbling Down," *Time,* August 17, 1992, p. 16; and T. E. Weber, "By the Numbers: Trade across a Continent," *The Wall Street Journal,* September 24, 1992, p. R12.

Figure 23–4
Where the markets are: multination trade groups and nations of major economic importance.

RANK BY GROSS NATIONAL PRODUCT	COUNTRY OR GROUP OF COUNTRIES	1989–91 GROSS NATIONAL PRODUCT (in billions of US dollars)	1991 POPULATION ESTIMATE (in millions)
1	12 European Community nations[a]	$6,720	345
2	3 NAFTA nations	6,420	368
3	Japan	3,626	122
4	Former Soviet Union[b]	2,460	289
5	7 European Free Trade Agreement nations[c]	989	90
6	4 Asian "Little Dragons" nations[d]	587	72
7	China	364	1,139
8	India	203	850
9	4 Eastern European nations[e]	118	64
10	4 South American Mercosur nations[f]	44	194

[a]Includes the United Kingdom, Ireland, Portugal, Spain, Denmark, Belgium, the Netherlands, Luxembourg, France, Germany, Italy, and Greece.

[b]Estimates are for the Soviet Union prior to break-up because no current data are available.

[c]Includes Norway, Sweden, Finland, Iceland, Austria, Switzerland, and Turkey.

[d]Includes Hong Kong, Singapore, South Korea, and Taiwan.

[e]Includes Poland, Hungary, the Czech Republic, and Slovakia.

[f]Includes Argentina, Brazil, Paraguay, and Uruguay.

Sources: *International Financial Statistics* (Washington, DC: International Monetary Fund, January 1993); *Population and Vital Statistics Report* (New York: United Nations, 1992); GNP data based on December 1991 exchange rates.

countries can no longer survive competing only in their domestic market if they are in global industries. Hence, Canadian manufacturers must not do business only in North America, but in Europe and Asia as well. For example, a British pharmaceutical expert estimates that in the 1970s it took four or five years and $16 million to develop a new drug. Today it takes up to 12 years and $250 million—a cost that is only possible for a global product in a global market.

Figure 23–4 also contains information on other multination trade groups (both formal and informal) and on individual countries that represent important markets of the 1990s. The seven European Free Trade Agreement (EFTA) countries (Austria, Switzerland, Norway, Sweden, Finland, Iceland, and Turkey) have tariff-free trade with the EC, but none of the political commitments. The four South American Mercosur countries (Argentina, Brazil, Paraguay, and Uruguay) planned to eliminate tariff barriers among their nations by December 31, 1994. The former Soviet Union doesn't qualify as a multination trade bloc, but it is included in Figure 23–4 anyway, to show its economic significance. The transition period into free-market economies will be traumatic for the republics of the former Soviet Union and other Eastern European countries, which face soaring inflation and unemployment as they redirect their economies.

Oblivious to many Canadian firms is the skyrocketing growth in East Asia—from Japan and the four "Little Dragons" (Hong Kong, Singapore, South Korea, and Taiwan) through Thailand, Malaysia, and Indonesia. Adding in China, these countries are likely to rival the gross domestic product of NAFTA or the European Community by the year 2000.[14]

ECONOMIC CONDITIONS

There are several important rules to international marketing in light of a country's economic conditions: the product must fit the needs of the country's consumers, and it must be sold where there is the income to buy it and there are effective means of distributing, using, and servicing it. Four aspects of these considerations are the country's stage of economic development, the country's economic infrastructure, consumer income, and currency exchange rates.

Stage of Economic Development   There are over 200 countries in the world today, each of which is at a slightly different stage of its economic development. However, they can be classified into two major groupings that will help the international marketer better understand their needs:

- *Developed* countries have somewhat mixed economies. Private enterprise dominates, although they have substantial public sectors as well. The United States, Canada, Japan, and most of Western Europe can be considered developed.
- *Developing* countries are in the process of moving from an agricultural to an industrial economy. There are two subgroups within the developing category: (1) those that have already made the move and (2) those that remain locked in a preindustrial economy. Countries such as Poland, Hungary, Australia, Israel, Venezuela, and South Africa fall into the first group. In the second

group are Pakistan, Sri Lanka, Tanzania, and Chad, where living standards are low and improvement will be slow. One third of the world's population is in this second group.

The stage of economic development significantly affects other economic factors, as discussed in what follows.

Economic Infrastructure   The **economic infrastructure**—a country's communication, transportation, financial, and distribution systems—is a critical consideration in determining whether to try to market to a country's consumers and organizations. Poor economic infrastructure is why many North American and European manufacturers of consumer goods have generally avoided China. But producers of primary goods such as wheat and coal and industrial product manufacturers are marketing in China. Companies in the transportation and communications fields are doing particularly well in selling products and services needed to develop China's infrastructure. This will eventually pave the way for more consumer goods manufacturers to serve China more effectively.

Parts of the infrastructure that North Americans or Western Europeans take for granted can be huge problems elsewhere, not only in developing countries but even in former Soviet-bloc nations where such infrastructure is assumed to be in place. Communications is an example. In 1992, there were only 100 international telephone lines going into Russia, so overseas dialing could take hours. In Warsaw it is not uncommon to dial a half dozen times before connecting with the desired number—the other five are busy or wrong numbers, because of the antiquated system. In Moscow, *Reader's Digest* learned to send its material by registered mail in plain brown envelopes—or by private delivery services—because attractive packages tend to get "lost" in the Russian postal system.[15] These communications problems have led to billions of dollars of investment to upgrade telecommunications and postal systems in Eastern European nations.

Even the legal system can cause problems. Emerging markets such as Indonesia and China lack a written, legal framework for business, so transactions in these nations rely more heavily on personal relationships. Also, because private property did not exist under communism, the legal red tape involved in obtaining title to buildings and land for new manufacturing operations has been a huge problem for Western firms trying to conduct business in former Soviet-bloc nations.

Consumer Income   A global marketer selling consumer goods also must consider what the average per capita income is among a nation's consumers and how the income is distributed. Per capita income is less than $200 annually in some of the developing countries. However, a country's distribution of income is also important, as it may give a more reliable picture of what a household's real discretionary income actually is. Because a consumer in a developing country has income and subsidies that provide for far more food, housing, and health care than in Western nations, global firms take great care in interpreting local economic data. That is why India, the chapter's opening example, holds increasing interest for global marketers. And while the average annual wage in China is less than $500, many Chinese have second jobs or bonuses not reported as income. With heavily subsidized housing, a large proportion of a Chinese consumer's income is disposable.[16]

Currency Exchange Rates   Fluctuations in exchange rates among the world's currencies are of critical importance in international marketing. Such fluctuations affect everyone—from international vacationers to global corporations. But in seeking to protect their investments, global corporations face even more frantic currency exchange problems than individual tourists. For example, global corporations have foreign currency traders whose job goes on 24 hours a day. Currency fluctuations can wipe out a firm's profit from regular operations, so decisions on when to buy or sell foreign currencies are critical. For example, in one four-year period in the 1980s, Kodak lost about $500 million because of currency fluctuations.

Some experts believe McDonald's rubles-only policy in its first Russian restaurant cost the company valuable revenue. At the nearby Pizza Hut, Russians without hard currency could buy pizza with rubles but had to take it away. To sit inside, you needed hard currency. McDonald's Canada established the rubles-only policy so Russian customers wouldn't feel like second-class citizens in their own country. The problem centres on the conversion rate on the ruble. The restaurant took in an estimated 117 million rubles in the first year. That would be fine, according to some experts, using the official rate of 1.8 rubles to the dollar. But at the black market rate of 25 rubles to the dollar, the revenues from the restaurant would be less than $5 million—not a lot of money compared with the $45 million capital investment for a processing plant and the restaurant. But McDonald's argues that it is looking at long-term profitability. It currently uses barter to generate hard currency, and now accepts other currency at its three Moscow restaurants.[17]

CULTURAL CONDITIONS

As discussed in Chapter 5, understanding a foreign nation's society and its culture is of vital importance. The culture of a country will influence what needs consumers have and how they go about satisfying them. *Reader's Digest* vice president Carole M. Howard gives some lessons that the company learned when its Russian and Hungarian editions were launched in 1991:[18]

1 Understand the local market, culture, and business environment. Russians may not arrive at work until 10:00 AM—not because they're lazy, but because they've been up since 5:00 AM standing in long lines shopping for food. So a big tote bag with the *Reader's Digest* logo in Russian was a hit as a giveaway at the news conference product launch.

2 Use traditional Western marketing and promotional techniques—with a dose of common sense. Direct mail is almost unknown in Hungary, so it can be *very* effective, but the quality of mailing lists is likely to be bad.

3 Stick to a back-to-basics approach. Do marketing research early to recover from surprises. The approach in both countries: use the *Reader's Digest* name and the phrase "World's most widely read magazine now on sale in Hungary (or Russia)" in every ad, mailing, and point-of-purchase display that appears.

4 Pay relentless attention to details. This gets down to such details as making sure your video plays in the host country's technical format and double-checking your translations with someone whom you trust—and who understands the local idiom.

5 Communicate, communicate, communicate. State things simply in all communications and put key items in writing to avoid misunderstandings. Talk frequently to be sure there's an easy, nonthreatening avenue for open communications.

Reader's Digest learned important lessons that apply to most global firms entering foreign markets when it launched its Russian and Hungarian editions. For those lessons, see the text.

These guidelines apply whenever a firm enters a new country, regardless of the good or service sold.

---

1 Why is analysis of the international marketing environment so important?

2 What are examples of trade barriers and trade incentives that global firms should consider when undertaking marketing activities in a new country?

3 What is a country's economic infrastructure?

EVALUATING ALTERNATIVES FOR GLOBAL OPERATIONS

Once a company has decided to enter the global marketplace, it must select a means of entry. The option chosen depends on its willingness and ability to commit financial, physical, and managerial resources. As Figure 23–5 demonstrates, the amount of financial commitment, risk, and profit potential increases as the firm moves from exporting to direct ownership. Host countries not only seek the benefits of additional products available for sale but are often even more interested in the number of good jobs available for local workers. Figure 23–5 shows that local employment increases significantly as a firm's financial commitment increases.

EXPORTING

Exporting is producing goods in one country and selling them in another country. This entry option allows a company to make the fewest changes in

▌*Figure 23–5*
Alternative methods for entering international markets.

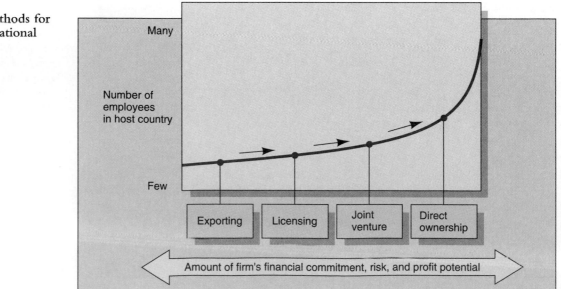

product, organization, and even corporate goals. Host countries usually do not like this practice, because it provides less local employment than alternative means of entry.

Indirect exporting is a firm's selling its domestically produced goods in a foreign country through an intermediary. It involves the least commitment and risk, but will probably return the least profit. This kind of exporting is ideal for the company that has no overseas contacts but wants to market abroad. The intermediary is often a broker or an agent that has the international marketing know-how and the resources necessary for the effort to succeed.

Direct exporting is a firm's selling its domestically produced goods in a foreign country without intermediaries. Most companies become involved in direct exporting when they believe their volume of sales will be sufficiently large and easy to obtain so that they do not require intermediaries. For example, the exporter may be approached by foreign buyers that are willing to contract for a large volume of purchases. Direct exporting involves more risk than indirect exporting for the company, but also opens the door to increased profits.

LICENSING

Under licensing, a company offers the right to a trademark, patent, trade secret, or other similarly valued items of intellectual property in return for a royalty or a fee. In international marketing, the advantages to the company granting the license are low risk and a capital-free entry into a foreign country. The licensee gains information that allows it to start with a competitive advantage, and the foreign country gains employment by having the product manufactured locally.

There are some serious drawbacks to this mode of entry, however. The licensor forgoes control of its product and reduces the potential profits gained from it. In addition, while the relationship lasts, the licensor may be creating its own competition. Some licensees are able to modify the product somehow and enter the market with product and marketing knowledge gained at the expense of the company that got them started. To offset this disadvantage, many companies strive to stay innovative so that the licensee remains dependent on them for improvements and successful operation. Finally, should the licensee prove to be a poor choice, the name or reputation of the company may be harmed.

Two variations of licensing, local manufacturing and local assembly, represent alternative ways to produce a product within the foreign country. With local manufacturing, a Canadian company may contract with a foreign firm to manufacture products according to stated specifications. The product is then sold in the foreign country or exported back to Canada. With local assembly, the Canadian company may contract with a firm in a foreign country to assemble (not manufacture) parts and components that have been shipped to that country. In both cases, advantage to the foreign country is the employment of its people, and the Canadian firm benefits from the lower wage rates in the foreign country.

JOINT VENTURE

When a foreign company and a local firm invest together to create a local business, it is called a **joint venture.** These two companies share ownership, control, and profits of the new company. Investment may be made by having either of the companies buy shares in the other or by creating a third and separate entity.

The advantages of this option are twofold. First, one company may not have the necessary financial, physical, or managerial resources to enter a foreign market alone. Second, a government may require or strongly encourage a joint venture before it allows a foreign company to enter its market.

The disadvantages arise when the two companies disagree about policies or courses of action for their joint venture or when governmental bureaucracy bogs down the effort. For example, Canadian firms often prefer to reinvest earnings gained, whereas some foreign companies may want to spend those earnings. Or a Canadian firm may want to return profits earned to Canada, while the local firm or its government may oppose this—the problem now faced by many potential joint ventures in Eastern Europe. For example, Gillette entered into a joint venture to produce razor blades with Leninets, a huge Russian holding company that agreed to provide buildings for its share of the joint venture. But with the breakup of the USSR, Gillette couldn't find the political entity to approve the transfer of the title of the buildings, a question that is still unresolved.[19]

DIRECT OWNERSHIP

The biggest commitment a company can make when entering the international market is **direct ownership,** a domestic firm's actually investing in and owning a foreign subsidiary or division. Examples of direct ownership are Toyota's automobile plant in Ontario and Hyundai's plant in Quebec. Many Canadian-based global corporations are also switching to this mode of entry. For example, Alcan opened a $30 million recycling plant in Worrington, England.

The advantages to direct ownership include cost savings, better understanding of local market conditions, and fewer local restrictions. Firms entering foreign markets using direct ownership believe that these advantages outweigh the financial commitments and risks involved.

Concept Check

1 **What mode of entry could a company follow if it has no previous experience in international marketing?**

2 **How does licensing differ from joint venture?**

TAILORING MARKETING PLANS TO THE COUNTRY

Marketing plans must be adapted to the international scene, not simply be duplicates of those at home. Three basic steps in adapting marketing plans for foreign marketing are selecting a country for entry, establishing the most effective organization for marketing on an international level, and designing the marketing plan to fit the market's needs.

SELECTING THE COUNTRY FOR ENTRY

In choosing a country for its international marketing efforts, a company must evaluate many factors, following these steps:

Specify the marketing objectives. These objectives should be achievable yet challenging. Profit levels, return on investment (ROI), sales, and competitive positions are all areas for which objectives are delineated.

Choose a single- or a multiple-country strategy. Choosing to enter a single country or several countries in a region is based on the product or products being sold and the sales potential. If several adjacent countries all want the same size or style of product, the marketing and production economies of scale may suggest a multiple-country strategy.

Specify the candidate countries or regions to consider. Alternative countries or regions that meet both the stated objectives for international marketing and the economic profile needed for success should be listed as potential candidates. Some special considerations in entering Eastern European countries are identified in the accompanying Ethics and Social Responsibility Alert.

Estimate the ROI for each of the candidates. To estimate the ROI, a company must project the size of the market, the expected revenues, the expenses, and the profits for each candidate country or region.

Ford targets Latin American markets.

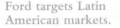

LA NATURALEZA DEL LÍDER.

La naturaleza de Grand Marquis tiene varias formas de expresar su poder. Una de ellas se comunica directamente con quien está al mando, para ofrecerle el más sofisticado y eficiente control e información de sus funciones, en un ambiente de sobriedad y buen gusto.
Su pánel de control digital, con computadora de viaje integrada, es tan sólo una muestra de que

Grand Marquis está diseñado con la tecnología electrónica más avanzada del mundo, para su mando. Su Sistema "Double-Airbag", primero y único en México, aumenta el nivel de seguridad de usted y su acompañante; respondiendo ante un posible impacto en tan sólo 55 milésimas de segundo.
Por supuesto, la naturaleza de un

automóvil así sólo puede conducirse con su poderoso motor V8 de 4.6 litros. Sólo puede disfrutarse a través de su transmisión automática con "overdrive", de su confortable suspensión independiente y de sus frenos de disco en las cuatro ruedas. Grand Marquis es el único automóvil que expresa, con naturaleza, el poder del hombre... para el hombre.

Grand Marquis 1993.
La Naturaleza del Líder.

EXCELENCIA
AUTOMOTRIZ

ETHICS AND SOCIAL RESPONSIBILITY ALERT

Should Western Firms Risk Investment in New Ventures in Eastern Europe?

What are a business firm's responsibilities to its shareholders and employees versus, say, assisting the economic development of Eastern Europe when undertaking new ventures may also provide jobs, decrease the likelihood of civil war, and increase the chances for world peace? This is a complex issue faced by hundreds of Western firms.

Western firms see huge opportunities to market both consumer and industrial products in Eastern countries like the former East Germany, Poland, Hungary, and Russia through joint ventures or marketing agreements with local firms. But two unanticipated problems are emerging that have scared off many potential Western companies: huge potential environmental and insurance liabilities from (1) taking title to factories and land that have some of the worst ground and water pollution in the world, and (2) retaining employees whose health problems from working in risky past conditions can be severe—life expectancy in some industrial regions of Eastern Europe is 8 to 11 years less than that in Western Europe.

Yet the host countries need these ventures badly for the jobs they can provide and the boost they can give to the local economy. And if Western firms take the risk and invest in such joint ventures that become total failures, have they dealt ethically with their responsibilities to present shareholders and employees?

What should Western firms do?

Sources: B. Hagerty, "Russia, Ukraine Brim with Quirky Laws," *The Wall Street Journal,* October 19, 1992, p. A13; and M. Simons, "Investors Shy Away from Polluted Eastern Europe," *The New York Times,* May 13, 1992, pp. A1, A4.

Select the one or more countries or regions to enter. The preceding analysis screens the candidates to provide a list of the one or more countries or regions that appear most likely to achieve the firm's objectives for its international marketing program.

Granted, these are all estimates and include some room for error. However, they will provide the necessary framework to enable the firm to make a knowledgeable choice among countries and regions.

ESTABLISHING THE MARKETING ORGANIZATION

After selecting a country for entry, the firm must establish an appropriate marketing organization. Its goal is to respond to the different needs of international marketing yet take advantage of the experience and knowledge of domestic marketers. Some alternative marketing organizations are discussed.

Export Department   When a company is simply exporting its goods, it typically does so through an export department. Made up of a manager and perhaps several assistants, this group handles the necessary paperwork.

Foreign Subsidiary   A wholly owned foreign subsidiary commonly has its own head of operations, who reports directly to the company president. Sales of Apple's Macintosh computer in Japan were slow until Apple established a subsidiary there. Sales began rising when the subsidiary developed a Japanese-language operating system for the Macintosh and announced that much of its software would use the new system.

International Division   When international sales become substantial or when modes of entry other than simple exporting are added, a company usually expands to include an international division. This division can be either geographically-based or product-based. All international marketing—the movement of products and also their marketing—is then handled by this group.

Worldwide Products Division   A worldwide products division is used when a company decides that it is no longer a company conducting international marketing, but a global firm marketing throughout the world. Like an international division, this structure can be divided by regions, with each division responsible for all products within a region, or it can be divided by products, with each division responsible for all markets where its product is sold. Most likely this structure is accompanied by a management base recruited from around the world.

DESIGNING AND IMPLEMENTING THE MARKETING PLAN

A global marketer goes through the same steps in designing a marketing plan as a domestic marketer. However, the global marketer must decide whether to use a global, customized, or glocalized approach. For years Procter & Gamble has generally used a global approach in Europe, using the same name for the product throughout much of the European community. Archrival Lever Europe—a division of Unilever—is trying to bring order out of its Teddy Bear (or Snuggle) fabric softener that is sold in 10 different European countries under seven brand names, often with different bottles, different marketing strategies, and occasionally different formulas.[20] Lever Europe's problems exemplify those faced by any firm trying to design a marketing plan upon entering a new country.

As mentioned earlier, careful marketing research must be done to help the international marketer decide whether to modify or maintain domestic product, price, place, and promotion strategies.

Product   The product may be sold internationally in one of three ways: in the same form as in the domestic market, with some adaptations, or as a totally new product.

- *Extension.* Selling the same product in other countries is an extension strategy. It works well for products like Coca-Cola, Wrigley's gum, General Motors cars, and Levi's jeans. However, it didn't work for Jell-O (a more solid gelatin was preferred to the powder in England) or Duncan Hines (which was seen as too moist and crumbly to eat with tea in England).

- *Adaptation.* Changing a product in some way to make it more appropriate for a country's climate or preferences is an adaptation strategy. Heinz baby food offers strained lamb brains for Australians and strained brown beans in the Netherlands. Exxon sells different gasoline blends based on each country's climate.
- *Invention.* Designing a product to serve the unmet needs of a foreign nation is an invention strategy. This is probably the strategy with the most potential, since there are so many unmet needs, yet it is actually the least used. National Cash Register has followed a reverse invention strategy by introducing crank-operated cash registers in some developing nations that have unreliable or inaccessible electric power.

In international markets—as in domestic ones—nothing succeeds like quality products that satisfy consumer needs and wants at reasonable prices. Honda motorcycles, Caterpillar construction equipment, Canon cameras, and Black & Decker power tools are examples.

Price   Most foreign countries use a cost-plus pricing strategy. For international firms this can mean their products are priced higher than the local goods. Why? International products must include not only the cost of production and selling, but also tariffs, transportation and storage costs, and higher payments to intermediaries.

Dumping is a firm's selling a product in a foreign country below its domestic price. This is most often done to build a share of the market by pricing at a competitive level. Another reason is that the products being sold may be surplus or cannot be sold domestically, and are therefore already a burden to the company. The firm may be glad to sell them at almost any price.

Some pharmaceutical firms sell penicillin, for example, at a lower price in foreign countries than at home. They justify this by saying that R&D costs are

Quality products: essential for entering foreign markets.

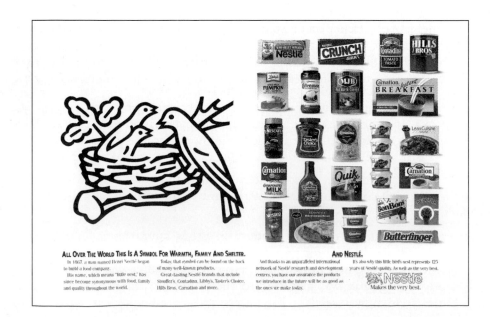

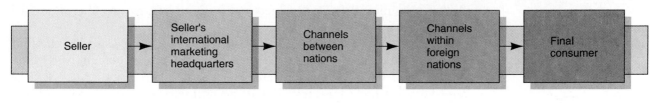

▌*Figure 23–6*
**International marketing
channel of distribution.**

not included in foreign prices. Japan has been accused of following a dumping strategy for some of its products in Canada and the United States.

An unusual pricing dimension of international marketing is **counter-trade,** using barter rather than money in making international sales, as mentioned in Chapter 5. Although countertrade accounts for only about 10–15 percent of world trade, it is growing in importance. An example was when Boeing sold ten 747 jet aircraft to Saudi Arabia in return for crude oil valued at 10 percent below posted world prices.

An unpleasant aspect of pricing is **bribery,** the practice of giving or promising something of value in return for a corrupt act. This is a common practice in many countries to reduce red tape and make sales. Although in many countries bribery is an accepted business practice in some international sales, it is officially illegal in all countries.

Place   An international marketer must establish a channel of distribution to meet the goals it has set. Figure 23–6 outlines the channel through which a product manufactured in one country must travel to reach its destination in a foreign country. The first step involves the seller; its headquarters is the starting point and is responsible for the successful distribution to the ultimate consumer.

The next step is the channel between the two nations, moving the product from the domestic market to the foreign market. Intermediaries that can handle this responsibility include resident buyers in the foreign country, independent merchant wholesalers who buy and sell the product, and agents who bring buyers and sellers together.

Once the product is in the foreign nation, that country's distribution channels take over. Foreign channels can be very long or surprisingly short, depending on the product line. In Japan fresh fish go through three intermediaries before getting to a retail outlet. Conversely, shoes go through only one intermediary. In other cases the channel does not even involve the host country. P&G sells its soap door-to-door in the Philippines because there are no alternatives in many parts of that country. The sophistication of the distribution channel increases with the economic development of the country. Supermarkets facilitate selling products in many nations, but they are not popular or available in many others where low incomes, culture, and lack of refrigeration dictate shopping on a daily rather than a weekly basis.

Promotion   Various aspects of promotion may have to be changed to reflect the differences in foreign markets. Advertising programs provide examples. Because values differ substantially from country to country, a product that is a luxury in one country may be a necessity in another. Creative messages in advertisements must then be designed to directly address the peculiarities within each market.

A recent study evaluating advertising across 16 countries found that only 5 percent of the ad campaigns studied were totally global, 5 percent were totally customized for the local market, and 90 percent were glocalized approaches where the advertising agencies tailored the umbrella strategy to the local market.[21] Regardless of the strategy, international advertisers have some strong "do" guidelines:[22]

- *Do* use TV commercials in which visuals are dominant over commercials that are "copy-heavy."
- *Do* enhance TV commercials with music—a powerful device that cuts across many cultures.
- *Do* test unique, distinctive approaches to see that they meet the basic rules and good taste guidelines of a culture.
- *Do* use brand symbols, trademarks, or logos—where possible—when the brand has stature and the symbol is meaningful.

Research also carries some promotional warnings: (1) a brilliant slogan in one language rarely translates to another with the same power and precision, so be careful, and (2) trying to please everyone in a culture and offend no one often gives bland, ineffective ads, just as it does domestically.

A common language helps Australia market itself to Canadian tourists.

Where there is a common language, many TV and print ads can be used both domestically and in a common-language country. For example, Australia markets vacations to Canada while Canada markets Canadian vacations to Australians—both often using domestic ad campaigns in the other country as well.

Concept Check

1 **What steps should a company follow to select appropriate international markets to enter?**

2 **What are the three international marketing product strategies, and when might each be used?**

3 **What is countertrade?**

Summary

1 International marketing, or trade between nations, is filled with risks and problems but promises profits to those who undertake it. The size of international marketing is large and growing—about 25 percent of Canada's GDP is exported.

2 When a firm takes one of its products into several foreign countries, it must decide whether to use a global, customized (or local), or "glocalized" strategy.

3 Although international and domestic marketing are based on the same marketing principles, many underlying assumptions must be reevaluated when a firm moves into international operations. Environmental variables such as political, economic, and cultural conditions must be carefully assessed to achieve successful operations.

4 International markets should be selected on the basis of their size, consumer income, potential market growth, cost of doing business in the country, competitive advantage that would be realized, and risk involved in entering them.

5 Four basic modes of entry into global marketing are exporting, licensing, joint ventures, and direct ownership. The relative difficulty of international marketing, as well as the amount of commitment, risk, and profit potential, increases in moving from exporting to direct ownership.

6 An organizational structure for international marketing should respond to the unique needs of international marketing, while still taking advantage of the experience and know-how of the domestic marketers.

7 Because foreign countries have different languages, customs, values, purchasing power, needs, and levels of economic development, a firm must take great care in deciding whether to use a global or a customized strategy.

8 Product, price, promotion, and place strategies can all be modified or adapted to reflect these differences and improve the chances of success in international markets.

Key Terms and Concepts

international marketing p. 586
global corporation p. 589
global approach p. 590
customized approach p. 590
glocalization p. 592
quota p. 593
blocked currency p. 593
duty p. 593
tariff p. 593
boycott p. 593

expropriation p. 593
economic infrastructure p. 597
exporting p. 600
indirect exporting p. 601
direct exporting p. 601
joint venture p. 601
direct ownership p. 602
dumping p. 606
countertrade p. 607
bribery p. 607

Chapter Problems and Applications

1 Ford introduced its Mondeo—for "world"—car in Europe in 1993 and introduced essentially the same model in Canada in 1994. Its cost: $6 billion. What are the advantages and disadvantages of this global approach?

2 A manufacturer of shoes has decided to enter the international market. As a point of entry, she has selected China. Her assumption is that with such a large population, a lot of shoes can be sold. Why might China be a good or bad market opportunity? What steps should the manufacturer follow to select the appropriate market?

3 What steps do some countries take to discourage trade? Why might they do this?

4 As a novice in international marketing, which alternative for global operations would you be likely to start with? Why? What other alternatives do you have for market entry?

5 What are the three product strategies a marketer can use in foreign market introductions? Which strategy has the most potential? Why? Can you think of any reverse inventions that might be successful?

6 Knowing that owning Western goods is a status symbol in Russia, what goods might you want to sell to that market? How would the current economic system in Russia affect your decision to enter this market?

7 Develop a SWOT analysis (see Chapter 2) for a Canadian company considering building a plant to produce consumer products in Eastern Europe to reach consumers living there.

8 Because English is the official language in Australia, many Canadian companies might select this market as an easy one to expand to internationally. Others, however, believe that this similarity in language could make it even harder to successfully engage in foreign trade. Who's right? Why?

9 Coca-Cola is sold worldwide. In some countries Coca-Cola owns the manufacturing facilities; in others it has signed contracts with licensees. When selecting a licensee in each country, what factors should Coca-Cola consider?

Marketing of Services

AFTER READING THIS CHAPTER YOU SHOULD BE ABLE TO:

▸ Describe four unique elements of services.

▸ Recognize how services differ and how they can be classified.

▸ Understand the way in which consumers view and judge services.

▸ Understand the important role of internal marketing in service organizations.

▸ Explain the role of the four Ps in the services marketing mix.

How Should I Do My Banking Today? Let Me Count the Ways!

It is becoming more and more convenient for you to do your banking these days. Chances are that one of the over 8,000 branches of chartered banks and trust companies across Canada is located near where you live or work. If you don't need the human contact, or would prefer to do your banking after hours, then there are over 15,000 automated teller machines (ATMs) available giving you 24-hour access to their money. Or, if you prefer, you could do your banking by phone. You could use voice- or computer-activated telephone banking services, or select a service with a living, breathing customer service officer, available by phone 24 hours a day. Canada Trust's Easyline both offers the convenience of automated banking by phone and allows the customer to talk to live personnel around the clock. If you needed money for shopping, on the other hand, you might not need to visit or contact your bank or use an ATM at all. You could go shopping these days without cash, checks, or credit cards. How? You simply use your debit card. With your debit card you can buy goods and services and the money will be taken directly from your bank account.

The banking industry is using these and other methods to deliver services to its customers. The type of delivery mode depends on the market and the customer. Some companies have closed branches in certain areas and replaced them with ATMs. ATMs can deliver high-volume services at less cost than physical branches. However, some markets will continue to require branch outlets, especially to serve those who prefer "personal banking" over "high-tech" banking.

But as the technology becomes simpler to use, many bank customers who are fearful of change, especially the elderly, may become encouraged to try the

ATM machines. In an effort to keep operating costs down and to provide customers with greater access to banking services, the banking industry is stepping up efforts to convince people that banking by ATM or telephone can be convenient and simple. So the next time you need to do some banking, you probably have to decide, Will I go to a branch, use an ATM machine, just give them a call, or just rely on my debit card.[1]

The marketing of services is unique and challenging. In this chapter we discuss how services differ from traditional products (goods), how service consumers make purchase decisions, and the ways in which the marketing mix is used.

THE UNIQUENESS OF SERVICES

As noted in Chapter 1, **services** are intangible items such as airline trips, financial advice, or telephone calls that an organization provides to consumers. Services are performances, acts, expertise, or deeds that consumers pay for with money or with something else of value, such as their own time.

Services have quickly become one of the most important components of the Canadian as well as the world economy. In Canada, about 60 cents out of every consumer dollar is spent on buying services. Seven of ten Canadians work in the services sector. In other words, more Canadians are doing things (performing services) than making things (producing goods). Figure 24–1 shows the actual trends in employment by the goods-producing versus the service sector from 1977 to 1990. It can easily be seen that the service sector has been outpacing the goods-producing sector in employment growth. Some experts argue that if the trend continues, all Canadians will be working in the service sector by 2025.[2]

▌ *Figure 24–1*
Employment by sector: trends in Canada.

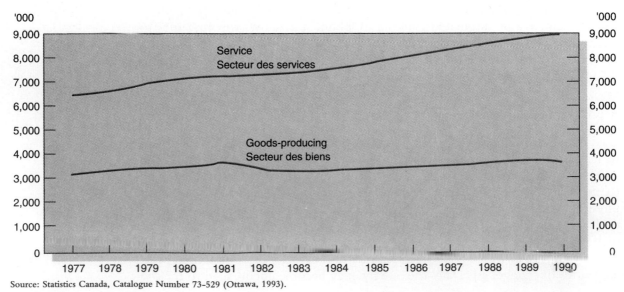

Source: Statistics Canada, Catalogue Number 73-529 (Ottawa, 1993).

The service sector in Canada includes *distributive services,* such as transportation, communications, and utilities; *consumer services,* such as accommodation and food services, personal services, entertainment, and recreational services; *producer services,* such as finance, insurance, and real estate; and *noncommercial* services, such as education, health services, and public administration.

New types of services are emerging all the time. These include grocery shopping services, pet-sitting and pet-walking services, house-watching services, voice mail and voice messaging services, and even a new fax message service. CompuFax, of Downsview, Ontario, offers automated fax services that eliminate the need for manual faxing and can send out any number of faxes, however long and varied, at a cost per page less than that of a postage stamp. Besides being able to send out the same fax to numerous customers simultaneously, CompuFax also offers two other services. Fax on demand enables customers to use their Touch-Tone phones to request information on a variety of products and services. A computer program at CompuFax reads the request and fills the order in seconds without a manual operator. The company will also set up an interactive program for a client. The targets for the services are financial institutions, insurance companies, publishers, and high-tech industries.[3]

THE FOUR I'S OF SERVICES

There are four unique elements to services: intangibility, inconsistency, inseparability, and inventory. These four elements are referred to as the **four I's of services.**

Intangibility   Services are intangible; that is, they can't be held, touched, or seen before the purchase decision. In contrast, before purchasing a traditional product, a consumer can touch a box of laundry detergent, kick the tire of an automobile, or sample a new breakfast cereal. A major marketing need for services is to make them tangible or show the benefits of using the service.[4] American Express emphasizes the year-end summary of charges it sends you, and a leading insurance company says, "You're in good hands with Allstate."

How inviting is your home?

Inconsistency   Marketing services is challenging because the quality of a service is often inconsistent. Since many services depend on people who provide them, their quality of service can vary with each person's capabilities and the day-to-day performance of the same individual. Inconsistency is much more of a problem in services than it is with tangible goods. Tangible products can be of good or bad quality, but with modern production lines the quality will at least be consistent.

On the other hand, one day the Toronto Maple Leafs look great, possible Stanley Cup winners, and the next day lose by 10 goals. Or a cello player with the Vancouver Symphony may not be feeling well and give a less-than-average performance. Whether the service involves tax assistance at Ernst & Young or guest relations at the Sheraton, organizations attempt to reduce inconsistency through standardization and training.[5] Standardization through automation is becoming increasingly popular, as, for example, in the use of ATMs by the banking industry.

Services are people.

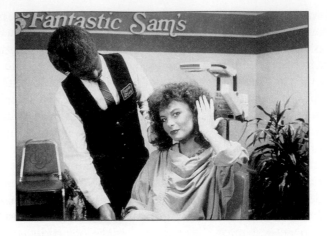

Inseparability   A third difference between services and goods, related to problems of consistency, is inseparability. In most cases the consumer cannot (and does not) separate the service from the deliverer of the service or the setting in which the service occurs. For example, to receive an education, a person may attend a university. The quality of the education may be high, but if the student has difficulty parking, finds counselling services poor, or sees little opportunity for extracurricular activity, he may not be satisfied with the educational experience.

Inventory   Inventory of services is different from that of goods. Inventory problems exist with goods because many items are perishable and, as noted in Chapter 16, there are costs associated with handling inventory. With services, inventory carrying costs are more subjective and are related to **idle production capacity,** or availability of the service provider when there is no demand. The inventory cost of a service is the cost of reimbursing the person used to provide the service along with any needed equipment. If a physician is paid to see patients but no one schedules an appointment, the fixed cost of the idle physician's salary is a high inventory carrying cost. In some service businesses, however, the provider of the service is on commission (a Merrill Lynch stockbroker) or is a part-time employee (a counterperson at McDonald's). Then, the inventory carrying costs can be significantly lower or nonexistent: the idle

▌*Figure 24–2*
Inventory carrying costs in services.

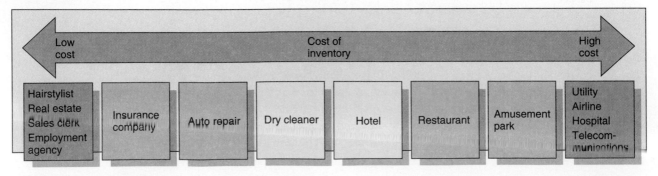

Low cost				Cost of inventory				High cost
Hairstylist Real estate Sales clerk Employment agency	Insurance company	Auto repair	Dry cleaner	Hotel	Restaurant	Amusement park		Utility Airline Hospital Telecommunications

production capacity is cut back through reduction of hours or there is no salary to pay because of the commission compensation system.

Figure 24–2 shows a sliding scale of inventory carrying costs represented on the high side by airlines and hospitals and on the low end by real estate agents and hairstylists. The inventory carrying cost of airlines is high because of high-salaried pilots and very expensive equipment. In contrast, real estate agents and hairstylists work on commission and need little expensive equipment to conduct business.

THE SERVICE CONTINUUM

The four I's differentiate services from goods in most cases, but many companies are not clearly service-based or good-based organizations. Is IBM a computer company or a service business? Does MacLean Hunter provide only goods when it publishes *Marketing* magazine, or does it consider itself a service because it presents up-to-date business information? As companies look at what they bring to the market, there is a range from the tangible to the intangible or good-dominant to service-dominant offerings referred to as the **service continuum** (Figure 24–3).

Teaching, nursing, and the theatre are intangible, service-dominant activities, and intangibility, inconsistency, inseparability, and inventory are major concerns in their marketing. Salt, neckties, and dog food are tangible goods, and the problems represented by the four I's are not relevant in their marketing. However, some businesses are a mix of intangible service and tangible good factors. A clothing tailor provides a service but also a good, the finished suit. How pleasant, courteous, and attentive the tailor is to the customer is an

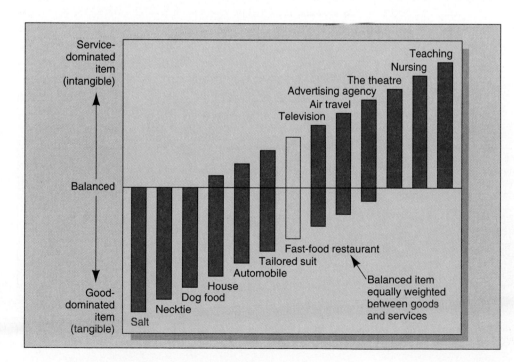

▌ *Figure 24–3*
Service continuum.

important component of the service, and how well the clothes fit is an important part of the product. As shown in Figure 24—3, a fast-food restaurant is about half tangible goods (the food) and half intangible services (courtesy, cleanliness, speed, convenience).

CLASSIFYING SERVICES

Throughout this book, marketing organizations, techniques, and concepts have been classified to show the differences and similarities in an organized framework. Services can also be classified in several ways, according to whether they are delivered by people or equipment, whether they are profit or nonprofit, or whether or not they are government sponsored.

Delivery by People or Equipment   As seen in Figure 24—4, companies offering services provided by professionals include management consulting and accounting firms. Skilled labour is required to offer services such as Sears appliance repair or Sheraton catering service. Unskilled labour such as that used by Brinks store-security forces is also a service provided by people.

Equipment-based services do not carry the marketing concerns of inconsistency, because people are removed from provision of the service. Electric utilities, for example, can provide service without frequent personal contact with customers. To keep in touch with their customers, many utility companies use newsletter inserts in their billing envelopes.

Profit and Nonprofit Organizations   Many organizations involved in services also distinguish themselves by their tax status as profit or nonprofit organizations. In contrast to *profit organizations, nonprofit organizations'* excesses in revenue

▌*Figure 24—4*
Service classifications.

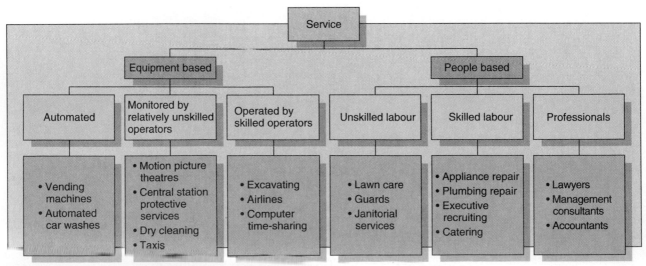

over expenses are not taxed or distributed to shareholders. When excess revenue exists, the money goes back into the organization's treasury to allow continuation of the service. Depending on the corporate structure of the nonprofit organization, it may pay tax on revenue-generating holdings not directly related to its core mission.

The Canadian Red Cross, United Way, Greenpeace, Second Harvest, and the University of Calgary are nonprofit organizations. Such organizations historically have not used marketing tactics, in the belief that they were inappropriate. In recent years, however, competitive pressures have forced these organizations to reevaluate their strategies.

Government Sponsored or Not   A third way to classify services is based on whether they are government sponsored. Although there is no direct ownership and they are nonprofit organizations, governments at the federal, provincial, and local levels provide a broad range of services. Many government departments and agencies have adopted marketing and promotion activities. The government of Canada has been one of the biggest advertisers in Canada, supporting initiatives such as NAFTA, or encouraging Canadians to stay fit or to quit smoking.

---

1 What are the four I's of services?

2 Would inventory carrying costs for an accounting firm employing chartered accountants be (*a*) high, (*b*) low, or (*c*) nonexistent?

3 To eliminate service inconsistencies, companies rely on _____ and _____.

Concept Check

HOW CONSUMERS PURCHASE SERVICES

Colleges, hospitals, hotels, and even charities are facing an increasingly competitive environment. Successful service organizations, like successful product-oriented firms, must understand how the consumer views a service and in what ways a company can present a differential advantage relative to competing offerings.

THE PURCHASE PROCESS

The intangible and inseparable aspects of services affect the consumer's evaluation of the purchase. Because services cannot be displayed, demonstrated, or illustrated, consumers cannot make a prepurchase evaluation of all the characteristics of services.[6] Similarly, because services are produced and consumed simultaneously, the buyer must participate in producing the service, and that participation can affect the evaluation of the service. Figure 24–5 portrays how different types of goods and services are evaluated by consumers. Tangible goods such as clothing, jewellery, and furniture have *search* qualities, such as colour,

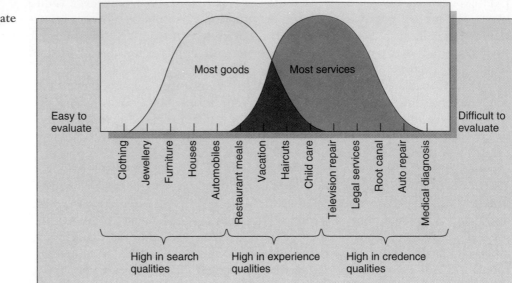

Figure 24–5
How consumers evaluate goods and services.

Easy to evaluate

Most goods   Most services

Difficult to evaluate

Clothing · Jewellery · Furniture · Houses · Automobiles · Restaurant meals · Vacation · Haircuts · Child care · Television repair · Legal services · Root canal · Auto repair · Medical diagnosis

High in search qualities

High in experience qualities

High in credence qualities

size, and style, which can be determined before purchase. Services such as restaurants and child care have *experience* qualities, which can only be discerned after purchase or during consumption. Finally, services provided by specialized professionals such as medical diagnosis and legal services have *credence* qualities, or characteristics that the consumer may find impossible to evaluate even after purchase and consumption.[7] To reduce the uncertainty created by these qualities, service consumers turn to personal sources of information such as early adopters, opinion leaders, and reference group members during the purchase decision process.[8]

PURCHASE EVALUATION

Once a consumer tries a service, how does she evaluate it? Primarily by comparing expectations about the service with the actual experience she has with the service. Differences between a consumer's expectations and experience are identified through **gap analysis.** This type of analysis asks consumers to assess their expectations and experiences on dimensions of service quality such as those described in Figure 24–6. Expectations are influenced by word-of-mouth communications, personal needs, past experiences, and promotional activities, while actual experiences are determined by the way an organization delivers its service.[9] The relative importance of the various dimensions of service quality varies by the type of service.[10] In the fast-food industry, Burger King is an example of a firm trying to implement gap analysis. According to Barry Gibbons, Burger King's CEO, the company is "measuring our performance against [customers'] expectations" by using a 24-hour hot line to receive 4,000 customer calls per day.[11] However, it is often difficult to get feedback from consumers about their service experiences, especially if they are unhappy. The

■ *Figure 24–6*
Dimensions of service quality.

DIMENSION AND DEFINITION	EXAMPLES OF SPECIFIC QUESTIONS RAISED BY STOCK BROKERAGE CUSTOMERS
Tangibles: Appearance of physical facilities, equipment, personnel, and communication materials	Is my stockbroker dressed appropriately?
Reliability: Ability to perform the promised service dependably and accurately	Does the stockbroker follow exact instructions to buy or sell?
Responsiveness: Willingness to help customers and provide prompt service	Is my stockbroker willing to answer my questions?
Competence: Possession of the required skills and knowledge to perform the service	Does my brokerage firm have the research capabilities to accurately track market developments?
Courtesy: Politeness, respect, consideration, and friendliness of contact personnel	Does my broker refrain from acting busy or being rude when I ask questions?
Credibility: Trustworthiness, believability, and honesty of the service provider	Does my broker refrain from pressuring me to buy?
Security: Freedom from danger, risk, or doubt	Does my brokerage firm know where my stock certificate is?
Access: Approachability and ease of contact	Is it easy to get through to my broker over the telephone?
Communication: Keeping customers informed in language they can understand, and listening to them	Does my broker avoid using technical jargon?
Understanding the customer: Making the effort to know customers and their needs	Does my broker try to determine what my specific financial objectives are?

accompanying Ethics and Social Responsibility Alert discusses the issue of consumer complaint behaviour.

CUSTOMER CONTACT AUDIT

Consumers judge services on the tangible aspects of their experience and on their interaction with the service provider. To focus on these experiences or "service encounters," a firm can develop a **customer contact audit**—a flowchart of the points of interaction between consumer and service provider.[12] This is particularly important in high-contact services such as hotels, educational institutions, and automobile rental agencies.[13] Figure 24–7 is a consumer contact audit for renting a car from Hertz. Look carefully at the sequence.

A Customer's Car Rental Activities   A customer decides to rent a car and (1) makes a telephone reservation (see Figure 24–7). An operator answers and

receives the information (2) and checks the availability of the car at the desired location (3). When the customer arrives at the rental site (4), the reservation system is again accessed and the customer provides information regarding payment, address, and driver's licence (5). A car is assigned to the customer (6), who proceeds by bus to the car pickup (7). On return to the rental location (8), the car is parked and the customer checks in, providing information on mileage, gas consumption, and damages (9). A bill is subsequently prepared (10).

Each of the steps numbered 1 to 10 is a customer contact point where the tangible aspects of Hertz service are seen by the customer. Figure 24–7, however, also shows a series of steps lettered A to E that involve two levels of inspections on the automobile. These steps are essential in providing a car that runs, but they are not points of customer interaction. To create a service advantage, Hertz must create a competitive advantage in the sequence of interactions with the customer.

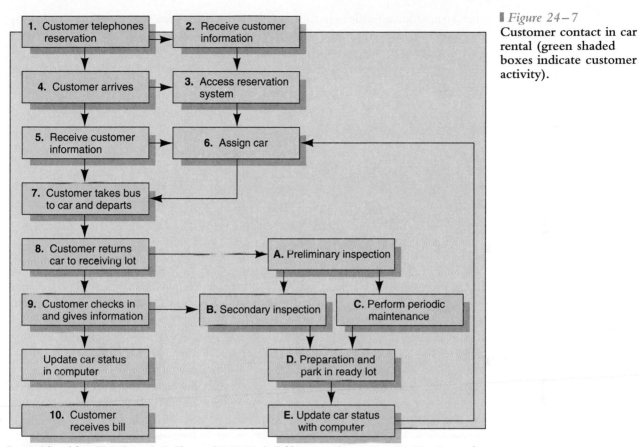

Figure 24–7
Customer contact in car rental (green shaded boxes indicate customer activity).

Source: Adapted from W. E. Sasser, R. P. Olsen, and D. D. Wyckoff, *Management of Service Operations: Text, Cases, and Readings* (Boston: Allyn & Bacon, 1978).

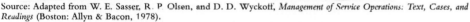

1 What are the differences between search, experience, and credence qualities?

2 Hertz created its differential advantage at the points of _____ in its customer contact audit.

Concept Check

MANAGING THE MARKETING OF SERVICES

Just as the unique aspects of services necessitate changes in the consumer's purchase process, the marketing management process requires special adaptation.[14] In services marketing, the employee often plays a central role in attracting, building, and maintaining relationships with customers.[15] This aspect of services marketing has led to a new concept—internal marketing.[16]

Internal marketing is based on the notion that a service organization must focus on its employees, or internal market, before successful programs can be directed at customers.[17] The internal marketing concept holds that an organization's employees will be influenced to develop a market orientation if marketing-like activities are directed at them. This idea suggests that employees and employee development through recruitment, training, communication, and administration are critical to the success of service organizations.[18]

Let's use the four Ps framework of the text for discussing the marketing mix for services.

PRODUCT (SERVICE)

To a large extent, the concepts of the product component of the marketing mix discussed in Chapters 11 and 12 apply equally well to Cheerios (a good) and to American Express (a service). Yet there are three aspects of the product/service element of the mix that warrant special attention: exclusivity, brand name, and capacity management.

Exclusivity   One favourable dimension in a new product is its ability to be patented. A patent gives the manufacturer of a product exclusive rights to its production. A major difference between products and services is that services cannot be patented. Hence the creator of a successful fast-food chain could quickly discover the concept being copied by others. Domino's Pizza now sees competitors copy its quick delivery advantage, which has propelled the company to the success discussed in Chapter 22.

Branding   An important aspect in marketing goods is the branding strategy used. However, because services are intangible, the brand name or identifying logo of the service organization is particularly important in consumer decisions because it is more difficult to describe what is being provided.[19] Many companies in the financial services industry in Canada, such as banks, trust companies, brokerage firms, and insurance companies, are now using branding, or are strengthening their existing branding efforts, in order to distinguish themselves in the minds of the consumers. Canada Trust and Bank of Montreal are two prime examples. Strong brand names and symbols are important for services marketers not only for differentiation purposes but also for conveying an image of quality. A service firm with a well-established brand reputation will also find it easier to market new services than firms without such brand reputations.[20]

Capacity Management   A key distinction between goods and services is the inseparability of services. To buy and simultaneously use the service, the customer must be present at the service delivery site. For example, a patient must be in the dental chair to "buy" a root canal, and a guest must be in a hotel to

Brand names and logos create service identities.

"buy" an accommodation. So the product/service component of the mix must be made available to the consumer by managing demand. This is referred to as **capacity management.**

Service organizations must manage the availability of the offering to (1) smooth demand over time so that demand matches capacity and (2) ensure that the organization's assets are used in ways that will maximize the return on investment (ROI).[21] Figure 24–8 shows how a hotel tries to manage its capacity during the high and low seasons. Differing price structures are assigned to each segment of consumers to help moderate or adjust demand for the service. Airline contracts fill a fixed number of rooms throughout the year. In the slow season, when more rooms are available, tour packages at appealing prices are used to attract groups or conventions, such as an offer for seven nights in Orlando at a reduced price. Weekend packages are also offered to buyers. In the high-demand season, groups are less desirable because guests who will pay high prices travel to Florida on their own.

PRICING

In the service industries, price is often referred to in various ways. Hospitals refer to charges, consultants, lawyers, physicians, and accountants to fees; airlines to fares; and hotels to rates.

Setting Prices   Two common methods of pricing services are cost plus percentage-of-cost and target ROI pricing.

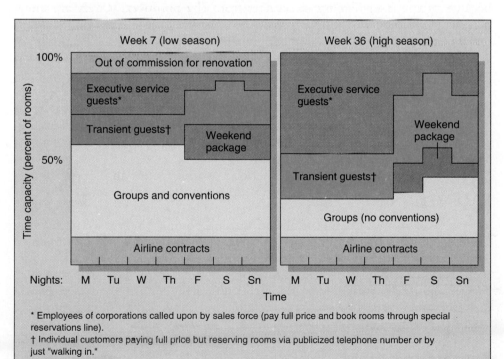

▌*Figure 24–8*
Balancing capacity management.

Source: Redrawn from C. H. Lovelock, *Services Marketing,* © 1991, p. 124. Reprinted by permission of Prentice Hall, Englewood Cliffs, NJ.

Cost plus percentage-of-cost pricing, discussed in Chapter 14, entails charging a customer for the cost of providing the service plus an additional fixed percentage. Professional service organizations such as accounting firms charge a fee based on a billable rate. The billable rate is the cost of the accountant (salary, benefits, training, and overhead) plus a markup. This pricing is common to most professional service organizations such as law, medicine, and consulting.

In *target ROI pricing,* the price for the service is based on a targeted ROI. This method of setting price is common in capital-intensive services such as airlines or public utilities.

Role of Pricing   Pricing plays two essential roles: to affect consumer perceptions and to be used in capacity management. Because of the intangible nature of services, price can indicate the quality of service. Would you be willing to risk a $10 dental surgery? Or a $50 divorce lawyer? Studies have shown that when there are few well-known cues by which to judge a product, consumers use price.[22]

The capacity management role of price is also important to movie theatres, hairstylists, restaurants, and hotels. Many service businesses use **off-peak pricing,** which consists of charging different prices during different times of day or days of the week to reflect variations in demand for the service. Restaurants offer luncheon specials, and movie theatres offer matinee prices.

PLACE (DISTRIBUTION)

Place or distribution is a major factor in developing service marketing strategy because of the inseparability of services from the producer. Rarely are intermediaries involved in the distribution of a service; the distribution site and service deliverer are the tangible components of the service.

Historically in professional services marketing, little attention has been paid to distribution. But as competition grows, the value of convenient distribution is being recognized. Hairstyling chains, legal firms, tax preparation companies, and accounting firms (such as Deloitte & Touche) use multiple locations for the distribution of services. In the banking industry, customers of participating banks using the Interac system can access any one of thousands of automated teller machines across Canada.

PROMOTION

The value of promotion, specifically advertising, for many services is in showing the benefits of purchasing the service. In services advertising it is important to stress attributes such as availability; location; consistent quality; efficient, courteous service; and assurances of satisfaction.[23] In addition, service firms must convey the proper image. Merrill Lynch's use of the bull in its ads contributes to image and positioning strategies.[24] Public relations is often a common tool used by organizations marketing services.[25]

Public Relations   Public relations has played a major role in the promotional strategy of nonprofit services and professional organizations. Many for-profit

service companies are also using a variety of public relations tools such as events sponsorship, or public-service activities. Nonprofit organizations, such as universities, hospitals, churches, and volunteer service agencies, generally use public relations alone to disseminate their messages. Specifically, public-service announcements tend to be the foundation of the public relations activities of nonprofit groups.[26] However, all types of organizations that market services are generally following the path set by packaged goods firms, that is, developing integrated marketing communications programs. Many churches—including the Catholic Church—concerned with low attendance at services are using integrated communications activities to bring the flocks in. Many professional services firms have also adopted integrated communications plans.[27]

SERVICES IN THE FUTURE

What can we expect from the services industry in the future? Technology, a significant trend that has affected product (goods) marketing, is also impacting on the services sector and will continue to do so in the future. The importance

M A R K E T I N G · A C T I O N · M E M O

Drive-Through Services Booming in Canada

Drive-through services are now booming all across Canada, and these services are not just for burgers and fries. In Calgary, drive-through phones have been around for 10 years, and the Alberta Treasury branch has had a drive-up teller service for just as long. Drive-through automated teller machines (ATMs) were launched by Canada Trust in 1991 in Ontario. Drive-through coffee shops originated in Vancouver in the early 1990s. According to experts, drive-throughs appeal to customers with special needs. Among them: lone diners who do not want to sit by themselves, consumers pressed for time, and parents who do not want to leave their children in the car or take them inside. Tim Barnes, a technical advisor for Alberta Government Telephones, suggests that women, couriers, and cabbies like the security of drive-through phones. Jim Elaschuk of Canada Trust says drive-throughs let businesses deliver services without having branches at every corner.

Drive-throughs also create business. McDonald's adopted drive-through service in the 1970s, and this service led to a significant increase in sales. When a Petro-Canada station added a drive-through service to its cappuccino and snack bar, incremental sales went up without significantly increasing costs or interfering with gas sales. A&W, which once offered only drive-in service, reports success with its new drive-through and will add new ones this year to existing units. Drive-throughs allow service businesses to provide an improved level of service, increased accessibility, and greater convenience that the customer of the 1990s is looking for. In the future, other service companies as well as traditional goods marketers are expected to offer more of these drive-through concepts. Soon, the consumer may be able to do most of his shopping without ever leaving the car.

Source: Adapted from T. Bullick, "Drive-Thru Services Thrive across the Country," *Marketing*, May 30, 1994, p. 2.

of relationship marketing and the technologies to pursue it will be applied more broadly in the service sector in the future. It has often been argued that relationship marketing in the services sector has been based on the notion that the employee is responsible for relationship building, at a very personal level. While employees will continue to be integral in cultivating long-term relations with customers, the advent of database and relationship marketing technologies will help enhance and solidify the personal efforts of service employees. For example, a computer support system at Toronto Dominion Bank now allows employees who interface with customers to deliver the full capabilities of the bank.

Consumers will put increased demand on services companies, expecting greater convenience, responsiveness, and access (see accompanying Marketing Action Memo). Technology will play a large role in satisfying those demands. Just as some product marketers are leveraging technology as a competitive advantage, so too will the service marketer. One service expert suggests that service firms that can balance "high tech with high touch" will be successful in the future.[28]

Do Your Banking In Your Pyjamas.

Do your banking at any time of day or night with TD Bankline.® Our bank-by-phone service allows you to obtain account balances and recent account activity, transfer money between accounts, and pay most personal bills. We'll even fax your account statement to you. It's fast, simple and convenient. Just call 1-800-465-BANK (2265) or in Toronto call 982-BANK. For a free trial run, press [1] for automated services and use the demonstration card number 4529-000-000-004.

TD BANK
Your Bank. Your Way.®

The impact of technology in services marketing.

As deregulation of service industries increases and entry barriers drop, the services market will become increasingly more competitive. Like product marketers before them, service firms will have to expend greater efforts to develop distinctive branding and positioning strategies. Services marketers will look to the experience of product marketers when making strategic marketing and management decisions. This can be valuable, since much of what is known about product marketing can be applied to services marketing.

But services marketing and management can be different, especially as the degree of intangibility increases. Service firms will have to recognize the differences and be prepared to develop marketing and management strategies beyond those currently used by product marketers. For example, one important area of distinction is the relative importance of the employee (as the provider and the service), especially in highly intangible, high-contact services. In this case, superior employee performance may be a source of competitive advantage for service firms, more so than in product marketing. But to leverage employees as a competitive advantage will take an innovative corporate culture that provides training, motivation, and employee empowerment. The challenge for services organizations in the future, according to Peter Drucker, will be how to organize and motivate their workers and how to provide them with dignity in their work.[29]

---

1 How does a movie theatre use off-peak pricing?

2 Smoothing demand is the focus of _____ management.

3 **Does a lawyer use cost plus percentage-of-cost or target return on investment pricing?**

Concept Check

Summary

1 Services have four unique elements: intangibility, inconsistency, insepara- bility, and inventory.

2 Intangibility refers to the difficulty of communicating the service benefits. Inconsistency refers to the difficulty of providing the same level of quality each time a service is purchased. Inseparability means that service deliv- erers represent the service quality. Inventory costs for services are related to the cost of maintaining production capacity.

3 Services can be classified in several ways. The primary distinction is whether they are provided by people or equipment. Other distinctions of services are in terms of tax status (profit versus nonprofit) or whether the service is provided by a government agency.

4 Consumers can evaluate three aspects of goods or services: search qualities, experience qualities, and credence qualities.

5 A gap analysis determines if consumers' expectations are different from their actual experiences.

6 A customer contact audit is a flowchart of the points of interaction be- tween a service provider and its customers, where competitive advantages should be created.

7 Internal marketing, which focusses on an organization's employees, is critical to the success of a service organization.

8 Because services cannot be patented, unique offerings are difficult to protect. In addition, because services are intangible, brands and logos (which can be protected) are particularly important to help distinguish among competing service providers.

9 The inseparability of production and consumption of services means that capacity management is important in the service element of the mix. This process involves smoothing demand to meet capacity.

10 The intangible nature of services makes price an important cue to indicate service quality to the consumer.

11 Inseparability of production and consumption in services eliminates in- termediaries in most service marketing. Distribution is important as a tangible component of a service offering.

12 Integrated marketing communications plans are important for successful promotion of services.

13 Service marketers can learn much from the experience of product marketers, but must recognize the differences in marketing and managing services.

Key Terms and Concepts

services p. 614

four I's of services p. 615

idle production capacity p. 616

service continuum p. 617

gap analysis p. 620

customer contact audit p. 621

internal marketing p. 623

capacity management p. 625

off-peak pricing p. 626

Chapter Problems and Applications

1 Explain how the four I's of services would apply to a branch office of the Royal Bank.

2 Idle production capacity may be related to inventory or capacity management. How would the pricing component of the marketing mix reduce idle production capacity for (*a*) a car wash, (*b*) a stage theatre group, and (*c*) a university?

3 What are the search, experience, and credence qualities of an airline for the business traveller and the pleasure traveller? What qualities are most important to each group?

4 Outline the customer contact audit for the typical deposit you make at your neighbourhood bank.

5 The text suggests that internal marketing is necessary before a successful marketing program can be directed at consumers. Why is this particularly true for service organizations?

6 Outline the capacity management strategies that an airline must consider.

7 Draw the channel of distribution for the following services: (*a*) a restaurant, (*b*) a hospital, and (*c*) a hotel.

8 How does off-peak pricing differ from the target return on investment or cost plus percentage-of-cost approach?

9 In recent years, many service businesses have begun to provide their employees with uniforms. Explain the rationale behind this strategy in terms of the concepts discussed in this chapter.

10 Look back at the service continuum in Figure 24–3. Explain how the following points in the continuum differ in terms of consistency: (*a*) salt, (*b*) automobile, (*c*) advertising agency, and (*d*) teaching.

Career Planning in Marketing

Getting a Job: The Process of Marketing Yourself

Getting a job is usually a lengthy process, and it is exactly that—a *process* that involves careful planning, implementation, and control. You may have everything going for you: a respectable grade point average (GPA), relevant work experience, several extracurricular activities, superior communication skills, and demonstrated leadership qualities. Despite these, you still need to market yourself systematically and aggressively; after all, even the best products lie dormant on the retailer's shelves unless marketed effectively.

The process of getting a job involves the same activities marketing managers use to develop and introduce products into the marketplace.[1] The only difference is that you are marketing yourself, not a product. You need to conduct marketing research by analyzing your personal qualities (performing a self-audit) and by identifying job opportunities. Based on your research results, select a target market—those job opportunities that are compatible with your interests, goals, skills, and abilities—and design a marketing mix around that target market. *You* are the "product"; you must decide how to "position" yourself in the job market. The price component of the marketing mix is the salary range and job benefits (such as health and life insurance, vacation time, and retirement benefits) that you hope to receive. Promotion involves communicating with prospective employers through written correspondence (advertising) and job interviews (personal selling). The place element focusses on how to reach prospective employers—at the campus placement centre or job fairs, for example.

This appendix will assist you in career planning by providing information about careers in marketing and outlining a job search process.

CAREERS IN MARKETING

The diversity of marketing opportunities is reflected in the many types of marketing jobs, ranging from purchasing to marketing research to public relations to product management. The growing interest in marketing among service and nonprofit organizations—such as hospitals, financial institutions, the performing arts, and government—has added to the numerous opportunities offered by traditional employers such as manufacturers, retailers, consulting firms, and advertising agencies. Examples of companies that may have opportunities for graduates with degrees in marketing include Procter & Gamble, Kraft General Foods, Bell Canada, Canada Life, General Motors, Air Canada, Bank of Montreal, and Unitel. Most of these career opportunities offer the chance to work with interesting people on stimulating and rewarding problems.

Comments one product manager, "I love marketing as a career because there are different challenges every day."[2]

Recent studies of career paths and salaries suggest that marketing careers can also provide an excellent opportunity for advancement and substantial pay. For example, a survey of chief executive officers (CEOs) of 1,000 publicly held companies revealed that marketing and finance were the most common career paths to their positions.[3] Similarly, reports of average starting salaries of college graduates indicate that salaries in marketing compare favourably with those in many other fields.[4] The future is likely to be even better. Research indicates that marketing and promotional services will be among the top 10 growth industries in the 1990s. In addition, intense domestic and foreign competition in both goods and services should continue to require greater marketing, sales, and public relations effort.[5]

Figure B–1 describes marketing occupations in six major categories: product management and physical distribution, advertising, retailing, sales, marketing research, and nonprofit marketing. One of these may be right for you! (Additional sources of marketing career information are provided at the end of this appendix.)

PRODUCT MANAGEMENT AND PHYSICAL DISTRIBUTION

Many organizations assign one manager the responsibility for a particular product. For example, P&G has separate managers for Tide, Cheer, Gain, and Bold. Product or brand managers are involved in all aspects of a product's marketing program, such as marketing research, sales, sales promotion, advertising, and pricing, as well as manufacturing. Managers of similar products typically report to a category manager.[6]

College graduates with bachelor's and master's degrees—often in marketing and business—enter P&G as brand assistants, the only starting position in its product or brand group. Each year students from campuses throughout Canada and the United States accept positions with P&G.[7] As brand assistants, their responsibilities consist primarily of selling and sales training.

After one to two years of good performance, the brand assistant is promoted to assistant brand manager, and after about the same period, to brand (product) manager. These promotions often involve several brand groups. For example, a new employee might start as brand assistant for P&G's soap products, be promoted to assistant brand manager for Crest toothpaste, and subsequently become brand manager for Pampers. The reason, as recruiter Henry de Montebello explains, is that "in the future everybody will have strategic alliances with everybody else, and the executives who thrive will be well-rounded."[8]

Several other jobs related to product management (Figure B–1) deal with physical distribution issues such as storing the manufactured product (inventory), moving the product from the firm to the customers (transportation), maintaining good relations with customers (customer service), and engaging in many other aspects of the manufacture and sale of goods. Prospects for these jobs are likely to increase in the 1990s as more firms adopt a marketing orientation and attempt to become more adept at meeting customers' needs.

PRODUCT MANAGEMENT AND PHYSICAL DISTRIBUTION

Product manager for consumer goods develops new products that can cost millions of dollars, with advice and consent of management—a job with great responsibility.

Administrative manager oversees the organization within a company that transports products to consumers and handles customer service.

Operations manager supervises warehousing and other physical distribution functions and often is directly involved in moving goods on the warehouse floor.

Traffic and transportation manager evaluates the costs and benefits of different types of transportation.

Inventory control manager forecasts demand for stockpiled goods, coordinates production with plant managers, and keeps track of current levels of shipments to keep customers supplied.

Administrative analyst performs cost analyses of physical distribution systems.

Customer service manager maintains good relations with customers by coordinating sales staffs, marketing management, and physical distribution management.

Physical distribution consultant is an expert in the transportation and distribution of goods.

SALES

Direct salesperson (door-to-door) calls on consumers in their homes to make sales.

Trade salesperson calls on retailers or wholesalers to sell products for manufacturers.

Industrial or semitechnical salesperson sells supplies and services to businesses.

Complex or professional salesperson sells complicated or custom-designed products to business. This requires understanding of the technology of a product.

NONPROFIT MARKETING

Marketing manager for nonprofit organizations develops and directs mail campaigns, fundraising, and public relations.

ADVERTISING

Account executive maintains contact with clients while coordinating the creative work among artists and copywriters. In full-service ad agencies, account executives are considered partners with the client in promoting the product and helping to develop marketing strategy.

Media buyer deals with media sales representatives in selecting advertising media and analyzes the value of media being purchased.

Copywriter works with art director in conceptualizing advertisements and writes the text of print or radio ads or the storyboards of television ads.

Art director handles the visual component of advertisements.

Sales promotion manager designs promotions for consumer products and works at an ad agency or a sales promotion agency.

Public relations manager develops written or filmed messages for the public and handles contacts with the press.

Specialty advertising manager develops advertising for the sales staff and customers or distributors.

RETAILING

Buyer selects products a store sells, surveys consumer trends, and evaluates the past performance of products and suppliers.

Store manager oversees the staff and services at a store.

MARKETING RESEARCH

Project manager for the supplier coordinates and oversees the market studies for a client.

Account executive for the supplier serves as a liaison between client and market research firm, like an advertising agency account executive.

In-house project director acts as project manager (see above) for the market studies conducted by the firm for which she works.

Marketing research specialist for an advertising agency performs or contracts for market studies for agency clients.

Source: D. W. Rosenthal and M. A. Powell, *Careers in Marketing,* © 1984, pp. 352–54. Adapted by permission of Prentice Hall, Englewood Cliffs, NJ.

▌*Figure B–1*
Twenty-six marketing occupations.

ADVERTISING

Although we may see hundreds of advertisements in a day, what we can't see easily is the fascinating and complex advertising profession. The entry-level advertising positions filled every year include jobs with a variety of firms. Advertising professionals often remark that they find their jobs appealing because the days are not routine but involve creative activities with many interesting people.

Advertising positions are available in three kinds of organizations: advertisers, media companies, and agencies. Advertisers include manufacturers, retail stores, service firms, and many other types of companies. Often they have an advertising department responsible for preparing and placing their own ads. Advertising careers are also possible with the media: television and radio stations, magazines, and newspapers. Finally, advertising agencies offer job opportunities through their use of account management, research, media, and creative services.

Most starting positions in advertising are as a media buyer, the person who chooses and buys the media that will carry the ad; or as a copywriter, the person responsible for the message, or copy, in an ad. From these positions, promotion to assistant account executive, who acts as a liaison between the client and the agency's creative department, may come quickly. Because the next position, account executive, requires a mind for business and an affinity for spotting an effective advertising idea, many of the large ad agencies now encourage employees who are advancing toward the position to pursue an MBA.[9] Students interested in advertising should develop good communications skills and try to gain advertising experience through summer employment or internships.

RETAILING

There are two separate career paths in retailing: merchandise management and store management (Figure B–2). The key position in merchandising is that of a buyer, who is responsible for selecting merchandise, guiding the promotion of the merchandise, setting prices, bargaining with wholesalers, training the sales force, and monitoring the competitive environment. The buyer must also be able to organize and coordinate many critical activities under severe time constraints. In contrast, store management involves the supervision of personnel in all departments and the general management of all facilities, equipment, and merchandise displays. In addition, store managers are responsible for the financial performance of each department and for the store as a whole.

Most starting jobs in retailing are trainee positions. A trainee is usually placed in a management training program and then given a position as an assistant buyer or assistant department manager. Advancement and responsibility can be achieved quickly because there is a shortage of qualified personnel in

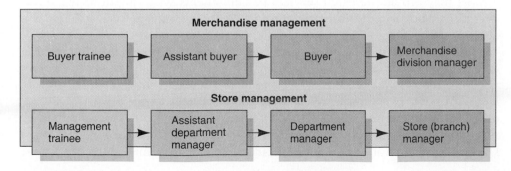

Merchandise management

| Buyer trainee | → | Assistant buyer | → | Buyer | → | Merchandise division manager |

Store management

| Management trainee | → | Assistant department manager | → | Department manager | → | Store (branch) manager |

Figure B–2
Typical retailing career paths.

retailing and because superior performance of an individual is quickly reflected in sales and profits—two visible measures of success.

SALES

College graduates from many disciplines are attracted to sales positions because of the increasingly professional nature of selling jobs and the many opportunities they can provide. A selling career offers benefits that are hard to match in any other field: the opportunity for rapid advancement (into management or to new territories and accounts), the potential for extremely attractive compensation, the development of personal satisfaction, feelings of accomplishment, and increased self-confidence, and independence—salespeople often have almost complete control over their time and activities. Many companies now offer two sales career paths—one for people who want to go into management, and another for those who want to remain in sales for the entire career.[10]

Employment opportunities in sales occupations are found in a wide variety of organizations, including insurance agencies, retailers, and financial service firms. Activities in sales jobs include *selling duties,* such as prospecting for customers, demonstrating the product, or quoting prices; *sales-support duties,* such as handling complaints and helping solve technical problems; and *nonselling duties,* such as preparing reports, attending sales meetings, and monitoring competitive activities. Salespeople who can deal with these varying activities are critical to a company's success.

MARKETING RESEARCH

Marketing researchers play important roles in many organizations today. They are responsible for obtaining, analyzing, and interpreting data to facilitate making marketing decisions. This means marketing researchers are basically problem solvers. Success in the area requires not only an understanding of statistics and computers but also a broad base of marketing knowledge[11] and an ability to communicate with management. Individuals who are inquisitive, methodical, analytical, and solution oriented find the field particularly rewarding.

The responsibilities of the men and women currently working in the market research industry include defining the marketing problem, designing the questionnaire, selecting the sample, collecting and analyzing the data, and, finally, reporting the results of the research. These jobs are available in three kinds of organizations. *Marketing research consulting firms* contract with large companies to provide research about their products or services. *Advertising agencies* may provide research services to help clients with questions related to advertising and promotional problems. Finally, some companies have an *in-house research staff* to design and execute their research projects.

Although marketing researchers may start as assistants performing routine tasks, they quickly advance to broader responsibilities. Survey design, interviewing, report writing, and all aspects of the research process create a challenging career. In addition, research projects typically deal with such diverse problems as consumer motivation, pricing, forecasting, and competition. A recent survey of research organizations suggested that to be successful in marketing research positions students should develop skills in written, oral, and interpersonal communication, statistics and analysis, research design, and logic. The survey also suggested that practical work experience (e.g., internships) provides a useful supplement to classroom education.[12]

INTERNATIONAL CAREERS

Many of the careers that have been described can be found in international settings—in multinational Canadian corporations, small- to medium-size firms with export business, and franchises. The dramatic changes in Europe and the need to rebuild the economies of the former Soviet republics may provide many opportunities. Variations of the permanent international career are also possible—for example, some companies may alternate periods of work at "headquarters" with "field" assignments in foreign countries.[13] Finally, a domestic international career—working for a foreign-owned company with an office in Canada—may be appealing.[14]

THE JOB SEARCH PROCESS

Activities you should consider during your job search process include assessing yourself,[15] identifying job opportunities, preparing your résumé and related correspondence, and going on job interviews.

ASSESSING YOURSELF

You must know your product—you—so that you can market yourself effectively to prospective employers. Consequently, a critical first step in your job search is conducting a self-analysis, which involves critically examining yourself on the following dimensions: interests, abilities, education, experience, personality, desired job environment, and personal goals.[16] The importance of performing this assessment was stressed by a management consultant:[17]

> Many graduates enter the world of work without even understanding the fact that they are specific somebodies, much less knowing the kinds of competencies and motivations with which they have been endowed . . . The tragedy of not knowing is awesome. Ignorant of who they are, most graduates are doomed to spend too much of their lives in work for which they are poorly suited . . . Self-knowledge is critical to effectively managing your career.

Asking Key Questions   A self-analysis, in part, entails asking yourself some very important and difficult questions (Figure B–3). It is critical that you respond to the questions honestly, because your answers ultimately will be used as a guide in your job selection. A less-than-candid appraisal of yourself might result in a job mismatch.

Identifying Strengths and Weaknesses   After you have addressed the questions posed in Figure B–3, you are ready to identify your strengths and weaknesses. To do so, draw a vertical line down the middle of a sheet of paper and label one side of the paper "strengths" and the other side "weaknesses." Based on your answers to the questions, record your strong and weak points in their respective

INTERESTS

How do I like to spend my time?
Do I enjoy being with people?
Do I like working with mechanical things?
Do I enjoy working with numbers?
Am I a member of many organizations?
Do I enjoy physical activities?
Do I like to read?

ABILITIES

Am I adept at working with numbers?
Am I adept at working with mechanical things?
Do I have good verbal and written communication skills?
What special talents do I have?
At which abilities do I wish I were more adept?

EDUCATION

How have my courses and extracurricular activities prepared me for a specific job?
Which were my best subjects? My worst? The most fun? The least?
Is my GPA an accurate picture of my academic ability? Why?
Do I aspire to a graduate degree? Before beginning my job?
Why did I choose my major?

EXPERIENCE

What previous jobs have I held? What were my responsibilities in each?
Were any of my jobs applicable to positions I may be seeking? How?
What did I like the most about my previous jobs? Like the least?

Why did I work in the jobs I did?
If I had it to do over again, would I work in these jobs? Why?

PERSONALITY

What are my good and bad traits?
Am I competitive?
Do I work well with others?
Am I outspoken?
Am I a leader or a follower?
Do I work well under pressure?
Do I work quickly, or am I methodical?
Do I get along well with others?
Am I ambitious?
Do I work well independently of others?

DESIRED JOB ENVIRONMENT

Am I willing to relocate? Why?
Do I have a geographical preference? Why?
Would I mind travelling in my job?
Do I have to work for a large, nationally known firm to be satisfied?
Must the job I assume offer rapid promotion opportunities?
If I could design my own job, what characteristics would it have?
How important is high initial salary to me?

PERSONAL GOALS

What are my short-term and long-term goals? Why?
Am I career oriented, or do I have broader interests?
What are my career goals?
What jobs are likely to help me achieve my goals?
What do I hope to be doing in 5 years? In 10 years?
What do I want out of life?

Figure B–3
Questions to ask in your self-analysis.

column. Ideally this cataloguing should be done over a few days to give you adequate time to reflect on your attributes. In addition, you might seek input from others who know you well (such as parents, close relatives, friends, professors, or employers) and can offer more objective views. They might even evaluate you on the questions in Figure B–3, and you can compare the results with your own evaluation. A hypothetical list of strengths and weaknesses is shown in Figure B–4.

Additional information about yourself can be obtained by developing a list of the five experiences or activities you most enjoy and analyzing what they have in common. Don't be surprised if the common characteristics are related to your strengths and weaknesses!

Taking Job-Related Tests Personality and vocational interest tests, provided by many colleges and universities, can give you other ideas about yourself. After

STRENGTHS	WEAKNESSES
Enjoy being with people	Am not adept at working with computers
Am an avid reader	Have minimal work experience
Have good communication skills	Have a mediocre GPA
Am involved in many extracurricular activities	Am sometimes impatient
	Resent close supervision
Work well with others	Work methodically (slowly)
Work well independently	Will not relocate
Am honest and dependable	Anger easily sometimes
Am willing to travel in the job	
Am a good problem solver	
Have a good sense of humour	
Am a self-starter, have drive	

▌ *Figure B–4*
Hypothetical list of job candidate's strengths and weaknesses.

tests have been administered and scored, test takers meet with testing service counsellors to discuss the results. Test results generally suggest jobs for which students have an inclination. If you have not already done so, you may wish to see whether your school offers such testing services.

IDENTIFYING YOUR JOB OPPORTUNITIES

To identify and analyze the job market, you must conduct some marketing research to determine what industries *and* companies offer promising job opportunities that relate to the results of your self-analysis. Several sources that can help in your search are discussed in the following.

College Placement Office   Your college placement office is an excellent source of job information. Personnel in that office can inform you about which companies will be recruiting on campus, alert you to unexpected job openings, advise you about short-term and long-term career prospects, offer advice on résumé construction, assess your interviewing strengths and weaknesses, and help you evaluate a job offer. In addition, the office usually contains a variety of written materials focussing on different industries and companies and tips on job hunting. Job postings may also be placed there.

Databases   Many companies no longer make frequent on-campus visits. Instead, they use a computerized résumé database service that allows them to review credentials of students. Database firms charge students or placement offices a nominal fee to create a database résumé that includes career and geographic preferences, academic and job history, and special skills and talents. Employers contact students directly when the candidate's qualifications meet their specific job requirments. The advantage of this system for students is that regardless of the size or location of the campus they are attending, many companies have access to their résumé.

Library   The public or college library can provide you with reference material that, among other things, describes successful firms and their operations, defines the content of various jobs, and forecasts job opportunities. For example, the Financial Post publishes *The Top 500 Canadian Companies* each year, and Dun & Bradstreet publishes directories of companies in Canada. *Careers in Marketing,* a publication of the American Marketing Association, presents career opportunities in marketing. Statistics Canada also provides projections for specific job prospects, as well as information pertaining to those jobs. A librarian can indicate reference materials that will be most pertinent to *your* job search.

Advertisements   Help-wanted advertisements provide an overview of what is happening in the job market. Local (particularly Sunday editions) and college newspapers, trade press (such as *Marketing*), and business magazines (such as *Sales and Marketing Management*) contain classified advertisement sections that generally have job opening announcements, often for entry-level positions. Reviewing the want ads can help you identify what kinds of positions are available and their requirements and job titles, which firms offer certain kinds of jobs, and levels of compensation.

Employment Agencies   An employment agency can make you aware of several job opportunities very quickly because of its large number of job listings available through computer databases. Many agencies specialize in a particular field (such as sales and marketing). The advantages of using an agency include that it reduces the cost of a job search by bringing applicants and employers together, often has exclusive job listings available only by working through the agency, performs much of the job search for you, and tries to find a job that is compatible with your qualifications and interests.[18] Employment agencies are much maligned because some engage in questionable business practices, so check with the Better Business Bureau or your business contacts to determine the quality of the various agencies.

Personal Contacts   An important source of job information that students often overlook is their personal contacts. People you know often may know of job opportunities, so you should advise them that you're looking for a job. Relatives and friends might aid your job search. Instructors you know well and business contacts can provide a wealth of information about potential jobs and even help arrange an interview with a prospective employer. They may also help arrange "informational interviews" with employers who do not have immediate openings. These interviews allow you to collect information about an industry or an employer and give you an advantage if a position does become available. It is a good idea to leave your résumé with all your personal contacts so they can pass it along to those who might be in need of your services. Student organizations (such as the student chapter of the American Marketing Association) may be sources of job opportunities, particularly if they are involved with the business community. Local chapters of professional business organizations (such as the American Marketing Association) can also provide job information; contacting the chapter president is a first step in seeking assistance from these organizations.

Employment Canada Office   Employment Canada offices have listings of job opportunities in their province and counsellors to help arrange a job interview for you. Although Employment Canada offices perform functions similar to employment agencies, they differ in listing only job opportunities in their province and in providing their services free.

Direct Contact   Another means of obtaining job information is direct contact—personally communicating to prospective employers (either by mail or in person) that you would be interested in pursuing job opportunities with them. Often you may not even know whether jobs are available in these firms. If you correspond with the companies in writing, a letter of introduction and an attached résumé should serve as your initial form of communication. Your major goal in direct contact is ultimately to arrange a job interview.

WRITING YOUR RÉSUMÉ

A résumé is a document that communicates to prospective employers who you are. An employer reading a résumé focusses on two key questions: What is the candidate like? and What can the candidate do for me?[19] It is imperative that you design a résumé that addresses these two questions and presents you in a favourable light. Personnel in your campus placement office can provide assistance in designing résumés.

The Résumé Itself   A well-constructed résumé generally contains up to nine major sections: (1) identification (name, address, and telephone number), (2) job or career objective, (3) educational background, (4) extracurricular activities, (5) work experience or history, (6) skills or capabilities (that pertain to a particular kind of job for which you may be interviewing), (7) accomplishments or achievements, (8) personal interests, and (9) personal references.[20] There is no universally accepted format for a résumé, but three are more frequently used: chronological, functional, and targeted. A *chronological* format presents your work experience and education according to the time sequence in which they occurred (i.e., in chronological order). If you have had several jobs or attended several schools, this approach is useful to highlight what you have done. With a *functional* format, you group your experience into skill categories that emphasize your strengths. This option is particularly appropriate if you have no

▌ *Figure B–5*
**Chronological résumé
format.**

SALLY WINTER

Campus address (until 6/1/95):   Home address:
Elm Street Apartments #2B   123 Front Street
College Town, Ont.   Vancouver, B.C. V1X 2A0
Phone: (416) 555-1234   Phone: (604) 555-4321

Education

B. Commerce, University of Toronto, 1995, Honours (3.6 GPA in major—
Marketing)

Work Experience

Paid for 70 percent of my college expenses through the following part-time and
summer jobs:
Legal Secretary, Smith & Smith, Toronto, Ontario—summer 1992

- Took dictation and transcribed tapes of legal proceedings
- Typed contracts and other legal documents
- Reorganized client files for easier access
- Answered the phone and screened calls for the partners

Salesclerk, College Varsity Shop, Toronto, Ontario—1991–1994 academic years

- Helped customers with buying decisions
- Arranged stock and helped with window displays
- Assisted in year-end inventories
- Took over responsibilities of store manager when she was on vacation or ill

Assistant Manager, Treasure Place Gift Shop, Vancouver, B.C.—summers and
Christmas vacations 1990–1993

- Supervised two salesclerks
- Helped select merchandise at trade shows
- Handled daily accounting
- Worked comfortably under pressure during busy seasons

Campus Activities

- Elected captain of the women's varsity tennis team for two years
- Worked as a reporter and night editor on campus newspaper for two years
- Elected Vice President, Commerce Society

Personal Interests

- Reading, listening to jazz, swimming

References Available on Request

Source: Adapted from C. R. Powell, "Secrets of Selling a Resume," in P. Schmidt, ed., *The Honda How to Get a Job Guide* (New York: McGraw-Hill, 1985), pp. 4–9.

experience or only minimal experience related to your chosen field. A *targeted* format focusses on the capabilities you have for a specific job. This alternative is desirable if you know what job you want and are qualified for it.[21] In any of the formats, if possible, you should include quantitative information about your accomplishments and experience, such as "increased sales revenue by 20 percent" for the year you managed a retail clothing store. A résumé that illustrates the chronological format is shown in Figure B–5.

Letter Accompanying a Résumé   The letter accompanying a résumé, or cover letter, serves as the job candidate's introduction. As a result, it must gain the attention and interest of the reader or it will fail to give the incentive to examine the résumé carefully. In designing a letter to accompany your résumé, address the following issues.[22]

- Address the letter to a specific person.
- Identify the position for which you are applying and how you heard of it.
- Indicate why you are applying for the position.
- Summarize your most significant credentials and qualifications.
- Refer the reader to the enclosed résumé.
- Request a personal interview, and advise the reader when and where you can be reached.

A sample letter comprising these five factors is presented in Figure B–6. Some students have tried creative approaches to making their letter stand out—sending a gift with their letter or using creative packaging, for example. Although these tactics may gain a recruiter's attention, most hiring managers say that a frivolous approach makes for a frivolous employee. As a general rule, nothing works better than an impressive cover letter and good academic credentials.[23]

INTERVIEWING FOR YOUR JOB

The job interview is a conversation between a prospective employer and a job candidate that focusses on determining whether the employer's needs can be satisfied by the candidate's qualifications. The interview is a "make or break" situation: if the interview goes well, you have increased your chances of receiving a job offer; if it goes poorly, you probably will be eliminated from further consideration.

Preparing for a Job Interview   To be successful in a job interview, you must prepare for it so you can exhibit professionalism and indicate to a prospective employer that you are serious about the job. When preparing for the interview, you need to perform several critical activities.

Before the interview, gather facts about the industry, the prospective employer, and the job. Relevant information might include the general description for the occupation; the firm's products or services; the firm's size, number of employees, and financial and competitive position; the requirements of the position; and the name and personality of the interviewer.[24] Obtaining this information will provide you with additional insight into the firm and help you formulate questions to ask the interviewer. The above information might be gleaned, for example, from corporate annual reports, the *Financial Post, Canadian Trade Index,* Standard & Poor's *Register of Corporations,* selected issues of *Canadian Business,* or other trade publications. If information is not readily available, you could call the company and indicate that you wish to obtain some information about the firm before your interview.

Preparation for the job interview should also involve role playing, or pretending that you are in the "hot seat" being interviewed. Before role-playing, anticipate questions interviewers may pose and how you might address

**▌ *Figure B–6*
Sample letter
accompanying a résumé.**

> Sally Winter
> Elm Street Apartments #2B
> College Town, Ont. M1X 2A0
>
> January 31, 1995
> Mr. J. B. Jones
> Sales Manager
> Hilltop Manufacturing Company
> Toronto, Ont. M1Z 2Z0
>
> Dear Mr. Jones:
>
> Dr. William Johnson, Professor of Business Administration at the University of Toronto, recently suggested that I write to you concerning your opening and my interest in a sales position. With a B. Commerce degree and courses in personal selling and sales management, I am confident that I could make a positive contribution to your firm.
>
> During the past several years I have been a salesclerk in a clothing store and an assistant manager in a gift shop. These two positions required my performing a variety of duties including selling, purchasing, stocking, and supervising. As a result, I have developed an appreciation for the viewpoints of the customer, salesperson, and management. Given my background and high energy level, I feel that I am particularly well qualified to assume a sales position in your company.
>
> My enclosed résumé better highlights my education and experience. My extracurricular activities should strengthen and support my abilities to serve as a sales representative.
>
> I am eager to talk with you because I feel I can demonstrate to you why I am a strong candidate for the position. I have friends in Toronto with whom I could stay on weekends, so Fridays or Mondays would be ideal for an appointment. I will call you in a week to see if we can arrange a mutually convenient time for a meeting. I am hopeful that your schedule will allow this.
>
> Thank you for your kind consideration. If you would like some additional information, please feel free to contact me. I look forward to talking with you.
>
> Sincerely,
>
> Sally Winter
>
> enclosure

them (Figure B–7). Do not memorize your answers, though, because you want to appear spontaneous, yet logical and intelligent. Nonetheless, it is helpful to practice how you might respond to the questions. You should also anticipate a substance abuse screening process—now common among a wide variety of organizations.[25] In addition, develop questions you might ask the interviewer that are important and of concern to you (Figure B–8).

When role-playing, you and someone with whom you feel comfortable should engage in a mock interview. Afterward, ask the stand-in interviewer to candidly appraise your interview content and style. You may wish to videotape

INTERVIEWER QUESTIONS

1   What can you tell me about yourself?
2   What are your strengths? Weaknesses?
3   What do you consider to be your most significant accomplishment to date?
4   What do you see yourself doing in 5 years? In 10 years?
5   Are you a leader? Explain.
6   What do you really want out of life?
7   How would you describe yourself?
8   Why did you choose your college major?
9   In which extracurricular activities did you participate? Why?
10 What jobs have you enjoyed the most? The least? Why?
11 How has your previous work experience prepared you for a job?
12 Why do you want to work for our company?
13 What qualifications do you think a person needs to be successful in a company like ours?
14 What do you know about our company?
15 What criteria are you using to evaluate the company for which you hope to work?
16 In what kind of city would you prefer to live?
17 What can I tell you about our company?
18 Are you willing to relocate?
19 Are you willing to spend at least six months as a trainee? Why?
20 Why should we hire you?

❚ *Figure B–7*
Questions frequently asked by interviewers.

the mock interview; ask the personnel in your campus placement office where videotaping equipment can be obtained for this purpose.

Before the job interview, you should attend to several details. Know the exact time and place of the interview; write them down—do not rely on your memory. Get the full company name straight. Find out what the interviewer's

❚ *Figure B–8*
Questions frequently asked by interviewees.

INTERVIEWEE QUESTIONS

1   Why would a job candidate want to work for your firm?
2   What makes your firm different from its competitors?
3   What is the company's promotion policy?
4   Describe the typical first-year assignment for this job.
5   How is an employee evaluated?
6   What are the opportunities for personal growth?
7   Do you have a training program?
8   What are the company's plans for future growth?
9   What is the retention rate of people in the position for which I am interviewing?
10 How can you use my skills?
11 Does the company have development programs?
12 What kind of image does the firm have in the community?
13 Why do you enjoy working for your firm?
14 How much responsibility would I have in this job?
15 What is the corporate culture in your firm?

name is and how to pronounce it. Bring a notepad and pen along on the interview, in case you need to record anything. Make certain that your appearance is clean, neat, professional, and conservative. And be punctual; arriving tardy to a job interview gives you an appearance of being unreliable.

Succeeding in Your Job Interview   You have done your homework, and at last the moment arrives and it is time for the interview. Although you may experience some apprehension, view the interview as a conversation between the prospective employer and you. Both of you are in the interview to look over the other party, to see whether there might be a good match. You know your subject matter (you); furthermore, because you did not have a job with the firm when you walked into the interview, you really have nothing to lose if you don't get it—so relax.[26]

When you meet the interviewer, greet him by name, be cheerful, smile, and maintain good eye contact. Take your lead from the interviewer at the outset. Sit down after the interviewer has offered you a seat. Do not smoke. Sit up straight in your chair and look alert and interested at all times. Appear relaxed, not tense. Be enthusiastic.

During the interview, be yourself. If you try to behave in a manner that is different from the "real" you, your attempt may be transparent to the interviewer or you may ultimately get the job but discover that you aren't suited for it. In addition to assessing how well your skills match those of the job, the interviewer will probably try to assess your long-term interest in the firm. William Kucker, a recruiter for General Electric, explains, "We're looking for people to make a commitment."[27]

As the interview comes to a close, leave it on a positive note. Thank the interviewer for his or her time and the opportunity to discuss employment opportunities. If you are still interested in the job, express this to the interviewer. The interviewer will normally tell you what the employer's next step is. Rarely will a job offer be made at the end of the initial interview. If it is and you want the job, accept the offer; if there is any doubt in your mind about the job, however, ask for time to consider the offer.

Following Up on Your Job Interview   After your interview, send a thank-you note to the interviewer and indicate whether you are still interested in the job. If you want to continue pursuing the job, "polite persistence" may help you get it. According to one expert, "Many job hunters make the mistake of thinking that their career fate is totally in the hands of the interviewer once the job interview is finished."[28] You *can* have an impact on the interviewer *after* the interview is over.

The thank-you note is a gesture of appreciation and a way of maintaining visibility with the interviewer. (Remember the adage, "Out of sight, out of mind.") Even if the interview did not go well, the thank-you note may impress the interviewer so much that his opinion of you changes. After you have sent your thank-you note, you may wish to call the prospective employer to determine the status of the hiring decision. If the interviewer told you when you would hear from the employer, make your telephone call *after* this date (assuming, of course, that you have not yet heard from the employer); if the interviewer did not tell you when you would be contacted, make your telephone call a week or so after you have sent your thank-you note.

As you conduct your follow-up, be persistent but polite. If you are too eager, one of two things could happen to prevent you from getting the job: the employer might feel that you are a nuisance and would exhibit such behaviour on the job, or the employer may perceive that you are desperate for the job and thus are not a viable candidate.

Handling Rejection   You have put your best efforts into your job search. You developed a well-designed résumé and prepared carefully for the job interview. Even the interview appears to have gone well. Nevertheless, a prospective employer may send you a rejection letter. ("We are sorry that our needs and your superb qualifications don't match.") Although you will probably be disappointed, not all interviews lead to a job offer, because there normally are more candidates than there are positions available.

If you receive a rejection letter, you should think back through the interview. What appeared to go right? What went wrong? Perhaps personnel from your campus placement office can shed light on the problem, particularly if they are in the custom of having interviewers rate each interviewee. Try to learn lessons to apply in future interviews. Keep interviewing and gaining interview experience; your persistence will eventually pay off.

SELECTED SOURCES OF MARKETING CAREER INFORMATION

The following is a selected list of marketing information sources that you should find useful during your academic studies and professional career.

BUSINESS AND MARKETING REFERENCE PUBLICATIONS

Britt, S. H.; and N. F. Guess (eds.). *The Dartnell Marketing Manager's Handbook.* 2nd ed. Chicago: Dartnell Corporation, 1983. This handbook contains 76 chapters on many important marketing topics, including organization and staffing, establishing objectives, marketing research, developing a marketing plan, putting the plan into action, promoting products and services, international marketing, and program appraisal.

Buell, V. P. (ed.). *Handbook of Modern Marketing.* 2nd ed. New York: McGraw-Hill, 1986. This handbook was designed to provide a single authoritative source of information on marketing and marketing-related subjects. Sections and chapters contain conceptual background material to aid the reader in overall understanding, followed by "how-to" information.

Business Periodicals Index (BPI). New York: H. W. Wilson Company. This is a monthly (except July) index of almost 300 periodicals from all fields of business and management.

Cochrane, C.; and K. L. Barasch. *Marketing Problem Solver.* 3rd ed. Radnor, PA: Chilton Book Company, 1989. A good reference for "how-to" problems, this handbook contains chapters on marketing research, marketing planning, product planning, pricing, advertising, trade shows, sales promotion, legal aspects of marketing, and other topics.

Cousins, J.; and L. Robinson (eds.). *The Online Manual.* Cambridge, MA: Blackwell Publishers, 1992. This manual is a practical tool to help both the experienced and inexperienced information user select from the thousands of databases now available on-line.

Daniells, L. M. *Business Information Sources.* 3rd ed. Berkeley, CA: University of California Press, 1993. This comprehensive guide to selected business books and reference sources is useful for business students, as well as the practising businessperson.

Rosenberg, J. M. *Dictionary of Business and Management.* 3rd ed. New York: John Wiley & Sons, 1992. This dictionary contains over 10,000 concise definitions of business and management terms.

Shapiro, I. J. *Dictionary of Marketing Terms*. 4th ed. Totowa, NJ: Littlefield, Adams & Company, 1981. This dictionary contains definitions of over 5,000 marketing terms.

Stansfield, R. H. *The Dartnell Advertising Manager's Handbook*. 3rd ed. Chicago: Dartnell Corporation, 1982. This handbook provides a practical review of advertising planning and practice. Topics include advertising department organization, campaign planning, agency selection, copywriting, media, and research.

CAREER PLANNING PUBLICATIONS

Bolles, R. N. *What Color Is Your Parachute? A Practical Manual for Job Hunters and Career Changers*. Berkeley, CA: Ten Speed Press, 1993.

Crowther, K. *Researching Your Way to a Good Job*. New York: John Wiley & Sons, 1993.

Jackson, T. *The Perfect Résumé*. New York: Doubleday, 1990.

Krannich, R. L.; and C. R. Krannich. *The Complete Guide to International Jobs and Careers*. 2nd ed. Woodbridge, VA: Impact Publications, 1992.

Leeds, D. *Marketing Yourself*. New York: HarperCollins, 1991.

Lewis, A. *How to Write Better Résumés*. 3rd ed. Hauppauge, NY: Barron's Educational Services, 1989.

Luke, R. H. *Business Careers*. Boston: Houghton Mifflin, 1989.

Rosenthal, D. W.; and Michael A. Powell. *Careers in Marketing*. Englewood Cliffs, NJ: Prentice Hall, 1984.

Schmidt, P J. *Making It on Your First Job: When You're Young, Inexperienced, and Ambitious*. Rev. ed. Princeton, NJ: Peterson's Guides, 1991.

SELECTED PERIODICALS

Advertising Age, Crain Communications, Inc. (semiweekly). Write to 965 E. Jefferson Ave., Detroit, MI 48207-3185 (subscription rate: $86).

Canadian Business (monthly) Write to 70 The Esplanade, 2nd Floor, Toronto, Ont. MSE 1R2 (subscription rate $25).

Financial Post Magazine (monthly). Write to 777 Bay Street, Toronto, Ont. M5G 2E4 (subscription rate $50).

Fortune, Time, Inc. (biweekly), Write to P.O. Box 60001, Tampa, FL 33660-0001 (subscription rate: $52.95).

Harvard Business Review, Harvard University (bimonthly). Write to Harvard Business Review Subscriber Service, P.O. Box 52623, Boulder, CO 80322-2632 (subscription rate: $75).

Industrial Marketing Management, Elsevier Science Publishing Co., Inc. (quarterly). Write to 655 Avenue of the Americas, New York, NY 10010 (subscription rate: $160).

Journal of the Academy of Marketing Science, The Academy of Marketing Science (quarterly). Write to JAI Press, Inc., 55 Old Post Rd. #2, P.O. Box 1678, Greenwich, CT 06836-1678 (subscription rate: $60).

Journal of Advertising Research, Advertising Research Foundation (bimonthly). Write to 3 E. 54th St., 15th Fl., New York, NY 10022 (subscription rate: $100).

Journal of Business and Industrial Marketing, MCB University Press (quarterly). Write to 60/62 Toller Ln., Bradford, West Yorkshire, England BD89BY (subscription rate: $60).

Journal of Consumer Marketing, MCB University Press (quarterly). Write to 60/62 Toller Ln., Bradford, West Yorkshire, England, BD89BY (subscription rate: $60).

Journal of Consumer Research, Journal of Consumer Research, Inc. (quarterly). Write to University of Chicago Press, Journals Division, 5720 S. Woodlawn Ave., Chicago, IL 60637 (subscription rate: $75 for nonmembers, $37 for members, $20 for students).

Journal of Health Care Marketing, American Marketing Association (quarterly). Write to 250 S. Wacker Dr., Suite 200, Chicago, IL 60606-5819 (subscription rate: $50 for nonmembers, $40 for members).

Journal of Marketing, American Marketing Association (quarterly). Write to 250 S. Wacker Dr., Suite 200, Chicago, IL 60606-5819 (subscription rate: $66 for nonmembers, $33 for members).

Journal of Marketing Education, University of Colorado (three per year). Write to University of Colorado, Graduate School of Business Administration, Campus Box 420, Boulder, CO 80309 (subscription rate: $30).

Journal of Marketing Research, American Marketing Association (quarterly). Write to 250 S. Wacker Dr., Suite 200, Chicago, IL 60606-5819 (subscription rate: $66 for nonmembers, $33 for members).

Journal of Personal Selling and Sales Management, Pi Sigma Epsilon (quarterly). Write to 155 E. Capitol Drive, Hartland, WI 53209 (subscription rate: $55).

Journal of Retailing, Institute of Retail Management (quarterly). Write to New York University, 202 Tisch Bldg., Washington Square, New York, NY 10003 (subscription rate: $30).

Marketing, MacLean Hunter (biweekly). Write to 777 Bay St., Toronto, Ont. M5W 1A7 (subscription rate: $60).

Marketing News, American Marketing Association (biweekly). Write to 250 S. Wacker Dr., Suite 200, Chicago, IL 60606-5819 (subscription rate: $60 for nonmembers, $30 for members).

Media Week, BPI Communications, Inc. (monthly). Write to 49 E. 21st St., New York, NY 10010 (subscription rate: $40).

Sales and Marketing Management, Bill Communications, Inc. (16 per year). Write to 633 Third Ave., New York, NY 10017 (subscription rate: $48).

PROFESSIONAL AND TRADE ASSOCIATIONS

American Marketing Association
250 South Wacker Drive
Chicago, IL 60606-5819
(312) 648-0536
Toronto Chapter
100 University Avenue
Toronto, Ontario M5W 1V8
(416) 593-7711

Canadian Advertising Foundation
350 Bloor St. E #402
Toronto, Ontario M4W 1H5
(416) 961-6311

Canadian Advertising Research Foundation
180 Bloor St. W #803
Toronto, Ontario M5S 2V6
(416) 964-3832

Canadian Association of Broadcasters
350 Sparks Street #306
P.O. Box 627 Stn. 8
Ottawa, Ontario K1P 5S2
(613) 233-4035

Canadian Direct Marketing Association
1 Concorde Gate #607
Don Mills, Ontario M3C 3N6
(416) 391-2362

Canadian Federation of Business and Professional
    Women's Clubs
56 Sparks Street #308
Ottawa, Ontario K1P 5A9
(613) 234-7619

Canadian Federation of Independent Business
4141 Yonge Street #401
Willowdale, Ontario M2P 2A6

Conference Board of Canada
255 Smyth Road
Ottawa, Ontario K1N 8M7
(613) 526-3280

Purchasing Management Association of Canada
2 Carlton Street #1414
Toronto, Ontario M5B 1J3
(416) 977-7111

Professional Marketing Research Society
2323 Yonge Street #806
Toronto, Ontario M4P 2C9
(416) 487-4893

Retail Council of Canada
210 Dundas St. W #600
Toronto, Ontario M5G 2E8
(416) 598-4684

Retail Merchants Association of Canada
1780 Birchmount Road
Scarborough, Ontario M1P 2H8
(416) 291-7903

VIDEO · CASE ONE
*Rollerblade, Inc.**

"*A*chieving success wasn't easy," reflects Mary Horwath. "It took months and years of hard work . . . and perhaps most of all, it took lots of imagination!"

THE SITUATION

But Horwath, now vice president of marketing services and international at Rollerblade, Inc., hears footsteps. Now in the 1990s, she summarizes Rollerblade's success:

> We had introduced a product and created a sport. We had arrived. By 1991 Rollerblade was rapidly becoming a part of the lives of many Americans and Canadians. But now we were faced with another challenge. It may have been a marketer's dream that people thought that in-line skating was "Rollerblading." But we knew that every skate wasn't a Rollerblade skate. And, for the first time, we had competition from other companies. We had always built brand identity during our years of building the sport. But now it was time to focus especially on marketing the Rollerblade brand. Of course we continued to build the sport because we knew that as the sport grew, so would Rollerblade, Inc.[1]

The future of the in-line skating industry looks good. A survey of leaders in the outdoor gear industry in the early 1990s placed in-line skating second only to family camping among outdoor activities expected to grow the most in the first half of the decade. Industry sales in 1993 were about $400 million. Optimists see the international in-line skate market perhaps reaching $1 billion in 1995 or soon after.

*This case was written by Linda Rochford of The University of Minnesota–Duluth and William Rudelius.

THE COMPETITION

Horwath's concern about competitors is genuine. When Rollerblade, Inc., was founded, it was the only manufacturer of in-line skates in the world. Today it has more than 30 direct competitors, most selling lower-priced skates than Rollerblade skates through mass merchandising chains like Wal-Mart and Kmart. Rollerblade, Inc., had historically avoided these types of outlets in favour of specialized sporting goods stores. But recently, the company has extended its distribution, for some of its skates, to major department stores and catalogue showroom-type retailers in order to compete more directly with the increased number of competitive brands looking to take market share away from Rollerblade, Inc.

MARKETS AND PRODUCTS

Horwath sees Rollerblade's primary target market as active adults aged 18 to 35. But from skating with skaters on Rollerblade skates Horwath has concluded that potential skaters are far more diverse than the mere 18- to 35-year-old target, and that skaters use Rollerblade skates for many different reasons: for racing, for fun, for exercise, for street hockey, for complex acrobatics, and even for transportation to and from work or college.

With these diverse markets, Rollerblade, Inc., develops a variety of in-line designs targeted at different market segments. Some examples:

- *Metroblade*™. A lightweight nylon and leather walking shoe that fits into a molded skate shell, for transportation that requires going into buildings.

- *Problade*™. Designed for serious racing for speed skaters with a low-cut leather boot and five oversize (80 mm) wheels.
- *Macroblade Equipe*™. Vented, moulded plastic shell that makes a lightweight, breathable skate.
- *Mondoblade*™. Skates for starting out in in-line skating.
- *Microblade*™. Skates with wild colours, for kids.

In addition, Rollerblade offers a complete line of skating accessories that includes knee pads, wrist guards, gloves, jerseys, shorts, T-shirts, and helmets.

Designing a high-quality in-line skate is a lot more complex than it may appear. In fact, Rollerblade, Inc., holds more than 185 patents for its in-line skating products. Its industry "firsts" include polyurethane boots and wheels, metal frames, dual bearings, heel brakes, buckle closures, ventilated shells, and breathable liners.

Because of the speeds involved in in-line skating, Rollerblade, Inc., has been an industry leader in promoting safety and the use of proper equipment. Both *Time* and *Fortune* named Rollerblade skates a "product of the year" in 1990.

GLOBAL ALLIANCES

To obtain financial strength for the future, in 1991 Rollerblade, Inc., developed an alliance with Italy's Nordica Sportsystem, a leading ski boot manufacturer. Nordica, owned by a Benetton family holding company, bought 50 percent ownership in Rollerblade, Inc. Besides capital, Nordica provides Rollerblade, Inc., with increased research, development, and manufacturing capabilities and access to global distribution networks. Today, Nordica is manufacturing four models of Rollerblade skates, including Macroblade Equipe—the first company model to incorporate Nordica's ski boot technology. Another Benetton company, Benetton Sportsystem Canada Inc., is the Canadian distributor for Rollerblade products. Located in Montreal, this company handles the warehousing, marketing, customer service, credit,

and accounting functions for Rollerblade, Inc., in the Canadian market.

QUESTIONS

1 What trends in the environmental forces (social, economic, technological, competitive, and regulatory) identified in Figure 1–2 in Chapter 1 *(a)* work for and *(b)* work against Rollerblade, Inc.'s, growth in the 1990s?

2 What are the differences in marketing objectives for Rollerblade, Inc., in *(a)* growing a new industry, as was its task in the 1980s, and *(b)* marketing its Rollerblade brand of in-line skates against competition, as it must do in the 1990s?

3 How should Mary Horwath translate the broad objectives identified in question 2 into specific marketing strategies and tactics for new product, price, promotion, and place actions?

4 Horwath believes significant opportunities exist for Rollerblade skates in global markets. To which countries or regions should she initially try to market Rollerblade skates? Why?

[1] Adapted from Mary Horwath, "Rollerblade: Creation of an American Original," a talk in Rome, Italy, November 1992.

*Cantel**

Cantel was incorporated in April 1983 for the purpose of applying for the licenses necessary to develop and operate a private cellular telephone network in Canada. It was formed by a consortium of Rogers Telecommunications Limited of Toronto, First City Financial Corporation Ltd. of Vancouver, and Telemedia Enterprises Inc. of Montreal. In December 1983, Cantel was selected by the Canadian Department of Communications, over five competitors, to receive the licenses. Cantel is the only Canadian company with a national license to provide cellular service, in competition with the cellular divisions of regional phone companies. Cantel's cellular network is what is known as "non-wire line" and operates in competition with the cellular subsidiaries of the "wire line" companies such as Bell Canada, Maritime Tel & Tel, Alberta Government Telephone, and BC Tel, which also offer conventional telephone services via telephone wires.

HOW CELLULAR PHONES WORK

A cellular phone uses radio signals instead of wires to transmit calls. The cellular networks are connected to the public wire line phone system, allowing cellular users to make calls to, or receive them from, virtually any other phone in the world. As a cellular network service provider, Cantel has erected hundreds of transmitters across the country; each transmitter serves an area called a *cell*. As a cellular subscriber uses a phone in a moving car, or walks down the street, a switching computer "hands off" the call from one cell to another without interruption of the call. Cellular's roots can be traced to the 1920s with the introduction of a mobile telephone service used by the Detroit police department.

But as mobile phones rapidly gained popularity, all the available channels for conventional mobile

transmission quickly became used up in many North American cities. This created a long waiting list of people wanting to subscribe to a mobile service. In addition, users found they could not always obtain a clear frequency to use the system (since there were only 12 to 25 channels available to service an entire city). Poor sound quality was also characteristic of early forms of mobile communications.

The concept of cellular communications was developed by AT&T's Bell Laboratories in 1947. It wasn't until 1962 that the first tests were conducted to explore commercial applications and it was recognized that by using low-powered transmitters covering cells one to eight miles in radius, the same set of frequencies could be reused several times within the same metropolitan area. The advent of computerized electronic switching technology in the 1970s made it possible to hand off calls as a vehicle with a cellular phone crossed the boundary between cells. In 1970, the US Federal Communications Commission set aside new radio frequencies for "land mobile communications." That same year, AT&T proposed to build the first high-capacity cellular telephone system, dubbed AMPS--Advanced Mobile Phone Service—in Chicago. In October 1983, the first cellular system began operation in Chicago, followed, in December, by a second system in Baltimore and Washington.

CANTEL

Cantel first launched cellular service in July 1985, in Montreal and Toronto. In July 1987, Cantel was the first cellular company to complete continuous coverage of the 1,200-kilometre corridor from Windsor, Ontario, through to Quebec City. This corridor has since almost doubled in length and now extends 2,000 kilometres through to the Atlantic coast, making it the longest cellular corridor in North America. Cantel's cellular network covers cities and corridors in all 10 Canadian provinces. Today, more than 87 percent of the Canadian population has access to Cantel service.

---

*The information in this case was supplied by Rogers Cantel Inc. Used with permission.

In 1989, Cantel became a wholly owned subsidiary of Rogers Communications Inc. of Toronto. Today, Rogers Communications Inc. maintains majority ownership in Rogers Cantel Mobile Communications Inc., a publicly traded company that is the holding company for Rogers Cantel Inc. and Rogers Cantel Mobile Inc. Besides operating Canada's only nationally licensed cellular company, Cantel also operates a chain of retail service centres and provides paging and data communication services. Cantel directly employs over 2,500 people and has indirectly created thousands of jobs in cellular sales and service. Cantel has over 531,000 cellular subscribers and more than 106,000 paging subscribers.

THE FUTURE

Now on the horizon is digital cellular transmission, which will allow the cellular carriers to make more efficient use of the radio frequency spectrum. Each radio channel that carries one call using today's analogue transmission system can carry three calls using digital technology. In later years, additional improvements will double that capacity to six calls per channel. The expansion of radio frequency capacity allows cellular carriers to continue increasing the number of cellular users without the risk of running out of calling capacity for current customers. Digital cellular transmission provides many benefits to cellular users, including enhanced privacy, fewer dropped calls, and less interference. The initial rollout of digital technology in North America is expected to take several more years.

Another innovation, PCN, or personal communications network, is also being researched by Cantel. PCN will provide an individual with the ability to call anyone, anywhere, anytime at a reasonable price. Using compact handsets based on the latest digital cordless telephone technology, Canadians will someday carry their personal phones in much the same way they now carry their keys or wallets. At home, in the office, or in urban public locations, the personal telephone will provide an inexpensive complement to cellular service, which provides full mobile capacity and wide service availability.

QUESTIONS

1 Segment the market for cellular phone subscribers. Who are the key targets?
2 Some suggest that a cellular phone is only as good as the network it's on. What would people be looking for in a cellular phone (product) and in a cellular network company (service)?
3 What message could Cantel use to induce people to use its cellular network?
4 Many people believe operating cellular phones while driving is a safety hazard. How can cellular companies ensure the safe use of cellular phones in this situation, particularly as more and more cars are being equipped with cellular phones?

VIDEO · CASE THREE
Nissan Canada*

SITUATION ANALYSIS

Nissan is the fourth-largest manufacturer of automobiles in the world. The company has been in Canada for 25 years and has approximately 200 dealerships across the country. Nissan employs about 4,000 people in Canada. The Canadian automotive market is highly competitive. Nissan's most direct competitors are the three other leading Japanese manufacturers: Honda, Toyota, and Mazda. Through the late 1980s, Nissan's sales had been slipping behind these competitors in a marketplace that as a whole was shrinking as the recession of the 1980s took its toll. The result: a declining sales volume (down 26 percent between

*The information in this case was supplied by the Television Bureau of Canada (TVB). We gratefully acknowledge the support of the TVB. Used with permission.

1987 and 1990) with at best a flat market share. As a consequence, Nissan, like many of its competitors, was increasingly being forced to resort to tactical offers and discounts to sell automobiles.

The underlying reasons behind this disappointing sales performance were clearly apparent in Nissan's quantitative tracking studies and readily seen in its qualitative research. Nissan had an unclear brand image with quality perceptions lagging behind the Japanese market leaders Honda and Toyota. Furthermore, its historical product strength in sports cars and trucks was falling out of step with the key "baby boomer" segment as they aged, started families, and—in keeping with the recessionary times—became more cautious in their purchasing. Increasingly, this segment was looking for more practical and proven family-oriented vehicles. However, they were not considering Nissan's sedans, family wagons, and sport utility vehicles when they did purchase. In short, consumers were overlooking Nissan's products in favour of more familiar and better-established competitive brands, which, in addition, were often offering more aggressive discounts.

MARKETING PROBLEM

Clearly, if Nissan were to achieve the ambitious sales and profit objectives it had set itself for the 1990s, it would have to find a way to get consumers to respond to its products. The company had to build a new long-term brand positioning that not only differentiated itself from its competitors but would be relevant to the changing needs and expectations of the baby boomers, a segment responsible for the bulk of sales activity in the auto market. Nissan did not want to be the biggest player in the market; rather, it wanted to be the best. Becoming the best was a long-term proposition, yet Nissan also had to obtain sales in the short term. Nissan was facing significant new product introductions from its closest competitors but had no major new product news of its own. Nissan also wanted to increase its profitability by reducing retail incentives and discounts. Finally, to further help profitability, the company would have to accomplish its new positioning with a static marketing and advertising budget in a category where expen-

diture was forecast to grow by 15 percent per annum.

STRATEGY DEVELOPMENT

After an extensive period of consumer research and a major internal review of its corporate values and business objectives, Nissan and its communications agency, Chiat/Day/Mojo, came to a series of key strategic conclusions:

1 With the differences between competitive products becoming more subtle, buying a car would be a decision based on more than the product merits alone. The 90s car buyers wanted and expected more; they were looking for a relationship with a car company that went beyond the car itself. They were concerned with the overall core values of a car company, its concern and position regarding the social issues of the day, and its willingness to stand behind its products. Increasingly, these were the "tangible differentiators," beyond the automobile, on which buyers would base their purchase decisions. The successful car companies in the 90s would be those that acknowledged and responded to these needs and expectations. To date, buyers felt no car manufacturer in Canada was fully meeting these expectations.

2 Nissan Canada was committed to truly delivering customer satisfaction—to the extent that it would even reorganize itself to establish a department of 36 people dedicated to customer satisfaction and introduce at no extra cost to the consumer an industry-leading warranty and owner support program: "the satisfaction commitment." It was going to try to establish a true relationship with its buyers.

3 Nissan Canada was committed to establishing a distinct Canadian identity that acknowledged its role and responsibility in Canada and to Canadian consumers in general. It wanted to stand for something in Canada. Nissan wanted to be more than just another Japanese import or US subsidiary.

Nissan was determined to transform itself culturally and operationally from being a product-driven or sales operation to a truly consumer-driven organization. For the first time, a car manufacturer was prepared to take full responsibility for its products and, perhaps most significant, to publicly declare and demonstrate this commitment. Nissan Canada's new positioning was "the car company with a commitment and responsibility to today's car buyers that goes beyond building state of the art cars."

To articulate and substantiate this new positioning, a two-pronged approach would be taken:

1 In all communications with the consumer, Nissan would demonstrate that it understood the reality of cars in people's lives in Canada today and that in this context it would take full responsibility for its products. In effect, Nissan would take cars off the typical, glossy pedestal and put them back on the streets of Canada, back in real life.

2 The "satisfaction commitment" would be launched as evidence of this responsibility. The objective was to establish something that was more than just another warranty program. Rather, it was further substantiation of Nissan's responsibility and commitment to buyers.

EXECUTION

Utilizing the existing theme line "Built for the human race," the new positioning was introduced. Nissan used a 60-second television spot called the "manifesto." This spot outlined Nissan's corporate values and dealt with issues such as safety, environmental responsibility, and driving in Canada today. Summing up, it suggests that Nissan's mission was to simply build "a car we can live with."

The "satisfaction commitment" was then introduced with a series of 30-second television commercials focussing on the assertion that Nissan "believes warranties are to protect the people who buy the cars, not the people who build them." Individual car line commercials, both 30- and 15-second, were also run as part of the mix. These television commercials echoed and expanded on the themes developed in the "manifesto" and featured the Sentra and Maxima sedans and the Pathfinder sport utility vehicle—the Nissan products that best exemplified the new positioning. In addition, a series of print ads were developed for newspapers and magazines.

In order to preempt competitive activity, the marketing and advertising campaign was launched in early September ahead of the industry's typical late September and early October new product launch activity. To fully maximize this advantage, the media plan used was front-loaded with very heavy TV for the first four weeks, following by sustaining two-week flights. The original intention was to run the "manifesto" for the first two weeks only and then rotate the "satisfaction" and the individual car line spots through the end of the year.

However, feedback from quantitative tracking and qualitative research indicated that the "manifesto" and "satisfaction" spots were having a much more powerful and immediate impact on consumer attitudes than expected. Therefore, the plan was revised and more weight was given to these spots. In the spring, a more detailed spot on the "satisfaction commitment" was used alongside individual car line spots. The manifesto was also used in special and high-profile television programs to reach lighter viewers.

RESULTS

While developed for the long term, the strategy had an impact on sales in the short term. Since the launch of the campaign, Nissan has posted market share gains in every month except one. In terms of actual sales volume, sales were up 1 percent in a market that was down by 10 percent. Tracking studies showed that the new campaign received some of the highest recall levels seen in the category, and buyer attitudes toward Nissan shifted positively on several key dimensions such as warranty protection, safety, and customer satisfaction.

QUESTIONS

1 When you buy (or will buy) an automobile, how important is the company behind the product (e.g., its image and reputation)?
2 Why do you think Nissan's new positioning strategy was so successful?
3 Much of Nissan's "satisfaction commitment" program, including the warranty and roadside assistance components, has been copied by several competitors. How can Nissan maintain its leadership role in the customer satisfaction area?

Pricing in the Pharmaceutical Industry*

*C*anadians spend billions of dollars annually for prescription drugs to treat acute and chronic ailments. The pharmaceutical industry in Canada has often been criticized for its pricing practices. Many public health officials, government departments or agencies, and consumer advocacy groups argue that, in many cases, the industry is charging too much money for its products. Pharmaceutical company executives have responded to such criticism by citing large research and development costs, extensive testing requirements to obtain government approval to market the products, and marketplace uncertainties as valid reasons for the prices they charge for their drugs.

FAIR AND REASONABLE PRICING

A central issue in the debate concerning prescription drug pricing relates to what is a "fair and reasonable price." Critics of drug pricing spotlight instances where they believe the prices charged are excessive. For instance, Ceredase, a drug for victims of a rare metabolic disorder, sells for $60,000 annually per patient. Clozapine, designed to treat schizophrenia, cost patients almost $9,000 per year. A drug to prevent an AIDS-related blindness, called Foscavir, costs $21,000 per patient annually.

Pharmaceutical firms counter critics' charges of excessive pricing using a variety of arguments. For example, the maker of Foscavir claimed the high price was necessary to recoup its financial investment in the drug. When Johnson & Johnson introduced a drug to treat colon cancer, the company cited some 1,400 studies involving 40,000 patients conducted over 25 years as the reason for

the $1,250 price for a one-year supply. The price for Retrovir, an antiviral drug to treat AIDS, was justified with a variety of considerations, including its maker's "responsibility to patients and shareholders, the very real remaining uncertainties in the marketplace, and the vital need to fund our continuing research and development programs."

Debate over what is a "fair and reasonable" price for drugs typically focusses on economic versus societal factors, and the relative importance of a firm's stakeholders in setting prices. Often the final pricing decision depends on the individual judgment and moral sensitivity of the managers making the decision.

PROLIFE: PRICING ADL

Issues in the pricing of ADL, a treatment for Alzheimer's disease, which affects the elderly, were recently faced by Prolife, a small pharmaceutical company. A task force of company executives was considering the pricing strategy for ADL. Two points of view were expressed: pursuing a high-price strategy designed to recoup the costs of the drug quickly and getting a jump on the competition, and pursuing a lower-price strategy to increase the drug's availability to victims of the disease.

Steve Vaughn, an assistant product manager at Prolife, was the principal proponent of a lower-price strategy. He argued that a less aggressive price strategy made sense even though it would take slightly longer to recoup the initial investment in ADL. Having a family member afflicted with Alzheimer's disease, Mr. Vaughn felt that the ability of victims and their families to pay for the drug should be considered in setting the price for ADL. He was overruled, however, by the task force members. Believing that his views deserved attention and action, and that "bottom line" considerations did not negate his position, he lobbied other task force members and has thought about expressing his opinion to senior executives at Prolife. He was cautioned by Bill Compton, a Prolife senior

*This case was based on "How Many Times Must a Patient Pay?" *Business Week,* February 1, 1993, pp. 30-31; "What's Up, Doc?" *U.S. News & World Report,* April 12, 1993, pp. 26-29; "Doctor Assails J&J Price Tag on Cancer Drug," *The Wall Street Journal,* May 14, 1990, pp. B1, B5; R. A. Spinello, "Ethics, Pricing, and the Pharmaceutical Industry," *Journal of Business Ethics,* August 1992, pp. 617-26; "The Big Pill," *The Economist,* March 6, 1993, p. 67; B. O'Reilly, "The Inside Story of the AIDS Drug," *Fortune,* Novemeber 5, 1990, pp. 112-29; *Wellcome PLC 1989 Annual Report* p. 13; and S. Tully, "Why Drug Prices Will Go Lower," *Fortune,* May 3, 1993, pp. 56-66.

product manager and his mentor, to reconsider his position. Compton noted that Prolife is a business and that "rocking the boat" might not be an advantage to Vaughn's career at Prolife.

QUESTIONS

1 Who are the primary stakeholders that must be considered in setting prices for prescription drugs?

2 How might the personal moral philosophies of moral idealism and utilitarianism be applied to prescription drug pricing in general and in the specific case of ADL?
3 How might the three concepts of social responsibility described in Chapter 4 be applied to prescription pricing in general and in the specific case of ADL?
4 If you were Steve Vaughn, what would you do in this situation?

VIDEO · CASE FIVE
Molson's Take Care Program*

Molson believes that drinking alcohol is both a social freedom and a responsibility. As Canada's largest brewery, Molson has made a commitment to being an industry leader promoting the responsible use of alcohol. Through the efforts of individuals and families, educators, social groups, health care professionals, police, government, and the brewing industry, the message of responsible use of alcohol is being heard.

TAKE CARE

Launched in 1989, Take Care is a multimillion-dollar national program encouraging responsible alcohol use by Canadians. The program includes broadcast, print, and outdoor advertising; promotions tied to Molson sports and entertainment properties across the country; educational initiatives in schools and colleges; and support to community and interest groups. The Take Care program goes beyond the issue of drinking and driving. Take Care addresses responsible drinking in the broader context of our work, our health, and our quality of life.

In May 1990, Molson launched the next phase of the program, the Take Care Team, featuring champion IndyCar racers Mario and Michael Andretti and Formula Atlantic racer

Claude Bourbonnais. The Take Care Team component of the Take Care program was designed to take the responsible use message to consumers through endorsements by celebrity race car drivers. The association was clear: if the best drivers in the world don't drink and drive, then others shouldn't either. In October 1990, Molson added another celebrity spokesperson to the Take Care Team: Canadian Alpine skier and Olympic athlete Brian Stemmle joined the celebrity race car drivers as a Take Care spokesperson promoting the responsible use of alcohol.

Molson added Canadian recording artist Colin James to its stable of spokespeople in July 1991. The two-time Juno Award winner's participation extended the campaign to include entertainment celebrities and to increase awareness of responsible drinking among a younger age group. In Quebec, La Brasserie Molson O'Keefe and the Quebec rock band Vilain Pingouin joined forces for the "Prends soin de toi" campaign. The campaign's theme, "*Garder le control, c'est rock & roll*" ("Stay in control, it's rock & roll"), was designed to increase young adults' awareness of responsible drinking.

Take Care commercials are seen regularly on prime-time Molson television properties. The campaign is "front and center" at many Molson sports and entertainment events, including the Molson Indy in Toronto and Vancouver, the Grand Prix Molson, and the Molson Canadian Rocks and Laurentide Rocks concert series.

*The information in this case was supplied by Molson Breweries. Used with permission.

OTHER TAKE CARE PROGRAMS SUPPORTED BY MOLSON

Some of the other Take Care programs supported by Molson include:

Working it Out. Working it Out is an educational video and companion guide intended to help families communicate their shared values, attitudes, and expectations about alcohol and to discuss the responsibilities associated with the decision to drink. Prepared in association with health professionals, family counsellors, and youth organizations, the program encourages families to make informed, responsible decisions.

Racers Against Drunk Drivers (R.A.I.D.). R.A.I.D. is an alcohol awareness program that was developed in conjunction with Young Drivers of Canada to promote responsible alcohol use among high school students. Through this program, professional race car drivers, with their cars, visit high schools and talk with the students about the effects of alcohol consumption. The emphasis is on preventing students from drinking and driving.

BACCHUS. Molson is a major corporate sponsor of BACCHUS Canada, a national nonprofit organization that promotes alcohol awareness activities on college and university campuses.

Public transit programs. During festive holiday seasons, Molson supports public transit programs that provide alternatives for people who have been drinking and do not want to drive. Molson transit programs were introduced in 1980 and have been offered in major cities, including Vancouver, Hamilton, London, Ottawa, Windsor, and Barrie.

Take Care pedicabs and rickshaws. Molson sponsors pedicabs and rickshaws during the summer and early fall in select communities, extending its Take Care message to users of environmentally friendly transportation services.

Community activities. Molson supports a variety of other community initiatives encouraging responsible use. Through its network of regional breweries, Molson assists community groups and organizations conducting preventive, rehabilitative, or educational alcohol-related programs. Funding is also provided to universities, health and welfare agencies, and youth organizations involved in research and education throughout Canada.

Educational theatre projects of Trinity Theatre. Molson provided financial support for *Youth and Alcohol,* a widely acclaimed theatrical presentation by Trinity Theatre. The presentation stresses the consequences of drinking and driving and addresses the social and peer group pressures that lead to underage drinking. Following the success of *Youth and Alcohol,* Molson supported the creation of a learning video developed by Trinity Theatre on peer counselling, for broader use in schools and colleges throughout Canada.

La tournée des fêtes Molson-O'Keefe. Molson sponsored the production of "*La tournée des fêtes Molson-O'Keefe,*" a one-hour prime-time variety special aired on Quebec's TVA network during the December holiday season. Using the slogan *"Prends soin de toi,"* the program presented dramatic, comic, and musical vignettes with responsible use messages delivered by Quebec sports and entertainment celebrities.

Industry programs. Molson is a major sponsor of brewing industry communications programs promoting responsible use, including safe driving campaigns, public awareness initiatives, and research on traffic safety. Among the better-known activities are the Responsible Use program of the Breweries Association of Canada, and the Brewers of Ontario and Brewers of Quebec safe driving and water safety programs.

Molson employee activities. Educational materials and responsible use messages are provided on a regular basis to Molson employees and their families. The company recognizes that alcohol- and drug-related problems are illnesses. Molson provides full assistance in the treatment of these conditions through confidential outside counselling.

CONCLUSIONS

Molson believes it must play a part in the challenge to promote responsible use of alcohol. Through the Take Care program and its support for education, research, and community action, Molson is making a contribution to public dialogue, understanding, and responsibility. Molson believes responsible drinking means knowing there's a price tag on our right to choose to drink. The price tag is that we're expected to exercise our right with fair play and respect for others and ourselves. Molson has accepted that responsibility, and its responsible drinking initiatives are symbols of that responsibility and public service.

QUESTIONS

1 Why would a company like Molson spend millions of dollars trying to convince people they shouldn't abuse its products?
2 Do you have any problem reconciling the fact that, on one hand, many brewers spend millions of dollars to advertise and promote their brands and then, on the other hand, spend millions more on messages to use their products responsibly?
3 Do a corporation's values and sense of ethics and social responsibility influence what brand of a product you select in the market? When you buy and consume beer, do you care about the type of company that produces and markets it?

VIDEO · CASE SIX
The Coca-Cola Company: Japan*

The Coca-Cola Company is the world's largest carbonated soft drink producer. In 1992, the company sold the equivalent of 10 billion cases of soft drinks worldwide. Approximately 75 percent of the company's soft drink revenues and 80 percent of soft drink operating income arise from sales outside North America. These statistics are not surprising since Coke and Coca-Cola are among the world's best-known trademarks.

THE COCA-COLA COMPANY: A GLOBAL ENTERPRISE

The global presence of the Coca-Cola Company is evident in numerous ways. Four of the world's top five carbonated soft drinks are sold by the company. These brands include Coca-Cola/Coca-Cola Classic, Diet Coke, Coca-Cola Light, Fanta, and Sprite. The company captured 45 percent of the worldwide market for carbonated soft drink flavour segments: cola, orange, and lemon–lime. Exhibit 1 illustrates the worldwide leadership position of Coca-Cola.

*This case was based on The Coca-Cola Company 1993 Annual Report; "We Got the Achtung Baby," Brandweek (January 18, 1993), pp. 23 and and "Cola War Bubbles in Japan." Advertising Age (March 23, 1992), p. 4.

One of the reasons for Coca-Cola's worldwide presence is its extensive, efficient, and effective bottling network. This bottling network, which includes company-owned bottlers, joint ventures with established bottlers in various countries, and franchised bottlers, allows for Coca-Cola/Coca-Cola Classic to be distributed in 195 countries, Fanta and Sprite in 164 countries, and Diet Coke/Coca-Cola Light in 117 countries.

COCA-COLA MARKETING IN JAPAN

The Coca-Cola Company sold its products in Japan as early as the 1920s. However, it did not establish a formal Japanese subsidiary until 1957. Since that time, the company has built a dominant position in the Japanese soft drink market. For example, Coca-Cola is sold in 1 million stores and some 700,000 vending machines in Japan. The Coca-Cola Company captures 32 percent of all carbonated and noncarbonated soft drinks sold in Japan. It is estimated that the Coca-Cola brand captures 70 percent of the $1.65 billion Japanese cola market; Coca-Cola Light captures 20 percent. Pepsi Cola captures less than 10 percent of this

■ *Exhibit 1*
Coca–Cola's market position in 15 countries (share of flavoured carbonated soft drink sales).

COUNTRY	MARKET LEADER	LEADERSHIP MARGIN	SECOND PLACE
Australia	Coca-Cola	2.8:1	Diet Coke
Austria	Coca-Cola	2.5:1	Fanta
Belgium	Coca-Cola	7.3:1	Coke Light
Brazil	Coca-Cola	3.7:1	Brazilian brand
Denmark	Coca-Cola	1.7:1	Danish brand
France	Coca-Cola	3.3:1	French brand
Germany	Coca-Cola	3.3:1	Coke Light
Great Britain	Coca-Cola	1.3:1	Diet Coke
Greece	Coca-Cola	2.8:1	Fanta
Italy	Coca-Cola	2.0:1	Fanta
Japan	Coca-Cola	1.5:1	Fanta
Korea	Coca-Cola	1.5:1	Korean brand
Norway	Coca-Cola	1.9:1	Coke Light
Spain	Coca-Cola	2.0:1	Spanish brand
Sweden	Coca-Cola	3.0:1	Fanta

Source: The *Coca-Cola Company 1993 Annual Report*, p. 29.

market. Industry executives estimate that advertising spending for the Coca-Cola brand is $80 million compared with $16 million of Pepsi Cola.

The successful entry into Japan by the Coca-Cola Company and subsequent performance provide valuable insights into global marketing in general and the need to consider cultural issues. For instance, company executives emphasize that adaptation to the local culture manifests itself in numerous ways. Its management practices focus on consensus and group building consistent with Japanese values. Customs such as lifetime employment for Japanese employees are adopted. Efforts to localize consumer communications are also evident in the language used in advertising and the group settings featuring consumption of the product.

QUESTIONS

1 How is the cultural dimension of individualism incorporated into the Coca-Cola Company's management and marketing practices in Japan?
2 After watching the videotape featuring television commercials for Coca-Cola in Japan, what similarities do you see with Coca-Cola commercials in Canada?

VIDEO · CASE SEVEN
Ganong Brothers*

Ganong Brothers, the candy-making company founded over 118 years ago and based in St. Stephen, New Brunswick, has accomplished a long list of firsts in its corporate history. The company is credited with inventing the chocolate nut bar in 1910. It also produced the first heart-shaped box of candy and invented a popular Maritime candy, the chicken bone. According to David Ganong, the fourth-generation Ganong head of the company, "Ganong Brothers is the only truly independent chocolate company left in Canada."

Ganong was looking for growth in the 1990s and saw the export market as the way to go. Ini-

*This case is based on information supplied by Ganong Brothers in 1994 as well as information adapted from an article by Sandra Porteous, "Bangkok's Ganong Tastes Oriental Success," *Marketing*, September 19, 1991, p. 15.

tially, Ganong Brothers focussed the majority of its export energy on the United States.But the company found the US market very difficult to break into, so it turned its attention to other markets. Ganong went to countries on the Pacific Rim and found the response to its high-quality chocolates very encouraging. Ganong constructed a $13 million plant in St. Stephen that provided the technologies to make the production of export goods possible. Next, Ganong built an off-shore manufacturing plant in Bangkok, Thailand, to provide smaller volume and more labour-intensive products for the Canadian market, the Pacific Rim, and other export markets. The company is now exporting its premium boxed chocolates to New Zealand, Romania, Taiwan, Singapore, and Argentina. But Japan is its largest export market; Ganong shipped about half a million boxes of chocolates to that country last year.

ENTERING THE JAPANESE MARKET

How did the company manage to penetrate the Japanese market, especially when candy has not been a popular item in Japan? First of all, Ganong recognized that more Japanese were vacationing in North America. Second, the Japanese believe in gift giving and have a custom dictating that a person on holidays should bring back a small gift to each of a long list of people. Third, while Japanese consumption of sugar is only a kilo compared with six to seven kilos per capita in North America, it is on the rise, particularly in the form of sweets and candies. Ganong decided to position its boxed chocolates as a quality gift item geared to the Japanese tourist.

Ganong began advertising in a Japanese catalogue that travellers read before starting a trip. The Japanese traveller could actually order the chocolates before vacationing and could have them delivered before arriving home. The Japanese could select from three tourist gift boxes: California Memories, Canadiana Gallery, and Maple Creams from Canada. All feature traditional scenes on the boxes including the Canadian and American flags. Chris Wilkinson, the company's export sales and marketing manager, suggests the tourist boxes are only the first step for the Japanese market. The

three products were designed for a niche discovered by the company. "The way that we went on these three does not represent the way to go in Japan," says Wilkinson. "These products have been successful because in the mind of the consumer they represent typical Canadian products that would be bought here." But the development of the tourist boxes has been a very good experience, according to Ganong. It allowed them to learn about the Japanese market and its complexities.

A MATTER OF CULTURE

It took some time for Ganong to learn about the Japanese taste for candy. The Japanese like milk chocolate, not dark chocolate, and they like nuts but not cream centres. They do not like candy such as toffee that sticks to your teeth, and they hate the taste of peppermint because they think it tastes like toothpaste. While they are developing a taste for candy, it still doesn't match the North American palate. For example, a one-pound box of chocolates has two layers of candy, and that is too much for the Japanese. They prefer big, empty boxes with a lot of packaging.

Ganong has also learned that the Japanese prefer quality over price. Quality of product, combined with service, and relationship building are very important to the Japanese. Ganong also found that the Japanese value family-owned businesses and respect firms with a history of providing quality products. Many Japanese firms, including those in the distribution business, are family owned, and this is a plus for a foreign family-owned company wanting to obtain distribution of products in Japan.

Ganong also discovered that the slow, traditional way of doing business on the east coast of Canada is much the way the Japanese operate. Patience, honesty, and willingness to build a long-term relationship were necessary to be successful in the Japanese market. According to Wilkinson, the potential for market growth in this part of the world is high "if we can take it [sugar consumption] from one kilo to two kilos."

Unfortunately, Ganong was not the only company to see potential in the Japanese market. Many European companies have also spotted this market and its emerging consumption trends.

While the market is growing, it is becoming awfully competitive there, says Wilkinson.

QUESTIONS

1 Many Japanese consumers believe their own products are superior to North American products. How could a firm like Ganong Brothers overcome such a hurdle?

2 The Japanese are much different, culturally, from Canadians. In what ways could Ganong Brothers have gathered "cultural intelligence" about the Japanese in order to plan and execute an appropriate strategy for marketing its chocolates to the Japanese?

3 While Ganong chocolates have been positioned as a gift item for the Japanese tourist to give to his family and friends, are there other ways Ganong can increase its sales of chocolates in Japan?

VIDEO · CASE EIGHT
*Claritin**

SITUATION

Schering Canada is one of the top 15 pharmaceutical companies in Canada. About 30 percent of its total business comes from allergy medication products. Schering has been in the antihistamine market for over 40 years with its product Chlor-Tripolon. The brand has benefited from strong physician endorsement and is well established among consumers. Chlor-Tripolon held over 50 percent of the OTC (over-the-counter) antihistamine market in the early 1980s. In 1988, Schering introduced its first nonsedating antihistamine, Claritin. The brand was detailed through physicians and pharmacists and was available to Canadian consumers only by prescription. As a result, Claritin was virtually unknown to the general public.

During the mid to late 1980s, the OTC nonsedating antihistamine segment of the market showed major growth. Unfortunately, Schering did not have a product competing in this segment. Claritin had been introduced as a prescription-only, nonsedating product, and Chlor-Tripolon did not possess the nonsedating attribute. In 1989, two competitors' nonsedating brands, Seldane and Hismanal, controlled over 60 percent of the total OTC volume (sedating and nonsedating). Schering felt it had to launch a nonsedating brand into the OTC market in order to recapture volume and market share lost to the competition. It was believed the best option would be to introduce Claritin as an OTC product while continuing efforts to promote the product through physicians and pharmacists.

MARKETING PROBLEM

Schering wanted to recapture its number one position in the allergy medication market in Canada. However, that would require Claritin to become an OTC player. The OTC market had well-established competitors, the market was price competitive, and high marketing communications costs would have to be incurred in order to be successful in this category. Additionally, Schering did not want to use discount pricing as a strategy to gain market share. In fact, it wanted to use premium pricing to establish a quality image in the category.

MARKETING COMMUNICATIONS CHALLENGE

The marketing communications challenge was to get Claritin into the awareness set and the evoked set of brands that allergy sufferers would consider purchasing, and to induce early trial of the brand.

*The information in this case was supplied by the Television Bureau of Canada (TVB). We gratefully acknowledge the support of the TVB. Used with permission.

While a new allergy sufferer often selects a brand based on physician recommendation, other users rely on personal experience and perceived brand effectiveness to make the purchase decision. Schering wanted to focus on the self-medication segment, those who had the experience with existing OTC products.

Efficacy—specifically, "fast and sustained action"—was the key attribute sought by the consumer when selecting allergy medication. However, establishing this functional difference (efficacy) between Claritin and competitive products through communications efforts would be difficult to achieve. The regulatory environment in Canada prohibited the use of comparative advertising and comparative claims between brands in this category. Schering and its agency, Cossette Communications, would have to find another way to demonstrate the efficacy of Claritin to Canadian consumers.

COMMUNICATIONS STRATEGY

Schering decided that the best way to break into this cluttered and regulated market was by differentiating itself through its "style of communications." To do so, it decided to use humour. This was a serious departure from the traditional communications used by other pharmaceutical companies. The aim was to break through the consciousness of the consumer even at the risk of alienating some potential consumers during the introductory phase. The strategy was intended to generate a high level of awareness for the product; build a distinct brand personality; create an image of brand effectiveness by associating the product with Chlor-Tripolon (consumers were aware of and liked Clor-Tripolon, and its image could be used to leverage the launch of Claritin); and induce quick trial of the brand.

Schering also felt it needed to "dominate" whatever communications media it chose. In other words, it wanted to "outmessage" competitive brands by at least a 2:1 ratio. It chose television as its primary communications vehicle. Television would be used to generate awareness and interest in the brand. But the company would also use other

communications tools, largely designed to induce trial. Direct mail, in-store coupons, and point-of-purchase material were selected to complete this task.

EXECUTION

1   ADVERTISING

Television advertising began in 1990. The advertising was concentrated in markets representing the highest volume opportunities. Efforts were made to ensure that there would be minimal cannibalization of the Chlor-Tripolon brand. Claritin was positioned directly against the leading brands Seldane (the market leader) and Hismanal. Schering sought to dominate the category in terms of messages (2:1 ratio) in order to quickly build brand awareness. The initial advertising campaign extended from April to August, the main allergy season. The television ads would also serve to support the other necessary components of the communications mix.

The two launch executions involved comparisons between annoying situations and allergy suffering. In the ads, Claritin was presented as the effective solution to allergy problems. Claritin was also closely associated with Chlor-Tripolon in the ads. Ongoing advertising tracking was conducted throughout the campaign. The results showed that Claritin had achieved high levels of awareness, but that about 50 percent of consumers "hated" the ads. Schering then turned to "testimonial" ads showing people who did hate the ads but who also liked the product.

The 1991 and 1992 campaigns were designed to entrench the brand's personality through the use of an unconventional and humorous presenter (or spokesperson). Several executions were developed, each relating to a specific allergy season. The slogan or signature "Claritin, everything you need to know about allergies" was designed to position Claritin as the best in the antihistamine category. The campaigns were extended beyond the traditional allergy season to cover the full year in order to promote the product to people who had perennial allergies (e.g., to cats or dust).

2 CONSUMER SALES PROMOTIONS

In 1990, two consumer sales promotions were used. High-value instantly redeemable coupons (IRCs) were offered to consumers at the store level. One offer was made in February and another in August. Coupon pads were used in Quebec, and on-package coupons were used in other regions in Canada. The second promotion involved a direct mail campaign to allergy sufferers offering a high-value trial coupon. Also, more detailed information about the product was distributed in this direct mail program. Three campaigns were used, one in April, one in June, and one in August. In 1991 and 1992, the programs were repeated, but this time, a new direct focus on Seldane users was used.

3 OTHER COMMUNICATIONS TOOLS

In addition to the advertising and consumer sales promotions, other forms of marketing communications were developed. Co-op ads were developed for use in the in-house publications of individual drugstores. Displays with pamphlets containing coupons and a mail-in offer with premiums were also deployed at the store level. Sponsorship of the Canada AM pollen report was also part of the communications program, and a small-scale newspaper campaign to support a 1-800 information line was carried out.

RESULTS

In less than three years after the launch into the OTC market, Claritin became the number two brand in the market. By 1993, Claritin became the category leader. With category leadership, Schering moved quickly to promote this fact, using it as "proof positive" that Claritin "does work." Chlor-Tripolon's share had also increased during that time. In 1993, Claritin held 41 percent of the market (up from 6 percent in 1989). At the same time, Seldane's market share dropped from 45 percent to 21 percent, while Hismanal's share dropped from 32 to 11 percent. Importantly, Claritin achieved its results while maintaining a premium pricing strategy in the category. The communications strategy had been successful in building short-term sales while allowing for long-term "quality image" building.

QUESTIONS

1 Why didn't Schering launch Claritin directly into the OTC market?
2 Claritin's growth in this market came as a direct result of taking share away from competitive products. One (market) share point in this category is valued at $750,000. Given Claritin's share of market in 1993, how does that translate in terms of dollar value or revenue?
3 Schering believed that if it could create more "noise," or outmessage the competitors in a particular medium (e.g., television), it would be successful in obtaining market share. But is it possible to outmessage the competition and not see it translate into market share results? In what situations?

VIDEO · CASE NINE
Certs Minis★

*W*arner-Lambert is a large multinational corporation with three divisions. One is a pharmaceutical division (Parke Davis), another is the Schick Razor division, and the other is Adams Brands (confections and consumer health care products). The Adams Brands division has some long-established brands in Canada such as Halls, Trident, Dentyne, Chicklets, Clorets, and Certs. The Certs brand has been around for 50 years, competing in what is called the portable breath freshener (PBF)

★The information in this case was supplied by the Television Bureau of Canada (TVB). We gratefully acknowledge the support of the TVB. Used with permission.

category. PBFs are defined as branded hard candy. The category includes such brands as Life Savers, Tic Tac, Breath Savers, Clorets, Trident Mints, Mentos, Jolly Rancher, Ganong, and others. If the category is expanded to include breath-related gum products like Dentyne, Excel, and Clorets, the category could be characterized as very crowded and very competitive. But Adams believed there were opportunities for growth in this category. The growth area in the PBF category was determined to be the "mini-mints" segment. For example, Tic Tac, a major competitive brand, had shown large market share increases since its entry into the category.

In turn, Adams had launched a few new mini-mint products into the category itself. Clorets Minis were launched in 1987 with good results. Similarly, Trident Minis, launched in 1990, were also doing well. However, Tic Tac continued to show growth, leading Adams to believe the overall category was growing. In 1992, Adams decided to launch the fourth entry in the mini-mint segment, Certs Minis. Certs Minis were designed to go head to head against Tic Tac in order to stop Tic Tac's growth and to wrestle share from this brand.

MINI-MINT ENVIRONMENT

Within the PBF category, the only growing segment was the mini-mints. The category was very underdeveloped in the 15–24 age group. This group tended to be gum users. The current brands in the mini-mint category, including Certs Minis, offer essentially the same benefits to the consumer: fresh breath and great taste. None of the brands in the segment could be considered significantly different from the others. Certs Minis, with their cherry and orange flavours, were not unique in the category. However, Certs Minis were the only PBF to offer only fruit flavours (all other PBFs offered both mint and fruit and tended to focus on cooling mint flavours). Buoyed by the success of Clorets and Trident Minis, it was believed that Certs Minis could make a successful entry into this category. Adams also believed that if Certs Minis could attract a younger target segment now, it could cultivate this group to become part of the franchise for the regular Certs product in the future.

POSITIONING

Product positioning in this category is somewhat difficult in that none of the recent players entering the market were real product innovations. The significant point of difference, or differentiation for a particular brand, was generally "created" through the marketing communications used. Realizing that Certs Minis were really a "me too" product, Adams would have to create a "perception of difference." Adams also wanted to differentiate Certs Minis from Certs, the base brand, while maintaining the benefits that the Certs name held in the minds of consumers. The company wanted to convince consumers (the 15–24 age group) that the product was a novel and interesting way to enjoy Certs. The positioning statement that was developed was that "Certs Minis is the fun, tangy way to enjoy Certs." The flavour of Certs Minis was a central component of the positioning strategy.

INITIAL CONSUMER RESEARCH

In order to gauge initial response to the product, Adams decided to use sampling. The company worked out an agreement with a partner, in this case, Pizza Hut, in order to get the product into the hands of the target group. Pizza Hut catered to the teen and young adult crowd, particularly during its lunch and day-part business. Adams and Pizza Hut teamed up to offer the target group a free sample of Certs Minis with a pizza purchase. This campaign was very successful. Consumers not only liked the product but also showed high purchase interest.

PROMOTION STRATEGY

Adams knew it could not match the spending of its major competitors when launching the product. Adams would need a compelling, entertaining, and easily understood message. The company also had to convince the target segment that Certs Minis were a "different" product, and not merely a line extension of Certs. The promotional message would focus on the tangy flavours of Certs Minis. The challenge now was to communicate an exciting new taste to a demanding and disbelieving market of young people. Television was selected as the primary medium to convey the message. The 15–24 age group were big viewers of television and liked to see products visually displayed. But conveying taste via television would not be easy.

But Adams's communications agency, BSB, had a method. It was a type of computer animation called "morphing." In the TV spot, a young person would be shown trying the product. He would be surprised and delighted when the Certs Minis, bursting with flavour, started ricocheting inside his mouth. Through the morphing technique, the viewing audience would be able to see his face distorted and stretched in response to all the activity going on inside his mouth. In this way, the taste of the product could be demonstrated to the audience.

The commercial spot, called "F/X," was pretested. Even though it was tested using only a rough version of the final production, it tested very well. Consumers who participated in the pretest not only understood that the main selling point in the ad was taste, but they also recognized the product as a Certs brand and showed favourable purchase intention. Adams spent $1.6 million over 11 months on television spots in both English and French Canadian markets, using a combination of network and specialty stations. Adams extended the television ad campaign to include point-of-purchase advertising (POP), which utilized key visuals from the television spot. In its first year, Certs Minis captured 4.1 percent of the overall PBF market, and 18 percent of the mini-mint segment.

QUESTIONS

1 Why would Adams brands want to launch a basic "me too" product into a crowded and competitive market?
2 Adams's initial sampling campaign with Pizza Hut was very successful. Wouldn't sampling on a larger-scale basis and concentrating on in-store distribution of the product be viable options to launch the product instead of advertising?
3 As the ad campaign concluded, the share of market held by Certs Minis began to decline. Why do you think this happened?

VIDEO CASE TEN
*Clearly Canadian**

*C*learly Canadian Beverage Corporation, a Vancouver-based company, had taken its products to the top of the new-age or alternative beverage category in just five years. *Beverage World,* a key industry journal, suggests that Clearly Canadian did not invent the new-age beverage category, "but through its pricing, packaging, distribution, positioning, formulating and financing it may have perfected it." But today, faced with increasing competition and fickle consumers, Clearly Canadian is attempting to maintain its leadership position in the new-age beverage category.

*The information used to prepare this case was supplied by Clearly Canadian Beverage Corporation.

THE NEW-AGE BEVERAGE MARKET

The new-age beverage market is valued at $1 billion in North America and is expected to grow between 8 and 15 percent annually. This compares with about 1 percent growth in the traditional soft drink business. However, the new-age segment is still very small compared with the traditional soft drink market, which is estimated to be valued at between $45 and $50 billion. Total new-age beverage *volume* is comparable to that of caffeine-free Diet Coke, the ninth best selling soft drink in Canada and the United States. However, impressive growth in this segment has attracted the attention of many new players, including marketing giants Coca-Cola, Seagram Co., and Perrier.

The new-age or alternative beverage segment is a catchall that includes almost anything that doesn't contain alcohol and isn't a traditional soda or soft drink. In general, the category includes "healthful" carbonated or noncarbonated flavoured waters and other beverages sold as an alternative to soft drinks. Beverage Marketing Corporation, a leading tracking company of new-age beverages, defines a beverage as new-age if it is relatively new in the market, is perceived by consumers as "good for me," and is all natural or generically perceived as such. Perception is nearly everything in this category. Crystal Pepsi, for example, doesn't meet Beverage Marketing's criteria, since it is marketed, more or less, as a cola. Within the new-age category, there are really three distinct product segments:

> *All-natural sodas.* Carbonated beverages containing a sugar concentrate base, which use or are perceived by the consumer to contain all natural ingredients and no artificial colours, flavours, or preservatives. This segment has a 49 percent share of the new-age beverage market. Beverage Marketing considers Clearly Canadian a natural soda. Some may argue the point and place Clearly Canadian as a sparkling flavoured water. But Clearly Canadian is a sweetened product and the company itself uses the term *soda*. Other products in this category would include Snapple, Coke's Nordic Mist, Seagram's Quest, and Perrier's Ice Mountain.
>
> *Sparkling flavoured waters.* A combination of unsweetened sparkling mineral or seltzer water and natural fruit essences. This segment holds 29 percent of the market. An example of a product in this category would be Tropicana Sparklers.
>
> *Sparkling juices.* A mix of sparkling mineral water and a percentage of natural fruit juices, up to 70 percent. This segment currently has 22 percent of the new-age beverage market. Products in this segment would include Crystal Geyser, Koala, and Ocean Spray Splash.

THE TARGET CONSUMER

In general, the people who are trying new-age beverages are doing so because they offer something different and, in most cases, something lighter, healthier, more natural. The baby boomers, for example, looking for a lighter, caffeine-free, less sweet drink have become consumers in this category. The target consumer for the category was originally thought to be someone who was health conscious and generally aged 26 to 45, on a middle to upper income level. But many of the new-age beverage marketers have discovered that there is a youth segment of the market: even children in elementary school consume the product. Additionally, the mature market (aged 50+), who are drinking less alcohol, have also been trying these new alternative beverages. Clearly Canadian, for example, sees its products selling beyond its initial 18–34 target segment who were demanding a healthier alternative to soft drinks or alcohol. In fact, Clearly Canadian believes its product is appealing to people of all ages, all walks of life, who want to think young and to stake out their own individuality.

CLEARLY CANADIAN'S SUCCESS

By 1992, Clearly Canadian was the number one brand in the growing new-age beverage market, with 17 percent of share of the overall category. Its sales were estimated at over $155 million. Why had Clearly Canadian been successful? Canada is home to one-fifth of all the world's freshwater, and it enjoys a worldwide reputation for having pure, clean, crystalline water. Clearly Canadian had been able to leverage that reputation to its advantage. Clearly Canadian also entered the market relatively early, seeing the trend toward healthier beverages. This allowed it to take an early leadership role. Innovative packaging that helped it stand out on crowded retail shelves was also a contributing factor. Premium pricing also helped in positioning Clearly Canadian as a quality product.

But many experts add that Clearly Canadian's distribution system was an integral part of its success. According to industry experts, the success of new-age beverages is largely tied to distribution. Clearly Canadian understood that. It used an innovative four-tier method of distribution—with master distributors (or licensees) working as the conduit between manufacturer and wholesaler to ensure the product got on the retail shelf. In fact, many new brands in this category have failed simply because of poor distribution. One distributor of new-age beverages comments that "forty-five brands have come and gone trying to compete with Clearly Canadian. In many cases it was because distributors couldn't get these products on the shelf." Clearly Canadian had achieved extensive market coverage in the United States and Canada and made continuing efforts to increase its presence at the retail level.

Clearly Canadian had also aggressively pursued a market development strategy and had expanded into Mexico, the Caribbean, England, and Ireland. It also secured a licensing arrangement in Japan with Asahi Breweries Ltd., Asia's third-largest beverage company, and signed a distribution agreement with Al-Magoul Trading of Saudi Arabia to distribute Clearly Canadian products throughout the Middle East.

THE CURRENT SITUATION

While Clearly Canadian had been largely responsible for the growth in the new-age beverage category, by 1993 both growth in the category and company sales started to level off. The reasons? Some experts suggested that the decline in growth was due to consumers' capricious tastes and the growing competition from other products such as the ready-to-drink iced teas. Others suggested that with the growing number of new brands, these so-called specialty drinks were no longer special enough to command the premium prices being charged by new-age beverage marketers. In fact, many new brands had used low-price strategies to secure market share, and this had undermined the premium-pricing strategies of the category leaders.

Clearly Canadian had lost some share to similar or "knockoff" products, but its more threaten-

ing competition appeared to be other alternative products such as bottled ice teas. Pepsi, for example, had joined with Lipton, and Coke had hooked up with Nestlé, to market ready-to-drink tea lines. These products, along with Snapple, were obtaining sales growth at the expense of Clearly Canadian and other brands in the new-age segment.

The drop in growth in the market surprised Clearly Canadian. It had continued to expand its market coverage and had launched some new products in 1992 and 1993. New flavours such as Summer Strawberry and Coastal Cranberry were added. A new 23-ounce multiserving bottle as well as four-packs and a 200-ml (6.6-oz) bottle were also launched. The 200-ml product was designed to help boost sales in the hospitality industry. The company also kept the size of its operations lean to help maintain profitability. In doing so, the company achieved one of the highest sales-per-employee figures in the industry.

The company also undertook new consumer promotion activities and a systemwide sales incentive program with Clearly Canadian sales representatives in order to achieve growth. Still, by mid-1993, supermarket sales for Clearly Canadian had actually shown a decline. This was in sharp contrast to the 240 percent increase in sales in 1991, and the 21 percent increase in 1992. Some experts believed the 1993 decline was part of an ongoing downhill trend for Clearly Canadian, and perhaps the category in general.

Industry experts have suggested that Clearly Canadian may have been complacent despite the entrance of far larger rivals into its category, and perhaps a little slow in bringing to market new products or line extensions to appeal to a broader and often fickle consumer base. By 1994, Clearly Canadian was attempting to get back on track. It developed new ad campaigns and launched new products including a ready-to-drink tea. Clearly Canadian's president, CEO, and cofounder, Doug Mason, insisted that the company would rebound.

QUESTIONS

1 Some experts suggest that the new-age beverage category is really just a fad and that growth in the cat-

egory cannot be maintained. As the category declines, so will Clearly Canadian. Comment.

2 Can new-age beverage marketers learn any lessons from wine cooler marketers?

3 In export markets, as the video points out, Clearly

Canadian strongly emphasizes the fact that the product is made from Canadian water. Why?

4 What are some of the basic ways a company can achieve growth in the new-age beverage market?

VIDEO · CASE ELEVEN
Lysol*

L&F is a North American business unit of the Kodak Corporation. It competes in the cleaning products market with such brands as Lysol, and in the home improvement category offering such brands as Thompson's Water Seal and Minwax. The long-term business strategy for L&F is managed growth, consistent and stable growth of the business over time. In order to achieve managed growth, L&F evaluates its product lines regularly. It upgrades the formulations of its products in order to improve their effectiveness and also introduces new products in order to improve sales and profitability. Often, L&F's United States sister company will bring out some new products, which, if successful, are then launched in Canada. An important brand for L&F is the Lysol product line. Most Canadian consumers are familiar with Lysol spray, but L&F wants to increase sales of not only the spray product, but the entire line of Lysol products. It is attempting to develop a strategy in Canada in order to market more of the entire line of Lysol products.

LYSOL

Lysol, primarily the spray, has a long brand heritage in Canada. The disinfectant benefit of the product is very distinctive. In the early 1990s, Lysol spray had 44 percent household penetration in Canada, but the other Lysol products—Lysol Basin, Tub & Tile Cleaner; Lysol Toilet Bowl Cleaner; and Lysol Liquid (All-Purpose) Cleaner—had much lower penetration. In fact, to many Canadians Lysol was known for its spray, and the other products did not

enjoy much familiarity. With little existing synergy between the products within the line, L&F wanted to bring these disparate products together. In doing so, L&F could achieve economies of scale in terms of marketing and promotion expenses. The company believed that by combining the marketing budgets for the four separate products, it could achieve a greater impact on the market. It was felt that one way to link the products together was through the unifying benefit of disinfection.

STRATEGY CONSIDERATIONS

L&F wanted to achieve greater market penetration with all four products. However, the overall household cleaning product category was not growing; it was mostly flat, and in some areas it was actually declining. Some industry people felt that the reasons for this were that many households were cleaning less and that the recession was also impacting on sales in the category. Therefore, new growth for Lysol would have to come at the expense of existing competitors. Given that L&F could probably not bring new consumers into the category, it would have to persuade existing consumers to switch brands. While all competitors were using advertising, couponing, and other forms of consumer promotion, the intensity of the battle was at the shelf level. Competitive firms were literally battling it out for shelf space in order to capture market share. This meant the use of extensive trade promotions, often in the form of price discounting.

L&F felt it shouldn't get more involved in trade discounts because of the squeeze it put on margins. It did believe, however, that limited use of consumer coupons should be part of its overall pro-

---

*The information in this case was supplied by the Television Bureau of Canada (TVB). We gratefully acknowledge the support of the TVB. Used with permission.

motional activity that would be consumer-focussed. L&F believed that the Lysol brand probably had a rather tired personality. The company wanted to give it a 1990s contemporary, interesting, and even provocative image.

The problem was that to most consumers, household cleaning products were really an uninteresting category. In fact, marketers would refer to this category as low-involvement. Thus, building consumer awareness of the entire line would not be possible without increasing consumer involvement level. The question was how to create interest in or involvement with the product line. A way had to be found to demonstrate the line and to have consumers pay attention. L&F knew that timing would be important. For example, interest in the category would be highest just before or during traditional spring cleaning time in Canada, which runs between late February and early May. Interest would also be high again in late fall or early winter. But if the product line itself could not be made interest-

ing or more involving, even good timing wouldn't help.

L&F had to determine an appropriate creative message for the consumer, select an appropriate communications medium, and consider other ways to build sales and market share for the line.

QUESTIONS

1 What would be the most appropriate communications medium for L&F to use in order to communicate with its market?
2 What would be a creative way to build consumer involvement with the product line? What would be the specific message and execution?
3 Besides the specific communications medium you recommended that L&F use in question 1, what other promotional activities would you recommend to build sales and market share for the Lysol line?
4 What type of communications schedule would you recommend L&F use during the year?

VIDEO · CASE TWELVE
Alcan *

*H*eadquartered in Montreal, Alcan Aluminium Limited is the parent company of a worldwide group of companies involved in all stages of the aluminum industry. Through subsidiaries and related companies around the world, Alcan's activities include bauxite mining, alumina refining, aluminum smelting, manufacturing, sales, and recycling. Since it was established in 1901, Alcan has developed a unique combination of competitive strengths with low-cost, owned hydroelectricity in Canada, proprietary process technology, and international diversification. Today, Alcan is one of the world's largest aluminum companies.

THE RECESSION OF THE EARLY 1980s

In the dark days of the 1982–1983 recession, while some industry players talked about broadening their asset bases and reducing their dependency on

what many experts believed to be a "mature" metal, Alcan Aluminium reaffirmed its commitment to the aluminum business. Alcan recognized that the glory days of aluminum were probably over given that the worldwide consumption rate of the metal was growing at only 2 to 3 percent a year. However, Alcan believed that there were opportunities in the aluminum business.

Alcan knew, however, a new strategy would be needed to exploit these opportunities. Primary producers of aluminum were generally at the mercy of metal market prices, which often fluctuated widely. To secure its future, Alcan would need to move away from simply being a supplier of ingots and sheets of aluminum and become involved in the market as a fabricator of finished aluminum products. Alcan streamlined its production and

---

*This case was prepared based on information supplied by Alcan Aluminium Limited including: *The World of Alcan, 1990; Alcan Aluminium Annual Report, 1993;* and *Alcan Facts, 1994.*

trimmed management in order to create a leaner operation that could survive slower growth in the primary markets and flucuating costs. It also embarked on a modernization plan to upgrade its facilities in order to compete in the manufactured aluminum products market.

Alcan enhanced existing resources and skills and developed new ones in order to develop a sustainable competitive advantage in the markets in which it intended to compete. Among those resources and skills were a broad manufacturing base, an advanced technology network, research and development expertise, and very important, low-cost energy. Alcan possessed hydroelectric facilities that generated electricity for two-thirds of its total smelting capacity worldwide. This is a key sustainable competitive advantage for a company competing in an industry that uses vast amounts of energy in the manufacturing process. This low-cost energy enabled Alcan to become one of the lowest cost primary producers of aluminum in the world. But Alcan didn't stop with its low-cost advantage. The company devoted time and money to R&D in order to develop new manufacturing processes and new product applications. The company moved to further penetrate the international primary aluminium market and to develop international markets for its fabricated products. Using a new product development strategy, the company designed new products for the automobile market and an innovative aluminium air battery, to replace existing standby battery systems.

While the company remained one of the world's largest producers of primary aluminum, it became one of the biggest producers of fabricated aluminum products serving the building and construction, containers and packaging, electrical, and transportation markets. Alcan was consistently one of the most profitable companies in Canada during the 1980s and early 1990s.

THE SITUATION IN 1993-94

In 1993, the pace of aluminum exports from the former Soviet Union accelerated, causing world inventories to rise even more steeply than during the previous two years. The deteriorating oversupply situation led to a further fall in prices for both ingot and fabricated products. Despite record production volumes, Alcan's revenues declined. In light of the persistent oversupply situation, Alcan announced a temporary cutback in production in 1994. The company also continued to reduce costs aggressively.

Sales at the end of 1993 were $6.9 billion, with fabricated aluminum and nonaluminum products sales totalling $5.8 billion and ingot sales totalling $1.1 billion. Over 80 percent of consolidated sales were accounted for by aluminum products. Other products included bauxite, alumina, specialty chemicals, and plastics, as well as magnesium, nickel alloys and stainless steel. Sales by market sector, in percent, were **building and construction** (e.g., sheet and extrusions)–24 percent; **containers and packaging** (e.g., beverage can and foil)–33 percent; **electrical** (e.g., bare and insulated conductor products)–9 percent, **transportation** (e.g., automotive castings and sheets and plate and extrusions for aerospace, marine, truck, and rail)–7 percent, and **other**–27 percent.

During this period, Alcan concluded an intensive study of the world aluminum market and of Alcan's competitive position in that market. Two conclusions were drawn: (1) that aluminum was a good and growing business to be in, provided a company is a really low-cost producer, and (2) that Alcan had the assets, technology, and market positions to prosper in a lower-price world, but it needed to revise some of its priorities in order to do so. Alcan identified five priorities as a result of the study:

1 Further reduce Alcan's already low primary smelter costs and bring material costs below the world average.
2 Take advantage of the new state-of-the-art rolling capacity coming onstream in Europe and North America to exploit growth markets.
3 Maintain investment only in those operations that create value for shareholders.
4 Focus R&D programs on core products and processes.
5 Continue to reduce overhead costs both in corporate offices and business units

To focus more effectively on these priority areas, Alcan's management structure was reorganized, essentially from a geographic to a product sector basis. Each sector, led by an executive vice president, would be responsible for developing and implementing the priorities.

The one exception to the product sector approach was the Asia/Pacific region, where one executive vice president would remain responsible to the overall stategy in that region. Alcan believes it can reshape its business in a market characterized by growth in demand, but at lower prices. The company views aluminum as one of the world's most useful materials. For Alcan, aluminum's versatility and its "environmentally friendly" nature, will mean a strong future.

QUESTIONS

1 Alcan has defined its business as aluminum, but what does this entail?
2 What are the competitive advantages that Alcan is leveraging or could leverage in the markets in which it competes?
3 What potential growth markets would you advise Alcan to explore in the future?
4 The recyclable nature of aluminum may be an advantage to exploit in an environmentally conscious world. Comment on how Alcan can use this attribute to secure new business.

VIDEO · CASE THIRTEEN
Second Harvest*

Second Harvest is a nonprofit agency that has been helping to alleviate the problems of hunger and food waste in Toronto since 1985. Second Harvest exists as a charitable food recovery program to locate and collect surplus perishable food and deliver it to social service agencies in Metro Toronto, to develop self-help initiatives for relief of hunger, and to increase public awareness of possible solutions to hunger and poverty. Second Harvest is not a food bank; it primarily handles perishable food. It does not warehouse food, but serves as a link between surplus food—food that would otherwise go to waste—and agencies that distribute food to hungry people.

Many social service agencies are having difficulty keeping up with the demand for emergency food assistance. In Toronto, it is estimated that 100,000 people depend on emergency food programs each month. Most of those people are single women and children. However, it is believed that perhaps as many as 400,000 people in Toronto may be in need of food each month. Ironically, while people are going hungry, more than 20 percent of all food produced in North America is wasted.

HISTORY OF THE ORGANIZATION

Second Harvest started in 1985 with a nonexistent budget and a few volunteers. The original objec-

tive was to redistribute surplus food, at no charge, to qualified agencies responsible for feeding the hungry. Such agencies included drop-ins or soup kitchens, pantries or food banks, residences or shelters, and subsidized housing developments. Second Harvest retrieved surplus food from any industry, group, or individual who regularly or occasionally had excess food, including food producers, farmers, retailers, wholesalers, restaurants, hospitals, production houses, and organizers of special events. In its first year of operation, Second Harvest redistributed over 250,00 pounds of food.

GROWTH OF THE ORGANIZATION

By 1990, Second Harvest had been able to put a board of directors in place consisting of community leaders and corporate executives. The basic day-to-day operations were being conducted out of a small office under an executive director working with a small staff and—primarily—a core group of volunteers. Through its small fleet of trucks, donated by good corporate citizens, Second Harvest was now able to redistribute close to 1 million pounds of food valued at over $1 million on an

*This case was prepared based on information supplied by Second Harvest.

annual basis, food that otherwise would have been wasted.

In 1993, the breakdown of the type of food redistributed by Second Harvest was bread, 34 percent; produce, 25 percent; prepared food, 18 percent; nonperishable items, 10 percent; meat, 7 percent; and dairy, 6 percent. About 40 percent of the food went to drop-ins or soup kitchens, 27 percent to pantries or food banks, 17 percent to residences or shelters, and 16 percent to subsidized housing. Over 300 food donors, occasional and regular, were involved in the food redistribution effort to more than 75 recipient agencies.

Currently, other organizations are assisting Second Harvest's redistribution efforts by sponsoring food drives. In addition to food donors, many individuals and organizations are supporting Second Harvest with financial contributions and gifts in kind. This support basically allows Second Harvest to run on a break-even basis.

In addition to its key food redistribution effort, Second Harvest has pushed forward with self-help initiatives. These include promoting the concept of community gardens and the publication of a cookbook that contains inexpensive, easy-to-prepare recipes designed to help those on fixed income who need to stretch their food dollars. Second Harvest has also expanded its role as an advocate for change in public policy as it pertains to hunger and poverty.

In order to achieve its three basic objectives, Second Harvest attempts to publicize the organization through literature, media exposure (public relations), and word-of-mouth communication. In 1993, Second Harvest launched a donor recognition and awareness campaign. Donor recognition stickers were provided to food and financial donors to display in their places of business. The stickers also help people identify establishments that are donating their surplus to Second Harvest. Second Harvest also ran a series of ads in community newspapers across Metro Toronto in order to raise awareness and to encourage potential donors to contact the organization.

Second Harvest recognizes that there is only so far it can go to meet the emergency need for a basic meal. This is why Second Harvest and other advocates for the poor are attempting to apply the necessary pressure that will result in a better community. The elimination of hunger and poverty through social change is the long-term solution. Yet, in the short term, Second Harvest must continue to meet the immediate needs of those who go hungry every day in Toronto.

QUESTIONS

1 How can Second Harvest motivate individuals and organizations to donate to its cause?
2 What specific promotion or communication tools should Second Harvest use to reach prospective donors?
3 What are some unique sources of surplus food that Second Harvest could tap into?

VIDEO · CASE FOURTEEN
McDonald's Canada Goes to Moscow*

McDonald's founder, Ray Kroc, built his food service business on the philosophy of QSC&V (quality, service, cleanliness, and value). All participants in the McDonald's system—corporate managers, store franchisees, and food suppliers—buy into the QSC&V concept and share common economic incentives. His formula for success worked. McDonald's quickly became the market leader in almost every trade area it operated in across the United States. By the late 1960s, with the maturation and saturation of the hamburger market in North America, McDonald's began to look for new opportunities for growth in the international marketplace. Now, in scarcely five decades, McDonald's Corporation has become the largest food service organization in the world. It is a $20 billion global corporation, operating about 3,000 restau-

*This case is based on information supplied by McDonald's Canada as well as information adapted from an article by P. Foster, "McDonald's Excellent Soviet Venture?" *Canadian Business,* May 1991, pp. 51–65.

rants in over 50 countries outside the United States, including Canada.

MCDONALD'S CANADA

George Cohon, a Chicago lawyer, came to Canada in 1968 and opened a McDonald's franchise. Within a few years he and a partner had 14 stores, but the business was undercapitalized and losing money. Cohon sold the stores back to McDonald's and became head of a wholly owned Canadian subsidiary. By 1986, Cohon turned Canada into the most successful of McDonald's international ventures. But Cohon, chairman, president, and CEO of McDonald's Canada, had a vision that went beyond the borders of Canada. He believed that the 290 million people living in the now-former Soviet Union would be interested in the McDonald's concept.

Cohon's dream of expansion actually began when he played host to a Soviet delegation at the Montreal Olympics in 1976. He followed up these contacts hoping to send mobile units to the 1980 Moscow games, but because of the Olympic boycott he put the dream on hold. But when Mikhail Gorbachev introduced the concepts of *glasnost* and *perestroika* to the Soviet Union and the world, Cohon saw an opportunity. Gorbachev's economic reforms would allow for joint ventures between Soviets and foreign companies. In April 1988, Cohon negotiated a 49/51 percent joint venture with the food service administration of the Moscow City Council. The agreement called for 20 restaurants and a huge food processing complex.

THE JOINT VENTURE

The McDonald's Canada and Moscow City Council joint venture involved two major departures from McDonald's normal practice. The joint venture was with an organization and not an individual, and the deal involved the development of a processing plant. All of McDonald's restaurants have historically depended on local suppliers for their food. However, the low quality and reliability of Soviet farm produce created the need for vertical integration—control over the manufactur-

ing of the food required for the restaurants. Sourcing food locally and setting up its own processing facilities would be a big task. McDonald's persuaded some of its largest suppliers to help out in improving the quality and productivity of selected Soviet farmers and to assist in building the processing plant.

European meat experts introduced new feed programs for the local cattle. Potato growers and processors from the Netherlands introduced strains preferred for frozen french fries and provided a system for processing them. Bakers from the United States, Canada, Sweden, and Germany developed the bun and pie systems. Dairy experts from Sweden set up a pasteurization process for a country where bacteria levels in milk were often six times higher than those permissible in the West. To construct the 10,000-square metre processing facility called McComplex, McDonald's used a Finnish company with a long history of dealing with the Soviets.

Although McComplex gave it control over the manufacturing of hamburger patties, buns, french fries, and fixings, McDonald's still needed its beef, flour, potatoes, and vegetables from a farm and food system renowned for its inefficiency. Moreover, McDonald's Canada had committed itself to operate with rubles. This currency was inconvertible, and thus any imports would have to be paid in hard currency generated within the Soviet system, or by diverting money directly from McDonald's Canada. The processing plant cost $40 million, almost 10 times the cost of the first restaurant, and was paid for in hard cash. Cohon is betting that someday the ruble will become a convertible currency. He argues that the joint venture is a long-term project and that he wanted the people of Moscow to be able to buy food at the restaurant in rubles, and not be treated like second-class citizens. (In contrast, Pizza Hut, with two locations in Moscow, allows only those with hard currency to eat inside its restaurants. People paying with rubles can buy food there but have to eat it outside.)

In addition to the concerns of currency and the quantity and quality of supplies, the joint venture also had to deal with the Soviet bureaucracy. Approvals to move the project ahead were long in coming and often caused frustration. One bright spot was that young Muscovites were eager to work at the restaurants. McDonald's received over 25,000 applications for the roughly 700 positions available at the first restaurant. McDonald's picked the best, and many were sent for training at the Institute of Hamburgerology in Toronto and to Hamburger University at world headquarters in Oak Brook, Illinois.

THE FIRST RESTAURANT OPENS

The McComplex was completed on schedule, and on January 31, 1990, the largest McDonald's restaurant in the world opened its doors. Its Gorky Street location was just 10 minutes from Red Square. The multilevel 700 seat restaurant would serve approximately 50,000 customers a day, making it not only the largest restaurant in the system, but the busiest. Demand forced the restaurant to almost double its staff. However, many people suggest the success of the first restaurant should be put into perspective. There is demand for any quality good in Moscow, and the people of this city often wait in long lines to buy any food that might be available. Indeed, the experts suggest, in these circumstances McDonald's would inevitably be successful.

The political uncertainty in Russia, however, has some experts suggesting that McDonald's may have jumped the gun. Still, the joint venture moves forward with the opening of its second and third restaurants and a new office tower. Cohon suggests that the "long view" is McDonald's approach and that Russia needs what McDonald's can provide: organizational infrastructure, technology transfer, managerial talent, agricultural improvement, and import substitution.

QUESTIONS

1 Why was McDonald's Canada so interested in securing a joint venture operation in Moscow?
2 With the disintegration of the Soviet Union and the prospect of Russia's falling back into the hands of communist hard-liners, many wonder about McDonald's bold move into Moscow. Was being the "first-in" a real advantage for McDonald's Canada?
3 What is the risk for McDonald's operating on a rubles-only basis?
4 The video points out the emphasis McDonald's places on training. Why is training so important to McDonald's?

VIDEO · CASE FIFTEEN
Royal Canadian Mint ★

CORPORATE BACKGROUND OF THE RCM

The Royal Canadian Mint (RCM) began operations in 1908 as a branch of the British Royal Mint. It became an agency of the Canadian government in 1931 and was established as a federal Crown corporation in 1969. Building on its original mandate to mint Canadian circulating coins, the RCM steadily diversified its activities to include other commercial and manufacturing operations. The RCM markets goods and services throughout

Canada and in over 60 countries around the world. The mint's head office is located in Ottawa. There is a plant in Winnipeg striking Canadian and foreign circulating coins. Over a billion foreign coins are produced there each year. The Ottawa plant handles specialized products such as Canadian and foreign numismatic coins, investment coins, refinery services, and medals. The RCM is the largest refiner of gold in the western hemisphere. Over 70 percent of Canada's gold production goes through the RCM every year to produce wafers, bars, granular gold, or whatever is specified by the mint's clients. But perhaps its most famous product is the Gold Maple Leaf, a gold bullion investment coin that is now the world's standard.

★The information in this case was supplied by the Royal Canadian Mint.

BACKGROUND ON THE GOLD MAPLE LEAF

The Gold Maple Leaf (GML) bullion investment coin was launched in 1979. This pure gold investment coin was a government initiative to stimulate the gold mining industry in Canada. The bullion market is a market for investors in precious metals. The investor is looking for liquidity and tradability and a form of financial insurance. The South African Krugerrand had been a well-entrenched competitor in this market for many years. The RCM decided to use product differentiation as part of its strategy to obtain market share for the GML. The Krugerrand was a 22-karat gold coin, while the GML was a 24-karat coin. In this market, purity of a gold bullion coin is a desired attribute among investors.

The strategy worked well for the RCM. During the initial three-year pilot period, over 3 million ounces of the GML were sold, primarily in North America and Europe. The RCM was committed to new market development as a strategy for growth and looked for market opportunities in Japan. With good distribution and promotion support, the entry into Japan was successful. By the mid-1980s, the Krugerrand was dropped in active trading on major gold markets. The Canadian GML quickly became the market leader and the standard upon which all other gold bullion coins were judged. Sales of the GML had reached 8 million ounces by the mid-1980s. The RCM decided it was ready to enter one of the largest gold bullion coin markets in the world, Hong Kong, in 1985.

MARKETING THE GML IN HONG KONG

SITUATION ANALYSIS

Hong Kong is basically operated by a free-enterprise, market-disciplined system. Low tax rates provide incentive for workers to work and for entrepreneurs to invest. Economic performance is high, with high GDP, modest inflation, improved employment, and a reduced trade gap. There are three gold markets operating in Hong Kong: the Chinese Gold and Silver Exchange Society Gold Bullion Market, the Loco London Market, and the Future Gold Market. Bullion coins occupy 7 percent of the entire gold market in Hong Kong, a market that was dominated by the Krugerrand. The size of the gold bullion coin market in Hong Kong was estimated at 500,000 ounces, with a market value of $1,194,573,410 HK. A dealer network consisting of over 400 outlets currently exists.

MARKETING THREATS

The South African Krugerrand, while not in active global trading, still dominated the Hong Kong market and was "the" bullion coin in Hong Kong. It had consistent and heavy advertising support. South Africa was expected to allocate a disproportionate amount of funding for the Krugerrand to counterattack the launch of the Gold Maple Leaf in order to block or restrict the GML's entry into the market.

The Krugerrand had established a good relationship with its retailers, and it seemed that it might be able to secure dominant point-of-sale space over the GML. Gold investment was also showing a decrease in popularity, since Hong Kong investors were hit hard in the past because of fluctuations in gold prices. In short, the GML was to be entering a market with some unfavourable resistance to the product.

MARKETING OPPORTUNITIES

The Gold Maple Leaf is an international coin with international liquidity. The GML is superior to the Krugerrand because it is a 24-karat 0.9999 pure gold product. The GML is legal tender and has a face value backed by the Canadian government. The Hong Kong market was already educated about the benefits of bullion coins. The Hong Kong people are highly mobile and would be concerned about the liquidity issue of the South African Krugerrand coin internationally. The GML originates from Canada, a Pacific trading partner of Hong Kong; Hong Kong people have a very favourable attitude toward Canada.

The RCM saw a possibility of having the Bank of China as a retail network, which would mean 200 selling points in addition to the 400 outlets currently dealing in the Krugerrand.

TARGET MARKET

The primary target market was to be Chinese males and females 25 years old and over, well educated, and with moderate to higher income. This target market had faith in gold as an investment and speculation tool and was fairly knowledgeable about the product. This group was pragmatic and interested in the ready tradability of the gold it bought. This group had an affinity for gold and often used it in gift giving.

MARKETING ASSUMPTIONS

The RCM assumed that a heavy counterattack would be launched from International Gold Corporation, the marketing arm for the Krugerrand. The RCM believed that gold was still considered one of the best ways to invest in Hong Kong. There was also an assumption that no drastic political or economic changes would occur that would lead to great fluctuations in gold prices.

The RCM also assumed that no government intervention would occur regarding the marketing of bullion coins and that no sudden bulk sales of gold from gold-producing countries like Russia would occur.

MARKETING OBJECTIVES

1 To introduce the GML to Hong Kong and to obtain a 5 to 6 percent market share or sales of 20,000 to 25,000 ounces.
2 To set up at least 300 retail outlets for the launch in September and 500 retail outlets by year-end (1985).
3 To build good relationships with retail partners.

ADVERTISING AND PUBLIC RELATIONS OBJECTIVES

1 To build awareness of the GML and its attributes among the target market.
2 To inform the target market of the advantages of this Canadian coin.

3 To persuade the target market to buy the GML as an alternative investment.
4 To establish investor awareness of the benefits of the GML.
5 To offer incentives to distributors to sell the GML.

MARKETING STRATEGY

The strategy was one of market development. The basic strategic and tactical decisions involving the four Ps were as follows:

1 *Product (positioning).* The GML was to be positioned as a natural alternative to the Krugerrand. The product was 1/10 oz to 1-oz coins of 0.9999 purity (24 K). It had high aesthetic value, international liquidity, and superior packaging.

2 *Place (distribution).* The network of the Bank of China was to be the first priority area. The Hong Kong Bank would also be solicited to participate in the GML's retail network. Other channels would be explored, such as department stores and hotels. By the end of year 1, the distribution levels were expected to be on a par with or better than the Krugerrand's.

3 *Pricing.* Retail banks would be persuaded to give a tight "spread" through an offer of a better merchandizing program than competitors offered.

4 *Promotion.* A total of $4 million HK was to be allocated for all promotional activities. All communications would clearly convey the unique product benefits of the GML over the Krugerrand. Advertising would receive the bulk of the promotional budget. Television would be used because of its high reach. Co-op advertising with major retail banks was considered. Point-of-sale materials would be tied closely with the television advertising. In terms of public relations, a trade and media launch was to be scheduled to announce the entry of the GML into the market; the president of the mint, who is also a minister of the Crown, was to officiate. Media relations were to be built when the RCM people were in Hong Kong for the launch. Consumer and trade sales promotion and incentive programs would also be used, including teller sales contests, bank client draws, and general consumer contests.

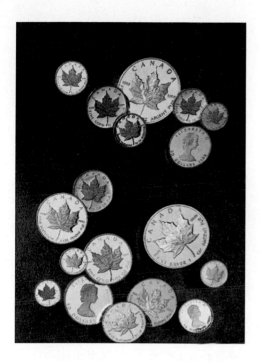

EVALUATION AND CONTROL

The success of the program was to be evaluated through a sales performance review, through prelaunch and postlaunch evaluation of promotion activities used, through awareness and tracking studies, and through market research of the target market.

QUESTIONS

1 Comment on the Royal Canadian Mint's marketing plan for entering the Hong Kong market. Why do you think the mint was successful in this market?
2 Ironically, one place the RCM has not had much success with its GML is Canada. Why?
3 If the RCM were to try to increase its penetration of the Canadian market, whom should it target?
4 Some suggest that the RCM owes its success in the gold bullion coin market to good luck. Explain.
5 The mint has introduced two new investment coins, the Platinum Maple Leaf and the Silver Maple Leaf. Who would be the appropriate targets for these products?

TEXT CASE ONE
Clean Windows, Inc.*

*I*t was January 1995. Terry Gill and John Kelly, partners of Clean Windows, Inc. (CW), were contemplating a marketing strategy for expanding their operations in the window cleaning market. Both were full-time students in the second year of their degree programs at the University of New Brunswick. They were committed to their studies and realized that their chosen strategy must allow them to complete their degree programs within the next two years.

They were optimistic that CW had the opportunity to grow very rapidly. Their optimism appeared justified, given the growth they had experienced in both residential and commercial contracts since they commenced operations in July 1994 (see Figure 1). Mr. Kelly attributed this growth to the "current lack of serious competition in the greater Fredericton area."

When questioned about balancing schoolwork and the responsibilities of his business, Mr. Gill commented:

> We know we have a really great concept here, but our study schedule could result in a lack of attention to customer demands and administrative details. I think that we can pull it off, but we need to make the right choices and develop an appropriate marketing strategy. John and I even considered franchising as our means of growth because we have to grow to maximize profitability.

*This case was prepared and revised by Professor E. S. Grant, University of New Brunswick, assisted by G. T. Clarke and K. Dunphy. Copyright 1989 and 1994.

Names of companies and people have been disguised. Some quantitative data have been adjusted, but relationships of data have been maintained. This case serves as a basis for discussion rather than an illustration of either effective or ineffective handling of an administrative situation.

INITIAL STRATEGY

Operations commenced June 20, 1994, with enough equipment for two cleaners. Initially, all labour activity was completed by Mr. Gill and Mr. Kelly. Business was relatively slow the first two months (see Figure 1), as most of the owners' time was spent cleaning windows, not on marketing and management activity. Advertising in these months was limited to the purchase of business cards and a direct mail campaign. The business cards were an important asset for business contacts, but the mail-out resulted in limited success. It was thought that this was due to poor timing.

One thousand five hundred photocopied flyers were distributed just prior to a long weekend in July. Both partners and employees delivered the flyers to private residences in the downtown area and to a few upscale neighbourhoods.

By the end of July a display ad was run in the business directory section of the local newspaper and free airtime was received on a local radio sta-

▌*Figure 1*
Monthly cleaning gross revenue.

MONTH	RESIDENTIAL	COMMERCIAL	TOTAL
July	$1,377	$ 37	$1,414
August	2,175	45	2,220
September	1,990	1,423	3,413
October	1,402	2,509	3,911
November	315	1,021	1,336
December	0	896	896

Source: Company records.

tion interested in promoting student businesses. Unfortunately, neither of these two media proved successful. Lawn signs and T-shirts displaying the company logo and phone number were purchased. These media, combined with word of mouth, accounted for close to 85 percent of all new cleaning contracts.

The promotions were responsible for business growth in August and September. With this additional business, the need for extra staff became apparent. By August, six cleaners were employed. An increase in demand through September and October was experienced, but it became difficult for both partners to cope with the increased volume as university commenced in September. By then, employment had decreased to two full-time employees who were responsible for reducing the partners' workload.

In early November, Mr. Gill and Mr. Kelly realized that the two full-time employees were not working out as anticipated. The decision was made to lay off both employees. This left only the partners to resume the labour-intensive duties of window cleaning. This was very difficult, since both maintained a rigorous cleaning schedule in addition to a full course load at the university.

With the summer quickly approaching, both partners agreed that this strategy would have to be reconsidered.

COMPETITION

When questioned about the competition, Mr. Kelly commented:

> There is only one firm that cleans residential windows, but we don't see them as a serious competitor. We know that they do have some business, but they cannot have much. We have phoned them several times, but our calls were never returned. There are two firms that service only commercial accounts. One of these firms cleans high-rise buildings only, but they operate out of Moncton, which is more than a two-hour drive. The other is a local firm; they are not equipped to clean high-rises but they have a very significant share of the local commercial market. We are certain that we can compete with them; almost all of our commercial clients have experienced their service and have expressed relief that there is now an alternative available.

Mr. Kelly had obtained information on all three of these competitors (see Figure 2). Fredericton had a number of maid and janitorial service companies. Most of these firms cleaned windows; however, none cleaned external window surfaces, and they cleaned interior window surfaces on an irregular basis.

Although Fredericton offers only a relatively small potential market size, both partners are certain that there is an attractive opportunity in both the residential and the commercial market.

▌ *Figure 2*
Competition in Fredericton window cleaning market.

COMPANY	CUSTOMER TYPE*	BONDED	LIABILITY INSURANCE	ESTIMATED PRICE
City Window Cleaners	Residential	?	?	?
Mr. Windows	Commercial	Yes	Yes	$15/hr
Gormay Cleaners	Commercial—high-rise buildings only	No	Yes	$40/hr
Other (janitorial and maid services)	Commercial† and residential†	NA	NA	NA

* Residential customers are defined as single dwellings only, all other accounts are defined as commercial.
† Clean only interior window surfaces.
? = unavailable.

Source: Telephone directory and telephone enquiries.

Many customers have indicated they would use CW's service again. One customer stated that she had seen the lawn sign and then decided to request CW's service. Unable to find the phone number (a business number was obtained in September), she claimed to have driven more than 50 miles before finding the law sign that she needed to find the number.

Mr. Gill believed that the most profitable opportunity would be to service what he calls high-rise buildings (all those that require staging). He estimates that there are more than 350 such buildings in the Fredericton area.

COST DATA

Cost data are given in Figures 3 and 4. All costs for 1994 (see Figure 3) were actual, based on the costs incurred to date. Costs for 1995 (see Figure 4) have been estimated by the partners. Transportation costs have been excluded. A small van belonging to Mr. Kelly's father had been used and John was confident that this vehicle would be available for at least another year. Although CW incurs no rental fee for the use of this van, fuel would have to be purchased.

All estimated costs were believed to be reasonably accurate. However, the pricing of window contracts had been much more arbitrary. Mr. Kelly sees the pricing decision as of key importance to CW's long-term profitability. To date, prices have been based on an estimated completion time for each potential contract.

The time estimate is multiplied by a charge-out rate of $15/hour per cleaner. Mr. Kelly confessed that the decision to use $15 per hour was arbitrary; however, he was confident that it was competitive and fair. This was thought to be the same charge-out rate used by Mr. Windows (see Figure 2). Mr. Kelly had difficulty deciding what to charge in the future. Although he believed their price was competitive, he had a hunch that many customers expected a lower charge-out rate given their status as students. He believed it was a serious issue and realized that many customers selected CW because of the altruistic satisfaction they received from supporting a student venture.

Enough equipment (ladders, staging, buckets, etc.) to operationalize three two-person crews had

▌ *Figure 3*
Actual costs—1994.

VARIABLE COSTS	PER HOUR	
Wages		
One two-person crew	(2 × $5.50 each)	$11.00/hour
Supplies		
Fuel	$ .75	
Cleaning fluids	.50	
Cleaning materials	.90	2.15
Total variable costs		$13.15
FIXED COSTS	**PER MONTH**	
Insurance (liability)	$ 15.00	
Telephone	55.00	
Advertising	110.00	
Bank charges	25.00	
Equipment depreciation	10.00	
Total fixed costs	$215.00	

Source: Company records.

Figure 4
Estimated costs—1995.

VARIABLE COSTS	PER HOUR	
Wages		
One two-person crew	(2 × $5.70 each)	$11.40/hour
Supplies		
Fuel	$ .80	
Cleaning fluids	.50	
Cleaning materials	.90	2.20
Total variable costs		$13.60

FIXED COSTS	PER MONTH
Insurance (liability)	$ 20.00
Telephone	60.00
Advertising	200.00
Bank charges	30.00
Equipment depreciation	20.00
Total fixed costs	$330.00

Source: Company estimates

Figure 5
Selected characteristics— Fredericton, NB.

Dwelling characteristics	
Single detached house	10,230
Apartment, five or more storeys	275
Movable dwelling	50
All other types	5,890
Total number of occupied private dwellings	16,445
Population characteristics	
By industry division	
All industries	24,095
Primary industries (SIC divisions A, B, C, and D)	440
Manufacturing industries (division E)	1,290
Construction industries (division F)	1,160
Transportation, storage, communication, and other utility industries (divisions G and H)	1,895
Trade industries (divisions I and J)	4,435
Finance, insurance, and real estate industries (divisions K and L)	950
Government service industries (division N)	4,565
Other service industries (divisions M, O, P, Q, and R)	9,365
Not applicable	480
Total labour force 15 years and over	24,570

Source: Statistics Canada, Cat. 94-107 and 108, 1986.

been acquired. It was estimated that additional equipment would cost $300 per crew, but it was uncertain whether or not it would be necessary to hire additional crews.

Additional investment would be necessary in order to clean high-rise buildings. Staging that would allow one person to safely manoeuvre up and down the side of a high-rise would cost approximately $4,500.

THE MARKET

Mr. Gill had evaluated the Fredericton market and concluded that it was sizable enough to allow CW to realize satisfactory profits. He had collected select statistics at the university's library (see Figure 5). Although Mr. Gill was uncertain how many households and commercial customers were likely to use his services, he was certain that his competitors were not satisfying the current demand.

In the past, CW's window contracts were largely concentrated within a small geographic area. Both partners were uncertain why this phenomenon existed. Mr. Kelly questioned, "Is this because our lawn signs were displayed more often in this area? Are these people different, or is it related to other, undetermined causes?"

THE FUTURE

The partners faced a number of important decisions. They had to decide whether or not their current strategy was appropriate for the situation. If it was not, they would have to agree on appropriate changes. These changes would have to be made in light of both partners' commitment to expansion. They believed they could create a student-owned franchise operation similar to College Pro Painters and University Painters. However, they were uncertain how they should proceed.

They would need to make some decisions very soon. Exams finished in April, and they anticipated that April and May would be extremely busy months, given that many people undertake an effort in the spring to clean their homes and businesses. They realized there would be little time available for analysis and strategic planning after late March. Time would be spent hiring employees, selling, cleaning, and perhaps even studying for final exams.

QUESTIONS

1 How can the market (commercial and residential) for window cleaning be segmented?
2 What types of promotional activities would you suggest CW, Inc., use? How can the firm encourage repeat usage of its service?
3 How feasible is the venture?
4 Would you recommend that the partners attempt to sell franchise agreements? Explain.

TEXT CASE TWO
National Hockey League*

*D*isney characters danced with hockey sticks, balloons and confetti filled the air, and NHL commissioner Gary Bettman, NHL chairman Bruce McNall, and Disney chairman Michael Eisner blew on duck calls. It wasn't hockey night in Canada, but the hatching of the Mighty Ducks, Disney's new expansion team, in Anaheim, California. The Mighty Ducks' entry into the 1993–94 NHL season was a signal that a new era had come to professional hockey. For the NHL, marketing had become the name of the game.

*This case was based on information supplied by the National Hockey League and a variety of secondary sources, including T. Falconer, "Hockey Hype," *Marketing*, March 22, 1993, p. 1, p. 3.

HISTORY

The National Hockey League traces its beginnings to November 22, 1917. It is the second-oldest league of four major team sports in North America, with only professional baseball pre-dating it. For most of its first decade, the NHL operated as a three-, four-, or five-team circuit. By 1926–27, however, the league had grown to 10 teams in two divisions, one Canadian, the other American. This marked the beginning of hockey's so-called modern era.

The two-division setup lasted for the next 12 seasons, but by the 1942–43 season, the league was left with six franchises, and it stayed that way for the next quarter century. The six franchises—New York Rangers, Toronto Maple Leafs, Boston Bruins, Chicago Blackhawks, Detroit Red Wings, and Montreal Canadiens—came to be known as the Original Six, and all are thriving today. By 1967–68, the NHL doubled its franchises from 6 to 12, with all six new teams located in the United States. The new teams were the California Seals, Los Angeles Kings, Minnesota North Stars, Philadelphia Flyers, Pittsburgh Penguins, and St. Louis Blues. All but the Seals survive today.

Six more expansions followed in the next 13 years, adding 14 more teams to the league. The Buffalo Sabres and Vancouver Canucks received franchises in 1970. The Atlanta Flames (later relocated to become the Calgary Flames) and the New York Islanders joined in 1972.

The Kansas City Scouts and Washington Capitals came on board in 1974, with the Kansas City franchise relocating to Colorado in 1976 and eventually becoming the New Jersey Devils in 1982. In 1979–80, the NHL added four teams—the Edmonton Oilers, Hartford Whalers, Quebec Nordiques, and Winnipeg Jets—in an amalgamation with the former World Hockey Association. The San Jose Sharks joined the league in 1991–92, followed by the Ottawa Senators and Tampa Bay Lightning in 1992–93. In 1993–94, the NHL welcomed the Florida Panthers (owned by Blockbuster Entertainment) and the Mighty Ducks of Anaheim (owned by Disney). The Minnesota North Stars relocated to Dallas, Texas, in the same season, to be known as the Dallas Stars.

Throughout its history, the NHL has been recognized for its ideas and innovations. For example, the NHL was the first major sports league to introduce a play-off system, one that has been adopted by all of the other major sports. The crown jewel trophy of team sports is considered the Stanley Cup, awarded each season to the play-off champion of the NHL. The Stanley Cup is the oldest trophy professional athletes in North America compete for, pre-dating even the historic Davis Cup of tennis. Originally, the Stanley Cup was competed for by amateur teams beginning in 1893. But the trophy became part of the NHL in 1926.

From its early beginnings through the mid-1960s, virtually all the NHL's players were Canadian. United States-born players began making the NHL in the 1960s, and soon after, European players started to emerge in the league, particularly from Sweden and Finland. Today, players from former Eastern bloc countries also play in the NHL.

PURPOSES AND OBJECTIVES OF THE NHL

The basic purposes and objectives for which the NHL is organized are as follows:

1 The perpetuation of hockey as one of the national games of the United States and Canada.
2 The promotion of the common interests of the members of the league, each member being the owner of a professional hockey club located in the United States or Canada.
3 The promulgation of rules governing the conduct of play of hockey games between the member clubs in the league, the relationships between players and member clubs, between member clubs and the league, and between the member clubs and other hockey clubs, to the end that the public may be assured of a high standard of skill and fair play, integrity, and good sportsmanship.
4 The arbitration and settlement of disputes between the member clubs and between member clubs and players.

5 The education of the public, through various forms of communication, to the end that professional hockey, as played according to the standards of the league, may gain popular support and acceptance as wholesome entertainment.

6 The development of youth in mind and body and the teaching of fair play and good sportsmanship through the medium of hockey.

MARKETING EMPHASIS

Historically, it could be argued, the NHL and many of the team owners have had a negative mind-set toward marketing. Marketing was actually considered unseemly. The general approach was to simply open the doors at the arenas and wait for the customers to come. But with NHL costs—particularly players' salaries—on the rise, the NHL needs a bigger audience, both at the games and on television, particularly in the United States. The league recognizes it needs to market itself. The culture at the top is now more marketing oriented than ever before. NHL Commissioner Gary Bettman, the former vice president of the NBA (National Basketball Association), leads the new marketing effort of the NHL.

The league is heavily involved in product licensing. Close to 245 licensees produce 1,000-plus products, and the NHL gets a percentage of the wholesale price. The league is aiming for the $1 billion mark in licensed product sales by 1996. The North American sports licensing market is valued at $12 billion, so the NHL believes there is opportunity for growth.

Corporate involvement and sponsorship in the NHL is also a priority with the league. Special events such as the annual all-star game are being used to bring in sponsorship dollars. Books and videos are used by the NHL for educational and promotional purposes.

South of the border, however, Canada's national pastime is popular only in certain regions. The NHL is attempting to build its geographic appeal and win national US television contracts. According to Steve Ryan, president of NHL Enterprises, the league's marketing arm, "TV not only puts people in the seats of the League's arenas, it sells licensed merchandise and makes it easier to get corporate sponsors. Television becomes our advertising vehicle for the game and drives the other components of our business." In the United States, the NHL faces a catch-22 situation. It needs franchises throughout the country to get a national TV contract. At the same time, it needs national TV coverage to sell the game to franchisees. With new teams in San Jose, Tampa Bay, Miami, and Anaheim, and the Minnesota franchise now in Dallas, the NHL is moving toward national coverage. Currently, the league has teams in 9 of the top 10 consumer markets in the United States, and other US teams play in markets considered to be in at least the top 50 consumer markets. This should help in building the profile of the NHL in the United States.

The NHL is also looking at the European market. ESPN, for example, is broadcasting NHL games on prime-time Swedish TV, and Europe is seen as a good market for licensing. In an effort to improve the entertainment value of the game for television viewers, the league is currently looking at how to improve the way the games are televised, from the use of different camera angles to a computer-enhanced puck that is easier to follow.

Marketing professional hockey in the United States may become a little easier with the selection of entertainment giants Disney and Blockbuster Entertainment as the league's Anaheim and Miami franchisees. Blockbuster offers NHL merchandise in its video outlets across Canada and the United States. Cross-marketing possibilities with Disney appear endless. For example, the Mighty Ducks' new arena, the Pond, is close to Disneyland, so vacation packages and other tie-ins with the theme park are certain. Disney's decision to name the team the Mighty Ducks, after the hockey movie that grossed $100 million US, not only gave the team instant name recognition, but helped enhance the profile of hockey in the southern United States.

The Mighty Ducks, in fact, had sold more than 10,000 season tickets even before the fans knew what players were on the team roster. Disney's sequel to the movie ran in the theatres in 1994 during the team's first season, and this helped maintain the interest in hockey at a national level in the United States.

WESTERN CONFERENCE		EASTERN CONFERENCE	
PACIFIC	CENTRAL	NORTHEAST	ATLANTIC
Anaheim	Chicago	Boston	Florida
Calgary	Dallas	Buffalo	New Jersey
Edmonton	Detroit	Hartford	New York Islanders
Los Angeles	St. Louis	Montreal	New York Rangers
San Jose	Toronto	Ottawa	Philadelphia
Vancouver	Winnipeg	Pittsburgh	Tampa Bay
		Quebec	Washington

▌*Exhibit 1*
National Hockey League team alignment.

The NHL believes that strong franchisees in the United States will help sell the game to a new generation of fans and ensure its long-term prosperity. As further evidence of the NHL's new approach to marketing, it has developed its first snack food product, potato chips, in partnership with Nalley's, Vancouver. The product is called NHL Super Crunch and is the first consumer product to feature an action photograph of NHL players.

THE FUTURE

The future looks promising for the league. Several teams are building new arenas, and some have been able to attract major corporate sponsors to be associated with the new complexes. Fan support for all of the participating 26 teams is likely to continue to be strong. This is based on the fact that game attendance has risen in each of the last 14 seasons. Projections are for more than 1,000 regular-season and play-off games to be played in 1994–95 in front of more than 16 million paying customers. "Hockey Night in Canada" remains one of the highest-rated television shows in Canada, and the NHL is available to more than 60 million US households through ESPN. The ABC network also currently carries NHL play-off games, and expanded coverage is possible in the near future.

The league realignment in 1993–94—two new conferences and four new divisions based on geography (see Exhibit 1), plus a conference-based format for the Stanley Cup play-offs—should also help the league's marketing efforts. The realignment was designed to better serve the interests of the teams, the players, the fans, and the media. It is also hoped the realignment will enhance rivalries among the teams as well as offer fans more variety in games involving their favourite teams. At present, hockey is an international game. Only soccer is played in more countries worldwide than hockey. The National Hockey League hopes that with great players and great teams, consumers will support and patronize professional hockey as a wholesome form of entertainment.

QUESTIONS

1 What is the "product" that the National Hockey League is really marketing to prospective fans? With whom is the NHL competing for fan attendance?
2 How does marketing hockey differ from marketing a consumer product like breakfast cereal?
3 Do some thinking or some research. Find out the basic demographic characteristics of the hockey fan.
4 Why does the NHL have to know the basic profile of the hockey fan? How could the NHL use this information?

The Florenceville Curling Club*

On an unseasonably hot New Brunswick June day, it seemed odd to be discussing the winter sport of curling, but that's what Ray Brennan and Clayton Buckingham found themselves doing in mid-1989. The two men had met at the Florenceville Curling Club (FCC) to discuss the future of the 32-year-old institution.

Looking through thick glass windows at an iceless surface, Clayton realized that it would be October before the familiar sound of corn brooms beating against cold ice was heard again. Ray, too, found the club strangely silent as he sat down in a well-worn armchair opposite Clayton. Both men were long-time members of the club; Ray had also served as president in the early 1970s. He was blunt and to the point with his friend. "The club can't survive another year with this kind of loss. We'd have to sell an awful lot of curling memberships to make up for this year's $12,000 shortfall."

Both men realized that drastic changes were needed if the 1989–90 season were not to be the FCC's last. Executive members of the club's management team were to meet in two weeks for their annual summer meeting. As senior members of the executive, Clayton and Ray had been given a mandate to come up with recommendations to guide the future of the Florenceville community facility, and to lead it out of its financial difficulties.

CURLING IN CANADA

Curling's status as a major Canadian sport is largely paradoxical. Many of the 753,000 Canadians who curl at least once a week are almost fanatically devoted to the sport. However, most other Canadians are either disinterested in or lack information about this winter game.

*This case was prepared by Professor Peter D Sianchuk of Mount Allison University for the Atlantic Entrepreneurial Institute as a basis for classroom discussion, and is not meant to illustrate either effective or ineffective management.

Curling is played by sliding 44-pound granite stones down a sheet of ice 14 feet wide and 138 feet long. Two teams, each with four members, typically play eight "ends" over a two-hour period. See Exhibit 1 for rules and Exhibit 2 for a description of curling terms.

The game originated on the frozen lochs of Scotland, but it was in Canada that it was developed and refined. In 1989 there were over 1,300 private and public curling rinks (or clubs) dotted across the Canadian landscape from the Inuvik Curling Club in the Northwest Territories to the Rattling Brook Club in Newfoundland. The majority of curling clubs were in the prairie provinces and Ontario.

Canada's national "grassroots" sport takes on an international dimension each year when the World Curling Championships are held. Although Canada has dominated the sport, other countries have enjoyed success including Norway, Sweden, Scotland, and Germany. The 1988 Women's World Championship team was from the Riessersee Curling Club in Garmisch-Partenkirchen, Germany.

The two major Canadian championships are the Labatt Brier (for male curlers) and the Scott Tournament of Hearts (for female curlers). Held in February or March of each year, these two tournaments bring together the top competitors from across the nation. At that time, curling receives its greatest media coverage. In 1987, 1.8 million Canadians tuned in to watch the Labatt Brier on TV. Estimates cited a cumulative TV rating of 5 million viewers for all televised curling events during 1987 (Exhibit 3). The 1986 Brier in Saskatoon set an attendance record of 151,538 spectators for the weeklong event.

Most participation in the sport is at the club level. In 1989, members typically paid between $100 and $300 for the right to curl for the season (each season usually lasts from October through early April). In 1989, the majority of curlers were in the 25- to 49-year-old age group (Exhibit 4) and were mostly male (66 percent).

Although the total number of participants in Canada had declined through the 1980s, there

❚ *Exhibit 1*
Basic rules of curling.

- Two four-member teams compete against each other on a long narrow sheet of ice (138 feet long by 14 feet wide).
- At each end large circular targets are painted under the ice.
- The outer circle is 12 feet in diameter.
- The outer circle houses three smaller circles: the 8-foot circle, the 4-foot circle, and the button (the button is the centre of the target, and is approximately 8 inches wide).
- Each member of the team throws two rocks up the ice toward the circles for a total of eight throws.
- Each team tries to put its rocks closest to the centre button.
- An offensive shot is one in which a team member tries to land his or her rock near the centre of the rings. A defensive shot involves trying to hit the opponents' rocks out of the circles, thus removing them from play.
- A team (or rink) is led by a skip, who sets the team game plan and throws the last two stones; the vice, who throws the two stones before the skip; and the lead and second, who throw the first and second sets of stones, respectively.
- To begin play, the skip goes to the far end of the ice and places his or her curling broom on the circles as a target for the lead, second, and vice to shoot at.
- After these three players have thrown their rocks, the skip returns to the throwing end of the ice to throw the last two stones.
- The 44-pound granite stones will spin to the left or to the right depending upon how they are released.
- By giving the stone a slight twist to the right or left (like turning the steering wheel of a car) the stone will "curl" to the right or left as it moves down the ice.
- The rock curls most as it begins to slow down (as it approaches the circles).
- By properly "curling" a rock, a player can curl the rock in behind another rock, thus providing protection from the other team, who may try to remove it.
- After both teams have thrown their 8 stones (for a total of 16), points are added up.
- The team with the stones closest to the button counts the points.
- Only one team can score in one "end."
- An "end" consists of 16 total rocks being thrown down the ice in one direction.
- After each end, the curlers come back down the ice in the opposite direction.
- Curling games usually consist of 8 or 10 ends.
- When a player throws a stone, two team members "sweep" down the ice (in front of the stone) with a brush or corn broom.
- The sweeping motion in front of a stone causes the ice to heat up very slightly; this in turn causes the rock to slide more.
- Proper sweeping can carry a stone an extra 8 to 12 feet down the ice surface; this allows more precise shots by sweeping when extra distance is needed.
- Sweeping also causes a stone to go straighter (as opposed to curling more), adding to the strategy of the game.

Source: Company files.

were increases in mixed competition. Mixed competition consists of teams of two male curlers and two female curlers. In contrast, competitive leagues often have teams made up of only one gender or age level. Most curlers play for social reasons, to keep fit, or for the competitive aspect of the game (in that order). Mixed competition seems to best satisfy all three of these criteria.

A 1987 study conducted by the national curling body, Curl Canada, revealed that the majority

Burned stone: If a team sweeping a stone down the ice happen to touch it with their brooms then it is "burned" and the other skip can take it off. This rule exists because the broom will cause the rock to change directions.

Button: The centre target of the curling circles. Each team tries to put its rocks as close as possible to the button.

Delivery: Occurs when the person throwing the stone releases toward the circles on the opposite end of the ice.

End: Occurs when each team has thrown its rocks in one direction up the ice. Points are tallied and then another end is played. Games of eight ends normally take two hours to play.

Hack: Rubber blocks in the ice similar to the starting blocks in a sprint race. The curler pushes off from the hack in order to slide upon the ice and deliver his or her rock.

Hog: After a rock is delivered, it must go a certain distance down the ice in order to be in play. The rock must cross the hogline. If it doesn't the player is said to have "hogged" the stone and it must be removed from play.

House: Another term for the circles or target area.

Lead: The first person on the team to throw two consecutive stones.

Rink: A team, or a curling club fielding a team, is often referred to as a rink.

Skip: The last person on the team to throw two consecutive stones. The skip calls the team's game plan.

Stone; rock: Terms for the 44-pound granite stone that is the key piece of equipment in a curling game.

Sweeping: The brushing movement in front of the stone that causes it to either go further, go straighter, or both.

Vice: Also referred to as a "mate," this is the second last person to throw stones, and often assists the skip with team strategy.

■ *Exhibit 2*
Basic curling terms.

Source: Company files.

COMPETITION	NUMBER OF VIEWERS (000S)		
	1987	1986	1985
Labatt Brier	1,800	1,300	1,200
Scott Tournament of Hearts	569	1,100	401
Men's World Championships	1,600	1,700	1,700
Ladies' World Championships	487	937	583
VIEWER COMPARISON PER SPORT (000S)	**1987**		
Curling (Labatt Brier)	1,800		
World Figure Skating Championships	1,700		
World Cup Downhill Ski Racing	800		
Grey Cup	3,900		
Stanley Cup	3,600		
Baseball	2,200		
NHL (Hockey Night in Canada)	2,000		
CFL	800		

*Annual viewership impressions reach approximately 5 million for all curling events on all channels; 1.1 million viewers are regular spectators.

■ *Exhibit 3*
Television viewership of major curling events.*

Source: Curl Canada—Three Year Promotional and Public Relations Plan, March 1988.

▌*Exhibit 4*
Demographic profiles of the average Canadian curler, 1987.

CATEGORY	%	CATEGORY	%
REGION		**MARITAL STATUS**	
Atlantic	6	Single	39
Quebec	8	Married	59
Ontario	30	Other	2
Mid West	23		
Alberta	23	**OCCUPATION**	
British Columbia	11	Professional	9
		Manager/owner	9
AGE		Sales	5
10 to 14 years	9	Clerical	10
15 to 19	16	Skilled labour	15
20 to 24	9	Unskilled labour	6
25 to 34	20	Farmer	6
35 to 49	27	Homemaker	6
50 years and older	19	Retired	7
		Student	26
SEX		Unemployed	2
Female	66		
Male	34	**HOUSEHOLD INCOME**	
		Under $20,000	13
EDUCATION		$20,000 to $34,999	27
Elementary school	12	35,000 to $49,999	24
High school	50	$50,000 or more	36
Tech school	15		
University	23		

Source: Curl Canada—A Profile of the Canadian Curler, July 1987.

of curlers in Canada (60 percent) were not members of a club, but played either as guests of a member, or in house leagues that rented ice to individual teams. The propensity to become a member tended to increase with age, frequency of play, and length of time an individual had curled.

HISTORY OF THE FLORENCEVILLE CURLING CLUB

The FCC began rather modestly in 1957 with two sheets of ice (which allowed two games—a total of 16 curlers—to be played at once) and a total construction cost of $6,951.80. Twenty individuals donated $100 each, generating a building fund of $2,000. Many of the original contributors had never even seen the game played. Additional funds were raised through the issue of $25 shares.

There were 65 members during the first year of operation, all male. On January 7, 1958, thirty-eight women met at the rink and formed the Florenceville Ladies' Curling Club, thus expanding the membership base to over 100. By the early 1970s membership had grown to 150 curlers and there was a pressing need for expansion. In 1974, the building was expanded so that two more sheets of ice could be added, but it wasn't until the 1976–77 season that all four sheets of ice were fully operational. The small club, which had a $1,850 mortgage in 1958, owed the Bank of Nova Scotia $122,400 by April of 1977. Expenses for the 1976–77 year totalled $53,009. With a revenue of $50,754, the club faced an operating loss of $2,255.

By the spring of 1979, the club was virtually bankrupt. Don Wishart, past president, blamed the financial problems on a lack of financial controls and too few curlers. The two problems were obviously related. Stopgap measures such as laying off both the bartender and the icemaker proved unsuccessful. This only put an increasing burden on the small contingent of volunteers who already kept the club in operation. In desperate need of cash, the club began an aggressive fundraising campaign in the autumn of 1979. A local company's $15,000 donation was matched through individual solicitations. New revenue-generating techniques, such as "Club 200,"* were instituted, and expenditures were tightened. No longer were free drinks given out by the club. Inventories were closely monitored and kept low. A better interest rate was negotiated with the bank. The club also invested $2,000 in a new electric duct heater, which would decrease the electricity bill by an estimated $2,000 per year (a special air refrigeration system is necessary to maintain curling ice, and as a result the FCC incurred electricity charges of between $1,400 and $1,800 per month in 1988–89).

The second problem, too few curlers, was more difficult to overcome. A committee was formed to ask former members why they no longer curled. People complained that the club was too competitive and cliquish and that they didn't feel welcome. To overcome this perception, a commercial or house league was established in 1980. Local companies, families, neighbours, or fellow employees could put a team into the league at a cost of $40 per season. If 10 people were on the team, then the cost to curl was $4 per person, rather than the normal membership of between $70 and $100. Rules were relaxed and everyone was encouraged to change positions in order to learn the intricacies of the game. The league turned out to be a great success with 18 teams composed of over 100 curlers enrolled in the first schedule and 26 teams in the second. By 1982–83, the FCC had reached its goal of getting more curlers into the club and showing them how much fun curling is. The FCC boasted 300[†] members by 1984, an all-time high. Taxes had been paid, and the mortgage was ahead by $38,380. The club had successfully weathered the recession of the early 1980s.

By 1989, the club once again found itself in financial difficulty. Memberships had decreased to 170 from the 1984 level of 300; this number still exceeded the 150 members (both social and curlers) who used the facilities in 1979. There was an increasing sentiment in the club that major operational changes were necessary. Volunteers had traditionally formed the backbone of the club, donating their time and energies to organize leagues, special events, and tournaments. Volunteers also performed all necessary business functions, ensuring bills and taxes were paid. Volunteer "burnout" was evident at the FCC. In addition, operating expenses had exceeded revenues by $12,000. Members like Ray Brennan and Clayton Buckingham, who had been curling at the club for many years, realized the seriousness of the situation.

THE FLORENCEVILLE AREA

Curling competes for consumer dollars with many other forms of entertainment. In Florenceville, competition includes other winter sports such as skiing, ice hockey, and snowmobiling; social activities such as those offered by clubs like the Legion, Elks, and Kinsmen; and in-home activities such as video rentals.

Although Florenceville had a population of only 725, it was surrounded by a number of small communities within easy driving distance, and from which its membership was drawn. The towns of Centreville, Bristol, Bath, and Stickney were all located within a 20-kilometre radius (Exhibit 5). Some membership was also drawn from Hartland, New Brunswick. These communities (including Florenceville) had a total population of 3,693.[‡] Outlying rural parishes from which the FCC might expect a few members included Aberdeen (population 1,192), Brighton (1,825), Peel (1,252), and Kent (2,248). Woodstock, the largest town in the area, was a half-hour drive up the Trans-Canada Highway and had its own curling club, so no FCC members were drawn from that area.

In 1989, Florenceville had one ice hockey arena, one video store, and one Legion hall. In Centreville there were a Kinsmen hall and an Elks

---

*The 200 people put in $40 each. Prizes totalling $5,000 were awarded during the curling season. The club retained the $3,000 difference between revenues and prize money and used it to pay the interest on the mortgage.

[†]Heating problems at the Florenceville hockey arena (located next door) resulted in fans coming over to the FCC to warm up between periods of hockey games. This increased the number of social members at the FCC. Approximately 110 members of the 300 total were social and not curling members.

[‡]Statistics Canada documents 94-107 and 94-108.

■ *Exhibit 5*

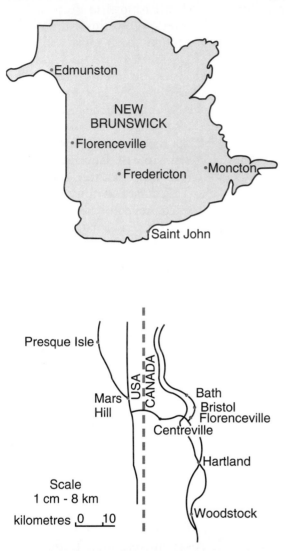

Source: Adapted from the *Atlantic Canada Vacation Guide Map.*

of the world's largest frozen foods producers with more than 30 manufacturing facilities in eight countries on three continents. Annual sales exceeded $1.5 billion. Other major employers were the Florenceville High School, Day and Ross Trucking Company in Hartland, and Thomas Farm Equipment in Centreville. Agriculture played a major role in the economic viability of the area. Potatoes grown in the Florenceville area were sold worldwide.

Florenceville had no radio station or newspaper. It was served by CJCJ-AM in Woodstock and WAGM-FM in Presque Isle, Maine. Besides large national newspapers such as the *Globe and Mail,* Florenceville residents read three local newspapers: *The Woodstock Bugle, The Hartland Observer,* and *The Victoria County Record* (Perth).

CLUB MANAGEMENT AND OPERATIONS

Like many other community-run, nonprofit organizations, the FCC was dependent upon volunteers for its existence. Members volunteered their time and effort in various capacities for the club's overall operation, sometimes as a club director. Usually a person with longstanding membership and experience would be elected president at the annual meeting. The president would be assisted by an elected vice-president, secretary, and treasurer, and by several other directors who would organize leagues or special events. These directors were nominated at the annual meeting. The nomination process was informal; rarely was a vote necessary to ratify a new director. The board of directors was made up of the elected officers and the directors nominated at the annual meeting.

Directors had individual responsibilities (such as organizing the entertainment for the year), leaving operational decisions to the president. Ideally, the president was to be advised by other executive members but was often left in a lone decision-making capacity. This became especially problematic when a strong-willed, individualistic person was elected as president. The club often found itself propelled in a direction based on the desires of one person. The club's history suggested one person

club, while a small Lions club operated out of Bath. Snowmobiling and skiing were two popular sports for the residents of the Florenceville Region. People could choose from three nearby ski hills: Mars Hill, Maine (½-hour drive), Crabbe Mountain, Fredericton (1¼-hour drive), and Mount Farlagne, Edmundston (1½-hour drive).

The largest employer in the area was the McCain Food Products company, which had its head office in Florenceville. From humble beginnings in 1957, McCain Foods had grown into one

▌*Exhibit 6*

Membership rate structure, Florenceville Curling Club, 1988–89.

Family	$160
Mens	110
Ladies	80
Commercial league	60 (per person)
Juniors	40
Seniors	40

Source: Company records.

should not run the club alone, and that the club often suffered when presidents attempted to do so.

The president had to carefully monitor the expenditures and revenues of the club. Revenues were generated from several sources. One of the most important revenue sources came from members' curling dues. See Exhibit 6 for a breakdown of fees. Income from dues declined from approxi-

mately $9,115 in 1988 to $8,708 in 1989. This reflected the declining membership figures for the club. Hall rentals also contributed significantly to revenues. Weddings, dances, bingos, and other activities were held at the club, mostly during the summer. This helped to provide some cash flow during the off-season. However, revenues from hall rentals plummeted from $20,104 in 1988 to $9,800 in 1989, severely weakening the financial state of the club. The 1987 figures were almost double those of 1989 at $16,614. Ray and Clayton agreed that this decline was a management issue, and that not enough effort had been put into utilizing club facilities. Other revenue was gained from bar services and the ladies' club. Bar sales were a significant part of most small clubs' revenues, since profit margins tended to be high. Financial statements for 1988 and 1989 are presented in Exhibits 7 to 9.

Past promotional efforts at the FCC were limited—most of them at the discretion of the

▌*Exhibit 7*

Florenceville Curling Club Ltd. Statement of Revenue and Expenditures Year Ended April 30.★

	1989	1988
Revenue		
Dues	$ 8,708	$ 9,115
Hall rentals, dances, bingo, and other	9,800	20,104
Total revenue	18,508	29,219
Expenditures		
Interest and bank charges	5,303	3,159
Repairs and supplies	7,320	12,530
Insurance	5,915	5,927
Taxes, licenses, and dues	5,446	4,465
Lights and heat	10,705	9,983
Telephone	548	501
Miscellaneous	566	732
Total Expenditures	35,803	37,297
Operating Income	(17,295)	(8,078)
Other contributions to expenditures		
Canteen and bar	3,111	11,014
Ladies' club	1,780	4,750
Total other contributions to expenditures	4,891	15,764
Excess of revenue over expenditures	$(12,404)	$ 7,686

★Unaudited.

Source: Company records.

	1989	1988
Assets		
Current assets		
Cash	$ 4,826	$ 3,869
Accounts receivable	2,125	1,655
Inventory, at cost	2,033	3,017
Prepaid expenses	6,838	7,318
Total current assets	15,822	15,859
Fixed assets	217,799	212,285
Total assets	$233,621	$228,144
Liabilities and shareholder equity		
Current liabilities		
Bank loan	$ 16,000	$ 0
Accounts payable and accrued liabilities	7,147	5,266
Current portion of long-term debt	6,120	6,120
Total current liabilities	29,267	11,386
Long-term liabilities	21,400	21,400
Total liabilities	$ 50,667	$ 32,786
Shareholder equity		
Authorized 800 common shares having a par value of $25 each		
Issued 661 common shares	16,525	16,525
Contributed surplus	32,600	32,600
Retained earnings	133,829	146,233
Total shareholder equity	182,954	195,358
Total liabilities and shareholder equity	$233,621	$228,144

*Unaudited.

Source: Company records.

▌ *Exhibit 8*
Florenceville Curling Club Ltd. Balance Sheet Year Ended April 30.*

	1989	1988
Cash from (for) operating activities		
Excess of revenues over expenditures	$(12,404)	$ 7,686
Net change in noncash working capital	2,875	(6,368)
Total cash from (for) operating activities	(9,529)	1,318
Cash from (for) investing activities		
Purchase of fixed assets	(5,514)	(1,800)
Total cash from (for) investing activities		
Increase (decrease) in cash and equivalents	(15,043)	(482)
Cash and equivalents of beginning of year	3,869	4,351
Cash (overdraft) and equivalents at year-end	$(11,174)	$ 3,869
Represented by		
Cash	$ 4,826	$ 3,869
Bank loan	(16,000)	0
	$(11,174)	$ 3,869

*Unaudited.

Source: Company records.

▌ *Exhibit 9*
Florenceville Curling Club Ltd. Statement of Changes in Financial Position for the Year Ended April 30.*

president. Early in the season, some advertising would be placed in *The Hartland Observer* and *The Victoria County Record* to solicit new members and promote special events during the season. Flyers and local posters were also used from time to time. Like other curling clubs in Canada, the FCC benefited from the high level of publicity generated in March by the Canadian and world championships. Non-curlers' interest peaked at this time due to media exposure on CBC, CTV, TSN, and radio and in print media. Very few clubs took advantage of this interest by having club promotions in the spring. Most clubs held promotions in the fall when the season was just beginning and interest was relatively low for curling, especially among non-curlers.

The FCC also benefited from the publicity generated by the McCain Super Spiel.★ Each year in early December, McCain Foods held this major national curling tournament in Florenceville. With prize money of over $15,000, the top names in Canadian curling came from across the country to compete for cash prizes in New Brunswick. In 1987 the Sports Network (TSN) broadcast the event, giving it national exposure. The Super Spiel gave the FCC an unprecedented level of publicity for a small-town curling rink.

THE PROBLEM

Clayton Buckingham slouched down comfortably in his chair as he listened to Ray Brennan's detailed description of the problems facing the FCC. Although the problems were connected, Ray summarized the discussion by dividing the topic into two areas. He prefaced his summary by stating, "We may only be a small community-run organization but our problems are no different from those of large companies like McCain's or Day and Ross.

"First, operations of the club need revamping, the executive structure of the club just doesn't work. We put too much reliance on one individual. I think all our presidents have been very capable but it's too much responsibility for one person. That's why we face so much 'volunteer burnout.' We heap too much on too few—there

needs to be greater sharing of duties and responsibilities. I'd like to see us operate with a new structure—a board of directors that would replace our current structure of a president and an executive. The new board would be chaired by someone who would organize and delegate tasks but wouldn't have to be setting up tables before a dance. The chairperson could make sure the club is on course without making unilateral operational decisions and getting their hands dirty with mundane tasks. All decision making would be funnelled through the chair, who would set regular meetings to deal with important operational problems. Smaller problems wouldn't have to be dealt with at the board level.

"A major part of this restructuring would be hiring a manager to run the club. I'm convinced the position could pay for itself through increased revenues and efficiencies. People would be more willing to help out if they knew there was someone else performing the bulk of the work."

Ray passed Clayton a neatly typed list of the potential duties for a club manager (Exhibit 10). He then handed Clayton another sheet of paper covered with rough, handwritten notes. It was a summary of the effects that a manager might have on overall operations. Clayton squinted at it and asked his friend to summarize the content.

Ray explained that the bar and canteen had traditionally been a strong revenue generator for the club and that extra effort was needed to ensure that it continued to generate a positive cash flow. A manager could supervise and administer this function. In 1987 sales were $11,215; they remained steady in 1988 at $11,014 but declined significantly in 1989 to $3,111.

"In addition to other duties," Ray said, "the club manager could act as a bartender and ensure that the bar money is being carefully monitored. A return to 1988 bar sales alone would almost pay the manager's salary.

"The Canada Employment Centre offers a one-time job development program. If we hire someone who has been drawing Unemployment Insurance benefits for at least 24 of the last 30 weeks then they'll pay us for up to 20 weeks of work at 40 hours per week. For 800 hours of work they'll give the club $6,000. I figure that the club would have to pay out approximately $9,000 in

---

★*Spiel* is a curling term to describe a tournament.

▌ *Exhibit 10*
**Proposed duties and
responsibilities of the
manager of the
Florenceville Curling
Club.**

1　To operate the club within the budget set down by the board of directors.
2　To supervise staff and ensure that required help is at hand to carry out any special functions.
3　To control incomes, expenditures, and inventories.
4　To utilize all ice available for rental.
5　To oversee the services provided by the kitchen and bar.
6　To promote activities within the club during the on and off season.
7　To ensure that the building and premises are well maintained.
8　To ensure proper records are kept; to keep committee chairpeople advised on progress made toward objectives; to advise the board of directors of committees' progress.
9　To see that sufficient supplies for the bar, kitchen, and building are on hand.
10　In coordination with the club treasurer, to ensure that the operating statement is made available to the board of directors.
11　To keep the board of directors informed of activities within the club.
12　To advise the board of directors or committee chairpeople of any deficiencies or wrongdoing, etc., of which they should be aware.
13　To select and train new staff members as required.
14　To meet all new members and give them guidance as required.
15　For each new curling season, to provide charts of different committees with corresponding chairpeople.
16　Provide posters, etc., to help members become aware of all future activities.
17　Advise committee chairpeople of special events and the financial and social results as soon as possible so chairpeople in turn can report to the board.
18　To control and inform prospective new curlers.
19　Coordinate the activities of committee chairpeople so as to avoid duplication of effort and misunderstandings.
20　Booking of the club for social functions; ensure the function is properly prepared.
21　Approve all expenditures and ensure that all income is accounted for.
22　Ensure all monies are properly deposited each day in the bank.
23　Make note of member and customer complaints, and advise committee chairpeople where necessary.

Source: Ray Brennan's rough notes, June 1989.

wages for the manager's first year. During the summer the manager could collect Unemployment Insurance benefits again.

"Bar profits have traditionally been in the 30 percent to 40 percent range. I estimate an extra $12,000 to $15,000 can be brought in during the first year with a manager. Since we'd only have to spend $9,000 ourselves, it would seem like a good deal."

The manager would really help to take more of the pressure off the other members," agreed Clayton.

Ray continued with his thoughts. "The second problem requiring attention is the way in which we plan things. Other than our financial statements, we have no record keeping so we really don't know what has worked in the past and what hasn't. New people come and go on the executive and we don't have any continuity of ideas. What advertising has been done in the past? Why was membership higher in 1984 than it is now? Why do people stop joining after several years? I don't know how we'd go about doing it, but I think we should put something down on paper; something we can look at from year to year, revise and use for planning the following year. Sometimes I feel we're running around in the dark when the light switch is close at hand. A proper analysis would surely help us to promote the club better; I don't think we've been nearly as effective as we could be. A club manager could play a major role in this process."

At the annual meeting in two weeks, Ray and Clayton would have to make the convincing argument that the future of the club depended upon their concrete recommendations to deal with these problems.

QUESTIONS

1 How are the operations of the Florenceville Curling Club similar to traditional profit-oriented businesses such as McCain Foods?
2 How would you evaluate the club's marketing performance to date?
3 What business is the FCC actually in?
4 What do you think about Ray Brennan's suggestion to hire a club manager?
5 What recommendations would you make in two weeks to the management team of the FCC?

TEXT CASE FOUR
Canadian Football League*

*T*he Canadian Football League (CFL) is the oldest professional football league in North America. Its history can be traced back to 1892. The league, as it exists today, broke loose from the amateur Canadian Rugby Union in 1958. But Canadian football is different from American football. The most notable differences are that the CFL has 12 men on the field per team, not 11; there are three downs instead of four; and the Canadian field is much larger than the American field. Unlike its American counterpart, the Canadian version of football offers a more wide open, often unpredictable style of play. The CFL went south of the border recently in an effort to obtain growth and to provide stability for the Canadian league. The big question was whether or not Americans would take to the CFL and accept the Canadian version of a "perceived" American game.

PREFACE TO US EXPANSION

Attendance at CFL games for three consecutive years averaged over 2 million fans. Regular-season television audiences on CBC and TSN averaged close to 600,000 in total, and the Grey Cup cham-

pionship game had over 2 million viewers, on average, over the three years. Still, the CFL has had a history of financial volatility. The historical poor financial performance of the league has created a perception or image problem for the CFL with various constituents, including sponsors, fans, and the media. The league is attempting to solve this problem through the implementation of tighter financial controls, including salary and spending caps within the league. In addition, the league is focussing on better event management to increase ticket sales and gross income at the gates. Better coordination between the league and local team ownership is being pursued, including relationships with the media. The goal is to put the league in a better position to secure sponsorship opportunities, attract more fans, and obtain better television contracts and new demand for franchises. The league is also involved in merchandising and licensing. Currently, over $6 million of CFL-licensed products are sold through licensee and retailer partnerships.

But first and foremost, the league believes that it must offer an excellent product to the fan. The league believes that by actively seeking expansion it can improve the product it offers as well as generate more revenues to help improve its financial position and its image. Thus, new team expansion is a cornerstone of the growth strategy being pursued by the league.

*The case is based on information supplied by the Canadian Football League. Used with permission.

THE EXPANSION TO THE UNITED STATES

The CFL had not expanded since 1954, with the entry of the British Columbia Lions. The league wanted to secure a franchise in Montreal to regain the original nine-team alignment. Other locations in Canada were also being considered, such as Halifax. But expansion into the United States was considered vital for the league if it was to grow and prosper in the future. The CFL believed there were several benefits that could be derived by expanding south of the border:

1 The new cities, partners, and expansion fees would increase the value of existing CFL franchises.
2 The new teams would help improve the perception of the product among fans, media, and sponsors.
3 The larger market would create opportunities for developing North American sponsors and North American television contracts.
4 There would be a reduction of costs on a pro rata basis to operate the league.
5 The fan base would be expanded.
6 The overall image of the CFL would improve.

CRITERIA FOR NEW CFL FRANCHISES

The league has targeted midsized cities, most with proximity to Canadian cities, that are unlikely to secure National Football League (NFL) franchises and are without professional big-league teams in other sports such as basketball or baseball. It is believed sports fans in such cities without other professional teams may more readily accept an imported version of the game of football. The CFL perceived a window of opportunity in the United States resulting from the demise of the World League Association of Football (WLAF). Presently, several cities that hosted WLAF teams are potentially ready to field professional football teams.

The league has several other criteria when evaluating potential franchises:

1 *Financial resources.* The ability to support the long-term commitment required to operate a sports franchise.

2 *Sports management expertise.* Because of the uniqueness of this business, it is preferable that potential franchises have either directly related experience or access to senior executives with this type of background.
3 *Local ownership and networking.* The league's experience has shown that local owners with strong networking capabilities usually have a superior chance of succeeding in the sports business.
4 *Stadium capacity.* Each applicant will be required to provide proof of the availability of a stadium with a seating capacity of 30,000 to 50,000.
5 *Sharing the vision of growth.* People with divergent objectives and agendas must strive for their personal success while participating in the big growth picture of the CFL.

The first US expansion team, the Sacramento Gold Miners, took the field in the 1993 season. This team had plenty of fan support playing out of Hornet Field on the campus of California State University, Sacramento. Three more teams—from Baltimore, Las Vegas, and Shreveport, Louisiana—joined the CFL for the 1994–95 season. But the question remains whether or not Canadian football can be effectively marketed in the United States. Interestingly enough, the CFL rule of having at least 20 Canadians on the 37-man roster was not enforceable in the United States, so the American-based teams can join the Canadian league with all-American rosters.

QUESTIONS

1 Essentially, the CFL has exported a differentiated style of football to the United States. How likely is it that American football fans will embrace this product?
2 An old marketing axiom is, If you build a better mousetrap, they'll beat a path to your door. One US sports reporter has suggested that the CFL brand of football is a "better mousetrap." Is this all that the CFL needs in order to make a successful expansion to the United States?
3 Comment on the league's criteria for evaluating potential franchises. What should be the most important things that the league looks for in a franchisee?
4 Not being able to enforce the Canadian content rule (20 Canadians on a 37-man roster) may be a blessing in disguise for the CFL expansion in the United States. Why?

TEXT CASE FIVE
Bookworms, Inc. *

*L*ate one August morning, Nancy Klein, co-owner of Bookworms, Inc., sat at her desk near the back wall of a cluttered office. With some irritation, she had just concluded that her nearby calculator could help no more. "What we still need," she thought to herself, "is estimates of demand and market share, but at least we have two weeks to get them."

Klein's office was located in the rear of Bookworms, Inc., an 1,800-square-foot bookstore specializing in quality paperbacks. The store carried over 10,000 titles and sold more than $520,000 worth of books. Titles were stocked in 18 categories, ranging from art, biography, and cooking to religion, sports, and travel.

Bookworms, Inc., was located in a small business district across the street from the boundary of Verdoon University (VU). VU currently enrolled about 12,000 undergraduate and graduate students majoring in the liberal arts, the sciences, and the professions. Despite national trends in enrollment, the VU admissions office had predicted that the number of entering students would grow at about 1 percent per year through the 1990s. The surrounding community, a city of about 350,000, was projected to grow at about twice that rate.

Bookworms, Inc., carried no texts, even though many of its customers were VU students. Both Klein and her partner, Susan Berman, felt that the VU bookstore had simply too firm a grip on the textbook market in terms of price, location, and reputation. Bookworms also no longer carried classical records, as of two months earlier. Klein recalled with discomfort the $15,000 or so they had lost attempting to market them. "Another mistake like that and the bank will be running Bookworms," she thought. "And, despite what Susan thinks, the copy service could just be that final mistake."

The idea for a copy service had come from Susan Berman. She had seen the candy store next door to Bookworms (under the same roof) go out of business in July. She had immediately asked the building's owner, Ed Anderson, about the future of the 800-square-foot space. Upon learning it was available, she had met with Klein to discuss her idea for the copy service. She had spoken excitedly about the opportunity: "It can't help but make money. I could work there part time and the rest of the time we could hire students. We could call it 'Copycats' and even use a sign with the same kind of letters as we do in 'Bookworms.' I'm sure we could get Ed to knock the wall out between the two stores, if you think it would be a good idea. Probably we could rent most of the copying equipment, so there's not much risk."

Klein was not so sure. A conversation the previous day with Anderson had disclosed his desire for a five-year lease (with an option to renew) at $1,000 per month. He had promised to hold the offer open for two weeks before attempting to lease the space to anyone else. Representatives from copying-equipment firms had estimated that charges would run between $200 and $2,000 per month, depending on equipment, service, and whether the equipment was bought or leased. The copy service would also have other fixed costs for utilities, interest, insurance, and the inventory (and perhaps equipment). Klein concluded that the service would begin to make a profit at about 20,000 copies per month under the best-case assumptions, and at about 60,000 copies per month under the worst-case assumptions.

Further informal investigation had identified two major competitors. One was the copy centre located in the Krismann Library on the west side of the campus, a mile away. The other was a private firm, Kinko's, located on the south side of the campus, also one mile away. Both offered service while you wait, on several machines. The library's price was about ½ cent per copy higher than Kinko's. Both offered collating, binding, colour copying, and other services, all on a seven-days-a-week schedule.

Actually, investigation had discovered that a third major "competitor" consisted of the VU de-

*This case was written by Professor J. E. Nelson, University of Colorado at Boulder. Used with permission.

partmental machines scattered throughout the campus. Most faculty and administrative copying was done on these machines, but students were allowed the use of some, at cost. In addition, at least 20 self-service machines could be found in the library and in nearby drugstores, grocery stores, and banks.

Moving aside a stack of books on her desk, Nancy Klein picked up the telephone and dialled her partner. When Berman answered, Klein asked, "Susan, have you any idea how many copies a student might make in a semester? I mean, according to my figures, we would break even somewhere between 20,000 and 60,000 copies per month. I don't know if this is half the market or what."

"You know, I have no idea," Berman answered. "I suppose when I was going to school I probably made 10 copies a month—for articles, class notes, old tests, and so on."

"Same here," Klein said. "But some graduate students must have done that many each week. You know, I think we ought to do some marketing research before we go much further on this. What do you think?"

"Sure. Only it can't take much time or money. What do you have in mind, Nancy?"

"Well, we could easily interview our customers as they leave the store and ask them how many copies they've made in the past week or so. Of course, we'd have to make sure they were students."

"What about a telephone survey?" Berman asked. "That way we can have a random sample. We would still ask about the number of copies, but now we would know for sure they would be students."

"Or what about interviewing students in the union cafeteria? There's always a good-sized line there around noon, as I remember, and this might be even quicker."

"Boy, I just don't know. Why don't I come in this afternoon and we can talk about it some more?"

"Good idea," Klein responded. "Between the two of us, we should be able to come up with something."

QUESTIONS

1 What sources of information should Klein and Berman use?
2 How should Klein and Berman gather data?
3 What questions should they ask?
4 How should they sample?

TEXT CASE SIX
Honeywell, Inc., Optoelectronics Division

After several years of developing fibre optic technology for the US Department of Defense projects, executives in the Optoelectronics Division of Honeywell, Inc., decided to pursue commercial applications for their products and technology. The task would not be easy, because fibre optics was a new technology that many firms would find unfamiliar. Fibre optics is the technology of transmitting light through long, thin, flexible fibres of glass, plastic, or other transparent materials. In its chief commercial applications, a light source emits infrared light flashes corresponding to data. Millions of light flashes per second send streams through a transparent fibre. A light sensor at the other end of the fibre "reads" the data transmitted. It is esti-

mated that sales of fibre optic technology could exceed $2 billion in 1992. Almost half the dollar sales volume would come from telecommunications, about 25 percent from government or military purchases, and about 25 percent from commercial applications in computers, robotics, cable TV, and other products.

Interest in adapting fibre optic technology and products for commercial applications had prompted Honeywell executives to carefully review buying behaviour associated with the adoption of a new technology. The buying process appeared to contain at least six phases: need recognition, identification of available products, comparison with existing technology, vendor or seller evaluation, the decision itself, and follow-up on technology performance. Moreover, there appeared to be several people within the buying organization who would play a role in the adoption of a new technology. For example, top management (such as the president and executive vice presidents) would certainly be involved. Engineering and operations management (e.g., vice presidents of engineering and manufacturing) and design engineers (e.g., people who develop specifications for new products) would also play a major role. Purchasing personnel would have a say in such a decision and particularly in the vendor-evaluation process. The role played by each person in the buying organization was still unclear to Honeywell. It seemed that engineering management personnel could slow the adoption of fibre optics if they did not feel it was appropriate for the products made by the company. Design engineers, who would actually apply fibre optics in product design, might be favourably or unfavourably disposed to the technology, depending on whether they knew how to use it. Top management personnel would participate in any final decisions to use fibre optics and could generate interest in the technology if stimulated to do so.

This review of buying behaviour led to questions about how to penetrate a company's buying organization and have fibre optics used in the company's products. Although Honeywell was a large, well-known company with annual sales exceeding $5 billion, its fibre optic technology capability was much less familiar. Therefore the executives thought it was necessary to establish Honeywell's credibility in fibre optics. This was done, in part, through an advertising image campaign that featured Honeywell Optoelectronics as a leader in fibre optics.

QUESTIONS

1 What type of buying situation is involved in the purchase of fibre optics, and what important buying criteria will be used by companies considering using fibre optics in their products?

2 Describe the purchase decision process for adopting fibre optics, and state how members in the buying centre for this technology might play a part in this process.

3 What effect will perceived risk have on a company's decision whether to use fibre optics in its products?

4 What role does the image advertising campaign play in Honeywell Optoelectronics' efforts to market fibre optics?

TEXT CASE SEVEN
Hasbro, Inc. ★

*H*ow does a toy company become number one in an industry marked by fads? Just ask the executives

★Based on "Hasbro's Hopes for Maxie Model Come to an End," *The Wall Street Journal,* February 12, 1990, p. B4; "For Video Games, Now It's a Battle of Bits," *The Wall Street Journal,* January 9, 1990, pp. B1, B4; "Barbie Is on the Front Line for Marketing Ethnic Dolls," *Dallas Times Herald,* August 30, 1990, pp. D1, D4; "It's Kid Brother's Turn to Keep Hasbro Hot," *Business Week,* June 26, 1989, pp. 152–53; "Toyland Turnaround," *Forbes,* January 9, 1989, pp. 168–69; A. Stone, "Toy Fair No Picnic for Toy Industry," *USA Today,* February 8, 1988, pp. B1–B2; A. Hagedorn, "Toy Firms Search for Next Blockbuster," *The Wall Street Journal,* September 12, 1986, p. 23; S. Weiner, "If a Toy Flops, It Can Be Tough Explaining Why," *The Wall Street Journal,* September 12, 1986, p. 23; L. M. Watkins, "Tapping Hot Markets: Toys Aimed at Minority Children," *The Wall Street Journal,* September 12, 1986, p. 23; "How Hasbro Became King of the Toymakers," *Business Week,* September 22, 1986, pp. 90–92; and "Marketing," *The New Yorker,* February 23, 1987, pp. 28–29.

at Hasbro, Inc., a market leader with worldwide sales of $1.4 billion and $100 million in profits. Recognizing that toy companies must replace 60 percent of their toy volume each year with new products, and that 80 percent of new toys introduced each year are failures, Hasbro executives know that the secret lies in deft product development.

HASBRO PRODUCT DEVELOPMENT AND MARKETING

Hasbro, Inc., looks for three qualities in new products: lasting play value, the ability to be shared with other children, and the ability to stimulate a child's imagination. In addition, the company provides different toys for the various stages of a child's development. Beginning with items for infants and preschool children, it also has toys and games for pre-adolescents of both sexes, and some adults (e.g., the game Scruples).

For example, preschool toys include Glo Worm and Teach Me Reader, young boys' toys include action figures like Transformers and G.I. Joe, and young girls have items such as My Little Pony. In addition, Hasbro markets stuffed toys like Yakity Yaks and Watchimals and games and puzzles including Candyland and Bed Bugs. An element of the company's marketing strategy includes reaching mothers at the time of the child's birth, for infant toys. As the child develops, toys such as G.I. Joe are promoted through Saturday morning cartoon shows where complementary toys (e.g., aircraft carriers) are advertised.

However, even Hasbro found it difficult to compete against Mattel, Inc.'s, Barbie doll for young girls. Two entries, Jem and Maxie, were both dropped after disappointing sales. Similarly, Hasbro's investment of $20 million in its Nemo video game, designed to compete against Nintendo, proved to be a failure.

TOY INDUSTRY

The toy industry produces an estimated $13 billion in sales annually. This figure has remained largely unchanged in recent years. A percentage breakdown of volume by toy category, excluding video games and children's books, is shown in Exhibit 1.

According to the editor of *Toy & Hobby World,* a trade publication, the toy industry is a "hit-driven business." Recent hits include Cabbage Patch Kids by Coleco, which produced estimated sales of $600 million in 1985 but fell to an estimated $115 million in 1987. Teddy Ruxpin, made by Worlds of Wonder, Inc., was the hit of 1986 and 1987. However, hits can quickly become disasters. For example, video games and software produced sales of $3.1 billion in 1982; 1985 sales were nearly zero. Video games rebounded again to $3.5 billion in 1990, with the popularity of Nintendo.

| Exhibit 1
Percentage of industry sales by toy category.

CATEGORY	PERCENTAGE OF MARKET
Dolls and action figures	31.6
Games and puzzles	11.6
Preschool and infant toys	10.1
Activity toys	9.5
Toy vehicles	9.0
Riding toys	8.6
Stuffed toys	7.6
Arts and crafts	4.2
Other	7.8
Total	100.0

Source: A. Hagedorn, "Toy Firms Search for Next Blockbuster," *The Wall Street Journal,* September 12, 1986, p. 23.

The search for hit products has resulted in the production of technologically advanced toys in recent years. These include Teddy Ruxpin-like talking toys and Lazer Tag (also produced by Worlds of Wonder, Inc.), where opponents shoot at one another with infrared light-emitting guns. Creating a hit also involves making large marketing expenditures. It is estimated that a full-scale introduction of a major toy requires $5 million to $10 million in advertising, plus $12 million to $15 million to produce a cartoon show featuring the toy or character.

In recent years, some toy companies have focussed on specific children. For example, some firms have recently produced Black, Hispanic, and Asian dolls and action figures to reach previously untapped buyers. Over 54 million (10 percent of the dolls' total volume) Black Cabbage Patch Kids have been sold since 1983. Other firms have produced dolls for disabled children. Mattel, for example, markets the Hal's Pals line, which includes a girl with leg braces and a cane and a boy in a wheelchair. The company donates the proceeds from Hal's Pals sales to disabled-children groups.

QUESTIONS

1 How do toy markets, including Hasbro, apply concepts from consumer behaviour in the marketing of toys?

2 What variables might be used to segment the toy market?

3 What might a product–market grid for Hasbro look like, and where are new product–market opportunities for the company?

4 What are your thoughts on the subject of marketing Lazer Tag, ethnic dolls and action figures, and dolls of disabled children?

TEXT CASE EIGHT
Field Furniture Enterprises

*E*dward Meadows, president of Field Furniture Enterprises, met with representatives of Kelly, Astor, & Peters Advertising (KAP) and Andrew Reed, Field's vice-president of marketing and sales, to discuss the company's advertising program for 1994. The KAP representatives recommended that Field Furniture increase its advertising in magazines (such as *Good Housekeeping* and *Better Homes and Gardens,* which feature home improvement ideas and new ideas in home decorating) by $250,000 and maintain the expenditures for other promotional efforts at a constant level during 1994. The rationale given for the increase in advertising was that Field Furniture had low name recognition among prospective buyers of furniture and it intended to introduce new styles of living and dining room furniture. Reed, however, had a different opinion as to how Field Furniture should spend the $250,000. He thought it was necessary to hire additional salespeople to call on the 30 new retail stores to be added by the company in 1994, increase the funds devoted to cooperative advertising, and improve the selling aids given to retail stores and salespeople.

THE COMPANY

Field Furniture is a medium-size manufacturer of medium- to high-priced living and dining room furniture. Sales in 1993 were $50 million. The company sells its furniture through 1,000 furniture stores nationwide, but not all stores carry the company's entire line. This fact bothered Meadows because, in his words, "If they ain't got it, they can't sell it!" The company employs 10 full-time salespeople, who receive a $40,000 base salary annually

and a small commission on sales. A company sales force is atypical in the furniture industry, since most furniture manufacturers use selling agents or manufacturer's representatives who carry a wide assortment of noncompeting furniture lines and receive a commission on sales. "Having our own sales group is a policy my father established 30 years ago," noted Meadows, "and we've been quite successful having people who are committed to our company. Our people don't just take furniture orders. They are expected to motivate retail salespeople to sell our line, assist in setting up displays in stores, coordinate cooperative advertising plans, and give advice on a variety of matters to our retailers and their salespeople."

In 1993, Field spent $2.45 million for total promotional expenditures, excluding the salary of the vice-president of marketing and sales. Promotional expenditures were categorized into four groups: sales expense and administration, cooperative advertising programs with retailers, trade promotions, and consumer advertising. Cooperative advertising allowances are usually spent on newspaper advertising in a retailer's city and are matched by the retailer's funds on a dollar-for-dollar basis. Trade promotion is directed toward retailers and takes the form of catalogues, trade magazine advertisements, booklets for consumers, and point-of-purchase materials such as displays for use in retail stores. Also included in this category is the expense of trade shows. Field Furniture is represented at two trade shows a year. Consumer advertising is directed to potential consumers through magazines. The typical format used in consumer advertising is to highlight new furniture and different living and dining room arrangements. Dollar allocation for each program in 1993 was as follows:

PROMOTIONAL PROGRAM	EXPENDITURE
Sales expense and administration	$ 612,500
Cooperative advertising	1,102,500
Trade advertising	306,250
Consumer advertising	428,750
Total	$2,450,000

THE INDUSTRY

The household wooden furniture industry includes hundreds of firms creating a fragmented market such that no one firm dominates the marketplace. Ontario and Quebec are the major furniture-producing areas. Industry sales were estimated at $1 billion.

The buying and selling of furniture to retail outlets centres on manufacturers' expositions at selected times and places around the country. At these marts, as they are called in the furniture industry, retail buyers view manufacturers' lines and often make buying commitments for their stores. However, Field Furniture's experience has shown that sales efforts in the retail store by company representatives account for as much as half the company's sales in a given year. The major manufacturer expositions are held in October and April. Regional expositions are also scheduled in June through August.

Company research on consumer furniture-buying behaviour indicated that people visit several stores when shopping for furniture and the final decision is made jointly by a husband and wife in about 90 percent of furniture purchases. Other noteworthy findings are:

- Eighty-four percent of buyers believe "the higher the price, the higher the quality" when buying home furnishings.
- Seventy-two percent of buyers browse or window-shop in furniture stores even if they don't need furniture.
- Eighty-five percent read furniture ads before they actually need furniture.

- Ninety-nine percent agree with the statement, "When shopping for furniture and home furnishings, I like the salesperson to show me what alternatives are available, answer my questions, and leave me alone so I can think about it and maybe browse around."
- Ninety-five percent get redecorating ideas from magazines.
- Forty-one percent have written for a manufacturer's booklet.
- Sixty-three percent need decorating advice for "putting it all together."

BUDGETARY ISSUES

After the KAP Advertising representatives made their presentation, Reed again emphasized that the incremental $250,000 should not be spent for consumer advertising. He noted that Field Furniture had set as an objective that each salesperson would make six calls per year at each store and spend at least four hours at each store on every call. "Given that our salespeople work a 40-hour week, 48 weeks per year, and devote only 80 percent of their time to selling due to travel time between stores, we already aren't doing the sales job," Reed added. Meadows agreed but reminded Reed that the $250,000 increment in the promotional budget was a maximum the company could spend, given other cost increases.

QUESTIONS

1 How might you describe furniture buying using the purchase decision process described in Chapter 6
2 How might each of the elements of the promotional program influence each stage in the purchase decision process?
3 What should Field's promotional objectives be?
4 How many salespeople does Field need to adequately service its accounts?
5 Should Field Furniture emphasize a push or a pull promotional strategy? Why?

TEXT CASE NINE
International Playtex, Inc. *

Will a single advertising campaign work in 12 separate countries? Executives at International Playtex, Inc., believe it will, at least for the Playtex WOW brand brassiere.

International Playtex, Inc., is one of the world's largest manufacturers of women's intimate apparel and personal care products. Company sales were $1.2 billion, of which intimate apparel accounted for $375 million. It is estimated that the company captures between 16 and 17 percent of the brassiere segment of the intimate apparel–undergarment category of women's clothing. Fully one-half of the company's sales of intimate apparel came from overseas markets.

Playtex is the leading advertiser of brassieres in the world. It accounts for 40 percent of the total media expenditures spent in the brassiere segment of the intimate apparel–undergarment category.

Coordinating an international advertising program for Playtex is not an easy task. In the past, Playtex managers and advertising agencies developed and executed advertising campaigns for individual countries. At one point, Playtex had 43 separate and distinct advertising campaigns running throughout the world at the same time. This practice proved to be costly. Moreover, as Playtex moved to streamline its international operations, it consolidated its advertising agency roster and awarded its worldwide advertising account to Grey Advertising, Inc., one of the world's largest advertising agencies. The WOW brand brassiere campaign would be the first global campaign assigned to Grey Advertising.

The WOW brand was the product of three years of research and development. The brand contained a new plastic that replaced wires that were used for support and shape. This feature would become the centrepiece of the global campaign because comfort, support, and shape had universal appeal to all women, according to one Grey Advertising executive.

The first step in developing the global campaign was selecting female models with universal appeal. After viewing dozens of models, three were selected—one blonde and two brunettes. These three models would be featured in commercials shown around the world.

Campaign implementation would involve dealing with a variety of specific circumstances. First, Playtex would have to overcome language differences. For example, the WOW brand would be called *Traumbügel* (dream wire) in German and *Alas* (wings) in Spanish. Addressing unique preferences of women would also have to be considered in presenting the brand. French women prefer lacy brassieres; American women prefer plain opaque styles. Adapting to governmental regulations and TV commercial standards in different countries would be a third hurdle. For instance, the commercial for Australia had to be produced in Australia, since Australian TV would show only locally produced commercials. In South Africa, TV standards precluded women from modelling bras; therefore fully clothed models would have to simply hold the item. Production constraints would be present as well. Again as a result of country differences, some commercials could be 30 seconds while others would be limited to 20 seconds. In addition, some countries required one second of no sound at the beginning of a commercial, while others did not.

QUESTIONS

1 Where would you place the WOW brand marketing strategy on a continuum from a pure globalization approach to a pure customized approach? Why?

2 Which environmental factors described in Chapters 5 and 23 would help or hinder a global marketing strategy for women's intimate apparel like that sold by Playtex?

3 What is the likelihood for success of the WOW brand marketing strategy? Why?

*Sources: Based on "Maintaining Modesty in Bra Commercials Is a Snap," *Ad Week*, May 4, 1987, p. 23; "Playtex Kicks Off a One-Ad-Fits-All Campaign," *Business Week*, December 16, 1985, pp. 48–49; and P. Sloan, "Smilow Moves to Keep Playtex in Top Position," *Advertising Age*, March 30, 1987, p. 3.

TEXT CASE TEN
Chalaga Mussel Farms*

*I*n July of 1994, mussel farmer Malcolm Wilson was examining the mussel industry in Atlantic Canada. As a mussel farmer, he was concerned about competition from two areas. One was the United States, particularly Maine, since it appeared to control the low end of the market. The other was Prince Edward Island where "Island Blue" Mussels were positioned at the high end of the market. Wilson was searching for an appropriate strategy that would make Chalaga Mussel Farms more competitive.

MALCOLM WILSON'S BACKGROUND IN MUSSEL FARMING

Malcolm Wilson worked part-time for a small mussel farming operation in Newfoundland in the late 1980s while attending the Marine Institute in St. John's. He quickly saw potential for the mussel industry and conducted some secondary research on the industry. His findings indicated that there was a future in owning and operating a mussel farm. However, he realized that several marketing issues needed to be given careful attention. For example, Wilson felt that Newfoundland was not a viable location, since there were difficulties with respect to distribution that, in turn, affected marketability. Wilson particularly wanted to enter the Minneapolis market since a previous visit to that region had been encouraging.

In January 1992, he relocated to Halifax, Nova Scotia, and he and a partner, who had some previous entrepreneurial experience, bought some mussels and equipment and started Chalaga Mussel Farms on the eastern shore of Nova Scotia.

Chalaga Mussel Farms was a small operation, and the two partners realized that they needed an increased sales volume in order to survive in an increasingly competitive marketplace. They felt that a steady supply of good-quality mussels was necessary for survival and to enhance market share. However, distribution posed a problem. One way to improve profit margins would be for them to own their own processing plant to clean, grade, and bag mussels, since this would permit them to market directly instead of being required to sell to others who had the ability to process.

The growing cycle of mussels requires approximately two years before the product can go to market, and Chalaga Mussel Farms needed to develop appropriate inventory and distribution channels in order to be competitive. By June, 1993 Chalaga Mussel Farms had begun production on a larger scale and was also examining distribution and pricing strategies. Chalaga Mussel Farms bought the appropriate equipment and set up a processing plant.

By late 1993 Chalaga Mussel Farms had sold 175,000 pounds of mussels directly to supermarkets, local brokers, and brokers in Quebec City, Montreal, and Toronto. The operation began to show a small profit and plans were made to increase production by 15 to 25 percent a year over the next three years.

Wilson was convinced that he would continue working in the mussel farm business and felt that having the right products in the right markets was the key to success. He then began to seek out more information on the mussel industry in Canada and the United States.

RESEARCH ON THE MUSSEL INDUSTRY

Wilson obtained several consulting reports, book and magazine articles on the mussel industry, and information from the Department of Fisheries and Oceans and *Canadian Aquaculture* magazine. To supplement his secondary research, Wilson conducted several interviews with mussel growers, brokers, and retailers in Canada and the United States, and conducted focus groups with pertinent individuals from Newfoundland, Nova Scotia, and Prince Edward Island who were knowledgeable about the mussel industry.

Data concerning mussel meat yield varied, but Wilson came up with an average percentage: whole mussel meats (16 percent recoverable yield) and broken meats (2 percent recoverable yield). Broken meats are often thrown away, but Wilson felt that they could be used for chowders and soups in the food service or institutional markets. From his research, Wilson decided that priority should be given to the development and expansion of Chalaga Mussel Farms product line, for example, whole meats could be individually quick frozen (IQF) or sold in 1 pound block form; a mussel salad could be developed to compete with other mussel salads currently on the market, such as Limfjord and Marina; smoked mussels could also be considered to compete with M'Lord brand; a yogourt pairing campaign might be undertaken (in Europe, cream based and yogourt based mussel salads are common), and recipes developed that paired mussel salad with yogourt.

The information Wilson gathered generally segmented the mussel market in three ways: geographically (United States and Canadian cities, Europe), by product type (wild, long-line cultured, and bottom-cultivated), and by sector (institutional or food service and restaurants versus consumer or retail); overall, 75 percent of fresh mussel product goes to the food service sector and 25 percent to the retail sector.

The volume consumed by the food service sector versus that consumed by the retail sector varied considerably by city. According to one of the studies that Wilson had reviewed, markets with a large retail sector volume offered good opportunities to long-line mussel growers because the retail sector catered to sophisticated consumers who could distinguish between the different types of mussels.

Another study suggested that the growth in North American demand for mussels in the 1980s could in part be traced to the dietary preferences of yuppies: mussels were high in protein, low in calories and cholesterol, and were considered "chic" to eat. Mussel consumption was clustered around large North American cities (see Exhibits 1 and 3). Growth was anticipated in the restaurant sector of these cities, because mussels were trendy and the high mark-up, particularly if bottom-cultivated mussels were used, made it attractive to restaurant managers. The retail trade was expected to have much slower growth.

The Canadian market, by industry sector, consisted of approximately 70 percent in the food service industry (mainly restaurants) and 30 percent in the retail trade (supermarkets, etc.). The retail trade was directed mainly at ethnic populations residing in large cities. The type of mussel consumed varied from city to city (see Exhibit 1).

Even though Quebec purchased a good deal of Prince Edward Island mussels, the 'Buy Quebec' preferential purchase policies limited the market

CITY	TONNAGE/YEAR	OTHER PERCENT	BOTTOM CULTIVATED PERCENT	LONG-LINE CULTURED PERCENT
Montreal	850	50	15	35
Quebec City	300	40	20	40
Ottawa	220	25	50	25
Toronto	810	10	75	15
Vancouver	220	10	55	35
City Total	2,400			

▌*Exhibit 1*
1994 Canadian market—institutional and retail combined selected cities—percent breakdown by city.

Source: Market Analysis Group (1994), Department of Fisheries and Oceans and estimates.

**❚ Exhibit 2
Price per pound.★
(1994).**

	WILD	CULTIVATED	LONG-LINE CULTURED		
			PEI	NFLD.	NS.
Wholesale	N/A	.35	1.20	.91	.95
Retail	N/A	.49	1.49	1.59	1.39

★All prices in Canadian dollars. Prices obtained from survey of wholesalers and retailers. Seasonal price fluctuations were wide.

potential. Other market segments Wilson considered were "value-added" products and export markets. Even though transportation costs limited the potential of these markets, Wilson knew that "Island Blues" were already being flown to Los Angeles and other US cities. He had to find a way to distribute his product more economically. Government research indicated that Europe was a mature market with few prospects for export; however, Wilson felt that there was still potential in Europe, particularly in the Baltic States and the Moscow region of Russia.

MUSSEL PROCESSING

There are basically three types of mussels marketed: long-line cultured, bottom-cultivated, and wild. Since the marketing approach for each type of mussel varied, Wilson had to pay particular attention to the different growing methods.

Chalaga Mussel Farms used the long-line suspension method of growing cultured mussels. This method involves the suspension of mussel "seed," small mussels from intertidal zones, stuffed in "socks" about three meters long. The socks are suspended on a line supported by buoys at the surface and attached to the bottom by weights. Fresh whole mussels are brought to the processing plant, which often houses two separate processing areas in one building: primary processing (fresh product) and secondary processing (value-added product). Tote boxes are used to carry the mussels with approximately 80 to 100 pounds per box.

The first stage of production includes declumping, grading, and debyssing. The mussels are manually shoveled into a hopper that leads to the

declumper, where they are drum rotated to break up the clumps. Next, they are separated by use of a bar grader and carried by conveyor belt to the debysser, constantly being sprayed with water during this process. The mussels are then debyssed and are put back in tote boxes while awaiting further processing or packaging for the fresh market.

Secondary processing requires that the mussels be cooked in a large steam kettle. This takes place in a separate area of the plant and here approximately 80 to 100 pounds are steamed for about 15 minutes per kettle load. The cooked mussels are then dumped on to a shaker that vibrates rapidly, thereby separating the meat from the shell. Mussel meats are then collected and placed in a tub of salted water where the meats float and the shells and other debris sink to the bottom. Finally, the mussel meats can be either marinated for a retail mussel salad product or stored in a chill room for later processing.

Compared to other types of mussels, the long-line mussel is cleaner (no pearls or grit), has a nicer shell and a higher meat yield. The market price for these mussels tends to be higher than the price for wild or bottom-cultivated mussels (see Exhibit 2).

In 1989, the Department of Fisheries and Oceans conducted some research on growing methods that Wilson considered very promising for long-line growers. New methods could improve growing yields and increase the industry margin of long-line cultured mussels between 30 and 35 percent at current wholesale prices.

Wild mussels were harvested from in-shore areas using bottom dredges. The mussels were then picked by hand from the dredged material. Like bottom-cultivated mussels, wild mussels had a re-

CITY	TONNAGE/YEAR	OTHER PERCENT	BOTTOM CULTIVATED PERCENT	LONG-LINE CULTURED PERCENT
New York	3,200	7	83	10
LA	450	2	93	5
Chicago	450	8	88	4
Atlanta	240	6	81	3
Seattle	265	N/A	50	50
Total	4,605			

■ *Exhibit 3*
1994 US—institutional and retail combined selected cities—percent breakdown by city.

Source: Market Analysis Group (1994), Department of Fisheries and Oceans and estimates.

duced meat yield and a higher content of sand and pearls than long-line cultured mussels. Quebec consumed a high proportion of wild mussels.

Once harvested, all mussel types had a shelf life of 7 to 14 days if properly stored. They had to be processed for market (cleaning, sorting, etc.) and handled carefully during transport. Mussels shipments usually constituted part of a mixed truckload of seafood products.

From his interviews with retailers, Wilson discovered that even though its shell appeared cleaner and the meat yield appeared higher to the average consumer, the long-line cultured mussel was difficult to distinguish from the wild mussel and the bottom cultivated mussel whether in or out of the shell.

US MARKETS

In 1993, the United States food service sector accounted for approximately 80 percent of mussel demand, while the retail sector accounted for 20 percent. The type of mussel consumed also varied from city to city (see Exhibit 3).

CANADIAN SUPPLY

In 1993, Canada supplied only between 2 and 3 percent of the world's mussels. In 1993, 2,885 tonnes of mussels (mostly long-line mussels) were produced in Canada. Exports represented 20 per-

cent, or 577 tonnes. In addition, 800 tonnes were imported from the United States. Almost all of the imported mussels were bottom-cultivated mussels. Most of the Canadian supply of mussels came from Atlantic Canada, but there were problems with distribution and not only to Canadian destinations. Canadian west coast production still faced technical difficulties.

Wilson had seen the mussel industry grow at a fast rate. He knew that the United States and Canadian markets were large, but he also felt that he was missing out on many other opportunities for export. A biologist's report mentioned that the environmental conditions in the Atlantic region could lead to a long-line cultured mussel capacity of 50,000 tonnes a year. This figure could double if bottom cultivated methods were considered.

US SUPPLY

Bottom cultivated mussels grown by Maine companies dominated the US mussel market. Maine mussels also had a strong presence in the Canadian market. In 1987, US growers produced 17,000 tonnes of mussels. Recent developments in Maine concerned Wilson—bottom-cultivating had been the prevalent growing method in the industry, but some growers were experimenting with long-line technology in anticipation of a more educated and demanding consumer. Most of the 20 US producers were on the east coast and four major operations (three in Maine) dominated the industry.

THE MUSSEL SCARE

Since 1989, mussel farming has been an industry plagued by inconsistent quality standards, seasonal supply, environmental hazards, and problems of mussel toxicity. The efforts of most of the private growers and producers who Wilson knew of, were directed towards preventing a repeat of the crisis of December 1987, when two deaths and 134 cases of illness were attributed to toxic molluscs from Prince Edward Island. On the United States east coast, the "Red Tide" (a marine condition that makes mussels toxic) had created havoc in the mollusc industry. Even though water temperature and other environmental conditions made the Red Tide a threat to Prince Edward Island waters but not to Nova Scotian waters, consumers assumed that all Atlantic products were at risk.

Industry self-regulation and government authorities had made improvements in quality control. The federal government had revamped its Shellfish Monitoring Program that included testing of water quality by Environment Canada, testing of the product by the Department of Fisheries and Oceans, and policing of growing areas by various agencies in order to prevent harvesting in closed areas. Wilson was prepared to support these activities. But, he also needed to make decisions about what products and what markets to pursue.

QUESTIONS

1   What type of products (growing methods) should be adopted by Chalaga Mussel Farms?
2   What markets should be pursued?
3   What pricing strategy must be adopted, given the products and markets that are selected?

Glossary

above-, at-, or below-market pricing Pricing based on what the market price is.

account management policies Policies that specify whom salespeople should contact, what kinds of selling and customer service activities should be engaged in, and how these activities should be carried out.

accumulated wealth Assets accumulated by households in the form of real property, financial securities, deposits, and pension funds.

action item list An aid to implementing a market plan, consisting of three columns: (1) the task, (2) the name of the person responsible for completing the task, and (3) the date by which the task is to be finished.

adaptive selling A need-satisfaction sales presentation involving adjusting the presentation to fit the selling situation.

advertising Any directly paid form of nonpersonal communication about an organization, good, service, or idea by an identified sponsor.

advocacy advertisements Institutional advertisements that state the position of a company on an issue.

all you can afford budgeting Allocating funds to advertising only after all other budget items are covered.

anchor stores Well-known national or regional stores that are located in regional shopping centres.

annual marketing plans Plans that deal with the marketing goals and strategies for a product, product line, or entire firm for a single year.

approach stage In the personal selling process, the initial meeting between the salesperson and the prospect, where the objectives are to gain the prospect's attention, stimulate interest, and build the foundation for the sales presentation.

attitudes Learned predispositions to respond to an object or a class of objects in a consistent manner.

average revenue The average amount of money received for selling one unit of a product.

baby boomers The generation of Canadians born between 1946 and 1964.

back translation The practice of retranslating a word or phrase into the original language by a different interpreter to catch errors.

balance of trade The difference between the monetary value of a nation's exports and imports.

barriers to entry Business practices or conditions that make it difficult for a new firm to enter the market.

barter The practice of exchanging goods and services for other goods and services rather than for money.

basing-point pricing Selecting one or more geographic locations (basing points) from which the list prices for products plus freight expenses are charged to buyers.

beliefs A consumer's subjective perception of how well a product or brand performs on different attributes; these are based on personal experience, advertising, and discussions with other people.

bidders list A list of firms believed to be qualified to supply a given item.

blended family Two families from prior marriages merged into a single household as spouses remarry.

blocked currency Currency that a government will not allow to be converted into other currencies.

boycott In international trade, the refusal by the government of one country to have dealings with another country, often to express disapproval for past actions.

brand equity The added value a given brand name provides a product beyond the product's functional benefits.

brand extension The practice of using a current brand name to enter a completely different product class.

brand loyalty A favourable attitude toward and consistent purchase of a single brand over time.

brand manager (see product manager)

brand name Any word or device (design, shape, sound, or colour) that is used to distinguish one company's products from a competitor's.

branding Activity in which an organization uses a name, phrase, design, or symbol, or a combination of these, to identify its products and distinguish them from those of a competitor.

breadth of product line The variety of different items a store or wholesaler carries.

break-even analysis An analysis of the relationship between total revenue and total cost to determine profitability at various levels of output.

break-even chart A graphic presentation of a break-even analysis.

break-even point (BEP) Output quantity at which total revenue and total cost are equal and beyond which profit occurs.

bribery The practice of giving or promising something of value in return for a corrupt act.

brokers Channel intermediaries that do not take title to merchandise and make their profits from commissions and fees by negotiating contracts or deals between buyers and sellers.

buildup forecast Summing the sales forecasts of each of the components to arrive at a total forecast.

bundle pricing The marketing of two or more products in a single "package" price.

business (see organization's business definition)

business analysis Stage of the new product process in which the features of the product are specified together with the marketing strategy needed to commercialize it and the necessary financial projections are made.

business audit The internal aspect of a situation analysis when conducted at the corporate level.

business culture The effective rules of the game within a company: the boundaries between competitive and unethical behaviour, and the codes of conduct in business dealings.

business firm A privately owned organization that serves its customers in order to earn a profit.

business marketing The marketing of goods and services to commercial enterprises, governments, and other profit and not-for-profit organizations for use in the creation of goods and services that they then produce and market to other business customers as well as individuals and ultimate consumers.

business portfolio analysis Analysis of a firm's strategic business units (SBUs) as though they were a collection of separate investments.

buy classes Groups of three specific buying situations organizations face: new buy, straight rebuy, and modified rebuy.

buying centre The group of persons within an organization who participate in the buying process and share common goals, risks, and knowledge important to that process.

buying objectives Goals set by the participants in the buying process to help them achieve their organization's goals; for a business firm, usually to increase profits through reducing costs or increasing revenues.

capacity management Managing the demand for a service so that it is available to consumers.

cash-and-carry wholesaler A limited-service merchant wholesaler that takes title to merchandise but sells only to buyers who call on it and pay cash for and transport their own merchandise.

category killers Specialty discount outlets that focus on one product category such as electronics or business supplies at very competitive prices.

cause-related marketing Tying the charitable contributions of a firm directly to the customer revenues produced through the promotion of one of its products.

caveat emptor A Latin term that means "let the buyer beware."

census metropolitan area (CMA) A geographic area with a continuous labour market of 100,000 or more people.

central business district The oldest retail setting; the community's downtown area.

channel captain A marketing channel member that coordinates, directs, and supports other channel members: may be a manufacturer, wholesaler, or retailer.

cluster sample A sample selected by dividing the population under study into groups or subgroups and then drawing a random sample of the groups.

code of ethics An organization's formal statement of its ethical principles and rules of conduct.

cognitive dissonance The feeling of postpurchase psychological tension or anxiety a consumer often experiences.

commercialization The final phase of the new product process, in which the product is positioned and launched into full-scale production and sales.

communication The sharing of meaning. Five elements—source, message, receiver, and the processes of encoding and decoding— are required for communication to occur.

community shopping centre A retail location that typically has one primary store (usually a department store branch) and 20 to 40 smaller outlets and serves a population base of about 100,000.

company forecast (see sales forecast)

comparative advertisements Advertisements that show one brand's strengths relative to those of competitors.

competition The set of alternative firms that could provide a product to satisfy a specific market's needs.

Competition Act Federal legislation that replaced the Combines Investigation Act, designed to protect and ensure competition and consumer interests.

competitive advertisements Advertisements that promote a specific brand's features and benefits.

competitive institutional advertisements Institutional advertisements that promote the advantages of one product class over another and are used in markets where different product classes compete for the same buyer.

competitive parity budgeting Matching the competitors' absolute level of spending or the proportion per point of market share.

computer-assisted retailing A retailing method whereby customers order products over computer linkups from their homes after viewing items on TV or on their computer monitors.

concept tests External evaluations of a product idea that consist of preliminary testing of the new product idea (rather than the actual product) with consumers.

conference selling A form of team selling in which a salesperson and other company resource people meet with buyers to discuss problems and opportunities.

consultative selling A need-satisfaction sales presentation in which the salesperson focusses on problem definition and serves as an expert on problem recognition and resolution.

consumer behaviour Actions of a person to purchase and use goods and services, including the mental and social processes that precede and follow these actions.

consumer ethnocentrism The tendency to believe that it is inappropriate, indeed immoral, to purchase foreign-made products.

consumer goods Products purchased by the ultimate consumer.

consumer socialization The process by which people acquire the skills, knowledge, and attitudes necessary to function as consumers.

consumerism A movement to increase the influence, power, and rights of consumers in dealing with institutions.

consumer-oriented sales promotion Sales tools used to support a company's advertising and personal selling efforts directed to ultimate consumers; examples include coupons, sweepstakes, and trading stamps.

continuity programs Sales promotions used to encourage and reward repeat purchases by acknowledging each purchase made by a consumer and offering a premium as purchases accumulate.

continuous innovation Introduction of new products that require no new learning to use.

contracting A strategy used during the decline stage of the product life cycle in which a company contracts the manufacturing or marketing of a product to another firm.

contribution margin analysis A form of profitability analysis that monitors controllable costs and indicates the contribution to profit of specific marketing factors.

control and evaluation Phase of the marketing plan in which the marketing manager (1) compares the results of the marketing plan with the marketing objectives to identify deviations and (2) acts on the deviations, correcting negative ones and exploiting positive ones.

convenience goods Items that the consumer purchases frequently and with a minimum of shopping effort.

convenience sample A nonprobability sample selected solely on the basis of convenience, as in person-on-the-street interviews.

cooperative advertising Advertising programs in which a manufacturer pays a percentage of the retailer's local advertising expense for advertising the manufacturer's products.

corporate chain A type of retail ownership in which a single firm owns multiple outlets.

corporate culture The shared values, beliefs, and purpose of employees that affect individual and group behaviour.

corporate objectives Specific, measurable goals a corporation hopes to achieve and by which it can measure its performance.

cost of goods sold Total cost of the products sold during a specified time period.

cost per thousand (CPM) The cost of reaching 1,000 individuals or households with an advertising message in a given medium. (M is the Roman numeral for 1,000.)

cost plus fixed-fee pricing A pricing method in which a supplier is reimbursed for all costs, regardless of what they may be, plus a fixed fee that is independent of the final cost of the project.

cost plus percentage-of-cost pricing Setting the price of a good or service by adding a fixed percentage to the production or construction costs.

countertrade Using barter rather than money in making international sales.

coupons Sales promotions that usually offer a discounted price to consumers.

cross tabulation Method of presenting and relating data on two or more variables to display summary data and discover relationships in the data.

cross-cultural analysis The study of similarities and differences between consumers in two or more nations or societies.

cue A stimulus or symbol perceived by the consumer.

cultural ethnocentricity The belief that aspects of one's culture are superior to another's.

cultural symbols Things that represent ideas and concepts to a society or nationality.

culture The set of values, ideas, and attitudes of a homogeneous group of people that are transmitted from one generation to the next.

customary pricing A method of pricing based on a product's tradition, standardized channel of distribution, or other competitive factors.

customer contact audit A flowchart of the points of interaction between a consumer and a service provider.

customer service The ability of a logistics system to satisfy users in terms of time, dependability, communications, and convenience.

customer value The unique combination of benefits received by targeted buyers that includes quality, price, convenience, on-time delivery, and both before-sale and after-sale service.

customized approach An international marketing strategy that assumes that the way the product is used and the needs it satisfies are unique to each country.

customs Norms and expectations about the way people do things in a specific country.

data The facts and figures pertinent to a problem, composed of primary and secondary data.

database marketing (see micromarketing)

deal A sales promotion that offers a short-term price reduction.

deceptive pricing A practice by which prices are artificially inflated and then marked down under the guise of a sale; illegal under the Competition Act.

decline stage The fourth and last stage of the product life cycle, when sales and profitability decline.

decoding Taking a set of symbols—such as a communicated message—and transforming them back to an abstract idea.

delayed-response advertising Advertising intended to influence the consumer in the near future, rather than right away, in making purchases or taking other actions.

deletion A strategy of dropping a product from the product line, usually in the decline stage of the product life cycle.

delivered pricing The practice of refusing a customer delivery of an article on the same trade terms as other customers in the same location.

Delphi forecast A type of survey of experts forecast in which people knowledgeable of the topic are polled to obtain a sequence of anonymous estimates.

demand curve The summation of points representing the maximum quantity of a product consumers will buy at different price levels.

demand factors Factors that determine the strength of consumers' willingness and ability to pay for goods and services.

demand-backward pricing Setting a price by estimating what consumers would be willing to pay and then adjusting production costs accordingly.

demographics Distribution of a population on selected characteristics such as where people live, their numbers, and who they are in terms of age, sex, income, or occupation.

dependent variable The change in the behaviour of what is studied in an experiment.

depth interviews Detailed individual interviews with people relative to a research project.

depth of product line The assortment of each item a store or wholesaler carries.

derived demand Sales of a product (typically industrial) that result from the sales of another item (often consumer).

desk jobber (see drop shipper)

development Phase of the new product process in which the idea on paper is turned into a prototype; includes manufacturing and laboratory and consumer tests.

differentiation positioning Positioning that avoids direct competition by stressing unique aspects of the product.

diffusion of innovation The process by which people receive new information and accept new ideas and products.

direct channel A marketing channel in which a producer and an ultimate consumer interact directly with each other.

direct exporting A firm's selling its domestically produced goods in a foreign country without intermediaries.

direct forecast An estimate of the value to be forecast without the use of intervening steps.

direct mail A form of direct marketing in which companies use mailing lists of consumers as both a communications and a distribution channel.

direct marketing (direct promotion) An approach in which promotional communications are delivered "directly" to consumers, who are asked to respond by phone, mail, or personal visit. Can involve personnel selling via telemarketing.

direct ownership In international trade, a domestic firm's actually investing in and owning a foreign subsidiary or division.

direct-response advertising Advertising that seeks to motivate consumers to take immediate action, such as a TV ad asking consumers to call a telephone number to place an order.

discontinuous innovation Introduction of new products that require totally new consumption patterns.

discounts Reductions from list price that a seller gives a buyer as a reward for some buyer activity favourable to the seller.

discretionary income The money that remains after taxes and necessities have been paid for.

disposable income The money a consumer has left after taxes to use for food, shelter, and clothing.

distinctive competencies An organization's unique resources and specials skills that form the basis for the firm's sustainable competetive advantage.

diversification A strategy of developing new products and selling them in new markets.

downsizing The practice of reducing the content of a package without changing package size while maintaining or increasing the package price.

drive A need that moves an individual to action.

drop shipper A merchant wholesaler that owns the merchandise it sells but does not physically handle, stock, or deliver; also called a *desk jobber.*

dual distribution (1)An arrangement in which a firm reaches buyers by employing two or more different types of channels for the same basic product. (2) A situation in which a manufacturer uses its own distribution channel in direct competition with its wholesalers and retailers.

dumping A firm's selling a product in a foreign country below its domestic price.

durable good An item that lasts over an extended number of uses.

duty Special tax on imports or exports.

dynamically continuous innovation Introduction of new products that disrupt the consumer's normal routine but do not require learning totally new behaviours.

early adopters The 13.5 percent of the population who are leaders in their social setting and act as an information source on new products for other people.

early majority The 34 percent of the population who are deliberate and rely on personal sources for information on new products.

economic infrastructure A country's communication, transportation, financial, and distribution systems.

economy The income, expenditures, and resources that affect the cost of running a business or a household.

80/20 rule The principle that 80 percent of sales (and costs) are generated by 20 percent of the items or customers, and vice versa, thus suggesting priorities.

elastic demand A situation where a percentage decrease in price produces a larger percentage increase in quantity demanded, thereby actually increasing sales revenue.

electronic data interchange (EDI) Transmission of documents such as purchase orders, bills of lading, and invoices by means of computers linked in two different firms.

elements of the marketing mix (see marketing mix).

encoding Transforming an abstract idea into a set of symbols for the purpose of communicating.

environmental factors The uncontrollable marketing factors involving social, economic, technological, competitive, and regulatory forces.

environmental scanning Acquiring information on events occurring outside the company and interpreting potential trends.

ethics The moral principles and values that govern the actions and decisions of an individual or a group.

euro-branding The strategy of using the same brand name for the same product across all countries in the European Community.

evaluative criteria Both the objective and subjective attributes of a brand important to consumers when evaluating different brands or products.

everyday low pricing (EDLP) The practice of replacing promotional allowances given to retailers with lower manufacturer list prices.

evoked set The group of brands a consumer would consider acceptable out of the set of brands in the product class of which she is aware.

exchange The trade of things of value between a buyer and a seller so that each is better off than before.

exclusive distribution A distribution strategy whereby a producer sells its products or services in only one retail outlet in a specific geographical area.

expense-to-sales ratio A form of ratio analysis in which the specific costs or expenses for a sales representative are expressed as a percentage of sales revenue.

experience curve pricing A method of pricing in which price often falls following the reduction of costs associated with the firm's experience in producing or selling a product.

experiment Obtaining data by manipulating factors under tightly controlled conditions to test for cause and effect.

experimental independent variable The causal condition manipulated or controlled by an experimenter.

exploratory research A preliminary examination of problem-specific information that may provide some insight into possible causes of and solutions to a problem.

exporting Producing goods in one country and selling them in another country.

expropriation The situation in which a foreign company or its assets are taken over by the host country.

external secondary data Published data from outside the firm or organization.

extraneous independent variable A causal condition that is the result of outside factors that an experimenter cannot control.

failure fee A penalty payment made to a retailer by a manufacturer if a new product does not reach predetermined sales levels.

family branding (see multiproduct branding)

family life cycle The concept that each family progresses through a number of distinct phases, each of which is associated with identifiable purchasing behaviours.

feedback The communication flow from receiver back to sender; indicates whether the message was decoded and understood as intended.

field experiment A test of marketing variables in actual store or buying settings.

field of experience A person's understanding and knowledge; to communicate effectively, a sender and a receiver must have a shared field of experience.

fixed cost An expense of the firm that is stable and does not change with the quantity of product that is produced and sold.

flexible-price policy Offering the same product and quantities to similar customers, but at different prices.

flighting schedule A scheduling approach in which periods of advertising are scheduled between periods of no advertising to reflect seasonal demand.

FOB (free on board) Designation for the point on the transportation route at which the seller stops paying transportation costs.

FOB origin pricing A method of pricing in which the title to goods passes to the buyer at the point of loading.

focus group An informal session of 6 to 10 current or potential users of a product in which a discussion leader seeks their opinions on the firm's or a competitor's products.

follow–up stage The phase of the personal selling process that entails making certain that the customer's purchase has been properly delivered and installed and that any difficulties in using the product are promptly and satisfactorily addressed.

form of ownership Who owns a retail outlet. Alternatives are independent, corporate chain, cooperative, or franchise.

form utility The value to consumers that comes from production or alteration of a good or service.

formula selling presentation The selling format that consists of providing information in an accurate, thorough, and step-by-step manner to persuade the prospect to buy.

four I's of services Four unique elements to services: intangibility, inconsistency, inseparability, and inventory.

four Ps (see marketing mix)

franchising A contractual agreement with a parent company that allows an individual or a firm (the franchisee) to operate a certain type of business under an established name and according to specific rules.

freight consolidators (see freight forwarders)

freight forwarders Firms that accumulate small shipments into larger lots and then hire a carrier to move them, usually at reduced rates.

frequency The average number of times a person in the target audience is exposed to a message or advertisement.

full warranty A statement of liability by a manufacturer that has no limits of noncoverage.

functional groupings Organizational groupings in which a unit is subdivided according to the different business activities within a firm, such as manufacturing, marketing, and finance.

gap analysis An evaluation tool that compares expectations about a particular service with the actual experience a consumer has with the service.

General Agreement on Tariffs and Trade (GATT) An international treaty intended to limit trade barriers and promote world trade through the reduction of tariffs.

general merchandise wholesaler A full-service merchant wholesaler that carries a broad assortment of merchandise and performs all channel functions.

generation X The label given to Canadians born in the mid-1960s to late 1970s.

generic brand A branding strategy that lists no product name, only a description of contents.

generic marketing strategies Strategies that can be adopted by any firm, regardless of the product or industry involved, to achieve revenue/growth.

geographical groupings Organization groupings in which a unit is subdivided according to geographical location.

global approach An international marketing strategy that assumes that the way a product is used and the needs it satisfies are universal.

global brand Using the same brand name personality and positioning for a product in all markets worldwide.

global competition A competitive situation that exists when firms originate, produce, and market their products and services worldwide.

global corporation A business firm that looks at the entire world as one market and conducts research and development, manufacturing, financing, and marketing activities wherever they can best be done.

glocalization An international marketing strategy that allows the local organization to tailor a firm's global umbrella strategy to the needs, customs, values, and lifestyles of the local market.

government units The federal, provincial, and local agencies that buy goods and services for the constituents they serve.

green marketing Marketing efforts to produce, promote, and reclaim environmentally sensitive products.

gross domestic product The monetary value of all goods and services produced in a country during one year.

gross income The total amount of money earned in one year by a person, family, or household.

gross margin Net sales minus cost of goods sold.

gross rating points (GRPs) A reference number for advertisers, created by multiplying reach by frequency.

growth stage The second stage of the product life cycle, characterized by rapid increases in sales and by the appearance of competitors.

harvesting A strategy used during the decline stage of the product life cycle in which a company continues to offer a product but reduces support costs.

head–to–head positioning Competing directly with competitors on similar product attributes in the same target market.

hierarchy of effects The sequence of stages a prospective buyer goes through from initial awareness of a product to eventual action (either trial or adoption of the product). The stages include awareness, interest, evaluation, trial, and adoption.

horizontal conflict Disagreements between intermediaries at the same level in a marketing channel.

hypermarket A large store (over 200,000 square feet) offering a mix of food products and general merchandise.

idea generation A phase of the new product process in which a firm develops a pool of concepts as candidates for new products.

idle production capacity A situation where a service provider is available but there is no demand.

inconsistency A unique element of services: variation in service quality because services are delivered by people with varying capabilities.

indirect channel A marketing channel in which intermediaries are situated between the producer and consumers.

indirect exporting A firm's selling its domestically produced goods in a foreign country through an intermediary.

industrial distributor A specific type of intermediary between producers and consumers that generally sells, stocks, and delivers a full product assortment and may provide financing.

industrial espionage The clandestine collection of trade secrets or proprietary information about a company's competitors.

industrial firm An organizational buyer that in some way reprocesses a good or service it buys before selling it again.

industrial goods Products used in the production of other items for ultimate consumers.

industry potential (see market potential)

inelastic demand A situation where a small percentage decrease in price produces a smaller percentage increase in quantity demanded.

infomercials Program-length advertisements, often 30 minutes long, that take an educational approach to communicating with potential customers.

information technology In marketing, design and management of computer and communication systems to satisfy an organization's requirements for information processing and access.

innovators The 2.5 percent of the population who are venturesome and highly educated, use multiple information sources, and are the first to adopt a new product.

inseparability A unique element of services: the fact that a service cannot be separated from the deliverer of the service or the setting in which the service occurs.

institutional advertisement Advertisements designed to build goodwill or an image for an organization, rather than promote a specific good or service.

intangibility A unique element of services: the fact that services cannot be held, touched, or seen before the purchase decision.

integrated marketing communications Developing and implementing various forms of persuasive communications tools with customers and prospects to influence their behaviour.

intensive distribution A distribution strategy whereby a producer sells goods or services in as many outlets as possible in a geographic area.

intermodal transportation Combining different transportation modes in order to get the best features of each.

internal marketing The notion that a service organization must focus on its employees, or internal market, before successful programs can be directed at customers.

internal secondary data Data that have already been collected and exist inside a business firm or organization.

international marketing Marketing across national boundaries.

intertype competition Competition between dissimilar types of retail outlets brought about by scrambled merchandising.

introduction phase The first stage of the product life cycle, in which sales grow slowly and profit is low.

inventory (1) Physical material purchased from suppliers, which may or may not be reworked and is available for sale to customers. (2) A unique element of services: the need for and cost of having a service provider available.

involvement The personal, social, and economic significance of a purchase to a consumer.

job analysis A written description of what a salesperson is expected to do.

joint venture In international trade, an arrangement in which a foreign company and a local firm invest together to create a local business.

judgment sample A nonprobability sample chosen by a researcher acting on the belief that the subjects will provide the needed information for study.

jury of executive opinion forecast An estimate by knowledgeable executives inside a firm of likely sales during a coming period.

jury test A pretest in which a panel of customers is shown an advertisement and asked to rate its attractiveness, how much they like it, and how much it draws their attention.

just-in-time (JIT) concept An inventory supply system that operates with very low inventories and requires fast, on-time delivery.

kidfluence The power children and adolescents exercise in the marketplace through (1) influencing parents' buying decisions, (2) carrying out family purchasing tasks, (3) spending their own money as they choose, and (4) forming habits that will affect their buying patterns as adults.

laboratory experiment A stimulation of marketing-related activity in a highly controlled setting.

laggards The 16 percent of the market who have fear of debt, use friends for information sources, and accept ideas and products only after they have been long established in the market.

late majority The 34 percent of the population who are skeptical, are below average in social status, and rely less on advertising and personal selling for information than do innovators or early adopters.

laws Society's values and standards that are enforceable in the courts.

lead time Lag from ordering an item until it is received and ready for use.

learning Those behaviours that result from (1) repeated experience and (2) thinking.

level of service The degree of service provided to the customer by the retailer: self, limited, or full.

licensing A contractual agreement whereby a company allows another firm to use its brand name, patent, trade secret, or other property for a royalty or fee.

lifestyle People's mode of living, identified by how they spend their time and resources (activities), what they consider important in their environment (interests), and what they think of themselves and the world around them (opinions).

line positions Job description of people—such as group marketing managers—who have the authority and responsibility to issue orders to the people who report to them, such as marketing managers.

local approach (see customized approach)

logistics management Organizing the cost-effective flow of raw materials, in-process inventory, finished goods, and related information from point of origin to point of consumption to satisfy customer requirements.

long-range marketing plans A marketing plan that deals with the marketing goals and strategies for a product, product line, or entire firm for two to five years into the future.

loss-leader pricing Deliberately pricing a product below its customary price to attract attention to it.

lost-horse forecast Starting with the last known value of the item being forecast, listing the factors that could affect the forecast, assessing whether they have a positive or a negative impact, and making the final forecast.

macromarketing The study of the aggregate flow of a nation's goods and services to benefit society.

maintained markup The difference between the final selling price and retailer cost; also called *gross margin*.

major account management The practice of using team selling to focus on important customers to build mutually beneficial, long-term, cooperative relationships.

make–buy decision An evaluation of whether a product or its parts will be purchased from outside suppliers or built by the firm.

management by exception A tool used by a marketing manager that involves identifying results that deviate from plans, diagnosing their causes, making appropriate new plans, and taking new actions.

manufacturer branding A branding strategy in which the brand name for a product is designated by the producer, using either a multiproduct or a multibranding approach.

manufacturer's agents Individuals or firms that work for several producers and carry noncompetitive, complementary merchandise in an exclusive territory; also called *manufacturer's representatives*.

marginal analysis Study of allocating resources in order to balance incremental revenues of an action against incremental costs.

marginal cost The change in total cost that results from producing and marketing one additional unit.

marginal revenue The change in total revenue obtained by selling one additional unit.

markdown Reduction in retail price usually expressed as a percentage, equal to the amount reduced divided by the original price and multiplied by 100.

market People with the desire and ability to buy a specific product.

market development A strategy of selling existing products to new markets.

market growth rate The annual rate of growth of the specific market or industry in which a firm or an SBU is competing; often used as the vertical axis in business portfolio analysis.

market modifications Attempts to increase product usage by creating new use situations, finding new customers, or altering the marketing mix.

market orientation An organization's situation if it has one or more departments (1) actively trying to understand customers' needs and the factors affecting them, (2) sharing this information across departments, and (3) using the information to meet these customer needs.

market penetration A strategy of increasing sales of present products in their existing markets.

market potential Maximum total sales of a product by all firms to a segment under specified environmental conditions and marketing efforts of the firms (also called *industry potential*).

market segmentation Aggregating prospective buyers into groups, or segments, that (1) have common needs and (2) will respond similarly to a marketing action.

market segments The groups that result from the process of market segmentation; these groups ideally (1) have common needs and (2) will respond similarly to a marketing action.

market share The ratio of sales revenue of a firm to the total sales revenue of all firms in the industry, including the firm itself.

market testing A phase of the new product process in which prospective consumers are exposed to actual products under realistic purchase conditions to see if they will buy.

market-based groupings Organizational groupings that assign responsibility for a specific type of customer to a unit.

marketing "The process of planning and executing the conception, pricing, promotion, and distribution of ideas, goods, and services to create exchanges that satisfy individual and organizational objectives."

marketing audit A comprehensive, unbiased, periodic review of the strategic marketing process of a firm or a strategic business unit (SBU).

marketing budget The assessment of costs/revenues of a strategic marketing plan, which takes into account the sales, expenses, and profits expected to result from implementation of the plan.

marketing channel People and firms involved in the process of making a good or service available for use or consumption by consumers or industrial users.

marketing concept The idea that an organization should (1) strive to satisfy the needs of consumers while (2) also trying to achieve the organization's objectives.

marketing mix The controllable factors of product, price, promotion, and place.

marketing organization Managers and employees within a firm who are responsible for bringing a marketing plan to fruition.

marketing objectives What a firm seeks to achieve with its marketing plan, especially with regard to sales, market share, and customer satisfaction.

marketing plan A written plan of action developed as a result of the strategic marketing process; it outlines objectives, and how to achieve them.

marketing public relations (MPR) Public relations efforts designed to influence perceptions of a firm, its activities, and its brands of products.

marketing research The process of defining a marketing problem and opportunity, systematically collecting and analyzing information, and recommending actions to improve an organization's marketing activities.

marketing strategy The means by which marketing objectives are to be achieved. It is characterized by what to do (generic marketing strategy), who is the focus of the strategy, and how to do it.

marketing tactics The detailed day-to-day operational decisions essential to the overall success of marketing strategies.

market-product grid Framework for relating market segments to products offered or potential marketing actions by a firm.

markup The amount added to the cost of goods sold to arrive at a selling price, expressed in dollar or percentage terms.

materials handling Moving goods over short distances into, within, and out of warehouses and manufacturing plants.

mature market Market consisting of people over age 50.

maturity phase The third stage of the product or retail life cycle, in which market share levels off and profitability declines.

merchandise line The number of different types of products and the assortment a store carries, distinguished by breadth and depth.

message The information sent by a source to a receiver in the communication process.

method of operation How and where a retailer provides services; the alternative approaches are an in-store or a nonstore format (mail, vending, computer-assisted, or teleshopping).

micromarketing An organization's effort to collect demographic, media, and consumption profiles of customers in order to target them more effectively.

mission (see organization's business definition)

missionary salespeople Sales support personnel who do not directly solicit orders but rather concentrate on performing promotional activities and introducing new products.

mixed branding A branding strategy in which the company may market products under its own name and that of a reseller.

modified rebuy An organizational buying situation in which the users, influencers, or deciders seek to change the product specifications, price, delivery schedule, or supplier.

moral idealism A personal moral philosophy that considers certain individual rights or duties universal regardless of the outcome.

motivation The energizing force that causes behaviour that satisfies a need.

multibranding A manufacturer's branding strategy in which a distinct name is given to each of its products.

multiple-zone pricing Pricing products the same when delivered within one of several specified zones or geographical areas, but with different prices for each zone depending on demand, competition, and distance; also called *zone-delivered pricing*.

multiproduct branding A branding strategy in which a company uses one name for all products; also called *blanket* or *family branding*.

national character A distinct set of personality characteristics common among people of a country or society.

need-satisfaction presentation A selling format that emphasizes probing and listening by the salesperson to identify needs and interests of prospective buyers.

new buy An organization's first-time purchase of a good or service, characterized by greater potential risk.

new product process The sequence of activities a firm uses to identify business opportunities and convert them to a salable good or service. There are seven steps: new product strategy, idea generation, screening and evaluation, business analysis, development, testing, and commercialization.

new product strategy development The phase of the new product process in which a firm defines the role of new products in terms of overall corporate objectives.

noise Extraneous factors that work against effective communication by distorting a message or the feedback received.

nonprobability sampling Using arbitrary judgments to select a sample so that the chance of selecting a particular element may be unknown or zero.

nonprofit organization A nongovernmental organization that serves its customers but does not have profit as an organizational goal.

nonprospects Nonusers of a product who are not considered likely to become users.

North American Free Trade Agreement (NAFTA) An agreement signed by Mexico, the United States, and Canada to lift many trade barriers.

objective and task budgeting A budgeting approach whereby the company (1) determines its advertising objectives, (2) outlines the tasks to accomplish these objectives, and (3) determines the advertising cost of performing these tasks.

observation Watching, either in person or by mechanical means, how people actually behave.

odd-even pricing Setting prices a few dollars or cents under an even number, such as $19.95.

off-peak pricing Charging different prices during different times of the day or days of the week to reflect variations in demand for the service.

off-price retailing Selling brand-name merchandise at lower than regular prices.

oligopoly A competitive setting in which a few large companies control a large amount of an industry's sales.

one-price policy Setting the same price for similar customers who buy the same product and quantities under the same conditions.

opinion leaders Individuals who exert direct or indirect social influence over others.

order cycle time (see lead time)

order getter A salesperson who sells in a conventional sense and engages in identifying prospective customers, providing customers with information, persuading customers to buy, closing sales, and following on customer experience with the good or service.

order taker A salesperson who processes routine orders and reorders for products that have already been sold by the company.

organizational buyers Units such as manufacturers, retailers, or government agencies that buy goods and services for their own use or for resale.

organizational buying behaviour The decision-making process that organizations use to establish the need for products and identify, evaluate, and choose among alternative brands and suppliers.

organizational buying criteria The factors on which buying organizations evaluate a potential supplier and what it wants to sell—the objective attributes of the supplier's products and services and the capabilities of the supplier itself.

organization's business definition (mission) A statement about the customers an organization wishes to serve, the specific needs of these customers, and the means or technology by which the organization will serve these needs.

organization's mission (see organization's business definition)

original markup The difference between retailer cost and initial selling price.

outsourcing Contracting work that formerly was done in-house by employees—such as those in marketing research, advertising, and public relations departments—to small, outside firms.

packaging The container in which a product is offered for sale and on which information is communicated.

panel A sample of consumers or stores from which researchers take a series of measurements over time.

parallel development An approach to new product development that involves the simultaneous development of the product and production process.

penetration pricing Pricing a product low in order to discourage competition from entering the market.

perceived risk The anxieties felt by the consumer because he cannot anticipate the outcome of making a purchase but sees that there might be negative consequences.

percent of sales budgeting Allocating funds to advertising as a percentage of past or anticipated sales, in terms of either dollars or units sold.

perception The process by which an individual selects, organizes, and interprets information to create a meaningful picture of the world.

perceptual map A graph displaying consumers' perceptions of product attributes across two or more dimensions.

personal selling The two-way flow of communication between a buyer and a seller, often in a face-to-face encounter, designed to influence a person's or a group's purchase decision.

personal selling process Sales activities occurring before, during, and after the sale itself, consisting of six stages: (1) prospecting, (2) preapproach, (3) approach, (4) presentation, (5) close, and (6) follow-up.

personality A person's consistent behaviours or responses to recurring situations.

physical distribution management Organizing the movement and storage of a finished product until it reaches the customer.

pioneering advertisements Advertisements that tell what a product is, what it can do, and where it can be found.

pioneering institutional advertisements Institutional advertisements about what a company is or can do or where it is located.

place utility The value to consumers of having a good or service available where needed.

place-based media Advertising media alternative that places messages in locations that attract a specific target audience such as airports, doctors' offices, and health clubs.

plan schedule A formal time-line chart showing the relationship through time of the various plan tasks.

planning gap The space on a graph between the projection of the path to reach a new goal and the projection of the path of the results of a plan already in place.

point-of-purchase displays Displays located in high-traffic areas in retail stores, often next to checkout counters.

population The universe of all people, stores, or salespeople about which researchers wish to generalize.

portfolio test A pretest in which a test ad is placed in a portfolio with other ads and consumers are questioned on their impressions of the ads.

possession utility The value of making an item easy to purchase through the provision of credit cards or financial arrangements.

posttests Tests conducted after an advertisement has been shown to the target audience to determine whether it has accomplished its intended purpose.

power centre A large strip mall with multiple anchor (or national) stores, a convenient location, and often a supermarket.

preapproach stage The stage of the personal selling process that involves obtaining further information about a prospect and deciding on the best method of approach.

predatory pricing Selling products at a low price to injure or eliminate a competitor.

premium A sales promotion that consists of offering merchandise free or at significant savings over retail.

prestige pricing Setting a high price so that status-conscious consumers will be attracted to the product.

pretests Tests conducted before an advertisement is placed to determine whether it communicates the intended message or to select between alternative versions of the advertisement.

price The money or other consideration exchanged for the purchase or use of a good, an idea, or a service.

price discrimination The practice of charging different prices to different buyers for goods of like grade and quality; illegal under the Competition Act.

price elasticity of demand The percentage change in quantity demanded relative to a percentage change in price.

price equation Price = list price − discounts and allowances + extra fees.

price lining Setting the price of a line of products at a number of different specific pricing points.

price-fixing A conspiracy among firms to set prices for a product.

pricing constraints Factors that limit a firm's latitude in the price it may set.

pricing objectives Goals relating to the role of price in an organization's marketing and strategic plans.

primary data Facts and figures that are newly collected for a research project.

primary demand Desire for a product class rather than for a specific brand.

private branding Selling of products under the name of a wholesaler or retailer rather than under the manufacturer's name.

probability sampling Using precise rules to select a sample such that each element of the population has a specific known chance of being selected.

problem definition The first step in marketing research: defining the nature and scope of a marketing problem or opportunity to be investigated.

product A good, service, or idea consisting of a bundle of tangible and intangible attributes that satisfies consumers and is received in exchange for money or some other unit of value.

product advertisements Advertisements that focus on selling a good or service and take three forms: (1) pioneering (or informational), (2) competitive (or persuasive), and (3) reminder.

product cannibalism A firm's new product gaining sales by stealing them from its other products.

product (plan) champion A person who is able and willing to cut red tape and move a product or a plan forward.

product class An entire product category or industry.

product development A strategy of selling a new product to existing markets.

product differentiation A strategy having different but related meanings; it involves a firm's using different marketing mix activities, such as product features and advertising, to help consumers perceive the product as different from and better than other products.

product form Variation of a product within a product class.

product life cycle The life of a product over four stages: introduction, growth, maturity, and decline.

product line A group of products closely related because they satisfy a class of needs, are used together, are sold to the same customer group, are distributed through the same outlets, or fall within a given price range.

product line groupings Organizational groupings in which a unit is responsible for specific product offerings.

product manager A person who plans, implements, and controls the annual and long-range plans for the products for which she is responsible.

product mix The number and variety of product lines offered by a company.

product modifications Strategies of altering a product characteristic, such as quality, performance, or appearance.

product positioning The place an offering occupies in a consumer's mind with regard to important attributes relative to competitive offerings.

production goods Products used in the manufacturing of other items that become part of the final product.

profit A business firm's reward for the risk it undertakes in offering a product for sale; the money left over after a firm's total expenses are subtracted from its total revenues.

profit equation Profit = total revenue − total cost.

profit responsibility The view that companies have a single obligation, which is to maximize profits for owners or stockholders.

profitability analysis Measuring the profitability of a firm's products, customer groups, sales territories, channels of distribution, and order sizes.

promotional allowance The cash payment or extra amount of "free goods" awarded sellers in the channel of distribution for undertaking certain advertising or selling activities to promote a product.

promotional mix The combination of one or more of the promotional elements a firm uses to communicate with consumers. The promotional elements include advertising, personal selling, sales promotion, public relations, and direct marketing.

prospecting stage In the personal selling process, the search for and qualification of potential customers.

prospects Nonusers of a product who are considered likely to become users.

protectionism The practice of shielding one or more sectors of a country's economy from foreign competition through the use of tariffs or quotas.

protocol In the new product development process, an early statement that identifies a well-defined target market; specifies customers' needs, wants, and preferences; and states what the product will be and do.

psychographics Characteristics represented by personality and lifestyle traits (activities, interests, and opinions).

public relations (PR) A type of mass communication consisting of an organization's indirectly paid presentations regarding its activities, products, or services.

publicity The creation and dissemination of information about a company or product in order to obtain favourable media coverage.

public-service announcement (PSA) A publicity tool that uses free space or time donated by the media.

pull strategy Directing the promotional mix at ultimate consumers to encourage them to ask the retailer for the product.

purchase decision process Steps or stages a buyer passes through in making choices about which products to buy.

push strategy Directing the promotional mix to channel members or intermediaries to gain their cooperation in ordering and stocking a product.

qualitative research A nonrigorous form of research that does not allow making statistical inferences or quantitative statements but is useful for hypothesis generation for quantitative research.

quality The totality of features and characteristics of a product or service that bear on its ability to satisfy stated or implied needs.

quantitative research Research based on numerical scores or measurements that can be used to draw conclusions about a population through statistical inference.

quantity discounts Reductions in unit costs for a larger order quantity.

quota In international marketing, a restriction placed on the amount of a product allowed to enter or leave a country.

quota sample A type of convenience or judgment sample for which a researcher chooses a prescribed number of respondents from each of a group of categories—for example, by age or income group or by gender.

rack jobber A merchant wholesaler that furnishes racks or shelves to display merchandise in retail stores, performs all channel functions, and sells on consignment.

rating (TV or radio) The percentage of households in a market that are tuned to a particular TV show or radio station.

reach The number of different people exposed to an advertisement.

reactive strategies New product strategies that result in new product development as a defensive response to competitors' new items.

rebate A sales promotion in which money is returned to the consumer based on proof of purchase.

receivers People—such as consumers—who read, hear, or see a message sent by a source in the communication process.

reciprocity An industrial buying practice in which two organizations agree to purchase products from each other.

reference group People to whom a person turns as a standard of self-appraisal or source of personal standards.

regional marketing A form of geographical segmentation that develops marketing mixes to reflect specific area differences in tastes, perceived needs, or interests.

regional rollouts Introducing a new product sequentially into limited geographical areas to allow production levels and marketing activities to build up gradually.

regional shopping centres Suburban malls with up to 100 stores that typically draw customers from a 5- to 10-mile radius, usually containing one or two anchor stores.

regulation The federal and provincial laws placed on business with regard to the conduct of its activities.

relationship marketing An organization's effort to develop a long-term cost-effective link with individual customers for mutual benefit.

relationship selling The practice of building ties to customers based on a salesperson's attention and commitment to customer needs over time.

relative market share The sales of a firm or an SBU divided by the sales of the largest firm in the industry; often used as a horizontal axis in business portfolio analysis.

reliability The ability of research results to be replicated under identical environmental conditions.

reminder advertisements Advertisements used to reinforce previous knowledge of a product.

replenishment time (see lead time)

repositioning Changing the place an offering occupies in a consumer's mind relative to competitive products.

reseller A wholesaler or retailer that buys physical products and resells them again without any processing.

restructuring (downsizing or streamlining) Striving for a more efficient corporation that can compete globally by selling off unsatisfactory product lines and divisions, closing down unprofitable plants, and laying off employees.

retail life cycle A concept that describes a retail operation over four stages: early growth, accelerated development, maturity, and decline.

retail positioning matrix A framework for positioning retail outlets in terms of breadth of product line and value added.

retailing All the activities that are involved in selling, renting, and providing goods and services to ultimate consumers for personal, family, or household use.

retailing mix The strategic components that a retailer manages, including goods and services, physical distribution, and communications tactics.

retromarketing Product differentiation based on consumer nostalgia for brands and packaging of an earlier time.

return on investment (ROI) The ratio of after-tax net profit to the investment used to earn that profit.

reverse marketing The effort by organizational buyers to build relationships that shape suppliers' goods services, and capabilities to fit a buyer's needs and those of its customers.

salad bowl A population of mixed ethnic origin in which the different groups do not blend but instead maintain their own traditions and values.

sales analysis A tool for controlling marketing programs in which sales records are used to compare actual results with sales goals and to identify strengths and weaknesses.

sales component analysis A tool for controlling marketing programs that traces sales revenues to their sources such as specific products, sales territories, or customers.

sales engineer A salesperson who specializes in identifying, analyzing, and solving customer problems and who brings technological expertise to the selling situations, but often does not actually sell goods and services.

sales force survey forecast An estimate by the firm's salespeople of sales during a coming period.

sales forecast What one firm expects to sell under specified conditions for the uncontrollable and controllable factors that affect sales.

sales management Planning, implementing, and controlling the personal selling effort of the firm.

sales plan A statement describing what salespeople are to achieve and where and how their selling effort is to be deployed.

sales promotion A short-term inducement of value offered to arouse interest in buying a good or service.

sales response function The relationship between the expense of marketing effort and the marketing results obtained. Measures of marketing results include sales revenue, profit, units sold, and level of awareness.

sampling error A measure of the discrepancy between results found from studying a sampled group and the results that could have been expected had a census been conducted.

scrambled merchandising Offering several unrelated product lines in a single retail store.

screening and evaluation The phase of the new product process in which a firm uses internal and external evaluations to eliminate ideas that warrant no further development effort.

sealed–bid pricing A method of pricing whereby prospective firms submit price bids for a contract to the buying agency at a specific time and place, with the contract awarded to the qualified bidder with the lowest price.

secondary data Facts and figures that have already been recorded before the start of the research project at hand.

selective distribution A distribution strategy whereby a producer sells its products in a few retail outlets in a specific geographical area.

self-concept The way people see themselves and the way they believe others see them.

self-regulation An industry's policing itself rather than relying on government controls.

selling agent A person or firm that represents a single producer and is responsible for all marketing functions of that producer.

seminar selling A form of team selling in which a company team conducts an educational program for a customer's technical staff, describing state-of-the-art developments.

semiotics The field of study that examines the correspondence between symbols and their role in the assignment of meaning for people.

sensitivity analysis Asking "what if" questions to determine how changes in a factor like pricing or advertising affect marketing results like sales revenues or profits.

service continuum A range from the tangible to the intangible or good-dominant to service-dominant offerings available in the marketplace.

services Intangible items such as airline trips, financial advice, or telephone calls that an organization provides to consumers in exchange for money or something else of value.

share points Percentage points of market share, often used as the common basis of comparison to allocate marketing resources effectively.

shelf life The time a product can be stored before it spoils.

shopping goods Products for which the consumer will compare several alternatives on various criteria.

shrinkage A term used by retailers to describe theft of merchandise by customers and employees.

simple random sample A type of sample for which all members of a population have an equal chance of being selected.

single-source data Information provided by a single firm on household demographics and lifestyle, purchases, TV viewing behaviour, and responses to promotions like coupons and free samples.

situation analysis Internal and external assessment of all the possible strategy-related factors that can mitigate or enhance an organization's opportunities for survival and growth.

situational influences A situation's effect on the nature and scope of the purchase decision process. These include (1) the purchase task, (2) social surroundings, (3) physical surroundings, (4) temporal effects, and (5) antecedent states.

skimming pricing A high initial price attached to a product to help a company recover the cost of development.

slotting fee Payment by a manufacturer to place a new product on a retailer's shelf.

social audit A systematic assessment of a firm's objectives, strategies, and performance in the domain of social responsibility.

social classes The relatively permanent and homogeneous divisions in a society of people or families sharing similar values, lifestyles, interests, and behaviour.

social forces The characteristics of the population, its income, and its values in a particular environment.

social responsibility The idea that organizations are part of a larger society and are accountable to society for their actions.

societal marketing concept The view that an organization should discover and satisfy the needs of its customers in a way that also provides for society's well-being.

societal responsibility The view that firms have obligations to preserve the ecological environment and benefit the general public.

source A company or person who has information to convey.

specialty merchandise wholesaler A full-service merchant wholesaler that offers a relatively narrow range of products but has an extensive assortment within the products carried.

specialty goods Products that a consumer will make a special effort to search out and buy.

staff positions Job description of people who have the authority and responsibility to advise people in line positions but cannot issue direct orders to them.

stakeholder responsibility The view that an organization has an obligation to all those constituencies that enable it to achieve its objectives and not only to its stockholders.

Standard Industrial Classification (SIC) system The federal government's system for classifying organizations on the basis of major activity or the major good or service provided.

standard markup pricing Setting prices by adding a fixed percentage to the cost of all items in a specific product class.

statistical inference Drawing conclusions about a population from a sample taken from that population.

stimulus–response presentation A selling format that assumes the prospect will buy if given the appropriate stimulus by a salesperson.

straight commission compensation plan A compensation plan in which salespeople's earnings are directly tied to their sales or profit generated.

straight rebuy An organization's reordering of an existing good or service from the list of acceptable suppliers, generally without checking with the various users or influencers.

straight salary compensation plan A compensation plan where the salesperson is paid a fixed amount per week, month, or year.

strategic alliances Agreements between two or more independent firms to cooperate for the purpose of achieving common goals.

strategic business unit (SBU) A decentralized profit centre of a large firm that is treated as though it were a separate, independent business.

strategic channel alliances A practice whereby one firm's marketing channel is used to sell another firm's products.

strategic corporate planning process The sum of all steps taken at an organization's corporate level to develop long-run master approaches for survival and growth.

strategic marketing process The steps taken at the product and market levels to allocate resources to viable marketing opportunities; involves phases of planning, implementation, and control.

stratified random sample A sample chosen by dividing the population into groups, or strata, and selecting a simple random sample of individuals from each group.

strip location A cluster of stores that serves people who live within a 5- to 10-minute drive in a population base of under 30,000.

subcultures Subgroups within the larger, national culture with unique values, ideas, and attitudes.

subliminal perception Seeing or hearing messages without being aware of them.

support goods Items used to assist in the production of other goods and services.

survey A study in which primary data are obtained by asking people questions.

survey of buyers' intentions forecast A method of forecasting sales that involves asking prospective customers whether they are likely to buy the product during some future time period.

survey of experts forecast A forecast of some future event based on the judgments of experts in the relevant field.

sustainable competitive advantage (SCA) A strength, relative to competitors, in the markets served and the products offered.

SWOT Acronym for internal corporate *strengths* and *weaknesses* and external *opportunities* and *threats*; a type of appraisal that can be made on the basis of the results of a situation analysis.

systematic sample A type of random sample in which respondents are chosen from a list. Typically, the researcher starts at random from a position on a list and chooses every *n*th item thereafter.

target market One or more specific groups of potential consumers toward which an organization directs its marketing mix.

target profit pricing Setting a price based on an annual specific dollar target volume of profit.

target return-on-investment pricing Setting a price to achieve a return-on-investment target.

target return-on-sales pricing Setting a price to achieve a profit that is a specified percentage of the sales volume.

tariff In international marketing, a government tax on goods or services entering or leaving a country.

team selling Using a group of professionals in selling to and servicing major customers.

technological forecast A forecast based on an estimate of when scientific breakthroughs will occur.

technology An environmental force that includes inventions or innovations from applied science or engineering research.

television home shopping A form of direct marketing in which consumers view products on their television sets.

test marketing The process of offering a product for sale on a limited basis in a defined area to gain consumer reaction to the actual product and to examine its commercial viability and the marketing program.

tied selling A seller's requirement that the purchaser of one product also buy another product in the line.

time poverty Condition resulting from the growth in dual-income families as the number of tasks to do expands while the time to do them shrinks.

time utility The value to consumers of having a good or service available when needed.

top-down forecast Subdividing an aggregate forecast into its principal components.

total cost The total expense a firm incurs in producing and marketing a product, which includes fixed cost and variable cost; in physical distribution decisions, the sum of all applicable costs for logistical activities.

total logistics cost All expenses associated with transportation, materials handling and warehousing, inventory, stockouts, and order processing.

total revenue The total amount of money received from the sale of a product.

trade feedback effect The effect of a country's imports on its exports and of its exports on its imports.

trade name The commercial name under which a company does business.

trademark Legal identification of a company.'s exclusive rights to use a brand name or trade name.

trade-oriented sales promotions Sales tools used to support a company's advertising and personal selling efforts directed to wholesalers, distributors, or retailers. Three common approaches are allowances, cooperative advertising, and sales force training.

trading down Reducing the number of features, quality, or price of a product.

trading up Adding value to a product by including more features or higher-quality materials.

trend extrapolation Extending a pattern observed in past data into the future.

truck jobber Small merchant wholesalers that usually handle limited assortments of fast-moving or perishable items that are sold directly from trucks for cash.

ultimate consumers People who use the goods and services purchased for a household; sometimes also called ultimate users.

uncontrollable factors (see environmental factors)

uniform delivered pricing A geographical pricing practice in which the price the seller quotes includes all transportation costs.

unit variable cost Variable cost expressed on a per unit basis.

unitary demand elasticity A situation where the percentage change in price is identical to the percentage change in quantity demanded.

universal product code (UPC) A number assigned to identify each product, represented by a series of bars of varying widths for scanning by optical readers.

unsought goods Products that the consumer does not know about or knows about and does not initially want.

usage rate Quantity of a product consumed or amount of patronage during a specific time period, a measure that varies significantly among different customer groups.

utilitarianism A personal moral philosophy that focusses on the "greatest good for the greatest number" by assessing the costs and benefits of the consequences of ethical behaviour.

utility The benefits or customer value received by users of a product.

Valdez Principles Guidelines that encourage firms to focus attention on environmental concerns and corporate responsibility.

validity The degree to which research has actually measured what it was intended to measure.

value Specifically, the ratio of perceived quality to price (value = perceived benefits/price).

value analysis A systematic appraisal of the design, quality, and performance requirements of an industrial purchase to reduce purchasing costs.

value consciousness Consumer concern for obtaining the best quality, features, and performance for a given price of a product or service.

value-based pricing The practice of simultaneously increasing service and product benefits and decreasing price.

values The beliefs of a person or culture regarding modes of conduct or states of existence.

variable cost An expense of the firm that varies directly with the quantity of product produced and sold.

venture teams Multidisciplinary groups of marketing, manufacturing, and R&D personnel who stay with a new product from conception to production.

vertical conflict Disagreement between different levels in a marketing channel.

vertical marketing systems Professionally managed and centrally coordinated marketing channels designed to achieve channel economies and maximum marketing impact.

want A felt need that is shaped by a person's knowledge, culture, and individual characteristics.

warehouse A location, often decentralized, that a firm uses to store, consolidate, age, or mix stock; to house product-recall programs; or to ease tax burdens.

warranty A statement indicating the liability of the manufacturer for product deficiencies.

wasted coverage People outside a company's target audience who see, hear, or read the company's advertisement.

wheel of retailing A concept that describes how new retail outlets enter the market as low-status, low-margin stores and change gradually in status and margin.

word of mouth The influence people have on each other through face-to-face conversations.

workload method A formula-based method for determining the size of a sales force that integrates the number of customers served, call frequency, call length, and available selling time to arrive at a sales force size.

youth market The market consisting of pre-teens, "tweens," and teenagers, or about 15 percent of Canada's population.

Chapter Notes

CHAPTER 1

1. From an interview with Michael Dingman, Benetton Sportsystems Canada Inc., Montreal, 1993.
2. Carrie Goerne, "Rollerblade Reminds Everyone That Its Success Is Not Generic," *Marketing News,* March 2, 1992, pp. 1–2.
3. Regis McKenna, "Marketing Is Everything," *Harvard Business Review,* January–February 1991, pp. 65–79.
4. "AMA Board Approves New Marketing Definition," *Marketing News,* March 1, 1985, p. 1.
5. Robert W. Ruekert and Orville C. Walker, Jr., "Marketing's Interaction with Other Functional Units: A Conceptual Framework and Empirical Evidence," *Journal of Marketing,* January 1987, pp. 1–19.
6. Richard P. Bagozzi, "Marketing as Exchange," *Journal of Marketing,* October 1975, pp. 32–39.
7. E. Jerome McCarthy, *Basic Marketing: A Managerial Approach* (Homewood, IL: Richard D. Irwin, 1960).
8. Carl P. Zeithaml and Valarie A. Zeithaml, "Environmental Management: Revising the Marketing Perspective," *Journal of Marketing,* Spring 1984, pp. 46–53.
9. Mary Horwath, "Rollerblade: Creation of an American Original," a talk in Rome, Italy, November 1992.
10. Lee Schaefer, "It's Not a Fad," *Corporate Report Minnesota,* April 1992, pp. 31–39.
11. For a contrary view, see Ronald A. Fullerton, "How Modern Is Modern Marketing? Marketing's Evolution and the Myth of the 'Production Era,'" *Journal of Marketing,* January 1988, pp. 108–25.
12. Ajay K. Kohli and Bernard J. Jaworski, "Market Orientation: The Construct, Research Propositions, and Managerial Implications," *Journal of Marketing,* April 1990, pp. 1–18.
13. "Mascara Study," *Marketing,* June 7, 1993, p. 19.
14. Donald P. Robin and R. Eric Reidenbach, "Social Responsibility, Ethics, and Marketing Strategy: Closing the Gap between Concept and Application," *Journal of Marketing,* January 1987, pp. 44–58.
15. Shelby D. Hunt and John J. Burnett, "The Macromarketing/Micromarketing Dichotomy: A Taxonomical Model," *Journal of Marketing,* Summer 1982, pp. 9–26.
16. Philip Kotler and Sidney I. Levy, "Broadening the Concept of Marketing," *Journal of Marketing,* January 1969, pp. 10–15.
17. Michael Treacy and Fred Wiersema, "Customer Intimacy and Other Value Disciplines," *Harvard Business Review,* January–February 1993, pp. 84–93.
18. George S. Day, *Market-Driven Strategy* (New York: Free Press, 1990), p. 175.
19. Angela Kryhul, "Canadian Products Rank Sixth in Worldwide Survey of Quality," *Marketing,* March 7, 1994, p. 5.

CHAPTER 2

1. James Pollock, "Breaking Away," *Marketing,* June 28, 1993, pp. 1, 3.
2. Roger A. Kerin, Vijay Mahajan, and P. Rajan Varadarajan, *Contemporary Perspectives on Strategic Marketing Planning* (Boston: Allyn & Bacon, 1990), Chapter 1; and Harper W. Boyd, Jr., and Orville C. Walker, Jr., *Marketing Management* (Homewood, IL: Richard D. Irwin, 1990), Chapter 2.

3. Theodore Levitt, "Marketing Myopia," *Harvard Business Review,* July–August 1960, pp. 45–56.
4. Kenichi Ohmae, *The Mind of the Strategist* (New York: McGraw-Hill, 1982), p. 91.
5. Roger A. Kerin and Robert A. Peterson, *Strategic Marketing Problems,* 6th ed. (Boston: Allyn & Bacon, 1993), pp. 4–5; and Derek F. Abell, *Defining the Business* (Englewood Cliffs, NJ: Prentice Hall, 1980), p. 18.
6. Arthur A. Thompson, Jr., and A. J. Strickland III, *Strategic Management,* 7th ed. (Homewood, IL: Richard D. Irwin, 1993), pp. 87–90.
7. H. Igor Ansoff, "Strategies for Diversification," *Harvard Business Review,* September–October 1957, pp. 113–24.
8. Leon Jaroff, "A Thirst for Competition," *Time,* June 1, 1992, p. 75.
9. Michael E. Porter, *Competitive Strategies: Techniques for Analyzing Industries and Competitors* (New York: Free Press, 1980); and George S. Day, *Market-Driven Strategy* (New York: Free Press, 1990).
10. Rahul Jacob, "Body Shop International: What Selling Will Be Like in the 90s," *Fortune,* January 13, 1992, p. 63; Lisa Herling, "The Body Shop: Company Profile," The Body Shop Communications Office, February 1992, pp. 1–5; and Martha T. Moore, "Body Shop: Profits with Principles," *USA Today,* October 10, 1991, p. 1.
11. Philip Elmer-DeWitt, "Anita the Agitator," *Time,* January 25, 1993, pp. 52–54.
12. Mark Maremont, "Getting the Picture," *Business Week,* February 1, 1993, pp. 24–26.
13. Mark Maremont, "The Hottest Thing since the Flashbulb," *Business Week,* September 7, 1992, p. 72.
14. Mark Maremont, "Smile, You're on Compact Disc," *Business Week,* August 10, 1992, p. 26; and Philip Elmer-DeWitt, "Can You Picture This?" *Time,* August 24, 1992, pp. 58–59.

CHAPTER 3

1. Michelle Hibler, "Classroom Commercials," *Canadian Consumer,* September–October 1991, pp. 8–12.
2. Jo Marney, "Focus on Kids," *Marketing,* October 28, 1991, p. 6.
3. "IBM Campaign Focuses on Kids," *Marketing,* April 1, 1991, p. 2.
4. Roger Sauve, *Canadian People Patterns* (Saskatoon: Western Producer Prairie Books, 1993); and Statistics Canada, *Market Research Handbook,* cat. 63-224 (Ottawa, 1994).
5. Douglas Bell, "Immigration Trends Shape Demand," *Marketing,* May 21, 1993, p. 29.
6. Statistics Canada, *Current Demographic Analysis,* cat. 91-209 (Ottawa, 1993).
7. Statistics Canada, *Population Projections for Canada,* cat. 91-520 (Ottawa, 1993).
8. This discussion is based on Scott Donaton, "The Media Wakes Up to Generation X," *Advertising Age,* February 1, 1993, pp. 16–17; and "Move Over Boomers," *Business Week,* December 14, 1992, pp. 74–82.
9. *Canadian Markets* (Toronto: The Financial Post, 1993).
10. Jan Larson, "Understanding Stepfamilies," *American Demographics,* July 1992, pp. 36–40.

11. Brian Briggs and Ray Bollman, "Urbanization in Canada," *Social Trends,* Summer 1991, pp. 8–12.
12. Douglas Bell (reference cited).
13. Ernst & Young, *Tomorrow's Customers,* 22nd ed. (Toronto, 1989), p. 7.
14. Gail Chiasson, "Slashed Food Prices as Strategy—Not a War," *Marketing,* January 25, 1993, p. 4.
15. Julia Moulden, "Even Greener Marketing," *Marketing,* February 8, 1993, pp. 1, 3.
16. Clarkson Gordon, *Tomorrow's Customers,* 20th ed. (Toronto, 1987), p. 9.
17. Statistics Canada, *Income Distribution in Canada,* cat. 13-207 (Ottawa, 1994.)
18. "America 2000," *Battelle,* May 3, 1983.
19. "BMW Puts a Backseat Driver on a Chip," *Business Week,* July 30, 1990, p. 20; and "New Plastic Is Promoted as a Natural," *The Wall Street Journal,* January 24, 1990, pp. B1, B2.
20. Michael Porter, *Competitive Strategy* (New York: Free Press, 1980).
21. Stan Sutter, "Molson Pours into U.S.," *Marketing,* January 25, 1993, p. 1.
22. Ron Stang, "Michigan Beer Drinkers Try Sleeman," *Marketing,* June 14, 1993, p. 5.
23. "The Best and Worst Deals of the 80s," *Business Week,* January 15, 1990, pp. 52–62.

CHAPTER 4

1. Adapted from information supplied by Molson Breweries, Public Affairs Department, Toronto, 1994.
2. For a discussion of the definition of ethics, see Gene Laczniak and Patrick E. Murphy, *The Higher Road: A Path to Ethical Marketing Decisions* (Boston: Allyn & Bacon, 1992), Chapter 1.
3. Verne E. Henderson, "The Ethical Side of Enterprise," *Sloan Management Review,* Spring 1982, pp. 37–47.
4. M. Bommer, C. Gratto, J. Grauander, and M. Tuttle, "A Behavioral Model of Ethical and Unethical Decision Making," *Journal of Business Ethics* 6 (1987), pp. 265–80.
5. "Just How Honest Are You?" *Inc.,* February 1992, p. 104.
6. "Business Week/Harris Poll: Is an Antibusiness Business Backlash Building?" *Business Week,* July 20, 1987, p. 71; and "Looking to Its Roots," *Time,* May 27, 1987, pp. 26–29.
7. "What Bosses Think about Corporate Ethics," *The Wall Street Journal,* April 6, 1988, p. 21.
8. N. Craig Smith and John A. Quelch, *Ethics in Marketing* (Homewood, IL: Richard D. Irwin, 1993).
9. "Special Report: Animal Uproar," *Advertising Age,* February 25, 1990, pp. S-1–S-11.
10. For a comprehensive review on marketing ethics, see John Tsalikis and David J. Fritzche, "Business Ethics: A Literature Review with a Focus on Marketing Ethics," *Journal of Business Ethics,* 8 (1989), pp. 695–743.
11. "Exporting Jobs and Ethics," *Fortune,* October 5, 1992, p. 10.
12. "It's All in the Cards," *Time,* November 7, 1988, p. 101.
13. "From the Mind of Minolta—Oops, Make That Honeywell," *Business Week,* February 24, 1992, p. 34; and "Where Trademarks Are Up for Grabs," *The Wall Street Journal,* December 5, 1989, pp. B1, B4.
14. Vern Terpstra and Kenneth David, *The Cultural Environment of International Business,* 3rd ed. (Cincinnati: South-Western Publishing, 1991), p. 12.
15. For an extended treatment of ethics in the exchange process, see Gregory T. Gundlack and Patrick E. Murphy, "Ethical and Legal Foundations of Business Marketing Exchanges," *AMA Winter Marketing Educators' Conference* (Chicago: American Marketing Association, 1990)
16. "Group Challenges Parts of Dalkon Shield Pact," *The Washington Post,* August 25, 1989, p. C2; and "Some Dalkon Shield Claimants Attack Trust's Settlement Policies," *The Wall Street Journal,* March 12, 1992, p. B4.
17. Lois Therrien, "Want Shelf Space at Supermarkets? Ante Up," *Business Week,* August 7, 1989, pp. 60–61.
18. Robert Johnson and Edward T. Pound, "Hot on the Trail of Trade-Secret Thieves, Private Eyes Fight All Manner of Snakes," *The Wall Street Journal,* August 12, 1992, pp. B1, B4.
19. "Corporate Spies Snoop to Conquer," *Fortune,* November 7, 1988, pp. 68–76.
20. "P&G Expected to Get about $120 Million in Settlement of Chewy-Cookie Lawsuit," *The Wall Street Journal,* September 11, 1989, p. B10.
21. Leonard J. Brooks, "Corporate Codes of Ethics," *Journal of Business Ethics* 8 (1989), pp. 117–29.
22. "Look What Ill Wind Is Blowing In," *Business Week,* April 16, 1990, p. 27.
23. "Doing the 'Right' Thing Has Its Repercussions," *The Wall Street Journal,* January 25, 1990, p. B1.
24. For an extensive discussion on these moral philosophies, see R. Eric Reidenbach and Donald P. Robin, *Ethics and Profits* (Englewood Cliffs, NJ: Prentice Hall, 1989); Shelby D. Hunt and Scott Vitell, "A General Theory of Marketing Ethics," *Journal of Macromarketing,* Spring 1986, pp. 5–16; and Donald P. Robin and R. Eric Reidenbach, "Social Responsibility, Ethics, and Marketing Strategy: Closing the Gap between Concept and Application," *Journal of Marketing,* January 1987, pp. 44–58.
25. James Q. Wilson, "Adam Smith on Business Ethics" *California Management Review,* Fall 1989, pp. 59–72; and Edward W. Coker, "Smith's Concept of the Social System," *Journal of Business Ethics* 9 (1990), pp. 139–42.
26. George M. Zinkhan, Michael Bisesi, and Mary Jane Saxton, "MBAs' Changing Attitudes toward Marketing Dilemmas," *Journal of Business Ethics* 8 (1989), pp. 963–74.
27. Alix M. Freedman, "Bad Reaction: Nestlé's Bid to Crash Baby-Formula Market in the U.S. Stirs a Row," *The Wall Street Journal,* February 16, 1989, pp. A1, A6; and Alix Freedman, "Nestlé to Drop Claim on Label of Its Formula," *The Wall Street Journal,* March 13, 1989, p. B5.
28. Milton Friedman, "A Friedman Doctrine: The Social Responsibility of Business Is to Increase Profits," *New York Times Magazine,* September 13, 1970, p. 126.
29. Richard A. Spinello, "Ethics, Pricing, and the Pharmaceutical Industry," *Journal of Business Ethics* 11 (1992), pp. 617–26.
30. "Can Perrier Purify Its Reputation?" *Business Week,* February 26, 1990, p. 45; and "Perrier Expands North American Recall to Rest of Globe," *The Wall Street Journal,* February 15, 1990, pp. B1, B4.
31. For an extended discussion on this topic, see P. Rajan Varadarajan and Avil Menon, "Cause-Related Marketing: A Coalignment of Marketing Strategy and Corporate Philanthropy," *Journal of Marketing,* July 1988, pp. 58–74. The examples given are found in this article and "McD's Ties to World Cup," *Advertising Age,* April 13, 1992, p. 17. See also Scott M. Smith and David S. Alcorn, "Cause Marketing: A New Direction in the Marketing of Corporate Responsibility," *The Journal of Consumer Marketing,* Summer 1991, pp. 19–35.
32. *Marketing,* May 3, 1993, p. 5.
33. These steps are adapted from J. J. Carson and G. A. Steiner, *Measuring Business Social Performance: The Corporate Social Audit* (New York: Committee for Economic Development, 1974); see also E. M. Epstein, "The Corporate Social Policy Process: Beyond Business Ethics, Corporate Social Responsibility, and Corporate Social Responsiveness," *California Management Review,* Spring 1987, pp. 99–114.
34. *Research Report: The Only Environment We Have: How Can We Save It?* (New York: Council on Economic Priorities, November 1989); and Rajib N. Sanyal and Joao S. Neves, "The Valdez Principles: Implications for Corporate Social Responsibility," *Journal of Business Ethics* 10 (1991), pp. 883–90.
35. "Business's Green Revolution," *U.S. News & World Report,* February 19, 1990, pp. 45–48.

36. For a listing of unethical consumer practices, see Robert E. Wilkes, "Fraudulent Behavior by Consumers," *Journal of Marketing,* October 1978, pp. 67–75; see also Catherine A. Cole, "Research Note: Determinants and Consumer Fraud," *Journal of Retailing,* Spring 1989, pp. 107–20.

37. "Coupon Scams Are Clipping Companies," *Business Week,* June 15, 1992, pp. 110–11; Paul Bernstein, "Cheating—The New National Pastime?" *Business,* October–December 1985, pp. 24–33; and "Video Vice: 1 in 10 Copy Videotapes Illegally," *USA Weekend,* February 9–11, 1990, p. 18.

38. Julia Moulden, "Even Greener Marketing," *Marketing,* February 8, 1993, pp. 1, 3; and "Consumers Keen on Green but Marketers Don't Deliver," *Advertising Age,* June 29, 1992, pp. S-2, S-4.

39. Stan Sutter, "The Challenge of the 1990's," *Marketing,* July 3, 1989, p. 2; and Derek Stevenson, "Buying Green," *Canadian Consumer,* February 1991, p. 47.

40. Julia Moulden (reference cited).

CHAPTER 5

1. Fred Weir, "Third Golden Arches Dawns Moscow Horizon," *The Male-Star,* July 6, 1993, p. B-6.

2. These estimates are based on statistics reported in "The World Economy," *The Economist,* January 5, 1991, p. 18; *International Financial Statistics Yearbook* (New York: International Monetary Fund, 1992); and trend projections by the authors.

3. Nathaniel Gilbert, "A Case for Countertrade," *Across the Board,* May 1992, pp. 43–45.

4. This discussion is based on Karl E. Case and Ray C. Fair, *Principles of Economics* (Englewood Cliffs, NJ: Prentice Hall, 1989), p. 930; "U.S. Firms Take Chances in Korea," *The Wall Street Journal,* June 15, 1992, pp. B1, B5; "Kodak Zooms In on Pro Photographers," *The Wall Street Journal,* February 27, 1991, pp. B1, B5; and "GM Finally Discovers Asia," *Business Week,* August 24, 1992, pp. 42–43.

5. *Canadian Markets* (Toronto: The Financial Post, 1993).

6. Statistics Canada, *Market Research Handbook,* cat. 63-224 (Ottawa, 1993).

7. Michael E. Porter, *The Competitive Advantage of Nations* (New York: Free Press, 1990), pp. 577–615; and Michael E. Porter, "Why Nations Triumph," *Fortune,* March 12, 1990, pp. 94–108.

8. Sandra Porteous, "Bangkok's Ganong Tastes Oriental Success," *Marketing,* September 19, 1991, p. 15.

9. For an extended discussion of this topic, see Robert Z. Lawrence and Robert E. Litan, "Why Protectionism Doesn't Pay," *Harvard Business Review,* May–June 1987, pp. 60–67.

10. Shawn Tully, "Europe 1992: More Unity Than You Think," *Fortune,* August 24, 1992, pp. 136–38; and "10,000 New EC Roles," *Business Week,* September 7, 1992, pp. 48–49.

11. The following discussion is based on "GATT Brief: The American Connection," *The Economist,* April 21, 1990, pp. 85–86.

12. North American Free Trade Agreement (Ottawa: Government of Canada, August 1992).

13. Ibid.

14. "The Search for Competitive Advantage: A New North American Free Trade Zone," Bank of Montreal, Economics Dept, April 1993.

15. For an extended discussion on cross-cultural analysis, see Vern Terpstra and Kenneth David, *The Cultural Environment of International Business,* 3rd ed. (Cincinnati: South-Western Publishing, 1991).

16. These dimensions were developed in Geert Hofstede, *Culture's Consequences* (Beverly Hills, CA: Sage Publications, 1980); and portions of this discussion are adapted from Michael R. Solomon, *Consumer Behavior* (Boston: Allyn & Bacon, 1992), pp. 478–80. For a recent application, see Carla Millar and Christine Restall, "The Embryonic Consumer of Eastern Europe," *Marketing Management,* Spring 1992, pp. 48–55.

17. Ford S. Worthy, "A New Mass Market Emerges," *Fortune* Pacific Rim Special Issue, Fall 1990, p. 57.

18. These examples are adapted from Terpstra and David (reference cited); Sergey Frank, "Global Negotiating," *Sales & Marketing Management,* May 1992, pp. 64–69; and "After Early Stumbles, P&G Is Making Inroads Overseas," *The Wall Street Journal,* February 6, 1989, p. B1.

19. See Terpstra and David (reference cited); "Valentine's Day in Japan: Ladies Don't Expect a Gift," *The Christian Science Monitor* (February 13, 1989), p. 6.

20. Roger E. Axtell, *Do's and Taboos around the World,* compiled by the Parker Pen Company (New York: John Wiley & Sons, 1985).

21. Joann S. Lublin, "Younger Managers Learn Global Skills," *The Wall Street Journal,* March 31, 1992, p. B1.

22. These examples are found in Solomon (reference cited), pp. 484–85; John C. Mowen, *Consumer Behavior,* 2nd ed. (New York: Macmillan, 1990), p. 604; and Richard Tansey, Michael R. Hyman, and George M. Zinkham, "Cultural Themes in Brazilian and U.S. Auto Ads: A Cross-Cultural Comparison," *Journal of Advertising* 19, no. 2 (1990), pp. 30–39.

23. "Greeks Protest Coke's Use of Parthenon," *Dallas Morning News,* August 17, 1992, p. D4.

24. "What Soviets Think: A Gallup Poll," *Advertising Age,* February 19, 1990, p. 46; and "The Japanese Talk about Themselves," *Fortune* Pacific Rim Special Issue, Fall 1990, p. 17.

25. Terpstra and David (reference cited), pp. 24–25.

26. These examples are adapted from Terpstra and David (reference cited), p. 21; David A. Ricks, Jeffrey S. Arpan, and Marilyn Y. Fu, "Pitfalls in Advertising Overseas," *Journal of Advertising Research,* December 1974, p. 48; and David A. Ricks, "Products That Crashed into the Language Barrier," *Business and Society Review,* Spring 1983, pp. 46–50.

27. Mark Magnier, "U.S Firms Sometimes Lose It in the Translation," *Dallas Morning News,* August 17, 1992, pp. D1, D4.

28. Terrence A. Shimp and Subhash Sharma, "Consumer Ethnocentrism: Construction and Validation of the CETSCALE," *Journal of Marketing Research,* August 1987, pp. 280–89.

29. Nancy Giges, "Europeans Buy Outside Goods, but Like Local Ads," *Advertising Age,* April 27, 1992, pp. I-1, I-26.

30. Sandra Vandermerwe and marc-André L'Huiller, "Euro-Consumers in 1992," *Business Horizons,* January–February 1989, pp. 34–40.

31. "From Cookies to Appliances, Pan-Euro Efforts Build," *Advertising Age,* June 22, 1992, pp. I-1, I-29.

32. This example is based on Shawn Tully, "Nestlé Shows How to Gobble Markets," *Fortune,* January 16, 1989, pp. 74–78; and "Nielsen/Ad Age Consumption Comparisons," December 10, 1990, p. 40.

CHAPTER 6

1. *Marketing,* March 29, 1993, p. 19.

2. "Car Dealers Give the Lady Some Respect," *American Demographics,* September 1992, p. 25.

3. James F. Engel, Roger D. Blackwell, and Paul Miniard, *Consumer Behavior,* 6th ed. (Hinsdale, IL: Dryden Press, 1990), p. 477. See also Gordon C. Bruner III and Richard J. Pomazal, "Problem Recognition: The Crucial First Stage of the Consumer Decision Process," *Journal of Consumer Marketing,* Winter 1988, pp. 53–63.

4. For interesting descriptions of consumer experience and expertise, see Stephen J. Hoch and John Deighton, "Managing What Consumers Learn from Experience," *Journal of Marketing,* April 1989, pp. 1–20; and Joseph W. Alba and J. Wesley Hutchinson, "Dimensions of Consumer Expertise," *Journal of Consumer Research,* March 1987, pp. 411–54.

5. For recent studies on external information search patterns, see Joel E. Urbany, Peter R. Dickson, and William L. Wilkie, "Buyer Uncertainty and Information Search," *Journal of Consumer Research,* September 1989, pp. 208–15; Narasimhan Srinivasan and Brian T. Ratchford, "An Empirical Test of a Model of External Search for Automobiles," *Journal of Consumer Research,* September 1991, pp. 233–42; and Julie L. Ozanne, Merrie Brucks, and Dhruv Grewal, "A Study of Information Search Behavior during the Categorization

of New Products," *Journal of Consumer Research,* March 1992, pp. 452–63.

6. For a description of the role of demographic and psychographic factors influencing the importance of information sources, see William E. Warren, "Demographic and Psychographic Dimensions as Predictors of Information Sources Used in Making a Consumer Decision," *Journal of Promotion Management* 1 (1991), pp. 43–55.

7. Engel, Blackwell, and Miniard, p. 479.

8. John A. Howard, *Consumer Behavior in Marketing Strategy* (Englewood Cliffs, NJ: Prentice Hall, 1989), pp. 176–77, 361. For an extended discussion on consumer choice sets, see Allan D. Shocker, Moshe Ben-Akiva, Bruno Boccara, and Prakesh Nedungadi, "Consideration Set Influences on Consumer Decision Making and Choice: Issues, Models, and Suggestions," *Marketing Letters,* August 1991, pp. 181–98.

9. Damon Darlin, "Although U.S. Cars Are Improved, Imports Still Win Quality Survey," *The Wall Street Journal,* December 12, 1985, p. 27.

10. "For Customers, More Than Lip Service?" *The Wall Street Journal,* October 6, 1989, p. B1; Patricia Sellers, "How to Handle Customers' Gripes," *Fortune,* October 24, 1988, pp. 88–89ff; and "For Marketers, No Peeve Is Too Petty," *The Wall Street Journal,* November 14, 1990, pp. B1, B6.

11. "Customers, 800-Lines May Not Connect," *The Wall Street Journal,* November 20, 1990, p. B1.

12. Many different definitions and perspectives on involvement exist. See, for example, Richard L. Celsi and Jerry C. Olson, "The Role of Involvement in Attention and Comprehension Processes," *Journal of Consumer Research,* September 1988, pp. 210–24; and Deborah J. MacInnis and C. Whan Park, "The Differential Role of Characteristics of Music on High- and Low-Involvement Consumers' Processing of Ads," *Journal of Consumer Research,* September 1991, pp. 161–73.

13. Carolyn Costley, "Meta Analysis of Involvement Research," in *Advances in Consumer Research,* vol. 15, ed. Michael Houston (Provo, UT: Association for Consumer Research, 1988), pp. 554–62.

14. J. Paul Peter and Jerry C. Olson, *Consumer Behavior: Marketing Strategy Perspectives,* 3rd ed. (Homewood, IL: Richard D. Irwin, 1993), pp. 239–41.

15. Del Hawkins, Roger J. Best, and Kenneth J. Coney, *Consumer Behavior: Implications for Marketing Strategy Perspectives,* 5th ed. (Homewood, IL: Richard D. Irwin, 1992), pp. 441–42; Peter and Olson, p. 240; and Engel, Blackwell, and Miniard, pp. 496–98.

16. Russell Belk, "Situational Variables and Consumer Behavior," *Journal of Consumer Research,* December 1975, pp. 157–63.

17. Representative studies on situational influences include Ronald Milliman, "The Influence of Background Music on the Behavior of Restaurant Patrons," *Journal of Consumer Research,* September 1986, pp. 286–89; Meryl Gardner, "Mood States and Consumer Behavior: A Critical Review," *Journal of Consumer Research,* December 1985, pp. 281–300; Robert Donovan and John Rossiter, "Store Atmosphere: An Environmental Psychology Approach," *Journal of Retailing,* Spring 1982, pp. 34–57; Richard F. Yalch and Eric Spangenburg, "An Environmental Psychological Study of Foreground and Background Music as Retail Atmospheric Factors," *AMA Educators' Conference Proceedings* (Chicago: American Marketing Association, 1988), pp. 106–10; and Sevgin A. Eroglu and Karen A. Machleit, "An Empirical Study of Retail Crowding: Antecedents and Consequences," *Journal of Retailing,* Summer 1990, pp. 201–21.

18. This perspective on motivation and personality is based on Hawkins, Best, and Coney, Chapter 10.

19. K. H. Chung, *Motivational Theories and Practices* (Columbus, OH: Grid, 1977). See also A. H. Maslow, *Motivation and Personality* (New York: Harper & Row, 1970).

20. Arthur Koponen, "The Personality Characteristics of Purchases," *Journal of Advertising Research,* September 1960, pp. 09 92.

21. Joel B. Cohen, "An Interpersonal Orientation to the Study of Consumer Behavior," *Journal of Marketing Research,* August 1967, pp. 270–78; and Rena Bartos, *Marketing to Women around the World* (Cambridge, MA: Harvard Business School, 1989).

22. Terry Clark, "International Marketing and National Character: A Review and Proposal for an Integrative Theory," *Journal of Marketing,* October 1990, pp. 66–79.

23. F. G. Crane and T. K. Clarke, *Consumer Behaviour in Canada: Theory and Practice,* 2nd ed. (Toronto: Dryden, 1994).

24. For further reading on subliminal perception, see F. G. Crane and T. K. Clarke, "Subliminal Perception," Chapter 5 in *Advertising, Law and the Social Sciences,* ed. Jack P. Lipton and Bruce Dennis Sales (New York: Plenum Publishing, 1994), pp. 129–154.

25. Robert Settle and Pamela Alreck, "Reducing Buyers' Sense of Risk," *Marketing Communications,* January 1989, pp. 34–40; and G. R. Dowling, "Perceived Risk: The Concept and Its Management," *Psychology and Marketing,* Fall 1986, pp. 193–210.

26. This description of learning principles is based on Hawkins, Best, and Coney, pp. 263–81; and David Loudon and Albert J. Della Bitta, *Consumer Behavior,* 3rd ed. (New York: McGraw-Hill, 1988), pp. 437–74.

27. "Shoppers Less Loyal, More Thrifty," *Marketing,* June 14, 1993, p. 14.

28. Gordon Allport, "Attitudes," in *Readings in Attitude Theory and Measurement,* ed. Martin Fishbein (New York: John Wiley & Sons, 1968), p. 3.

29. Peter and Olson, pp. 195–98. See also Richard J. Lutz, "Changing Brand Attitudes through Modification of Cognitive Structure," *Journal of Consumer Research* 2 (1975), pp. 49–59.

30. Henry Assael, *Consumer Behavior and Marketing Action,* 3rd ed. (Boston: Kent Publishing, 1990), p. 275.

31. For an extended discussion of self-concept, see M. Joseph Sirgy, "Self-Concept in Consumer Behavior: A Critical Review," *Journal of Consumer Research,* December 1982, pp. 287–300. For a broader perspective, see Russell Belk, "Possessions and the Extended Self," *Journal of Consumer Research,* September 1988, pp. 139–68.

32. This description of the VALS Program is based on *The VALS 2 Segmentation System* (Menlo Park, CA: SRI International, 1989); Martha Riche, "Psychographics for the 1990s," *American Demographics,* July 1989, pp. 25–31, 53; and "SRI's New Psychographic Typology Reasserts Old Stereotypes of Aging," *Maturity Market Perspective,* September–October 1989, pp. 1, 6.

33. This discussion of the Goldfarb Segments was adapted from *The Goldfarb Segments: A Marketing Tool,* (Toronto: Goldfarb Consultants, March 1992).

34. See for example, Laurence F. Feick and Linda Price, "The Market Maven: A Diffuser of Marketplace Information," *Journal of Marketing* 51 (January 1987), pp. 83–97; and Peter H. Block, "The Product Enthusiast: Implications for Marketing Strategy," *Journal of Consumer Marketing* 3 (Summer 1986), pp. 51–61.

35. Crane and Clarke, *Consumer Behaviour in Canada.*

36. Meg Cox, "Ford Pushing Thunderbird with VIP Plan," *The Wall Street Journal,* October 17, 1983, p. 37.

37. "Importance of Image," *The Wall Street Journal,* August 12, 1985, p. 19; and "What Soviets Think: A Gallup Poll," *Advertising Age,* February 28, 1990, p. 46.

38. Representative work on positive and negative word of mouth can be found in Jacqueline Brown and Peter H. Reingen, "Social Ties and Word-of-Mouth Referral Behavior," *Journal of Consumer Research,* December 1987, pp. 350–62; Marc Weinberger and Jean B. Romeo, "The Impact of Negative Product News," *Business Horizons,* January–February 1989, pp. 44–50; Barry L. Bayers, "Word of Mouth: The Indirect Effects of Marketing Efforts," *Journal of Advertising Research,* June–July 1985, pp. 31–39; and Marsha L. Richins, "Negative Word of Mouth by Dissatisfied Consumers: A Pilot Study," *Journal of Marketing,* Winter 1983, pp. 68–78.

39. "Pork Rumors Vex Indonesia," *Advertising Age,* February 16, 1989, p. 36.

40. Crane and Clarke, *Consumer Behaviour in Canada,* pp. 152–53.

41. William O. Beardon and Michael G. Etzel, "Reference Group Influence on Product and Brand Choice," *Journal of Consumer Research,* September 1982, pp. 183–94; and Terry L. Childers and Akshay R. Rao, "The Influence of Familial and Peer-Based Reference Groups on Consumer Decisions," *Journal of Consumer Research,* September 1992, pp. 198–211.

42. "Honda Revs Up a Hip Cycle Campaign," *The Wall Street Journal,* July 31, 1989, p. B1.

43. For an extended discussion on consumer socialization, see George P. Moschis, *Consumer Socialization,* (Lexington, MA: Lexington Books, 1987). See also Laura A. Peracchio, "How Do Young Children Learn to Be Consumers? A Script-Processing Approach," *Journal of Consumer Research,* March 1992, pp. 425–40.

44. Patrick E. Murphy and William A. Staples, "A Modernized Family Life Cycle," *Journal of Consumer Research,* June 1979, pp. 12–22.

45. Research describing the purchasing roles and influence of husbands and wives is found in Sidney C. Bennett and Elnora W. Stuart, "In Search of Association between Personal Values and Household Decision Processes: An Exploratory Analysis," *AMA Educators' Conference Proceedings* (Chicago: American Marketing Association, 1989), pp. 259–64.

46. Ken Riddell, "On Promotions, Pizza and YTV," *Marketing,* September 27, 1993, p. 8.

47. This discussion was adapted, in part, from Robert B. Settle and Pamela L. Alreck, *Why They Buy* (New York: John Wiley & Sons, 1989), pp. 197–219.

48. Milton Yinger, "Ethnicity," *Annual Review of Sociology* 11 (1985), pp. 151–80.

49. Michel Laroche, Annamma Joy, Michael Hui, and Chankon Kim, "An Examination of Ethnicity Measures: Convergent Validity and Cross-Cultural Equivalence," *Advances in Consumer Research,* vol. 18, ed. Rebecca H. Holman and Michael R. Solomon (Provo, UT: Association for Consumer Research, 1991), pp. 150–157.

50. Adapted from François Vary, "Quebec Consumer Has Unique Buying Habits," *Marketing,* March 23, 1992, p. 28. See also "Today's Media Are More Than Messages," *Marketing,* April 12, 1993, p. 14.

51. Alex Sakiz, "Values, Not Language, Make the Canadians in Quebec Different," *Marketing,* May 13, 1991, p. 6.

52. Anne Darche, "Differences Getting Too Much Attention," *Marketing,* March 25, 1991, p. 35.

53. Ann Boden, "Aiming at the Right Target," *Marketing,* January 28, 1991, p. 6.

54. Ibid.

55. Sharifa Khan, "Communication Is Key to Crossing Cultures," *Marketing,* June 17, 1991, p. 23.

CHAPTER 7

1. Interview courtesy of Bob Procsal, Honeywell, MICRO SWITCH Division.

2. Peter LaPlaca, "From the Editor," *Journal of Business & Industrial Marketing,* Summer 1992, p. 3.

3. Peter LaPlaca, "From the Editor," *Journal of Business & Industrial Marketing,* Winter 1988, p. 3.

4. Statistics Canada, *Market Research Handbook,* cat. 63-224 (Ottawa, 1993).

5. Statistics Canada, *Standard Industrial Classification Manual* (Ottawa, 1986).

6. An argument that consumer buying and organizational buying do not have important differences is found in Edward F. Fern and James R. Brown, "The Industrial/Consumer Marketing Dichotomy: A Case of Insufficient Justification," *Journal of Marketing,* Spring 1984, pp. 68–77. However, most writers on the subject do draw distinctions between the two types of buying. See, for example, Robert W. Eckles, *Business Marketing Management* (Englewood Cliffs, NJ: Prentice Hall, 1990), p. 6; and Robert W. Haas, *Business Marketing Management* (Boston: PWS-Kent Publishing Company, 1992), p. 31.

7. Figure 7–3 is based on Robert R. Reeder, Edward G. Brierty, and Betty Reeder, *Industrial Marketing,* 2nd ed. (Englewood Cliffs, NJ:

Prentice Hall, 1991), pp. 8–22; Robert W. Eckles, *Business Marketing Management* (Englewood Cliffs, NJ: Prentice Hall, 1990), pp. 20–26; Frank G. Bingham, Jr., and Barney T. Raffield III, *Business to Business Marketing Management* (Homewood, IL: Richard D. Irwin, 1990), pp. 6–14; Michael D. Hutt and Thomas W. Speh, *Business Marketing Management,* 3rd ed. (Hinsdale, IL: Dryden Press, 1989), pp. 6–12; and Michael H. Morris, *Industrial and Organizational Marketing* (Columbus, OH: Merrill Publishing Company, 1988), pp. 21–28.

8. For a recent study of evaluative criteria used by industrial firms, see Daniel H. McQuiston and Rockney G. Walters, "The Evaluative Criteria of Industrial Buyers: Implications for Sales Training," *Journal of Business & Industrial Marketing,* Summer to Fall 1989, pp. 65–75.

9. David L. Blenkhorn and Peter M. Banting, "How Reverse Marketing Changes Buyer–Seller Roles," *Industrial Marketing Management,* August 1991, pp. 185–90; and Michiel R. Leenders and David L. Blenkhorn, *Reverse Marketing: The New Buyer–Supplier Relationship* (New York: Free Press, 1988).

10. J. William Semich and Somerby Dowst, "How to Push Your Everyday Supplier into World Class Status," *Purchasing,* August 17, 1989, p. 76.

11. Richard N. Cardozo, Shannon H. Shipp, and Kenneth Roering, "Proactive Strategic Partnerships: A New Business Markets Strategy," *Journal of Business & Industrial Marketing,* Winter 1992, pp. 51–63.

12. For a discussion of JIT, see Gary L. Frazier, Robert E. Spekman, and Charles R. O'Neal, "Just-in-Time Exchange Relationships in Industrial Markets," *Journal of Marketing,* October 1988, pp. 52–67; Paul A. Dion, Peter M. Banting, and Loretta M. Hasey, "The Impact of JIT on Industrial Marketers," *Industrial Marketing Management,* February 1990, pp. 41–46; and Steve McDaniel, Joseph G. Ormsby, and Alicia Gresham, "The Effect of JIT on Distributors," *Industrial Marketing Management,* May 1992, pp. 145–49.

13. Shirley Cayer, "Welcome to Caterpillar's Quality Institute," *Purchasing,* August 16, 1990, pp. 81–84.

14. Mary C. LaForge and Louis H. Stone, "An Analysis of the Industrial Buying Process by Means of Buying Center Communications," *Journal of Business & Industrial Marketing,* Winter–Spring 1989, pp. 29–36.

15. "Where Three Sales a Year Make You a Superstar," *Business Week,* February 17, 1986, pp. 76–77.

16. Bingham and Raffield, p. 11.

17. Thomas V. Bonoma, "Major Sales: Who Really Does the Buying?" *Harvard Business Review,* May–June 1982, pp. 111–19. For recent work on buying groups, see Ajay Kohli, "Determinants of Influence in Organizational Buying: A Contingency Approach," *Journal of Marketing,* July 1989, pp. 50–65; and John R. Ronchetto, Jr., Michael D. Hutt, and Peter H. Reingen, "Embedded Influence Patterns in Organizational Buying Systems," *Journal of Marketing,* October 1989, pp. 51–62.

18. Carl R. Ruthstrom and Ken Matejka, "The Meaning of 'Yes' in the Far East," *Industrial Marketing Management* 19 (1990), pp. 191–92; John L. Graham and Yoshiro Sano, "Across the Negotiating Table from the Japanese," *International Marketing Review,* Autumn 1986, pp. 58–71; and Peter Banting, Jozsef Beracs, and Andrew Gross, "The Industrial Buying Process in Capitalist and Socialist Countries," *Industrial Marketing Management,* May 1991, pp. 105–13.

19. Julia M. Bristor, "Influence Strategies in Organizational Buying: The Importance of Connections to the Right People in the Right Places," *Journal of Business-to-Business Marketing* I (1993), pp. 63–98; Herbert E. Brown and Roger W. Brucker, "Charting the Industrial Buying Stream," *Industrial Marketing Management,* February 1990, pp. 55–61; and Melvin R. Mattson, "How to Determine the Composition and Influence of a Buying Center," *Industrial Marketing Management* 17 (1988), pp. 205–14.

20. These definitions are adapted from Frederick E. Webster, Jr., and Yoram Wind, *Organizational Buying Behavior,* Englewood Cliffs, NJ: Prentice Hall, 1972, p. 6.

21. For an extensive description of 18 industrial purchases, see Arch G. Woodside and Nyrem Vyas, *Industrial Purchasing Strategies: Recommen-*

dations for Purchasing and Marketing Managers (Lexington, MA: Lexington Books, 1987).

22. For insights into buying industrial services, see James R. Stock and Paul H. Zinszer, "The Industrial Purchase Decision for Professional Services," *Journal of Business Research,* February 1987, pp. 1–16.

23. Patrick J. Robinson, Charles W. Faris, and Yoram Wind, *Industrial Buying and Creative Marketing* (Boston: Allyn & Bacon, 1967).

24. Recent studies on the buy-class framework that document its usefulness include Erin Anderson, Wujin Chu, and Barton Weitz, "Industrial Purchasing: An Empirical Exploration of the Buy-Class Framework," *Journal of Marketing,* July 1987, pp. 71–86; Morry Ghingold, "Testing the 'Buy-Grid' Buying Process Model," *Journal of Purchasing and Materials Management,* Winter 1986, pp. 30–36; P. Matthyssens and W. Faes, "OEM Buying Process for New Components: Purchasing and Marketing Implications," *Industrial Marketing Management,* August 1985, pp. 145–57; and Thomas W. Leigh and Arno J. Rethans, "A Script-Theoretic Analysis of Industrial Purchasing Behavior," *Journal of Marketing,* Fall 1984, pp. 22–32. Studies not supporting the buy-class framework include Joseph A. Bellizzi and Philip McVey, "How Valid Is the Buy-Grid Model?" *Industrial Marketing Management,* February 1983, pp. 57–62; and Donald W. Jackson, Jamey E. Keith, and Richard K. Burdick, "Purchasing Agents' Perceptions of Industrial Buying Center Influences: A Situational Approach," *Journal of Marketing,* Fall 1984, pp. 75–83.

25. See, for example, Gary L. Lilien and Anthony Wong, "An Exploratory Investigation of the Structure of the Buying Center in the Metal Working Industry," *Journal of Marketing Research,* February 1984, pp. 1–11; and Wesley J. Johnston and Thomas V. Bonoma, "The Buying Center: Structure and Interaction Patterns," *Journal of Marketing,* Summer 1981, pp. 143–56. See also Christopher P. Puto, Wesley E. Patton III, and Ronald H. King, "Risk Handling Strategies in Industrial Vendor Selection Decisions," *Journal of Marketing,* Winter 1985, pp. 89–98.

26. Gerald Levitch, "Sitting Pretty," *Marketing,* June 21, 1993, pp. 1, 3.

27. Ibid.

28. Ibid.

29. Ibid.

CHAPTER 8

1. Robert A. Peterson, *Marketing Research,* 2nd ed. (Plano, TX: Business Publications, Inc., 1988), pp. 2–3.

2. "New Marketing Research Definition Approved," *Marketing News,* January 2, 1987, pp. 1, 14.

3. Joe Mandese, "Video Technology Foils Measurement," *Advertising Age,* March 9, 1992, p. 30.

4. Kate Fitzgerald, "Fisher-Price Suffers from Turmoil in Toyland," *Advertising Age,* November 20, 1989, p. 12; and "Fisher-Price: Fighting to Reclaim the Playpen," *Business Week,* December 24, 1990, pp. 70–71.

5. Calvin L. Hodock, "The Decline and Fall of Marketing Research in Corporate America," *Marketing Research,* June 1991, pp. 12–22.

6. Ken Riddell, "Shoppers Adds Life to Pop Market," *Marketing,* July 26, 1993, p. 2.

7. Patrick E. Murphy and Gene R. Laczniak, "Emerging Ethical Issues Facing Marketing Researchers," *Marketing Research,* June 1992, pp. 6–11.

8. This section on advantages and disadvantages of cross tabulations was adapted from Roseann Maguire and Terry C. Wilson, "Banners or Cross Tabs? Before Deciding, Weigh Data—Format, Pros, Cons," *Marketing News,* May 13, 1983, pp. 10–11.

9. For a discussion on marketing research as a continuous process, see Eugene Del Vecchio, "Marketing Research as a Continuous Process," *Journal of Consumer Research,* Summer 1990, pp. 13–19.

10. Robert A. Peterson, *Marketing Research,* 2nd ed.

CHAPTER 9

1. "Reebok High Steppers," *Fortune,* July 1, 1991, p. 84.

2. Jean Sherman, "No Pain, No Gain," *Working Woman,* May 1987, p. 92; "Can Reebok Sprint Even Faster?" *Business Week,* October 6, 1986, pp. 74–75; and "Sneakers That Don't Specialize," *Business Week,* June 6, 1988, p. 146.

3. "Reebok's Pump Is Patent-Primed," *Business Week,* November 9, 1992, p. 52; Edward C. Baig, "Products to Watch: Reebok Pump," *Fortune,* January 1, 1990, p. 97; and "Where Nike and Reebok Have Plenty of Running Room," *Business Week,* March 11, 1991, pp. 56–60.

4. "What Recession? Reebok Introduces High-Priced Pumps for the 'Serious Athlete,' " *Marketing News,* March 16, 1992, p. 3; and "The 'Blacktop' Is Paving Reebok's Road to Recovery," *Business Week,* August 12, 1991, p. 27.

5. "Stalking the New Consumer," *Business Week,* August 28, 1989, pp. 54–62; and "From the Publisher," *Time,* January 14, 1991, p. 4.

6. Clay Chandler and Michael Williams, "A Slump in Car Sales Forces Nissan to Start Cutting Swollen Costs," *The Wall Street Journal,* March 3, 1993, pp. A1, A4; and James Cook, "Where's the Niche?" *Forbes,* September 24, 1984, pp. 54–55.

7. *'93 Ford Thunderbird* (Dearborn, MI: Ford Motor Company, August 1992), pp. 6–7, 14–15.

8. Issues in using market segmentation studies are described in William Rudelius, John R. Walton, and James C. Cross, "Improving the Managerial Relevance of Market Segmentation Studies," in *1987 Review of Marketing,* ed. Michael J. Houston (Chicago: American Marketing Association, 1987), pp. 385–404.

9. Example supplied by Allison Scolieri, Goldfarb Consultants, Toronto, March 10, 1992.

10. Julia Moulden, "Making a Better Butter," *Marketing,* May 10, 1993, pp. 1, 3.

11. F. G. Crane and T. K. Clarke, "Attitudes toward Milk: A Canadian View," *British Food Journal,* November–December 1989, pp. 6–9.

12. *Simmonds 1990 Study of Media and Markets: Restaurants, Stores and Grocery Shopping Poll* (New York: Simmonds Market Research Bureau, Inc., 1990), pp. 0001–0003.

13. Lois Therrien, "McRisky," *Business Week,* October 21, 1991, pp. 114–22; and Kathleen Deveny, "Firms See a Fat Opportunity in Catering to Americans' Quest for 'Easy' Lunches," *The Wall Street Journal,* November 3, 1992, pp. B1, B4.

14. Robert Metz, "Apple Now a Strong Investment," *Minneapolis Star Tribune,* October 1, 1987, p. 2M.

15. Andrew Kupfer, "Apple's Plan to Survive and Grow," *Fortune,* May 4, 1992, pp. 68–72.

16. John Markoff, "Apple to Offer a 2-in-1 Computer," *New York Times,* October 19, 1992, pp. C1, C4.

17. Edward W. Desmond, "Byting Japan," *Time,* October 5, 1992, pp. 68–69; and Neil Gross and Kathy Rebello, "Apple? Japan Can't Say No," *Business Week,* June 29, 1992, pp. 32–33.

18. Catherine Arnst, "PC Makes Head for 'Soho,' " *Business Week,* September 28, 1992, pp. 125–26; and Ken Yamada and Stephen Kreider Yoder, "Apple Is Joining PC Wars with Price Cut and a New Line," *The Wall Street Journal,* August 5, 1992, pp. B1, B6.

19. Kathy Rebello, "Apple's Daring Leap into the All-Digital Future," *Business Week,* May 25, 1992, pp. 120–22.

20. "An Apple of a Deal," *Marketing,* July 26, 1993, p. 2.

21. George S. Day, *Market-Driven Strategy* (New York: Free Press, 1990), p. 168.

22. Carolyn Green, "Remaking Xerox Canada," *Marketing,* April 5, 1993, pp. 1, 3.

23. A. Ries and J. Trout, *Positioning: The Battle for Your Mind* (New York: McGraw-Hill, 1981).

CHAPTER 10

1. Richard S. Teitelbaum, "Reader's Digest: Are Times Tough? Here's an Answer," *Fortune,* December 2, 1991, pp. 101–2.

2. Adapted from David Shani and Sujana Chalassani, "Exploiting Niches Using Relationship Marketing," *Journal of Consumer Marketing,* Summer 1992, pp. 33–42.

3. Teitelbaum (reference cited).

4. Stan Sutter, "Winds of Change Blowing," *Marketing,* February 8, 1993, p. 14; and *Marketing,* June 28, 1993, p. 8.

5. Kathleen Deveny, "Segments of One," *The Wall Street Journal,* March 22, 1991, p. B4; Thomas McCarroll, "Grocery-Cart Wars," *Time,* March 30, 1992, p. 49; and Frederick E. Webster, Jr., "The Changing Role of Marketing in the Corporation," *Journal of Marketing,* October 1992, pp. 1–17.

6. Michael E. Porter and Victor E. Millar, "How Information Gives You Competitive Advantage," *Harvard Business Review,* July–August 1985, pp. 149–60; and Benn R. Konsynski and F. Warren McFarlan, "Information Partnerships—Shared Data, Shared Scale," *Harvard Business Review,* September–October 1990, pp. 114–20.

7. Faye Rice, "How to Deal with Tougher Customers," *Fortune,* December 3, 1990, pp. 39–48.

8. Frank Rose, "Now Quality Means Service Too," *Fortune,* April 22, 1991, pp. 99–100; Patricia Sellers, "What Customers Really Want," *Fortune,* June 4, 1990, pp. 58–68; and Ann B. Fisher, "What Consumers Want in the 1990s," *Fortune,* January 29, 1990, pp. 108–12.

9. Rose, p. 102.

10. Gary Levin, "Media Ads Blasted for Loss of Impact," *Advertising Age,* November 2, 1992, p. 14.

11. Gary Levin, "Package-Goods Giants Embrace Databases," *Advertising Age,* November 2, 1992, pp. 1, 37.

12. Stan Sutter, "Winds of Change Blowing."

13. "Today's Media Are More Than Messages," *Marketing,* April 12, 1993, p. 14.

14. Levin, "Package-Goods Giants Embrace Databases," p. 37.

15. Dom Del Prete, "Advances in Scanner Research Yield Better Data Quicker," *Marketing News,* January 7, 1991, p. 54.

16. Laurence N. Gold, "High Technology Data Collection for Measurement and Testing," *Marketing Research,* March 1992, pp. 29–38.

17. Joe Schwartz, "Back to the Source," *American Demographics,* January 1989, pp. 22–26; and Felix Kessler, "High-Tech Shocks in Ad Research," *Fortune,* July 7, 1986, pp. 58–62.

18. W. Steven Perkins and Ram C. Rao, "The Role of Experience in Information Use and Decision Making by Marketing Managers," *Journal of Marketing Research,* February 1990, pp. 1–10.

19. Howard Schlossberg, "Marketers Moving to Make Data Bases Actionable," *Marketing News,* February 18, 1991, p. 8.

20. "Analyzing Promotions: The Free-Standing Insert Coupon," *Nielsen Researchers* 4 (1982), pp. 16–20.

CHAPTER 11

1. "HDTV Coming of Age: How Will It Affect Us?" *Maine Sunday Times,* May 30, 1993, p. 7A.

2. Ibid.

3. Definitions within this classification are from Committee on Definitions, *Marketing Definitions: A Glossary of Marketing Terms* (Chicago: American Marketing Association, 1960).

4. Ibid.

5. Brian Dumaine, "Closing the Innovation Gap," *Fortune,* December 2, 1991, pp. 56–62.

6. Brenton R. Schlender, "How Sony Keeps the Magic Going," *Fortune,* February 24, 1992, pp. 76–84.

7. Dumaine, p. 56.

8. F. G. Crane and T. K. Clarke, *Consumer Behaviour in Canada: Theory and Practice,* 2nd ed. (Toronto: Dryden, 1994).

9. Clare Ansberry, "Eastman Kodak Is Pulling Plug on Its Ultralife," *The Wall Street Journal,* April 10, 1990, pp. B1, B2.

10. Ronald Baily, "Sweet Technology, Sour Marketing," *Forbes,* May 1, 1989, p. 140.

11. " 'Smokeless' Cigarette Test Turns to Ashes," *Boston Globe,* March 1, 1989, p. 43.

12. Dumaine, pp. 58–59.

13. "Marketers Blunder Their Way through the 'Herb Decade,' " *Advertising Age,* February 13, 1989, pp. 3, 66.

14. Claire Poole, "Sweating It Out," *Forbes,* October 16, 1989, p. 274.

15. R. G. Cooper and E. J. Kleinschmidt, "New Products—What Separates Winners from Losers?" *Journal of Product Innovation Management,* September 1987, pp. 169–84.

16. *New Products Management for the 1980s* (Booz, Allen & Hamilton, Inc., 1982).

17. "Masters of Innovation: How 3M Keeps Its New Products Coming," *Business Week,* April 10, 1989, pp. 58–63.

18. *Marketing,* June 7, 1993, p. 2.

19. Laura Medcalf, "Of Ice and Men," *Marketing,* July 26, 1993, pp. 1, 3.

20. *Marketing,* June 7, 1993, p. 2.

21. "P&G Rewrites the Marketing Rules," *Fortune,* November 6, 1989, pp. 34–38.

22. Gail Chiasson, "A Sobering Mouthwash Pitch," *Marketing,* June 28, 1993, p. 2.

23. "Masters of Innovation," *Business Week,* April 10, 1989, pp. 58–63; and P. Ranganath Nayak and John M. Ketteringham, *Breakthroughs!* (New York: Rawson Associates, 1986), pp. 50–73.

24. Dumaine, p. 57; Schlender, p. 78.

25. Brian Dumaine, "Corporate Spies Stoop to Conquer," *Fortune,* November 7, 1988, pp. 68–76.

26. Susan Caminiti, "What the Scanner Knows about You," *Fortune,* December 3, 1990, pp. 51–52.

27. Sak Onkvisit and John J. Shaw, *Product Life Cycles and Product Management* (New York: Quorum Books, 1989), p. 26.

28. Paul Ingrassia, "Industry Is Shopping Abroad for Good Ideas to Apply to Products," *The Wall Street Journal,* April 29, 1985, p. 1.

29. "Step by Step with Nike," *Business Week,* August 13, 1990, pp. 116–17.

30. Melvin Prince, "Choosing Simulated Test Marketing Systems," *Marketing Research,* September 1992, pp. 14–16; and Christopher Power, "Will It Sell in Podunk? Hard to Say," *Business Week,* August 10, 1992, pp. 46–47.

31. "Pinning Down Costs of Product Introductions," *The Wall Street Journal,* November 26, 1990, p. B1.

32. "How Managers Can Succeed through Speed," *Fortune,* February 13, 1990, pp. 54–59.

33. Ibid.

34. W. Christopher Musselwhite, "Time-Based Innovation: The New Competitive Advantage," *Training and Development,* January 1990, pp. 53–56.

CHAPTER 12

1. Laura Medcalf, "Selling Clearly Canadian in the U.S.," *Marketing,* July 19, 1993, p. 3; and *Annual Report* (Vancouver: Clearly Canadian Beverage Corporation, 1992).

2. For an extended discussion of the generalized product life cycle curve, see David R. Rink and John E. Swan, "Product Life Cycle Research: A Literature Review," *Journal of Business Research,* September 1979, pp. 218–42; and David M. Gardner, "Product Life Cycle: A Critical Look at the Literature," in *Review of Marketing 1987,* ed. Michael Houston (Chicago: American Marketing Association, 1987), pp. 162–94.

3. Joseph Pereira, "Name of the Game: Brand Awareness," *The Wall Street Journal,* February 14, 1991, pp. B1, B4.

4. "The Sun Chip Also Rises," *Advertising Age,* April 27, 1992, pp. S-2, S-6; and "Gillette to Launch Women's Sensor," *Advertising Age,* February 10, 1992, p. 36.

5. Orville C. Walker, Jr., Harper W. Boyd, Jr., and Jean-Claude Larréché, *Marketing Strategy* (Homewood, IL: Richard D. Irwin, 1992), p. 251.

6. Portions of the discussion on the fax machine industry are based on "U.S. SemiCon Corporation: Facsimile Technology Program," in *Strategic Marketing Problems: Cases and Comments,* ed. Roger A. Kerin

and Robert A. Peterson, 6th ed. (Boston: Allyn & Bacon, 1993), pp. 489–502; and Ruth Ann Gardner, "Facsimile Forecast: 1991 through 1995," *Dataquest Perspective,* March 13, 1991, pp. 8–11.

7. Lawrence P. Feldman and Albert L. Page, "Harvesting: The Misunderstood Market Exit Strategy," *Journal of Business Strategy,* Spring 1985, pp. 79–85.

8. William Qualls, Richard W. Olshavsky, and Ronald E. Michaels, "Shortening of the PLC—An Empirical Test," *Journal of Marketing,* Fall 1981, pp. 76–80.

9. The terms *high-* and *low-learning life cycles* were developed by Chester R. Wasson, *Dynamic Competitive Strategies and Product Life Cycles* (Austin, TX: Austin Press, 1978).

10. "Ninja Turtle Man Has a New Concept He Thinks Will Sell," *The Wall Street Journal,* August 7, 1992, pp. A1, A8.

11. Everett M. Rogers, *Diffusion of Innovations,* 3rd ed. (New York: Free Press, 1983).

12. S. Ram and Jagdish N. Sheth, "Consumer Resistance to Innovation: The Marketing Problem and Its Solution," *Journal of Consumer Marketing,* Spring 1989, pp. 5–14.

13. "Everyone Is Bellying Up to This Bar," *Business Week,* January 27, 1992, p. 84.

14. Carlee R. Scott, "Car Batteries Go for New Gadget to Charge Sales," *The Wall Street Journal,* March 1, 1990, pp. B1, B6.

15. "Modified Screwdrivers May Prevent Slips," *The Wall Street Journal,* December 19, 1990, p. B1.

16. Alecia Swasy, "How Innovations at P&G Restored Luster to Washed Up Pert and Made It No. 1," *The Wall Street Journal,* December 6, 1990, pp. B1, B6; and "Tossing Its Head at P&G, Helene Curtis Styles Itself No. 1 in the Hair-Care Market," *The Wall Street Journal,* November 19, 1992, pp. B1, B16.

17. Elaine Underwood, "Retro Brands: Tastykake and Ritz Get a Legacy Look by Returning to Ghosts of Packages Past," *Adweek Marketing,* October 4, 1991, p. 18; and *Marketing,* June 7, 1993, p. 3.

18. "But I Don't Want to Play Nintendo Anymore!" *Business Week,* November 19, 1990, pp. 52–53; and "Mario vs. Sonic Dog in $30M Pre-Holiday Clash," *Brandweek,* October 26, 1992, pp. 1, 6.

19. "P&G Plans Big New Ivory Push," *Advertising Age,* November 23, 1992, p. 12; and "P&G's Soap Opera: New Ivory Bar Hits the Bottom of a Tub," *The Wall Street Journal,* October 23, 1992, p. B11.

20. Bob Geiger, "Liquid Yogurts Pour in the U.S.," *Advertising Age,* June 1, 1987, pp. 3, 62.

21. Cyndee Miller, "Beef, Pork Industries Have Met the Enemy—and It's Chicken," *Marketing News,* August 5, 1991, pp. 1, 7.

22. "Et Tu, Brut?" *Consumer Reports,* March 1992, p. 203; and John B. Hinge, "Critics Call Cuts in Package Size Deceptive Move," *The Wall Street Journal,* February 5, 1991, pp. B1, B8.

23. "Xerox Fights Trademark Battle," *Advertising Age,* April 27, 1992, p. I-39.

24. For an extended treatment of brand equity, see Peter H. Farquar, "Managing Brand Equity," *Marketing Insights,* Summer 1990, pp. 58–64; and David A. Aaker, *Managing Brand Equity* (New York: Free Press, 1991).

25. David A. Aaker, *Managing Brand Equity.*

26. Tim Falconer, "Hockey Hype," *Marketing,* March 22, 1993, pp. 1, 3.

27. *Annual Report* (Vancouver: Clearly Canadian Beverage Corporation, 1992).

28. "Ruffles Makes Waves in Israel," *Advertising Age,* November 23, 1992, p. J-12.

29. Daniel L. Doden, "Selecting a Brand Name That Aids Marketing Objectives," *Advertising Age,* November 5, 1990, p. 34.

30. Kim Robertson, "Strategically Desirable Brand Name Characteristics," *Journal of Consumer Marketing,* Fall 1989, pp. 61–71.

31. "Multiple Varieties of Established Brands Muddle Consumers, Make Retailers Mad," *The Wall Street Journal,* January 24, 1992, pp. B1, B5.

32. For a review of brand extensions, see David A. Aaker and Kevin Lane Keller, "Consumer Evaluations of Brand Extension," *Journal of Marketing,* January 1990, pp. 27–41.

33. "Baby Boom in Toiletries Hits J&J," *Advertising Age,* January 21, 1991, p. 16; and "J&J Sets Nighttime Tylenol," *Advertising Age,* February 18, 1991, pp. 1, 46.

34. Warren Keegan, Sandra Moriarty, and Tom Duncan, *Marketing,* (Englewood Cliffs, NJ: Prentice Hall, 1992), p. 467.

35. "Low Threat Labels," *Marketing,* June 14, 1993, p. 9.

36. Ron Suskind, "Minolta Puts Name on Polaroid," *The Wall Street Journal,* June 29, 1990, pp. B1, B8.

37. Michael J. McCarthy, "Food Companies Fear Pressure on Prices," *The Wall Street Journal,* December 10, 1990, pp. B1, B5.

38. Alecia Swasy, "Sales Lost Their Vim? Try Repackaging," *The Wall Street Journal,* October 11, 1989, p. B1.

39. Carl McDaniel and R. C. Baker, "Convenience Food Packaging and the Perception of Product Quality," *Journal of Marketing,* October 1977, pp. 57–58.

40. Swasy, p. B1.

41. "P&G to Tout Recycled Packages," *Advertising Age,* April 19, 1990, p. 42; and "Heinz to Unveil Recyclable Bottle for Its Ketchup," *The Wall Street Journal,* April 4, 1990, p. B3.

42. This discussion is based on "Germany's New Packaging Laws: The 'Green Dot' Arrives," *Business America,* February 24, 1992, pp. 36–37; and "The Last to Go Green: U.S. Lags in Eco-Labeling," *Business International,* March 30, 1992, pp. 93–94.

43. This example is based on John A. Quelch, "The Procter & Gamble Company: The Lenor Refill Package," Harvard Business School Case N9-592-016; "Procter and Gamble, Inc.: Downy Enviro-Pak," University of Western Ontario Case 9-90-A006; and "Downy Refill Makes a Splash on Shelves," *Advertising Age,* July 8, 1991, p. 16.

44. Sonia L. Nazario, "Microwave Packages That Add Crunch to Lunch May Also Pose Chemical Risks," *The Wall Street Journal,* March 1, 1990, pp. B1, B6.

45. Robert E. Wilkes and James B. Wilcox, "Limited versus Full Warranties: The Retail Perspective," *Journal of Retailing,* Spring 1981, pp. 65–77.

CHAPTER 13

1. Interview with Dwight R. Riskey, vice president of marketing research and new business, Frito-Lay, Inc. Used with permission.

2. "Small Firms Short on Cash Turn to Barter," *The Wall Street Journal,* November 26, 1990, pp. B1, B2; Arthur Bragg, "Marketing Comes of Age," *Sales and Marketing Management,* January 1989, pp. 61–63; and Jack G. Kaikati, "Marketing without Exchange of Money," *Harvard Business Review,* November–December 1982, pp. 72–74.

3. "Chrysler's '92 Dodge Viper Rolls into Dallas for the First Time," *Dallas Morning News,* June 25, 1992, p. 2D.

4. Adapted from Kent B. Monroe, *Pricing: Making Profitable Decisions,* 2nd ed. (New York: McGraw-Hill, 1990), Chapter 4. See also David J. Curry, "Measuring Price and Quality Competition," *Journal of Marketing,* Spring 1985, pp. 106–17.

5. Joseph B. White, "Value Pricing Is Hot as Shrewd Consumers Seek Low-Cost Quality," *The Wall Street Journal,* March 12, 1991, pp. A1, A5; and *Marketing News,* January 1, 1991, p. 1.

6. Numerous studies have examined the price–quality–value relationship. See, for example, Jacob Jacoby and Jerry C. Olson, eds., *Perceived Quality* (Lexington, MA: Lexington Books, 1985); Kent B. Monroe and William B. Dodds, "A Research Program for Establishing the Validity of the Price-Quality Relationship," *Journal of the Academy of Marketing Science,* Spring 1988, pp. 151–68; Akshay R. Rao and Kent B. Monroe, "The Effect of Price, Brand Name, and Store Name on Buyers' Perceptions of Product Quality: An Integrative Review," *Journal of Marketing Research,* August 1989, pp. 351–57; William B. Dodds, Kent B. Monroe, and Dhruv Grewal, "Effects of Price, Brand, and Store Information on Buyers' Product Evaluations," *Journal of Marketing Research,* August 1991, pp. 307–19; and Roger A. Kerin, Ambuj Jain, and Daniel J. Howard, "Store Shopping Experience and Consumer Price-Quality-Value Perceptions," *Journal of Retailing,*

Winter 1992, pp. 235–45. For a thorough review of the price–quality–value relationship, see Valarie A. Zeithaml, "Consumer Perceptions of Price, Quality, and Value," *Journal of Marketing,* July 1988, pp. 2–22. Also see Jerry Wind, "Getting a Read on Market-Defined 'Value,' " *Journal of Pricing Management,* Winter 1990, pp. 5–14.

7. These examples are from Roger A. Kerin and Robert A. Peterson, "Throckmorten Industries (A)," *Strategic Marketing Problems: Cases and Comments,* 6th ed. (Boston: Allyn & Bacon, 1993), p. 293; and "Software Economics 101," *Forbes,* January 28, 1985, p. 88.

8. Thomas T. Nagle, *The Strategy and Tactics of Pricing* (Englewood Cliffs, NJ: Prentice Hall, 1987), p. 107.

9. Barbara J. Coe, "Shifts in Industrial Pricing Objectives," *AMA Educators' Conference Proceedings* (Chicago: American Marketing Association, 1988), pp. 9–14. See also Barbara Coe, "Strategy in Retreat: Pricing Drops Out," *Journal of Business & Industrial Marketing,* Winter–Spring 1990, pp. 5–26.

10. "Pepsi, Coke Say They're Loyal to NutraSweet," *The Wall Street Journal,* April 22, 1992, p. B1.

11. David Wessel, "The Price Is Wrong, and Economists Are in an Uproar," *The Wall Street Journal,* January 2, 1991, pp. B1, B6.

12. For a review of pricing objectives, see Saeed Samiee, "Pricing in Marketing Strategies of U.S.- and Foreign-Based Companies," *Journal of Business Research,* February 1987, pp. 1–16.

13. "Price War Is Raging in Europe," *Business Week,* July 6, 1992, pp. 44–45.

14. "Made Just for Him," *Time,* April 16, 1990, p. 49.

15. Michael Garry, "Dollar Strength: Publishers Confront the New Economic Realities," *Folio: The Magazine for Magazine Management,* February 1989, pp. 88–93; Cara S. Trager, "Right Price Reflects a Magazine's Health Goals," *Advertising Age,* March 9, 1987, pp. 5–8ff; and Frank Bruni, "Price of Newsweek? It Depends," *Dallas Times Herald,* August 14, 1986, pp. S1, S20.

16. For an overview of price elasticity studies, see Ruth N. Bolton, "The Robustness of Retail-Level Elasticity Estimates," *Journal of Retailing,* Summer 1989, pp. 193–219; and Gerald J. Tellis, "The Price Elasticity of Selective Demand: A Meta-Analysis of Econometric Models of Sales," *Journal of Marketing Research,* November 1988, pp. 331–41.

17. See, for example, Susan L. Holak and Srinivas K. Reddy, "Effects of a Television and Radio Advertising Ban: A Study of the Cigarette Industry," *Journal of Marketing,* October 1986, pp. 219–27; Rick Andrews and George R. Franke, "Time-Varying Elasticities of U.S. Cigarette Demand, 1933–1987," *AMA Educators' Conference Proceedings* (Chicago: American Marketing Association, 1990), p. 393; and Judith Waldrop, "No Smoking Please," *American Demographics,* June 21, 1993, p. 1, 3.

18. Kent B. Monroe, *Pricing: Making Profitable Decisions,* 2nd ed. (New York: McGraw-Hill, 1990), pp. 24–26. See also David W. Nylen, *Marketing Decision-Making Handbook* (Englewood Cliffs, NJ: Prentice Hall, 1990), pp. G237–G239.

19. For illustrations of break-even analysis that document its use and versatility, see Thomas L. Powers, "Break-Even Analysis with Semifixed Costs," *Industrial Marketing Management,* February 1987, pp. 35–41; and "Break-Even Analysis," *Small Business Report,* August 1986, pp. 22–24.

CHAPTER 14

1. Based on "Sonic Boom," *The Economist,* January 25, 1992, p. 69; "Nintendo, Sega Zap Prices As Video-Game Heats Up," *The Wall Street Journal,* May 5, 1992, p. B1; and "Nintendo, Sega Slash Price of Videogames," *Advertising Age,* June 8, 1992, p. 44.

2. "IBM Introduces Line of Workstations: Industry Analysts Impressed by Prices," *The Wall Street Journal,* February 16, 1990, p. B3.

3. For an extended treatment of skimming and penetration pricing, see Joel Dean, "Pricing Policies for New Products," *Harvard Business Review,* November–December 1976, pp. 141–53; and Hermann Simon, "Pricing Opportunities—and How to Exploit Them," *Sloan Management Review,* Winter 1992, pp. 55–63.

4. "PC Prices Cut in Japan," *The Wall Street Journal,* October 21, 1992, p. B7.

5. Jeffrey H. Birnbaum, "Pricing of Products Is Still an Art, Often Having Little Link to Costs," *The Wall Street Journal,* November 25, 1981, p. 25.

6. See, for example, V. Kumar and Robert P. Leone, "Measuring the Effect of Retail Store Promotions on Brand and Store Substitution," *Journal of Marketing Research,* May 1988, pp. 178–85.

7. Robert C. Blattberg and Scott A. Neslin, *Sales Promotion: Concepts, Methods, and Strategies* (Englewood Cliffs, NJ: Prentice Hall, 1990); and Kent B. Monroe, *Pricing: Making Profitable Decisions,* 2nd ed. (New York: McGraw-Hill, 1990).

8. Gerald Levitch, "Sitting Pretty," *Marketing,* June 21, 1993, pp. 1, 3.

9. For an excellent review of bundle pricing, see Joseph P. Guiltinan, "The Price Bundling of Services: A Normative Framework," *Journal of Marketing,* April 1987, pp. 74–85; and Thomas T. Nagle, *The Strategy and Tactics of Pricing* (Englewood Cliffs, NJ: Prentice Hall, 1987), pp. 170–72.

10. "Lawyers Start to Stop the Clock," *Business Week,* August 17, 1992, p. 108.

11. For a recent discussion on the experience curve, see William W. Alberts, "The Experience Doctrine Reconsidered," *Journal of Marketing,* July 1989, pp. 36–49.

12. "IBM's Personal-Computer Strategy: At Any Price," *The Economist,* October 10, 1992, pp. 82, 84.

13. "Store-Brand Pricing Has to Be Just Right," *The Wall Street Journal,* February 14, 1992, p. B1.

14. For a review of quantity discounts, see George S. Day and Adrian B. Ryans, "Using Price Discounts for a Competitive Advantage," *Industrial Marketing Management,* February 1988, pp. 1–14; and James B. Wilcox, Roy D. Howell, Paul Kuzdrall, and Robert Britney, "Price Quantity Discounts: Some Implications for Buyers and Sellers," *Journal of Marketing,* July 1987, pp. 60–70.

15. "Burger King in Big Blow to Pepsi, Is Switching to Coke," *The Wall Street Journal,* May 2, 1990, pp. B1, B6.

16. Michael Levy and Charles Ingene, "Retailers Head Off Credit Cards with Cash Discounts," *Harvard Business Review,* May–June 1983, pp. 18–22.

17. Rockney G. Walters, "An Empirical Investigation in Retailer Response to Manufacturer Trade Promotions," *Journal of Retailing,* Summer 1989, pp. 258–72; and Ronald C. Curhan and Robert J. Kopp, "Obtaining Retailer Support for Trade Deals: Key Success Factors," *Journal of Advertising Research,* December–January 1987–1988, pp. 51–60.

18. "P&G Plays Pied Piper on Pricing," *Advertising Age,* March 8, 1992, p. 6.

CHAPTER 15

1. Steve Kichen, "Pick a Channel," *Forbes,* March 2, 1992, pp. 108, 110; "A Surprise Lift for Computer Retailers," *Business Week,* October 19, 1992, pp. 63–64; "Everyone Loves a Bargain—Europeans Included," *Business Week,* February 10, 1992, pp. 118–19; "At Any Price," *The Economist,* October 10, 1992, pp. 82, 84; and "Computers Plug into Mass Merchandising," *Advertising Age,* November 9, 1992, pp. S-1, S-6; and Angela Kryhul, "Distributing Dell," *Marketing,* April 19, 1993, p. 1.

2. "Pepsi, Concerned about Market Share in France, Will Break with Local Bottler," *The Wall Street Journal,* November 7, 1989, p. A12.

3. For an extensive review of industrial channel and distribution systems, see E. Raymond Corey, Frank V. Cespedes, and V. Kasturi Rangan, *Going to Market: Distribution Systems for Industrial Products* (Boston: Harvard Business School Press, 1989).

4. Michael D. Hutt and Thomas W. Speh, *Business Marketing Management,* 4th ed. (Hinsdale, IL: Dryden Press, 1992), pp. 314–15.

5. James D. Hlavacek and Tommy J. McCuistion, "Industrial Distributors—When, Who, and How?" *Harvard Business Review,* March–April 1983, pp. 96–101.

6. John A. Quelch, "Why Not Exploit Dual Marketing?" *Business Horizons,* January–February 1987, pp. 52–60. See also Gary L. Frazier and Tassaddug A. Shervani, "Multiple Channels of Distribution and Their Impact on Retailing," in *The Future of U.S. Retailing,* ed. Robert A. Peterson (New York: Quorum Books, 1992), pp. 217–37.

7. "Looks Like Hot Summer for Iced Tea," *Advertising Age,* May 4, 1992, p. 4.

8. The examples are described in "GM Says Sales Arm Plans to Distribute Saab Cars in Canada," *The Wall Street Journal,* May 10, 1990, p. B2; and Rustan Kosenko and Don Rathz, "The Japanese Channels of Distribution: Difficult but Not Insurmountable," *AMA Educators' Conference Proceedings* (Chicago: American Marketing Association, 1988), pp. 233–36.

9. This discussion of direct selling and direct marketing was adapted, in part, from Courtland L. Bovée and John V. Thill, *Marketing* (New York: McGraw-Hill, 1992), p. 393.

10. For an extended treatment of direct marketing, see Mary Lou Roberts and Paul D. Berger, *Direct Marketing Management* (Englewood Cliffs, NJ: Prentice Hall, 1989); and Herbert Katzenstein and William S. Sachs, *Direct Marketing* (Columbus, OH: Merrill, 1986).

11. Adapted from Louis W. Stern, Adel I. El-Ansary, and James R. Brown, *Management in Marketing Channels* (Englewood Cliffs, NJ: Prentice Hall, 1989), pp. 99–108; Kenneth G. Hardy and Allan J. Magrath, *Marketing Channel Management* (Glenview, IL: ScottForesman, 1988), pp. 3–5, 310–34; and Bert Rosenbloom, *Marketing Channels,* 3rd ed. (Hinsdale, IL: Dryden Press, 1987), pp. 44–47.

12. For research on similarities and differences among agents, merchant wholesalers, and sales offices and branches, see James R. Moore, Donald W. Eckrich, and Vijay Bhasim, "Industrial Channels Design and Structure: An Empirical Investigation," *Journal of Midwest Marketing,* Fall 1988, pp. 87–98; and Ronald D. Michman, "Managing Structural Changes in Marketing Channels," *Journal of Business & Industrial Marketing,* Summer–Fall 1990, pp. 5–14.

13. For recent research on manufacturer's agents, see Donald M. Jackson and Michael E. d'Amico, "Products and Markets Served by Distributors and Agents," *Industrial Marketing Management,* February 1989, pp. 27–33.

14. Louis W. Stern and Adel I. El-Ansary, *Marketing Channels,* 4th ed. (Englewood Cliffs, NJ: Prentice Hall, 1991).

15. "Clothing Makers Don Retailers' Garb," *The Wall Street Journal,* July 13, 1989, p. B1.

16. Frank V. Cespedes, "Channel Management Is General Management," *California Management Review,* Fall 1988, pp. 98–120.

17. "Fuller Brush Hopes to Clean Up by Expanding to Retail Stores," *Dallas Times Herald,* September 15, 1987, pp. C1, C5.

18. "Distributors: No Endangered Species," *Industry Week,* January 24, 1983, pp. 47–52.

19. Angela Kryhul, "Distributing Dell."

20. This exhibit is based on discussions in "Mass Market Transforms PC Retailing," *The Wall Street Journal,* December 18, 1990, p. B1; "More Computer Marketers Taking the Direct Approach," *Marketing News,* October 26, 1992, p. 6; and "A Surprise Lift for Computer Retailers," *Business Week,* October 4, 1992, pp. 63–64.

21. "Liquid Paper Corporation," in *Strategic Marketing Problems: Cases and Comments,* ed. Roger A. Kerin and Robert A. Peterson, 6th ed. (Boston: Allyn & Bacon, 1993), pp. 362–79.

22. Richard Green, "A Boutique in Your Living Room," *Forbes,* May 7, 1984, pp. 86–94.

23. Carla Rapoport, "You Can Make Money in Japan," *Fortune,* February 12, 1990, pp. 84–92; and "Avon Launches a $90 Million Offer to Buy Back Shares in Japanese Unit," *The Wall Street Journal,* September 15, 1992, p. B4.

24. "Car Dealers Try to Dent $5 Billion Quick Lube Market," *Marketing News,* April 13, 1992, p. 9.

25. Philip Kotler *Marketing Management,* 7th ed. (Englewood Cliffs, NJ: Prentice Hall, 1991), p. 568; and Michael R. Czinkota and Jon

Woronoff, *Unlocking Japanese Markets* (Chicago: Probus Publishing Co., 1991), pp. 92–97.

26. "Gillette Tries to Nick Schick in Japan," *The Wall Street Journal,* February 4, 1991, pp. B3, B4.

27. This discussion is based on Czinkota and Woronoff.

28. For examples of channel conflict, see Allan J. Magrath and Kenneth G. Hardy, "Avoiding the Pitfalls in Managing Distribution Channels," *Business Horizons,* September–October 1987, pp. 29–33; and Rogert J. Calantone and Jule B. Gassenheimer, "Overcoming Basic Problems between Manufacturers and Distributors," *Industrial Marketing Management,* August 1991, pp. 215–21.

29. "Heinz Struggles to Stay at the Top of the Stack," *Business Week,* March 11, 1985, p. 49.

30. Studies that explore the dimensions and use of power and influence in marketing channels include Gul Butaney and Lawrence H. Wortzel, "Distributor Power versus Manufacturer Power: The Customer Role," *Journal of Marketing,* January 1988, pp. 52–63; Kenneth A. Hunt, John T. Mentzer, and Jeffrey E. Danes, "The Effect of Power Sources on Compliance in a Channel of Distribution: A Causal Model," *Journal of Business Research,* October 1987, pp. 377–98; John F. Gaski, "Interrelations among a Channel Entity's Power Sources: Impact of the Exercise of Reward and Coercion on Expert, Referent, and Legitimate Power Sources," *Journal of Marketing Research,* February 1986, pp. 62–67; Gary Frazier and John O. Summers, "Interfirm Influence Strategies and Their Application within Distribution Channels," *Journal of Marketing,* Summer 1984, pp. 43–55; Sudhir Kale, "Dealer Perceptions of Manufacturer Power and Influence Strategies in a Developing Country," *Journal of Marketing Research,* November 1986, pp. 387–93; George H. Lucas and Larry G. Gresham, "Power, Conflict, Control, and the Application of Contingency Theory in Channels of Distribution," *Journal of the Academy of Marketing Science,* Summer 1985, pp. 27–37; and F. Robert Dwyer and Jule Gassenheimer, "Relational Roles and Triangle Dramas: Effects on Power Play and Sentiments in Industrial Channels," *Marketing Letters* 3 (1992), pp. 187–200.

CHAPTER 16

1. Kay Ritta and Burton Hall, "Delivering Quality," *BMW* magazine, February 1983, pp. 64–67.

2. Definition provided by the Council of Logistics Management, Chicago, 1986. Emphasis added.

3. Elizabeth Edwardson, "Workers at L. L. Bean Busy as Santa's Elves Filling Christmas Orders," *Minneapolis Star Tribune,* December 23, 1992, p. 5D.

4. Herbert W. Davis, "Physical Distribution Costs—1991," in *Proceedings of Council of Logistics Management 1991,* pp. 359–64.

5. James Pollock, "Breaking Away," *Marketing,* June 28, 1993, p. 3.

6. "Why Federal Express Has Overnight Anxiety," *Business Week,* November 9, 1987, pp. 62–66.

7. Martin Keller, "Changing Channels," *Express* magazine, Winter 1990, pp. 2–4.

8. "Europeans Think Alike When It Comes to Customer Service," *International Ambassador,* August 1990, p. 25; and "The European Customer Service Survey: Results," *Europa,* September 1990, p. 1.

9. John J. Coyle, Edward J. Bardi, and C. John Langley, Jr., *The Management of Business Logistics,* 5th ed. (St. Paul, MN: West Publishing, 1992), pp. 85–90.

10. Coyle, Bardi, and Langley, p. 90.

11. George Stalk, Philip Evans, and Lawrence Shulman, "Competing on Capabilities: The New Rules of Corporate Strategy," *Harvard Business Review,* March–April 1992, pp. 57–69 (especially pp. 61–62). Also see Hank Gilman, "Rural Retailing Chains Prosper by Combining Service, Sophistication," *The Wall Street Journal,* July 2, 1984, p. 1.

12. George S. Day, *Market-Driven Strategy* (New York: Free Press, 1990), p. 180.

CHAPTER 17

1. Angela Kryhul, "Superstore Concept Expands," *Marketing,* June 28, 1993, p. 4.
2. Peter Bloch, Nancy Ridgeway, and Daniel L. Sherrell, "Extending the Concept of Shopping: An Investigation of Browsing Activity," *Journal of the Academy of Marketing Science,* Winter 1989, pp. 13–22.
3. *Canadian Markets* (Toronto: The Financial Post, 1993), pp. 26–40; Statistics Canada, *Market Research Handbook,* cat. 63-224 (Ottawa, 1993), p. 170; and Statistics Canada, *Employment Statistics,* cat. 72-002 (Ottawa, 1993).
4. Derek Stevenson, "Cross-Border Dispute," *Canadian Consumer,* July–August 1991, pp. 8–15.
5. "New Spots Planned," *Marketing,* February 8, 1993, p. 29; and James Pollock, "Craft Chain Comes North," *Marketing,* July 26, 1993, p. 1.
6. "World's Top Stores," *Marketing,* March 1, 1993, p. 18.
7. Stan Sutter, "Sears Move Stuns Industry," *Marketing,* February 15, 1992, p. 1; and "Sears Adds Value to Its Catalogues," *Marketing,* February 15, 1993, p. 8.
8. Jennifer S. Stack and Joseph E. McKendrick, "Franchise Market Expands As Rest of Economy Slumps," *Marketing News,* July 6, 1992, p. 11.
9. Robert E. Bond and Christopher E. Bond, *The Source Book of Franchising Opportunities* (Homewood, IL: Dow Jones-Irwin, 1991).
10. Bob Mackin, Jr., "Designer Coffee a Hot Item on the West Coast," *Marketing,* June 28, 1993, p. 12.
11. Angela Kryhul, "Superstore Concept Expands."
12. Jo Marney, "Consumers Now Driven by Need, Not Want," *Marketing,* March 1, 1993, p. 7.
13. Helen Keeler, "Shopping a la Carte: Everything You Want to Know about Catalogue Shopping," *Canadian Consumer,* November–December 1991, pp. 25–27.
14. Statistics Canada, *Market Research Handbook,* cat. 63-224 (Ottawa, 1993), p. 105.
15. "Trade Exec's 'Crystal-Ball' Outlook for the 1990s," *Vending Times,* December 1989, pp. 1, 3, 8.
16. Phil Fitzell, "Opening the Floodgates," *Beverage World,* January 1990, pp. 48–58.
17. David Fryxell, "How to Succeed in Executive Shopping," *Link-Up,* March–April 1992, pp. 8–10; Gary Robins, "On-Line Service Update," *Stores,* February 1990, pp. 24–29; and "Computer Formats Spur Variety in ER," *Discount Store News,* July 3, 1989, p. 116.
18. Kathy Haley, "Keys Are Interactive TV and Channel Expansion," *Advertising Age,* February 22, 1993, p. C16; Richard Zoglin, "An Old Fox Learns New Tricks," *Time,* March 1, 1993, pp. 52–54; and R. Fulton MacDonald, "Capitalizing on the Coming Revolution," *Retail Control,* January 1990, pp. 22–29.
19. Erich Linke, "New Home-Shopping Technologies," *The OECD Observer,* October–November 1992, pp. 17–19.
20. The following discussion is adapted from William T. Gregor and Eileen M. Friars, *Money Merchandising: Retail Revolution in Consumer Financial Services* (Cambridge, MA: Management Analysis Center, Inc., 1982).
21. William Lazer and Eugene J. Kelley, "The Retailing Mix: Planning and Management," *Journal of Retailing,* Spring 1961, pp. 34–41.
22. Francis J. Mulhern and Robert P. Leon, "Implicit Price Bundling of Retail Products: A Multiproduct Approach to Maximizing Store Profitability," *Journal of Marketing,* October 1991, pp. 63–76.
23. William B. Dodds, "In Search of Value: How Price and Store Name Information Influence Buyers' Product Perceptions," *Journal of Consumer Marketing,* Spring 1991, pp. 15–24.
24. Faye Rice, "What Intelligent Consumers Want," *Fortune,* December 28, 1992, pp. 56–60; and Gary Strauss, "Warehouse Clubs Heat Up Retail Climate," *USA Today,* September 7, 1990, pp. 1B, 2B.
25. Adrienne Ward, "Department Stores Play the Outlet Game," *Advertising Age,* January 27, 1992, pp. 5–6; and Adrienne Ward, "New Breed of Mall Knows: Everybody Loves a Bargain," *Advertising Age,* January 27, 1992, p. 55.
26. Barry Brown, "Edmonton Makes Size Pay Off in Down Market," *Advertising Age,* January 27, 1992, pp. 5–4.
27. Eric Peterson, "Power Centers! Now!" *Stores,* March 1989, pp. 61–66; and "Power Centers Flex Their Muscle," *Chain Store Age Executive,* February 1989, pp. 3A, 4A.
28. Pierre Martineau, "The Personality of the Retail Store," *Harvard Business Review* 36 (January–February 1958), p. 47.
29. Howard Barich and Philip Kotler, "A Framework for Marketing Image Management," *Sloan Management Review,* Winter 1991, pp. 94–104; Susan M. Keaveney and Kenneth A. Hunt, "Conceptualization and Operationalization of Retail Store Image: A Case of Rival Middle-Level Theories," *Journal of the Academy of Marketing Science,* Spring 1992, pp. 165–75; and James C. Ward, Mary Jo Bitner, and John Barnes, "Measuring the Prototypicality and Meaning of Retail Environments," *Journal of Retailing,* Summer 1992, p. 194. For a review of the store image literature, see Mary R. Zimmer and Linda L. Golden, "Impressions of Retail Stores: A Content Analysis of Consumer Images," *Journal of Retailing,* Fall 1988, pp. 265–93.
30. Mary Jo Bitner, "Servicescapes: The Impact of Physical Surroundings on Customers and Employees," *Journal of Marketing,* April 1992, pp. 57–71.
31. Jans-Benedict Steenkamp and Michel Wedel, "Segmenting Retail Markets on Store Image Using a Consumer-Based Methodology," *Journal of Retailing,* Fall 1991, p. 300, and Philip Kotler, "Atmosphere as a Marketing Tool," *Journal of Retailing,* Winter 1973–74, p. 61.
32. *Marketing,* June 21, 1993, p. 2.
33. Bob Mackin, Jr., "The Bay Goes Back to Basics," *Marketing,* August 16, 1993, p. 3.
34. The wheel of retailing theory was originally proposed by Malcolm P. McNair, "Significant Trends and Development in the Postwar Period," in *Competitive Distribution in a Free, High-Level Economy and Its Implications for the University,* ed. A. B. Smith (Pittsburgh: University of Pittsburgh Press, 1958), pp. 1–25. See also Stephen Brown, "Guest Commentary: The Wheel of Retailing—Past and Future," *Journal of Retailing,* Summer 1990, pp. 143–49; and Malcolm P. McNair and Eleanor May, "The Next Revolution of the Retailing Wheel," *Harvard Business Review,* September–October 1978, pp. 81–91.
35. William R. Davidson, Albert D. Bates, and Stephen J. Bass, "Retail Life Cycle," *Harvard Business Review,* November–December 1976, pp. 89–96.
36. Richard Gibson, "Discount Menu Is Coming Back to McDonald's as Chain Tries to Win Back Customers," *The Wall Street Journal,* November 20, 1990, pp. B1, B10; and Lois Therrien, "McRisky," *Business Week,* October 21, 1991, pp. 114–22.
37. Gretchen Morgenson, "Here Comes the Cross-Shoppers," *Forbes,* December 7, 1992, pp. 90–101.
38. Martin Mayer, "Scanning the Future," *Forbes,* October 15, 1990, pp. 114–17; and James M. Sinkula, "Status of Company Usage of Scanner-Based Research," *Journal of the Academy of Marketing Science,* Spring 1986, pp. 63–71.
39. Stephanie M. Shern, Robert J. Verdisco, and Murray Forseter, "Loss Prevention Trends in Retail: An Executive Overview," *Chain Store Age Executive,* January 1992, pp. 6–13. "Kiddie City Beefs Up Security at Urban Store," *Chain Store Age Executive,* February 1989, p. 36; and "Employee Involvement Is Key to Store Security," *Chain Store Age Executive,* April 1989, p. 80.

CHAPTER 18

1. *Marketing,* April 12, 1993, p. 8; Jennifer Lawrence, "P&G Customizes Ads to Plug Retailers," *Advertising Age,* February 8, 1993, p. 38; Jennifer Lawrence, "Jager: New P&G Pricing Builds Brands," *Advertising Age,* June 29, 1992, pp. 13, 49; Glen Heitsmith, "Try It, You'll Like It," *Promo,* September 1992, pp. 6–7; "Stalking the New Consumer," *Business Week,* August 28, 1989, pp. 54–62; "100 Leading National Advertisers," *Advertising Age,* January 4, 1992, p. 16; and Cyndee Miller, "Moves by P&G, Heinz Rekindle Fears That Brands Are in Danger," *Marketing News,* June 8, 1992, pp. 1, 15.

2. Kate Fitzgerald, "Vision System Takes Marketing to Checkout," *Advertising Age,* November 30, 1992, p. 35; Robert C. Blattberg and John Deighton, "Interactive Marketing: Exploiting the Age of Addressability," *Sloan Management Review,* Fall 1991, pp. 5–14; and Brian Dumaine, "P&G Rewrites the Marketing Rules," *Fortune,* November 6, 1989, pp. 34–48.

3. Jeffrey McElnea, "Pretest 'Blue-Sky' FSIs to Minimize Risk" *Marketing News,* May 11, 1992, p. 15; Joanne Lipman, "Procter and Gamble to Demote Promotions," *The Wall Street Journal,* July 17, 1989, p. B4; and Julie Liesse Erickson, "FSI Boom to Go Bust?" *Advertising Age,* May 1, 1989, pp. 1, 82.

4. Wilbur Schramm, "How Communication Works," in *The Process and Effects of Mass Communication,* ed. Wilbur Schramm (Urbana, IL: University of Illinois Press, 1955), pp. 3–26.

5. E. Cooper and M. Jahoda, "The Evasion of Propaganda," *Journal of Psychology* 22 (1947), pp. 15–25; H. Hyman and P. Sheatsley, "Some Reasons Why Information Campaigns Fail," *Public Opinion Quarterly* 11 (1947), pp. 412–23; and J. T. Klapper, *The Effects of Mass Communication* (New York: Free Press, 1960), Chapter VII.

6. David A. Ricks, Jeffrey S. Arpan, and Marilyn Y. Fu, "Pitfalls in Advertising Overseas," *Journal of Advertising Research,* December 1974, pp. 47–51.

7. This discussion in IMC is based on Don E. Schultz, Stanley I. Tannenbaum, and Robert F. Lauterborn, *Integrated Marketing Communications* (Chicago: NTC Books, 1993); and Don E. Schultz, "Integrated Marketing Communications: Maybe Definition Is in the Point of View," *Marketing News,* January 18, 1993, p. 17.

8. Don E. Schultz, *Marketing News.*

9. B. C. Cotton and Emerson M. Babb, "Consumer Response to Promotional Deals," *Journal of Marketing,* July 1978, pp. 109–13.

10. Robert George Brown, "Sales Response to Promotions and Advertising," *Journal of Advertising Research,* August 1974, pp. 33–40.

11. Siva K. Balasubramanian and V. Kumar, "Analyzing Variations in Advertising and Promotional Expenditures: Key Correlates in Consumer, Industrial, and Service Markets," *Journal of Marketing,* April 1990, pp. 57–68.

12. Dunn Sunnoo and Lynn Y. S. Lin, "Sales Effects of Promotion and Advertising," *Journal of Advertising Research,* October 1978, pp. 37–42.

13. J. Ronald Carey, Stephen A. Clique, Barbara A. Leighton, and Frank Milton, "A Test of Positive Reinforcement of Customers," *Journal of Marketing,* October 1976, pp. 98–100.

14. James M. Olver and Paul W. Farris, "Push and Pull: A One-Two Punch for Packaged Products," *Sloan Management Review,* Fall 1989, pp. 53–61.

15. Ken Riddell, "Advertising Sees Share of Pie Dwindling," *Marketing,* January 7, 1994, p. 2; and Ken Riddell, "The Need for Leadership," *Marketing,* June 14, 1993, p. 15.

16. Joseph Weber, "Drug Ads: A Prescription for Controversy," *Business Week,* January 18, 1993, pp. 58–60.

17. "Category Management: Marketing for the 90s," *Marketing News,* September 14, 1992, pp. 12–13; "Where the Promotion Dollar Goes," *Adweek's Marketing Week,* June 19, 1990, p. 10; and Arthur Shapiro, "Advertising versus Promotion: Which Is Which?" *Journal of Advertising Research,* June–July 1990, pp. RC13–RC16.

18. Magid M. Abraham and Leonard M. Lodish, "Getting the Most Out of Advertising and Promotion," *Harvard Business Review,* May–June 1990, pp. 50–60; Steven W. Hartley and James Cross, "How Sales Promotion Can Work for and against You," *Journal of Consumer Marketing,* Summer 1988, pp. 35–42; Robert D. Buzzell, John A. Quelch, and Walter J. Salmon, "The Costly Bargain of Trade Promotion," *Harvard Business Review,* March–April 1990, pp. 141–49; and Mary L. Nicastro, "Break-Even Analysis Determines Success of Sales Promotions," *Marketing News,* March 5, 1990, p. 11.

19. "Donnelley Marketing's 14th Annual Survey of Promotional Practices," *Promo,* May 1992, p. 24.

20. Ken Riddell, "Taking the Clipping Out of Couponing," *Marketing,* April 12, 1993, p. 11.

21. Kapil Bawa and Robert W. Shoemaker, "Analyzing Incremental Sales from a Direct-Mail Coupon Promotion," *Journal of Marketing,* July 1989, pp. 66–78.

22. Roger A. Strang, "Sales Promotion—Fast Growth, Faulty Management," *Harvard Business Review,* July–August 1976, pp. 115–24; and Ronald W. Ward and James E. Davis, "Coupon Redemption," *Journal of Advertising Research,* August 1978, pp. 51–58. Similar results on favourable mail-distributed coupons were reported by Alvin Schwartz, "The Influence of Media Characteristics on Coupon Redemption," *Journal of Marketing,* January 1966, pp. 41–46.

23. Ken Riddell, "The Need for Leadership."

24. Kerry J. Smith, "Sing-Along Fever Runs High," *Promo,* August 1992, pp. 22, 46.

25. James Pollock, "The Poop on Ultra Diapers," *Marketing,* November 22, 1993, p. 4.

26. Gary McWilliams and Mark Maremont, "Forget the Green Stamps—Give Me a Ticket to Miami," *Business Week,* February 24, 1992, pp. 70–71; Glenn Heitsmith, "Credit Cards Form Hub of Loyalty Programs," *Promo,* October 1992, pp. 30, 56; and Howard Schlossberg, "Frequency Programs Work Best When Data Are Leveraged Properly," *Marketing News,* November 9, 1992, pp. 3, 5.

27. "New Handy Snack Display Is Dandy," *Marketing News,* October 9, 1987, p. 15.

28. Cyndee Miller, "P-O-P Gains Followers As 'Era of Retailing' Dawns," *Marketing News,* May 14, 1990, p. 2.

29. Kathleen Deveny, "Displays Pay Off for Grocery Marketers," *The Wall Street Journal,* October 15, 1992, pp. B1, B5; "VideOcart Is Rolling Again," *Promo,* August 1991, pp. 1, 36; and Bradley Johnson, "Retailers Check Out In-Store," *Advertising Age,* December 16, 1991, p. 23.

30. Marvin A. Jolson, Joshua L. Wiener, and Richard B. Rosecky, "Correlates of Rebate Proneness," *Journal of Advertising Research,* February–March 1987, pp. 33–43.

31. Alison Fahey, "Rebate Program Rings Wright Bell," *Advertising Age,* May 21, 1990, p. 44.

32. This discussion is drawn particularly from John A. Quelch, *Trade Promotions by Grocery Manufacturers: A Management Perspective* (Cambridge, MA: Marketing Science Institute, August 1982).

33. Michael Chevalier and Ronald C. Curhan, "Retail Promotions as a Function of Trade Promotions: A Descriptive Analysis," *Sloan Management Review,* Fall 1976, pp. 19–32.

34. G. A. Marken, "Firms Can Maintain Control over Creative Co-Op Programs," *Marketing News,* September 28, 1992, pp. 7, 9.

35. Jerry White, "Integrated Marketing," *Marketing,* June 14, 1993, p. 15.

36. This discussion on MPR was based, in part, on Mark Clemente, *The Marketing Glossary* (New York: AMACOM, 1992), pp. 283–85.

37. Howard Schlossberg "Sports Marketing," *Journal of Promotion Management* 1, no. 1 (1991), pp. 119–22.

38. *Marketing,* January 25, 1993, p. 11.

39. Hugh Filman, "Specialists Prove They Can Boost Retailers' Sales and Profiles," *Marketing,* February 15, 1993, p. 15.

CHAPTER 19

1. Gary Burandt and Nancy Giges, "Moscow Meets Madison Avenue," *Advertising Age,* September 28, 1992, pp. 16, 31, 44; Laurel Wentz and Elena Bowes, "Unification Spurs Multinational Intros in Europe," *Advertising Age International,* January 18, 1993, pp. I3, I30; and "World Brands," *Advertising Age,* July 13, 1992, pp. 51–58.

2. "Global Media and Marketing," *Advertising Age,* December 14, 1992, pp. 51–58.

3. David A. Aaker and Donald Norris, "Characteristics of TV Commercials Perceived as Informative," *Journal of Advertising Research,* April–May 1982, pp. 61–70.

4. William Wilkie and Paul W. Farris, "Comparison Advertising: Problems and Potentials," *Journal of Marketing,* October 1975, pp. 7–15.

5. Jennifer Lawrence, "P&G Ads Get Competitive," *Advertising Age,* February 1, 1993, p. 14; Jerry Gotlieb and Dan Sorel, "The Influence of Type of Advertisement, Price, and Source Credibility on Perceived Quality," *Journal of the Academy of Marketing Science,* Summer 1992, pp. 253–60; and Cornelia Pechman and David Stewart, "The Effects of Comparative Advertising on Attention, Memory, and Purchase Intentions," *Journal of Consumer Research,* September 1990, pp. 180–92.

6. For a discussion of institutional or corporate advertising, see F. G. Crane, "The Need for Corporate Advertising in the Financial Services Industry: A Case Study Illustration," *Journal of Services Marketing* 4, no. 2 (1990), pp. 31–37.

7. Robert J. Lavidge and Gary A. Steiner, "A Model for Predictive Measurement of Advertising Effectiveness," *Journal of Marketing,* October 1961, p. 61.

8. John Philip Jones, "Ad Spending: Maintaining Market Share," *Harvard Business Review,* January–February 1990, pp. 38–42; and Charles H. Patti and Vincent Blanko, "Budgeting Practices of Big Advertisers," *Journal of Advertising Research,* December 1981, pp. 23–30.

9. James A. Schroer, "Ad Spending: Growing Market Share," *Harvard Business Review,* January–February 1990, pp. 44–48.

10. Jeffrey A. Lowenhar and John L. Stanton, "Forecasting Competitive Advertising Expenditures," *Journal of Advertising Research,* April 1976, pp. 37–44.

11. Daniel Seligman, "How Much for Advertising?" *Fortune,* December 1956, p. 123. Also see F. G. Crane, "The Promotion Intelligence Quotient of Small Business Owners," *Journal of Small Business and Entrepreneurship,* July–September 1992, pp. 14–18.

12. James E. Lynch and Graham J. Hooley, "Increasing Sophistication in Advertising Budget Setting," *Journal of Advertising Research,* February–March 1990, pp. 67–75.

13. Jimmy D. Barnes, Brenda J. Muscove, and Javad Rassouli, "An Objective and Task Media Selection Decision Model and Advertising Cost Formula to Determine International Advertising Budgets," *Journal of Advertising* 11, no. 4 (1982), pp. 68–75.

14. Bob Garfield, "Allstate Ads Bring Home Point about Mortgage Insurance," *Advertising Age,* September 11, 1989, p. 120; and Judann Dagnoli, " 'Buy or Die' Mentality Toned Down in Ads," *Advertising Age,* May 7, 1990, p. S-12.

15. Gail Chiasson, "Tracking Shows Why Most Ads Fail," *Marketing,* July 19, 1993, p. 8.

16. Janet Meyers and Laurie Freeman, "Marketers Police TV Commercial Costs," *Advertising Age,* April 3, 1989, p. 51; John Pfeiffer, "Six Months and a Half a Million Dollars, All for 15 Seconds," *Smithsonian,* October 1987, pp. 134–35; and Alex Ben Block, "Where the Money Goes," *Forbes,* September 21, 1987, pp. 178–80.

17. Cleveland Horton, "Wieden & Kennedy: Keeping Ad Game Fresh," *Advertising Age,* April 13, 1992, pp. S3, 50.

18. Gail Chiasson, "Tracking Shows Why Most Ads Fail."

19. Canadian Media Directors' Council (CMDC), *Media Digest* (Toronto, 1993–94), p. 7.

20. Ibid., p. 9.

21. Surendra N. Singh and Catherine Cole, "The Effects of Length, Content, and Repetition on Television Commercial Effectiveness," *Journal of Marketing Research,* February 1993, pp. 91–104.

22. Canadian Media Directors' Council, *Media Digest,* p. 7; and *Marketing,* June 14, 1993, p. 3.

23. *Marketing,* May 31, 1993, p. 36.

24. Dan Plashkes, "The Bottom Line in Direct-Response TV," *Marketing,* November 22, 1993, p. 23.

25. Canadian Media Directors' Council, *Media Digest,* pp. 15–16.

26. Ibid., pp. 23–25.

27. Julia Collins, "Image and Advertising," *Harvard Business Review,* January–February 1989, pp. 93–97.

28. "Apple Launches Disk Ad Inserts," *Marketing,* March 22, 1993, p. 2.

29. Canadian Media Directors' Council, *Media Digest,* pp. 18–22.

30. Arch G. Woodside, "Outdoor Advertising as Experiments," *Journal of the Academy of Marketing Science,* Summer 1990, pp. 229–37.

31. John Cortez, "Growing Pains Can't Stop the New Kid on the Ad Block," *Advertising Age,* October 12, 1992, pp. 5–28; Allen Banks, "How to Assess New Place-Based Media," *Advertising Age,* November 30, 1992, p. 36; and John Cortez, "Media Pioneers Try to Corral On-the-Go Consumers," *Advertising Age,* August 17, 1992, p. 25.

32. Sehoon Park and Minhi Hahn, "Pulsing in a Discrete Model of Advertising Competition," *Journal of Marketing Research,* November 1991, pp. 397–405.

33. "Professor Claims Corporations Waste Billions on Advertising," *Marketing News,* July 6, 1992, p. 5.

34. The discussion of posttesting is based on Courtland L. Bovée and William F. Arens, *Contemporary Advertising,* 2nd ed.(Homewood, IL: Richard D. Irwin, 1988), p. 209.

35. David A. Aaker and Douglas M. Stayman, "Measuring Audience Perceptions of Commercials and Relating Them to Ad Impact," *Journal of Advertising Research,* August–September 1990, pp. 7–17; and Ernest Dichter, "A Psychological View of Advertising Effectiveness," *Marketing Management* 1, no. 3 (1992), pp. 60–62.

36. Dave Kruegel, "Television Advertising Effectiveness and Research Innovation," *Journal of Consumer Marketing,* Summer 1988, pp. 43–51; and Laurence N. Gold, "The Evolution of Television Advertising-Sales Measurement: Past, Present, and Future," *Journal of Advertising Research,* June–July 1988, pp. 19–24.

37. F. G. Crane, "Consumers' Attitudes toward Advertising: A Canadian Perspective," *International Journal of Advertising* 10 (1991), pp. 111–16.

38. S. M. DeYoung and F. G. Crane, "Females' Attitudes toward the Portrayal of Women in Advertising: A Canadian Study," *International Journal of Advertising* 11 (1992), pp. 249–55.

39. James Pollock, "The New Reality," *Marketing,* July 19, 1993, p. 13; and *Marketing,* April 19, 1993, p. 24.

40. F. G. Crane, Carolyn Meacher, and T. K. Clarke, "Lawyers' Attitudes toward Legal Services Advertising in Canada," *International Journal of Advertising* 8 (1989), pp. 71–78.

CHAPTER 20

1. Statistics Canada, *Canada Year Book,* cat. 11–402E (Ottawa, 1993).

2. Paul S. Busch and Michael J. Houston, *Marketing: Strategic Foundations* (Homewood, IL: Richard D. Irwin, 1985), p. 706.

3. For different perspectives on relationship selling, see Robert F. Dwyer, Paul H. Schuer, and Sejo Oh, "Developing Buyer–Seller Relationships," *Journal of Marketing,* April 1987, pp. 11–27; Lawrence A. Crosby, Kenneth R. Evans, and Deborah Cowles, "Relationship Quality in Services Selling: An Interpersonal Influence Perspective," *Journal of Marketing,"* July 1990, pp. 68–81; and Barry J. Farber and Joyce Wycoff, "Relationships: Six Steps to Success," *Sales & Marketing Management,* April 1992, pp. 50–56.

4. For a perspective on types of selling, see Thomas R. Wotruba, "The Evolution of Personal Selling," *Journal of Personal Selling & Sales Management,* Summer 1991, pp. 1–12.

5. "1992 Sales Manager's Budget Planner," *Sales & Marketing Management,* June 22, 1992, pp. 68, 73.

6. Cathy Hills, "Making the Team," *Sales & Marketing Management,* February 1992, pp. 55–57.

7. Marvin A. Jolson and Thomas R. Wotruba, "Prospecting: A New Look at This Old Challenge," *Journal of Personal Selling & Sales Management,* Fall 1992, pp. 59–66.

8. James Pollock, "In Pursuit of Privacy," *Marketing,* January 4, 1993, pp. 1, 4.

9. Gerrard Macintosh, Kenneth A. Anglin, David M. Szymanski, and James W. Gentry, "Relationship Development in Selling: A Cognitive Analysis," *Journal of Personal Selling & Sales Management,* Fall 1992, pp. 23–34.

10. For a variation on the "canned presentation," see Marvin A. Jolson, "Canned Adaptiveness: A New Direction for Modern Salesmanship," *Business Horizons,* January–February 1989, pp. 7–12.

11. Research on these formats can be found in Barton A. Weitz, Harish Sujan, and Mita Sujan, "Knowledge, Motivation, and Adaptive Behavior: A Framework for Improving Selling Effectiveness," *Journal of Marketing,* October 1986, pp. 174–91; Thomas W. Leigh and Patrick F. McGraw, "Mapping the Procedural Knowledge of Industrial Sales Personnel: A Script-Theoretic Investigation," *Journal of Marketing,* January 1989, pp. 16–34; David M. Szymanski, "Determinants of Selling Effectiveness: The Importance of Declarative Knowledge to the Personal Selling Concept," *Journal of Marketing,* January 1988, pp. 64–67; and Rosann L. Spiro and Barton A. Weitz, "Adaptive Selling: Conceptualization, Measurement, and Normological Validity," *Journal of Marketing Research,* February 1990, pp. 61–69.

12. Based on Ronald D. Balsley and E. Patricia Birsner, *Selling: Marketing Personified* (Hinsdale, IL: Dryden Press, 1987), pp. 261–63.

13. An extensive listing of closing techniques is found in Robin T. Peterson, "Sales Representative Perceptions on Various Widely Used Closing Tactics," *AMA Educators' Conference Proceedings* (Chicago: American Marketing Association, 1988), pp. 220–24.

14. Theodore Levitt, *The Marketing Imagination* (New York: Free Press, 1983), p. 111.

15. William A. O'Connell and William Keenan, Jr., "The Shape of Things to Come," *Sales & Marketing Management,* January 1990, pp. 36–41.

16. See, for example, Troy A. Festervand, Stephen J. Grove, and Eric Reidenbach, "The Sales Force as a Marketing Intelligence System," *Journal of Business & Industrial Marketing,* Winter 1988, pp. 53–60; Douglas M. Lambert, Howard Marmorstein, and Arun Sharma, "Industrial Salespeople as a Source of Market Information," *Industrial Marketing Management* 19 (1990), pp. 141–48; and Lawrence B. Chonko, John F. Tanner, and Ellen Reid Smith, "The Sales Force's Role in International Marketing Research and Marketing Information Systems," *Journal of Personal Selling & Sales Management,* Winter 1991, pp. 69–79.

17. For a brief article on this topic, see Edwin E. Bobrow, "The Question of Reps," *Sales & Marketing Management,* June 1991, pp. 32–34.

18. Benson Shapiro, *Sales Program Management: Formulation and Implementation* (New York: McGraw-Hill, 1977), pp. 250–55.

19. For an extended treatment of major account management, see Jerome A. Colletti and Gary S. Turbridy, "Effective Major Account Management," *Journal of Personal Selling & Sales Management,* August 1987, pp. 1–10; and Richard Cardozo and Shannon Shipp, "New Selling Methods Are Changing Industrial Sales Management," *Business Horizons,* September–October 1987, pp. 23–28.

20. Walter J. Talley, "How to Design Sales Territories," *Journal of Marketing,* January 1961, pp. 7–13.

21. Several variations of the account management policy grid exist. See, for example, Gilbert A. Churchill, Jr., Neil M. Ford, and Orville C. Walker, Jr., *Sales Force Management: Planning, Implementation, and Control,* 4th ed. (Homewood, IL: Richard D. Irwin, 1993), p. 249; and David W. Cravens, Thomas N. Ingram, and Raymond W. LaForge, "Evaluating Multiple Channel Strategies," *The Journal of Business & Industrial Marketing,* Fall 1991, pp. 37–48.

22. For research on job analyses, see William C. Montcrief III, "Selling Activity and Sales Position Taxonomies for Industrial Salesforces," *Journal of Marketing Research,* August 1986, pp. 261–70.

23. Neil M. Ford, Orville C. Walker, Jr., Gilbert A. Churchill, Jr., and Steven W. Hartley, "Selecting Successful Salespeople: A Meta-Analysis of Biographical and Psychological Selection Criteria," in *Review of Marketing 1987,* ed. Michael J. Houston (Chicago: American Marketing Association, 1988), pp. 90–131.

24. Earl D. Honeycutt, Jr., Clyde E. Harris, Jr., and Stephen B. Castleberry, "Sales Training: A Status Report," *Training and Development Journal,* May 1987, pp. 42–47.

25. Churchill, Ford, and Walker, p. 530; and Douglas J. Dalrymple and William L. Cron, *Sales Management,* 4th ed. (New York: John Wiley & Sons, 1992), p. 444.

26. See, for example, William L. Cron, Alan J. Dubinsky, and Ronald E. Michaels, "The Influence of Career Stages on Components of Salesperson Motivation," *Journal of Marketing,* January 1988, pp. 78–92; Pradeep K. Tyagi, "Relative Importance of Key Job Dimensions and Leadership Behaviors in Motivating Salesperson Work Performance," *Journal of Marketing,* Summer 1985, pp. 76–86; Richard C. Beckerer, Fred Morgan, and Lawrence Richard, "The Job Characteristics of Industrial Salespersons: Relationship to Motivation and Satisfaction," *Journal of Marketing,* Fall 1982, pp. 125–35; and Walter Kiechel III, "How to Manage Salespeople," *Fortune,* March 14, 1988, pp. 179–80.

27. Gilbert A. Churchill, Jr., Neil M. Ford, and Orville C. Walker, Jr., "Personal Characteristics of Salespeople and the Attractiveness of Alternative Rewards," *Journal of Business Research* 7 (1979), pp. 25–50; and Neil M. Ford, Orville C. Walker, Jr., and Gilbert A. Churchill, Jr., "Differences in the Attractiveness of Alternative Awards among Industrial Salespeople: Additional Evidence," *Journal of Business Research* 13 (1985), pp. 124–28. See also Lawrence B. Chonko, John F. Tanner, Jr., and William A. Weeks, "Reward Preferences of Salespeople," *Journal of Personal Selling & Sales Management,* Summer 1992, pp. 67–75.

28. "Types of Employee Awards," *Sales & Marketing Management,* June 22, 1992, p. 73.

29. For statistics and research on salesperson turnover, see "Turnover Rates by Industry Group," *Sales & Marketing Management,* June 22, 1992, p. 71; "Sales Force Turnover Has Managers Wondering Why," *Marketing News,* December 4, 1989; George H. Lucas, Jr., A. Parasuraman, Robert A. Davis, and Ben Enis, "An Empirical Study of Salesforce Turnover," *Journal of Marketing,* July 1987, pp. 34–59; and René Y. Darmon, "Identifying Sources of Turnover Costs: A Segmental Approach," *Journal of Marketing,* April 1990, pp. 46–56. See also Edward F. Fern, Ramon A. Avila, and Dhruv Grewal, "Salesforce Turnover: Those Who Left and Those Who Stayed," *Industrial Marketing Management* 18 (1989), pp. 1–9; and Thomas R. Wotruba and Pradeep K. Tyagi, "Met Expectations and Turnover in Direct Selling," *Journal of Marketing,* July 1991, pp. 24–35.

30. Donald W. Jackson, Jr., Janet E. Keith, and John Schlacter, "Evaluation of Selling Performance: A Study of Current Practice," *Journal of Personal Selling and Sales Management,* November 1983, pp. 43–51. See also Erin Anderson and Richard L. Oliver, "Perspectives on Behavior-Based versus Outcome-Based Salesforce Control Systems," *Journal of Marketing,* October 1987, pp. 76–88; and Daniel A. Sauers, James B. Hunt, and Ken Bass, "Behavioral Self-Management as a Supplement to External Sales Force Controls," *Journal of Personal Selling & Sales Management,* Summer 1990, pp. 17–28.

31. Jerry McAdams, "Rewarding Sales and Marketing Performance," *Management Review,* April 1987, pp. 33–38. See also Gilbert A. Churchill, Jr., Neil M. Ford, Steven W. Hartley, and Orville C. Walker, Jr., "The Determinants of Salesperson Performance: A Meta-Analysis," *Journal of Marketing Research,* May 1985, pp. 103–18.

CHAPTER 21

1. Alexander Ross, "The Alcan Success in Canada," *Canadian Business,* June 1989, pp. 30–34; and *Annual Report* (Montreal: Alcan Aluminium, 1993).

2. Ronald Henkoff, "How to Plan for 1995," *Fortune,* December 31, 1990, pp. 70–79.

3. Andrew J. Parsons, "Building Innovativeness in Large U.S. Corporations," *Journal of Consumer Marketing,* Spring 1992, pp. 35–50; Stanley F. Stasch and Patricia Langtree, "Can Your Marketing Planning Procedures Be Improved?" *Journal of Marketing,* Summer 1980,

pp. 79–90; and David S. Hopkins, *The Marketing Plan* (New York: The Conference Board, 1981), p. 24.

4. Brian Dumaine, "P&G Rewrites the Marketing Rules," *Fortune,* November 6, 1989, pp. 35–48.

5. Joseph Weber, "A Big Company That Works," *Business Week,* May 4, 1992, pp. 124–32.

6. Stewart Toy, Mark Maremont, and Ronald Grover, "An American in Paris," *Business Week,* March 12, 1990, pp. 60–64; and "Mickey Mess," *Time,* June 22, 1992, p. 30.

7. The discussion on sustainable competitive advantage was adapted, in part, from Sundar G. Bharadwaj, P. Rajan Varadarajan, and John Fahy, "Sustainable Competitive Advantage in Service Industries: A Conceptual Model and Research Propositions," *Journal of Marketing,* October 1993, pp. 83–99; Michael E. Porter, *Competitive Advantage* (New York: Free Press, 1985); and Jay Barney, "Firm Resources and Sustained Competitive Advantage," *Journal of Marketing,* March 1991, pp. 99–120.

8. See Bharadwaj, Varadarajan, and Fahy (reference cited).

9. George S. Day, *Market-Driven Strategy* (New York: Free Press, 1990). Also see Michael E. Porter, *Competitive Advantage.*

10. Sundar G. Bharadwaj, P. Rajan Varadarajan, and John Fahy (reference cited).

11. Murali K. Mantrala, Prabhakant Sirha, and Andris A. Zoltners, "Impact of Resource Allocation Rules on Marketing Investment-Level Decisions and Profitability," *Journal of Marketing Research,* May 1992, pp. 162–175.

12. James Pollock, "Kraft GF Comes of Age with Nabisco Acquisition," *Marketing,* January 11, 1993, p. 2.

13. Philip Kotler, *Marketing Management,* 7th ed. (Englewood Cliffs, NJ: Prentice Hall, 1991), pp. 38–39.

14. Roger A. Kerin, Vijay Mahajan, and P. Rajan Varadarajan, *Contemporary Perspectives on Strategic Market Planning* (Boston: Allyn & Bacon, 1990), p. 52.

15. George S. Day, "Diagnosing the Product Portfolio," *Journal of Marketing,* April 1977, pp. 29–38.

16. Stratford Sherman, "How Intel Makes Spending Pay Off," *Fortune,* February 22, 1993, pp. 57–61; and Robert Hof, "Inside Intel," *Business Week,* June 1, 1992, pp. 86–94.

17. Strengths and weaknesses of the BCG technique are based largely on Derek F. Abell and John S. Hammond, *Strategic Market Planning: Problem and Analytic Approaches* (Englewood Cliffs, NJ: Prentice Hall, 1979); and Yoram Wind, Vijay Mahajan, and Donald Swire, "An Empirical Comparison of Standardized Portfolio Models," *Journal of Marketing,* Spring 1983, pp. 89–99.

18. Rick Brown, "Making the Product Portfolio a Basis for Action," *Long Range Planning,* February 1991, pp. 102–10.

19. Robert D. Buzzell, Bradley T. Gale, and Ralph G. M. Sultan, "Market Share—A Key to Profitability," *Harvard Business Review,* January–February 1975, pp. 97–106; Carolyn Y. Woo and Arnold C. Cooper, "The Surprising Case for Low Market Share," *Harvard Business Review,* November–December 1982, pp. 106–13; and Robert Jacobson and David A. Aaker, "Is Market Share All That It's Cracked Up to Be?" *Journal of Marketing,* Fall 1985, pp. 11–22.

20. Derek F. Abell, *Defining the Business: The Starting Point of Strategic Planning* (Englewood Cliffs, NJ: Prentice Hall, 1980), Chapter 8.

21. Regis McKenna, "Marketing in an Age of Diversity," *Harvard Business Review,* September–October 1988, pp. 88–95.

22. Robert Linneman and John Stanton, "Mining for Niches," *Business Horizons,* May–June 1992, pp. 43–51.

23. Michael G. Harvey and Roger A. Kerin, "Diagnosis and Management of the Product Cannibalism Syndrome," *University of Michigan Business Review,* November 1979, pp. 18–24.

24. Thomas J. Peters and Robert H. Waterman, Jr., *In Search of Excellence: Lessons from America's Best-Run Companies* (New York: Harper & Row, 1982); and Michael E. Porter, "From Competitive Advantage to Corporate Strategy," *Harvard Business Review,* May–June 1987, pp. 43–59.

25. Fahri Karakaya and Michael J. Stahl, "Underlying Dimensions of Barriers to Market Entry in Consumer Goods Markets," *Journal of the Academy of Marketing Science,* Summer 1992, pp. 275–78; Gary E. Willard and Arun M. Savara, "Patterns of Entry: Pathways to New Markets," *California Management Review,* Winter 1988, pp. 57–76; and Fahri Karakaya and Michael J. Stahl, "Barriers to Entry and Market Entry Decisions in Consumer and Industrial Goods Markets," *Journal of Marketing,* April 1989, pp. 80–91.

26. Mary T. Curren, Valerie S. Folkes, and Joel H. Sheckel, "Explanations for Successful and Unsuccessful Marketing Decisions: The Decision Maker's Perspective," *Journal of Marketing,* April 1992, pp. 18–31; and Spyros Makridakis, "What Can We Learn from Corporate Failure?" *Long Range Planning,* August 1991, pp. 115–26.

27. Stratford Sherman, "How Intel Makes Spending Pay Off," *Fortune,* February 22, 1993, pp. 57–61.

28. George S. Day and Liam Fahey, "Valuing Marketing Strategies," *Journal of Marketing,* July 1988, pp. 45–57; Mary Anne Raymond and Hiram C. Barksdale, "Corporate Strategic Planning and Corporate Marketing: Toward an Interface?" *Business Horizons,* September–October 1989, pp. 41–48; Walter Kiechel III, "Corporae Strategy for the 1990s," *Fortune,* February 29, 1988, pp. 34–42; and Enrique R. Arzac, "Do Your Business Units Create Shareholder Value?" *Harvard Business Review,* January–February 1986, pp. 121–26.

29. Lee Ginsburg and Neil Miller, "Value-Driven Management," *Business Horizons,* May–June 1992, pp. 23–27.

CHAPTER 22

1. Much of the Domino's Pizza material is taken from Bernie Whalen, " 'People Oriented' Marketing Delivers a Lot of Dough for Domino's," *Marketing News,* March 15, 1984, pp. 4ff; by permission of the American Marketing Association.

2. Stan Sutter, "A New Topping for Domino's," *Marketing,* January 25, 1993, p. 2; John P. Cortez, "New Direction for Domino's," *Advertising Age,* January 4, 1993, pp. 34–35; John P. Cortez, "Domino's to Beef Up Menu Items," *Advertising Age,* November 23, 1992, p. 25; and Lisa Driscoll and David Woodruff, "With Tom Monaghan Back Can Domino's Deliver?" *Business Week,* October 28, 1991, pp. 136, 140.

3. William Taylor, "Message and Muscle: An Interview with Swatch Titan Nicolas Hayek," *Harvard Business Review,* March–April 1993, pp. 99–110; and Robert Hof, "NeXT's Black Box May Be the Next to Go," *Business Week,* January 25, 1993, p. 38.

4. Thomas V. Bonoma, "Making Your Marketing Strategy Work," *Harvard Business Review,* March–April 1984, pp. 69–76.

5. Larry Armstrong and Karen Lowry Miller, "Toyota's New Pickup: Oops" *Business Week,* February 15, 1993, pp. 37–38.

6. Zachary Schiller, "After a Year of Spinning Its Wheels, Goodyear Gets a Retread," *Business Week,* March 26, 1990, pp. 56, 58.

7. Larry Hirschhorn and Thomas Gilmore, "The New Boundaries of the 'Boundaryless' Company," *Harvard Business Review,* May–June 1992, pp. 104–15; Jack Welch, "How Good a Manager?" *Business Week,* December 14, 1987, p. 95; and Thomas Moore, "Goodbye, Corporate Staff," *Fortune,* December 21, 1987, pp. 65–74.

8. Thomas V. Bonoma and Victoria L. Crittenden, "Managing Marketing Implementation," *Sloan Management Review,* Winter 1988, pp. 7–14.

9. Paul S. Adler, Henry E. Riggs, and Steven C. Wheelwright, "Product Development Know-How: Trading Tactics for Strategy," *Sloan Management Review,* Fall 1989, pp. 7–17.

10. Jon Katzenbach and Douglas Smith, "The Discipline of Teams," *Harvard Business Review,* March–April 1993, pp. 111–20; and Jon Katzenbach and Douglas Smith, *The Wisdom of Teams* (Boston: Harvard Business School Press, 1992).

11. Don Frey, "Learning the Ropes: My Life as a Product Champion," *Harvard Business Review,* September–October 1991, pp. 46–56.

12. Thomas J. Peters and Robert H. Waterman, Jr., *In Search of Excellence: Lessons from America's Best-Run Companies* (New York: Harper & Row, 1982).

13. Tim Falconer, "A Classic Comes of Age," *Marketing,* September 13, 1993, pp. 1, 3.

14. David Woodruff, James Treece, Sunita Bhargava, and Karen Miller, "Saturn: GM Finally Has a Real Winner," *Business Week,* August 17, 1992, pp. 86–91; James Treece, "Here Comes GM's Saturn," *Business Week,* April 9, 1990, pp. 56–62; and S. C. Gwynne, "The Right Stuff," *Time,* October 29, 1990, pp. 74–84.

15. David Woodruff, "Saturn: Labor's Love Lost?" *Business Week,* February 8, 1993, pp. 122–24; and Raymond Serafin, "The Saturn Story," *Advertising Age,* November 16, 1992, pp. 1, 13, 16.

16. The scheduling example is adapted from William Rudelius and W. Bruce Erickson, *An Introduction to Contemporary Business,* 4th ed. (New York: Harcourt Brace Jovanovich, 1985), pp. 94–95.

17. Robert Howard, "The CEO as Organizational Architect," *Harvard Business Review,* September–October 1992, pp. 107–21; and Christopher Bartlett and Sumantra Ghoshal, "Matrix Management: Not a Structure, a Frame of Mind," *Harvard Business Review,* July–August 1990, pp. 138–45.

18. Betsy Spethmann, "Category Management Multiples," *Advertising Age,* May 11, 1992, p. 42; "Focus on Five Stages of Category Management," *Marketing News,* September 28, 1992, pp. 17, 19; and Kevin T. Higgins, "Category Management," *Marketing News,* September 25, 1989, pp. 2, 19.

19. Philip Kotler, *Marketing Management,* 7th ed. (Englewood Cliffs, NJ: Prentice Hall, 1991), pp. 691–92.

20. Robert W. Ruekert and Orville W. Walker, Jr., "Marketing Interaction with Other Functional Units: A Conceptual Framework and Empirical Evidence," *Journal of Consumer Marketing,* Spring 1987, pp. 1–19.

21. Steven Lysonski, Alan Singer, and David Wilemone, "Coping with Environmental Uncertainty and Boundary Spanning in the Product Manager's Role," *Journal of Consumer Marketing,* Spring 1989, pp. 33–43.

22. John A. Quelch, Paul W. Farris, and James Olver, "The Product Management Audit: Design and Survey Findings," *The Journal of Consumer Marketing,* Summer 1987, pp. 45–58.

23. Robert S. Eckley, "Caterpillar's Ordeal: Foreign Competition in Capital Goods," *Business Horizons,* March–April 1989, pp. 80–86.

24. Bill Saposito, "Campbell Soup Gets Piping Hot," *Fortune,* September 9, 1991, pp. 142–48.

25. Thomas V. Bonoma, "Marketing Performance—What Do You Expect?" *Harvard Business Review,* September–October 1989, pp. 44–48.

26. Angela Kryhul, "A Timely Turnaround," *Marketing,* September 6, 1993, p. 1.

27. Stanley J. Shapiro and V. H. Kirpalani, *Marketing Effectiveness: Insights from Accounting and Finance* (Boston: Allyn & Bacon, 1984); Leland L. Bick and Stephen L. Busby, "Profitability Analysis by Market Segments," *Journal of Marketing,* July 1973, pp. 48–53; V. H. Kirpalani and Stanley J. Shapiro, "Financial Dimensions of Marketing Management," *Journal of Marketing,* July 1973, pp. 40–47; and Paul Fischer and W. J. E. Crissy, "New Approaches to Analyzing Marketing Profitability," *Journal of Marketing,* April 1974, pp. 43–48.

28. Debbie Berlant, Reese Browning, and George Foster, "How Hewlett-Packard Gets Numbers It Can Trust," *Harvard Business Review,* January–February 1990, pp. 178–83.

29. G. David Hughes, "Computerized Sales Management," *Harvard Business Review,* March–April 1983, pp. 102–12.

30. Philip Kotler, William Gregor, and William Rogers, "The Marketing Audit Comes of Age," *Sloan Management Review,* Winter 1977, pp. 25–43.

CHAPTER 23

1. Adapted from Rahul Jacob, "India Is Opening for Business," *Fortune,* November 16, 1992, pp. 128–30.

2. Jacob, pp. 128–30.

3. *General Agreement on Tariffs and Trade: What It Is, What It Does* (Geneva, Switzerland: GATT Information and Media Relations Division, 1990), pp. 1–3. For a discussion of problems with GATT mentioned in the text, see Paul Magnusson, "GATT Is on Its Feet—But Far from Steady," *Business Week,* December 7, 1992, pp. 36–37; and "GATT's Gordian Knot Proves Difficult to Cut," *The Wall Street Journal,* October 8, 1990, p. A1.

4. *The Financial Post 500* (Toronto: The Financial Post Company, 1992).

5. Kenichi Ohmae, "Planting for a Global Harvest," *Harvard Business Review,* July–August 1989, pp. 136–45.

6. *The North American Free Trade Agreement* (Ottawa: The Government of Canada, 1992).

7. Theodore Levitt, "The Globalization of Markets," *Harvard Business Review,* May–June 1983, pp. 92–102; and Theodore Levitt, "The Pluralization of Consumption," *Harvard Business Review,* May–June 1988, pp. 7–8.

8. Joanne Lipman, "Marketers Turn Sour on Global Sales Pitch Harvard Guru Makes," *The Wall Street Journal,* May 12, 1988, pp. 1, 10.

9. Lipman, pp. 1, 10.

10. Peter Foster, "McDonald's Excellent Soviet Adventure," *Canadian Business,* May 1991, pp. 51–65; "Moscow's Big Mak Attack," *Time,* February 5, 1990, p. 51; and Scott Hume, "How Big Mac Made It to Moscow," *Advertising Age,* January 22, 1990, pp. 16, 51.

11. S. Tamer Cavusgil, "Guidelines for Export Market Research," *Business Horizons,* November–December 1985, pp. 27–33.

12. "The Barriers Come Tumbling Down," *Time,* August 17, 1992, pp. 15–16; David Aikman and Laura Lopez, "MEGAmarket," *Time,* August 10, 1992, pp. 43–44; Paul Magnusson, "Free Trade? They Can Hardly Wait," *Business Week,* September 24, 1992, pp. 24–25; George Anders, "Heading South," *The Wall Street Journal,* September 24, 1992, pp. R1, R7; and Randolph Heaster and Charles R. T. Crumplex, "NAFTA's Downside," *Minneapolis Star Tribune,* December 16, 1992, pp. 1D, 2D.

13. Carla Rapoport, "Europe Looks Ahead to Hard Choices," *Fortune,* December 14, 1992, pp. 144–49; Barbara Rudolph, "The Grapes of Wrath," *Time,* November 23, 1992, p. 50; and William Drozdiak, "European Leap to Unity Falls Short of Deadline," *Minneapolis Star Tribune,* December 31, 1992, pp. 4A, 5A.

14. Louis Kraar, "Asia 2000," *Fortune,* October 5, 1992, pp. 111–42; Cyndee Miller, "Economic Reform in China Holds Promise for Western Marketers," *Marketing News,* December 7, 1992, pp. 1, 15; and Gaylon White, "The New Consumerism, Asian Style," *Express* magazine, Summer 1992, pp. 10–14.

15. Carole M. Howard, "*Reader's Digest* Meets Eastern Europe," *Express* magazine, Spring 1992, pp. 28–31.

16. James Sterngold, "The Awakening Chinese Consumer," *New York Times,* October 11, 1992, pp. F1, F6.

17. Peter Foster, "McDonald's Excellent Soviet Adventure."

18. Carole M. Howard, p. 29.

19. Bob Hagerty, "Russia, Ukraine Brim with Quirky Laws," *The Wall Street Journal,* October 19, 1992, p. A13.

20. E. S. Browning, "In Pursuit of the Elusive Euroconsumer," *The Wall Street Journal,* April 23, 1992, pp. B1, B3.

21. Alan T. Shao, "Standardized Advertising Campaigns: Impediments Encountered by European Agencies," *Journal of Promotion Management* 1, no. 2 (1993), pp. 39–52.

22. "Global Advertising: Standardized or Multi-Cultural?" *Journal of Advertising Research* July–August, 1992.

CHAPTER 24

1. James McElgunn, "Banks Start to Rethink Delivery of Services," *Marketing,* May 31, 1993, pp. 1, 2; and James McElgunn, "Banking by Phone Catching On Fast," *Marketing,* February 1, 1993, p. 2.

2. Herbert G. Grubel and Michael A. Walker, *Service Industry Growth* (The Fraser Institute, 1989).

3. *Marketing,* June 14, 1993, p. 2.

4. Leonard Berry, "Big Ideas in Services Marketing," *Journal of Consumer Marketing,* Spring 1986, pp. 47–51.

5. Frederick F. Reichheld and W. Earl Sasser, Jr., "Zero Defections: Quality Comes to Services," *Harvard Business Review,* September–October 1990, pp. 105–11; "Standardized Services Run Gamut from Mufflers to Wills," *Marketing News,* April 10, 1987, pp. 17, 43; and Valarie A. Zeithaml, Leonard Berry, and A. Parasuraman, "Communication and Control in the Delivery of Service Quality," *Journal of Marketing,* April 1988, pp. 35–48.

6. Keith B. Murray, "A Test of Services Marketing Theory: Consumer Information Acquisition Activities," *Journal of Marketing,* January 1991, pp. 10–25.

7. Valarie A. Zeithaml, "How Consumer Evaluation Processes Differ between Goods and Services," in *Marketing of Services,* ed. James H. Donnelly and William R. George (Chicago: American Marketing Association, 1981).

8. Keith B. Murray, "A Test of Services Marketing Theory."

9. Valarie A. Zeithaml, A. Parasuraman, and Leonard L. Berry, *Delivering Quality Service* (New York: Free Press, 1990); and Stephen W. Brown and Teresa Swartz, "A Gap Analysis of Professional Service Quality," *Journal of Marketing,* April 1989, pp. 92–98.

10. J. Joseph Cronin, Jr., and Steven A. Taylor, "Measuring Service Quality: A Reexamination and Extension," *Journal of Marketing,* July 1992, pp. 55–68.

11. "Burger King Opens Customer Hot Line," *Marketing News,* May 28, 1990, p. 7.

12. Mary Jo Bitner, Bernard H. Booms, and Mary Stanfield Tetreault, "The Service Encounter: Diagnosing Favorable and Unfavorable Incidents," *Journal of Marketing,* January 1990, pp. 71–84; Eberhard Scheuing, "Conducting Customer Service Audits," *Journal of Consumer Marketing,* Summer 1989, pp. 35–41; and W. Earl Sasser, R. Paul Olsen, and D. Daryl Wyckoff, *Management of Service Operations* (Boston: Allyn & Bacon, 1978).

13. "Services Marketers Must Balance Customer Satisfaction against Their Operational Needs," *Marketing News,* October 10, 1986, pp. 1, 14.

14. Leonard L. Berry, Jeffrey S. Conant, and A. Parasuraman, "A Framework for Conducting a Services Marketing Audit," *Journal of the Academy of Marketing Science,* Summer 1991, pp. 255–68.

15. Patriya Tansuhaj, Donna Randall, and Jim McCullough, "A Services Marketing Management Model: Integrating Internal and External Marketing Functions," *Journal of Services Marketing,* Winter 1988, pp. 31–38.

16. Christian Gronroos, "Internal Marketing: Theory and Practice," in *Services Marketing in a Changing Environment,* ed. Tim Bloch, G. D. Upah, and V. A. Zeithaml (Chicago: American Marketing Association, 1984).

17. Ibid.

18. Scott W. Kelly, "Developing Customer Orientation among Service Employees," *Journal of the Academy of Marketing Science,* Winter 1992, pp. 27–36; Sybil F. Stershic, "Internal Marketing Campaign Reinforces Service Goals," *Marketing News,* July 31, 1989, p. 11; James L. Heskett, "Lessons in the Service Sector," *Harvard Business Review,* March–April 1987, pp. 118–26; Leonard Berry, "Big Ideas in Services Marketing," *Journal of Consumer Marketing,* Spring 1986, pp. 47–51; and Ray Lewis, "Whose Job Is Service Marketing?" *Advertising Age,* August 3, 1987, pp. 18, 20.

19. Dan R. E. Thomas, "Strategy Is Different in Service Businesses," *Harvard Business Review,* July–August 1978, pp. 158–65.

20. Sundar G. Bharadwaj, P. Rajan Varadarajan, and John Fahy, "Sustainable Competitive Advantage in Service Industries: A Conceptual Model and Research Propositions," *Journal of Marketing,* October 1993, pp. 83–99.

21. Christopher Lovelock, *Services Marketing* (Englewood Cliffs, NJ: Prentice Hall, 1991), pp. 122–27.

22. Kent B. Monroe, "Buyer's Subjective Perceptions of Price," *Journal of Marketing Research,* February 1973, pp. 70–80; and Jerry Olson, "Price as an Informational Cue: Effects on Product Evaluation," in *Consumer and Industrial Buying Behavior,* ed. A. G. Woodside, J. N. Sheth, and P. D. Bennett (New York: Elsevier-North Holland Publishing, 1977), pp. 267–86.

23. Robert E. Hite, Cynthia Fraser, and Joseph A. Bellizzi, "Professional Service Advertising: The Effects of Price Inclusion, Justification, and Level of Risk," *Journal of Advertising Research,* August–September 1990, pp. 23–31; William R. George and Leonard L. Berry, "Guidelines for the Advertising of Services," *Business Horizons,* July–August 1981, pp. 52–56; and Eugene M. Johnson, Eberhard E. Scheuing, and Kathleen A. Gaida, *Profitable Service Marketing* (Homewood, IL: Dow Jones-Irwin, 1986).

24. Sak Onkvisit and John J. Shaw, "Service Marketing: Image, Branding, and Competition," *Business Horizons,* January–February 1989, pp. 13–18.

25. William A. Mindak and Seymour Fine, "A Fifth P: Public Relations," in *Marketing of Services,* ed. James H. Donnelly and William R. George (Chicago: American Marketing Association, 1981), pp. 71–73.

26. Joe Adams, "Why Public Service Advertising Doesn't Work," *Ad Week,* November 17, 1980, p. 72.

27. F. G. Crane, *Professional Services Marketing: Strategy and Tactics* (New York: The Haworth Press, 1993).

28. Leonard Berry, "Big Ideas in Services Marketing," *Journal of Consumer Marketing,* Spring 1986, pp. 47–51.

29. Stan Sutter, "Advertising That's a Step Ahead of the Times," *Marketing,* January 25, 1993, p. 7.

APPENDIX B

1. Denny E. McCorkle, Joe F. Alexander, and Memo F. Diriker, "Developing Self-Marketing Skills for Student Career Success," *Journal of Marketing Education,* Spring 1992, pp. 57–67.

2. Nicholas Basta, "The Wide World of Marketing," *Business Week's Guide to Careers,* February–March 1984, pp. 70–72.

3. "The Corporate Elite," *Business Week,* October 12, 1992, pp. 119–46.

4. Tony Lee, "Bursting the Salary Bubble," *Managing Your Career,* Spring 1993, pp. 22–23, 32; and *CPC Salary Survey* (Bethlehem, PA: College Placement Council, Inc., September 1992), pp. 2–3.

5. David Gumpert, "Reaching for the Best Opportunity: 10 High-Flying Businesses to Join in the 90s," *Managing Your Career,* Spring 1992, pp. 4–6.

6. "Focus on Five Stages of Category Management," *Marketing News,* September 28, 1992, pp. 17, 19; and Sandy Gillis, "On the Job: Product Manager," *Business Week's Guide to Careers,* April–May 1988, pp. 63–66.

7. Phil Moss, "What It's Like to Work for Procter & Gamble," *Business Week's Guide to Careers,* March–April 1987, pp. 18–20.

8. David Kirkpatrick, "Is Your Career on Track?" *Fortune,* July 2, 1990, pp. 38–48.

9. Vincent Daddiego, "Making It in Advertising," in Robert H. Luke, *Business Careers* (Boston: Houghton Mifflin, 1989), pp. 189–91.

10. Milan Moravec, Marshall Collins, and Clinton Tripoli, "Don't Want to Manage? Here's Another Path," *Sales and Marketing Management,* June 1990, pp. 62–72.

11. Michael R. Wukitsch, "Should Researchers Know More about Marketing?" *Marketing Research,* Winter 1993, p. 50.

12. Joby John and Mark Needel, "Entry-Level Marketing Research Recruits: What Do Recruiters Need?" *Journal of Marketing Education,* Spring 1989, pp. 68–73.

13. Susan B. Larsen, "International Careers: Reality, Not Fantasy," *CPC Annual: A Guide to Employment Opportunities for College Graduates,* 36th ed. (Bethlehem, PA: College Placement Council, Inc., 1992), pp. 78–85.

14. John W. Buckner, "Working Abroad at Home," *Managing Your Career,* Spring 1992, pp. 16–17.

15. Hugh E. Kramer, "Applying Marketing Strategy and Personal Value Analysis to Career Planning: An Experiential Approach," *Journal of Marketing Education,* Fall 1988, pp. 69–73.

16. Ronald B. Marks, *Personal Selling* (Boston: Allyn & Bacon, 1985), pp. 451–52; Alan Deutschman, "What 25-Year-Olds Want," *Fortune,* August 27, 1990, pp. 42–50; and Dawn Richerson, "Personality and Your Career," *Career Woman,* Winter 1993, pp. 46–47.

17. Arthur F. Miller, "Discover Your Design," in *CPC Annual,* vol. 1 (Bethlehem, PA: College Placement Council, Inc., 1984), p. 2.

18. Marks, pp. 461–62.

19. John L. Munschauer, "How to Find a Customer for Your Capabilities," *CPC Annual,* vol. 1 (Bethlehem, PA: College Placement Council, Inc., 1984), p. 24.

20. C. Randall Powell, "Secrets of Selling a Résumé," in *The Honda How To Get a Job Guide,* ed. Peggy Schmidt (New York: McGraw-Hill, 1984), pp. 4–9.

21. Ibid., p. 4.

22. Arthur G. Sharp, "The Art of the Cover Letter," *Career Futures* 4, no. 1 (1992), pp. 50–51.

23. Perri Capell, "Unconventional Job Search Tactics," *Managing Your Career,* Spring 1991, pp. 31, 35.

24. Julie Griffin Levitt, *Your Career: How to Make It Happen* (Cincinnati: South-Western Publishing, 1985).

25. Deborah Vendy, "Drug Screening and Your Career," *CPC Annual* (Bethlehem, PA: College Placement Council, Inc., 1992), pp. 61–62.

26. Marks, p. 469.

27. Terence P. Pare, "The Uncommitted Class of 1989," *Fortune,* June 5, 1989, pp. 199–210.

28. Bob Weinstein, "What Employers Look For," in *The Honda How to Get a Job Guide,* ed. Peggy Schmidt (New York: McGraw-Hill, 1985), p. 10.

Name Index

Company Index

Subject Index

Credits